A World History

A WORLD

OXFORD UNIVERSITY PRESS ·

HISTORY

THIRD EDITION

William H. McNeill

1979   New York · Oxford

Copyright © 1967, 1971, 1979 by Oxford University Press, Inc.

Library of Congress Cataloging in Publication Data

McNeill, William Hardy, 1917-
  A world history.

  Includes bibliographies and index.
  1. World history.   I. Title.
D21.M32   1980   909   78-27518
ISBN 0-19-502554-7
ISBN 0-19-502555-5 pbk.

10 11 12 13 14 15 16 17 18 19 20

Printed in the United States of America

Preface

Human societies, distinguished from one another by differing styles of life, are very numerous, and have existed from pre- and proto-human times throughout mankind's history. Civilizations are unusually massive societies, weaving the lives of millions of persons into a loose yet coherent life style across hundreds or even thousands of miles and for periods of time that are very long when measured by the span of an individual human life. Being both massive and long-lived, civilizations must perforce also be few. Indeed, from the time when human societies first attained civilized complexity and size, no more than four different major civilized traditions ever co-existed in the Old World; and in the New, where Amerindian development remained always weak and retarded, no more than three distinct civilizations ever emerged.

These facts allow an overview of the history of mankind as a whole. To be sure, the effort to hold simultaneously in mind what was happening in widely separated parts of the earth requires us to focus attention on certain aspects of reality and to pass others by. The same is true of the study of more detailed segments of the human past—think, for instance, of the local peculiarities of each town and village that are so ruthlessly neglected in our standard national histories! As in cartography, each scale has advantages and shortcomings, and an appropriate amount of detail. Too much information will obscure the whole; too little will deprive history of its verisimilitude and disguise the open-ended surprisingness of human experience. Historians of the nineteenth century erected a frame for national histories that continues to command general assent; and in the twentieth century, American textbook writers arrived at a rough consensus concerning the history of something called Western Civilization. But for world history, an agreed criterion has not yet appeared. What to omit and what to pay attention to remain very much matters for debate and disagreement.

Because of these disagreements, it seemed worthwhile to write this brief account of mankind's past. The success of my book *The Rise of the West* (Chicago, 1963) made it plausible to believe that a shorter work would make my personal vision of the whole history of mankind more accessible to students and to general readers—a vision which, however imperfect, still has the virtue of being cohesive and intelligible, something that can be grasped and remembered and reflected upon afterwards.

The organizing idea is simple: in any given age the world balance among cultures was liable to disturbance emanating from one or more centers where men succeeded in creating an unusually attractive or powerful civilization. Neighbors and neighbors' neighbors were then tempted or compelled to change their own traditional ways of life, sometimes by outright borrowing of techniques or ideas, but more often by adjusting and changing things to suit the local scene more smoothly.

In successive ages the major centers of such disturbance to the world altered. It therefore becomes possible to survey the epochs of world history by studying first the center or centers of primary disturbance, and then considering how the other peoples of the earth reacted to or against what they knew or experienced (often at second or third hand) of the innovations that had occurred in the main centers of cultural creativity.

In such a perspective, geographical settings and lines of communication between different civilizations became critically important. Archaeology, technology, and art history provide important clues to ancient relationships which the surviving literary record sometimes disguises.

This book was written during the summer of 1964 and revised in the summer of 1965; the text was revised in the summer of 1970 for a second edition, enlarging the final part substantially. A few relatively minor changes to take account of new archaeological discoveries and other data were incorporated into the third edition in 1978. The Carnegie Corporation helped to finance the book's preparation and the reproduction of a set of readings for an experimental course in world history. I owe special thanks also to Professor John A. Wilson of the University of Chicago, who read Part I, and to Professor Immanuel Hsu of the University of California at Santa Barbara, who checked the passages dealing with the Far East. Both detected errors and infelicities which I hope have been removed. In the preparation of the second edition I was helped greatly by Allan M. Schleich of Creighton University, Professor David Jones of the University of Minnesota, and Professor Bill B. Brayfield of the University of Hartford, who gave me detailed reports based on their experiences with the first edition, which they used in world history courses. Professor Jones, John Hord, and Hugh Scogin performed a similar service for the third edition; Hugh Scogin also took responsibility for revising the Bibliographical Essays.

Chicago, Illinois   W.H.M.
June 1978

Contents

‡‡‡ TEXT MAPS

Drawn by Vaughn Gray

✝✝✝ *CHRONOLOGICAL CHARTS*

✝✝✝ *LIST OF PLATES*

The Development of Greek Sculpture

BETWEEN PAGES 176 AND 177

1: Stele of Aristion
2: Poseidon
3: Head of the Athena Lemnia
4: Portrait of an Unknown Roman
5: Portrait of a Roman Lady

Chinese, Mongol, Persian, and Mughal Painting

European Art and Society

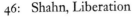

PART I

Emergence and Definition of the Major Old World Civilizations to 500 B.C.

T HE *first great landmark of human history was the development of food production. This permitted an enormous multiplication of human numbers, and laid the basis for the emergence of civilizations. How, when, and where hunting and gathering gave way to farming and pastoralism is uncertain. One of the earliest and most important instances of this transition took place in the Middle East, between about 8500 and 7000 B.C. Thence, through migrations and borrowings, few of which can be reconstructed by modern scholars, grain cultivation spread into Europe and India, China, and parts of Africa. The Americas, monsoon Asia, and west Africa probably saw the independent invention of agriculture, though this is not certain.*

The second great landmark in mankind's history was the emergence of skilled and complex societies we call civilized. Here the primacy of the Middle East is undisputed. Man's earliest civilized communities developed in the valleys of the Tigris-Euphrates and the Nile between about 3500 and 3000 B.C. The Indus valley followed suit soon afterwards. At first civilized complexity required very special geographical conditions. Only on irrigated land could rich crops be harvested year after year from the same fields; and only where irrigation was needed did large numbers of men find it necessary to co-operate in digging and diking. An agricultural surplus that could support specialists, together with habits of social organization embracing large numbers of men, thus could and did emerge in the flood plains of the principal Middle Eastern rivers, and, until much later, not elsewhere.

About a thousand years thereafter, men began to extend civilized complexity to rain-watered land. The invention of the plow was here fundamental. It permitted ancient farmers to harness the strength of animals to the tasks of cultivation, and thereby allowed the individual farmer to increase his food production very substantially. This made available an agricultural surplus such as had previously been produced only on irrigated land. In addition, civilization demanded a distinctive social order. Rulers had to find ways to compel the cultivators to hand over their surplus crops in order to support the new courts and palace cities. A significant variation depended on sea trade, which allowed rulers of such an island as Crete to gather the fruits of the entire Mediterranean coastline and sustain a palace city at Knossos on the strength of trading profits.

A fourth great change in human relationships brought steppe pastoralists and warriors to the fore for the first time. This happened soon after 1700 B.C., when techniques of chariot warfare were perfected somewhere along the northern fringes of Mesopotamia. Chariots gave dominion to warriors who knew how to tame horses, and since the great center of horse raising was on the steppes, it was warrior tribes of central Asia and the Ukraine, speakers of Indo-European tongues, who reaped the principal advantage. These warriors overran all of Europe, western Asia, and India. Others, who had somehow acquired the techniques of chariot warfare, also conquered the peasants of the Yellow river valley in China.

In Europe, India, and China, interaction between pre-existing agricultural peoples and the new masters of the land laid the groundwork for the emergence of three new and enormously successful styles of civilization. The pace of their development was roughly comparable, so that by 500 B.C. a distinctive European type of civilization had emerged in Greece; an equally distinctive Indian style of civilization had appeared in the Ganges river valley; and along the middle reaches of the Yellow river, Chinese civilization had likewise asserted itself.

The Middle East had a more complicated history. The effect of the chariot conquest on Mesopotamia and Egypt was comparatively superficial, since local peoples soon learned how to use chariots to oust their conquerors. Three civilized empires, based in Egypt, Asia Minor, and northern Mesopotamia, then competed for supremacy in the Middle East until a new wave of barbarian invasion struck. The newcomers were equipped with iron (actually soft steel) weapons, and the great empires of the Bronze Age broke under the attack of tribesmen armed with the new and more abundant metal. But once again the effect of barbarian conquest was transitory. New empires arose, climaxing in the unstable political unification of the entire civilized area of the ancient Middle East, first under the Assyrians and then under the Persians.

As a result of this tangled development, what had once been separate civilizations in Egypt and Mesopotamia, as well as various satellite civilizations that had arisen on rain-watered land around and between

B.C.	EUROPE	EGYPT AND AFRICA	SYRIA, PALESTINE	MESOPOTAMIA, IRAN	INDIA	CHINA	OTHER

By 500,000 B.C. Emergence of various types of men and proto-men.
  30,000   Appearance of fully modern human types—*Homo sapiens*
   7500   Beginning of grain agriculture in Middle East.

3500

(left vertical margin: N E O L I T H I C   A G E | B R O N Z E   A G E | I R O N   A G E)

- **EUROPE**: neolithic grain farming
- **MESOPOTAMIA, IRAN**: **EMERGENCE OF CITIES IN SUMER**; *calendar*

3000
- **EGYPT AND AFRICA**: Menes; first dynasty; *solar calendar* — OLD KINGDOM
- **MESOPOTAMIA, IRAN**: *cuneiform writing*
- **OTHER**: root and rice cultivation in southeast Asia; maize in Mexico (perhaps earlier)

2500
- **EUROPE**: Kuban graves; *megalithic missionaries*; MINOAN CIVILIZATION
- **CHINA**: neolithic farmers in Yellow river valley
- **EGYPT AND AFRICA**: OLD KINGDOM

- **MESOPOTAMIA, IRAN**: Sargon of Akkad beginning of empire
- **EGYPT AND AFRICA**: MIDDLE KINGDOM
- **INDIA**: INDUS CIVILIZATION

2000
- **SYRIA, PALESTINE**: emergence of satellite civilizations on rain-watered land: Hittite, Canaanite, Elamite, Hurrian, etc.; Abraham leaves Ur for Canaan
- **EGYPT AND AFRICA**: Hyksos
- **MESOPOTAMIA, IRAN**: Hammurabi; Kassites

B A R B A R I A N   C H A R I O T E E R S
- **SYRIA, PALESTINE**: Mitanni

1500
- **EUROPE**: Achaeans; Mycenaean civilization; sack of Troy
- **EGYPT AND AFRICA**: *Akhnaton and Atonism*; sea peoples — NEW KINGDOM
- **SYRIA, PALESTINE**: Hittite empire; *Alphabetic Writing*; Hebrews, Philistines
- **MESOPOTAMIA, IRAN**: first Assyrian empire
- **INDIA**: Aryan invasion; "heroic age"
- **CHINA**: Shang dynasty; Anyang

I R O N   A G E   I N V A S I O N S

1000
- **EUROPE**: Dorians; Etruscans; *Homer?*
- **SYRIA, PALESTINE**: King David; King Solomon; foundation of Carthage
- **CHINA**: Chou dynasty; western Chou

A S S Y R I A N   E M P I R E
- **EUROPE**: Scyths; Celts; *Thales*; *Pythagoras*
- **INDIA**: Gangetic kingdoms
- **CHINA**: sack of Loyang; eastern Chou
- **SYRIA, PALESTINE**: *Hebrew prophets*

C A V A L R Y   R E V O L U T I O N
- **MESOPOTAMIA, IRAN**: Cyrus; Zoroaster

500

P E R S I A N   E M P I R E
- **EUROPE**: *Aeschylus*, *Pericles*, *Plato*, *Aristotle*
- **MESOPOTAMIA, IRAN**: Darius; Xerxes
- **INDIA**: **Buddha**
- **CHINA**: **Confucius**; warring states

A L E X A N D E R' S   E M P I R E
- **EUROPE**: Ptolemies
- **MESOPOTAMIA, IRAN**: Seleucids
- **INDIA**: **Mauryan Empire**
- **OTHER**: Dongson culture in southeast Asia

Hellenistic science
- **CHINA**: Shih Huang-ti; **HAN EMPIRE**
- **MESOPOTAMIA, IRAN**: Parthian Empire

R O M A N   E M P I R E

F I R S T   C L O S U R E   O F   T H E   E C U M E N E

the two great river valleys, all began to merge into a new cosmopolitan Middle Eastern style of life. A decisive formulation of a Middle Eastern world-view appropriate to this cosmopolitan civilization took place among the Jews, whose religion, as shaped by the prophets of the eighth to sixth centuries B.C., *was as vital and persuasive as the Buddhism of India, the Confucianism of China, or the philosophy of Greece, all of which also found their initial expression before the end of the sixth century* B.C. *With the clear and emphatic fourfold patterning of Old World civilization that thus came into focus by 500* B.C., *an initial, constitutive phase of world history came to a close.*

The aim of Part I of this book will be to explore this initial period of civilized history, when the main patterns of thought and conduct that governed most men's lives in later ages printed themselves upon human minds and feelings for the first time.

CHAPTER 1

In the Beginning

Human history begins with the emergence of *Homo sapiens* from proto-human populations. The process was undoubtedly very slow, but by about 100,000 years ago scattered hunting packs of biologically modern kinds of man roamed the savanna lands of Africa and perhaps also inhabited regions with suitably mild climates in Asia as well. These earliest human communities depended in large part on skills inherited from their proto-human ancestors. The use of wood and stone tools, for example, seems to have started long before fully human populations had come into existence. Elementary language, and habits of co-operation in the hunt, were also proto-human in their origin. So, perhaps, was the use of fire.

A longer infancy and childhood was what mainly distinguished fully human populations from the man-like creatures who flourished before them. This meant a longer time when the young depended on parents, and a correspondingly longer time when the elders could teach their offspring the arts of life. From the child's side, slower maturation meant prolonged plasticity and a much-increased capacity to learn. Enlarged learning capacities, in turn, increased the frequency of intentional preservation of inventions and discoveries made, presumably, more or less by accident. When this occurred cultural evolution began to outstrip the slow pace of biological evolution. Human behavior came to be governed far more by what men learned in society than by anything individuals inherited biologically through the marvelous mechanisms of the DNA molecules. When cultural evolution took over primacy from biological evolution, history in its strict and proper sense began.

The Earliest Men

‡‡‡ Nothing is known for sure about the spread of the earliest human populations from their cradleland, if indeed there was a single geographical center where modern man first evolved. Minor biological variations certainly arose—witness the racial differences among existing mankind. But when and where modern races defined themselves is unclear. Fortunately the historian can afford to neglect such questions because the variables that change human conduct through time do not seem to be related in any calculable way to biological variations among different human populations.

Even cultural differentiation may not at first have been very conspicuous. At any rate, hand axes and other stone tools show remarkable uniformity over wide areas of the Old World and across comparatively vast periods of time. Indeed, about nine-tenths of *Homo sapiens'* time on earth saw men confined to the life of hunters and gatherers, using simple tools of wood and stone, familiar with fire, and living so far as we can tell in an almost unchanging way from generation to generation.

Surviving stones, shaped to human purposes by skilled chipping and flaking, cannot reveal much about the life of their makers. Presumably, as long as men lived mainly by hunting, and supplemented animal flesh with whatever they could pick up—grubs and insects, edible roots, stalks, and seeds—they lived a roving life, like the few surviving primitive hunters of modern times. Very likely bands were small, numbering from twenty to sixty persons. Occasional contact with neighbors was certainly a feature of primitive life. Probably such contacts became regular ceremonies, when neighboring bands came together to celebrate the fact of survival and to transact unusual business. On such occasions, marriages might be arranged between members of different groups, and rare objects like cowry shells were certainly exchanged. Hostilities between neighboring bands probably also occurred, at least occasionally, but evidence is really lacking since surviving stone blades and axe heads could be used equally well for hunting animals or for killing other men.

Ecological Influences

‡‡‡ The apparent stability of the earliest hunting style of life suggests that adjustment to the environment became very exact. Each band inherited adequate customary responses to every situation that might arise. In the absence of important changes in the ecological balance of plants and animals within which early human hunters found their niche, human life might still adhere to the patterns of behavior appropriate to small, roving bands of hunters and gatherers. If so, human cultural evolution would have assumed a vastly slower pace, more akin to the rhythms of biological development from which it emerged than to the headlong rush of history.

In some important parts of the earth, however, the natural environment did not remain stable. Instead, climatic changes along the northern limits of human (and proto-human) habitation transformed the ecological background drastically and repeatedly, and in doing so presented men with a series of critical challenges to their powers of adaptation and invention. This in all probability was what unleashed the potentialities of cultural evolution from the tight mesh of use and wont that defined but also restricted the lives of ancient hunters.

The ecological changes that triggered human history are all related to the latest retreat of continental ice from the northern hemisphere. Glacial ice began to melt back from Europe and northern Asia and America about 30,000 years ago. On the bared ground, tundra and thin forest first developed. Along the Atlantic face of the Old World the drift of cyclonic storms across the warm waters of the Gulf Stream established a comparatively moist and equable climate in western Europe. As a result, vegetation grew lushly and sustained a large population of sub-arctic herbivores: mammoth, reindeer, bison, and many more. This in turn constituted a rich food resource for primitive men and other large-bodied predators to feed upon.

But before men could take advantage of these possibilities some basic inventions were needed. In particular, men had to learn how to sew skins together to make an artificial pelt that might keep even hairless humans warm in a very chilly landscape. This in turn required awls and something to serve as "thread"—perhaps sinews or thongs of raw hide. The necessary inventions were made, allowing bands of hunters who were skeletally all but indistinguishable from modern men to invade the tundra and forest of western Europe some 25–30,000 years ago. Earlier human or para-human populations, the so-called Neanderthal men, whose skeletal structure differed substantially from that of any surviving population, disappeared as the newcomers advanced.

Tools and weapons of stone are not the sole evidences of their life which these invading hunters left behind. For it was they who made the famous cave paintings of southern France, and who left other traces of their magico-religious ceremonies in the earth's dark recesses. What may have been the ideas that led hunters of perhaps 18,000 years ago to put images of their prey on the walls of deep dark caves cannot be known today. Very likely elaborate myths explained the relationships of men to the animals they killed. Perhaps the rites of caves were intended to encourage the animal spirits to increase and multiply on the face of the earth; but we can only guess.

The arctic big-game hunters of western Europe depended on the herds, and the herds depended on grass, mosses, and other vegetation. When the further retreat of the ice and the warming of the climate allowed thick forests to form, these food resources were cut off. The great herds disappeared and a new style of human life had to be worked out. The caves were abandoned and the men who had used them perhaps followed the dwindling sub-arctic herds northward and eastward as the ice retreated. In western Europe, forest browsers, like deer and cattle, arrived with the trees, and human hunters (perhaps new arrivals) quickly learned to prey upon them. But the hunting bands that spent their life pursuing deer and wild cattle left comparatively few traces in the archaeological record. Other populations, however, learned to exploit aquatic food resources by inventing simple boats, nets, and fish hooks. Geographically fixed communities thus developed, since boats had to come back to harbor and there were only certain spots where suitable shelter from storms could be found. Great rubbish piles, composed mainly of the remains of shellfish, accumulated on such sites. They allow modern archaeologists to study the sequence of occupation and to trace changes in tool assemblages through time.

Other parts of the world are far less well explored than western Europe, and it is not yet possible to reconstruct in any detail what happened elsewhere while these changes were taking place along the Old World's northwestern fringe. It seems probable that changes were not so drastic. Western Europe's shifting balance between glacial ice and the Gulf Stream induced far more radical alterations of climate and biosphere than occurred elsewhere; and so far as the still rather limited exploration allows us to guess, it appears that changes in human occupancy and modes of life in other parts of the world were correspondingly less drastic. An exception, perhaps, should be made for the Americas, for it was the melting back of the glacial ice that permitted bands of hunters to move up the Pacific coast of Asia and cross to Alaska. Thence they drifted southward until they penetrated all parts of the American continents and adjacent islands. Dates for the first human occupation of the New World are in dispute, but it is likely that the earliest hunting bands began to spread through North America about 20,000 years ago. Human occupation of the world's other habitable continent, Australia, appears to be much older, and probably goes back to a time when a land bridge united that continent with southeast Asia.

Changes Brought by Agriculture

‡‡‡ Primitive hunting bands had only recently reached Tierra del Fuego at the southernmost tip of South America at the time a new style of human life achieved clear definition in the general region of the Middle East. For it was probably between 8500 and 7000 B.C. that a few human communities located in the hilly region to the north and east of Mesopotamia began to reshape their natural environment by cultivating plants and domesticating animals. Wheat and barley were their most important crops; sheep and goats, their principal domesticated animals. The first food-producing communities preferred wooded ground. It was easy to kill any number of trees by cutting through the bark all round their trunks. This exposed the forest floor to sunlight, so that seeds planted in the loose leaf mold around the standing trunks of the dead trees could grow and flourish. Then after two or three crops had depleted the soil, fertility could be renewed by burning the dried-out trees and scattering the ashes over the ground. Nothing primitive

farmers could do prevented weeds from taking root in the plots they had cleared from the forest; and after a few years the self-seeded weeds began to crowd out the crop. The only response was to move on, clear a new plot from the forest, and start the cycle over again, letting the abandoned fields grow back to woods and slowly return to something like their original state. This sort of cultivation still survives in a few remote parts of the world. Geographers call it slash and burn agriculture.

The first farmers needed three implements which had been unimportant for hunters: an axe to cut into the trees, a hoe to stir the leaf mold for the reception of seed, and a sickle to harvest the ripened grain. A serviceable hoe could be made entirely of wood, and a sickle needed sharp cutting edges, not fundamentally different from those hunters needed for cutting and scraping animal carcasses. But the axe had to be tough enough to withstand the shock of heavy blows without shattering. Flint, which hunters had long been accustomed to chip into arrow heads and knife blades, was useless for such purposes for it was too brittle. Other kinds of rock, mainly granites and basalts, that were too tough to chip, had to be shaped into axe heads by a slow process of grinding and polishing. This created a distinctive "neolithic" or New Stone Age style of tool.

In addition, neolithic farmers developed a number of other important additions to the hunter's tool kit. Baskets and clay pots for storing grain and other possessions became important and, for people who were no longer constantly on the move, possible. Mudbrick houses, looms for making cloth, oven-fired pottery suitable for boiling cereals and other foods, and the arts of baking and brewing all came rapidly into use. The village community replaced the roving band as the fundamental unit of human society. The discipline of regular and laborious work in the fields, together with the need for measurement of time to identify the right season for planting, distinguished the farmer's from the hunter's style of life. Foresight and restraint were also needed, for even in a time of hunger it was necessary to save a proper amount of seed grain to assure future harvests. Courage and habits of violence, so necessary for hunters, had little importance for farmers.

Finally, human numbers vastly increased when men ceased to be mere predators upon the natural environment. Instead of remaining a rather rare species, men became numerous enough to alter the natural balance of plant and animal life radically, partly by intention and partly in ways quite unforeseen and unintended.

Somewhere in monsoon Asia a type of agriculture centered upon root crops seems to have arisen independently of the Middle Eastern style of grain-centered cultivation. Many experts also suppose that food production originated independently in the Americas, in east Asia, and in west Africa. Archaeological investigation has not yet shown clearly when and how cultivation began in these regions, and since the earliest farmers usually left very slight traces behind them, it may never be possible to reconstruct the geographical and chronological facts precisely.

The Earliest Civilization

‡‡‡ Nevertheless, Middle Eastern grain agriculture and domesticated animals deserve to be accorded a special place in human history, for it was from this style of life that the first civilization emerged.

The earliest known settlements that surpassed simple villages were located at places in the ancient Middle East where unusually precious and rare commodities could be found. Jericho, for example, commanded access to the salt of the Dead Sea; and when men shifted to a cereal diet they began to need salt to maintain fluid balances in their bodies. Access to such a vital commodity became precious enough that a walled city grew up at Jericho almost as soon as farming spread widely through adjacent regions; that is, after about 7000 B.C. Another early center was in Asia Minor at Catal Hüyük, where volcanic glass, known as obsidian, could be found. Obsidian, when fractured, produced unusually sharp cutting edges, and was therefore also precious. Accordingly, a trade center much resembling Jericho arose at this site about 6000 B.C.

Yet these isolated "cities" were intrinsically incapable of expansion, depending, as they did, on a monopoly or near-monopoly of some rare commodity. Civilization, to be capable of spreading, needed a broader ecological base than anything attainable at Jericho or Catal Hüyük. This the land of Sumer provided. It lay along the lower reaches of the Tigris and Euphrates rivers on the flat alluvial plain bordering the Persian Gulf. Primitive farming techniques had to be radically altered before the annually renewed river silt from which the land of Sumer was built could be made to produce rich crops. In the forested hills of the Middle East enough rain fell in early summer to sustain the growing grain until the harvest. This was not the case further south, where summer rains almost never fell. Hence, only by bringing river water to the fields to irrigate the crops could a harvest be assured. But the construction and maintenance of irrigation canals and dikes called for the massed labor of hundreds or thousands of men and for a much tighter social discipline than had prevailed in the earliest farming communities. In neolithic villages it is likely that the small biological family constituted the ordinary working unit. Each family normally consumed the produce of its own plot or plots of cropland, and there was no need of organized co-operation among larger numbers, save perhaps on ceremonial, religious occasions. Everyone was equally enslaved to the vagaries of the weather, and all were equally free, since the principal dif-

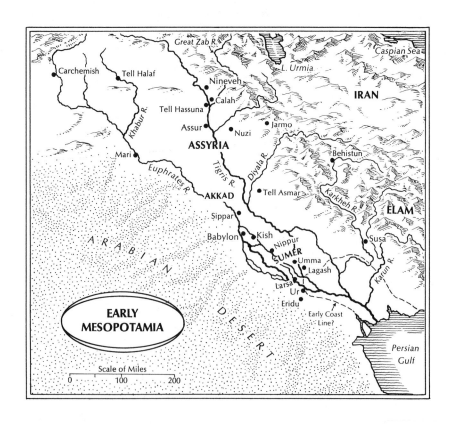

ferentiation was between age groups and the two sexes. This simple social structure altered radically in the river bank environment. For the scale of human effort necessary for controlling the river's waters required that the labor of the majority of the people be directed by some sort of managerial elite.

How a managerial class first arose is not certain. Conquest of one people by another may have divided society between masters and servants, managers and managed. On the other hand, experts in the supernatural, whose special status was certainly age-old in human society, may have begun a far-ranging process of functional specialization. In subsequent times Mesopotamian myths explained that gods had created men to be their slaves, so that food and clothing and the other necessities of a well-appointed divine household—i.e. a temple—would be provided for the god's enjoyment without his having to take the trouble of producing them.

We also know a little about how these ideas were applied in practice. Thus, at Lagash an inscription divides the land of the city into three categories, depending on what sort of dues its possessors owed the god. Very likely the heaviest dues did not leave the farmers enough to eat. This then made it necessary for them to work for the god during part of the year, i.e. to labor on irrigation works or at some other project planned by the priests. In this way some of the grain and other agricultural products paid into the temple by farmers were paid out again as wages for work that was done at the direction of the god's personal servants, i.e., the priests.

Such a system obviously permitted the labor of thousands of men to be concentrated for carrying through big projects. It also permitted specialization, for many different experts—dancers, singers, goldsmiths, cooks, carpenters, architects, clothmakers—employed all their skills in feeding, dressing, amusing and worshipping the god with the sort of pomp and luxury needed to assure the divine good pleasure. Because they no longer had to spend any time producing their own food, these experts were able to develop skills and knowledge far greater than men had ever before attained. Civilization thereby came into existence in a short thousand years, between about 4000 B.C., when the first settlements appeared in the lower Tigris-Euphrates valley, and 3000 B.C., when written records that can be read by modern scholars start to cast a fitful light upon the social and intellectual sides of Sumerian culture.

Sumerian Inventions

‡‡‡ Technical developments were at first very rapid. Bronze metallurgy, wheel-spun pottery, wheeled vehicles, sailing vessels, sculpture, monumental buildings, and—perhaps most important of all—the plow, appear almost simultaneously in the archaeological record. A distinctive art style, best exemplified for us by the thousands of surviving seal engravings, also defined itself rather quickly. Other skills that left no traces for modern archaeologists certainly accompanied these developments. Weaving and dying of woolen textiles, for example, which later provided Mesopotamian cities with a major export commodity, and the elaborate pageantry of temple services must date back to the very beginning of Sumerian civilization. In addition, the arts of measurement assumed unparalleled importance and precision. Construction of canals and dikes and of monumental temple structures, raised high above the plain like artificial mountains, called for precise measurement and careful planning.

Far more critical, however, was the measurement of time, for the fundamental rhythm of the farming year depends on knowing when to plant. The moon's waxing and waning is the most conspicuous marker of elapsed time; but the cycles of the moon do not fit evenly into the solar year, and the priests had therefore to observe, measure, and correlate the movements of both the sun and the moon before a reliable calendar could be created. The maintenance of such a calendar may, indeed, have been the most important service priests offered early cultivators. Knowledge necessary to maintain a calendar also constituted an important basis for priestly pre-eminence in society. Ordinary farmers perhaps felt that men who could foreknow the seasons thereby demonstrated their special relation with the gods and deserved to be obeyed. It is possible that the organization of irrigation works, with all the technical and social consequences that flowed from that departure, was begun under the direction of priests whose social leadership rested, in large part, on their ability to predict the seasons.

Religion

‡‡‡ Another basis of priestly power and prestige was the fact that they knew all about the gods and how to please them—or, if that proved

impossible, how to appease them. Sacred songs and how to sing them; holy rituals and how to perform them: these were the main elements of priestly lore. But the Sumerian priests were not simply content to repeat what others had said and done before. At some time, probably near the beginning of civilized development, they worked out a systematic doctrine about how the gods ruled the world. We know about their ideas from poems written down much later, and it is possible that only concepts that appealed to men about 1800 B.C.—when most of such texts were first put into writing—were recorded. But even if ancient Sumerian religion may have included some crude and primitive elements—we know, for instance, that an early king of Ur was accompanied to his grave by wives and courtiers who seem to have been buried alive—it still remains true that the ancient priests worked out a consistent theological system to explain both natural and human phenomena.

The basic idea was simple. Major natural forces were personified —treated, that is, as though they were human, but with enormously greater power, including the power of eternal life. Each such personified force or god took his (or her) place in a divine political society, ruled over by Anu, god of the sky. Each year the great gods met on New Year's day to decide what would happen that year. Individual gods might be overruled. For example, some disaster might be decreed for a particular city, even though the god resident in that city was well disposed toward the people who served him and did not wish to see them hurt. But even a god had to give in to the will of the whole community of gods; and when fate for the year had been decided, not even a god could undo it. Enlil, god of Storm and of Thunder, was the chief executor of the gods' will. He punished and brought disaster according to the decision made each New Year.

Each god was thought of as entirely human in his character. He lived in a house—the temple; and inhabited a cult statue just as a man's soul inhabited his body. Sometimes the god's spirit might be away—as a man's soul might wander in dreams; but there were ways to call the absent god back to his statue when some particularly important question had to be asked of him. He replied by signs and omens: such things as the flight of birds or the shape of a sacrificed sheep's liver could tell the experts what the god meant. Every day he had to be fed, amused, praised. In special festivals there were extra rituals in which the people as a whole might take part as spectators. And if the signs and omens pointed to disaster, there were still other rituals that might turn away the god's wrath in time.

As long as one accepts the basic assumption about the nature of the gods and their relations among themselves and with men, the system was self-confirming. A ready explanation for everything that could happen was at hand: if signs and omens promised a disaster that did not come, it only proved that the preventive measures the priests had taken were effective; and if disaster came unannounced, it merely meant that the god had not chosen to forewarn his people.

Such a set of beliefs proved very powerful. For three thousand years priests in Mesopotamia continued to elaborate upon ideas and rituals worked out by the Sumerians at the beginning of civilized history. Moreover, numerous barbarian peoples were convinced that the great gods of the Sumerian pantheon did indeed rule the world. Among them were the ancient inhabitants of the steppe lands of eastern Europe and western Asia whose descendants—Greeks, Romans, Celts, Germans, and Slavs—continued to honor gods of sky, thunder, sun, moon, and the rest whose powers and character had first been defined by the speculations of ancient Sumerian priests.

Writing

‡‡‡ From the point of view of subsequent history, the most remarkable priestly invention traceable to Sumer was the discovery of means whereby spoken words could be recorded. This was done by making marks on soft clay with a sharp reed end. If a permanent record was wanted, an all but indestructible document could easily be produced by baking the freshly imprinted clay in a hot oven. It is to such baked clay tablets that we owe all our detailed knowledge of ancient Mesopotamia. The script that slowly emerged from this practice is called cuneiform, i.e. wedge-shaped.

At first, Sumerian priests used writing mainly to record deposits in and withdrawals from temple storehouses. A persistent problem for this kind of record keeping was how to find ways to keep track of the names of the men who engaged in these transactions. Eventually the problem was solved by punning. Syllables in a man's name that sounded like an easily pictured word were written down. Soon such picture signs came to mean the sound, not the thing, and could be used to record the appropriate syllable-sound in any context. By developing enough standard syllable pictures the scribes could then record all the sounds of ordinary speech. Writing of complete sentences, and of sacred stories, religious invocations, laws, contracts, and many other sorts of documents thus became possible soon after 3000 B.C.

Conventionally, and not without reason, historians use the invention of writing to mark the divide between prehistory and history. Since writing that can be read by modern scholars allows a much deeper insight into the activities of men long since vanished from the earth, this distinction still makes sense, despite all the advances of archaeology which have recently blurred the sharp demarcation that once existed between these epochs.

It is possible, and some think probable, that all known forms of writing derive directly or indirectly from the Sumerian script. Whether or not that is the case, it remains true that the effort Sumerian priests made to record unambiguously just who had and had not paid his debts to the god called forth the world's earliest known form of writing, thereby vastly increasing human capacity to store and retrieve accurate information. Effective management of civilized societies subsequently depended in large measure on the enhanced capacity for information processing that writing allows.

Irrigation

‡‡‡ By about 3000 B.C., when written records begin to allow a more detailed knowledge of ancient Sumer, water engineering had attained very considerable elaboration. All the readily irrigable land had already been brought under cultivation. A dozen or more cities, each with several thousand inhabitants, dotted the irrigated landscape, and within each city the god's house or temple constituted by far the largest and grandest structure. Nippur appears to have enjoyed a certain primacy among Sumerian cities. Priests from all parts of Sumer probably gathered there from time to time at the temple of Enlil, god of the storm. Exchange of news and views, and the transaction of all sorts of business affecting neighboring cities, presumably took place on such occasions. The cohesion and uniformity of Sumerian civilization could scarcely have been maintained in any other fashion.

When quarrels broke out between adjacent cities, no doubt the conferences of priests attempted to adjudicate the points of dispute. But as Sumerian water engineering approached its geographical and technical limits, quarrels were bound to become really serious, because as irrigation canals became larger and longer every new withdrawal from the rivers began to affect the water supply available downstream. Peaceable adjudication of disputes over water rights, which in a dry season might quickly become a matter of life and death, was therefore not always possible. As a result, war between neighboring cities, and presently among rival coalitions of cities, became an important and recurring feature of Sumerian life. In addition, defense against outer barbarians was always difficult. The river valleys lay wide open on all sides to hostile assault, and the wealth so spectacularly accumulated through irrigation and specialization of artisan skills made the Sumerian cities worthwhile objects of attack.

Military Force and Monarchy

‡‡‡ As a result, by 3000 B.C. Sumerian cities had developed a military organization that rivaled priestly leadership. Kingship may initially have been based upon a theory that the gods delegated someone as their representative among men. In times of peace such a dignitary would be chief priest; but in time of war he had either to lead the army in person or else find some younger and more vigorous man to do so on his (and the gods') behalf. When warlike relations between adjacent cities became normal, the importance of military leadership increased at the expense of ritual and other peacetime functions. Sometimes frictions arose between priestly and military leaders. War's demands were insatiable when rivals still threatened and decisive victory had not been won. But clearly, there was no possibility of decisive victory as long as the separate cities of the Sumerian plain maintained their independence. Only a single administration empowered to distribute water and settle other quarrels among the various cities could end civil strife. Such an imperial state might also reasonably be expected to hold the barbarians of the borderlands in awe through the overwhelming force it could assemble in case of provocation.

The great difficulty lay in devising means whereby a single monarch could effectively control distant parts of his domain. The earliest great conquerors appear to have kept a large military household around their persons at all times. In order to maintain a following of several thousand armed men, rulers like Sargon of Akkad (*c.* 2350 B.C.) found it necessary to travel from place to place all the time. A steady income of plunder from hostile communities was probably also essential. Such a predatory regime was inherently precarious. Any military reverse encouraged local communities to refuse to admit the monarch's armed men when next they knocked at the city gates. But the only alternative was to scatter garrisons out among the subject communities to assure their obedience; and this meant the dispersal of the monarch's striking force, and endangered his superiority in the field over local rivals. Moreover, garrisons stationed for long periods of time away from the king's person might cease to obey the distant monarch's commands, even when such commands could be reliably transmitted to them.

In the face of such difficulties ancient Sumer never attained peace for very long. Deep-seated local loyalties to the separate cities within which Sumerian civilization had originally developed undermined all efforts at imperial unification, and shifting coalitions and alliances among rival cities failed to balance each other off so exactly as to prevent frequent resort to war. Thus the problem of maintaining peace at home and an effective guard against outsiders was never solved. Nevertheless, just because the problem remained critically important, it provided the principal growing point for Sumerian as well as for later Mesopotamian civilization. Improved weapons and more massive, better organized military forces were one result. Administrative and political devices for controlling men at a distance were another. Some of these Sumerian inventions have remained fundamental to civilized governments ever since, for such basic elements as published law codes, bureaucratic appointment to office, and official postal services all date back to ancient Mesopotamia. There are even traces of official propaganda designed to convince people that the land of Sumer had "always" been united under the supreme jurisdiction of one god and one king.

Long before the inadequacy of these devices for maintaining peace and order had been fully demonstrated, important aspects of Sumer's civilization attracted the attention of neighbors far and near and stimulated them to alter their own ways in the light of Sumerian achievements. A survey of the first phase of the impact of Sumerian civilization upon strangers and foreigners will therefore engage our attention in the next chapter.

CHAPTER 2

Diffusion of Civilization:
First Phase to 1700 B.C.

Between about 4000 and 1700 B.C. human societies were affected by the spread of two concentric disturbances. It was as though at about a three-thousand-year interval stones had been dropped into the middle of a pond. Geographical and social irregularities meant that the propagation of the two successive waves did not follow an exact geometric pattern, but instead darted ahead here, lapped round an island of conservatism there, or somewhere else stopped short in face of an impenetrable climatic barrier. Yet despite such complexities, the simile is useful. Within all the variety of landscape in Europe, Asia, and Africa, the Middle Eastern sort of slash and burn farming continually spread to new ground, wherever temperature, rainfall, and natural forest cover permitted. Then, some distance behind, more complex societies which we can properly call civilized also established themselves successfully on new, especially hospitable ground.

Pastoralism

‡‡‡ As slash and burn grain cultivation spread, and the number of persons dependent on this mode of life increased, two important modifica-

tions of the earliest farming pattern assumed major importance. First, in the great steppe region of Eurasia, lying north of the hill and mountain zone where agriculture had arisen initially, there were few trees and correspondingly few locations naturally suited to slash and burn cultivation. On the other hand, the wide grasslands that gave the steppe its special character were particularly well suited for the maintenance of herds of domesticated animals. Hence, hunters of the steppe, when confronted with the array of skills the earliest farmers had developed, were making an effective adjustment to their geographical environment when they accepted animal domestication and rejected the laborious digging and harvesting which grain cultivation required.

A distinctive pastoral style of life thus emerged, acquainted with agriculture but disdainful of it. A similar, though hotter and dryer, environment existed south of the mountains, where the grasslands shade off into desert throughout a great arc north of the Arabian peninsula. In this zone too, pastoralism developed as a variant of neolithic farming techniques. The assortment of domesticated animals in the southern region tended to differ from the larger-bodied beasts favored in the north. Sheep, goats, and donkeys could better withstand the shortages of summer fodder inherent in a semi-desert climate than could cattle and horses, whose greater size helped them to survive the winter cold of the northern steppe.

The emergence of pastoralism as a distinct mode of life on the northern and southern flanks of the agricultural world cannot be dated precisely. Probably no large number of people lived as pastoralists before 3000 B.C. Long after that time, adaptation to nomadic life on the steppe was not complete. Such an apparently simple technique as riding on horseback, for example, did not become common until after 900 B.C., perhaps because a life in the saddle demanded a breed of horse that could be trained to allow men on their backs without taking fright—and of men who kept on trying to break horses for riding, even when the first result was nothing but wild bucking and a nasty fall onto the ground.

Pastoralists, like hunters, were parasites upon herbivores. They were like hunters, too, in pursuing a wandering life, moving comparatively large distances in search of grass for their animals. Pastoralists often followed a more or less regular migration pattern, moving from lowland to upland pastures with the seasons of the year. Above all else, shepherds and herdsmen had to protect their herds from rival carnivores, whether those rivals were animals or other men. Such a life required a chief, who could decide the route of march and take command of the entire community in time of emergency whenever rivals attempted to invade the community's traditional pasture lands or attack the flocks and herds.

Warlike organization and habits of violence characteristic of successful big-game hunters remained near the surface of such a life, whereas the earliest farming communities were remarkably peaceable

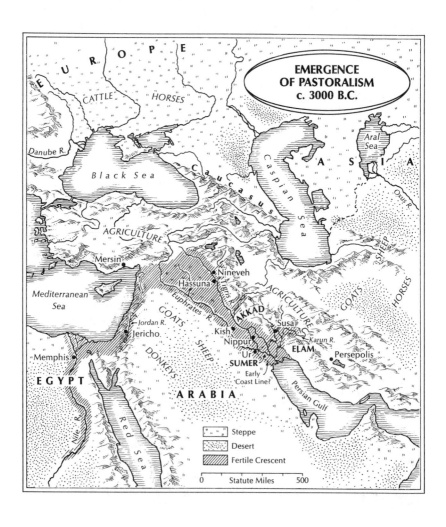

and egalitarian. This contrast gave pastoralists a distinct advantage in any military collision with farmers. Indeed, pastoralists enjoyed so great an advantage that they were always tempted to try to domesticate their fellow men by conquering and exploiting them as they did their animals.

The subsequent history of mankind in the Old World turned upon an interplay between the superior numbers made possible by farming and the superior politico-military organization required by pastoralism. This balance tipped sometimes in favor of one side, sometimes in favor of the other, depending on ups and downs of social organization and cohesion, and on developments in technology. The occasional appearance of a great conqueror and empire builder or the outbreak of devastating plague also played their part in disturbing the balance from time to time. Everywhere and always major shifts in the relation between farmers and herdsmen harrowed and disturbed human society, but bloody collisions between the two divergent ways of life also pricked men on to make experiments in living they might otherwise have never ventured. After about 3000 B.C. the pace of social evolution all across the Old World was, therefore, vastly accelerated.

The Plow

‡‡‡ The invention of the plow also altered and diversified the texture of human life in a very significant way. Somewhere, sometime before 3000 B.C, but perhaps not long before, men learned how to harness the strength of their animals to the tasks of tillage. This had several important consequences. It united grain growing and animal husbandry as never before, making each dependent on the other. It also imparted to the Middle Eastern style of farming—which thus achieved a mature definition—some important advantages over other types of cultivation.

First of all, the plow allowed grain-growers to settle permanently in one spot. Obviously as the number of farming communities multiplied, forest land suitable for slash and burn cultivation became more and more difficult to find. One response was to migrate from the original centers in the hilly country of the Middle East, thus spreading agriculture in all directions. But the farming communities that remained behind had to return at more and more frequent intervals to fields that had already been tilled. Under such circumstances the luxuriant fertility of virgin soil could no longer be expected. Plowing, however, allowed men to cultivate far more land than they could hope to do with hoes and digging sticks, so that by gathering a less abundant crop from more land the farmer could maintain or even increase his food supply.

Moreover, it was soon discovered that a fallow field, i.e. a field that was plowed but not planted with grain, could grow a satisfactory crop of grain the next year, since competing weeds could be destroyed by plowing the fallow before they had time to seed themselves. By alternating cropland and fallow, therefore, a plowman could maintain himself indefinitely in one spot. The lessened fertility of plowed acres as compared with the virgin soil used by slash and burn cultivators was partly made up for by a more systematic and convenient layout of fields. Stumps, after all, seriously obstruct uniform, careful cultivation, even with a hoe. Indeed, what we conceive a field to be—a comparatively smooth, uniformly cultivated piece of land in which a single kind of seed is usually planted—was the creation of the plow, whose size and awkwardness in turning, together with its inability to adjust to the small hummocks and hollows characteristic of a forest floor, required men to remake the landscape far more drastically than the forest farmers had done.

Small, rectangular fields began to appear all over the Middle East as a result of plowing the same soil time after time. As this occurred, Middle Eastern farmers often found themselves able to raise a considerable surplus of food even on land not refreshed by river silt or watered by irrigation channels. In such societies animal power had so effectually begun to supplement merely human muscles that a few men could be spared from the immediate tasks of feeding themselves. This made civilization possible, even beyond the limits of irrigation. And it was not long, as we shall see presently, before the new possibility of creating and sustaining civilized types of society on rain-watered land was acted upon in regions suitably close to the original seat of civilized life.

Thus between 3500 and 2500 B.C. the rise of pastoral communities on the one hand and of plowing villages on the other greatly enriched the variety of human styles of life and prepared the ground for a geographically massive spread of civilization to all regions of the Eurasian continent and North Africa where temperatures and rainfall permitted the growing of grain on a large scale.

Egyptian Civilization

‡‡‡ Prior to about 2500 B.C., however, the spread of civilized forms of society required very special geographical circumstances. Only in irrigable river valleys could the techniques then known support the corps of specialists needed if civilized levels of skill and knowledge were to be attained. Several smallish rivers within fairly short range of Sumer met these requirements. The Jordan, for example, and the Karun river, which today flows into the Tigris near its mouth but in ancient times made its independent way to the Persian Gulf, both saw very ancient cities rise along their banks; and it is probable that archaeologists will uncover others like them elsewhere. But these river valleys were too small to become seats of a society massive enough to stand comparison with Sumer, or with the other antique civilizations that were arising simultaneously in the Nile and Indus valleys.

Until the 1930's, the civilization of Egypt was believed to be the most ancient of the earth. But Egyptologists now agree that Sumer, whose antiquity was first uncovered in the 1920's, came first. The traditional beginning of Egyptian history was the unification of Upper and Lower Egypt under King Menes. This occurred sometime between about 3000 B.C. and 2850 B.C., at a time when Sumerian cities already had several centuries of development behind them.

Small but unmistakable traces of Sumerian influence upon the earliest phases of Egyptian civilized development have been recognized. It seems probable, therefore, that seafarers from the head of the Persian Gulf made their way around Arabia to the Red Sea and there came into contact with the peoples inhabiting the narrow Nile valley. Techniques and ideas already familiar to the Sumerians were of particular value to the early Egyptians, who were living in an environment similar to that of the lower Tigris-Euphrates. Irrigation, metallurgy, writing, the plow, wheeled vehicles, and monumental buildings had all appeared in Mesopotamia by the time of Menes. All, in short order, were fitted to Egyptian use by a dramatically rapid process of imitation and adaptation.

Egypt's political unification promoted rapid acceptance of those el-

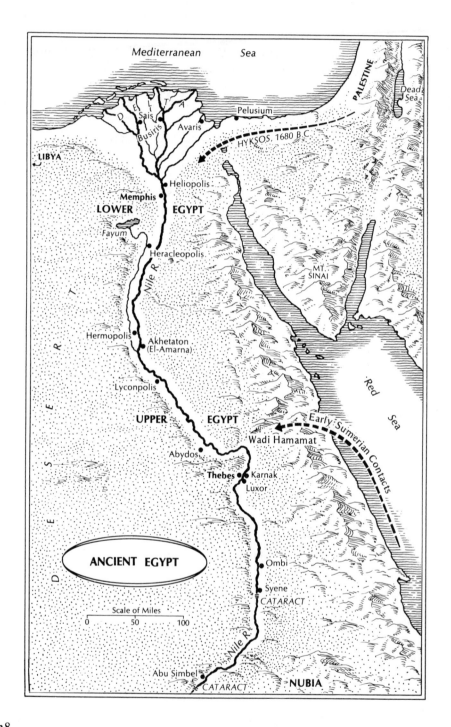

Mediterranean Sea

PALESTINE

Dead Sea

DELTA

Sais

Busiris

Avaris

Pelusium

HYKSOS, 1680 B.C.

LIBYA

Heliopolis

Memphis

LOWER **EGYPT**

Fayum

Heracleopolis

MT. SINAI

Nile R.

Hermopolis

Akhetaton
(El-Amarna)

Lyconpolis

DESERT

UPPER **EGYPT**

Wadi Hamamat

Early Sumerian Contacts

Red Sea

Abydos

Thebes · Karnak

Luxor

DESERT

ANCIENT EGYPT

Ombi

Syene

CATARACT

Scale of Miles

0   50   100

Nile R.

Abu Simbel

CATARACT

NUBIA

ements in the Sumerian tool kit that appealed to the Egyptians, while elements incompatible with local tradition or geographical conditions were repudiated. In other words, Egyptian civilization came rapidly into existence, with a stylistic coherence and institutional framework of its own. What had taken a thousand years or longer in Mesopotamia required less than half as much time in Egypt, thanks to the advantage the Egyptians had of being able to profit from Sumerian experience.

The Egyptians did not simply imitate Sumerian models; they adapted and altered everything to fit local taste. This is well illustrated by the differences between early Egyptian writing, known as hieroglyphic, and the cuneiform of Sumer. Egyptians used different materials for writing and a different set of syllabic signs as well. As a result, there is no resemblance at all in actual forms of the script. The only link is the idea of how to record sounds by breaking abstract words into syllabic elements. Egyptian art is similarly independent of Sumerian models, sharing only the idea of monumental, mathematically exact structures and sculpture in stone. Similar stylistic uniqueness ran through all aspects of Egyptian high culture.

In general, one may say that deep-seated differences between Egyptian and Sumerian social structures made the early expressions of Egyptian civilization both more nearly perfect and more fragile. Everything in Egypt focused upon the court of the god-king or Pharaoh. In Sumer, the gods were believed to be invisible, though man-like in their needs and traits of character and behavior. The Egyptians, on the other hand, declared their king to be a god. Immortal himself, he could also confer immortality upon other men. Here was a powerful motive for obeying the Pharaoh, since a grateful god-king might be expected to reward those who had served him well in this life by graciously allowing them to share his divine immortality as ever faithful servants. Defiance of the Pharaoh, on the other hand, forfeited all hope of life after death.

The Old Kingdom

‡‡‡ The peculiar geographical conditions of the Nile valley also helped political centralization. Barren deserts on both flanks of the Nile made the valley almost immune from any really dangerous foreign attack. Occasional raids by the Nubians from the south or by Libyans

from the west lacked the weight of numbers that made barbarian attack such a serious problem in Mesopotamia. Moreover, within the valley itself, the slow, stately Nile current could carry boats northward
without difficulty, while the return trip could be made almost as simply by raising sails to catch the north-to-northeast wind that blows
across Egypt nearly all the time. Shipping up and down the Nile was
so easy that it eclipsed all other forms of transport. No part of the fertile soil was far from the river's edge, and from almost any place along
the bank a ship could carry goods or men upstream or downstream all
the way from the marshy delta at the river's mouth to the first cataract. Under these circumstances, to control the shipping on the river
was to control the entire country. And it is in the nature of things that
vessels moving upstream and downstream are easier to manage and
check up on than is any form of overland transport that does not have
to follow definite routes. Hence, devices for upholding a central, imperial administration which were painfully and imperfectly developed in
Mesopotamia were not really needed in Egypt. The divine ruler, with
a few obedient and eager servants stationed at intervals along the river,
could command the entire country without difficulty.

When Menes first united Upper and Lower Egypt, two separate
royal households managed their respective portions of the kingdom;
but eventually Egypt's two halves were brought under a single administration. In effect, the divine Pharaoh's household acted like a Sumerian
temple, concentrating surplus agricultural products from up and down
the navigable length of the Nile river in a single spot. Thereby, overwhelming power could be sustained at Pharaoh's court. Egypt thus
solved the problem of internal peace and order which proved so stubbornly insoluble in Sumer.

The Pharoah's household also constituted the principal framework
within which Egyptian civilization took form. Artisans and administrators attached to the god-king's household summoned the pyramids into
being and originated the scarcely less wonderful conventions of Egyptian art within three to four hundred years after Menes' conquest.
Hieroglyphic writing, glazed tiles and pots, exquisite carpentry, together with music and dancing and other skills less well known from
archaeological remains, all grew up within the same royal household. If
such skills existed elsewhere at all, they did so only in pale and imperfect provincial forms.

Such concentration upon a single center had the advantages that large-scale enterprise always has. The great pyramids, for example, could be built only by mustering the rural manpower of all Egypt during the season of the year when no work needed to be done in the fields; and only a single commanding center such as the Pharaoh's court could do so. On the other hand, the rigorously centralized regime of ancient Egypt was inevitably fragile too. Everything depended on the willingness of men far removed from the Pharaoh's presence to obey him or his agents. Throughout a period of about four hundred years, during the period of the Old Kingdom (*c.* 2600–2200 B.C.), this appears nonetheless to have been effectively the case, save for brief periods of transition from one dynasty to another.

Even at the height of the Old Kingdom, sharp local diversity lay just beneath the surface of Pharaonic power. This is particularly evident in the religious confusion of ancient Egypt. Local gods, often conceived in animal or semi-human forms, commanded local loyalties, and nothing like the coherence of the Sumerian pantheon ever emerged. Local sanctuaries and priesthoods presumably preserved these incompatible pieties. In course of time some of them began to develop elaborate ceremonies and started to construct buildings comparable in scale to those of the ancient temples of Mesopotamia.

Nevertheless, it was not disobedient priesthoods but rebellious local officials who ultimately disrupted the centralization of the Egyptian government. The educated class of scribes, who recorded their dismay at the disintegration of Pharaonic order, felt that the political break up of Egypt was profoundly wrong. Nevertheless, for more than a century after 2200 B.C. the country remained politically divided, as Mesopotamia had been almost always.

A sharp decay of most aspects of the Egyptian civilization resulted. Local rulers did their best to maintain high art and other attributes of the Pharaonic dignity, but lesser resources meant the decay of luxury and often of expertise as well. Yet even in time of outward disorder and political division, memories of Pharaonic civilization survived. The splendors of the Old Kingdom had rooted its ideals firmly in the soil of the Nile valley.

The Middle Kingdom

‡‡‡ Hence it is not surprising that after nearly two centuries of political division, Egypt was again united (*c.* 2000 B.C.) by a new conqueror

from the south who made his capital not at Memphis, near the apex of the Nile delta, but far upstream, at Thebes. The so-called Middle Kingdom, thus established, lasted until about 1800 B.C. when the land of Egypt once again broke up into local and competing sovereignties, each ruler claiming to be the legitimate Pharaoh of all the land.

Art styles and other records suggest that the rulers of the Middle Kingdom set out deliberately to model themselves on the achievements of the Pharaohs of the Old Kingdom. Yet there were important differences. Temple architecture became more and more elaborate. Local landlords and magnates, whether priests or laymen, continued to enjoy far greater importance than had been the case in the days of the Old Kingdom. Egyptian society and civilization therefore became less dependent upon a single center, and correspondingly more capable of surviving political disaster. Yet these advantages were purchased at the cost of the loss of the supreme artistic refinement and stylistic coherence which had characterized the culture of the Old Kingdom at its height (i.e. c. 2600–2400 B.C.).

In view of the fact that the next major landmark of Egyptian history was conquest in force by barbarian strangers from Asia known as Hyksos, this dispersion of cultural leadership during the Middle Kingdom was probably critically important for the survival of the Egyptian style of civilization. Had a single Pharaonic household still, as in the days of the Old Kingdom, comprised the entire circle of Egyptian expertise, its destruction might also have destroyed Egyptian civilization: but before the Hyksos appeared, this risk had been removed through multiplication of lesser centers of specialized skill and knowledge within the structure of Egyptian society itself.

The Indus Civilization

‡‡‡ Far less is known of the other great civilization that emerged in the third millennium B.C. in the Indus valley. The script used by the Indus peoples cannot be read by modern scholars, so that an all-important avenue for understanding the Indus culture is still closed. Archaeological investigation of Indus sites is also incomplete, and some of the digging that was done was done poorly. Nevertheless, certain deductions seem legitimate from what has already been discovered. The Indus civilization had two great urban capitals, one located at Harappa

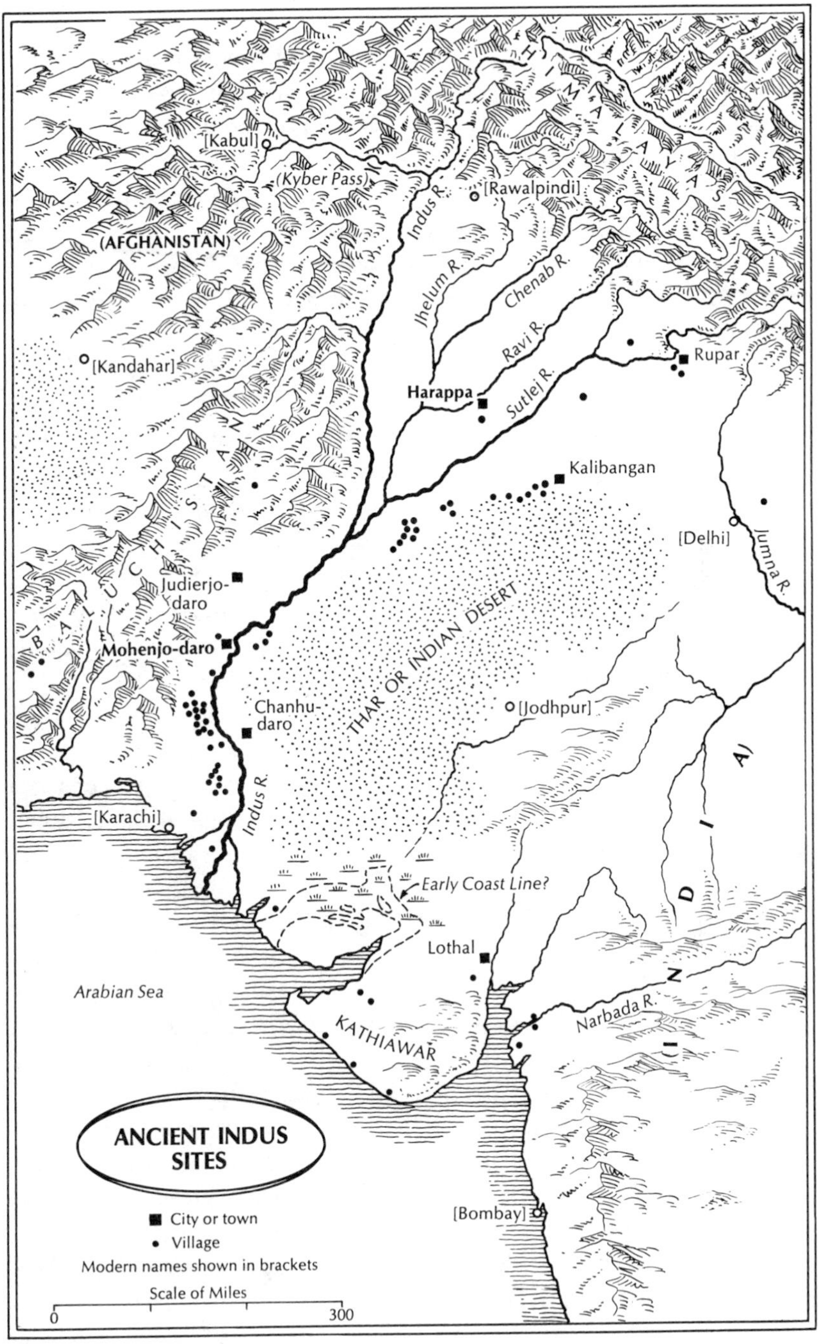
[Kabul]
(Kyber Pass)
[Rawalpindi]
HIMALAYAS
(AFGHANISTAN)
Indus R.
Jhelum R.
Chenab R.
Ravi R.
Sutlej R.
[Kandahar]
Harappa
Rupar
Kalibangan
BALUCHISTAN
[Delhi]
Jumna R.
Judierjo-daro
Mohenjo-daro
THAR OR INDIAN DESERT
Chanhu-daro
[Jodhpur]
[Karachi]
Indus R.
Early Coast Line?
Lothal
Arabian Sea
KATHIAWAR
Narbada R.
(INDIA)
ANCIENT INDUS SITES
City or town
Village
Modern names shown in brackets
[Bombay]
Scale of Miles
0
300

and the other several hundred miles downstream at Mohenjo-daro. Political unification, analogous to that of Egypt in the days of the Old Kingdom, offers the best explanation for the remarkable uniformity that characterizes these two cities.

Contact with Sumer is certain, since seals and other small objects of Indus manufacture have been discovered in Mesopotamia in strata dating from about 2500 B.C. In all probability sea-borne contact with Sumer therefore played the same role in accelerating the growth of Indus civilization as it did in the earliest stage of Egyptian development. Just as in Egypt, the art style and mode of writing developed by the Indus peoples apparently bore no relation to Sumerian models. Stimulus to develop their own distinctive styles of life was what Egyptian and Indus peoples took from the Sumerians. Only at the very start, before local styles had been defined, can traces of direct imitation or awkward mimicry of Sumerian techniques be expected. Examples of such imitiation have been found in Egypt, but ground water has so far prevented archaeologists from penetrating to the lowest levels at Harappa and Mohenjo-daro, where similar evidences of direct imitation might perhaps be found.

Both Mohenjo-daro and Harappa are divided between an elevated citadel or sanctuary and lower-lying blocks. Some areas contained long rows of identical rooms—sleeping quarters for some sort of conscript or slave labor perhaps. More than this can scarcely be deduced about the social structure of ancient Indus society. The analogy of both Egypt and Sumer suggests that a society organized by priestly colleges for the service of the gods was probably at the heart of Indus civilization; but we cannot be sure.

The chronological span represented by the mounds of rubble constituting the two capital sites can be stated with fair assurance, since cross dating with Sumer through seals and other imports at either end is possible. On this basis it seems probable that Indus civilization flourished from about 2500 to 1500 B.C. The two great cities were destroyed by attackers who, having slaughtered the inhabitants and burned the towns, did not care to take up residence there themselves. Almost certainly, Aryan-speaking tribesmen from the north were the barbarians who thus destroyed the Indus cities and disrupted Indus civilization. The destruction was nearly complete. Only the elements of Indus civilization which were familiar to simple villagers survived into later times. The special knowledge and high skills once possessed by the (presumably priestly) leaders vanished when the barbarians killed or dispersed them, between 1500 and, at the latest, 1200 B.C. A similar fate might have overtaken Pharaonic Egypt had not the political development of the Middle Kingdom spread the skills and knowledge required to maintain Egyptian civilization to numerous temples and noble households, long before the Hyksos attacked and overran the land.

Mesopotamian Civilization, 2500–1700 B.C.

‡‡‡ While these great changes transformed the life of Egypt and the Indus valley, civilized life did not remain stable and constant in Mesopotamia. Yet nothing so fundamental as had taken place between 3500 and 2500 B.C. in the land of Sumer could recur in the centuries that followed. The problem of frontier guard against barbarians eager to plunder the riches of the irrigated plain was never solved for long. The no less intractable problem of keeping peace among the cities themselves was solved only by a common subjection to the alien, and often hated, rule of some barbarian or half-barbarian conqueror.

Amid unending political and military turmoil, two important changes should be noted. First, soon after 2000 B.C., the Sumerian language ceased to be spoken on ordinary occasions. It was supplanted by various Semitic languages, of which Akkadian was the first to achieve literary definition. The displacement of Sumerian from everyday usage seems to have taken place gradually. Semitic speakers from the desert fringes must have moved in in such numbers as gradually to reduce the Sumerian language to the status of a sacred tongue, to be learned in schools and intoned at religious festivals. The obvious necessity of addressing the gods in their familiar language, however, preserved Sumerian for many centuries. The fact that the priests had to learn Sumerian, as we might learn Latin today, required them to create bilingual word lists and other school helps. This, in turn, permitted modern scholars to decipher and read Sumerian once they had mastered Akkadian with the help of bilingual inscriptions using old Persian.

Secondly, little by little and despite frequent setbacks, territorially extensive political empires gained in coherence and stability. Development of three devices of fundamental importance for later political systems made this possible: bureaucracy, law, and market prices. The principle of bureaucracy is so much taken for granted today that we find it hard to imagine a human society in which an individual's public or business role does not depend on the offices or appointive posts he happens to hold. But when the idea was new it took a lot of getting used to. A stranger who arrived with a document appointing him governor in the king's name had to be treated differently from other strangers. Judges, army officers, tax collectors, and still other officials also had special roles to play—and they had to persuade perfect strangers to co-operate by accepting the claim that they were acting in an official capacity. But when the idea did gain acceptance, it made it possible for a king to rule distant lands through his officers and officials. Effective co-operation across long distances became possible, even without such special links as the Nile provided in the land of Egypt.

Law that could be applied to particular cases at any place under the king's rule had a similar effect. It made human relations more nearly predictable—as the bureaucratic principle did too. Strangers could deal with one another with some confidence in the result. And if someone did fail to live up to his obligations there was a chance to bring him to book through the king's law and judges. The most famous early law code was promulgated by Hammurabi, king of Babylon (c. 1700 B.C.), though it is not clear from records of surviving cases that the provisions of this law code were in fact enforced.

Market prices, and rules for buying and selling that could be enforced in courts of law, also made effective co-operation among strangers possible. In ancient Mesopotamia, prices were calculated in barley to begin with. Later silver bars served the same purpose for large transactions; but common people seldom did any trading. When they did, they went in for barter and never had to use a common standard.

A majority of the population always remained poor peasants who worked in the fields and counted themselves lucky when the tax and rent collectors left them enough to eat. They had little or nothing to do with the king's officials, the king's law, or interregional markets. But among the wealthy, who by hook or crook concentrated surplus agricultural and other commodities in their hands, the gradual development of bureaucracy, law, and market prices did allow co-ordination of effort across hundreds of miles of space and through years or even decades of time.

Yet political empires in ancient Mesopotamia were never secure for long. Local loyalties remained very strong; communications were slow and costly; and only a very energetic ruler like Hammurabi, many of whose letters to his subordinates still survive, could extend effective control over the whole of Mesopotamia. Centers of political power tended to migrate upstream. This was so partly because salting of the soil as a result of evaporation damaged and eventually destroyed the fertility of the oldest fields in the extreme south of Mesopotamia. In addition, in any military collision the city upstream always had the advantage, since it could cut off the canals and interrupt the water supply of those downstream. As a result Akkad began to dominate Sumer by the time of Sargon (c. 2350 B.C.); and Babylon, still further north, became the capital of Mesopotamia by the time of Hammurabi.

In Hammurabi's time, too, Babylonian priests boldly reworked Sumerian and Akkadian learning to exalt the name and powers of Marduk, Babylon's divine proprietor and protector. Thus, for example, the so-called "Creation Epic" (which recounts how the world was made in terms echoed later by the Book of Genesis), makes Marduk the chief of the gods. This was done by substituting his name for that of Enlil, the storm god of Nippur, who had played a primary role among the gods in the Sumerian original. In other respects also, scribes and mathematicians in Hammurabi's age proved themselves unusually venturesome. For example, complex arithmetic calculations appear for the first time in tablets from this age; and then for more than a thousand years nothing new of any significance in mathematics is to be found.

The geographical shift from Sumer to Akkad and from Akkad to Babylonia, and the linguistic transformation that accompanied this northward migration of the center of wealth and power, did not much modify the fundamental continuity of Mesopotamian civilization. The ideas first worked out by Sumerian priests to explain the world and man's relation to the gods stood the test of time. So did the early technological adjustments to life in the river flood plains. Remarkably small change came to either of these aspects of Mesopotamian civilization. Invention and slow improvement tended to concentrate instead on political and military matters where, as we have seen, the arts of imperial administration were gradually elaborated.

Transition to Rain-watered Lands

‡‡‡ Geographical enlargement of the civilized area of the Mesopotamian valley itself, together with the rise of Egyptian and Indus styles of civilization in the distant river valleys of the Nile and Indus, obviously constituted an important reinforcement to the ranks of human civilization. Yet as long as such complicated societies required irrigated river valleys for their sustenance, they had, perforce, to remain rare and exotic forms of human life, islanded in a sea of barbarism. Only when rain-watered land could also be made to sustain specialists in sufficient numbers to make civilized societies possible could civilizations dominate the globe. This was a process that took nearly four thousand years to come to its completion, starting not long before 2000 B.C. and finally accomplished only in the nineteenth century of the Christian era.

All details of how the transition to rain-watered land first occurred are unknown, although the fact is indisputable. By about 2000 B.C., for example, Mesopotamia had come to be ringed around by a series of satellite civilizations, or proto-civilizations, of which the Hittite society in Asia Minor and the Canaanite in Syria and Palestine are by far the best known. Egypt's deserts forbade any comparable development on the flanks of the Nile valley, but it is possible, perhaps probable, though not yet attested to archaeologically, that elements of Indus civilization filtered southward and eastward to affect the lives of non-irrigating peoples in southern and central India.

It is not difficult to state what was needed for civilization to be able to flourish on rain-watered land. First, farmers had to be able to produce a surplus of food. Second, some social mechanism had to transfer food surpluses from the hands of the farmers who produced them to an array of specialists, who could then begin to elaborate high skills and secret knowledge without having to spend most of their time working in the fields, like the peasant majority.

We have already seen how the spread of plowing enabled ordinary farmers on many soils and in most seasons to produce an agricultural surplus. This was an indispensable preliminary to the establishment of civilization beyond the limits of irrigation. Yet the exact origin and early diffusion of plow agriculture is quite unclear. Equally the origin and nature of the social mechanisms that transferred food from

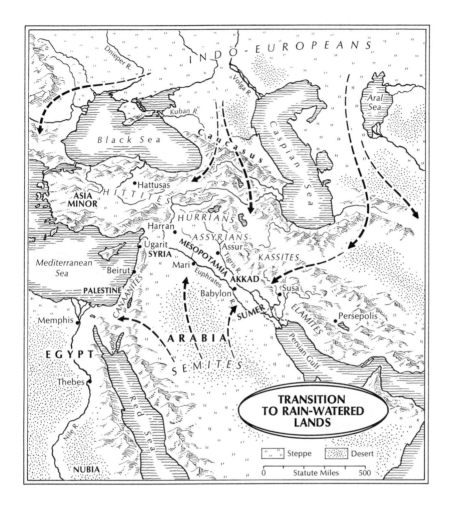

its producers to specialized consumers really escape modern knowledge. Conquest and trade were probably the two principal factors. But conquerors and merchants acted variously upon pre-existing forms of social leadership to produce rather considerable structural variations among the civilized and proto-civilized societies that began to grow up beyond the limits of river valley irrigation.

In northeastern Asia Minor, for example, the discovery of a number of clay tablets written by Assyrian merchants about 1800 B.C. allows a glimpse of emergent Hittite civilization. At that time local rulers had already begun to gather a following of soldiers, priests, merchants, and artisans—thus anticipating on a small scale the courtly life that developed a century or so thereafter at the Hittite capital of Hattusas. Many aspects of Hittite life were direct importations from Mesopotamia. Cuneiform writing, for example, and some of the myths of Mesopotamian religion were borrowed outright. At the same time, important elements from local tradition survived. The result was an amalgam of Mesopotamian provincialism and local uniqueness. Hittite art sensitively reveals the resulting cultural position, for despite a close relation with Mesopotamian models, the sculpture of Hattusas has an unmistakable, rather clumsy, style of its own.

Hittite society comprised several different ethnic groups, and it seems likely that conquest of one group by the other lay at the bottom of the social differentiation upon which Hittite civilization depended. Only after local chiefs and rulers had a certain amount of wealth or labor power at their disposal could civilized merchants really begin to do business. The goods produced in distant civilized areas were likely to be too expensive to interest ordinary farmers, and the things civilized merchants sought in exchange—e.g. metals, timber, or other raw materials—often required rather elaborate operations for their transport or other preparation. It seems altogether likely that the men who organized local manpower for such enterprises and who bought cloth, metal goods, and other wares from civilized traders were able to do so by virtue of wealth and power they had initially acquired as leaders of one ethnic group in the conquest of another. The prominence of armed men, and the squat heaviness characteristic of Hittite sculpture, certainly suggest the heavy tread of conquerors, who found themselves in a position to require rents and services from their victims on a scale sufficient to maintain small cities in which artisans and other specialists could cater to the conquerors' tastes.

Substantially the same pattern of social evolution appears to have occurred in other parts of Mesopotamia's borderland. Canaanites on the west may have been more mercantile, less military; but in the hill country north and east of the Tigris valley, Hurrians and Elamites developed their own variations on the civilized Mesopotamian style of life by following a predominantly military route—or so our very imperfect information suggests.

At a still further remove, in the steppe country beyond the mountains, pastoralists were particularly interested in metal that might improve their weaponry or enhance the splendor of their dress. By about 2500 B.C., for example, chieftains of the Kuban valley, north of the Caucasus mountains, began to furnish their graves with handsome bronze weapons and jewelry. Bronze made the already warlike barbarians of the steppe even more formidable. They proved able, in fact, to conquer their neighbors far and wide. Thus, for example, during the following six to seven hundred years, bronze-wielding barbarians swarmed from the steppe and overran all of western Europe, conquering and in time absorbing pre-existing populations. Habits of violence and admiration of the military virtues were implanted deeply into the European consciousness by these Bronze Age barbarian invasions. Europe also became Europeanized in speech, since, except for Finns, Estonians, Magyars, and Basques, all the modern inhabitants of Europe speak languages derived from an ancient tongue (or closely related tongues) brought from the western steppelands of Eurasia by the Bronze Age conquerors.

This family of languages is called Indo-European because its various branches are spoken not only in Europe but in Persia and northern India as well. This modern distribution attests to the fact that when their rude prowess had been reinforced by the possession of up-to-date bronze weapons, the steppe barbarians also found it possible to conquer eastward and southward. In the Middle East, for example, small bands of warriors, speaking Indo-European tongues appear to have established themselves as rulers among the hill people called Hurrians; the same was true of the Kassites further east. Even the Hyksos, whose main ethnic component was Semitic in speech, also may have incorporated a few Indo-European speakers into their ranks. The Aryan conquest of the Indus valley and the destruction of the ancient Indus civilization which ensued constituted one extreme wing of this barbarian migration. Other less well-known tribes (Tocharians) moved even further eastward, perhaps at a later date, as far as the borders of China.

Further consideration of the character and consequences of this vast movement of peoples will be reserved for the next chapter.

Sea-borne Civilization

‡‡‡ While interaction between civilized techniques and barbarian societies was producing these striking changes in the ethnic map of Eura-

sia, another, less massive but not unimportant, sea-borne contagion also transformed human lives and cultures in the Mediterranean and along the Atlantic coast.

Minoan Crete offers the principal example of an early sea-borne civilization. The island itself was not settled much before 4000 B.C., when Mediterranean seafaring presumably began. Cretan rubbish piles betray clear signs of commerce with Egypt by about 3000 B.C. Full-scale civilization emerged on the island over a thousand years later, for the famous palace of Minos was first built about 1900 B.C. By about the same time an as yet undeciphered form of writing, together with metallurgy, magnificent pottery, a charmingly naturalistic art style, and all the other appurtenances of archaic civilization had put in their appearance.

The wealth required to maintain the artisans and other specialists who created the splendors of Minoan civilization came mainly from sea commerce—or so it seems. Minoan ships traveled widely in the Mediterranean. Search for the copper and tin needed to make bronze may have been the main lure to distant voyaging. At any rate, traces of Minoan settlements have been discovered in Sardinia, near old copper mines. Crete itself exported timber and olive oil to the Syrian coast and to Egypt. In addition Minoan merchants probably served as middlemen between civilized artisans of the eastern Mediterranean and raw-material producers of the north and west.

Exactly how Minoan society was organized remains beyond the scope of modern knowledge. Minos was probably a title like Pharaoh, and the ruler's powers were probably based more on his religious than on his military or administrative role. Warfare was clearly far less important than it was on the mainland. So far as can be discovered, Knossos, the capital, was not defended by any wall; and arms and armor are not in the least prominent among Cretan remains.

The religion upon which Minos' power rested was related to cults that survived into historic times in Asia Minor. The central deity appears to have been a "Great Mother" goddess, whose special symbol was the double axe. In addition, bulls and snakes were objects of special reverence. Bull-dancing, i.e. acrobatic religious performances in which youths seized the charging animal's horns and leaped high over his back, was an important rite. Spanish bullfighting may descend from this ancient religious sport.

As compared with the severe, stolid character of Hittite sculpture, Minoan art strikes a modern observer as light, graceful, spontaneous. Naturalistic pictures of fish and other aquatic forms of life, and a conventionalized but vivacious portrayal of human beings, suggest a gayer and less violent outlook than that revealed by Hittite and other continental societies, where military struggles and harsh oppression of conquered peoples were the central realities of civilized and proto-civilized existence.

Further west in the Mediterranean, when Cretan civilization was at its height, another center of high culture existed on the island of Malta. This island appears to have been the site of the "mother church" of a "megalithic" religion. All that is known for sure is that a large number of tombs and other structures made of very large rocks came to dot the coastlands of western Europe and north Africa all the way from Morocco to southern Sweden. Why men took the trouble to make such structures cannot now be determined. Presumably missionary-priests persuaded the local inhabitants that such efforts were worthwhile, and both organized the necessary manpower and taught local peoples the skills needed to construct these massive monuments. In all probability the teachers of this religion held out hope of an immortal existence in islands of the blessed lying far to the west beyond the sunset. The tombs and other megalithic structures presumably helped to assure such happy immortality. It seems probable that the ideas of megalithic religion were related in some way to Egyptian cults of the dead; but exactly how this linkage may have been forged is not clear. Indeed, since written records do not exist, the doctrines of the megalithic religion may only be guessed at on the basis of Irish and other Celtic folklore of much later times.

The geographical distribution of megalithic remains in Europe and Africa makes it clear that the bearers of this culture traveled by water, and must, indeed, have been rather expert seamen. In all probability their vessels were simple coracles, i.e. wickerwork covered by hides to keep out the sea. With such light, simple boats it was possible to sail long distances by hugging the shores and landing whenever a storm threatened. Accidental voyages across the open sea obviously could occur whenever a boat got caught in an unexpected storm. It is possible, for example, that the Canary Islands were populated as a result of just such an accidental voyage. At any rate, a Stone Age people who may have been descendants of megalith builders inhabited those remote islands when Europeans first discovered them in the fourteenth century of the Christian era. As a matter of fact, voyages all the way across the Atlantic, sailing as Columbus was later to do before the northeast trades, were technically possible even with such simple vessels as those the ancient megalith-makers possessed.

The expansion of megalithic proto-civilization to the Far West occurred between about 3000 and 1700 B.C. By the later date, barbarian conquerors descended from pastoralists of the Eurasian steppe reached the Atlantic shores of Europe, and there subdued the peaceable megalith builders. Occasionally, the new masters of the land used the old megalithic skills to erect structures like Stonehenge in England. These standing stone circles, of which several besides Stonehenge exist, probably represent a monumental version in stone of a style of religious architecture that had originated as a circle of tree trunks. One purpose was calendrical. The great stones were arranged in such a way that at key dates of the solar year the rising and setting sun (and some bright stars as well) lined up with gaps between the stones. In this way the longest and shortest day of the year could be determined very accurately.

East Asia and the Americas

‡‡‡ Elsewhere in the world we know much less about changes in human life between 3000 and 1700 B.C. Along the middle reaches of the Yellow river valley, where Chinese civilization was soon to take its rise, a rather dense farming population formed, which depended mainly on millet for its food. These farmers cultivated a special kind of soil, known as loess, which was easily dug since it had been formed by deposition of wind-blown dust during the Ice Age. The loess region was not forested, and techniques of cultivation therefore had nothing in common with Middle Eastern slash and burn methods. For this reason, and because millet was not an important crop elsewhere, most scholars argue that Chinese farming arose independently of Middle Eastern agriculture, despite the fact that wheat and barley, distinctive Middle Eastern crops, were also cultivated on the loess soils at a very early time.

Further south, in the big river valleys of southeast Asia, a quite

different type of garden cultivation also acquired much greater importance during the third millennium B.C. In these regions the monsoon is
the dominating fact: for half the year it rains, practically every day,
and for the rest of the year there is drought. Sharp alternation between
wet and dry seasons meant local floods and then a gradual drying off
of the land. Various root crops were well adapted by nature to this
condition; so was rice, which became the staple of monsoon agriculture.

In its mature form, the rice cultivation of monsoon Asia differed
from the Middle Eastern styles of grain agriculture in three important
respects: (a) rice plants were transplanted from special seed flats (i.e.
treated like roots or other plants that can be propagated by transplantation of offshoots); (b) animal power was not vitally necessary to supplement human muscles in the work of cultivation; and (c) rice fields
or paddies had to be kept under a shallow sheet of water for several
months while the rice plants matured. These differences meant that the
southeast Asian garden style of cultivation was more intensive and
much more labor-consuming than field agriculture of the Middle Eastern type. In particular, it took an enormous amount of work and considerable skill to build rice paddies, except on land that was naturally
flooded for part of the year. Elsewhere it was necessary first to level
off the surface exactly and build low dikes to keep the water evenly
spread. Then a stream had to be diverted from its natural course and
made to flow onto the field, just enough to maintain the water level at
a height suitable for the growing rice. Yet where this kind of remodeling of the land surface could be carried through, the yield from well-
tended rice fields was very large, enough to maintain the labor power
needed for the paddies. As a result, very dense peasant populations
could develop in the monsoon regions of Asia on the basis of rice paddy
farming; but to begin with, such communities stuck close to river banks
where natural flooding made the work of the paddy farmers much
lighter. It was only later, after Chinese civilization had come into existence, that higher, hilly ground was also brought under rice cultivation
on any large scale.

Nevertheless, between 3000 and 1500 B.C. a series of populous
human communities arose along the river banks and coastal plains of
southeast Asia, spreading all the way from Bengal to China. These societies depended on rice and root crops for their food and developed

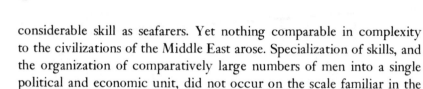

considerable skill as seafarers. Yet nothing comparable in complexity to the civilizations of the Middle East arose. Specialization of skills, and the organization of comparatively large numbers of men into a single political and economic unit, did not occur on the scale familiar in the Middle East, perhaps because the climatic conditions of the monsoon region made the common effort required for large-scale irrigation unnecessary, and indeed, in wetter regions, absurd.

How far early Asian seafarers may have penetrated among the islands of the Pacific cannot be said, since archaeological study of those parts is very spotty. Migration, perhaps geographically more extensive than anything the megalithic folk of Europe accomplished, probably occurred, for seafaring in regions ruled by the predictable monsoons and trade winds is relatively easy, even for primitive craft; whereas the storm-beset north Atlantic is one of the most unruly oceans of the entire world.

In the New World, the roving bands of hunters who had come across Bering Strait with the retreat of the glaciers occupied all of North and South America by about 8000 B.C. This is attested by the discovery of chipped stones in Tierra del Fuego at the tip of South America, dating from about that time. But hunting and gathering did not long remain the only way these American populations lived. Shortly before the first hunters reached Tierra del Fuego, traces of maize cultivation had been found in central Mexico, the southwestern United States, and perhaps also in Peru and some other parts of South America. Yet the earliest cultivated forms of maize were not much like later forms of the plant, and perhaps early yields and nutritional value were small. At any rate, the dawn of agriculture in the Americas did not quickly lead to the rise of cities and the beginning of civilization. Until a few centuries before the Christian era, simple village life was all there was, even in the most advanced regions of the New World.

Despite many uncertainties and glaring gaps in our information, it is clear that mankind's achievements by 1700 B.C. were impressive. By comparison with the rates of cultural advance which had prevailed in earlier ages, the pace of social change had assumed a dizzying rapidity. Within less than two thousand years, three irrigation civilizations had arisen in the central region of the Old World; a large number of lesser, satellite civilizations had grown up on rain-watered land, and echoes of civilized achievements had reached both the barbarian warriors of the northern steppelands and shore dwellers of the Mediterranean, the Atlantic, and, perhaps, also the Indian Ocean. A less complex, less supremely skilled, and far less well-known cultural advance had also taken place in monsoon Asia and in the loess region of the Yellow river valley.

In short, civilized history, in all its complexity, was well launched. Civilized and semi-civilized adventurers, pioneers, warriors, traders, missionaries, mining prospectors, and land grabbers had already shown their power to disturb other, weaker peoples and to penetrate new and ever more distant regions of the earth.

CHAPTER 3

Cosmopolitanism in the

Middle East 1700-500 B.C.

 During a period of about three hundred years, beginning soon after 1700 B.C., the civilized world was overrun by barbarian conquerors. Hill peoples living north and east of Mesopotamia, tribesmen from the desert fringes of Syria, Palestine, and northern Arabia, together with wide ranging war bands originating from the northern steppe combined in varying proportions to attack all existing centers of civilized life. The range of these barbarian conquests was never again equaled. In outlying civilized areas where the social structure sustaining specialized skills was not very tough, the barbarian conquests destroyed most of what had been achieved. At the two extreme edges of the civilized world, in Crete and in India, little but smoking ruins survived the Achaean and Aryan assaults, both of which probably reached their climax between 1500 and 1400 B.C.

Nearer the center, where civilized styles of life were more deeply rooted, the consequences of barbarian conquest were less drastic. Mesopotamian and Egyptian civilizations survived with only local and temporary setbacks. The barbarians who took power in each land (Hyksos in Egypt about 1680 B.C., Kassites in Mesopotamia at about the same time) were interested in enjoying what they had conquered. They therefore needed help from priests, scribes, and other experts to keep both gods and men in order so that rents, taxes, and luxury goods produced by specially skilled workmen might continue to flow in. As a result, the structure of society upon which civilization depended did not break down. Indeed, traditional forms of Mesopotamian and Egyptian culture underwent surprisingly little change.

Technique of Chariot Warfare

‡‡‡ The range and force of these barbarian conquests was closely linked with an important advance in the technique of warfare. The barbarian conquerors possessed light war chariots and fast horses to pull them. From the security of a galloping chariot they were able to launch a shower of arrows against any opposing military array with almost complete impunity. Battle tactics were to feint a charge a few times, showering the enemy with arrows on each approach, and then mount a final attack in which all the chariots charged home at once and overran the opposing forces.

The advantages enjoyed by chariotry in the seventeenth century B.C. may be compared to the advantage of a tank force when pitted against unsupported infantry in the second quarter of the twentieth century A.D. Mobility, firepower, and armor, three prime determinants of battle, all favored the charioteers. Their greatest weakness lay in the fact that chariots, and the equipment needed by a chariot warrior, were very expensive. Bronze weapons and armor, horses, and the skilled carpentry, leather-work, and other artisan crafts required to construct a serviceable chariot added up to an enormous cost. Chariots had consequently to remain comparatively few. The chariot age was therefore an age of aristocracy, when military supremacy, as well as economic and political control, rested in the hands of a very small elite.

When and where the full elaboration of chariot warfare originated is not certain. Iran or Azerbaijan, where civilized artisan skills, above all the art of the wheel-wright, were accessible to tribes of horse-raising pastoralists, would appear to be the most likely places for the initial development of chariot warfare. The most likely date is shortly after 1700 B.C., for it was then that the rapid expansion of barbarian conquest got under way.

As the chariot's advantages became fully apparent, the new master weapon acquired an enormous prestige. Even in regions where wooded landscapes made bow fighting largely ineffective, e.g. in northern and western Europe, barbarian tribes hastened to acquire the best chariots they could. This appears to have been the case in Greece, for example. Certainly the tactics of the Achaean warriors before the walls of Troy as reported by Homer make no sense. Homer's heroes do not use bows, but instead dismount before fighting and use their chariots merely as conveniences in getting to and from the field of battle. This deprived the chariot of any but ceremonial significance. Further east, however, more open landscapes made the bow a practicable weapon. The Aryans who invaded India, as well as those other charioteers who established their rule in China's Yellow river valley before 1400 B.C., used the chariot rationally, as a moving platform from which to launch a shower of arrows.

With the perfection of techniques of chariot warfare, barbarian horse raisers began to enjoy enormous military advantages. Conquest became easy, even with only a handful of chariots. Landed aristocracies of the sort which had begun to build provincial civilizations all around the flanks of Mesopotamia shortly before 2000 B.C. became much easier to establish, for the difference in military power between a few men with chariots and everybody else had become enormous. As a result, after an initial period of mere destructiveness, which brought both the Indus and the Cretan civilizations low, the barbarian conquerors began to construct their own rougher, militarily more formidable, style of civilization in both Greece and India. Classical Greek and Indian civilizations took their origin in this way. The same appears to be true of distant China, where the arrival of chariot warriors probably inaugurated the Shang dynasty. (Traditional Shang dates according to the shorter chronology are 1525–1028 B.C.) The Shang, to be sure, were the second dynasty recorded in Chinese tradition, and the Hsia dynasty had laid down many of the fundamentals of Chinese civilization before their arrival. Nevertheless, the Shang charioteers gave important new impulse and direction to Chinese society and government.

It therefore appears that the invention of the chariot, and the great differentiation this introduced on the battlefield between mounted and

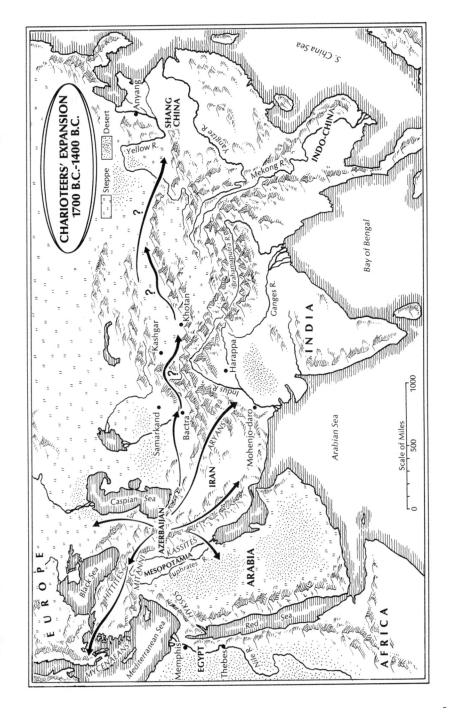

CHARIOTEERS' EXPANSION
1700 B.C.-1400 B.C.

Steppe
Desert

S. China Sea

Anyang

SHANG
CHINA

Yellow R.

Yangtze R.

INDO-CHINA

Mekong R.

?

?

Brahmaputra R.

Bay of Bengal

Khotan

Kashgar

Ganges R.

?

Harappa

INDIA

Indus R.

Samarkand

Bactra

ARYANS

Mohenjo-daro

Caspian Sea

IRAN

AZERBAIJAN

Arabian Sea

Scale of Miles

1000

500

0

KASSITES

Black Sea

HITTITES

MITANNI

MESOPOTAMIA

Euphrates R.

ARABIA

AFRICA

MYCENAEANS

Mediterranean Sea

HYKSOS

Memphis

EGYPT

Thebes

Nile R.

Red Sea

EUROPE

unmounted men, set the stage for new beginnings of each of the three great outlying civilizations of the Old World. The military and aristocratic governments of Mycenaean Greece, Aryan India, and Shang China, and the approximate simultaneity with which these regimes arose, created a loose kinship that extended across the entire breadth of Eurasia. The indirect influence from Mesopotamia, along whose flanks the war chariot was first perfected, also established a real if remote interrelationship among all the great civilizations of the Old World.

Three Middle Eastern Empires

‡‡‡ The significance of the chariot conquerors for the old and firmly rooted civilizations of the Middle East itself was not so great. Victorious barbarian invaders promptly created extensive but loosely administered feudal empires. The members of each war band scattered out across the countryside and set themselves up as landlords and masters of the pre-existing populations. Rather rapidly the conquerors adopted at least some of the ways of civilization. The Hyksos, for example, whom the Egyptians hated as foreigners, went very far toward accepting the manners and rituals of ancient Egyptian religion and civilization. In Mesopotamia the assimilation of the Kassite barbarians was even more complete.

Despite this fact, the ancient peoples of the Middle East did not willingly accept subjugation to barbarian masters. It was not long before local leaders, beginning sometimes on a very small scale, borrowed the techniques of chariot warfare in order to throw off what was still felt to be an alien yoke. In Egypt, for example, a local princeling of Thebes in the south led a rebellion against the Hyksos, and drove them entirely from the Nile valley by about 1570 B.C. In Mesopotamia it was the king of Assyria, far to the north, who led the "native reaction" by throwing off barbarian overlordship (about 1380 B.C.). The Hittites too recovered from the initial shock of exposure to the new type of warfare by acquiring chariots for themselves, and soon became a third great power, disputing distant Syrian borderlands with Egypt, the strongest single state of the age, and with Assyria.

The discovery of an Egyptian file of diplomatic records from the fourteenth century B.C. allows modern scholars a vivid glimpse of the international aristocratic life of these three great empires. Akkadian cuneiform was the language of diplomacy. Kings' daughters were given and accepted in marriage to seal alliances, thus incidentally spreading styles of courtly life and civilization to new ground. Professional charioteers, gathered into garrisons, constituted the core of the fighting forces. They were paid both with booty and with gold or other valuables that accrued to the ruler by taxation. Egypt, whose coffers were replenished by gold mines in Nubia beyond the first Nile cataracts, had the largest supply of gold and therefore could afford to maintain the best army. Pharaoh recruited mercenaries from every borderland of the Nile.

Noble warriors, tamers of horses and masters of the battlefield, were unruly subjects. A warrior king might indeed persuade them to follow his banners toward almost any sort of reckless adventure; but no well-ordered bureaucracy could flourish in states built around the rude consensus of aristocrats of the chariot. Hence, the Egyptian, Hittite, and first Assyrian empires were loosely consolidated states, chronically liable to local rebellion. Whenever a princeling or landed magnate took offense at the central authority he could defy the distant king and his agents with ease, and could only be brought to book if a majority of his fellow aristocrats sided against him and with the king. The chariot nobility did this in the most practical of all possible ways, either by obeying the royal summons to come into the field against a rebel or by refusing to do so. The king's power was thus very effectively restricted by the consensus of his mighty men. The same rude consensus restrained individual nobles from random revolt or disobedience.

Chivalric courtesies among fighting men, and a ruthless oppression of mere peasants and servitors, characterized the cosmopolitanism of these Bronze Age empires. In the long run the lack of sympathy between the ruling warriors and the rest of society constituted a profound weakness. But as long as ordinary men could not bring any armaments into the field of battle that could stand against the tactics of chariot warfare, aristocratic cosmopolitan chivalry prevailed.

The Iron Age

‡‡‡ Soon after 1200 B.C., however, the widespread use of a new and much cheaper metal than the bronze upon which aristocratic chari-

oteers had depended changed the military balance drastically. Once again numbers began to tell on the battlefield. The new metal was iron, produced from ores that were far more abundant than those of copper and especially those of tin, needed to make bronze. The technique for working iron was, however, far more difficult.

Both copper and tin are easily reduced from their ores. The alloy bronze (copper alloyed with about 3 to 10 percent tin) is easily melted and can be cast into molds either directly to the form of the desired object, or into ingots to be hammered to shape. The metallurgy of iron is different in many ways. It does not melt except at temperatures far above those of any primitive fire, although its ores are easily reduced in the solid state by heating when surrounded by charcoal. This yields a metallic sponge which can be consolidated without melting by hammering at a white heat, a process that also squeezes out most of the slaggy remains of the rocky impurities in the ore. Once consolidated, iron is extremely malleable when hot and can be easily forged to shape, while pieces can be solidly joined together by hammer-welding.

Prolonged heating of iron when embedded in a charcoal fire enables it to absorb carbon (between 0.1 and 1.0 percent) and it becomes steel. Steel differs from iron in that it acquires extreme hardness when quenched from a red heat in water, but it is brittle unless the quench is delicately interrupted to prevent too rapid cooling or unless the quenched object is gently reheated to partially soften it. The latter process did not become common until after 1000 A.D., and the earlier iron tools were extremely variable in properties. The best products were rare and their makers famed. Very little iron was uniformly carburized to make steel, and only a small fraction was used in hardened form. Early iron was *not* superior to bronze in its properties and its dominance was mainly rooted in the ready availability of iron ores.

The metal iron appears around 2000 B.C., probably as an accidental by-product of smelting of copper or lead. Its purposeful production commenced about 1200 B.C., but iron tools and weapons did not become widespread until four centuries later.

The first major consequence of this technical advance was another general wave of barbarian invasion which lapped round the great empires of the ancient Middle East and toppled them one after another between 1200 and 1000 B.C. The military success of the Iron Age barbarians rested upon the psychological cohesion of rudely egalitarian

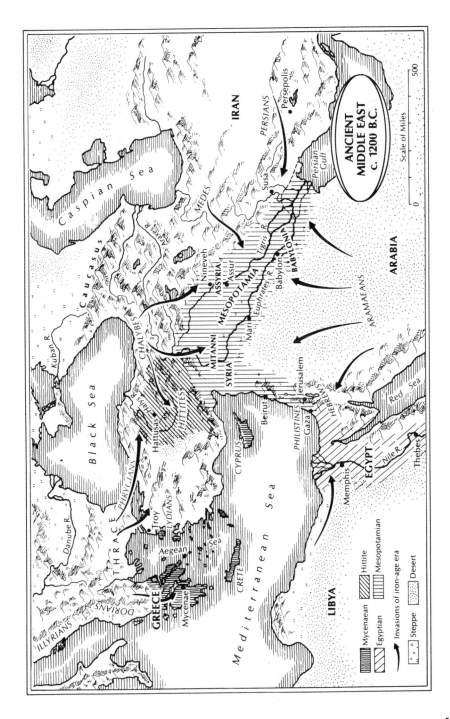

ANCIENT MIDDLE EAST c. 1200 B.C.

Scale of Miles

0   500

Caspian Sea

IRAN

PERSIANS

Persepolis

Persian Gulf

MEDES

Susa

ARABIA

Nineveh

ASSYRIA

Assur

MESOPOTAMIA

BABYLONIA

Babylon

Tigris R.

Euphrates R.

Mari

ARAMAEANS

Araxes R.

Caucasus

CHALYBES

MITANNI

SYRIA

Kuban R.

Black Sea

HITTITES

Hattusas

Halys R.

PHRYGIANS

Beirut

Jerusalem

PHILISTINES

HEBREWS

Gaza

Red Sea

CYPRUS

Danube R.

THRACE

Troy

LYDIANS

Aegean Sea

CRETE

EGYPT

Memphis

Nile R.

Thebes

DORIANS

GREECE

Mycenae

ILLYRIANS

Mediterranean Sea

LIBYA

Mycenaean

Egyptian

Invasions of iron-age era

Hittite

Mesopotamian

Steppe   Desert

communities in which every man could be an effective soldier because there was no deep division between masters and their subjects like that which had long prevailed in the civilized regions of the world. Aristocratic charioteers, necessarily few in number, surrounded by sullen subjects and weakened by traditional rivalries among themselves, were no match for such a massed assault.

The new invaders of the Middle East came from the same border regions as their predecessors of the Bronze Age: the steppe and mountain regions to the north and east, and the desert fringes on the south. Many peoples later to become famous were among these migrant bands: Medes and Persians in Iran; Philistines, Hebrews, and. Aramaeans in Syria and Palestine; Phrygians and Dorians in the Aegean area. Most of the invaders were organized tribally. Each tribe established its own local political institutions, sometimes (as among the Hebrews) linked informally into a broader confederation that came into operation in time of unusual emergency.

Effects of Iron

‡‡‡ The use of iron had important economic as well as political and military effects. The new metal was sufficiently abundant to make it possible for farmers to have sickle blades, plow shares, and other agricultural tools made of iron. This gave an increased efficiency to farming, especially in regions where clayey soils made breaking the earth comparatively difficult.

In some parts of the Middle East the free peasantries that sprang up after the Iron Age invasions were in a position to trade some of their crops for artisan products—including, first and foremost, iron tools and weapons, but also such things as wheel-spun, kiln-baked pottery and spoked cart wheels, whose manufacture required special skills beyond the reach of any ordinary farmer. Even when landlords and tax gatherers reasserted themselves in Middle Eastern society—a phenomenon not long delayed—this sort of local circulation of goods between town and country continued to exist. A group of humble town artisans, possessing skills and producing goods needed by the peasantry, came permanently into existence. No matter what military or political disasters and disruptions subsequently visited the region, this local specialization survived or quickly re-established itself.

As the advantages of economic specialization thus penetrated down to the very bottom of the social scale in the Middle East, civilization became fully and firmly indelible for the first time. No important segment of the population any longer remained entirely outside the network of exchange and interdependence. Everyone benefited tangibly from specialization, even the poorest peasant who now started to go to market for the purchase of essential tools, if nothing else. This was, perhaps, the greatest achievement of the Iron Age. Social differentiation and specialization which had originally been the product of most unusual geographical and social circumstances became permanently part of the agricultural society of the Middle East. Civilized social complexity and specialization had finally, after some two thousand years, become endemic.

By contrast, the political arrangements resulting from the Iron Age invasions were very unstable. Struggles among local tribes and tribal confederations soon led to the reappearance of large territorial states. The Assyrians were the most successful empire builders. They were able to draw fighting men from among a hardy and numerous local peasantry. Other assets were the imperial tradition and governmental techniques of ancient Mesopotamia whose cultural heirs and defenders the Assyrian kings consciously felt themselves to be. Egypt, on the other hand, having barely been able to repel three successive hosts of would-be invaders (1220 to 1165 B.C.), remained on the defensive within the boundaries of the Nile valley, intent only upon keeping intruders at arm's length and preserving the cultural inheritance of the most ancient Pharaohs.

Despite ruthless and almost incessant warfare, the Assyrian empire never became really secure. Subject peoples like the Israelites and Babylonians rebelled repeatedly. Drastic retaliation, such as the removal of all leading families from the kingdom of Israel to Babylonia (722 B.C.), did not prevent the renewal of disorder as soon as a plausible opportunity presented itself. Yet not rebellion from within but another major revolution in the technique of warfare was what finally overthrew the Assyrians. This military revolution occurred between 850 and 700 B.C., and its major center was upon the steppes. In essence it was absurdly simple: during these centuries steppe nomads began habitually to ride on horseback. They thereby became cavalrymen, with all the advantages of mobility conferred by this simple method of exploiting the strength and speed of horseflesh.

The Cavalry Revolution

‡‡‡ We are so accustomed to the idea of riding on horseback that it is likely to seem the most natural way to use a horse. Why then did it take men so long to become habitual riders? As a matter of fact, men had occasionally mounted on horses' backs long before 2000 B.C. But there were serious difficulties. In the crisis of military action, a mounted bowman had to have both hands free for shooting. Any unexpected change in his horse's motion put the rider in danger of falling off his mount at the very feet of his foe. Charioteers solved this problem by entrusting driving to one man, shooting to another. Cavalrymen had to do both at once. This required a division of labor not between two men but between the lower torso, which controlled the horse, and the upper, which controlled the bow. Under these circumstances only long habituation on the part of both horse and rider could secure the sort of reliable co-ordination needed to make riding safe. The centaur of Greek legend and the cavalryman of history thus constituted a remarkable symbiosis between very different biological species, and we should not be surprised that it took a long time for riding to become important.

But when riding did become common, its military effect was similar to the earlier invention of chariotry. By mounting their horses' backs, bow in hand, whole tribes of nomads acquired a mobility and striking power superior to what any infantry army, however well organized and disciplined, could attain. Hit-and-run raids from the steppes became safe and easy. Only an equally mobile, better disciplined, or more numerous cavalry force could hope to stop such raids. This the Assyrians could not supply. Their homeland was not good horse-raising country, lacking enough grass. Horses therefore remained comparatively rare, the pride of rulers and nobles but far beyond the reach of the Assyrian rank and file.

Soon after 700 B.C. peoples known to the Greeks as Cimmerians and Scythians exploited the new power of the steppe by launching extensive raids against the Middle East. Successful cavalry raids encouraged revolt in the rear. Hence, rebellious Babylonians from the south, Medes from the Iranian highlands to the east, and Scythians from the northern steppe combined their forces for the final overthrow of the Assyrian state in 612 B.C. The victors divided the spoils: the Scythians returning homeward to the northern steppe, their horses laden with plunder, while the Medes and Babylonians divided up the Assyrian empire with a newly ambitious Egypt.

The victors soon fell to quarreling among themselves. In particular Babylonia and Egypt started a struggle for control of Palestine and Syria, in the course of which the small kingdom of Judah, having chosen alliance with Egypt, roused the ire of King Nebuchadnezzar of Babylon (ruled 605–561 B.C.). Babylonian armies captured Jerusalem in 587 B.C., destroyed the city, and deported its inhabitants to Babylon. This episode, in itself not specially remarkable, turned out to be critically important for the evolution of Judaism.

The Persian Empire, 559–330 B.C.

‡‡‡ Within less than half a century, a new conqueror, Cyrus the Persian (ruled 559–530 B.C.), emerged from the eastern highlands and united nearly all of the Middle East under his sovereignty. His successors, Cambyses (ruled 530–521 B.C.) and Darius the Great (ruled 521–486 B.C.), added Egypt and northwest India to the Persian empire. The Persians protected the critical steppe frontier by hiring border tribes of horse nomads to check raids from the more distant grasslands. When this arrangement threatened to break down, both Cyrus and Darius led the full muster of the Persian field army out into the steppe, in hope of over-awing if not of defeating the nomad cavalrymen. Cyrus lost his life in such frontier warfare, and the great Darius met with only indifferent success when in 513 B.C. he invaded Europe and penetrated the Scythian homeland by invading what is today part of southern Russia.

In the civilized heartland of the Middle East itself the Persians at first undertook to restore local freedoms and traditional religious and legal systems to all the peoples they annexed to their empire. Cyrus accordingly allowed the Jews to return to Jerusalem, and a few did so. He simultaneously restored or recognized the authority of the ancient priesthoods of Egypt and Babylon on condition that they support his regime. But Cambyses, the son of Cyrus, and Darius found it necessary to withdraw such special privileges when local pieties and priestly aspirations proved fertile seedbeds for revolt. As a result, Cyrus' successors abandoned his policy of liberation, and the old techniques of Assyrian

THE CAVALRY REVOLUTION
800 B.C.—500 B.C.

Steppe Desert Persian Empire about 500 B.C.

administration were quickly revived and even improved on. Disheartened by repeated failures to secure effective local independence, the resistance of the Middle Eastern peoples to the political supremacy of an alien but distant overlord tended to weaken. Nevertheless, the Persian empire survived only a little more than two hundred years, and was destroyed in the end (330 B.C.) not by native revolt but by attack from a still semi-barbarous Macedonia, lying on the distant western fringe of the empire.

Before we leave the Middle East and turn our attention to India, Greece, and China, we should consider, if only briefly, three key developments of Middle Eastern civilization which these long and tumultuous centuries brought into much sharper focus than before. The first of these was the evolution of techniques of empire; the second was the invention of alphabetic writing; the third, the rise of ethical monotheism.

The Techniques of Empire

‡‡‡ Generally speaking, the basic devices of imperial government had all been worked out in ancient Mesopotamia before the Bronze Age invasions of the eighteenth century B.C. A political order dominated by bureaucrats, i.e. by administrators whose powers depended upon their offices rather than their persons, had been well developed under Hammurabi. The same principle was revived by the Assyrians and adopted by the Persians with no important changes. The network of appointive officials remained quite thin on the ground. A royal governor responsible for a comparatively large territory could not oversee or control what happened in all parts of the province entrusted to him. In practice he had to deal with a wide variety of local authorities—temple priesthoods, city magistrates, territorial princelings, tribal chieftains, or some other type of local power-wielding elite.

Use and wont defined most such relationships quite closely: the amount and nature of any tax payments or military service local authorities rendered to the governor; legal jurisdictions of king, governor, and local authority; religious and other ceremonial observances required to keep good relations with the gods; in short, any matter that brought officialdom into contact with local life tended to become thickly encrusted by custom. Thereafter, either partner found it difficult to alter the relationship. This meant both a limit upon the ability of the king and his governors to mobilize the resources of the entire society for war or any other purpose, and a guarantee of stability for the imperial government itself, since traditional tributes and services could more or less be counted upon without having to be renegotiated or forcibly collected each year.

Such principles of government were not new in the first millennium B.C., but the Assyrians, Babylonians, Medes, and Persians applied them to larger territories and for longer periods of time than had ever been done before. The main reasons for their success lay in the military superiority enjoyed by the rulers of large territories against lesser rivals. Important improvements in military administration lay behind this imperial preponderance. The Assyrians, for example, developed something approximating a professional officer corps, and formed regular units, arranged into tens and hundreds. A successful officer might expect promotion from lesser to greater commands at the will and discretion of his superiors. Radical rationality had far greater scope in such a system than in the civil administration proper. Moreover, annual or almost annual campaigns kept the imperial army in good fighting trim, easily capable of overcoming any improvised local resistance and of over-awing most threats from across distant borders.

In Sargon of Akkad's day (c. 2350 B.C.) the maintenance of a standing army had presented enormous difficulties since goods could not be concentrated at any one place on a sufficient scale to maintain a sizable force. But distributing armed men across the countryside, wherever food could be found, risked dissolution of the central power. Sargon had met this dilemma by sustaining his army on the basis of perpetual plundering of conquered territories. Hammurabi had stationed his soldiers on landed estates, and tried to enforce regular service by keeping careful records of each man's military obligations. Under the Assyrians and Persians the ancient dilemma remained, but improvements in transport and communication had blunted its horns. It was now possible for the imperial court to attract toward itself a sufficient flow of goods to allow a large force—the royal bodyguard —to be maintained at all times. The full imperial muster could not be kept under arms, but had to be scattered across the countryside between campaigns, and then summoned for service when needed. But as the size and professionalism of the royal bodyguard increased to the scale of the Persians' 10,000 "Immortals," the central imperial authority acquired an automatic military superiority over any ordinary rival. The mere existence of such a royal bodyguard compelled even distant provinces to obey the imperial summons to arms, since everyone knew beforehand that disobedience would bring swift and overwhelming retaliation. Only some quite unusual constellation of forces, such as that represented by the Scythian cavalry raids in the seventh century B.C. or by the well-organized Macedonian army that Alexander led into Persia in the fourth century B.C., could upset the military advantage such an imperial establishment normally enjoyed.

Herein lay the secret of Assyrian and Persian political-military successes. And in the larger frame of world history the development of such a fundamental instrument of power as a standing army, supplemented by a semi-professional militia for campaigns, certainly marks a major landmark of political evolution. Both Roman and modern European armies based themselves on the administrative principles first worked out by the ancient Assyrians and Persians.

Behind the rise of a professional standing army lay economic and technological advances that allowed concentration of goods on a scale sufficient to maintain large numbers of men under arms year in and year out. Systematic road building helped. The Assyrian army regularly built highways suitable for use by wheeled vehicles. This facilitated supply service for the troops, and vastly accelerated their marches toward distant flanks of the empire. Roads also cheapened and speeded movements of men and goods in time of peace.

In addition, a series of legal and customary definitions of merchants' rights and privileges facilitated trade over comparatively long distances and between mutually alien and distrustful populations. Babylonian law in the second millennium B.C. had already taken account of the needs of merchants, and in their days of imperial greatness the Assyrians and Persians continued to accord important legal protection to traders. Merchants, for example, were exempt from military service. Important cities where merchants and artisans lived enjoyed surprisingly extensive rights of self-government in return for payments of money tribute. Even more important, the roads were—in principle if not always in practice—policed by the imperial government. Hence any local robber who tried to plunder passing caravans could expect punishment from imperial officials commanding local garrisons, or at the hands of detachments of the field army itself. Interregional traders and the imperial armies thus supported one another in a more or less conscious and deliberate alliance. The two constituted the principal growth points of ancient Middle Eastern society between 1700 and 500 B.C.

Alphabetic Writing

‡‡‡ The growing preponderance of a single central political authority had wide and complex ramifications. For example, merchants, officials, and other participants in interregional affairs required a common language. They found it after about 1000 B.C. in Aramaic. They also needed a simpler mode of writing. From its inception in Sumerian temples, the art of writing had been confined to a learned few, who had to go to school for long years in order to master the numerous syllabic symbols employed to represent spoken language. But before 1300 B.C. radical simplification of the art made writing quite easy to learn. This in turn opened the possibility of literacy to much broader segments of society.

Experimentation with simpler modes of writing seems to have concentrated along the eastern Mediterranean coast, from Sinai to the Taurus mountains. This region lay between Egypt and Mesopotamia, where the completely different hieroglyphic and cuneiform styles of writing offered themselves as models, but where the elaborate school systems required to train boys to full mastery of those complicated scripts did not exist. Under these circumstances, half-educated scribes, with no vested interest in ancient correctness, dabbled freely with simplified ways of recording speech. Their efforts produced numerous "alphabets" based on the principle that if a single sign is used to symbolize each distinguishable consonantal sound, then about thirty signs suffice to record human speech. For the Semitic languages which were spoken in the region, vowels sounds do not really have to be written down, since it is easy to supply the correct vowels for insertion between written consonants. Even today Arabic and Hebrew continue to omit vowels.

The precise time at which alphabetic writing originated cannot be established with certainty. By about 1300 B.C. it had become common in Syria and Palestine. The discovery of numerous potsherds used to record very ordinary transactions suggests that alphabetic literacy soon percolated fairly widely through the urban society of the region. Scribes of Mesopotamia and Egypt of course repudiated the new styles of writing, and for sacred uses the older cuneiform and hieroglyphic scripts continued to be employed until near the Christian era. But for ordinary affairs, alphabets, slightly adjusted to fit different languages, spread in every direction from their Syrian place of origin and offered a new medium through which more popular literatures could attain a degree of permanence.

The importance of the invention of alphabetic writing may be compared to the importance of the introduction of iron which occurred at roughly the same time. Iron tools and weapons democratized warfare and society by making the distinction between rich and poor less sharp. It also, as explained above, made civilization really endemic for the first time by bringing rural peasants and urban artisans into a mutually beneficial exchange relationship. Similarly, alphabetic writing democratized learning by allowing ordinary men to master the rudiments of literacy. Through the alphabet the higher intellectual traditions of civilized society, which had formerly been the preserve of special colleges of priests and highly trained scribes, became accessible to laymen and commoners as never before. Even more important, alphabetic writing made it far easier for laymen and commoners to contribute to the literary heritage of civilized communities, thus widening and increasing the variety of that heritage very considerably. Without the existence of alphabetic writing, for example, it seems unlikely that the utterances of a simple shepherd like Amos (or of any of the other Hebrew prophets) would have been preserved to influence men's thoughts and conduct from that day to this.

The effect of iron and of alphabets, therefore, was to establish civilized styles of life far more securely than ever before, by making a fuller participation in the economic and intellectual pursuits of civilization accessible to a larger proportion of the total population than before. Yet one must not exaggerate. The gap between town and country remained very great, and with only rare exceptions, the peasantries of the Middle East entered only passively and as victims into political affairs. Equally, they shared very little in the high culture of the cities, clinging stubbornly to local folkways, pieties, and resentments against harsh tax collectors, dishonest merchants, and greedy landowners whose ways were not their ways and whose very existence seemed, to peasant eyes, an evidence of profound injustice and unrighteousness.

The Rise of Monotheism

‡‡‡ Alienation of the peasantry was only part of the problem confronting the cultural leaders of the Middle East between 1700 and 500 B.C. Old styles of thought and feeling, frozen into fixed forms by the priestly piety and learning of ancient Mesopotamia and Egypt, were not adequate to account for facts newly apparent in a cosmopolitan age. Thus, for example, when Egyptian armies and diplomats crisscrossed Asia, Syria, and Palestine, sometimes successfully and sometimes not, it became impossible to believe that the divine Pharaoh's will was everywhere and always supreme among men, as a god's will ought to be. And when political power and economic wealth moved up the Tigris-Euphrates valley, first to Babylon and then to Nineveh, leaving the once flourishing cities of Sumer to decay or utter desolation, religious hymns and rituals which treated Sumer as the center of the world and the gods' principal concern no longer commanded easy and automatic assent. Such discrepancies between present facts and the inherited pieties were even more acute for lesser peoples inhabiting the regions between Egypt and Mesopotamia, for they found themselves more and more at the mercy of foreign armies and alien masters, who knew little and cared less for the myths, rituals, and deities that local priesthoods honored.

Generally speaking these discrepancies provoked one of two opposing responses. Some men explained the gap between pious expectation and reality by saying that the gods were displeased by failure to perform traditional rites properly. What was needed therefore was a more faithful adherence to ancient precedents, whereupon the gods might be expected to set things right once more. Rigid conservatism and conscious archaism, seeking to discover and revive old forms that had been lost and forgotten, was the appropriate behavior for those who accepted this explanation.

Others argued that earlier ideas about the gods and man's relation to them needed to be emended or even replaced by new revelation.

Yet even radical religious reformers often claimed to be restoring forgotten truths that had been obscured with the passage of time. And, on the other side, conservative archaists could become revolutionaries, if their version of the truth and correct service of the gods conflicted in some important respect with current religious practice. As a matter of fact, the really important movements that made lasting changes in men's world outlook combined the appeal of a return to a better (sometimes fictitious) past with an appeal to the authority of new revelation.

The intellectual and religious evolution of ancient Middle Eastern society tended toward ethical and transcendental monotheism. But only the Jews were able consistently to carry the trend to a logical, unambiguous conclusion. Other peoples, even when they exalted one deity above others and magnified the power of some particular god until it extended over the entire universe, nevertheless could not throw away traditional polytheisms altogether.

In Babylonia, for example, the priests claimed universal dominion for Marduk. Old hymns and rituals were "corrected" to eliminate everything which had become out of tune with the priests' opinions. Thus, for example, passages in Sumerian hymns referring to the divinity of kings were simply omitted. But after this sort of purification of ancient texts, further alteration stopped, and a fixed body of sacred literature, derived for the most part from ancient Sumer itself, endured throughout Assyrian times with almost no change at all. The antiquity and authority of such a religion was no doubt impressive, yet it offered little to comfort individual persons adrift in the great cosmopolitan empires of the age.

Egypt's religious evolution was more stormy. When the Egyptians, having driven the Hyksos invaders from their land, embarked on their imperial venture into Asia, they had to take account of the strange foreign ways they encountered outside the Nile valley. Old ideas that made the Nile and the Pharaoh central to the entire universe did not seem to fit the outside world very well. Accordingly, in the fourteenth century B.C. a clique of reformers and religious radicals arose, who argued that the traditional gods of Egypt and other lands were all false. Only Aton, the glorious sun, everywhere the same and everywhere beneficent to men, together with Pharaoh who, like the sun, was also beneficent and—at least in principle—also universal, seemed to the reformers to bear the true marks of divinity. When the Pharaoh Amenhotep IV (1379–62 B.C.) came to the throne he espoused these ideas. Renaming himself Akhnaton, he set out to use all the traditional powers of his office to overthrow the old rites and pieties of Egypt. This roused a counter-fanaticism among priests and conservatives, so that after Akhnaton's death the Atonist faith was persecuted as energetically as it had briefly persecuted the older forms of Egyptian religion. Thereafter the Egyptians gave up all effort to reorganize their religious tradition to take account of the new realities that contacts with distant peoples had brought to the fore. Rigid conservatism in all things, treasuring each jot and tittle of ancient learning because of its immemorial antiquity, became the prevailing attitude of mind. The older the better, so that in art, for example, sculptors copied Old Kingdom works, and did so with such skill that modern scholars cannot always be sure which are from the third millennium B.C. and which were made two thousand years later!

The political history of the ancient Middle East reinforced this psychological turn. After 1100 B.C. Egyptian power shrank back to the narrow valley of the Nile, whose natural defenses gave pause even to the Assyrians and made the Persian control over Egypt persistently insecure. Egypt, in short, both in thought and deed, turned her back upon the rest of the world, and by so doing was able to preserve her age-old political and cultural identity until Roman times.

Early Judaism

‡‡‡ The really fruitful thinking of the first millennium B.C. occurred not in either of the ancient centers of Middle Eastern civilization, but in two marginal areas: Palestine and Iran. Palestine lay between Egypt and Mesopotamia. Its inhabitants were aware of the cultural traditions of both but shared fully in neither. In similar fashion, eastern Iran lay on the cultural watershed between Mesopotamia and the rising civilization of India. Hence, in both Palestine and eastern Iran when local conditions stimulated men to try to explain afresh the working of the universe, they found not one but two competing systems of thought at hand. Under these circumstances simple assimilation or modest adjustment of civilized myths to suit local needs and traditions was not really satisfactory. Instead, a freer and more radical religious revelation be-

came possible. Serious and sensitive men in both places set out to wrestle with the perennial problems of human life without being able to rely upon ready-made, self-authenticated, and immemorially ancient bodies of doctrine.

In this struggle to define anew men's relations to the supernatural, the Judaic tradition, centered in Palestine and recorded in the Hebrew scriptures, proved critically important, for it became the seedbed not only of modern Judaism, but of Christianity and of Islam as well.

Biblical tradition traced the Hebrews back to Abraham, who left the Sumerian city of Ur (perhaps about 1900 B.C.) to take up a nomadic life along the desert fringes of Mesopotamia and Syria. Abraham reputedly migrated the length of the fertile crescent that curves to the north of the Arabian desert until he and his followers arrived in the land of Canaan, later called Palestine. There is nothing intrinsically improbable about this traditional account.

The next major episode in Hebrew history, the Egyptian bondage, is more puzzling, for Egyptian records and chronology are difficult to reconcile with the Biblical story. Perhaps some Hebrews migrated into Egypt with the Hyksos, and were later subjugated by native Pharaohs; but no Egyptian record says so. Moses, the leader of the Exodus, may have been in touch with Atonist religion; but of this there is no evidence, other than his Egyptian name. The Biblical account of how the oppressed Hebrews left Egypt and resumed a nomadic life in the Sinai peninsula may be based on historical happenings. The covenant with Yahweh and Moses' law-giving at the foot of Mt. Sinai seem, indeed, exactly what a people who had forgotten customary ways of living in the desert would require.

Most modern scholars are of the opinion that the Hebrews who invaded Canaan and occupied the hill country of Palestine soon after 1200 B.C. came freshly from the desert, and that only a few of them (perhaps one or two of the twelve tribes) had been in Egypt or acknowledged the religion of Moses. Nevertheless, a codified law and a god of battles who had proved his power by protecting his people from the wrath of Egypt were clearly assets to tribesmen who lacked political or cultural cohesion. Hence, it is not surprising that the religion of Yahweh became the rallying point for military operations against the Canaanites. On the other hand, as soon as the Hebrews

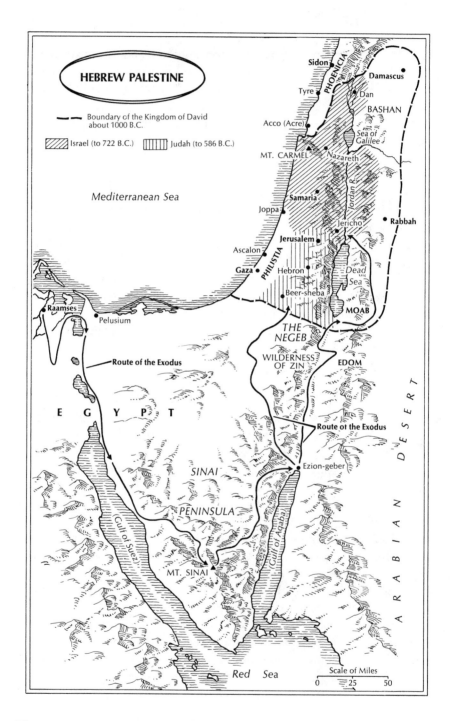

HEBREW PALESTINE

- - - Boundary of the Kingdom of David
about 1000 B.C.

Israel (to 722 B.C.)   Judah (to 586 B.C.)

Mediterranean Sea

Sidon
PHOENICIA
Damascus
Tyre   Dan
BASHAN
Acco (Acre)
Sea of
Galilee
MT. CARMEL   Nazareth
Jordan R.
Samaria
Joppa
Jericho
Rabbah
Jerusalem
Ascalon
PHILISTIA
Hebron   Dead
Gaza   Sea
Beer-sheba
MOAB
Raamses
Pelusium
THE
NEGEB
WILDERNESS
OF ZIN   EDOM
Route of the Exodus
E G Y P T
Route of the Exodus
Ezion-geber
SINAI
PENINSULA
Gulf of Suez
Gulf of Aqaba
A R A B I A N   D E S E R T
MT. SINAI
Red Sea
Scale of Miles
0   25   50

began to settle down to agriculture, they naturally resorted to the gods of the land, the baals, whose power to guard the crop and fertilize the fields had been attested by long experience.

The worship of Yahweh never merged into the fertility cults of Canaan. Memories of the desert and of the good old days when Yahweh's followers smote the Canaanites and destroyed their idols kept old antagonisms alive. Hence, when the need for defense against Philistines and other neighbors compelled the Hebrews to unite under the leadership of a king, the mighty men who fought first for Saul and then for David naturally rallied under Yahweh's warlike banner. The rapid expansion of David's kingdom (c. 1000–961 B.C.), however, opened the way for courtly luxury and closer relations with neighboring states. This in turn provoked bands of prophets to denounce, in Yahweh's name, all the new-fangled corruptions resulting from the inroads of civilization and to renew attack on the baals. Elijah was the most famous of these early prophets.

Prophecy took a new turn when individuals, inspired by a burning sense of God's power and will, denounced social injustices in passionate poetry, which was then recorded and preserved. The earliest of these literary prophets was Amos (c. 750 B.C.). During this period, the Hebrew prophets remoulded the religion of Yahweh, universalizing Yahweh's power rather than regarding him as a tribal war god, which had been the tendency during the time of the invasion of Canaan. At the same time, they declared that God was both just and merciful, punishing wrongdoers yet ready also to forgive those sinners who repented in time.

Yahweh had always been a jealous god, requiring the undivided loyalty of his people and repudiating all rivals. It was therefore comparatively easy for the Hebrew prophets to develop the worship of Yahweh into an uncompromising monotheism. No other people of the Middle East could become monotheists and also remain true to their traditional faith, for they had all inherited polytheistic pantheons. Yet monotheism seemed the only really satisfactory explanation of a world in which distant monarchs and unforeseeable events originating hundreds of miles away profoundly affected local affairs. In such an age, religious localism no longer accorded with common sense and everyday experience. Traditional rites rang hollow; only the Hebrews were able to give full expression to the widely felt need for religious universalism. Their definition of ethical monotheism constituted therefore one of the greatest and most enduring achievements of ancient Middle Eastern civilization.

The institutional form that the worship of Yahweh assumed was also of great importance for subsequent religious development. As long as the Hebrews enjoyed political independence, the cult of Yahweh centered upon temple rituals conducted in the capital. Temple ritual reached its peak under King Solomon, David's son and successor (reigned *c.* 961–*c.* 922 B.C.), who built a splendid new temple to Yahweh at Jerusalem. Hebrew political strength weakened after King Solomon's death (*c.* 922 B.C.) when the kingdom split into two parts: Israel in the north with its capital at Samaria, and the smaller kingdom of Judah in the south with Jerusalem for its capital. Then, as we have seen, when Israel was conquered by the Assyrians in 722 B.C., its leading families were deported, and a similar fate befell Judah at the hands of the Babylonian conqueror, Nebuchadnezzar, in 587 B.C.

The exiles from Israel lost their identity (the ten "Lost Tribes") and merged into the general population of the Middle East. In the northern kingdom, therefore, the religion of Yahweh survived only on a simple peasant level. Adherents of this faith were later known as Samaritans. Jews, who inherited the far richer tradition of Judah, despised the Samaritans as men who had allowed true religion to become mixed with superstition.

A far different fate befell the exiles from Judah. Not long before the conquest of Jerusalem (587 B.C.) a strenuous effort had been made to purify the worship of Yahweh. In the course of this reform the sacred scriptures were organized into the books of the Old Testament, almost as known today. Hence, when the leading families of the land found themselves exiled in Babylon, far from Yahweh's temple, they at least possessed the sacred texts and could read and study them. Weekly meetings of the faithful at which a teacher (rabbi) explained the scriptures replaced temple services, and became the central cult act of what we may henceforth properly call the Jewish religion. Even when Cyrus the Persian permitted the exiles to return to Jerusalem (only a few actually did so), services in the restored temple did not displace local weekly meetings for reading the scriptures. Most Jews could not attend the temple, for many remained scattered in distant lands among alien peoples. They nevertheless retained the full belief in their religion, reinforcing their hopes by pondering the promises of the holy texts.

Religion was thus separated from locality. Jews could in most outward things behave like the people around them, speak diverse languages, and dress and act in different ways while yet remaining faithful to Yahweh. Religion, in short, became disentangled from other aspects of human culture. Instead of depending upon priests to conduct services in the temple at Jerusalem, or requiring its adherents to live in a single area and follow more or less uniform customs, the Jewish faith became capable of flourishing wherever a few worshippers of Yahweh might gather to study and meditate upon the scriptures.

The exile also worked an important change in the emotional tone of the Jewish faith. Emphatic predictions of a future righting of wrongs had always been a prominent feature of prophecy. But the experience of the exile in Babylon gave the future an even greater importance. Jews were compelled to ask themselves: Why does God allow the wicked to prevail? Why does He punish his faithful servants so harshly? Two theories emerged from this questioning. Some, like Ezra and Nehemiah, emphasized the need for an even more scrupulous adherence to God's will as revealed in the scripture, since present sufferings were obviously due to God's displeasure with shortcomings of the past. But others, in particular the great poet Isaiah, developed the idea that God was purging his people, trying their patience and testing their fortitude, in order to reward the remnant on a great "Day of Judgment" when the world would come to an end and all its injustices be finally swept away. To men buoyed by such a vision, the greater the sufferings of the present, the nearer seemed the Day of Judgment, and the more important it was to adhere carefully to God's prescriptions as recorded in scripture.

Since different passages of the holy books seemed to contradict one another on many points, and since there were many personal problems which no scriptural instruction seemed to meet, the rabbis had to exert much ingenuity in applying scripture to daily life. Doing so they gradually evolved a code of conduct that answered almost every problem a man could raise, and gave everyday life meaning and value. Such a belief and such a moral code was like a beacon amid the flaccid cultural landscape of the ancient Middle East, whose great cities were populated in large measure by men who had lost their ancestral religious values without acquiring any real convictions or new moral codes that were adequate to urban conditions. In the major cities, therefore, where other faiths broke down, Judaism flourished, and amid all uncertainties and hardships of the age, strengthened its hold on its adherents' minds.

The canon of scripture was not closed until long after 500 B.C. and the rabbinical commentaries upon the sacred texts did not attain definitive form until several centuries after the Christian era. Nevertheless, by 500 B.C. the peculiar emphasis and unique vitality of Judaism had become clearly apparent.

Zoroastrianism

‡‡‡ Meanwhile, far to the east, on the other flank of the Mesopotamian world, another religious movement attained major importance in the sixth century B.C. The reform of Persian religion associated with the name of Zoroaster differed from the development of Judaism in being the work of a single great prophet, who repudiated and denounced the traditions of his people and sought to make all things new. The Parsis of modern India trace their religion back to Zoroaster, but the connecting links are obscure. It is not certain, for example, what if any of the sacred writings preserved by the Parsis should be attributed to Zoroaster himself. The most ancient part of those writings, the *Gathas*, are written in a crabbed form of the Persian language, many passages of which remain almost unintelligible to modern scholars.

It is difficult therefore to know details of what Zoroaster taught. Dispute also rages as to where and when he preached. The only indisputable landmark is the fact that King Darius of Persia (d. 486 B.C.) used Zoroastrian phrases in some of his inscriptions. This suggests that he was himself an adherent of the faith. It seems likely that in Darius' time the Zoroastrian doctrine was still fresh-minted, the work of a man seeking to explain and order the changing world in which the Persians found themselves as they launched their imperial career.

Zoroaster's message was lofty and abstract. He preached the glory of a supreme, incorporeal, and universal deity, Ahura Mazda. Mazda was locked in cosmic strife with Ahriman, the principle of evil. Every good man's duty, clearly, was to enlist on the side of Light and obey Ahura Mazda's instructions, transmitted through the prophet Zoroaster. These involved modest cultic observances (blood sacrifice was expressly forbidden) and moral conduct toward other men. As reward, Zoroaster promised prosperity in this world and immortality hereafter. He also seems to have believed that the end of the world would come in due season, at which time Ahura Mazda would signify his triumph by sending a purifying freshet of molten metal to engulf the wicked. The forces of Light, divine and angelic as well as human, would then rejoice together and forever in their victory.

Zoroastrianism never became the faith of any people who were not Persian; and even among the Persians probably only a limited circle of aristocrats and courtiers espoused the prophet's doctrine in its entirety. After the time of Xerxes (d. 465 B.C.), for example, inscriptions left by Persian monarchs referred to deities and concepts that contradict Zoroaster's teachings (as reconstructed by modern scholars anyhow). Hence it does not appear that strict Zoroastrianism long prevailed even in the Persian court. Yet the political power the Persians won under Cyrus and stabilized under Darius meant that the religion of Zoroaster became at least vaguely known to all the various peoples whom the Persians ruled over. Thus certain features of later Judaism —for example, such concepts as angels and a fiery damnation of the wicked—were either borrowed from or influenced by Zoroastrian doctrine.

Zoroastrianism had no such world-transforming career as Judaism and its two daughter religions, Christianity and Islam, were to have. Yet Zoroaster's teaching deserves to rank with the utterances of the great Hebrew prophets as a serious and fervent effort to give religious direction and order to the flux and uncertainty of the cosmopolitan world of the ancient Middle East. Zoroastrian dualism explained evil more plausibly than any strictly monotheistic faith could do. Dualisms which traced their origins indirectly to Zoroaster have therefore cropped up repeatedly in the Judeo-Christian-Moslem traditions; but Zoroastrianism itself barely survives, and not without extensive later emendation, among the Parsi community of India.

CHAPTER 4

The Definition of Indian

Civilization to 500 B.C.

 The warlike invaders who destroyed the Indus cities about 1500 B.C. inaugurated a dark and barbarous age in India. It is likely that several waves of Aryan invaders drifted southward across the mountains, requiring as much as three hundred years to complete their migration. During all this time, rival bands of warriors wandered with their cattle from place to place, stopping to reap a crop from time to time, before again moving on. The wanderers fought one another and subjugated the native populations they found on the ground. Bands gradually penetrated to new parts of India, spreading Aryan speech and breaking down the earlier isolation of forest peoples in the interior, whom the newcomers easily overpowered because of their warrior habits and better armament.

By slow degrees, however, the wanderers began to settle down to a more stable agricultural life. Herding ceased to have the pre-eminence it had enjoyed in the heroic days of roving and conquest. The more laborious tasks of working in the fields supplanted the leisured routine of warrior herdsmen. But even after the invaders had become fully agricultural, Aryan expansion into the further reaches of southern and eastern India continued. Their style of slash and burn cultivation required sporadic migration to new ground when old fields had become too choked with weeds.

Remains from the "heroic age" of Indian history are few. Lacking well-built cities or permanent places of residence, the early Aryans left little for archaeologists to discover. To be sure, there are literary texts descended from this age. But these owe their preservation to the fact that priests later adapted them for use in religious rituals. In the process, the original texts underwent repeated changes as they were passed orally from one generation to the next. As a result, it is often impossible to know what is genuinely ancient and what may have been added later. Nevertheless, both the *Rig Veda*, the holiest and probably the oldest collection of Sanskrit poems that has been preserved, and the *Mahabharata*, a vast epic poem, include passages that describe how noble archers engaged in duels with rival heroes by exchanging volleys of arrows while galloping across the field of battle in horse-drawn chariots. Such passages attest that India, like Greece and the Middle East, experienced an aristocratic chariot age.

Then, about 900 B.C. chariot tactics ceased to prevail in India. Iron spread to the subcontinent and, just as it did in the Middle East, allowed poor men who could not afford to keep horses and chariots to protect themselves with armor. The coming of iron therefore overthrew aristocratic predominance. As iron altered the balance of forces on the battlefield, small states arose in which each fighting man had his share in making political decisions. Evidence for the existence of these armed, rudely egalitarian communities comes mainly from the north, especially amid the foothills of the Himalayas; but it is possible that similar political arrangements had once had a much wider distribution before the great centralized monarchies of the Ganges valley began to overpower such local communities. It is indeed only when these old-fashioned clan republics succumbed to the forces of some great king —a process in full career about 600 B.C.—that we hear of their existence.

Shift to the Ganges

‡‡‡ Iron had another important effect on Indian life. Tools made of the new metal facilitated clearing the jungle, especially in the Ganges valley, where the heavy rains of the monsoon sustained lush vegetation

and made the soil, once cleared of its trees, into unusually fertile farm land. Rice, which, as we saw, was probably first domesticated by garden cultivators of southeast Asia, added greatly to the productivity of the Ganges valley. Wheat and barley, the two staples of Middle Eastern agriculture, yielded far less food per acre of crop land than did rice. Denser populations could therefore be sustained in lands suited to rice. Permanent occupation of particular fields went along with rice farming, for the artificial flooding and draining of a rice paddy eliminated nearly all weeds by altering the moistness of the field drastically. Moreover, the diking, digging, and terracing needed to bring irrigation water to the paddy fields was too laborious to make moving to a new location seem in the least attractive. Thus fully settled agriculture, with permanent village and town centers and a population that could be taxed easily because it could not afford to flee into jungle clearings, all arose in the Ganges region as a result of the establishment of rice cultivation.

By about 800 B.C., therefore, the Ganges valley had achieved the prerequisites for a fresh growth toward civilized complexity. This time the Indus valley was left far behind. Old-fashioned shifting cultivation still prevailed in the Indus region. No firm, large-scale political structure could be raised upon the backs of a population that could melt off into the forest whenever a royal agent came to demand taxes or some sort of labor service. To the east, on the contrary, the rice paddies both tied their cultivators down and gave them such a productive type of agriculture that they could afford to part with considerable quantities of their crop and still survive.

Several great monarchies served by professional administrators and by professional soldiers therefore began to develop in the Ganges valley at a time when the Indus (and presumably also south India about which we know nothing) were still divided among innumerable tribal groupings, united, if at all, only by the unstable suzerainty of some high king, who lacked real administrative authority beyond his own immediate circle of personal followers. In the Ganges region, however, the development of effectively centralized monarchies supported the rise of courtly centers, where high artisan skills could and did develop rapidly. Interregional trade also became important, and even lapped over from its center in the Ganges region to add a new and potentially very significant element to Indus valley life. Archaeological evidence shows that sea-borne trade with Mesopotamia was resumed by about 800 B.C.

In all these respects, the development of India differed from that of the Middle East only in being somewhat retarded and somewhat less well recorded. Yet the new style of life which began to emerge in India after 800 B.C. was quite different from that prevailing in the cosmopolitan world of the Assyrian and Persian empires north and west of the Hindu Kush. The unique character of the emergent Indian civilization centered on the institution of caste and the ascetic transcendental emphases of Indian religion. Each of these requires a little explanation.

Caste

‡‡‡ A modern caste is a group of persons who will eat with one another and intermarry, while excluding others from these two intimacies. In addition, members of any particular caste must bear some distinguishing mark, so that everyone will know who belongs and who does not belong to it. Definite rules for how to behave in the presence of members of other castes also become necessary in situations where such contacts are frequent. When an entire society comes to be organized on these principles, any group of strangers or intruders automatically becomes another caste, for the exclusive habits of the rest of the population inevitably thrust the newcomers in upon themselves when it comes to eating and marrying. A large caste may easily break into smaller groupings as a result of some dispute, or through mere geographical separation over a period of time. New castes can form around new occupations. Wanderers and displaced individuals who find a new niche in society are automatically compelled to eat together and marry one another by the caste-bound habits of their neighbors.

How or when Indian society came to be organized along these lines remains unclear. Perhaps the Indus civilization itself was built upon something like the caste principle. Or perhaps the antipathy between Aryan invaders and the dark-skinned people whom they attacked lay at the root of the caste system of later India. But whatever the origins of caste, three features of Indian thought and feeling were mobilized to sustain the caste principle in later times. One of these was the idea of ceremonial purity. Fear of contaminating oneself by contact with a member of a lower, "unclean" caste gave Brahmans and others near the top of the pyramid strong reasons for limiting their association with low-caste persons.

From the other end of the scale, too, the poor and humble had strong reasons for clinging to caste. All but the most miserable and marginal could look down upon somebody, a not unimportant psychological feature of the system. In addition, the humbler castes were often groups that had only recently emerged from primitive forest life. They naturally sought to maintain their peculiar customs and habits, even in the context of urban or mixed village life, where men of different backgrounds and different castes lived side by side. Other civilized societies usually persuaded or compelled newcomers to surrender their peculiar ways, and assimilated them in the course of a few generations to the civilized population as a whole. In India, on the contrary, such groups were able to retain their separate identities indefinitely by preserving their own peculiar customs within the caste framework, generation after generation.

The third factor sustaining the caste principle was theoretical: the doctrine of reincarnation and of "varna." The latter declared that all men were naturally divided into four castes: the Brahmans who prayed, the Kshatriyas who fought, the Vaisyas who worked, and the Sudras who performed unclean tasks. Official doctrine classified the first three castes as Aryan, the last as non-Aryan, and put much stress on caste rank, from Brahmans at the top to Sudras at the bottom. Reality never corresponded even remotely to this theory. As far back as we can tell there were hundreds if not thousands of castes in India, rather than the four recognized in Brahmanical teaching. But the theory was important because apparent injustices and anomalies disappeared when the doctrine of reincarnation was combined with the doctrine of varna. The idea of reincarnation, indeed, gave logical explanation and justification to the system by explaining that caste was a divinely established institution, hereditary from father to son, and designed to reward and punish souls for their actions in former lives. This undoubtedly helped to stabilize the confused reality. A man of unblemished life, born into the lowest caste, could hope for rebirth higher up the ladder. Conversely, a man of high caste who failed to conform to proper standards could expect rebirth in a lower caste. A really wicked man even risked reincarnation as a worm or beetle.

Clearly, the caste system as observed today did not exist in ancient India. Yet modern castes are the outgrowth of patterns of social organization that are as old as the oldest records. Early Buddhist stories, for instance, reveal many episodes turning upon caste distinctions, and passages in the *Rig Veda* and other ancient writings imply caste-like practices and attitudes. By 500 B.C. we can at least be sure that the seeds from which the modern caste organization of society grew had already sprouted luxuriantly on Indian soil.

Caste lessened the significance of political, territorial administration. Everyone identified himself first and foremost with his caste. But a caste ordinarily lacked both definite internal administration and distinct territorial boundaries. Instead, members of a particular caste mingled with men of other castes, observing the necessary precautions to prevent contamination of one by the other. No king or ruler could command the undivided loyalty of people who felt themselves to belong to a caste rather than to a state. Indeed, ordinary caste members regarded rulers, officials, soldiers, and tax collectors as troublesome outsiders, to be neglected whenever possible and obeyed only as far as necessary. The fragile character of most Indian states resulted in large part from this fact. A striking absence of information about war and government is characteristic of all early Indian history; and this, too, presumably reflects Indian peoples' fundamental emotional disengagement from the state and from politics.

Caste also made it easy for Indian civilization to bring new groups within the pale. No very radical adjustment of previous customs and habits was required of the newcomers, who simply became one more among the already innumerable castes of the land. Correspondingly, very primitive and ancient patterns of thought and behavior remained half-hidden within the fabric of Indian society, perpetuated by peoples who in adjusting themselves to the necessity of living amid strangers had nevertheless, through the device of caste, retained their primitive ancestors' magical rites, charms, and habits of thought.

Transcendental Religion

‡‡‡ Disregard for war and politics and tolerant hospitality for widely divergent customs accorded well with India's unique religious evolution. Until quite recently in India, religious doctrine was transmitted

exclusively by word of mouth from teacher to pupil. Any earnest inquirer after truth might sit at the feet of more than one teacher. Hence, all sorts of blending and interlacing of different doctrines easily occurred. Moreover, there are no dates to help sort out the development of religious thought. The bulky religious literature that has survived contains remarkably few references to events or personages that can be identified with a particular time and place. Any effort to disentangle strands of thought must therefore be logical rather than historical. Nevertheless, the logical sequence may match the historical stages of development. We simply cannot be sure.

Surviving records are, of course, all written in Sanskrit, the language of the Aryan invaders. They brought with them a pantheon of deities, among whom the principal war leader and strongest personality was Indra, destroyer of cities and god of thunder and storm. Other gods embodied other natural elements and forces—sky, air, earth, water, and the like. A priesthood accompanied the invaders also. Its function was to invoke the gods, offer sacrifice, and by other appropriate rituals to ward off divine displeasure. Prosperity in peace and in war, long life, and good health were the goals of these pious observances.

Nothing in this religion seems notably different from the aims and attitudes of other barbarian tribes of Indo-European speech: Greeks, Latins, Celts, Germans, Iranians, Slavs, and the rest. All of them revered aspects of nature which had been endowed with more or less definite personalities. Details of the pantheon varied from case to case, but it seems clear that the fundamental world view expressed by these early Indo-European religions had been built up by priestly specialists who were at least vaguely aware of how the Mesopotamians conceived the divine rulers of the universe as a quarrelsome company of capricious personalities. The pervasive though inexact resemblances between the Sumerian pantheon and those of the different Indo-European peoples cannot be accounted for in any other way.

The Vedas and Brahmanas

‡‡‡ Our knowledge of Aryan religion derives from the Vedas. The Vedas, used as handbooks of religious ritual, consist of songs that were

recited aloud during sacrifices, together with other passages instructing the priests what to do during the ceremony. In course of time, the language of the Vedas became more or less unintelligible, even to priests. A great effort was thereupon made to preserve details of accent and pronunciation, by insisting on exact memorization of texts from master to pupil across the generations. Every jot and tittle of the inherited verses was felt to matter, since a misplaced line or mispronounced word could nullify a whole sacrifice and might even provoke divine displeasure.

Preoccupation with correctness of detail speedily shifted emphasis from the gods of the Aryan pantheon to the act of worship and invocation itself. Aryan priests may also have learned about magical powers claimed by priests of the Indus civilization. At any rate, some Brahmans began to argue that by performing rituals correctly they could actually compel the gods to grant what was asked of them. Indeed, proper sacrifice and invocation created the world of gods and men anew, and stabilized afresh the critical relation between natural and supernatural reality. In such a view, the importance and personalities of the separate gods shrank to triviality, while the power and skill of the priesthood was greatly magnified. These extravagent priestly claims were freely put forward in texts called Brahmanas. These were cast in the form of commentaries on the Vedas, purportedly explaining what the older texts really meant, but often changing meanings in the process.

The Upanishads, Mysticism, and the Beginning of Hinduism

‡‡‡ Priestly claims to exercise authority over gods and men were never widely accepted in ancient India. Chiefs and warriors might be a bit wary of priestly magic, but they were not eager to cede to the priests the primacy claimed by the Brahmanas. Humbler ranks of society also objected to priestly presumption. This is proved by the fact that a rival type of piety took hold in India and soon came to constitute the most distinctive element in the whole religious tradition of the land. Another body of oral literature, the Upanishads, constitutes our evidence of this religious development. The Upanishads are not sys-

tematic treatises nor do they agree in all details. Yet they do express a general consensus on important points.

First of all, the Upanishads conceive the end of religious life in a radically new way. Instead of seeking riches, health, and long life, a wise and holy man strives merely to escape the endless round of rebirth. Success allows his soul to dissolve into the All from whence it had come, triumphantly transcending the suffering, pain, and imperfection of existence.

In the second place, holiness and release from the cycle of rebirths were attained not by obedience to priests nor by observance of ceremonies. The truly holy man had no need of intermediaries and, for that matter, no need of gods. Instead, by a process of self-discipline, meditation, asceticism, and withdrawal from the ordinary concerns of daily life, the successful religious athlete might attain a mystic vision of Truth—a vision which left the seer purged and happy. The nature and content of the mystic vision could never be expressed in words. It revealed Truth by achieving an identity between the individual soul and the Soul of the universe. Such an experience, surpassing human understanding and ordinary language, constituted a foretaste of the ultimate bliss of self-annihilation in the All, which was the final goal of wise and holy life.

The themes and attitudes expressed in the Upanishads are so different from the worldly and practical tone of the Vedas and Brahmanas that anyone who is not himself a mystic is likely to ask how the change can be accounted for. Perhaps ascetic practices had been known to the priests and holy men of India before the Aryan invasion. If so, the Upanishads' recipe for the religious life may represent the recognition in Sanskrit literature of attitudes and ascetic disciplines which were of pre-Aryan origin. But since we have no evidence of what pre-Aryan religion was like, this explanation remains speculative.

A second sort of explanation points to the changing social scene of India as a cause for the spread of mysticism. It seems to be true that the ascetic, other-worldly emphasis of the Upanishads began to attract attention among the speakers of Aryan tongues only when the small, more or less egalitarian communities of free men, which had arisen in northern India during the Iron Age, began to crumble before the greater power of centralized bureaucratic kingdoms of the Ganges valley. Perhaps, therefore, men who found their familiar way of life no longer possible were attracted to asceticism precisely because strangers and agents of distant rulers had destroyed the social and political order their fathers had known. On such a hypothesis, men who were descended from warriors and rulers found a substitute for their own lost liberties in the private and personal pursuit of holiness, conducted, for the most part, in the freedom of forest retreats, far from the ordinary haunts of men. It was in such places that the Upanishads were created, when a master of ascetic discipline attempted to pass on to others the secret of his experience.

Still a third explanation is physiological. Skeptics of course have no difficulty in proving that prolonged fasting, sleeplessness, and deliberate repression of breathing can produce unusual bodily sensations. When men are prepared by an eager expectation to interpret sensations experienced under such circumstances as a confrontation with some divine, ultimate reality, the experience acquires overwhelming emotional and personal importance.

Yet to anyone who has experienced a mystic vision such explanations are simply irrelevant. Initiates who share a memory and who live in hope of the renewal of their spiritual transport know the self-validating force of the experience. Justification is unnecessary, explanation impossible, doubt inconceivable—or so the words and behavior of thousands upon thousands of mystics strongly suggest.

The godless asceticism recommended by the Upanishads and the meticulous performance of rituals demanded by the Brahmanas certainly seem opposed. Yet the Brahman priests of ancient India found an easy way to reconcile these contradictory ideals. They argued that the way of the Upanishads was appropriate toward the end of a man's life, after he had spent his youth honoring priests, observing ceremonial prescriptions, and raising a family. In this fashion the doctrines of the Upanishads were accepted into Brahmanical religion, and the priests, whose pretensions to authority were directly assailed by the teachings of the Upanishads, serenely survived as purveyors of religious ritual for ordinary people.

The merger of Vedic and Upanishadic religious traditions marks the birth of Hinduism, one of the great religious systems of the world. An enormous variety of religious practice and belief was, and continued to be, part of Hinduism; and the entire system kept on evolving in response to the rival demands of priestly ritual and mystical aspiration.

Encounters with other, more systematic religions were another important stimulus to Hinduism's on-going development.

Jainism and Buddhism

‡‡‡ About 500 B.C., the emergence of Buddhism and of Jainism presented Hinduism with the first such external challenge. These two religions had historical founders, both of whom were probably alive in the year 500 B.C. although exact dates are not known in either case. Jainism was established, or reformulated, by Mahavira; Buddhism arose around the charismatic figure of Prince Gautama. The two religions had much in common. Both in a sense popularized the ideas that had been abstractly expressed in the Upanishads. Both Mahavira and Gautama, the Buddha, made personal annihilation and escape from the cycle of rebirth the supreme goal of religious striving. But the two religions differed in some important details of doctrine, and Jainism never attained Buddhism's popularity. It remained a faith for an elite, demanding strenuous asceticism, even to the point of starvation unto death, of its initiates.

Buddhism, on the contrary, was built around a moderate regimen. In his youth, Gautama tried asceticism, but he then decided that severe maltreatment of the body was not the way to escape from the suffering of existence. Instead he recommended a quiet middle way between ordinary self-indulgence and the severities of the practicing ascetic. He himself, and his numerous followers, divided their time between contemplation, religious discussion, and begging. During the rainy season, Gautama was fond of remaining in the same spot with a group of like-minded men around him. In the dry season he wandered from place to place, living on alms. Annihilation of suffering by annihilating the self was Buddha's ultimate goal. That goal—Nirvana—was, however, a distant one for most of mankind. In the meanwhile, Buddha urged his followers to cultivate inner holiness by pursuing the "noble eightfold path," that is, the cultivation of right views, right aspirations, right speech, right conduct, right livelihood, right effort, right mindedness, and most important of all, right rapture. Gautama, the Buddha, never made explicit what the word translated as "right" in these phrases meant. He taught by example, not abstractly. His followers attempted to model their own lives on his, and observed the rules he laid down from time to time when particular problems came up.

During Gautama's lifetime, therefore, a body of followers arose who found the way of life he prescribed to be so satisfying that even after his death (*c.* 483 B.C.) they continued to live in communities that followed his rules, and honored the holy Buddha as embodied by Prince Gautama. Writers of English ordinarily call such communities "monasteries." The later Christian monasteries did in fact resemble them quite closely, since many Buddhist communities came in time to possess buildings and income-producing property donated by pious laymen who felt the need for holy men's aid along the path of salvation.

In this fashion, what had begun as a temporary association between master and followers attained a corporate durability which has lasted uninterruptedly until our own time. Buddha's teachings, to be sure, underwent great elaboration and radical change in the course of time, but the institutional continuity of communities of monks remains unbroken. The lives, feelings, and acts of hundreds of millions of men have been affected by these communities and by the religious ideals they preached and embodied. Despite the fact that the land of its birth later repudiated Buddhist forms of piety, India's main impact upon peoples outside her borders came in the guise of missionaries who spread the doctrine and the practices of the Buddhist religion into China, Japan, Korea, and almost all the lands of southeast Asia.

In India itself, during the first centuries of its existence, Buddhism popularized, moderated, and defined the Upanishadic style of religious life. Thereby, Buddhism helped to imprint a distinctive other-worldly, mystical, and ascetic tradition upon Indian civilization as a whole, and defined directions of growth from which later Indian thinkers and holy men never departed. Yet despite its early successes, Buddhism did not in the end prevail. Instead, a revived and transformed Hinduism proved capable of winning and holding the allegiance of most Indians. How this happened must be reserved for later consideration, but it is worth pointing out the practical weakness in Buddhism that made this great reversal possible. In its early forms, Buddhism had no rituals for the ordinary emergencies of human life—birth, death, marriage, coming of age, and the like. The texture of ordinary life therefore continued to call for the services of the Brahmans, and the need for Brahmans kept alive Vedic learning and priestly practices in all their complexities. The Buddhist way of life offered a complete guide only to the unusual individual who renounced normal family life and devoted himself entirely to the pursuit of holiness. Others could not afford to do without traditional rites and priestly assistance. For the ordinary crises of life early Buddhism had nothing to offer. India therefore never became a thoroughly Buddhist land, and Indian civilization never entirely fitted itself to a Buddhist mould.

Nevertheless, it seems fair to say that by about 500 B.C., when caste and the characteristic emphases of Indian religion had both come into focus, Indian civilization as a whole had defined its enduring character and special bent. Great elaboration and cumulatively great transformations of course lay ahead, yet a cultural identity recognizably the same links contemporary India with the ancient India of Buddha's time.

CHAPTER 5

The Definition of Greek

Civilization to 500 B.C.

 While India worked its way toward the definition of a new and distinctive civilization on one flank of the ancient Middle East, on its other flank another new civilization was also emerging: the Greek. The principal stages of early Greek history closely resemble what we know or can surmise about Indian development. But the end product differed fundamentally. The Greeks valued political organization into city-states above all other bases of human association, and attempted to explain the world and man not in terms of mystic illumination but through laws of nature. Thus despite a similar start, when fierce "tamers of horses"—like those of whom Homer later sang—overran priest-led agricultural societies, the Indian and Greek styles of civilization diverged strikingly by 500 B.C.

Mycenaean Vikings

‡‡‡ One great difference existed from the first. The Aryans of India remained landsmen, whereas the earliest Greek invaders of the Aegean region took readily to the sea, infiltrating Knossos in Minoan Crete and

establishing themselves among the Aegean islands as well as on the Greek mainland. The first Greek-speaking rulers of Knossos made very little change in the archaeological remains of Minoan civilization, although they did develop a new script (Linear B), which recorded an archaic form of the Greek language. About 1400 B.C., however, Knossos was destroyed, perhaps by some piratical raid launched from the new-sprung capital at Mycenae on the Greek mainland. For the next two hundred years a series of sea raids—alternating perhaps with more peaceable trade—carried Mycenaean ships to almost all the coasts of the Mediterranean. We know from Egyptian records of three separate attacks launched against Egypt by a coalition of "sea peoples" in which Mycenaean Greeks probably took a minor part. In the year 1190 B.C., however, the Egyptians successfully repelled the last of these ventures, and a remnant of the invading host settled in Palestine to become the Philistines of Biblical history. A similar raid (traditionally dated 1184 B.C.) against Troy at the mouth of the Dardanelles became the focus around which Homer's tales of heroism clustered.

The City-state

‡‡‡ Soon after 1200 B.C. these far-flung enterprises came to an end. A new wave of invaders, Greek-speaking Dorians, came down from the north and overran the centers of Mycenaean power. With the Dorians or very soon after came iron, with all the usual political consequences. Aristocratic charioteers, who had controlled war and politics in the days of Mycenae's greatness, were overthrown by wandering tribes of iron-wielding warriors. Such groups were always ready to migrate to any new spot where better crop land or pasture could be found. The Dorian invasions therefore proceeded piecemeal, and involved many secondary displacements of peoples. In particular, refugees from the Greek mainland took ship and established a series of new settlements across the Aegean on the coast of Asia Minor. These regions were subsequently known as Ionia and, further north, Aeolia. For protection against the native inhabitants the Greek settlements clustered on defensible peninsulas and other suitable places on the coast. Since the refugees (like the Hebrews of the Exodus) had no pre-existing pattern of leadership or code of custom to which all unthinkingly subscribed, they had to invent a visible set of laws and system of government to

assure effective co-operation in the new settlements. In so doing, they created the earliest Greek city-states.

Moses had faced a similar problem a century or two before, when he led the children of Israel from Egypt into the desert. The legislation with which he organized the Hebrew community in its new environment became the kernel of later Judaism. The self-governing city-states created by Greeks on the coast of Asia Minor had almost as great an importance in world history. For by inventing the city-state or *polis* (hence our word "politics"), the Greeks of Ionia established the prototype from which the whole Western world derived its penchant for political organization into territorially defined sovereign units, i.e. into states. The supremacy of citizenship over all other forms of human association is neither natural nor inevitable, as the Indian caste principle may remind us. Hence, if we Westerners owe our religion to Hebrew refugees from Pharaoh, we also owe our politics to Greek refugees from the Dorians, who had to reorganize and rationalize their traditional society in order to survive in a new and hostile environment just about two centuries after Moses had done the same for his followers.

Development on the mainland toward supremacy of the polis was slower. Semi-migratory tribes had first to settle permanently on some particular piece of land, and then had to combine with neighbors into a single territorial unit to constitute a polis. The line of evolution is fairly clear. Violence diminished, population grew, land became scarce and fixed farming became the rule. As the population settled down, local chieftains found it convenient to settle disputes by sitting in council under the presidency of a high king. When the full council could not be in session it often seemed desirable to appoint individuals to look after matters of common concern, and to check the king in any attempt he might make to extend his authority. In this fashion magistrates arose, who were appointed for a limited term and entrusted with a delegated and, in course of time, legally defined authority. In some of the emergent city-states the kingship itself became a magistracy; in other cases kingship remained hereditary in a particular family.

Colonization and Trade

‡‡‡ As population continued to grow, emigration overseas offered a solution for some of those who lacked enough land to live on at home.

Political struggles also encouraged emigration because defeated factions sometimes decided to take ship and found a new polis of their own in a place where suitable land could be found. In ancient times, emigration was not usually an individual or family affair, but was organized by groups of several hundred persons at a time. Numbers were needed for protection. Numbers also permitted new settlements to retain a fully Greek character amid barbarian populations even as far away as Sicily and southern Italy, or along the northern Aegean and Black Sea coasts. Greek colonies were fully self-governing from the start, although religious ties with the mother city were always maintained.

Colonization helped trade, for the new cities often acted as middlemen between up-country barbarians and the older Greek cities. Long-distance trade got an enormous fillip when a few Greek cities began to specialize in producing wine and olive oil. These were comparatively precious products and they required special climate and skills. Oil and wine could, however, be quite easily stored and shipped in jars. Barbarians within reach of Greek navigation quickly learned to value these products, and could offer grain, timber, or other raw materials in exchange. It soon became obvious that vintners and olive-growers had a great advantage in such trade. Barbarian nobles would pay a lot to get what they could not produce at home. They were therefore ready to supply far greater quantities of grains and other raw materials to the Greek cities where this sort of commercial agriculture took root than these same cities could possibly raise on the land that lay within their own boundaries. Population, in other words, could increase beyond the limits set by local grain supplies as long as a vigorous export of wine and oil could be maintained.

Coined money, invented first in the Kingdom of Lydia during the sixth century B.C., was an important lubricant to this Greek style of economic exchange. Coins of copper as well as of silver were needed to allow common people to buy and sell on an everyday basis. Indeed, in the biggest and most important Greek cities a large proportion of the entire population actually had to buy the food they ate, most of which had been imported by ship. Services came to be reckoned in money values—so many coins per day. So did commodities of every kind, including land and taxes.

The spread of market relations downward to the very bottom of society occurred for the first time in such cities. It meant a far greater flexibility than earlier societies had ever known. Rising prices could pull men and material resources toward any given line of activity; falling prices shifted manpower and resources away from overcrowded or inefficient kinds of activity. And prices rose and fell in response to supply and demand, partly evened out by official efforts to assure the food supply by regulating storage and distribution of grain. This kind of flexibility meant that Greeks and others tied into their price net could react more quickly and effectively to any sort of economic change than earlier societies had ever been able to do.

Export of oil and wine in return for grain and raw materials was a pattern of exchange that had fundamental importance for all later Greek and Roman history.

First of all, it made possible the creation of comparatively large cities in olive- and vine-growing coastlands, for such cities could feed themselves on imported grain. Secondly, it brought farmers into the commercial life of the towns as active and absolutely vital participants. In the older Middle Eastern societies, agricultural surpluses came onto the urban markets largely in the form of economically unrequited rents and taxes. A passive and withdrawn peasantry, regarding rulers and townspeople as their oppressors and natural enemies, was an inescapable consequence of such a relationship. Not so in Greece. The farmer with his wine and oil regarded himself and was regarded by others as the ideal type of citizen, entering the market freely as a buyer and seller, and expecting also to play his part in public affairs when the dry season interrupted the tasks of cultivation and permitted him the needful leisure.

Effects of the Phalanx

‡‡‡ About 650 B.C. a momentous change in military tactics gave a secure basis to the common farmer's participation in political life. This was the invention of the phalanx—a densely massed infantry formation eight ranks deep whose members were trained to run and charge in unison. A skillful charge delivered by several thousand armored men moving as a single mass proved capable of sweeping cavalry or any other kind of opposing force off the field. As this became obvious, every city had to organize and train as big a phalanx as possible from among the citizenry. Anything that interfered with strengthening the

phalanx endangered the city. If danger became acute, as happened for example in Sparta in the seventh century B.C., when a revolt of enslaved subjects threatened the Dorian rulers with disaster, the response could be drastic. The Spartans actually made themselves into a perpetual garrison in their own land, requiring that each citizen between the ages of twenty and thirty live in a barracks and eat in a military mess. No other city reacted so extremely as Sparta did, but no other Greek city was able to develop so professional a fighting force either. Others contented themselves with remodeling older aristocratic institutions in such a way as to give decisive weight to an assembly of all who were able to equip themselves for the phalanx with shield, helmet, sword, and spear.

The introduction of the phalanx had still another pervasive and profound influence. Every young man who could afford to buy the necessary armor and weapons spent long hours with his fellow youths practicing the rhythms and skills needed to fight effectively in the phalanx. Speed, strength, and courage were only part of what was required. In addition every man had to learn to keep time to the beat set up by the war chant, so that the wall of shields would not break when the phalanx charged across the field of battle. Every man's safety depended upon his neighbor keeping his place in the ranks, for each man's shield helped to cover the right side of the man next to him. Conspicuous personal feats of arms were as much out of place in such a situation as cowardice or inability to keep pace with the rhythm of the charge, for anything that broke the line threatened immediate disaster.

As the drill sergeants of every modern army know, hour after hour spent in rhythmic exercises with other men has an extremely powerful emotional effect. In all probability such exertions rouse instinctive resonances inherited by all men from extremely remote ancestors, who by dancing around their camp fires presumably both expressed and at the same time created the socio-psychological solidarity required for effective co-operation in the hunt. The aim and climax of the phalanx drill was battle; and this, too, roused fiercely primitive impulses deriving directly from experiences of human and proto-human hunting packs.

Perhaps because of these resonances with the most elemental level of human sociality, every Greek citizen and soldier who endured the long hours of training needed for successful phalanx fighting, and who

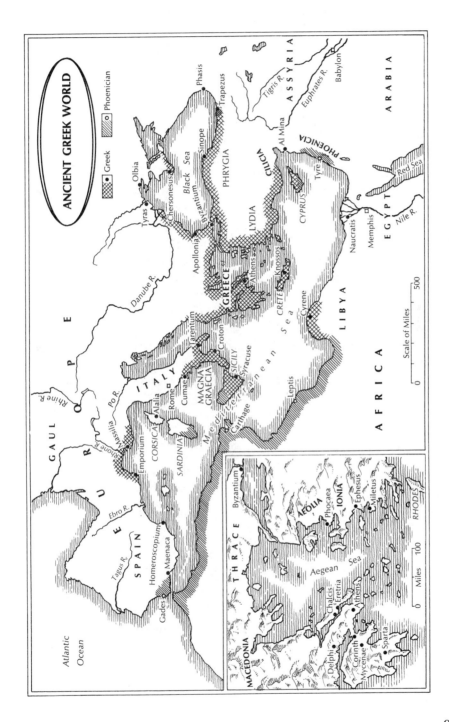

ANCIENT GREEK WORLD

• Greek
○ Phoenician

Scale of Miles
0   500

Miles
0   100

had then undergone the fatigues and dangers of a campaign and known the fierce joys and sudden exertions of battle emerged from such adventures marked for life by a deep sense of solidarity with all those who had shared these experiences with him. This intense sentiment became the basis for a collective pride in the greatness and glory of the city to which all equally belonged, and in whose service all might find personal fulfillment. In this way, by what only superficially seems to be a paradox, the Greek polis was able to create citizens who attained an unusually vivid sense of personal freedom by submitting to a common rhythm and a severely demanding regimen.

It is not therefore surprising that with the introduction of the phalanx the Greeks altered their ideal of personal behavior. In the earlier aristocratic age, individual self-assertion and conspicuous consumption had been generally admired. Feats of individual prowess, such as those celebrated by Homer, and personal display of luxury went hand in hand. The phalanx, however, made close conformity to a norm absolutely mandatory in military matters. This principle was soon carried over into civil life as well, so that it became ill-mannered, un-Greek, improper, to live luxuriously or, indeed, to differ in any conspicuous way from one's fellows. Competitive self-assertion was instead transferred to the collective concerns of the polis. To be sure, athletic contests offered a residual outlet for individual competitiveness. These took place as part of religious celebrations at a number of Panhellenic shrines of which Olympia (hence our Olympic Games) was the most famous. But in ordinary everyday life the conformity and cooperation required by good citizenship eclipsed individual assertiveness—in principle if not always in practice.

Dominance of the Polis in Greek Culture

‡‡‡ So powerful and compelling was the psychological pull of the polis that almost every aspect of Greek cultural activity was speedily caught up in and—as it were—digested by the new master institution of Greek civilization. Religion, art, literature, philosophy, took shape or acquired a new accent through their relationship with the all-engulfing object of the citizens' affection. A few remarks about each of these facets of Greek life will make their relationship to the polis clearer.

First, religion. In the dark age following the Dorian invasions, each local king and clan chieftain conducted religious observances on behalf of his household and followers. Later, these traditional religious duties were often treated as magistracies, to be occupied temporarily by one or another high-born aristocrat. Such religious functionaries were usually quite indifferent to the vast discrepanies of doctrine they had inherited. Greek religion had been compounded of two distinct elements. Stories associated with the gods who were believed to live on top of Mount Olympus, and whom the Greeks had brought with them from the north (a pantheon resembling the pantheon which the Aryans brought to India), confronted other myths associated with the ancient goddesses of fertility who had been worshipped in the land before the Greeks arrived.

Priests of the oracle at Delphi together with poets who regarded themselves and were regarded by others as divinely inspired did something to bring order into this confusion. Hesiod (eighth century B.C.) in particular attempted to organize the various myths into a coherent whole. But Hesiod and his predecessor, the mighty but theologically unsystematic Homer, could not really reconcile the innumerable contradictions that resulted from the combination of two incompatible religious systems. This logical disarray opened wide the gate for private speculation about the nature of the world and man's place in it. In this way philosophy was born.

Religious development moved in another direction. Ordinary men and politicians were not seriously troubled by the obvious conflicts among traditional myths. As long as traditional modes of invocation and worship of each deity were reasonably clear it was enough to know that one god was appropriate for one occasion and another for a different occasion. But as the wealth of Greek cities increased, and especially when it became common for rich men to vie with one another in financing public worship, a great deal of inventiveness was devoted to the elaboration of traditional rites into impressive spectacles. In the course of this ritual elaboration, elements of the Olympian worship and elements derived from the older cults of the land were intermingled. This was conspicuously the case in Athens, for example, where during the Panathenea—one of the religious high points of the year—a great procession symbolically linked the ancient mystery cult center at Eleusis to the Acropolis by going from one to the other. Similarly, the worship of Dionysus—a johnny-come-lately among the gods who had no place among the Olympians—became the occasion for dramatic presentations of myths drawn indiscriminately from the Olympian and from the pre-Olympian religious traditions. In this practical fashion the rising polis, through public cult ceremonies, mingled and, by mingling, effectively disguised the discordancies of the Greek religious heritage.

Art, too, or at least those monuments that survive, came largely within the polis frame during the sixth century B.C. Construction of public temples gave employment to masons and architects. The creation of cult statues for such temples, not to mention the embellishment of temple walls and pediments, offered scope for sculptors. Classical Greek art was fundamentally shaped by the requirements of this sort of public use. Individual portraits were quite inappropriate to an art aiming at the portrayal of gods and heroes. Instead, an ideal type of human beauty was called for, and Greek artists succeeded in achieving it with a surety of touch that has stirred admiration ever since.

It was not until after 500 B.C. that the rise of the drama set the polis mark upon Greek literature. Prior to that time, poetry had been shaped to aristocratic tastes, and tended to glorify individual self-assertion and aggrandizement. This was pre-eminently true of the greatest and most influential of all Greek poets: Homer. Homer probably lived sometime between 850 and 700 B.C. in Asia Minor; but his poems deal with Mycenaean heroes, and reproduce a good deal of quite correct information about that age which must have been transmitted orally, perhaps by a bardic tradition. Modern archaeological discovery has tended to increase the plausibility of Homer's account of the wrath of Achilles and of Odysseus' travels; but the *Iliad* and *Odyssey* also contain clear anachronisms to prove that the poet lived much later, as the Greeks of the classical age themselves always believed. Homer's statement of the heroic ideal, combining fierceness and joy in action with a haunting sense of the inevitability of eventual defeat and death, entered fundamentally into the Greek view of life. For just as a well-trained phalanx rushed into battle like a single being, animated by a single will and inspired by a common ferocity, so each individual Greek of the classical age tended to regard his particular polis as though it were one of Homer's heroes, and was easily persuaded to strive for the collective gain and glory of his city regardless of personal costs or consequences. In this simple fashion the Greeks were able to reconcile the self-effacement required by the phalanx with the older, aristocratic, and self-assertive ideal enshrined in Homer's poetry. To harness heroic violence and unbridled self-assertiveness to the service of the polis as the Greeks were thus able to do was really quite as remarkable as the simultaneous transvaluation of values taking place in India with the rise of the ascetic, mystical idea at the expense of earlier Aryan this-worldliness.

Despite the general success of the polis ordering of things, a few individuals fretted over the logical inconsistencies of Greek religion and traditional world view. As trade developed, opportunities to learn about the wisdom of other peoples multiplied. Inquiring Greeks soon discovered that among the priestly experts of the Middle East there was no agreement about such fundamental questions as how the world was created or why the planets periodically checked their forward movement through the heavens and went backward for a while before resuming their former motion. It was in Ionia that men first confronted this sort of question systematically enough to bother recording their views. These, the first philosophers, sought to explain the phenomena of the world by imaginative exercise of their power of reason. Finding conflicting and unsupported stories about the gods to be unsatisfactory, they took the drastic step of omitting the gods entirely, and boldly substituted natural law instead as the ruling force of the universe. To be sure, the Ionian philosophers did not agree among themselves when they sought to describe how the laws of nature worked, and their naïve efforts to explain an ever wider range of phenomena did not meet with much success.

Nevertheless, their attempts at using speculative reason to explain the nature of things marked a major turning point in human intellectual development. The Ionian concept of a universe ruled not by the whim of some divine personality but by an impersonal and unchangeable law has never since been forgotten. Throughout the subsequent history of European and Middle Eastern thought, this distinctively Greek view of the nature of things stood in persistent and fruitful tension with the older, Middle Eastern theistic explanation of the universe. Particular thinkers, reluctant to abandon either position entirely, have sought to reconcile the omnipotence of the divine will with the unchangeability of natural law by means of the most various arguments. Since, however, the two views are as logically incompatible with one another as were the myths from which the Ionian philosophers started, no formulation or reconciliation ever attained lasting and universal consent. Men always had to start over again to reshape for themselves a more satisfactory metaphysic and theology. Here, therefore, lay a growing point for all subsequent European thought which has not yet been exhausted.

Indeed, the recent successes of natural science seem to have vindicated the Ionian concept of natural law in ways and with a complexity that would have utterly amazed Thales (d. *c.* 546 B.C.) or any of his successors, who merely voiced what turned out to be amazingly lucky guesses. How did they do it? It seems plausible to suggest that the Ionians hit upon the notion of natural law by simply projecting the tight little world of the polis upon the universe. For it was a fact that the polis was regulated by law, not by the personal will or whim of a ruler. If such invisible abstractions could govern human behavior and confine it to certain roughly predictable paths of action, why could not similar laws control the natural world? To such a question, it appears, the Ionians gave an affirmative answer, and in doing so gave a distinctive cast to all subsequent Greek and European thought.

Limitations of the Polis

‡‡‡ It would be a mistake to leave the impression that all facets of Greek life fitted smoothly and easily into the polis frame. The busy public world left scant room for the inwardness of personal experience. Striving for purification, for salvation, for holiness, which found such ample expression in the Indian cultural setting, was almost excluded. Yet the Greeks were not immune from such impulses. Through the ancient mystery religions, as well as through such an association as the "Order" founded by Pythagoras, the famous mathematician and mystic (d. *c.* 507 B.C.), they sought to meet these needs. But when such efforts took organized form, a fundamental incompatibility between the claims of the polis to the unqualified loyalty of every citizen and the pursuit of personal holiness quickly became apparent. This was illustrated by the stormy history of the Pythagorean Order. Either the organized seekers after holiness captured the polis, as happened for a while in the city of Croton in southern Italy, or the magistrates of the polis persecuted the Order, as happened in Pythagoras' old age. There seemed no workable ground of compromise in this, the earliest recorded instance of conflict between church and state in Western history.

The fundamental difference between Greek and Indian institutions as shaped by about 500 B.C. was made apparent by this episode. The loose federation of cultures allowed by the caste principle in India experienced no difficulty at all in accommodating organized seekers after holiness such as the communities of Buddhist monks. By contrast, the exclusive claim upon the citizens' time, effort, and affection which had been staked out by the Greek polis allowed no sort of corporate rival.

Enormous energies were tapped by the polis. A wider segment of the total population was engaged in cultural and political action than had been possible in any earlier civilized society, and the brilliant flowering of classical Greek civilization was the consequence. Yet the very intensity of the political tie excluded ranges of activity and sensitivity that were not compatible with a territorial organization of human groupings, and sowed seeds of civil strife between the Greek cities which soon proved disastrous. But every achievement involves a surrender of alternatives: it is merely that the Greek achievement, by its very magnitude, casts an unusually clear light upon what it also excluded.

The Definition of Chinese

Civilization to 500 B.C.

 In the Yellow river's middle reaches the great stream leaves the barrenness of the Inner Mongolian steppe and cuts through soft loess soil on its way toward the flood plain below. Rain falls sporadically in this region of fertile, easily worked soil, sometimes in cloudbursts that bring flash floods; but there are many seasons of scant rainfall when the crops suffer from drought, and occasional years when the rains, which depend upon the furthest northward reach of the monsoon, simply fail to arrive.

In this precarious environment neolithic farmers began raising crops of millet before 3000 B.C. Later, wheat and barley from the Middle East and rice from monsoon Asia also became known to the farmers of the Yellow river. But in a region where water was likely to be critically short, rice could never displace the less productive but more drought-resistant millet, wheat, and barley.

Three distinct types of neolithic settlements have been discovered in this mid-region of the Yellow river valley. One of them, the so-called "Black pottery" culture, developed rather large villages, sometimes protected by stout earthen walls. Such details as the shapes of their large ceremonial pots closely resemble elaborate bronze vessels dating from the early period of Chinese civilization. Hence it seems likely that the Black pottery people were ancestral to the historical Chinese, although it would be unwarranted to assume that the peoples who produced the other, different pottery styles did not also contribute to the emergent Chinese civilization.

In essentials, Chinese civilization arose independently. The unique natural environment of semi-arid loess soil meant that everyday routines of agriculture were different from elsewhere; and this provided a basis for a correspondingly unique higher culture that began to develop about 2000 B.C. Yet at an early stage of its history, Chinese civilization seems to have been affected by contact with invaders who derived some essential skills, at least indirectly, from western Asia.

This is attested by archaeological discoveries at Anyang, one of the capitals of the Shang dynasty, dating from about 1400–1100 B.C. Anyang revealed some important differences from the material remains left behind by the farming folk of the Black pottery villages. In particular, royal graves contained horse skeletons, bronze weapons and accoutrements, and chariots. Such features are, of course, strongly reminiscent of the nearly contemporary chariot conquerors of the Middle East, Greece, and India. Two other telltale traces are the compound bow (specially strengthened to make it short yet powerful and thus useful in the confined space of a chariot) and the rectangular layout of the city itself, with two main streets crossing at right angles in the center of the walled area.

Some scholars are so impressed by the uniqueness of Chinese civilization and by the distances separating the Yellow river valley from western Asia as to repudiate the idea that there could be any important connection between Chinese and Middle Eastern affairs in such early times. The peculiarities of Chinese writing and the high technical virtuosity of Chinese bronze casting also impress those who deny that Chinese civilization was fundamentally affected by what happened far to the westward. But once chariots had been perfected, men who knew how to use this new and overwhelming weapon must have found it easy to subdue peaceable cultivators of oases in central Asia, just as other charioteers were able to conquer Mesopotamia, Egypt, India, and the Aegean lands. Moreover, oases of varying size were strung out all across central Asia, being located wherever a stream came plunging down from the high snow-capped mountains into the deserts that lay at the feet of the Himalayan, Altai, and Tien Shan ranges. Indeed, the Yellow river valley was in a sense no more than the largest and most easterly of these oases, being located on a stream that was powerful enough to break through the desert barrier, regain rain-watered land, and penetrate at last to the ocean itself.

Chronological relationships are compatible with the idea of diffsion of chariot technology eastward as well as west and south, for there is about a two-hundred-year gap between the time when conquering charioteers first appeared in the Middle East and the time when similar military equipment is known to have reached China. But archaeological investigation of the oasis sites, where traces of the passage of chariot conquerors might be expected, remains elementary and has not turned up any evidence of charioteers. This means that connections with western Asia attributed to the rulers of Anyang must remain hypothetical.

The Shang Dynasty

‡‡‡ Later tradition gave the name Hsia to the first human rulers of China. No archaeological finds can be definitely attached to the Hsia, unless, indeed, the Black pottery villages represent the material remains of that age. Anyang, on the other hand, definitely belongs to the second dynasty recorded in Chinese history, the Shang. The shorter of the two traditional chronologies assigns the dates 1523–1028 B.C. to the Shang dynasty, and modern scholarship can find no reason to question the correctness of this record.

Clearly, caution is called for in interpreting incomplete archaeological data. Conquerors, if indeed they came by the oasis route through central Asia, probably intermarried with local women, sent their sons' sons onward to the next oasis and the next, during a period of some two centuries. Hence one need not assume any massive influx of Indo-European barbarians, such as flooded into India at about the time the Shang dynasty established itself in China. Moreover, it seems clear that the conquerors soon adopted much of the culture of their new subjects; or to express the matter more precisely, it seems probable that when the Shang aristocracy established itself over the farming populations of the Yellow river valley, the rulers began to collect rents and used part of their income to support a body of artisans, whose skills rapidly improved as they became professional. Some of the skills seem to have been new to China, e.g. bronze-founding and wheel-making—both of them vital to the charioteers' armament. But new skills could be harnessed to old uses, as the elaborate bronze ceremonial vessels which have been dug in thousands from Shang graves prove. For these pots conform in many cases to shapes already familiar among the Black pottery folk. The incised patterns of geometrically distorted animal shapes, which decorate these pots, may also derive from an older wood-carving art style familiar to the Black pottery people.

An important feature of the discoveries at Anyang was a great collection of "oracle bones." These are bones or sometimes tortoise shells that were consulted by priestly diviners of that ancient society in the hope of finding the answers to various urgent questions about the future. "Will it rain?" and "Will the barbarians attack?" are the sort of questions asked. The diviners, being conscientious professionals, anxious to improve their skills in interpreting the signs vouchsafed by the gods, sometimes recorded both the question and the answer. They did so in a style of writing directly ancestral to modern Chinese ideographic script—so much so that modern scholars found no great difficulty in reading the oracle bones from the time when they were first discovered.

Not much can be deduced about Shang society and government from the brief records inscribed on the oracle bones. Nor do other archaeological materials tell us much more than that Shang society was warlike and aristocratic, and supported a small group of highly skilled artisans who produced objects of great refinement for their noble masters. The great bulk of the population labored at the tasks of cultivation without taking any active part in the life of the court and noble households. It seems probable that the Shang "empire" was parceled out among warrior chieftains who were only remotely controlled by any superior central authority. But evidence is really too scant to permit definite conclusions.

The inscriptions on the oracle bones do provide somewhat fuller information about Shang religious ideas. The names of several gods and goddesses appear, though their function is seldom made explicit. Some seem to be embodiments of a mountain, river, lake, or of a similar natural feature. In other cases, symbols whose exact meaning cannot really be recovered probably refer to ancestral spirits. Human sacrifice was practiced by the Shang, and a dead king was followed to his grave by a whole retinue of followers and courtiers. Such traits as these, repugnant to later Chinese sensibilities, remind us of how close to barbarism Shang society remained.

The Chou Dynasty

‡‡‡ In 1028 B.C. or thereabouts the Shang dynasty was overthrown by the Chou, who were conquerors come from the western borderlands of China in the Wei valley of modern Kansu. There is no reason to doubt the essential accuracy of Chinese traditional history, which divided the Chou period into two halves: the early or western Chou (1028–771 B.C.) when the capital remained the Wei valley, and the later or eastern Chou (770–256 B.C.) when the capital was located near the center of the Chinese world at Loyang.

During the first of these periods, the central administration may have been able to exert more or less effective control over a considerable area of northern China. But in 771 B.C. a sudden barbarian attack overwhelmed the capital, destroyed the direct imperial line, and paralyzed the central authority. In the following year, when a scion of the ruling house assumed the imperial office at Loyang, thus inaugurating the eastern Chou dynasty, an effective central authority was not restored. Instead a series of rival local princes disputed power and precedence with one another, engaging in an unending series of diplomatic and warlike encounters. Their struggles gradually became more ruthless as rival princes extended and strengthened their power through improvements in the arts of administration and war.

The end of this period, traditionally called the age of the "warring states" (403–221 B.C.), saw a rather rapid geographic expansion of Chinese civilization. Refugees from the increasing violence at the center helped to spread Chinese culture and skills to surrounding peoples, and in doing so sucked them into the political vortex. Princely efforts to find new allies among the barbarians had the same effect. These processes brought the coastal regions of north China into the circle of Chinese culture for the first time, and extended the frontier of the Chinese style of life as far south as the Yangtse valley. China, in short, was rapidly becoming geographically recognizable as the China of later ages.

In another and even more important sense China was also becoming her historic self in the age of the Chou. For it was under this dynasty that the ideas that became basic to all later Chinese civilization found their first clear expression. In addition, in the later Chou period, arts of bureaucratic government and a system of society hospitable to bureaucratic centralization emerged in each of the rival states into which China divided. To be sure, idea and practice did not come into reasonable harmony until after the establishment of the Han dynasty (202 B.C.), yet the main elements and emphasis of the Chinese style of civilization had become manifest some three centuries earlier, i.e. by about 500 B.C.

From the very beginning, the Chou conquerors appear to have eliminated some of the more barbarous aspects of Shang religion. Human sacrifice and ritual slaughter ceased. Very likely the conquerors explained their usurpation of supreme power by claiming a mandate from Heaven. This idea certainly became a cornerstone of later Chinese political thought, and may, as Confucius believed, date back to the propaganda of the first Chou conquerors. As later developed, the theory held that Heaven, which was conceived as a vaguely anthropomorphic supreme deity, granted rule over earth to a specially selected agent, the "Son of Heaven" or emperor. As long as he behaved piously and correctly, the Son of Heaven could expect to continue to remain in office. Impiety or rude, improper behavior, on the other hand, invited the withdrawal of Heaven's mandate, whereupon some other man might be chosen for the role of ruler on earth.

Rulership involved the exercise of magical powers among the Chou. The monarch was expected to bring rain, for example, by performing appropriate rites whenever rain was needed. This sort of thing was gradually elaborated into a cosmological theory, fully developed only in Han times, which traced parallels between heaven and earth in great detail. As the heavens turned on the pole star, for example, earthly affairs were supposed to turn upon the emperor, who was responsible not only for matters of war and politics but for all terrestrial phenomena that might affect human activity. A good emperor brought peace and good harvests, a bad one brought the reverse. Behavior in accordance with carefully prescribed rites constituted the essence of the emperor's duty. Only so could earth and Heaven attain the harmony which was necessary for human welfare.

Such ideas as these both exalted and severely limited the emperor's power. One clear implication was that there could be only one Son of Heaven. All other rulers must derive authority from him through some sort of delegation, real or fictitious. In the early Chou period, the emperor's power was real enough to create no serious problem for theorists. Local noble families held land on a sort of feudal tenure, which quickly became hereditary. The centrifugal tendency inherent in such a system was counteracted by palace schools in which the sons of no-

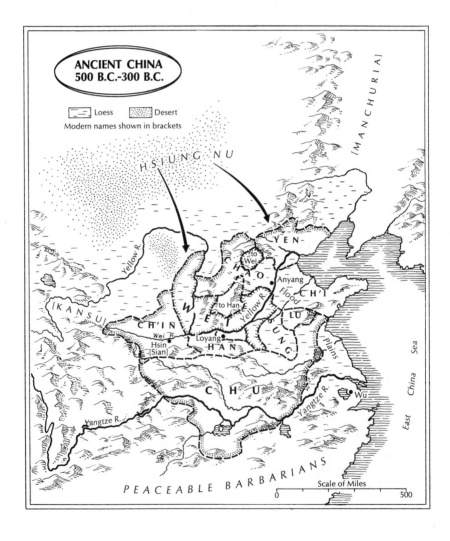

bles were trained not solely in military skills like archery but also to a knowledge of the rites they would have to perform when they became heads of families and responsible for the welfare of all under their command. Knowledge of these rites implied also familiarity with the ideas behind them, i.e. with the theory of political legitimacy and human social order that made the Son of Heaven supremely responsible for all that happened on earth. Proper performance of the necessary rites also required literacy, so that the young nobles of Chou China had to learn at least the rudiments of the difficult Chinese script. They thus combined the skills and duties of ruler, warrior, priest, and scribe, and in their own persons performed functions which in Middle Eastern society had long since been distributed among separate professions.

After 770 B.C., however, reality and theory began to diverge from one another in distressing degree. The later Chou rulers no longer enjoyed the practical authority their predecessors had in fact exercised. The titular Son of Heaven became one of the weaker rulers of a small state near the center of the Chinese world, while upstart princes near the frontier built far more powerful kingdoms for themselves, and professed only the merest lip service—if that—to the old pieties of Chou religion and cosmology. Effective efforts to collect larger amounts of taxes and to mobilize more dependable armies became the price of survival in the age of the warring states. This required princes to find men to serve them who were willing to go beyond precedent and treat others as mere instruments for the realization of the purposes of state. It required, in short, the elaboration of civil and military bureaucracy.

Confucianism and Taoism

‡‡‡ Recurrent and increasingly violent war, with all the pressures toward maximization of state power which such contests created, accorded ill with the older belief that correct observance of traditional rites was the key to all good order among men and to earthly prosperity as well. Outright repudiation of the pieties of the past was one possible response. This point of view was ruthlessly advanced by a number of practical statesmen and men of affairs, known collectively as "Legalists." But their radical repudiation of traditional ideas did not prevail in the end. Instead, it was the stoutly conservative yet modu-

lated piety of Confucianism that put a stamp on Chinese society which lasted until our own time.

Such an outcome was far from clear in Confucius' own lifetime (551–479 B.C.). The Sage, indeed, regarded himself as a failure, for he was never called upon to govern; and he believed that an educated man's virtue could only find its full expression through the exercise of power and responsibility. It is ironical to reflect that through his disciples he governed China for a vastly longer period and in a more profound and important sense than could possibly have been the case had Confucius been entrusted, as he always desired, with the conduct of affairs in one of the competing states that existed during his own lifetime.

Even his eventual success would have seemed absurd to Confucius, for he believed that he added nothing to the wisdom of the ancients. In a sense he was perfectly correct in denying that his ideas were new. For Confucius looked back with deepest nostalgia to the days of the early Chou, and beyond that to the Shang, Hsia, and to the legendary age of the divine emperors. Then, he felt, times had been good because Heaven and earth had stood in correct relationship to each other. This vision of the past set the stage for Confucius to wrestle with the central problem of his day: How could a good man live well in a bad world? For if the harmonious relationships which ought to prevail between Heaven and earth were lacking, as was all too evidently the case, what should a wise man do?

Confucius' answer was cool, unsystematic, moderate. A good man, he said, should pursue virtue in all the ordinary circumstances and confrontations of life. He should know and observe ancient rites whenever possible. He should be good, wise, and brave, whenever possible. He should respect superiors, and expect deference from his inferiors in rank. He should be prepared to govern wisely and well when entrusted with office, but should not demean himself by departing from the gentlemanly code exemplified and described by Confucius in order to attain power improperly. Such power was incompatible with virtue, and virtue, according to Confucius, was always the supreme end of human life.

Confucius did not believe that nobility was necessarily hereditary. On the contrary, he seems to have thought that a proper education could make the right sort of young man into a gentleman even if his father had come from some humble walk of life. Education, building upon a natural aptitude, might thus open a path whereby ambitious and capable men could hope to rise toward the top of the social scale. This was to become a very prominent and important aspect of traditional Confucian China, and constituted a break with the hereditary aristocracy of earlier Chou times.

Confucius flatly declined to speculate about the realm of the spirits. He never doubted their reality or power, but when the world of men was in such confusion and disorder, he preferred to direct attention to the human aspect of things, dismissing the mysteries of Heaven and of ancestral spirits as improper objects of scrutiny. Better to learn traditional rites by which good men of the past had dealt with Heaven and the ancestors than to speculate vainly upon divine nature or powers!

Confucius' disciples recorded his sayings and passed them on to later ages, perhaps in edited form, as the wisdom of their revered master. Tradition credits Confucius with arranging the "Five Classics" of later Chinese learning, but this is almost certainly fictitious. Nevertheless, the codification of a body of traditional Chinese writings into five classical texts had great importance later, since study of the classics became the mark of the well-educated man, and ability to quote aptly from one or another of these books and to use the written language in a pure, classical style became the hallmarks of Chinese gentlemen. Intense study of a limited number of texts (including of course such works as the *Analects* in which Confucius' sayings were collected) gave the Chinese of later generations a common core of shared experience defining fundamental attitudes and values which became the cement of Chinese civilization.

Confucian emphasis upon decorum and self-control could not satisfy everyone. Too much was left out: the depths of human passion and the mysteries of nature had no place in a well-regulated Confucian world. Other schools of thought that took these aspects of reality seriously commanded considerable attention in China. The most important of these was Taoism. This was an ill-defined tradition built around a body of more or less secret knowledge. Taoists emphasized magical charms and rituals that were supposed to impart health and long life, and might confer other and more unusual powers over human and natural forces, e.g. the ability to fly through the air. In a later age, and partly under the stimulus of Buddhism, Taoism attained something approaching a doctrinal definition. But in Confucius' time Taoists appear to have been more like Siberian shamans or the medicine men of the Amerindian tribes than like the philosophers of Greece or the holy men of India.

Nevertheless, the existence of Taoist adepts gave a balance to the ancient Chinese world view that Confucianism alone could not supply. Moderation and self-discipline needed its complement of mystery and magic to satisfy the ordinary range of human needs and to express the fluctuating feelings of men who lived in hard and uncertain times. By complementing each other, the one supplying precisely what the other lacked, Confucianism and Taoism constituted an unusually stable pattern of thought, which lasted, with many changes and later enrichment yet without fundamental interruption, from Confucius' time until the twentieth century of the Christian era. No other cultural tradition has lasted so long and governed the lives of so many millions of men. China's comparative isolation from other high cultures helped to assure such stability; but the intrinsic attractiveness of the Chinese way, combining common sense with endless subtlety, contributed to its long and brilliant success.

CHAPTER 7

Changes in the Barbarian World

1700–500 B.C.

 The cosmopolitan massiveness of Middle Eastern civilization and the rise of three new high cultures in India, Greece, and China obviously increased the variety of civilized influences playing upon the barbarian world. In the remoter habitable regions of the earth, so far as anyone knows, no very important changes occurred. In Australia, for example, an age-old style of hunting life maintained the even tenor of its way, unaffected by anything occurring elsewhere. In the Americas, also, no very dramatic developments can be discerned from the archaeological record. Cultivation of maize and other crops became more and more important, and centers of comparatively dense population began to arise on the central plateau of Mexico and further south in what is today Guatemala. Events along the west coast of South America are more obscure, owing to unsettled questions of chronology, but it seems probable that Peru lagged somewhat behind Mexico in developing centers of dense agricultural population.

Sub-Saharan Africa also remained apart from the rest of the world. In all probability, cultivation of edible roots and other crops made considerable progress in west Africa, while the east coast of the continent was visited at least occasionally by seafarers from civilized ports. The Egyptian style of civilization penetrated some distance up the

Nile into Nubia, but what if any contact there may have been between Nubia and the deeper interior of the continent, is simply not known. Extensive archaeological investigation will be necessary before anything approaching a reliable picture of the ancient history of sub-Saharan Africa will become possible.

The Mediterranean

‡‡‡ In the part of the Old World closer to the main centers of civilized developments, we are better able to discover major landmarks of change. The western Mediterranean, for example, was the scene of successful colonization not merely by the Greeks, but by representatives of Middle Eastern civilization, the Phoenicians and Etruscans, as well. The most successful Phoenician colony was Carthage, in north Africa, established not long before 800 B.C. Other Phoenician colonies dotted the north African coast and occupied the southern and western portions of Sicily. A second civilized people from the east, the Etruscans, whose exact origin is one of the standing puzzles of ancient history, also appeared in the western Mediterranean about 800 B.C., and established a series of towns in central and northern Italy. These outposts of Middle Eastern styles of civilization, together with the numerous Greek colonies in eastern Sicily and southern Italy, spread familiarity with the advantages of civilized life to all the coasts of the Mediterranean. From these centers, knowledge of and admiration for at least some aspects of the life of the coastal cities tended to seep inland along trade routes.

Westward from the Steppes

‡‡‡ This geographically modest sea-borne extension of civilized influence was dwarfed by the continuing expansion of the formidable steppe warrior peoples. We have already encountered steppe warriors as conquerors of civilized populations: Kassites, Hyksos, Mycenaeans, Aryans, and the rest. Other steppe warriors exercised their prowess in the conquest of less-developed lands, above all in Europe where a long series of westward displacements from the steppe into forested land gathered momentum a little before 2000 B.C. The final result, as we saw above, was to impose upon the whole continent a barbarian level of culture.

The spread of cavalry tactics after about 900 B.C. brought the steppe peoples into much closer relation to the Middle Eastern centers of civilization than before. Successful raids such as those made by the Scythians in the seventh century B.C. introduced rude warriors and pastoralists to the luxuries and delights of civilization. Border wars and hit-and-run raids became normal thereafter. This meant that the steppe tribesmen were under constant temptation to organize themselves into stronger and more cohesive units in order to make their raiding more formidable. The Scythians, for example, after migrating from central Asia to southern Russia (probably just before 700 B.C.), erected a tribal empire in the Ukraine, and soon entered into extensive trade relations with the rising Greek world to the south. The basic exchange was Scythian grain for the oil and wine produced in the city-states of the Aegean coastlands. As a result of such trade, by 500 B.C. the Scythian aristocracy of southern Russia was beginning to acquire a very sophisticated taste for Greek luxuries.

Further to the west, Celtic-speaking tribes exploited the mobility that came from riding horseback to expand their dominion widely through western Europe. The center of Celtic dispersion was what is now southern Germany. This was a region where tribes that had been squeezed from the westernmost bay of the Eurasian steppe—i.e. the central plain of Hungary—had to adjust their habits to a new, forested environment. The main problem was that the bow, the standard weapon of steppe nomads, could not be used very successfully in a forested landscape, since arrows too often would be deflected from their target by twigs and branches. The ancient Celtic warriors solved this problem by inventing a great two-handed sword, designed to be used from horseback. Armed with these great blades, the Celts overrode earlier occupants of France, Spain, Britain, Ireland, and northern Italy. They also raided sporadically even further afield into such regions as Greece, Asia Minor, and central Italy.

Like the Scythians, the new masters of western Europe were often interested in the luxuries of Mediterranean civilization, so far as they could get hold of them. In Spain, for example, Carthaginian traders and colonists allied themselves with the Celts and subjugated the earlier inhabitants of the land. In what later became France, Greek trade with still other Celtic barbarians began to reach northward from the port of Massilia (modern Marseilles) after about 600 B.C. The pattern of exchange was similar to that in southern Russia.

The militarization of society that these conquests by peoples deriving ultimately from the steppe brought to Europe created one of the basic conditions of later European development. Yet it also cost the destruction of some of the megalithic achievement of an earlier age. Long voyages in small craft could not be undertaken safely when the masters of the shoreline were inclined to treat a stranger as an enemy to be robbed and killed if he did not seem too strong. On the other hand, much of the megalithic priestcraft probably survived perhaps in modified forms, among the Celtic Druids.

What happened on the eastward flank of the steppe world is not nearly so well known as are events in Europe. This is because archaeological study of central Asia is still in a most imperfect state, and rash guesswork remains the only alternative to complete ignorance. It seems likely that the arts of horsemanship and the skills of nomadry spread eastward through the grasslands rather slowly. One people after another, living in or near the steppe, picked up the necessary skills from neighbors further west. Any tribe already equipped to live the life of a full-fledged nomad would migrate eastward only as a last resort, since this meant moving from better pasture land to worse. The reason is that rainfall and temperature both decline as one moves eastward along the Eurasian steppe toward Mongolia.

As a result of this geographic fact, by the time all the steppe had been filled by nomad groups—not until about 400 B.C.—a regular and very powerful east-west gradient came into operation. The high plateau of Mongolia constituted a very harsh environment and required great hardihood of both man and beast. Westward the steppe extended all the way to the Hungarian plain, becoming warmer and better watered as the altitude decreased and the rain-bearing Atlantic winds came nearer. Any political disturbance of life on the steppe therefore was likely to impel fugitives and/or conquerors westward, where better grass and a better climate beckoned. Hence, across the centuries a steady drift westward manifested itself. Scythians, starting in the Altai, moved to the Ukrainian steppe. Turkish tribes replaced them in central Asia, only to follow the Scyths westward in time, making room for the Mongol-speaking peoples who came pressing in on the Turks' rear.

Steppe warriors, owners of herds of horses and accustomed from childhood to life in the saddle, were very formidable fighting men. Raiding the civilized regions lying to the south of the steppe zone was a richly rewarding occupation. Any weakening in the guard which civilized rulers maintained against such raids was quickly discovered by casual parties of nomad horsemen, probing southward on the lookout for whatever they could pick up. A few striking successes in small-scale raids quickly induced thousands of nomads to join a successful captain. Nomad harassment could therefore quickly snowball into a massive assault, unless civilized resistance could somehow be organized in time. In western Asia, the principal early example of this phenomenon was the Scythian participation in the siege and sack of Nineveh, the Assyrian capital, in 612 B.C. But, as we have already seen, soon thereafter the Medes and the Persians found a way of coping with the steppe danger, by hiring tribes of nomads to stand guard against their fellows along the frontier of the Middle East.

Eastward from the Steppes

‡‡‡ In the Far East it is possible that the sack of the Chou capital in 771 B.C. was also the work of nomad raiders, operating from a base somewhere in central Asia. Unfortunately, information about this episode in Chinese history is too scant to tell whether steppe nomads, mounted and equipped for cavalry warfare, were the destroyers of the western Chou dynasty or not.

Some modern scholars think that raiders from the steppe penetrated all the way to the Pacific, reaching the coast near the southern border of modern China. By about 700 B.C. a proto-civilization had arisen in this region, based in large part on seafaring. The archaeological remains left by these "Dongson" peoples show some surprising similarities to archaeological materials from the western steppe region of Eurasia. Perhaps therefore when the arts of cavalry warfare were still new a few venturesome horsemen did move southward from the Altai region through Szechuan and overran the coastal Dongson peoples, whose seamanship had permitted the accumulation of enough wealth to make them tempting objects of attack.

Exactly how far Dongson seamen may have penetrated is an unsolved problem. The winds and waters of the south Pacific are comparatively quiet and dependable during the greater part of the year. Even with small craft and inexact navigation, it is possible to travel long distances across such an ocean. The Malay peoples of Borneo and the southern Philippines probably descend from these early seafarers. Not long before the Christian era they sent a stream of colonists to the island of Madagascar at the other side of the Indian Ocean—a fact attested by the survival today of a Malay tongue as the main speech of that distant island. It is also possible that other seamen may have penetrated far into the Pacific. Traces of Dongson seafarers have been found in New Guinea, and it is even possible that a few vessels may have reached the American coast. Perhaps these men taught the Amerindians how to smelt tin and copper to make bronze.

Such a transoceanic contact would account for the otherwise very puzzling resemblances between Amerindian art from early Mexico and Peru and the art of the southeast coastland of the Asian mainland. Other ideas, the association of the four points of the compass with colors, for example, also crop up on both sides of the Pacific and may attest some early transoceanic contact. On the other hand, the crops upon which Amerindian civilizations were based were not derived from the Old World, and some scholars think that even if a few boatloads of castaways crossed the ocean successfully at an early date they contributed nothing of importance to the emergence of Amerindian civilizations. Such a view assumes that the art of bronze casting and the other resemblances that seem to link the Old World with the New arise from independent inventions.

Whatever the truth may be in this matter, the fact remains that the level of culture and technical skill possessed by the Amerindians never caught up with the achievements of the Old World. The major centers of innovation and the most important seats of civilization continued to be in Eurasia, where no fewer than four major civilizations had defined themselves by 500 B.C.

Summary

‡‡‡ Between 1700 and 500 B.C. the geographic area within which the influences of high cultures began to make a difference in how men lived became much larger. The rise of new centers of civilization was accompanied by the development of a high barbarism in the steppes and in such favored regions as western Europe, southern China, north Africa, and (although we know almost nothing about it) in southern

India too. Civilization had indeed become endemic, capable of establishing itself wherever reasonably fertile agricultural land was to be found.

The story of the next two thousand years, from 500 B.C to A.D. 1500 is the story of, among other things, an ever renewed though not always successful expansion of civilized styles of life at the expense of neighboring barbarisms. It is also a story of rough equilibrium between the four major centers of civilization in the Middle East, India, Europe, and China. The second part of this book will undertake to sketch the main turning points and leading characteristics of this era of cultural balance.

Bibliographical Essay, Part I

An historical atlas and a dictionary of dates are valuable reference works for anyone interested in history. The best atlas for world history is *Westermanns Atlas zur Weltgeschichte* (Braunschweig, 1956), which has unfortunately never been issued in an English edition. William Robert Shepherd, *Historical Atlas*, 9th ed. (New York 1964) is the standby for the English-speaking world. William L. Langer, ed., *An Encyclopedia of World History*, rev. ed. (Boston, 1972), is standard and very useful for checking dates and refreshing one's memory about the sequence of events.

Numerous books purport to deal with world history. Some are collective works, like the Cambridge histories: *The Cambridge Ancient History*, 12 vols. (Cambridge, 1923–39), *The Cambridge Medieval History*, 8 vols. (Cambridge, 1913–36), and *The Cambridge Modern History*, 13 vols. (Cambridge, 1902–12). Others bear the stamp of an individual mind and therefore, though more coherent, are also controversial, since no one man can master the learning of every field of history. Four such books have some claim to a general reader's interest: H. G. Wells, *The Outline of History* (London, 1920); Oswald Spengler, *The Decline of the West*, 2nd ed. rev., 2 vols. (New York, 1931); Arnold J. Toynbee, *A Study of History*, 10 vols. (London, 1934–54); and William H. McNeill, *The Rise of the West* (Chicago, 1963). Toynbee's work has also appeared in abridged form, D. C. Somervell, ed., *A Study of History*, 2 vols. (London, 1946, 1957) and in an illustrated abridgement, Arnold Toynbee, *A Study of History* (New York, 1972).

Two sorts of additional reading obviously clamor for a student's attention: translations of ancient texts and modern studies of the past. Translations of the Bible and of classics like Homer are very numerous and, with generations of scholarship, have attained a high precision. It therefore seems captious to try to recommend one translation against another for works of this sort. Other civilized traditions are not nearly as richly represented in English translation. For the ancient Middle East, James B. Pritchard, ed., *Ancient Near Eastern Texts Relating to the Old Testament*, rev. ed. (Princeton, 1969) offers an excellent and arresting selection of documents, as does James B. Pritchard, *The Ancient Near East, New Anthology of Texts and Pictures* (Princeton, 1975). N. K. Sandars, tr., *The Epic of Gilgamesh* (Penguin, 1960) is an inexpensive, easily available edition of Mesopotamia's chief literary monument. Hans Goedicke, tr., *The Report about the Dispute of a Man with his Ba* (Baltimore, 1970) provides an insight into Egyptian views on life and death. For Indian culture, W. T. DeBary, Jr. et al., eds., *Sources of Indian Tradition* (New York, 1958) gives a fine selection of passages from the Vedas, Upanishads and other early texts. Johannes A. B. van Buitenen, *The Mahabharata* (Chicago, 1973–) has begun a scholarly translation of India's greatest epic. W. T. DeBary, Jr. et al., eds., *Sources of Chinese Tradition* (New York, 1960) does well in assembling and excerpting from early Chinese texts. In addition, Arthur Waley, tr., *The Analects of Confucius* (New York, 1939), Arthur Waley, tr., *Shih Ching, Book of Songs* (Boston, 1937), and Richard Wilhelm, tr., *The I Ching, or Book of Changes*, 3rd ed. (Princeton, 1967), are worth attention.

Many works dealing with ancient times lard their pages with translated extracts from ancient texts. Interplay between translation and commentary often gives a better introduction to the subject than unsupported translations, particularly when the culture under consideration is deeply unfamiliar. Good examples of this literary genre for the ancient Middle East are: Samuel Noah Kramer, *Sumerian Mythology* (Philadelphia, 1944); Henri Frankfort et al., *Before Philosophy* (Penguin, 1941); J. A. Moulton, *Early Zoroastrianism* (London, 1913). For Indian culture, Edward Conze, *Buddhism: Its Essence and Development* (New York, 1959); Sir Charles Eliot, *Hinduism and Buddhism: An Historical Sketch*, 3 vols. (London, 1921); and Heinrich Zimmer, *Philosophies of India* (New York, 1951 are all helpful. The same may be said of Fung Yu-lan, *History of Chinese Philosophy*, 2 vols. (Princeton, 1952). Two works on early Greek thought belong here: John Burnet, *Early Greek Philosophy*, 4th ed. (London, 1930), is a sober, standard and painstaking account; whereas F. M. Cornford, *From Religion to Philosophy: A Study in the Origins of Western Speculation* (London, 1912) stands at the opposite pole, being brilliant, speculative and provocative.

Perusal of photographs of ancient works of art and other material remains constitutes a second and very valuable avenue along which a student of the ancient past may travel. It has the great advantage that no translator stands between you and the original work. In addition, relatively large numbers of works may be passed before one's eyes easily in a short period of time simply by turning the pages of a well-illustrated book. This allows comparisons, and comparisons may generate insights into changing modes of sensibility across both space and time—if the student takes the pains to keep in mind a loose space-time grid within which to fit each particular work of art. As a supplement and corrective to the often excessive verbalism of historians—whose sources after all are usually written—serious attention to art and art history is to be recommended highly. For prehistoric art, H. G. Bandi et al., *Art of the Stone Age* (New York, 1961) is good. For the art of the ancient Middle East, consult the following: André Parrot, *Sumer: The Dawn of Art* (New York, 1961); André Parrot, *Arts of Assyria* (New York, 1962); Henri Frankfort, *The Art and Architecture of the Ancient Orient* (Penguin, 1959); W. Stevenson Smith, *Art and Architecture of Ancient Egypt* (Penguin, 1958). H. A. Groenewegen-Frankfort and Bernard Ashmole, *Art of the Ancient World* (New York, n.d.) is a standard introduction to the art of the ancient Middle East and Mediterranean.

The magnificent volume, Heinrich Zimmer and Joseph Campbell, *The Art of Indian Asia*, 2nd ed., 2 vols. (New York, 1955) demonstrates better than any text the radiation of Indian culture into southeast Asia. Ludwig Bachhofer, *A Short History of Chinese Art* (London, 1947) offers a technical yet convincing stylistic analysis of the early Chinese bronzes. An even more striking work of stylistic analysis is Henri Frankfort, *Cylinder Seals* (London, 1939), who uses the one object from ancient Mesopotamia which survived abundantly to relate changing artistic motifs to alterations in the social and political order of that ancient society. A more telling illustration of the relationship between art history and social development as a whole could scarcely be imagined.

Unfortunately, heavily illustrated art books are bound to be expensive, and this limits their utilization. An easy, though not entirely satisfactory, alternative is provided by University Prints, an agency which sells individual photographs of a wide variety of art objects for very modest sums. If a teacher wishes to equip all members of a class with the same photographs in order to be able to study and discuss them easily, University Prints offers a flexible and readily accessible resource. Their address is 15 Brattle Street, Cambridge, Mass., 02138.

Books of modern scholarship may be grouped by subject as follows:

HUMAN EVOLUTION AND PREHISTORY. W. E. Le Gros Clark, *The Antecedents of Man* (Chicago, 1960); Kenneth P. Oakley, *Man the Tool-Maker*, 5th ed. (London, 1976); Robert Ardrey, *African Genesis* (London, 1961); Sol Tax, ed., *Evolution after Darwin*, 3 vols. (Chicago, 1960); Carleton S. Coon, *The Origin of Races* (New York, 1962); M. F. Ashley Montague, ed., *Culture and the Evolution of Man* (New York, 1962); James Mellaart, *The Neolithic of the Near East* (New York, 1976); and Grahame Clark, *World Prehistory, A New Outline* (Cambridge, 1969). Theoretical rather than historical, but a very thoughtful little book, is Robert Redfield, *The Primitive World and its Transformations* (Ithaca, N.Y., 1953).

ANCIENT MIDDLE EAST. Henri Frankfort, *The Birth of Civilization in the Near East* (Bloomington, Ind., 1951); V. Gordon Childe, *What Happened in History* (Penguin, 1943); Samuel Noah Kramer, *The Sumerians: Their History, Culture and Character* (Chicago, 1963); John A. Wilson, *The Burden of Egypt: An Interpretation of Ancient Egyptian Culture* (Chicago, 1951); A. Leo Oppenheim, *Ancient Mesopotamia, Portrait of a Dead Civilization* (Chicago, 1964); Karl W. Butzer, *Early Hydraulic Civilization in Egypt: A Study in Cultural Ecology* (Chicago, 1976); W. Stevenson Smith, *Interconnections in the Ancient Near East: A Study of the Relationships between the Arts of Egypt, the Aegean and Western Asia* (New Haven, Conn., 1965); O. R. Gurney, *The Hittites*, rev. ed. (Penguin, 1961); George Steindorff and Keith C. Seele, *When Egypt Ruled the East*, rev. ed. (Chicago, 1957); A. T. Olmstead, *A History of Assyria* (Chicago, 1923); Donald Harden, *The Phoenicians* (New York, 1962); William F. Albright, *The Archeology of Palestine*, rev. ed. (Penguin, 1960); T. H. Robinson and W. O. E. Oesterly, *History of Israel*, 2 vols. (Oxford, 1932); H. H. Rowley ed., *The Old Testament and Modern Study* (Oxford, 1951); A. T. Olmstead, *A History of the Persian Empire* (Chicago, 1948); R. C. Zaehner, *The Dawn and Twilight of Zoroastrianism* (New York, 1961); Jack Finegan, *Light from the Ancient Past: The Archeological Background of Judaism and Christianity*, 2nd ed. (Princeton, 1959); David Diringer, *The Alphabet: A Key to the History of Mankind*, 2nd ed. rev. (London, 1953); Ignace J. Gelb, *A Study of Writing*, rev. ed. (Chicago, 1964); Otto Neugebauer, *The Exact Sciences in Antiquity* (Leiden, 1950); Charles Singer et al., eds., *A History of Technology, I: From Early Times to Fall of Ancient Empires* (Oxford, 1954); and R. J. Forbes, *Metallurgy in Antiquity* (Leiden, 1950).

EUROPE. J. G. D. Clark, *Prehistoric Europe: The Economic Basis* (New York and London, 1952); C. F. C. Hawkes, *The Prehistoric Foundations of Europe to the Mycenean Age* (London, 1940); V. Gordon Childe, *The Dawn of European Civilization*, 6th ed. (New York, 1958); John Boardman et al., eds., *The European Community in Later Prehistory: Studies in Honor of C. F. C. Hawkes* (Totowa, N.J., 1971); J. D. Evans, *Malta* (New York, 1959); J. D. S. Pendlebury, *The Archeology of Ancient Crete* (London, 1939); R. W. Hutchinson, *Prehistoric Crete* (Penguin, 1962); Sinclair Hood, *The Minoans: The Story of Bronze Age Crete* (New York, 1971); A. R. Burn, *Minoans,*

Philistines and Greeks, B.C. *1400–900* (London, 1930); Chester G. Starr, *Origins of Greek Civilization, 1100–650* B.C. (New York, 1961); M. I. Finley, *The World of Odysseus* (New York, 1954); Eric R. Dodds, *The Greeks and the Irrational* (Boston, 1957); Alfred E. Zimmern, *The Greek Commonwealth,* 5th ed. rev. (Oxford, 1931); M. I. Finley, *Early Greece: The Bronze and Archaic Ages* (New York, 1970); M. Pallottino, *Art of the Etruscans* (London and New York, 1955); Raymond Block, *Origins of Rome* (New York, 1960); T. G. E. Powell, *The Celts* (New York, 1958); B. H. Warmington, *Carthage* (London, 1960); and Marija Gimbutas, *The Slavs* (New York, 1971).

THE EURASIAN STEPPE. V. Gordon Childe, *The Aryans: A Study of Indo-European Origins* (New York, 1926); Tamara Talbot Rice, *The Scythians* (London, 1957); M. Rostovtzeff, *Iranians and Greeks in South Russia* (Oxford, 1922); George Vernadsky, *Ancient Russia* (New Haven, 1943); William M. McGovern, *The Early Empires of Central Asia* (Chapel Hill, N.C., 1939); Charles Burney and David M. Lang, *The Peoples of the Hills, Ancient Ararat and Caucasus* (New York, 1972); and V. M. Masson and V. I. Sarianidi, *Central Asia: Turkmenia before the Achaemenids* (New York, 1972).

INDIA. Stuart W. Piggott, *Prehistoric India to 1000* B.C. (Penguin, 1950); R. E. M. Wheeler, *Early India and Pakistan, to Ashoka,* rev. ed. (London, 1968); R. E. M. Wheeler, *The Indus Civilization, The Cambridge History of India,* supp. vol. (Cambridge, 1953); R. E. M. Wheeler, *The Indus Civilization* (Cambridge, 1968); R. C. Majumdar and A. D. Pusalker, eds., *History and Culture of the Indian People, I: The Vedic Age* (London, 1951); Bridget and Raymond Allchin, *The Birth of Indian Civilization: India and Pakistan before 500* B.C. (Penguin, 1968); and J. H. Hutton, *Caste in India: Its Nature Functions and Origins* (Cambridge, 1946).

CHINA. Ping-ti Ho, *Cradle of the East* (Chicago, 1975); Herrlee G. Creel, *The Birth of China* (London, 1936; reissued 1951); Li Chi, *The Beginnings of Chinese Civilization* (Seattle, 1957); Cheng Te-k'un, *Archeology in China, I: Prehistoric China* (Cambridge, 1959); Cheng Te-k'un, *Archeology in China, II: Shang China* (Cambridge, 1960); Cheng Te-k'un, *Archeology in China, III: Chou China* (Cambridge, 1964); Chang Kwang-chih, *Archeology of Ancient China,* rev. ed. (New Haven, 1977); Chang Kwang-chih, *Early Chinese Civilization: Anthropological Perspectives* (Cambridge, Mass., 1976); William Watson, *China: Before The Han Dynasty* (New York, 1961); Herrlee Creel, *The Origins of Statecraft in China, I: The Western Chou Empire* (Chicago, 1970); L. C. Goodrich, *A Short History of the Chinese*

People, 3rd ed. (New York, 1959); and three controversial but fascinating works, Herrlee G. Creel, *Confucius, the Man and the Myth* (New York, 1949; new title, *Confucius and the Chinese Way* (New York, 1960); Joseph Needham, *Science and Civilization in China,* multivolumed (Cambridge, 1954–); and G. F. Hudson, *Europe and China* (London, 1931).

OTHER PARTS OF THE WORLD. Most of the rest of the world barely enters the historic record before 500 B.C. Three works on African prehistory, however, deserve mention here: Sonia Cole, *The Prehistory of East Africa* (New York, 1954); J. Desmond Clark, *The Prehistory of Southern Africa* (Penguin, 1959); and George Peter Murdock, *Africa: Its Peoples and Their Cultural History* (New York, 1959). As for the New World and southeast Asia, it seems best to suggest relevant works as part of the bibliographical essay appended to part II of this book.

Equilibrium Among the Civilizations 500 B.C.–A.D. 1500

FOR about 2000 years, between 500 B.C. and A.D. 1500, no single center of civilized life enjoyed definite preponderance in the world. Before that time, the Middle East had taken first place, influencing neighbors and neighbors' neighbors, even across long distances, because aspects of the way of living familiar to men in the Middle East struck others as definitely superior to what they themselves had previously known. But as the civilizations of India, Greece, and China assumed distinctive shapes, the bearers of these civilizations ceased to feel inferiority vis-à-vis the Middle East and became correspondingly indifferent to influences issuing from such an alien source. On the margins, barbarians now had several variant models of civilized life from which to choose, and they often mixed elements of one civilization with those of another.

The four distinctive civilized styles of life which had arisen in the Old World by 500 B.C. were roughly equivalent to each other. Throughout the ensuing centuries, growth and modification within each of these civilizations never ceased. The area of the earth occupied by each civilization tended to expand. This, of course, increased the bulk and variety within each civilized heartland and reduced the insulating barbarian zones between. Contact from one end of Eurasia to the other tended, despite some setbacks, to increase in frequency as the centuries passed. This permitted leaders of one culture to borrow or adapt items from other civilizations which happened to interest them. Such cross-cultural borrowing was, indeed, one of the principal stimuli to innovation within each separate civilization. Yet such borrowings were always voluntary, spontaneous, never forced.

In other words, each of the major civilizations of the Old World retained its autonomy for a two-thousand-year period. The relationship between the four may be thought of as an equilibrium. Any important disturbance tended to affect other parts of the system, but no one civilization ever attained such scale or power as fundamentally to alter the fourfold balance of the whole.

The equilibrium among the world's civilizations did, nonetheless, suffer a series of shocks which constitute the major bench marks of

A chronological chart.

B.C. / A.D.	WESTERN EUROPE	EASTERN EUROPE	MIDDLE EAST AND NORTH AFRICA	EURASIAN STEPPE	CHINA	INDIA AND SOUTHEAST ASIA	OTHER
400	Celtic expansion	Persian wars — Xerxes — PERSIAN EMPIRE — Athenian empire — Peloponnesian war — Hippocrates	PERSIAN EMPIRE		*Confucius*	*Buddha*	
300	Gauls sack Rome	Plato — Aristotle — MACEDONIAN EMPIRE	MACEDONIAN EMPIRE		warring states	Alexander's conquest — MAURYAN EMPIRE	
200	Rome unites Italy — Hannibal's war	Euclid — Praxiteles — Aristarchus of Samos	SELEUCIDS — PTOLEMIES		Shih Huang-ti unites China	Asoka	
100	RISE OF ROME — FIRST CLOSURE — Hipparchus			PARTHIANS — HSIUNG-NU	HAN DYNASTY — Ssu-ma Ch'ien		
1 AD	Lucretius — Cicero — JULIUS CAESAR — Vergil — AUGUSTUS	CAESAR — CRUCIFIXION	THE ECUMENE			spread of Indian culture to southeast Asia	
100	Claudius — St. Paul — Domitian — Tacitus — Trajan	Jewish revolt: destruction of the temple — Gospels written — Jewish revolt		KUSHANS — TURKISH DOMINANCE			
200	Marcus Aurelius — civil war and invasion — Plotinus	codification of Greek science: Galen, Ptolemy — Mani				reinvigoration of Hinduism	
300	restoration of Roman empire — CHRISTIANITY BECOMES OFFICIAL RELIGION — Huns			EPHTHALITES — SANIAN DYNASTY — Attila — JUAN-JUAN	barbarian invasions	decimal numbers — SPREAD OF BUDDHISM	"classic" period in Amerindian civilizations begins
400	GERMANIC INVASIONS — sack of Rome — St. Augustine — St. Patrick — Clovis					classical Sanskrit Kalidasa — GUPTAS	Ghana in West Africa

Vertical axis labels: HELLENIC EXPANSION ... INDIAN EXPANSION

Banner text across the chart: RISE OF ROME — FIRST CLOSURE OF THE ECUMENE

Timeline chart (500–1400 A.D.)

Dates (left margin): 500, 600, 700, 800, 900, 1000, 1100, 1200, 1300, 1400

Vertical labels (left margin): SION · ISLAM · EXPANSION

Europe

- St. Benedict
- partial or
- JUSTINIAN restoration of Roman Byzantine empire
- Slav infiltration into Balkans
- AVARS
- Austrasian invasion
- Moslems in Spain
- battle of Tours
- Leo III, the Isaurian Moslem repulse
- iconoclastic controversy
- Charlemagne, Roman emperor
- BULGARS
- Viking, Magyar, Arab raids and invasions
- Cluniac reform
- conversion of Magyars and of Norway
- conversion of Rus
- Basil II
- Byzantine recovery
- Papal reform
- final East-West schism
- battle of Manzikert
- FIRST CRUSADE
- St. Anselm
- Abelard
- Hellenic Renaissance
- St. Francis
- fourth crusade
- Alexander Nevsky
- MONGOL DOMINANCE
- collapse of the Hohenstaufen empire
- St. Thomas Aquinas
- BLACK
- battle of Kossovo
- TURKISH DOMINANCE
- Papacy at Avignon
- Dante
- Great Schism
- Hundred Year's war
- Italian Renaissance
- capture of Constantinople by Turks
- capture of Granada

Islam

- SASS
- Mohammed ISLAMIC CONQUESTS
- OMMAYADS
- ABBASID CALIPHATE
- TURKISH DOMINANCE
- ibn-Sina
- al-Ghazali
- Omar Khayyam
- ibn-Rushd
- Rumi
- MONGOL
- DEATH
- Hafiz
- ibn-Khaldun
- Persian art at its peak

Central Asia / China

- SUI DYNASTY
- CHINA REUNITED
- T'ANG DYNASTY
- Chinese control of oases of central Asia
- Li Po
- printing invented
- overthrow of Buddhism
- Uighur empire
- Tibet
- battle of Talas
- Islamic conversion of steppe tribes
- TURKISH DOMINANCE
- Genghis Khan
- SUNG DYNASTY
- compass, gunpowder invented
- Chu Hsi
- EMPIRE
- DEATH
- EPIDEMIC
- Tamerlane
- MING DYNASTY
- Cheng-ho voyages to India

India

- Moslems in Sind
- Shankara
- Mohammed of Ghazni; conquest of northern India
- slave sultanate of Delhi
- TURKISH DOMINANCE
- Kabir

East Asia / Americas / Africa

- Buddhism established in Japan
- Polynesian dispersal begins
- Nara period in Japan
- end of classic period of Amerindian culture
- Lady Murasaki
- Moslem conquests in West Africa
- Chichen Itza in Yucatan
- Aztecs in Mexico
- Incas in Peru

*world history during this period. First Greek and then Indian civiliza-
tion spread widely beyond their original borders. Yet the Hellenization
of the Middle East, like the Indianization of China and Japan, proved
in the end to be only a superficial, temporary phenomenon. In both
cases strong native reactions eventually repudiated most of the alien elements accepted eagerly in earlier generations. Then for a third time
the world's balance seemed threatened by the sudden rise of Islam and
its successive stages of expansion, first throughout the ancient Middle
East, north Africa, and Spain (632–1000), and then into India, eastern
Europe, and central Asia (1000–1453). Hindu India eventually (1565)
lost political independence. As a result, Moslem overlords and rulers
joined forces with converts to Islam (who were drawn mainly from the
lower castes) to put Hinduism under restrictions and pressures that
profoundly affected its subsequent development.*

*Still a fourth disturbance, emanating this time from western Eu-
rope, finally upset the cultural balance of the earth. The process began
after A.D. 1500 when European enterprise first opened the Americas
and explored the rest of the earth's habitable coastlines. Yet in a real
sense, it was not until 1850 that the Western world attained such
crushing superiority over the other major civilizations of the earth as
to compel the leaders of all non-Western societies to abandon their
ancestors' time-tested ways and surrender their traditional, cultural autonomies in order to enter upon a desperate effort to "modernize" by
borrowing skills from the West.*

*Consideration of these modern periods of world history will be
reserved for the third and fourth parts of this book. In Part II we will
deal with the intervening period, when more definitely than at earlier
or in later times, each separate part of the civilized world went its own
way, paying only marginal attention to what was happening elsewhere.*

CHAPTER 8

The Flowering of Greek Civilization 500-336 B.C.

In 499 B.C. the Greek cities of Ionia rebelled against the Persian rule they had acknowledged since 546 B.C. when Cyrus the Great had wrested Asia Minor from King Croesus of Lydia. Five years later the revolt was suppressed. Miletus, the leading city of the Ionian coast, was sacked. Victory in this first round of war between Greeks and Persians rested clearly with the latter. Nevertheless, King Darius was not satisfied, for Athens and Eretria, two obscure Greek cities, had dared to send a few ships from across the Aegean to aid the rebels. A punitive expedition, sent in 490 B.C., plundered Eretria but failed to capture Athens. To be sure, the Persians did land at Marathon, twenty-six miles from Athens, expecting treason from within to open the city's gates. But the scheme failed. The Athenians won a brisk skirmish at Marathon by attacking the Persians as they reembarked on their ships, and a runner brought the news to Athens before the Persian fleet could arrive (hence our modern "marathon" races). As a result, when the Persian ships did show up the traitors in Athens made no move, and the discomfited invaders then withdrew across the Aegean.

These clashes were the prelude to a serious attempt on the part of the Persians to conquer European Greece. In 480 B.C., Xerxes, King

Darius' son and successor, mustered his imperial field army, some 60,-000 strong, for the attempt. The Persians made very elaborate preparations indeed. A floating bridge was constructed across the Hellespont, supplies were stored at depots all along the north coast of the Aegean sea, and diplomatic missions were sent to persuade the Greeks to submit. Many cities and the influential Greek oracle at Delphi decided to accept Persian terms before it was too late. But some twenty cities, loosely confederated under Spartan leadership, refused to yield. A Spartan detachment vainly attempted to stop the Persian host at Thermopylae in the north. Then, as Xerxes' army marched south, the Athenians were compelled to evacuate their city, which was plundered and burned by the advancing Persians.

Yet until the Greeks submitted, such victories remained indecisive, for the Persians had great difficulty in supplying their army in an unfriendly and ravaged land. Xerxes therefore tried to bring matters to a head by attacking the Greek fleet, which had taken refuge in the Bay of Salamis just west of Athens. In the narrow strait between the island of Salamis and the mainland the superior numbers of the Persian fleet could not be brought to bear, so that the Greeks, by skillful and resolute maneuvering, were able to win a decisive victory (480 B.C.). After this failure, Xerxes decided that he and the larger part of his army would have to return to Persia, since supplies sufficient to feed the entire force over the winter were simply not available in Greece.

Next spring, accordingly, a sharply reduced Persian force confronted the combined armies of the Greek cities at Plataea, where, once again, victory rested with the Greeks (479 B.C.). Simultaneously, the Athenians carried the war across the Aegean, where the mere appearance of their warships encouraged a number of Ionian cities to revolt.

The Persians never again undertook full-scale operations against Greece. Hostilities dragged on until 446 B.C. Almost annually the leagued Greek cities dispatched a fleet early in the summer to attack Persian strongholds along the Aegean coast; and each fall the fleet came back, almost always with some new success to its credit. Athens took the lead in these operations since Sparta, the greatest land power of the Greek world, refused to continue active operations after the immediate threat of Persian invasion faded.

Effects of Athenian Naval Warfare

‡‡‡ The indefinite prolongation of naval warfare brought great changes to the internal balance of the Athenian polis. Citizens who owned little or nothing could always serve as rowers in the warships. They thus rendered a military service to their polis that became just as important as service in the phalanx. The fleet, in other words, gave a major military role even to the poorest citizens, who had formerly been unable to afford the equipment needed to fight with the phalanx. Moreover, the pay for rowing service, together with the chance of picking up some rich booty from the sack of a new-won town, became, for a large number of Athenian citizens, a very welcome addition to their annual income.

Even before the great Persian invasion, Athens had become a democratic city. But at first the voting rights of the poorer citizens were insecure, being more the result of efforts by aristocratic politicians to find new support among the lower classes than of any effective strength or organization among the poor themselves. But when rowing in the fleet became a normal summer's occupation, the poor took on a military role that entitled them to be heard in affairs of state. The democratic constitution thus became secure for the first time. Old-fashioned farmer-infantrymen were pushed to the margins of Athenian political life. They lived too far from the city to attend the meetings of the assembly regularly, whereas when the fleet was at home, the urban poor often had little else with which to occupy their time.

Very soon Athens' eager pursuit of aggressive naval war alarmed some of the more conservative Greek cities. In 467 B.C., for example, the island of Naxos declined to send the usual contingent of ships and men to war against the Persians. The Athenians interpreted this as treason. They turned their armament against Naxos, defeated the islanders, and assessed a money tribute. Subsequently other allies were treated in the same way. As a result, what had begun as a free league of cities against Persia by degrees became an Athenian empire, which at its height exercised dominion over some fifty cities, great and small, scattered all around the Aegean.

Despite the democratic form of Athenian public life, for a long time the city's leaders and military commanders continued to come

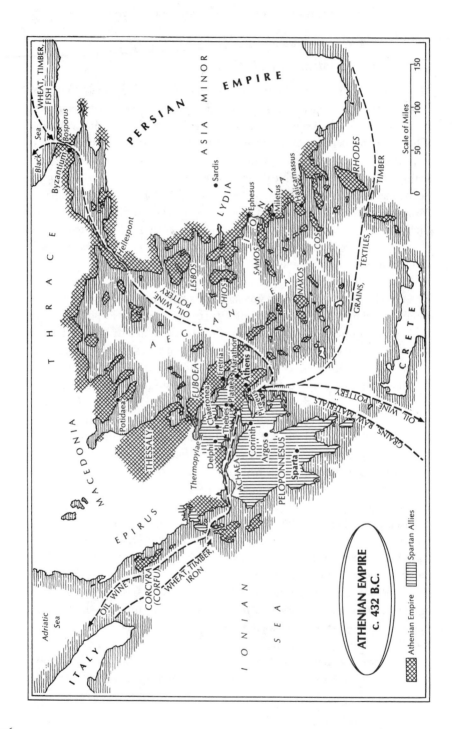

ATHENIAN EMPIRE
c. 432 B.C.

▨ Athenian Empire ▥ Spartan Allies

PERSIAN EMPIRE

ASIA MINOR

Black Sea

Bosporus

WHEAT, TIMBER, FISH

Byzantium

Hellespont

THRACE

Sardis

LYDIA

Ephesus

Miletus

Halicarnassus

RHODES

TIMBER

GRAINS, TEXTILES,

C R E T E

I O N I A

A E G E A N   S E A

LESBOS

CHIOS

SAMOS

NAXOS

COS

OIL, WINE, POTTERY

MACEDONIA

THESSALY

Potidaea

EUBOEA

Chaeronea

Marathon

Eretria

Plataea

Thebes

Athens

Eleusis

Piraeus

Thermopylae

Delphi

ACHAEA

Corinth

Argos

Sparta

PELOPONNESUS

OIL, WINE, POTTERY

GRAINS, RAW MATERIALS

EPIRUS

CORCYRA (CORFU)

OIL, WINE

WHEAT, TIMBER, IRON

I O N I A N   S E A

Adriatic Sea

ITALY

Scale of Miles
0   50   100   150

from aristocratic families with traditional claims to political eminence. This was true even of democrats like Pericles, who dominated the political scene in Athens between 460 and 429 B.C. and gave his name to Athens' greatest age. After his death, during the long and bitter Peloponnesian war against Sparta and her allies (431–404 B.C.), the division of interest between farmer-soldiers and the landless rowers of the fleet became so serious that old-fashioned aristocratic leadership foundered. Thus Pericles was succeeded by Cleon, a capable and unscrupulous commoner. After Cleon's death in battle (422 B.C.) the aristocratic monopoly of political leadership was never entirely restored.

A more portentous change was the decay of polis loyalty. This change was felt throughout the Greek world, wherever the old simplicities, which required and permitted nearly every adult male to farm and fight in the phalanx beside his fellows, gave way to more complex social differentiations among such groups as merchants, artisans, farmers, soldiers, sailors, slaves, foreigners, landowners, and sharecroppers. The long struggle of the Peloponnesian war drastically accelerated this process. Everywhere (even within Athens itself) the rich and conservative tended to support Sparta, while democrats sympathized with Athens. Since outside intervention on behalf of one or the other party was always a possibility, both the temptation and the opportunities for treason multiplied. The old idea, according to which private interest and ambition should be subordinated to the welfare of the polis as a whole, could not withstand such pressures. One after another the separate cities of Greece lost their internal cohesion as party rivalry degenerated into wholesale resort to threat, assassination, and exile.

The Classical Age

‡‡‡ But before the polis world dissolved into squalid civil strife, for a period of almost fifty years, from the time of Xerxes' great disaster in 480–79 B.C. until the outbreak of the Peloponnesian war in 431 B.C., Athens in particular and the Greek world at large experienced a golden age which was more concentrated in time and space and more perfect in its expression than any comparable period of human history.

After their surprising success against the imperial majesty of Persia, the Greeks came to feel extraordinary confidence in themselves and in their way of life. Awed no longer by the pomp and secret wisdom of the East, sublimely sure of themselves and eager to explore the world within and about them, Athenians in particular, and other Greeks in somewhat lesser degree, found themselves able to combine thought and action in such a way that each supported and urged the other onward. Who, after all, could doubt the essential goodness and excellence of Athenian institutions when the city had won and continued to win such successes overseas? And yet who could doubt that there was much to learn from the new experiences, strange new products, and novel ideas that converged upon a city that had so suddenly become the mistress of the eastern Mediterranean? The Athenians were proud of their past, committed to their present, and eager to explore anything new in their future. Imbued with supremely venturesome confidence, they proceeded to give classical expression to almost every aspect of Greek culture: drama, philosophy, history, rhetoric, architecture, and sculpture.

Drama

‡‡‡ "Goat songs" honoring the god of wine, Dionysus, were sung by masked choruses in several Greek cities, but only in Athens did these crude beginnings develop into tragedy. In the course of the fifth century B.C. music, staging, costumes, and dancing all became much more elaborate. Choruses began to undergo prolonged training when it became customary to conduct competitions for the best performance at the great festivals of Dionysus. Antiphonal singing between leader and chorus developed into dramatic dialogue. Presently, two actors were presented on the stage simultaneously, later as many as three. With this development, the chorus retreated from the center of attention and assumed a secondary role, commenting, warning, or setting the mood for the action of the play whose main thread was now carried by the actors.

The tragic performances of ancient Athens presented a magnificent spectacle. All male citizens could attend freely, for the festivals were still regarded as public acts of worship. The cost of putting on each performance was met by rich men who found satisfaction in competing for the prize. Even the most stupid citizen could respond to the rhythms of dance, song, and language—for the words were sung by the chorus and the actors' lines also conformed to poetic meters. These aspects of Greek drama are almost entirely lost to moderns. All that survives is the texts of a few of the plays, together with a number of fragments of others. Yet these mutilated remains continue to arouse admiration, partly because of their poetic power, partly because of the ideas they express. This admiration is and remains genuine because the tragic poets of ancient Athens took advantage of the traditional celebrations handed down to them to construct stories that confronted fundamental problems of human life. In doing so they touched upon themes that command perennial interest, being in some sense universal to all men.

Three great poets worked this remarkable transformation of the ancient goat songs: Aeschylus (525–456 B.C.), Sophocles (495–405 B.C.), and Euripides (484 or 480–406 B.C.). For their subject matter they drew on the common stock of stories about gods and men which had been handed down from immemorial antiquity—what we call myth, but what the Greeks themselves thought of as ancient history. But the tragic poets seem to have felt free to alter details of the traditional stories if it suited their purposes to do so. They exercised their own personal insight and imagination even more freely in trying to explain the relations of gods to men, of fate to free will, and of private to public duty—to mention only a few of the themes they dealt with.

Yet although all three of the great tragedians remained faithful to conventional forms and limits, it does not take much penetration to recognize that with Euripides tragedy was beginning to lose its usefulness for the exploration of serious moral and theological questions. The older poets, Aeschylus and Sophocles, shared traditional pieties with the majority of their audience. The changes, adjustments, subtleties, and queries they brought to bear upon traditional moral and religious ideas did not disrupt but rather enlarged and reconfirmed the general structure and validity of old viewpoints by giving them poignant and sophisticated expression. Not so Euripides. He had grown up in a later generation, when traditional convictions had already eroded among intellectually inclined young Athenians. Yet in public Euripides had to conform—or pretend to conform. Anything else would have been felt as a desecration of what was, after all, a religious ceremony. He solved his problem by almost scornfully bringing forth some formula of conventional piety. This served to unravel the plot or save a situation which, on the human dramatic level, Euripides often presented in a way that implicitly contradicted the glib and easy answers his divine messengers and oracles provided for the difficulties of life.

Clearly, what had happened was that the intellectual elite of Athens no longer shared the presuppositions of the mass of the citizenry. A man like Euripides no longer believed in the reality or powers of a god like Dionysus, whose festival he, as a tragic poet, was required to celebrate! Small wonder, therefore, that after his time no other great poet rose in Athens to carry on the tragic tradition. Instead, it soon became customary to revive the classic tragedies. Fresh dramatic creation was confined to comedy, where wit, suspense, and the foibles of human character could be explored without raising any of the deeper issues of the human condition as the tragedians had, throughout the fifth century, been able and eager to do.

Philosophy

‡‡‡ Philosophers took over where the tragedians left off. This is attested by the dialogue form assumed by most of Plato's writings. The great advantage of philosophic dialogue was that it need not confrom to outworn conventions, nor did it have to appeal to the entire citizen body of the Athenian polis. Any reflective, leisured man familiar with Attic Greek and curious about the nature of things could read what Plato wrote: he could agree or disagree, read and reread the dialogues, or discard them as futile. But neither author nor reader depended on the assent of the crowd and the approval of public officials who were responsible for arranging traditional religious celebrations. Dramatic poets were bound by all these ties. Hence when a pervasive and basic rapport between the mass public and the most advanced thinkers of Athens ceased to prevail—a circumstance already hampering Euripides—further investigation into the nature of man and his place in the world could only occur through the more private, personal medium of philosophic dialogue.

Athens had not been an important early center of Greek thought. But when she became mistress of the Aegean, philosophers as well as other strangers converged upon the city. The temper of the Athenian populace was distrustful. Thus, for example, a famous philosopher and personal friend of Pericles, named Anaxagoras, was exiled for impiety, having argued that the sun was not a god but merely a red-hot stone.

Another group of wise men, the sophists, met a much warmer reception in Athens. Their profession was to train young men in the art of rhetoric. Speaking well was, of course, very necessary for a political career in a democratic city such as Athens, for nothing important could be done without persuading the Assembly of the citizens. But when teachers and pupils began to think and talk about words and speeches, they soon became aware of the fact that language and argument had rules and were themselves subject to analysis. This was a very exciting discovery. Some of the sophists appear to have believed that a thorough mastery of the rules of logic and its embodiment in language would unlock all the mysteries of the universe if men had but the wit and daring to do so.

The sophists distrusted mere custom and habit. Such an attitude could be very disruptive, for in the cold light of logic, what binding force was there in the polis law itself, which varied from city to city and from nation to nation in an utterly illogical way? Why should not a bold and courageous man penetrate the veil of convention and base his action upon the nature of things, to be discovered through precise manipulation of the logical tools of language? Indeed why not? Especially if the bold young man in question happened to belong to a political faction or social class that had little chance of winning control of the government through constitutional procedures. Hence it was mainly young men of wealth who felt the fascination of the radical sophist challenge to the legal frame within which public life proceeded. Sophistry justified them in their withdrawal of loyalty from the polis. They were the men who found the demands placed upon them by the vulgar democrats of Athens to be a more and more unwelcome burden—especially during the disastrous years of the long war with Sparta (431–404 B.C.).

During these same years another enigmatic figure wrestled with the moral and political questions that had been raised by the sophists. His name was Socrates (d. 399 B.C.), a native Athenian, who served as soldier and magistrate when called upon to do so, and who yet could not persuade himself that the laws and government of Athens were really just, wise, or good. Socrates spent his time arguing in public places with anyone who cared to risk the shock of discovering, under Socrates' insistent and incisive questioning, how inadequate his opinions and convictions really were.

Socrates wrote nothing. He is known to us mainly through Plato's dialogues, in which he almost invariably plays the role of questioner. Plato's portrait may be retouched to make Socrates conform to Plato's own views and preferences. The comic poet Aristophanes (d. 385 B.C.) and the historian Xenophon (d. 354 B.C.) also left literary portraits of Socrates that bear small resemblance to Plato's protagonist. Yet despite obscurities, it is clear that Socrates, like his disciple Plato, was a radical conservative. In effect, he attempted to use the sophists' tools of linguistic and logical analysis to support traditional values, hierarchies, and standards by finding a universal truth or reality behind mere conventions of the here and now. It is far from clear whether or not Socrates ever satisfied himself that he had found such universal truths. Yet when a group of democratic politicians brought him to trial in 399 B.C. on the charge of having corrupted the youth and of not believing in the gods of Athens, he preferred to die rather than repudiate his mode of life. He asserted that he must obey the dictates of justice first and always, even at the risk of colliding with man-made laws such as those according to which the Athenians condemned and executed him.

Plato (427–347 B.C.) was a young man when Socrates took poison and died according to Athenian law. Like many of the other Athenian young men who had gathered around Socrates to hear him deflate the pretensions of upstarts, Plato was of noble birth, and even claimed descent from Athens' early kings. Perhaps for this reason, the great issue for Plato was always political: how to put things right so that good men would rule and justice prevail. But true reform required true knowledge, without which one man's opinion was no better than another's, and there could be no escape from the harsh party strife which was tearing Athens apart. To the pursuit of this sort of knowledge he therefore dedicated his life. In doing so, he brought together almost all the strands of earlier Greek thought and gave to subsequent Western philosophy much of its vocabulary and many of its most central problems: for example, the relation of soul and body, knowledge and opinion, idea and reality, and naïve but necessary questions as to the nature of the Good, the True, and the Beautiful.

Plato wrote two dialogues in which he sketched an ideal state founded upon truth and justice; but when he tried to translate his ideas into practice he met with utter failure. This happened at Syracuse in Sicily, for the statesman who had invited Plato to come proved unable to persuade the youthful ruler of that city to submit to the regimen of studies Plato prescribed. Toward the end of his life Plato appears to have found in intellectual activity and writing a partial substitute for political leadership, which he felt belonged to him by right, but which his rigid and unpopular views made impossible in a democratic city like Athens. The Academy which he established became a center for philosophic, mathematical, and scientific work. It maintained itself as a going concern for more than 900 years—longer than any modern university has yet done—and for most of that time the Academy made Athens the major center of higher education in the classical world.

Aristotle (384–322 B.C.) was a member of the Academy for many years before he set up his own school, the Lyceum. He took naturally to the life of a professional thinker. No question under the sun—or above it for that matter—lay outside the scope of Aristotle's interest. He worked out a comprehensive, closely reasoned philosophy that provided moderate, common-sense answers to everything of importance, and left remarkably few loose ends for his followers to cope with.

After Aristotle's time, the Greek cities lost real independence, and the political spark went out of Greek life. Philosophy more and more became a guide to life, attuned to the needs of the rich and well-educated men of the Greek world. Really disturbing new thoughts and new information became taboo when the central thrust of philosophy became the task of defining a reasonable code of conduct for the well-born. With this change, the first greedy reach after truth—the eager ambition of the sophists, the tenacious search for certainty to which Socrates and Plato devoted their lives, and the voracious appetite for new knowledge which had inspired Aristotle's intellect—all faded away. The great age of Greek philosophy thus came to a close. Yet the body of ideas the philosophers had expressed, and the variety of questions about the nature of the world and of human thought, belief, and knowledge they had raised, remained to haunt later generations and inspired them with a degree of sophistication about the complexities of truth which earlier thinkers, and men unacquainted with the Greek tradition of philosophy, could never equal. The bold effort to apprehend the world by use of human reason, which the Ionian philosophers had launched in the sixth century B.C., and which was broadened and deepened so energetically in Athens during the fifth and fourth centuries B.C., was therefore not in vain, despite the eventual fraying out of faith in the powers of human reason which became apparent after Aristotle's death.

Science, Rhetoric, History

‡‡‡ The main development of Greek science came after the Macedonian conquest (338 B.C.) had brought Athens' great age to a close. Nevertheless, geometry and geometric astronomy attracted the serious attention of Plato and other philosophers, and Aristotle very persuasively systematized physics. Simultaneously, Hippocrates of Cos (*c.* 460–370 B.C.) founded an influential school of medicine which emphasized careful observation and diagnosis, and interpreted disease not as a result of seizure by evil spirits—the usual Middle Eastern view —but as the consequence of an imbalance of fluids (known as "humors") within the body.

Rhetoric enjoyed a very high place in Greek education. Skilled public speaking was a political necessity in democratic states and continued to be much admired even after it lost its practical political function. Study and practice of the art of speaking generated rules of correctness, and in the end elegant and graceful elocution became an object of admiration for itself, whether or not the speaker had anything important to say. Degeneration of rhetoric into a polite accomplishment only occurred after polis sovereignty had ended. Until that time (and sporadically afterward) citizen assemblies had to deal with pressing matters which provided rhetoricians with an urgent and inescapable subject matter.

History as a distinct discipline was created by the researches of Herodotus of Halicarnassus (d. *c.* 425 B.C.). Herodotus composed a charming and discursive account of the Persian wars, in order, as he himself says, to give "due meed of glory" to both Greeks and barbarians. He portrayed the war as a struggle between freedom and slavery and clearly believed that the surprising Greek victory proved the superiority of free, self-governing communities over even the greatest of monarchies, where all men had to bow before the will of the king. Athens was the hero of Herodotus' story, but he was always aware that men remained under the gods, and were subject to a fate which they could not control. Boasting and vainglory invited divine retribution—a theme that recurs over and over again in Herodotus' pages and which he used to explain the failure of Xerxes' invasion.

Thucydides (d. *c.* 400 B.C.), the second master historian among the Greeks, grew up in Athens when sophistry and rationalism were in full career. He could not believe with Herodotus that the gods intervened directly in human affairs. Instead, Thucydides thought that the body politic was like the human body, liable to disordering disease through imbalance of its parts. His subject was the long, fratricidal struggle between Athens and Sparta that began in 431 B.C. Its tortuous course, provoking civil strife on top of inter-city war, gave him ample opportunity to observe distempers in the public life of the Greek cities.

Thucydides was not at first a passive observer of the war. In 424 B.C. the Athenians elected him general, but then exiled him when he failed to prevent a serious military setback. Thereafter Thucydides took no active part in public affairs. Instead he set out to discover precisely what had been said and done on either side, in the hope perhaps of diagnosing the evils of the body politic as a necessary preliminary to being able to cure them.

Thucydides never became a cool and dispassionate observer. Nor could he simply dismiss morals and belief in the supernatural ordering of human affairs. Toward the end, as Athens entered its death struggle, Thucydides the Athenian probably began to believe that he was witnessing the punishment meted out by inscrutable divine power to a city that had defied justice, being puffed up with an overweening pride that fed upon its own success. When Thucydides saw his theme conforming to this pattern, he began to recast his narrative, giving Athens the role of tragic hero, betrayed by flaws inherent in her own greatness. He thus applied the tradition of the tragedians to contemporary history, using the medium of prose. Herodotus had similarly carried forward the epic tradition with his history of the latest collision between Europe and Asia, one of whose earlier incidents Homer's *Iliad* had chronicled.

By combining exactitude of detail with penetrating analysis and an intense controlled passion at the spectacle presented by Athens' downfall, Thucydides made a reality of his proud claim to have written "not a prize essay for the moment, but a possession forever."

Architecture and Sculpture

‡‡‡ Among the Greeks of the classical age monumental architecture was almost entirely limited to the construction of temples and other

public buildings. Traditional forms confined the architect's task to the refinement of proportion and perfection of detail. But care expended on such matters as the slight curvature of the profile of the columns and of the floor upon which they rested, gave the finished structure an optical precision and grace that could not otherwise have been attained.

Enough original sculpture survives from the fifth and fourth centuries B.C. to allow us to perceive for ourselves the technical mastery Greek sculptors attained. Later critics hailed Phidias (d. *c.* 431 B.C.) as the greatest of all sculptors, but nothing that can be certainly assigned to his hand survives, although he planned the sculptural decorations of the Parthenon and may have executed some of them. His masterworks, the cult statues of Athena in Athens and of Zeus at Olympia, were finished in ivory and gold. They both, being precious, have utterly disappeared. But literary descriptions make it clear that Phidias gave these great statues an aloof majesty and serene beauty that left a strong impression even in later ages when men had ceased to take the gods of Olympus seriously. Like Sophocles the tragedian or Herodotus the historian, Phidias lived at the point in time when old beliefs and pieties still seemed valid, needing only a more precise and adequate expression. Phidias did with gold and ivory what the others did with words: reshaping and enriching older conceptions, and attuning them to the more sophisticated age in which he lived.

Later sculptors continued to command extraordinary skill, but the serene self-confidence and inner harmony which Phidias had expressed could not be recaptured by later generations. A more self-conscious, theatrical style came in, which aimed to surprise or amaze the observer. Late portraits of the gods, such as the famous Hermes of Praxiteles (d. *c.* 320 B.C.), entirely lack Phidias' majesty. The grace and beauty of idealized humanity were thoroughly within Praxiteles' reach. Yet his Hermes seems neither great nor powerful—more a pretty plaything of the imagination than a ruler of the world.

In every field of endeavor of which we have record, therefore, Athenian certainties and self-confidence, so buoyant during the first years after the Persian wars, developed toward a more diverse, divided, and complicated outlook. Division brought dissension and sometimes provoked disillusionment. But energies that had been raised so high took a long time to dissipate themselves, and Greek cultural forms remained capable of affecting other peoples for many centuries after the first bloom of Athens' great age had faded.

Social Change After the Peloponnesian War

‡‡‡ The political and social evolution of Greece confirmed, perhaps even provoked, this cultural transformation. After the Peloponnesian war ended (404 B.C.), muted hostility between rich and poor became chronic in most Greek cities. Distrust and fear divided one class from the other. The old psychological solidarity nurtured by common service in the phalanx disappeared as citizens ceased, save in unusual circumstances, to take direct part in military campaigns.

Athenian dominion gave way to Spartan supremacy. Despite their claim to have fought for the "liberty of the Greeks," the Spartans proved themselves taskmasters at least as harsh as the Athenians had been. Athenian power therefore soon revived; but it was the city of Thebes that first crushed Sparta on the battlefield (371 B.C.) and thus inaugurated a short-lived Theban supremacy over Greece. Intervention of the still semi-barbarian kingdom of Macedon then brought a far stronger political unit into the very center of Greek politics. But even after Macedonian military superiority had been definitively demonstrated at the battle of Chaeronea (338 B.C.), the Greeks continued to nurse a stubborn longing for local autonomy and polis independence, so that any weakening of Macedonian power stirred hope of liberation from what was in fact an extremely light yoke.

Yet after 338 B.C. the scale of economic and military organization had changed, so that separate city-states no longer exercised genuine sovereignty. A well-trained phalanx remained indispensable, but could best be had for hire. The old-fashioned citizen army depended, after all, on the sense of mutuality among the members of the phalanx. Since citizens no longer fully trusted one another, thanks to the bitterness fostered during the party struggles that everywhere accompanied the Peloponnesian war, most citizen armies could no longer function effectively. Professional troops therefore began to supplement and then to supplant citizen armies, especially for expeditions to distant parts where the campaign might last for several years. Citizens who owned enough land or other income-producing property to support themselves preferred to stay at home and gave up the hard, heroic role their forefathers had believed to be the only one suitable for free men and responsible citizens.

As this occurred, a private sphere of life began to widen its claims on men's attention, and politics relaxed its all-engulfing hold on the Greek imagination and emotion. Poor, disenfranchised citizens, landless men, refugees, foreigners, and slaves became more numerous in the Greek world. Even citizens who continued to have a legal voice in public affairs found the privilege increasingly hollow. Single and separate cities, where the citizens' voices could perhaps still be heard, had lost control of their own fates. Greece as a whole, for that matter, had become a mere pawn on a military and diplomatic chess board which was dominated by governments commanding professional armies and navies and financial resources vastly greater than any single city could hope to match.

With the decisive loss of local polis sovereignty—an event signalized by the Macedonian conquest in 338 B.C.—Greek civilization and culture lost much of its initial *élan*. Only an elite could share the refinements of philosophy as elaborated by Plato, or understand the nuances of disbelief expressed by Praxiteles' statue. The humble, uneducated, poverty-stricken multitude went one way while the rich and well-born went another; and the polis solidarities which had briefly linked them into a single whole survived only weakly and in memory, not as living reality.

Greek civilization had still a brilliant future ahead, and its power of geographical expansion had, in fact, barely begun to manifest itself when this inner erosion set it. The greatness of the initial achievement was such that men in far parts of the earth and living long afterward continued and still continue to respond with a special vibrancy to the surviving monuments of the Athenian golden age. Fundamental and enduring lines of subsequent European thought and sensibility had found their first and clearest expression in the work of these few Greeks.

Such innovation did not go unnoticed at the time. We shall therefore next turn to the manner in which neighboring peoples reacted to the Greek achievement, and in reacting forwarded the expansion of a Hellenistic style of civilization.

CHAPTER 9

The Spread of Hellenistic

Civilization 500 B.C.–A.D. 200

We have already seen how traders brought aspects of Greek civilization to the attention of barbarian chieftains in such backwoods regions of the Mediterranean world as Scythia, northern Italy, and Gaul. (See above, pp. 114 and 115.) Closer to the Aegean center, the kingdom of Macedon acquired a somewhat deeper tincture of the Greek style of life as a prelude to conquering the heartland of Greek civilization itself. How this happened is quite instructive, for other border states have often been able to profit, like Macedon, from a position on the margins of a civilization by building a territorially large and therefore militarily strong power, capable, when organized with civilized efficiency, of conquering smaller rivals nearer the old center of culture.

Macedonian Conquest

‡‡‡ Macedonian kings made their courts into a school of Greek manners. The tragedian Euripides, for example, spent some time as an honored guest at the royal court of Macedon, and Aristotle tutored Alexander the Great. No doubt the Macedonian kings felt genuine admiration for Greek civilization for its own sake. But their policy of

Hellenization* had additional advantages. Young Macedonian noblemen on coming to court naturally acquired Greek tastes; but having done so, soon discovered that they could not lead the life of their choice anywhere but at court and in the king's service. The reason for this was that the Macedonian countryside was inhabited by a free and sturdy peasantry whose chiefs might indeed lead them into battle but could not extract heavy rents and dues from them. Hence a backwoods noble had no source of cash income such as was needed if imported Greek wares were to be paid for privately. The monarchy, deriving money income from mines and from conquered cities near the coast, was able to import the luxuries required to live in a civilized way, and to distribute them among deserving servants of the king. In this way the Macedonian kings created a group of loyal and obedient yet proudly free and noble officers and royal agents.

When such officers of the crown undertook to teach Macedonian peasants the tactics of Greek phalanx warfare, they quickly created a very efficient military machine. The Macedonians were numerous, hardy, and tough. They were also accustomed to obeying their superiors, who now, for the first time, were willing to follow the king and give up the fierce local feuds which had previously made the Macedonian nobility utterly ungovernable. King Philip of Macedon (ruled 359–336 B.C.) was the first to reap the full benefit of the new configuration of forces within his country. He conquered neighboring barbarous lands—Illyria, Thrace—and then turned upon Greece. Everywhere his army met with success, presaging the even more brilliant victories that came to Macedonian arms under his son Alexander (ruled 336–323 B.C.).

Alexander's career directed Hellenism eastward. His army marched against Persia in 334 B.C. and everywhere consciously championed Greek ways. After 330 B.C., when the last Persian monarch, Darius III, was killed by his own followers, Alexander claimed to be the

* Terminology is confusing. Our word "Greek" comes from Roman usage and was unknown to the ancient Greeks before they met the Romans. When the ancient Greeks wanted to refer to themselves collectively they used the word "Hellenes." Hence, "Hellenic" means of or pertaining to the ancient Greeks, and "Hellenism" is often used as a shorthand for their civilization. "Hellenization," however, means becoming like the ancient Greeks in some way or other, and "Hellenistic" means being similar, but not quite identical to them.

legitimate successor and avenger of the murdered monarch. Yet he did not thereby abandon his role as founder of cities—on the Greek model—and exemplar of the Greek heroic ideal. Alexander aspired to conquer the whole world, and was bitterly disappointed when his weary troops, after subduing the easternmost reaches of the Persian empire and invading northwestern India, refused to press forward into the Ganges valley. After a difficult return trip, in the course of which Alexander and his soldiers followed the Indus to its mouth and then marched overland to Babylon, the ever-victorious Macedonian died suddenly of a fever (323 B.C.).

Alexander's unexpected death, less than twelve years after he had launched his army on its great venture, became a signal for the outbreak of strife among his generals. His posthumous son and heir was among the early victims. Only after nearly half a century of warfare did three more or less stable monarchies emerge, each ruled by a Macedonian general's descendants: the Ptolemies in Egypt, the Seleucids in Asia, and the Antigonids in Macedonia. Of the three, Ptolemaic Egypt was at first the strongest. As a sea power the Ptolemies disputed control of the Aegean with the Antigonids, while on land they quarreled with the Seleucids for primacy in Palestine and Syria.

Greek Emigration

‡‡‡ Both the Ptolemaic empire and the Seleucid empire depended in considerable part upon Greek immigrants. Thousands of Greeks swarmed out of their homeland in the wake of Alexander's conquest in hope of finding fortunes in foreign parts. Some became government officials and administrators, others entered military service and some settled as farmers in special military colonies. But the great majority became city folk, pursuing hundreds of different occupations both in government service and in business and the free professions— working as merchants, doctors, architects, scribes, tax farmers, professional athletes, actors, and the like.

Massive emigration was both a symptom and a cause of economic setback in Greece itself. Within a century of Alexander's conquest we hear of deserted fields and empty villages. More and more the Greek countryside was abandoned by citizen farmers. Slaves and foreigners took their place. In a sense these changes simply made the society of

Greece conform to a pattern already age-old in the Middle East. The close linkage between farmers and city folk, which had prevailed for a while during the first flowering of Greek culture, disappeared. A wide and all but unbridgeable social and psychological gap opened between the upper classes of the towns (many of them now landowners, drawing rents from the country) and the rude peasantry. Almost as great a gap also divided the poor of the city from the rich and educated classes who more and more dominated the political as well as the economic scene.

Such polarization of society had long been familiar in the Middle East. It was, indeed, the price of civilization, for technical limitations upon production and transportation made it necessary for some men to go without if others were to have the leisure to acquire and elaborate high culture. The classical age itself had not really escaped this limiting condition. Athens had been, in its days of greatness, a predator upon weaker communities all round the Aegean and Black Sea coasts. Citizens of Athens acted together to exploit their advantage, and used their wealth and leisure for public display rather than for private consumption. But collective exploitation at a distance is not necessarily milder than the pressure of a landlord upon peasants close by; and a society of cultivated landlords, with their servitors, attendants, educators, and providers of other professional services, is not necessarily less humane or less civilized than an imperial community of equals whose equality is dependent in great part upon an unceasing flow of tribute, plunder, and the gains to be had from such services as the administration of justice among subject peoples.

As Greek high culture came to be the possession of an urban upper class whose income depended primarily upon land rents or government salaries, it became far more readily exportable. Very special circumstances were required to produce a city like Athens or Sparta. But any landlord, if he commanded a sufficiently large cash income, could acquire a Greek education, learn Greek manners, and become in all respects a Greek without having to alter the social structure of his community as a whole.

As the Greeks penetrated the Middle East, therefore, the increasingly urban, upper-class character of Greek civilization at home facilitated its spread abroad among the landlords and other men of means who had long dominated local society. The Greek style of life, which included such things as athletics in the nude and dancing girls as well as philosophy and poetry, appealed strongly to many of these men. Greeks, as a rule, were willing to admit such recruits to their circle as soon as the neophytes acquired a suitably Greek education and set of manners. Even humbler folk found it convenient or necessary to learn Greek, which rapidly became the dominant language of the entire eastern Mediterranean, displacing Aramaic from that position within two or three centuries of Alexander's victories.

Religious Changes

‡‡‡ At first everything seemed to go one way. Middle Eastern peoples borrowed arts and manners from the Greeks while the conquerors found little in the life of their subjects to admire or imitate. Nevertheless, before very long cultural borrowing became a two-way street. In particular, the lower classes of the towns found in Middle Eastern religions a far more adequate explanation of the world than anything available to them from the Greek tradition. No one any longer took the gods of Olympus very seriously. Their worship was inextricably tied up with public ceremonies and city-wide celebrations, whereas the poor and humble of the great cities of the Mediterranean needed a religion that could comfort them in time of personal distress, and help them to hope for a better future, if not in this life then in the next.

Educated gentlemen might still prefer the careful arguments of philosophers, who, despite important differences in detail, all agreed that wisdom required a man to refrain from extremes and not to care about anything too much, lest by caring he allow some outside attachment to disturb his personal calm and self-control. As long as life presented no really serious crises, such a prescription for leading a private life made excellent sense in an age when public affairs were in the hands of distant monarchs and their unscrupulous servants. But when disaster came, which for the Hellenistic gentlemen of the eastern Mediterranean meant when crude Roman soldiers and governors trampled their gardens and demanded bigger taxes, bribes, and ransoms than they could pay, the comforts of philosophy were distant and too cold to be effective. Under these circumstances the upper classes, too, began to feel the need for a more personal and emotionally vibrant faith.

Several religions combining Greek with Middle Eastern elements met this need. A few Greeks were attracted to Judaism, which retained its full vigor and emotional conviction. But the hatred pious Jews felt for some of the Greek habits and customs—in particular the nudity of the gymnasium deeply shocked Jewish sensibility—made any sort of halfway house between the two cultures difficult. Other cults, like those of Mithra, for example, and of Serapis, proved more flexible, and permitted the close marriage of Greek with Middle Eastern ideas and religious rituals. A general turn toward a theistic interpretation of the world therefore became evident among the Greeks even before the Roman conquest drastically altered the political order of the eastern Mediterranean.

Hellenistic Sciences and Arts

‡‡‡ A second fruitful interaction between Middle Eastern and Greek cultures occurred in the field of astronomy. For several centuries Babylonian observers had accumulated accurate observations of such events as eclipses, and had developed a workable way of locating objects in the sky by means of a spherical grid. When the Greeks discovered these tables, they eagerly set out to explain Babylonian data by constructing geometric models of the heavens. Aristarchus of Samos (d. *c.* 230 B.C.) proposed the idea that the earth revolved around the sun, but because the stellar parallax was too small to be observed with the instruments then available, this idea was discredited. Instead, Hipparchus of Nicaea (d. *c.* 126 B.C.) proposed the scheme which became standard in later centuries. He assumed that the stars and planets were embedded in transparent spheres which revolved around the earth at varying speeds. To account for the regular reversal of the apparent motion of the planets he assumed that a smaller sphere revolved around a point on the surface of the earth-centered sphere and carried the fiery planet on its surface. The observed motion was therefore the sum of two independent motions which sometimes reinforced each other and sometimes worked in opposite directions. This system had the advantage that any new refinement of observation could be accounted for by inventing another sphere whose size, speed, and axis of rotation could be adjusted to produce the observed phenomena.

We are so steeped in Copernican astronomy that it is perhaps hard to understand the enthusiasm with which men accepted this geometric explanation of the heavenly motions. Such complicated machinery seems inherently implausible today; but what impressed everyone at the time and for centuries afterwards was the mathematical precision of the scheme, which actually allowed prediction of planetary motions. The ability to determine where the wandering lights of the firmament would in fact find themselves at a particular time in the future (or where they had been in the past) seemed a certain guarantee of the correctness of the whole system.

The success of Hellenistic astronomy was further reinforced by its astrological application. The fundamental idea of astrology was that events in the heavens foreshadowed events on earth. After the linkage of Greek mathematics to Babylonian observational records it did in fact become possible to calculate the relative position of the planets at any time—past or future. With such skill, it therefore seemed possible to predict what would happen on earth. By making the assumption that the position of the planets at the time of a man's birth affected his whole life's span, a single calculation gave the key to the future for any individual. This seemed enormously impressive to the ordinary un-mathematical mind. Consequently, almost from its inception—mainly at Alexandria in Egypt—the new science of astrology attained enormous and enduring popularity. Reciprocally, the demand for men who could cast horoscopes correctly kept mathematical astronomy alive through all succeeding ages. In Roman times the astronomer Ptolemy (second century A.D.) distilled Greek mathematical astronomy into a single book, which we know by its Arabic title, *Almagest*. A little later Galen (d. *c.* A.D. 200) codified Greek medicine for later ages, just as Euclid (*fl. c.* 300 B.C.) had done earlier for geometry.

Other aspects of Hellenistic culture diversified older Greek tradition but cut no strikingly new paths. This was true of sculpture and architecture, city planning and the arts of fortification, for example. Literature tended to become academic—full of learned references —or artificial—populated by silly shepherdesses and the like. History degenerated into a branch of rhetoric, while the rhetoricians preferred a good phrase to a good idea. Such refinement and artificiality appealed of course only to the educated. The poor and vulgar also found a quasi-literary voice through the mime. This was a form of popular theater which preserved something of the bawdy tradition of Athenian comedy.

The Rise of Rome

‡‡‡ A new and politically important strand was added to the mixture of peoples and cultures in the eastern Mediterranean with the Roman conquest, first of Macedonia and Greece (146 B.C.), then of Seleucid Asia (64 B.C.), and finally of Egypt (30 B.C.). Rome began its political career as the leader of a federation of Latin cities in central Italy. A period of royal Etruscan rule ended with the establishment of an aristocratic republic (509 B.C.). The Republic was at first very strongly committed to the preservation of a simple rural Latin way of life in reaction against the corruptions of both Greek and Etruscan brands of civilization. For more than a century, Romans engaged in border wars, slowly expanding their territory, but also suffering occasional setbacks as when a raiding body of Gauls sacked the city and almost captured the capitol (390 B.C.). Rapid expansion began soon thereafter so that by 265 B.C. all of Italy south of the Apennines was united under Roman leadership.

Rome's success rested partly on a numerous and hardy peasantry, disciplined and led by a hard-bitten and tenacious aristocracy that long remained profoundly distrustful of the corrupting luxury and wealth they saw among their more civilized neighbors. Additionally, the native peoples of Italy were but loosely organized into tribes and districts, sometimes with and sometimes without a definite urban headquarters. No stubborn defense of local autonomy hindered the Romans in fastening their military and political leadership upon these peoples, especially since they were already familiar with federal arrangements within their own local political systems. Hence it proved possible to unite Italy under a single city's government without much trouble, whereas the Greeks struggled endlessly among themselves and never managed to combine local loyalties with stable attachment to any larger political whole.

Rome's rise brought on collision with the imperial city of Carthage in north Africa. Sicily, where Greeks and Carthaginians had been fighting one another for centuries, was the first bone of contention. Before they were able to defeat the Carthaginians, the Romans had to build a fleet, thus becoming a naval power for the first time. By 241 B.C. the Carthaginians were driven from Sicily. The island became the first

Roman province governed by a special magistrate or governor and required to pay taxes to Rome.

A second and far more severe test of Roman strength came between 218 and 201 B.C., when Hannibal, a skillful Carthaginian general, marched an army from Spain to Italy. Roman efforts to defeat Hannibal all failed. After a particularly severe defeat at Cannae (216 B.C.) the Romans decided to avoid battle, but kept armies in the field to shadow every move Hannibal made. The Carthaginians had expected most of the subjected cities and peoples of Italy to rise in revolt against the Romans. A few cities did indeed welcome Hannibal as liberator, but most of Rome's subjects and allies in Italy preferred a Roman to a Carthaginian master. Consequently, after twelve years in Italy, during which time he was never defeated in the field, Hannibal was compelled to embark for home because in the mean time a Roman expeditionary force had turned the tables on him by provoking revolt among natives of north Africa against their Carthaginian masters. At Zama in north Africa the Romans with their African allies won a final battle (202 B.C.). They forced Carthage to make a humiliating peace, transferring Spain from Carthaginian to Roman control. Thereafter the Romans remained without rival in the western Mediterranean.

Long years of war brought devastation to much of Italy. The simple farming folk who had constituted the backbone of Roman strength were particularly hard hit. As a result, the constitutional development of the city changed direction. Up to the time of the wars with Carthage, Roman government had been conducted by magistrates who were elected by two different popular assemblies, while still a third kind of assembly met to pass laws. This clumsy system was held together by the Senate, which was the body that gave real continuity to official action. Magistrates consulted the Senate about all important matters and seldom went against the advice they got. Old patrician families dominated the Senate, but "new men," who qualified themselves by winning election to the more important magistracies, were also let in. This gave an ever increasing political weight to commoners (Latin: *plebs*) in the period before the Hannibalic war.

That war changed Rome's political structure as well as its society and economy. Popular leaders, as it happened, met defeat at Hannibal's hands early in the war, and Rome was saved by generals from old patrician families. This discredited plebeian leadership. Plebeian politicians lost support, also, when the small farmers left the land after the war. Instead, generals took over as the most important group of political leaders. Their power depended increasingly on personal loyalty of the troops to their commander. But for a while the Senate retained great authority, for it was only with Senate approval that a magistrate could be appointed general (Latin: *imperator*) with the legal right to raise an army and make war. Political careers came to depend upon being able to cultivate favor in the Senate so as to get a military command, and then to cultivate favor among the soldiers, so as to compel the magistrates and Senators at home to do whatever had to be done to advance the imperator's career still further. Commanders, soldiers, and, often, the Senate all had an interest in keeping the troops busy far away from home. Hence Rome began to make war often and with little provocation, more because of domestic difficulties than because of dangers abroad.

Breakdown of the Republic

‡‡‡ Involvement in the wars of the east came without delay; but for half a century the Senators held back from assuming direct political control over any part of the Hellenistic world of the eastern Mediterranean. This policy was abandoned in 146 B.C., when Macedon (already thrice defeated in battle) was made into a province and Greece was "liberated" by a foreign conqueror for the last time. Very rapidly Roman governors, soldiers, and tax collectors acquainted themselves with the refinements and luxuries of Hellenistic civilization. New tastes flowed into Rome with the new wealth derived from plunder. Simultaneously, Roman society underwent a catastrophic differentiation between rich and poor, similar to the crisis that the Peloponnesian war had brought nearly three centuries earlier to Greece.

Civil war between rival generals, commanding increasingly professionalized troops, fastened a military dictatorship upon the Roman state. Julius Caesar (d. 44 B.C.), the conqueror of Gaul and champion of the lower classes in Rome, was the first man who seized and held extra-legal power for more than a brief period. His expressed intention of reorganizing the Roman government roused bitter opposition among

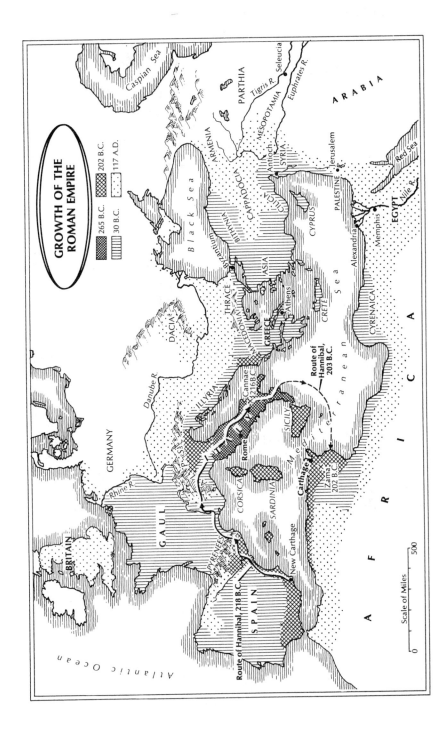

GROWTH OF THE ROMAN EMPIRE

265 B.C.   202 B.C.
30 B.C.   117 A.D.

Atlantic Ocean

BRITAIN

GERMANY

GAUL

Rhine R.

SPAIN

Route of Hannibal, 218 B.C.

PYRENEES

New Carthage

CORSICA

SARDINIA

Danube R.

DACIA

ILLYRIA

ITALY

Rome

Cannae
216 B.C.

SICILY

Carthage

Zama
202 B.C.

Route of
Hannibal, 203 B.C.

Mediterranean Sea

THRACE

MACEDONIA

GREECE

Athens

CRETE

Black Sea

BITHYNIA

ASIA

CAPPADOCIA

CILICIA

ARMENIA

PARTHIA

Tigris R.

Euphrates R.

Seleucia

MESOPOTAMIA

SYRIA

Antioch

CYPRUS

PALESTINE

Jerusalem

Caspian Sea

ARABIA

Red Sea

Nile R.

EGYPT

Memphis

Alexandria

CYRENAICA

A F R I C A

Scale of Miles

0   500

his fellow Senators. They thought of him as a tyrant and usurper and so slew him on the steps of the Senate house. But their act, intended to restore the Republic, merely plunged the Roman world into another round of civil war, from which Caesar's adopted son, Augustus, emerged victorious (30 B.C.).

Having won undisputed sovereignty over the Mediterranean, Augustus proceeded to borrow his defeated enemies' slogans by claiming in 27 B.C. to have "restored the Republic." He did reinstate republican forms and even entrusted the government of some of the provinces of the empire to the Senate. But Augustus was careful to keep military command in his own hands, and behind the scenes he exercised very effective control over elections and set limits on the deliberations of the Senate. Nevertheless, the forms of republican government were not completely empty, if only because the emperor (from Latin *imperator*) was at pains to avoid hurting senatorial feelings.

The pretense of republicanism made transmission of authority from one emperor to another rather awkward. The hereditary principle was an affront to republican theory, which held that free elections should determine political leadership. Nevertheless, the custom whereby a reigning emperor designated his successor usually worked smoothly, for all men dreaded a recurrence of civil war. As a result, for more than two hundred years after Augustus' victory the Roman world remained internally at peace, with the exception of one disastrous year (A.D. 69) when soldiers from different armies proclaimed no fewer than three emperors in rapid succession and the imperial rivals fought out their claims in the heart of the empire. Frontier wars continued. Augustus, for example, pushed his frontiers to the Rhine and the Danube; the Emperor Claudius (reigned A.D. 41–54) began the conquest of Britain; Domitian (reigned A.D. 81–96) occupied the part of Germany lying between the upper Rhine and Danube, and Trajan (reigned A.D. 98–117) conquered both Dacia (in modern Hungary and Rumania) and Mesopotamia. Two fierce Jewish revolts in Palestine also engaged Roman arms (A.D. 66–70 and A.D. 132–35) and various wars against the Parthians to the east and the Germans to the north kept Roman armies from idleness. Yet these struggles had little effect in the interior of the empire, where peace and orderliness prevailed as never before or since.

Hellenism in the Roman Empire

‡‡‡ During this long period of peace, the Roman empire witnessed a massive transplantation of Hellenistic civilization westward to Italy, Gaul, and Spain. To be sure, Latin rather than Greek became the prevailing language of these regions, so that it was Hellenistic culture in a Latin dress that rooted itself in the western provinces. Sculptors learned to carve with all the skill of their Hellenistic contemporaries, but Roman taste, emphasizing realistic portraiture, gave Roman sculpture its own distinctive character. Similarly in the field of literature, Lucretius (d. 55 B.C.), Cicero (d. 43 B.C.), and Vergil (d. 19 B.C.)—to name only the most distinguished—developed Latin into a language capable of expressing most of the Greek philosophic, rhetorical, and poetic refinements. Yet Latin could never become Greek. Latin letters and thought therefore retained always a distinctive accent, even when faithfully patterned on Greek originals or inspired by Greek example.

Within the framework of imperial administration, the provinces of the empire were organized into a series of city-states, each possessing its own local version of the public institutions, buildings, and governmental procedures which had once constituted the frame of existence for Greek and early Roman life. During the long Roman peace, provincial cities came to be dominated by local landowners. Their progress in the refinements of civilization was made at the direct cost of the peasants round about who tilled the soil and paid them rents. Gentility, but also a certain vapidity and cultural fragility, were inevitable consequences. Only a comparative handful of the population knew or cared much about the high Greco-Roman culture of the great Mediterranean world, and these favored few owed their security to the obedience of distant frontier garrisons to an emperor whom most of the soldiers had never seen. Under the circumstances it is surprising that peace lasted as long as it did, and that the privileged social position of a demilitarized landed class was not challenged until after A.D. 193, when civil wars and barbarian invasions once more began to ravage the empire.

To begin with, Roman imperial rule left most local institutions pretty much alone. By degrees, however, dealings that ran across older lines of jurisdiction acquired greater importance, and a new legal system became necessary to regulate such affairs. Roman magistrates took the lead in elaborating legal principles that could be applied everywhere to everyone; and when the Emperor Caracalla, in a move to make more people taxable, declared that every free man should be counted as a Roman citizen (A.D. 212), the Roman law, as elaborated across preceding centuries, became universally applicable within the empire's borders.

The central notion of this system of law was that human relations ought to be regulated by contracts that were freely entered into and enforceable in courts of law. A second basic idea was that property in any form ought to have a single, definite owner who was fully empowered to enter into contracts with respect to such property. This obviously facilitated commerce, and made for a society in which individuals might rise and fall in wealth and status depending on the contracts they entered into. A third principle declared that the political sovereign could make new law at will. This meant that the entire legal system could continue to develop across time to fit new needs and circumstances.

The efficiency and flexibility of Roman law surely helped to maintain the empire as a viable socioeconomic system, both before and after the breakup of the Roman peace in A.D. 193. Even though various local forms of customary law later asserted their jurisdiction in many parts of Europe, the Roman law was never forgotten, and its principles could be and were revived when need arose. This facilitated enormously the re-emergence of commercial activity in later ages and constituted one of the enduring legacies of the Roman empire to modern times.

Christianity

‡‡‡ Behind the Hellenized façade of Roman life great changes were under way during the first two centuries of the Christian era. The interaction between Middle Eastern and Greek cultures, which had begun before the Romans appeared on the scene, continued apace. The Roman state, with its rapidly developing bureaucracy, tax collectors, legal system, postal services, and standing army, borrowed heavily from ancient Middle Eastern examples of imperial administration. More important still were changes in religion, for it was in these centuries that Christianity—a faith that combined Jewish and Greek elements with a new and most persuasive revelation—created a force that was destined to shape men's minds and feelings for millennia. Yet, until after A.D. 200, Christianity, as well as other competing "mystery reli-

gions" that offered salvation from the hardships and tribulations of the world, remained relatively obscure, since it was the poor and humble of the cities who first found solace in the Christian gospel.

Despite the Greek language in which the Gospels were couched, and despite the Greek ring to some of St. Paul's (d. *c.* A.D. 64) phrases about sin and atonement, Christianity was basically a reaffirmation of the Middle Eastern view of the nature of the world and man. The early Christians' concern for God and salvation, and their vivid expectation of a speedy end of the world, stemmed from Jewish roots, and these aspects of the new faith carried greater emotional power than did the abstract complexities of trinitarian theology or other distinctively Greek aspects of the new religion.

Such analysis of the antecedents of Christianity should not disguise the fact that the events so simply narrated in the Gospels and in Acts generated something new and enormously appealing. Jesus and his disciples clearly expected God to intervene speedily and with power to set the wicked world aright. When instead the Roman authorities in Jerusalem arrested and crucified Jesus (*c.* A.D. 30), these expectations seemed at first to have proved false. But soon afterwards the dispirited Apostles gathered in an "upstairs room" and suddenly felt again the heartwarming presence of their Master. This seemed absolutely convincing evidence that Jesus' death on the cross had not been the end but rather a beginning. With a great rush of renewed hope, his followers concluded that he would soon return in glory to inaugurate the long-awaited Day of Judgment. Their friend and Master, Jesus, it now seemed certain, was indeed the Messiah, prophesied from of old, who had been sent by God to save whoever heeded his teaching, and would soon return on clouds of fire to judge the quick and the dead.

Such surprising news could not be kept quiet. On the contrary, the Apostles bubbled over with excitement and tried to explain to anyone who would listen all that had happened and was going to happen. Around this tiny kernel of excited missionaries the vast fabric of historical Christianity gradually formed—a process as surprising and worldshaking as the similarly pervasive changes of behavior provoked by Buddha, Confucius, or any of the other great teachers of mankind.

In one important respect, however, the career of historic Christianity differed from that of any other great religion. From the beginning, learned and respectable Jews refused to accept the idea that Jesus was the Messiah. Only a small minority of Jews ever accepted the new gospel. But St. Paul and others found willing listeners among pagans of the Hellenized cities of Syria and Asia Minor. Men who longed for a savior, but were not prepared to accept the ceremonial rules of Judaism, found the Christian message perfectly convincing. It was early decided that such converts would not have to conform to the Jewish Law. Faith in Christ (a Greek term meaning "The Anointed One" and equivalent to the Hebrew "Messiah") and a reformed life as a member of the Christian community were enough. As a result, after the Jewish Christians of Jerusalem had been dispersed in the course of the Jewish revolt of A.D. 66–70, Christian communities of the Greek-speaking cities of the eastern Mediterranean severed their ties with Judaism entirely. No other great religion underwent such a change of environment in infancy, for Greek ideas and religious inheritance were not at all the same as Jewish, yet pagan converts inevitably brought with them many of their former habits of thought.

In particular, the combination of divine and human traits in a single person was a thoroughly familiar idea among Greeks. The idea that Jesus Christ was a man and yet the Son of God, and therefore divine, appealed to Greek-thinking and Greek-speaking converts very strongly. The divine aspect of Christ's existence tended therefore to attract greater emphasis. Similarly, Greek habits of logical argument demanded clearer definition of the relationship between God the Father, God the Son, and God the Holy Spirit, for the Holy Spirit continued to visit and inspire Christian congregations from time to time, just as it had visited the Apostles in Jerusalem after the crucifixion. From this emerged the subtleties of trinitarian theology. But before the abstract definition of dogma became critically important, Christians felt the need for a dependable record of Jesus' life on earth. Accordingly, the four Gospels, each recording a somewhat divergent recollection of the Master's words and deeds, were written down between A.D. 70 and 100. Soon thereafter, St. Paul's letters and several other texts of exhortation or of prophecy were brought together to form the New Testament. Weekly readings from these sacred texts, as well as from the Jewish Scriptures, together with singing and a ritual meal commemorating Jesus' last supper with his disciples, maintained the faith of the growing communities of Christians.

The willingness of members of these groups to help one another, especially in time of sickness or other unusual hardship, was another very powerful support for the early church. Despite the distrust with which Roman rulers inevitably viewed a semi-secret society which preached the early end of the world and the overthrow of Roman authority, the Christian churches continued to attract converts among the poor and disinherited.

The success of Christianity, coupled with the general petering out of Greek pagan energies, was a sign that Hellenism was at long last losing its expansive power. By that time, however, peoples in Asia and Europe had transformed, borrowed, and made their own, aspects of Hellenistic civilization which seemed worth while to them. Echoes of this process extended to India and even to distant China. This we will explore in the next chapter, which will consider the development of these civilizations during the years of Hellenism's triumphs, and survey the repercussions of civilized achievements upon the barbarian world as a whole.

CHAPTER 10

Asia 500 B.C.-A.D. 200

While Hellenism was outgrowing its Aegean cradle-land and becoming a diffusely genteel mode of existence, the other civilizations of the Old World did not stand still. The Macedonian and Roman conquests had consequences beyond Hellenistic and Roman frontiers, particularly in India. Simultaneously, in Mongolia the rise of the first really powerful nomad confederation triggered far-ranging migrations along the steppe. The upshot was that more intimate and regular communication than ever before was established among all civilized and many of the semi-civilized peoples of Eurasia. Despite fundamental cultural conservatism in all the main centers of civilization, the new frequency of contact across the entire Eurasian continent did stimulate peoples in critical crossroads areas to unusual creativity, especially in the field of religion.

The Mauryan Empire of India

‡‡‡ When Alexander led his army into the Indus valley (327 B.C.), most of the Ganges region had already been consolidated under a single kingdom of Magadha. By disrupting local defenses and alliances the Macedonian invasion of northwestern India perhaps prepared the way for Chandragupta Maurya, king of Magadha (reigned *c.* 321–297 B.C.), to add the Indus region to his domain. Under his grandson,

Asoka (reigned *c.* 274–36 B.C.), central and southern India too, save for the extreme tip, was annexed to the Mauryan empire.

This vast state borrowed a good deal from Persian and Hellenistic models. Mauryan sculpture may have been produced by workmen im-

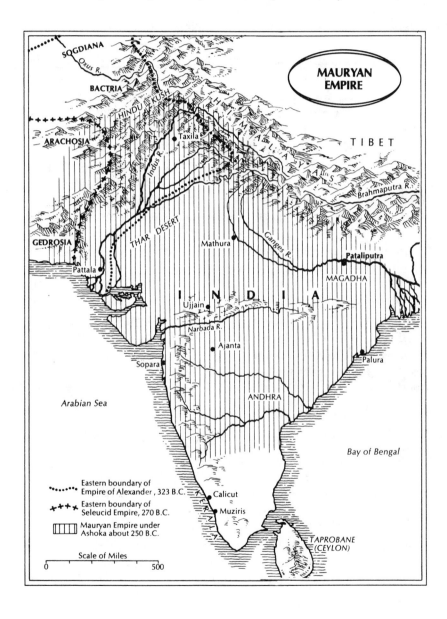

ported from beyond the Hindu Kush. Chandragupta's palace appears to have closely resembled the Persian palace at Persepolis. Asoka's famous pillar edicts, which he set up in widely scattered parts of his empire, seem to have been inspired by the Persian royal inscriptions carved into the cliffs at Behistan. Perhaps even the Mauryan concept of universal empire owed something to the Persian and Macedonian examples.

Yet Asoka, after youthful indulgence in war and conquest, became a pious Buddhist, and devoted the rest of his life to spiritual conquests. He sent missionaries to all parts of his realm, as well as abroad. He also erected several shrines to house portions of Buddha's ashes. For a while it seemed as though Buddhism would sweep all before it, but official patronage, even when supplemented by invocations of the Buddha, pilgrimages to holy places, alms-giving, and other pious observances, could not overcome the original weakness of the religion. Despite such inventiveness, it remained true that only for monks could Buddhism provide a complete way of life. Ordinary men in ordinary walks of life were still compelled to resort to Brahmans for rites appropriate to birth, marriage, and death, not to mention all the lesser crises of human life.

Very soon after Asoka's death his empire split into warring fragments. Fresh waves of invaders came through the passes from central Asia: Greeks, Shakas, Kushans, and Parthians. These invasions were related to flights and removals on the steppe which were triggered in turn by the clash between a newly united China and the Turkish-speaking pastoralists of Inner and Outer Mongolia.

The Unification of China

‡‡‡ All this widespread upheaval among the peoples of the steppe was started by China's unification. This was the work of the ruler of the state of Ch'in. In 221 B.C. his armies, tempered in long border wars against steppe barbarians, completed the overthrow of all rivals within China, and he assumed the title of First Emperor (Shih Huang-ti) of a new dynasty, the Ch'in. The new emperor used his position to reorganize Chinese administration radically and ruthlessly. The country was divided into provinces and prefectures, on lines that lasted until modern times. He prescribed a uniform script, which also took hold and

soon made older books more or less indecipherable. He completed the construction of the Great Wall to keep the nomads in check, and created an efficient system of posts and roads within China to allow him to rush troops to any threatened frontier or rebellious province.

This great autocrat and conqueror recklessly overrode local tradition, repudiating anything that set limits on his power. This meant, among other things, collision with Confucian doctrine, which sought to confine the emperor to governing according to traditional rites. Shih Huang-ti therefore prohibited Confucian teaching and ordered all Confucian books burned, save for a single copy of each work, which

was to be preserved in the imperial archives. This decree won Shih Huang-ti the undying hatred of later generations of Confucians. More important at the time, his massive conscription of Chinese manpower for state service created general discontent, and when the great conqueror died in 210 B.C. his heir proved unable to maintain his father's power. Fresh civil war broke out, ending in 202 B.C., when the founder of the Han dynasty secured hegemony over all China. Except for one brief usurpation (A.D. 9–22) his descendants continued to occupy the imperial office until A.D. 220.

The early Han emperors allied with the class of landowners who had become the dominant element in Chinese society. Sons of these families, educated in a predominantly Confucian mould, were recruited into the imperial bureaucracy. This established a pervasive harmony of outlook between officials and landowners. They often combined to keep peasants and other subordinate ranks of society in their proper place. One sign of the stabilization of Chinese society along these lines was a decline of intellectual controversy, which had been a prominent feature of the period of the warring states. Shih Huang-ti, for example, was identified with the Legalist school that emphasized the rights of the state over all rivals, whereas the Han emperors soon accepted Confucianism as an official ideology. Rival doctrines were repressed, more through official disapproval than by intellectual refutation, until, by degrees, a remarkable uniformity of outlook arose among the educated classes of imperial China.

Governments in Central Asia

‡‡‡ Long before this aspect of China's stabilization had time to work itself out, the military strength of a united China was made manifest abroad. Shih Huang-ti lost no time in taking the offensive and drove a number of tribes from Inner Mongolia across the Gobi desert to the sparse grasslands of Outer Mongolia. These refugees formed the kernel of a barbarian steppe confederation, called Hsiung-nu by the Chinese, which presently became so formidable as to constitute a military equal even to the mass of a united China. The first Han emperor, for example, nearly lost his life on a campaign against the Hsiung-nu (200 B.C.). After this sobering experience he signed a treaty agreeing to pay trib-

ute to the leaders of the confederation and recognizing their restored dominion over Inner Mongolia.

The Hsiung-nu thereupon set out to extend their control westward across the steppe. In doing so they dislodged various Iranianspeaking peoples who fled toward the southwest, where they overthrew the Greek kingdom of Bactria, an interesting but little-known state that arose in the region between the decaying Seleucid and Mauryan empires, far to the east of other Greek-speaking kingdoms. Yet after a period of confusion, during which successive waves of invaders crossed the Himalayas and overran much of northwestern India, a more stable regime returned to the oases and pasture lands of central and western Asia. In 102 B.C. Chinese armies traveled westward and established the suzerainty of the Son of Heaven as far as the Jaxartes river. Some time later (exact dates are disputed), a comparatively strong monarchy ruled by Kushan kings established itself where the Greek kingdom of Bactria had formerly been, i.e. in modern Afghanistan and across the mountains into modern Pakistan. The Kushans were descendants of the Iranian tribesmen whom the Hsiung-nu drove away from China's western frontier. Still further west, another group of Iranian newcomers from the steppe, the Parthians, also erected a fairly stable empire which lasted from 171 B.C. until A.D. 226.

Changes in Warfare and Trade

‡‡‡ This widespread stabilization of civilized governments in central Asia became possible because of an important development in the technique of cavalry warfare. Before 100 B.C. the Parthians discovered that by feeding horses on alfalfa, specially planted and harvested, they could develop a larger, stronger, and more beautiful breed than the shaggy steppe ponies known previously. Such a horse, in turn, was able to carry a much heavier load of armor. This was important because a well-armored man and horse could render the arrows of light steppe cavalry ineffective. A company of such heavy cavalrymen could in fact return arrow for arrow, and then, when the steppe cavalrymen's quivers had been emptied, could drive them from the field and harass their retreat. Seldom, however, could armored cavalry overtake light horse. The result, therefore, was to create a stalemate between

civilized heavy cavalry and the light cavalry of the steppe nomads. Neither could prevail in the other's environment. The big horses could not find sufficient nourishment in the slim pickings of the wild steppe, whereas on agricultural ground the unarmored nomads could no longer prevail against the new style of heavy armored cavalry.

Agricultural communities capable of sustaining the big horses— they could eat hay and grain when the irrigated fields needed for alfalfa were lacking—therefore had the possibility of defending themselves against nomad raiding. But the expense was great, for horse and armor, not to mention the trained professional fighting man required to use these instruments effectively, all were costly. Another difficulty was that local institutions often had to be adapted in order to concentrate enough income in the hands of individual fighting men to permit them to purchase and maintain such elaborate equipment. This usually meant subordinating a village, or several villages, to a single strong-armed warrior. But when a truly formidable class of such paladins formed in the countryside, it meant that the will of the central government could not prevail, save on sufferance and with the concurrence of this new military class. Since monarchs, peasants, and townsmen all had reason to regret such a transformation, civilized societies did not accept the new heavy-armor technology of warfare very rapidly, except in regions exposed to constant raiding from the steppes, i.e. in Iran and central Asia.

Nevertheless, the shield against the steppe nomads which thus was raised in central Asia allowed civilized governments and merchants to collaborate in establishing an organized trade route, linking China with Rome by means of a well-appointed, regularly policed, and heavily taxed caravan route. Shipments of Chinese silk traveled westward to Roman Syria along this "Silk Road," while a variety of goods made the return trip—metals, glass, and considerable quantities of coin.

Almost simultaneously, Greek-speaking sea captains operating from the Red Sea discovered how to take advantage of the regular monsoon winds of the Indian Ocean to travel across the ocean from the straits of Aden all the way to southern India. Similar voyages were soon undertaken across the Bay of Bengal, linking the east coast of India to Malaya. A short portage across the isthmus of Kra then brought the voyagers into touch with Chinese vessels operating along the southeast Asian coasts. Thus a sea route, broken only by the portage across the neck of Malaya, also came to link Rome with China shortly before the Christian era.

Hundreds, perhaps thousands of persons made a living by traveling to and fro along these routes: camel drivers, sailors, guards, merchants, porters, and other common folk. They seldom left much trace in the literary record. Yet talk around campfires and in port taverns, we may well believe, spread information and misinformation about every part of the known world throughout the bazaars of Asia, all the way from Syria to China and from southern India to the Aral Sea.

Developments in the Arts

‡‡‡ No fundamental modification of any of the four major civilizations of the Old World resulted from this increase of communication and travel between China, India, and the Middle East. We have already seen how the Greek style of life penetrated the upper strata of Middle Eastern society, interacted with European barbarism to civilize all of Mediterranean Europe, and contributed a distinctive imprint to emerging Christianity as well. But contact with the other civilizations of the Old World did not add much more than the luxury of silk clothes to the life of Greco-Roman gentlemen.

Much the same was true elsewhere. The mainstream of Chinese culture, for example, was not affected in any important fashion by contact with the rest of the civilized world. Scholars and officials, steeped in the classics of Confucian scholarship, were as impervious to the silly notions of lowly trading folk as were their Roman equivalents, for whom a novel superstition like Christianity mattered as little as did the discredited deities of Olympus. We know far less about the lives of upper-class Brahmans in India, but they too may be presumed to have found little of interest in the gossip and tall stories of the ports and caravanserais, where the most fertile interchange between Greek, Indian, and Middle Eastern civilizations took place.

The established civilizations of the Old World, in other words, continued on their course as before. In China the years between Confucius' death (479 B.C.) and Shih Huang-ti's final conquest in 221 B.C. were particularly fertile. Various rival schools of learning arose to dispute preeminence with Confucianism and Taoism; but after the Han dynasty established peace in the land, these rivals withered or were absorbed into

Confucianism. The process of absorption brought much which had originally been skipped over by Confucius into his followers' traditional learning. The usual course was to read all sorts of new notions into the Confucian classics by treating them as allegories or anagrams, which hinted at truths available only to the learned and ingenious scholar who could decipher their full meaning. In this way, as men were later to do with the Christian scriptures, a host of new ideas could be fitted within the framework of Confucianism without difficulty.

Chinese learning was further enhanced by the inauguration of history as a distinct form of literary composition. The great pioneer was Ssu-ma Ch'ien (145–87 B.C.), who compiled a multi-volumed record of all the past known to him, from the beginning of things until his own lifetime. He organized China's history around the idea that each dynasty began with an especially virtuous ruler chosen by Heaven for the task, and then by degrees dissipated its initial virtue until Heaven lost patience and withdrew its mandate from the last unworthy ruler. He fitted the data of China's past into this scheme so persuasively that it became standard for all later Chinese historical writing.

We are much less well informed about the development of Indian literary and intellectual culture. The linkage of priestcraft, courtly elegance, and ascetic discipline, which achieved a classical expression in the Gupta age (c. A.D. 320–535), was presumably maturing; but when all dates are unsure it seems best to reserve a discussion of Indian thought and literature to a later chapter.

The Iranian regions remain tantalizingly obscure. The replacement of the Seleucid by Parthian overlordship in Iran and Mesopotamia (171 B.C.) does not appear to have had any drastic cultural consequences, at least initially. The Parthian monarchs, like the Seleucids, drew major tax revenues from the Hellenized cities of Mesopotamia and accordingly adopted a generally phil-Hellenic point of view. In the countryside, however, where the Zoroastrian faith survived, a more purely Iranian way of life persisted. This came clearly to political expression with the establishment of the Sassanian or New Persian empire in A.D. 226.

Art reflects exposure to new visual experiences far more sensitively than literature responds to contact with another learned tradition. This is so because it is not necessary to translate a work of art before strangers and outsiders can react to it. Literary culture, by contrast, is utterly unintelligible to the uninitiated. This is well illustrated by the manner in which contact with Greek sculpture stimulated Indian artists to perfect their own independent style of carving within a very short period. The earliest-known Indian sculpture dates from the time of Asoka. Within no more than two centuries a rich, mature style developed, well illustrated by the elaborate carving of the great Buddhist stupa at Sanchi. Art historians still debate exactly how much Indian artists were indebted to the Greeks. Yet the generally naturalistic character of Indian sculpture, its free use of Mediterranean decorative motifs, and the certainty that Indian stonecutters had ample opportunity to see numerous examples of Greek sculpture (at least as exported in cheap copies from Alexandria), all point to a real connection between the two sculptural traditions.

Astride the Hindu Kush a hybrid art style arose, using Greek forms to body forth Buddhist saviors. Buddhist missionaries spread this art across central Asia and brought it into China toward the end of the period we are now considering. As this style of art traveled eastward, Greek conventions were misunderstood. The spirit was also transmuted: what had begun as a naturalistic portrait statue of Apollo ended as a stylized evocation of other-worldly aspiration. Greco-Buddhist art really affected China only after the end of the Han dynasty (A.D. 220), when it entered deeply into and quite transformed earlier Chinese art. In this indirect fashion, we may literally watch Greek art styles spread across Asia, altering their meaning and symbolic significance as they progressed.

New, Cosmopolitan Religions

‡‡‡ The propagation of art styles was not, however, the most significant cultural consequence of the opening of regular communication between the separate civilizations of the Old World. Rather, in the regions where men of different cultures met and chaffered in the bazaars, there arose communities of rootless wanderers and lost souls who strove to make the harsh world in which they found themselves more tolerable by religious innovation of a sort that proved fundamental and very attractive to millions of men elsewhere throughout all later ages.

Three regions proved particularly fertile. One was in southern

India, a second in northwestern India, and the third lay in the Greek-speaking regions of the Roman empire. Christianity was of course the great religious creation of the Greek-speaking populations of the eastern Mediterranean cities. A reformulated Hinduism emerged almost simultaneously in southern India, while Mahayana Buddhism was doing the same in northwestern India. All three regions were active centers of long-distance trade, with big new cities where rootless men congregated. All three also were zones where several quite different older religious and cultural traditions overlapped, stimulating sensitive individuals to reorder their belief in the light of new inspiration, mystic experience, elaboration of ritual, and logic.

Something has already been said of Christian beginnings, and of the mingling of Jewish and Greek traditions that provided the new religion with its early setting.

In southern India, Hinduism achieved a much sharper definition during the first Christian centuries in an environment where Aryan, Dravidian, and Greco-Roman influences met and overlapped. The change came gradually, for no one prophet or preacher deliberately or consciously transformed the traditional faiths of India. Rather, through a process of ritual invention, the various myths concerning the innumerable deities honored by different Indian castes began to coalesce around the figures of two rival yet complementary deities, Shiva and Vishnu. Their worshippers believed that each of these gods chose to appear to human gaze in many different forms, suited to the understanding and sensibility of particular persons. Hence, almost any primitive cult or local peculiarity of worship could readily be attached to the cult of Vishnu or of Shiva, since every local god who in fact attracted worship was shown by that very fact to be a valid instance of divine incarnation.

Such a doctrine, nevertheless, introduced a new sort of order and system into Hinduism, since, when a local cult had been identified as a form of the worship of one of the two high gods of the Hindu pantheon, worshippers could begin to share in the more sophisticated service of a god whom they had previously known only in one of his particular guises.

The really important feature of the new form of Hinduism lay in this: worshippers of Vishnu and Shiva believed that these deities were saviors, able and ready to rescue them from the toils of their present life and raise them up the scale of being toward a blissful, perfect state.

The Development of Greek Sculpture

A POLIS WARRIOR AND CITIZEN

Aristion (the name, engraved on the base, means "good" or "noble") is wearing body armor and holds a spear, but lacks the helmet, sword, and shield that completed a hoplite's panoply.

The style of fighting and of living that made a nobleman like Aristion voluntarily dismount and join as an equal the ranks of ordinary farmer-citizens in Athens' phalanx inaugurated the classical age of Greece. The classical style of art, here seen emerging from archaic stiffness, balanced naturalism (observe the muscles of the forearm) with convention (drapery, hair, and beard) through the exercise of technical skill analogous perhaps to the political skill that kept precarious balance between heroic egoism and personal subordination to the polis during Athens' golden age.

Hirmer Fotoarchiv Munich

Stele of Aristion, 510-500 B.C.,
from Velanidesa in Attica.
National Museum, Athens.

PLATE 1

Poseidon, 470-450 B.C., found in the sea off Cape Artemision. National Museum, Athens.

CLASSIC GREEK BEAUTY

Accidents of preservation permit modern eyes to experience the aesthetic force of classical Greek sculpture at its peak only through this (and a few other) minor

PLATE 2

Head of the Athena Lemnia. Museo Civico, Bologna.

works. The bronze Poseidon (left) cannot be assigned to any of the famous sculptors of the fifth century B.C. In all probability we here confront a routine product of Athenian workshops of that age. The Lemnian Athena (right) copies a statue that may have come from the hand of Phidias. It was made centuries afterwards, when Roman taste had fixed on the fifth century B.C. as the most admired period of Greek art.

PLATE 3

Portrait of an Unknown Roman, 1st cent. B.C. Museum of Fine Arts, Boston.

THE REPUBLIC AND EMPIRE OF ROME

These two portraits of unknown Romans show what happened when Greek sculptors put their virtuosity to work to please the Roman taste for family portraiture. Through

PLATE 4

Portrait of a Roman Lady, A.D. 54-117. Palazzo Capitolino, Rome.

its simplicity and apparent realism the head on the left (first century B.C.) expresses the energy, self-discipline, and habit of command which made Rome great. The second bust dates from about a century later, when the elegant artificiality of imperial court life had superimposed itself upon the sterner virtues of the past, just as the lady's towered and patterned curls distract attention from but cannot hide the strong and haughty face beneath.

PLATE 5

Crowned Female Head, 2nd cent. A.D., from Vienne, France. Lyon Museum, France.

HOW CLASSICISM WORE ITSELF OUT

Classicism had become a genteel accomplishment for a landowning few by the second century A.D. when these two heads were made. The crowned female represents the "spirit" of a provincial town in Gaul—a conventional personification

PLATE 6

Bust of Marcus Aurelius, 2nd cent. A.D. Avenches Museum, Switzerland.

invented in the Hellenistic east a full five centuries before. The skill with which the sculptor duplicated ancient motifs and style was undiminished; but his work looks backward. The bust of the Stoic philosopher and emperor, Marcus Aurelius (right), is technically less accomplished, yet manages to convey a sense of yearning for something better to believe in than worn-out gods and personified cities (like the lady opposite).

PLATE 7

Portrait of Eutropus, 3rd-5th cent. A.D. Kunsthistorisches Museum, Vienna.

THE END OF CLASSICISM

A new style, the Byzantine, begins to define itself in a bust such as this, carved sometime between the third and fifth centuries A.D. The rise of Christianity, barbarian invasions, and the breakup of the Roman Empire coincided with the shift in art illustrated here. Indeed, this bust seems to express disillusion with the world of men and a striving after transcendental truth of the sort upon which early Christianity throve.

PLATE 8

The Radiation and Transformation of Greek Sculpture

Photo Jean Roubier

Helvetian head from Aventicum. Avenches Museum, Switzerland.

MINGLING OF STYLES WESTWARD

This head was found in Switzerland at a Roman site. Some mingling and cross fertilization of Greco-Roman skills and style with a native art tradition (perhaps in wood?) must lie behind this strange and striking work.

PLATE 9

Athena or Roma, 2nd-3rd cent. A.D.
Lahore, Pakistan.

Buddha, 4th cent. A.D.
Lahore, Pakistan.

MINGLING OF STYLES EASTWARD

As an art style travels in time and space it alters in surprising ways. The four figures reproduced here were chosen to illustrate relationships running across all of Eurasia and some three to four centuries of time, beginning about A.D. 100 when a provincial participant in or missionary of Greco-Roman culture carved the buxom Athena (or Roma) that gazes at us from the left above. Provincial Greco-Roman art may be seen put to new uses in a second statue which comes from the same region and about the same time (above right). Here the artist used Greco-Roman motifs like the topknot and toga to portray the Buddha. In turn, Chinese sculptors seized upon the models offered by Indo-Greek Buddhist art to produce first a hybrid Chinese (opposite above) and then a fully Sinified (opposite below) version of the Buddha. Observe how the naturalistic thrust of Greek art alters and is in the end completely contradicted by the Chinese sculptor who reduced not merely the drapery but Buddha's foot itself to a flat, decorative, and delightful pattern of curves.

PLATE 10

Buddha from Shensi,
5th cent. A.D.
Gallery Sabauda, Turin.

Buddha from Honan, 5th cent. A.D.
Museum of Fine Arts, Boston.
Gift of Denman Waldo Ross
in memory of Okakura Kakuzo.

PLATE 11

Siddhārta Fasting, A.D. 300-400, from Sikri. Lahore, Pakistan.

PLATE 12

Didargañj Yakshi, Mauryan dynasty, front and back views. Patna Museum, India.

THE TWO FACES OF INDIA

Asceticism and sensuality, often carried to the extreme limits set by human physiology, complemented and perhaps even sustained one another within the hospitable matrix of Indian culture. These two statues offer a dramatic, visual statement of the polarity.

PLATE 13

The Development and Radiation of Indian Architecture

Temple No. XVII, 5th cent. A.D. Sānchī.

AN ARCHITECTURAL MIRROR OF INDIAN SOCIETY

The photographs on this and succeeding pages illustrate the elaboration of Indian temple architecture between the fifth and thirteenth centuries A.D. An entrance porch, an enclosed room to house the cult image, and, excepting Plate 14, a tower rising above the spot where the image normally resided can be detected in each of these photographs, despite the great variations of ground plan and scale that characterize the temple structures.

The loose cohesion of the temples' over-all plan and their abundance of decorative and sculptural detail (compare Plates 18 and 19) hold a mirror to Indian society itself, whose central institution—caste—protected the peculiar ways and customs of an endless number of sub-groupings, and could always make room for newcomers, whether they came as humble converts from primitive hunting folk or as mighty conquerors from afar. In the same way, another gate, tower, or group of statues added to one of these temples simply enriched without upsetting the structure as a whole.

PLATE 14

Mālegitti Śivālaya Temple, *c.* A.D. 625. Bādāmī.

PLATE 15

Paraśurāmeśvara Temple, c. A.D. 750. Bhuvaneśvara.

PLATE 16

The doctrine of rebirth remained central. The simple believed that pious acts and gifts to the gods would assure rebirth in a higher caste. The educated, on the other hand, could still proclaim, with the Upanishads, that annihilation of self in the supreme reality of which even Vishnu and Shiva were but appearances, remained the goal of religious striving. Thus, by combining high metaphysics with vulgar superstition, Hinduism offered something for everyone. The combination was immensely powerful, and eventually displaced Buddhism from the land of its birth.

Before that fate overtook Buddha's followers, however, a remarkable development of the Buddhist faith took place, mainly in the northwest part of India, where Indian, Greek, Persian, and steppe peoples met and mingled. This religious development probably occurred at the time when the Kushan empire bestrode India's northwest frontier (1st century B.C. to 2nd century A.D.). The greatest Kushan monarch, Kanishka, was reputed in later Buddhist tradition to have been a patron of some of the most important theological pioneers of the new faith. Once again, the central innovation was belief in the existence of divine yet incarnate saviors, called bodhisattvas. A bodhisattva was a soul which, though it had attained a state of holiness deserving the release of Nirvana, nevertheless declined that privilege in order to aid others on the road to salvation. In the meanwhile, these saviors lived a spiritual existence in a super-celestial heaven where prayers and other invocations could reach them, and where they could aid struggling humanity by a sort of spiritual sympathy.

The exponents of these ideas termed their doctrine *Mahayana*, that is, the Great Way or Vehicle, thus distinguishing it from the older *Hinayana*, or Lesser Way. The development certainly carried Buddhism very far from the metaphysical pessimism and ideal of dissolution of self which its founder (presumably) preached. Instead, the worshipper, by appropriate prayer and ritual invocation of a bodhisattva of his choice, could hope to become a bodhisattva himself (though perhaps only after innumerable incarnations) and thus attain a blessed life after death not entirely unlike that promised by Christianity.

Perhaps the resemblances between Christianity, Mahayana Buddhism, and the new forms of Hinduism are to be attributed to the spirit of the times. We can readily believe that persons caught up in great trading and administrative centers of western Asia, often far from home and thrown amid strangers, welcomed the prospect of salvation. Christianity, Mahayana Buddhism, and Hinduism—not to mention a number of other less influential cults like Mithraism, the worship of Isis, Cybele, and others—gave men of the most various backgrounds courage to persevere even in the face of disappointment and hardship, since all these faiths held forth the hope of a future in which present injustices would be righted gloriously and forever. Moreover, these religions were independent of any particular locality or community. Like post-exilic Judaism, wherever a few of the faithful gathered together the hope of salvation burned bright. Short of that ultimate bliss, the everyday fellowship of the religious community itself provided a not ineffective solace for hardship or loneliness. All of these religions were therefore well attuned to the requirements of urban living, as no earlier faith except Judaism had been. Since injustices and hardship were inseparable from civilized life, the appearance of such faiths very likely made the long-term survival of civilization far easier than would otherwise have been the case.

Diseases and Empires

‡‡‡ Another consequence of the intensification of contact across the Old World had a very different effect. Goods, ideas, and techniques were not the only things that traveled from one community to another. Disease germs also were transmissible, and as contacts multiplied it seems likely that various types of infection which had before been largely confined to one or the other part of Eurasia and Africa spread to new regions. Among a previously unexposed population, disease germs may cause very heavy mortality. Records from both China and Rome show that a series of severe plagues hit in the first and second centuries A.D. Many parts of the Roman empire, indeed, began to suffer from depopulation, and lack of manpower became a chronic problem for the Roman authorities from A.D. 200, if not before. It is therefore not fantastic to suggest that epidemic disease, resulting from closer contact across the entire span of Eurasia and much of Africa, may have been a major factor in the collapse of the Roman and Han empires. Of course there were other factors: brute barbarian attack and internal social tensions clearly played major roles.

Yet even after the Roman peace and the Han imperial administration were both irremediably broken, the three great world religions that had come to birth in the first centuries of the Christian era— Christianity, Mahayana Buddhism, a reformulated Hinduism—continued to flourish and attracted to themselves much of the high cultural life of the troubled age that succeeded. Of all the achievements of antiquity, none remains more vigorously alive today.

CHAPTER 11

The Flowering and Expansion

of Indian Civilization

A.D. 200–600

 By A.D. 200 Hellenism had lost its power to attract. The polite, cool, and moderate style of life recommended by Greek philosophers to Roman gentlemen no longer seemed to fit the needs of the time, especially when the long Roman peace suffered violent disruption in A.D. 193 and, after a brief rally, disintegrated squalidly between A.D. 235 and 284 into a long series of civil wars, barbarian invasions, and disputed successions to the imperial office. Simultaneously, Confucian China suffered similar disasters. The last decades of the Han dynasty were disfigured by civil wars and barbarian invasions, and the final overthrow of the dynasty in A.D. 220 simply made public the political and military confusion which had already divided China into a number of competing local states.

In the center of the civilized world, however, matters wore a very different aspect. From the Caspian to the Hindu Kush the serried array of the Iranian baronage stood guard against the raiding steppe cavalry. Their heavy horses, heavy armor, and powerful bows, together with their readiness at a moment's notice to take the field in order to protect the peasants upon whose rents they themselves depended, provided a most effective defense for the heartlands of Middle Eastern and Indian civilization. Any raiding party had to penetrate through a continuously protected countryside where the most technologically formidable warriors of the age lay in wait. Few made the attempt; fewer still repeated it.

Secure behind this barrier, both Indian and a revived Persian civilization attained new levels of elegance, sophistication, and religious virtuosity. India in particular entered upon a golden age which remained "classical" for subsequent Indian generations. Far less is known about the cultural attainments of Sassanian Persia. Unsympathetic Moslem and Christian reports of Zoroastrian and other forms of religious heterodoxy constitute the principal basis for what little we know of Sassanian literary and religious history; and the art of the age has survived only in a very damaged state. Yet Sassanian influence upon Rome and Central Asia was almost as great as Indian influence upon southeast Asia and the Chinese Far East. It seems well, therefore, to divide the history of the centuries between A.D. 200 and A.D. 600 into two "fields of force," and consider the Indian and Sassanian achievements and influence in successive chapters, even though they coincided in time. This chapter will therefore describe the flowering and expansion of Indian civilization, and the next will deal with the achievements of Sassanian Persia.

The Gupta Empire

‡‡‡ In A.D. 320 an energetic Indian king of the lower Ganges, named Chandra-gupta,* crowned himself in a special ceremony as "universal ruler." To make good his title he then launched a series of conquests. Within less than a century, his heirs brought all of northern India from the Bay of Bengal to the Arabian Sea under their suzerainty. The Gupta empire, thus established, endured until about A.D. 535. During much of this time, warfare and major political violence seem to have been unimportant in India. We have record of only a single raid from

* The name is identical with that of the founder of the Mauryan empire, who lived about 650 years before. To distinguish the two, it is customary to print the first Chandragupta's name as a single word and to hyphenate the second.

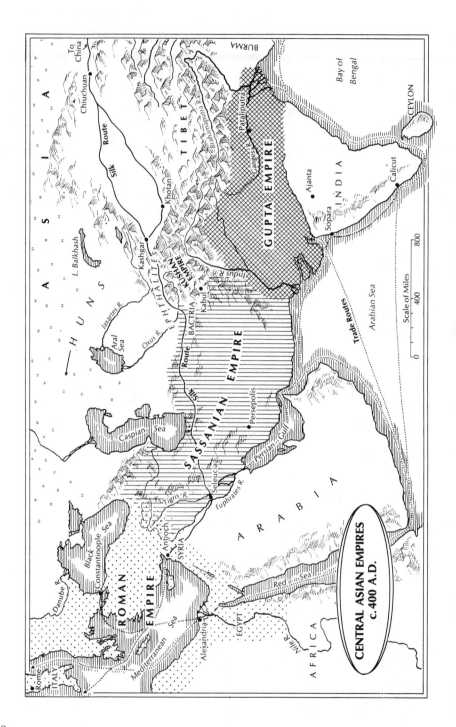

CENTRAL ASIAN EMPIRES
c. 400 A.D.

across the mountains, which struck about A.D. 455. The cohesion of the Gupta empire never entirely recovered from this raid, yet ensuing disorders were not incompatible with continued cultural creativity. Seemingly, within India itself chivalric conventions and religious injunctions tamed the destructiveness of warfare to an unusual degree. It was under these conditions that Indian civilization flowered in such a fashion that the Gupta age has ever since remained, in the estimation both of Hindus and of foreigners, the high point of the Indian past.

Despite the vastness of their realm, the Gupta rulers left scant trace behind them in the Sanskrit literary tradition. Hence what information we have is nearly all derived from reports written by Chinese, Ceylonese, and other Buddhist pilgrims. Precise political, military, geographic, and chronological facts are therefore nearly as unclear for this great age of India's history as they are for far less distinguished periods. The absence of political information is itself of course indicative of the strongly apolitical bent which Indian society and culture had manifested for nearly a thousand years before the rise of the Gupta empire.

The Gupta sovereigns themselves probably shared traditional Indian values so completely that they expected the realm of politics and of the state to remain relatively superficial. Thus, for example, the Gupta conquerors appear to have made it a policy to allow defeated rulers (or their close relatives) to remain in control of their accustomed lands. On a day-to-day basis, Gupta interests could be adequately cared for by a resident stationed at the vassal king's court; and on state occasions, ceremonial deference kept the Gupta emperors well content.

The Gupta kings also patronized a revivified Hinduism, and as a part of that religious policy presumably accepted the Hindu notion of law which accorded remarkably little scope to mere rulers. Instead, Hindu doctrine held that the Vedas were the highest source of authority, followed in order by commentaries on the Vedas (i.e. the Brahmanas), the example of holy men, and last of all, personal inclination, i.e. the edicts of a king or other public authority.

These views found expression in law books, called *Dharma shastras*, which were compiled during the Gupta era. They became basic for Hindu life thereafter. For example, the *Dharma shastras* defined the institution of caste by spelling out in detail how men of different castes should behave in a great variety of particular circumstances. Faithful performance of caste duties in this life, it was asserted, would prepare the soul for incarnation further up the ladder of being. Moral conduct during a series of lives would finally allow the soul to penetrate permanently into the realm of reality where all is One and one is All. But in the meantime, it was every man's moral duty to conform to the traditions of his caste and to observe the rites and practices of the group into which he had been born, no matter how crude, simple, or rationally inexplicable such customs might be.

Thus religion, law, mystical metaphysics, and crude superstition were all tied tightly together so that each reinforced the other, and—so far as we know anything at all of public and political life of the Gupta period—it appears that affairs of state also fitted neatly into the same bundle.

Sanskrit Learning

‡‡‡ Three institutions stimulated the cultural efflorescence of the age. The royal court patronized artists, writers, musicians, astrologers, astronomers, doctors, and other professional experts. Temples rivaled the courts as centers for cultural activity, for appropriately sumptuous service of the god—Shiva, Vishnu, or one of the *avatars* (incarnations) of either of them—called for the same sorts of activities as sustained the grandeur of merely human monarchs. Third, behind both court and temple stood an ancient school system whereby the bulky accumulation of lore bodied forth in Sanskrit oral literature was passed on from generation to generation.

In these schools, the central relationship was between a holy man and a group of disciples who came to him to learn by heart whatever traditional wisdom he had to impart. Memorization of the Vedas and other holy texts, with careful attention to correct accent and grammar, constituted the core of the educational system. Commentaries on the texts, and commentaries on commentaries, had long since proliferated beyond the limits established by even the most capacious memory, so that specialists, grouped into more or less stable "schools," divided the domain of Sanskrit learning among them.

The prestige and practical importance of the school system was tellingly demonstrated in the Gupta era by the revival of Sanskrit. In Buddha's time, Sanskrit had become a learned language, intoned by Brahman priests at religious ceremonies, but otherwise forgotten. Early Buddhist writing was couched in literary versions of the popular languages of the day, all of which were derived from Sanskrit but differed from it much as French and Spanish differ from Latin. Similarly, the Mauryan empire used a number of local languages for administration. All this altered by the time of the Guptas. Sanskrit became again a living literary language, in which fresh work of utmost refinement and polish was composed.

One reason for Sanskrit's remarkable comeback may have been the growing difficulty of bridging the gap between the various local dialects. As regional differences in the everyday, uneducated forms of speech increased, the need for a *lingua franca* intelligible to all became far more acute than in the days of Asoka, when relatively small variations made differences of dialect not too difficult to overcome.

But the central fact that permitted Sanskrit's revival was the school system whereby any man aspiring to knowledge could learn Sanskrit. A corps of men speaking the same language, and attuned to the same intellectual wave lengths, was thus maintained generation after generation. In Gupta times, this corps of educated men took over leadership in practically every branch of cultural activity. Thereby, of course, they displaced the Buddhists, who in an earlier time had discarded Sanskrit learning as useless baggage for the soul. Some of the reasons for Buddhism's ultimate failure in India have already been suggested in Chapter IV. The readiness of Brahman Sanskritists to react energetically to the foreign stimuli that had come into India from the Greek and Iranian worlds during the preceding three or four centuries was another factor that allowed them to eclipse the increasingly wealthy, insulated, and withdrawn Buddhist monks.

The enlarged horizons of Sanskrit learning were most apparent in astronomy and medicine, where the Greek imprint became clear and unmistakable. Yet the appropriation of Greek notions about the mechanics of planetary motion, together with the mathematical skills needed for casting horoscopes, did not freeze Sanskrit learning into rigid, alien moulds. On the contrary, one of the great inventions of the human mind, the decimal place system of numerical notation, emerged in India by A.D. 270. The simple numerical system of notation which we call "Arabic," and which the Arabs correctly attributed to India, ranks with alphabetic writing as one of the master keys of human inventiveness. Once the notation had been invented, calculation became comparatively easy and rapid. As a result, both the affairs of the market place and the abstruse concerns of theoretical mathematicians were enormously facilitated. All the same, the perfected notation spread rather slowly. For a long time it remained a mathematical toy for experts, who continued to employ their old notations too. Use for everyday calculations spread among the Arabs only in the tenth century A.D. and reached Latin Christendom two centuries later still.

Sanskrit Literature

‡‡‡ The heart of Sanskrit learning lay not in natural science but in literary and linguistic labors. Preoccupation with an antique, learned, and sacred language led to the development of grammatical science. Panini wrote a grammar of Sanskrit which became classical; but when he lived is quite uncertain.

Similarly, the precise literary history of India's two great epic poems is irrecoverable, since oral transmission and elaboration across centuries left few definite traces for modern scholars to analyze. Nevertheless, it seems certain that both the *Mahabharata* and the *Ramayana* achieved their final form during the Gupta period. The *Mahabharata* is an enormously lengthy poem, roughly three and a half times as long as the entire Christian Bible. It contains a great variety of matter. At the core is an ancient story of heroic warfare between rival coalitions of noble charioteers, which must descend from very ancient bardic songs of Aryan times. Recitation of these songs somehow became part of Brahman religious ceremonies. The priests saw fit to interlard the bloody violence of the traditional tales with all sorts of sermons and stories teaching religious lessons. If the Christian fathers had reworked Homer to make the *Iliad* into a handbook of Christian doctrine, the effect would be similar. In addition, folk tales and fairy stories interrupt the narrative from time to time. Sometimes stories within stories suspend the main theme across hundreds of printed pages. The *Ramayana* is shorter and more tightly organized. It is a story of the hero Rama and his wife Sita, and of the trials and tribulations that separated them through a long series of adventures until a final reunion ends the tale.

Both the *Mahabharata* and the *Ramayana* became very popular in India, and remain so to the present. Innumerable episodes provided a mine of material for subsequent literary elaboration, much as the Greek playwrights exploited Homer and Hesiod for their plots, or as Shakespeare used Italian and classical authors for many of his. The entire subsequent literary tradition of India has been shaped by this device. Between them, the two poems created a literary frame of reference and universe of discourse that still survives.

No author can be assigned to either the *Mahabharata* or the *Ramayana;* and it is clear that the texts of both poems evolved over a lengthy period of time before achieving their final shape in the Gupta period. The history of Sanskrit drama is very different, for the plays that survive usually have an author's name attached to them and bear every indication of having been composed by a single man for presentation at the royal court. The use of some Greek technical stage terms proves that Greek models had some importance for the Sanskrit theater. How much is hotly disputed, since Sanskrit drama has its own conventions and the Indian playwrights usually drew their plots from the traditional materials of the epics.

Kalidasa (*c.* A.D. 400–455) is the acknowledged master of Sanskrit literature. His plays rank as classics, and his epic and lyric poetry bespeak an elegant sensibility, perhaps just a little too self-conscious and contrived to appeal strongly to twentieth-century Western taste. These aspects of Kalidasa's work were elaborated after his time by other courtly writers, until verbal complexity and ingenuity outbalanced and even obscured meaning.

Gupta Art

‡‡‡ Accidents of preservation make a fair judgment of the state of the plastic arts in Gupta times very difficult. Moslem conquerors later systematically destroyed the temples of northern India on the ground that they were seats of idolatry. Hence little distinctively Hindu art survives from the centers of Gupta power, which lay in the north. A few carvings from the south can be dated to Gupta times, but they are rather crude and artistically unsatisfactory. Obviously, artists faced a difficult task in giving visual form to gods whose essence was the mutability of their form, since the numerous deities of the Hindu pantheon were all linked together as successive incarnations of Vishnu or Shiva. So far as surviving monuments allow us to judge, this problem was not successfully solved during the Gupta period.

Buddhist art, on the other hand, attained a finish and perfection it never subsequently equaled. The paintings of the caves of Ajanta are deservedly famous, reflecting an elegant luxury and refinement characteristic of all aspects of Gupta culture. A few examples of Buddhist sculpture also survive, and exhibit the same artistic mastery—with just a hint of decadence—that is characteristic of the Ajanta paintings.

Religion was never separable from other aspects of India's cultural life. The law books, the two great epics, monumental temples, cult statues, and other works of visual art, not to mention the irrecoverable arts of music and dancing, were all part of Hinduism in the sense that all dealt with the relations between men and the supernatural and each in its own way helped to give definition to this critical frontier of human experience. The definitive doctrinal elaboration of Hinduism, however, came only some centuries after the end of the Gupta era, when Shankara (c. A.D. 788–850) propounded a monistic, transcendent philosophy that later defenders of Hinduism regularly resorted to when arguing against Moslem and Christian critics of India's traditional faith.

The perfection achieved in Gupta times in so many branches of cultural endeavor gave an enduring stamp to Hindu and Sanskrit culture, yet did so without injecting anything radically different or new. Maximal perfection and balance can, presumably, be attained only by refraining from major innovation. This the writers and scholars of the Gupta age faithfully did, and, by remaining gladly within the limits their predecessors had defined for them, they were able to polish and improve what had been handed down in a fashion later generations never surpassed.

Eastern Spread of Indian Civilization

‡‡‡ The Gupta golden age was felt far beyond India's border. The principal carriers of Indian culture were merchants and missionaries, not soldiers like those who had brought Hellenism to the Middle East, or Greco-Roman civilization to Gaul. In southeast Asia, Indian civilization abutted upon a region where no pre-existing culture offered much competition. Here, therefore, a Greater India arose. Between about A.D. 100 and A.D. 600 a series of local states and royal courts in such areas as Burma, Sumatra, Java, Malaya, Siam, and Viet Nam ea-

gerly strove to import as much of Indian civilization as they could.

North of the mountains, Indian merchants and missionaries confronted very different conditions. Chinese, Persian, and Greco-Roman populations were not prepared to jettison their pasts *in toto*, even when they were irresistibly attracted to some of the aspects of Indian culture—above all to the techniques of mystical asceticism which Indian holy men had long cultivated. Hence it was only selected aspects of Indian culture that took root and flourished in other parts of the civilized world, whereas Indian influence on southeast Asia was diluted only by the residual barbarisms and village simplicities of that region.

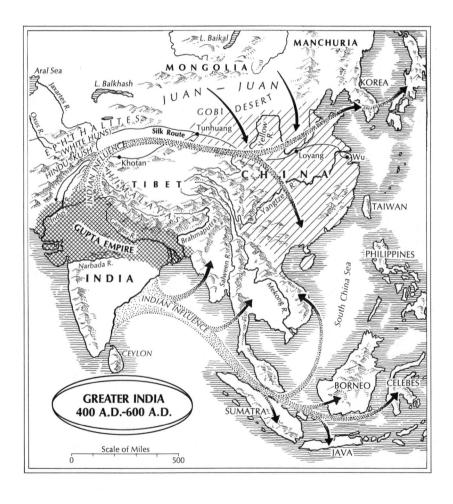

GREATER INDIA
400 A.D.-600 A.D.

In southeast Asia legends provide some information about how Indian styles of life penetrated the peaceable village communities that existed along the shores and river banks of the Bay of Bengal and the South China Sea. Typically, a merchant from India married into a chieftain's family, and from that vantage point began to exercise cultural-political leadership over surrounding settlements until a small state emerged. Royal power in such states rested largely upon magical ideas which tied fertility of the fields to the potency of royal persons and a ceremonial stone symbol thereof (i.e. a stone phallus)—the so-called "linga." Temple and palace structures designed to house the royal person and the linga in fitting splendor soon gave fuller expression to these notions. At first the local rulers tried to reproduce Indian court life and furnishings as lavishly and correctly as possible. They even imported monumental statues and other ceremonial gear from India. Shortly before A.D. 600, however, independent stylistic development, presaging the magnificent architecture and sculpture of later centuries, demonstrated the emancipation of southeast Asian courts from their earlier tutelage.

It should perhaps be emphasized that the great bulk of the population of southeast Asia was very slightly affected by the introduction of these new styles of court life and architecture from India. Heavier labor service and taxes were perhaps the only difference villagers could notice. But the same might of course be said of the village populations of Roman Gaul and Britain, who scarcely shared the Hellenized culture of their masters in any respect. Indian expansion into southeast Asia was geographically a good deal more extensive than the westward movement of Hellenism, and also may perhaps be said to have affected more people, since the imprint of Indian models on native cultures of that part of the world has lasted until our own time.

Buddhist Missions to the Far East

‡‡‡ Buddhists played a part in the earliest phase of Indian penetration of southeast Asia, but it was Hindu religious ideas and cult practices that prevailed in most of the region, perhaps because Hinduism was more hospitable to local religious traditions than Buddhism could be. North of the mountains Hinduism never made any important impression. Buddhism, on the contrary, flowed like a mighty torrent into

China and lapped over into Korea and Japan between A.D. 200 and 600.

The reception of Buddhism in China constituted a conscious break with Confucian traditions and values. Nothing, indeed, could be more alien to the cool, this-worldly moderation of Confucianism, with its emphasis upon family and political duties, than Indian Buddhism, which sought escape from the world and preached ascetic withdrawal from all ordinary human ties. Perhaps it was just this antithesis that appealed to the Chinese. For when the Han government began to lose its grip on the country as a whole, and barbarian invasion added a fresh dimension of violence to the miseries of civil war, the sage advice of Confucians, recommending moderation and decorum, must have sounded as hollow as the consolations of Greek philosophy did to Roman ears in the same age. Stronger medicine for the soul was needed in such times. The Romans found the answer in Christianity, the Chinese in Buddhism. Yet although Buddhism came to command a wide following among the Chinese, adepts in the older Confucian lore never disappeared and never surrendered their distrust of a doctrine so subversive of ordinary life and political discipline as Buddhism—at least if taken literally—appeared to be.

Efforts to get correct knowledge and true images of Buddha led several Chinese pilgrims to travel to India and visit the scenes of Buddha's life. Some of them brought back whole libraries of Buddhist texts and proceeded to organize systematic translation. But by about A.D. 600 the initial phase of eager appropriation of Buddhist learning had been pretty well completed.

Chinese Buddhists never paid much attention to the sectarian differences that divided the Indians, nor did the complex metaphysical speculations to which the Indian monks devoted their intellectual energies appeal to the Chinese. Mystical enlightenment, however, and the retreat from civil society into a community of like-minded, disciplined seekers after peace of mind did meet a need that neither the Confucian nor the Taoist traditions of China knew how to cope with. Chinese Buddhism therefore soon began to evolve in directions of its own, essentially independent of the declining curve of Buddhism in India.

Buddhism brought a distinctive new kind of art into China. Greek and Indian elements had already blended in central Asia to produce a stately, impressive style. In China, Buddhist art underwent rapid adjustment to the Chinese environment, so that by A.D. 600 an effective and unmistakably Chinese version had developed. Before the reception of Buddhism, Chinese art had been mainly decorative and geometrical. Buddhist art brought a notable enrichment to the Chinese artistic naturalistic portrayal of bodhisattvas, that is, of divine helpers of mankind clothed in human form. In addition, Buddhist wall paintings and carvings often tried to tell a story which required the artist to suggest spatial and other relationships between his figures. These aspects of Buddhist art represented a notable enrichment of the Chinese artistic tradition and remained of great importance even after Buddhism itself had been rejected by most of the Chinese population.

The impact of Buddhism on Korea and Japan was of a profounder character. Those lands boasted no very impressive pre-existing high culture. They found themselves on the extreme edge of the Chinese sphere of influence in the period when China proper was eagerly absorbing Buddhism. Hence it was Chinese civilization in Buddhist dress that attracted the kings and courtiers of Korea who, between A.D. 372 and 528, made Buddhism into a state religion in each of the kingdoms into which Korea was then divided. Japan, being more remote, was less ready to grasp the latest modes of Chinese civilization. Nevertheless, a Buddhist mission that reached the land of the Rising Sun in A.D. 552 met with important success. From that time onward the Japanese islands joined the circle of the civilized (and semi-civilized) nations clustering around the imposing bulk of China.

Indian Influence upon the West

‡‡‡ Indian influence on the Iranian and Roman parts of the civilized world was far less evident than it was in the Far East and central Asia. Indeed, scholars are far from agreed that there was any important Indian impact on Europe and western Asia. The trouble is that records are lacking. If Christian and other religious ascetics of the Iranian and Roman worlds were influenced in any important ways from India, they failed to say so; and, in the nature of the case, we cannot expect records to have been made. Assuredly, humble folk traveling back and forth between India and Alexandria had ample opportunity to exchange tales about the wondrous powers attributed to Indian ascetics. Indeed, we know that at least one Indian holy man reached the Mediterranean, because he burned himself publicly in Athens and by doing so

excited enough wonderment that his deed was recorded. But Christian monks who saw visions and interpreted them as encounters with God could not be expected to know or admit that Indian idolators had done the same centuries before. Nevertheless, the resemblances between certain details of Christian ascetic practices and the devotions of Indian sages are striking, and the style of holiness embraced so fervently by the early monks of Egypt and Syria bore a general resemblance to much more ancient Indian ascetic disciplines and withdrawal from the world. That some early Christian monks may have picked up useful hints about how to be holy from tales or personal study of Indian ascetic practices seems entirely possible, but remains unproven.

In the field of philosophy itself—once the pride and arcanum of Greek pagan rationalism—the new themes and mystical emphasis introduced by Plotinus (d. A.D. 270) resembled ideas long familiar to students of the Upanishads. At the very least, Plotinus and his contemporaries were aware that Indian philosophy existed, and that it was as sophisticated and massive as the Greek tradition itself.

A Westerner is always likely to underestimate the magnitude of a cultural movement which affected his own past in disguised and limited ways. It is therefore well to underline the fact that the expansion of Indian civilization to southeast Asia and its impact on Chinese, Korean, and Japanese styles of life imbued the civilization of more than half the human race with a common tint. Insofar as Asia has any community of cultural tradition uniting the Indian with the Chinese, Japanese, Korean, Mongolian, Tibetan, Burmese, Cambodian, and Ceylonese peoples, it is due to the contagion of ancient Indian civilization, especially in its religious manifestation.

The achievement of Hellenism was no greater.

CHAPTER 12

Barbarian Invasions and

Civilized Response A.D. 200-600

 While Indian religiosity and courtliness were winning converts in southern and eastern Asia, in the north the harsh shouting of warriors and the clash of arms resounded all along the length of the frontier between steppe barbarism and the civilized communities of Europe and Asia. Both in China and in Europe, civilized defenses were beaten back by advancing barbarians, but in the center of the long line the Iranians held the steppe peoples at bay. China proved capable of absorbing her invaders, and re-established imperial unity (A.D. 589) after some three and a half centuries of division and disorder. By contrast, the Roman empire was never reconstituted after the great barbarian breakthroughs of the period A.D 378–511.*

The Iranians met a more suprising fate. After their long and suc-

---

* But the fiction carried on. In western Europe, for example, the last "Roman" emperor abdicated in 1806 and adopted the more accurate title "Emperor of Austria." In the Balkans, Greek-speaking Roman emperors reigned uninterruptedly from the "New Rome" of Constantinople until 1204. After A.D. 565 these Roman emperors are commonly termed Byzantine, but they referred to themselves as Romans, and the last claimant to the title disappeared only in 1453, when the Turks conquered Constantinople.

cessful struggle against steppe barbarians and a series of hard-fought but indecisive wars against the Romans of Constantinople, the Persian empire of the Sassanids collapsed before Arab invaders from the south. The conquerors were newly converted to the faith of Mohammed, which armed them with theological weapons that proved at least as effective as their (quite ordinary) horsemen, bows, and lances. Yet before the Iranians merged their cultural identity into the world of Islam, their military success against the steppe peoples and against more civilized neighbors compelled or induced Romans on the west and oasis dwellers of central Asia on the east to borrow much from them, in the process becoming what Western historians have long been accustomed to call "medieval."

During the period between A.D 200 and 600, therefore, the northern parts of the civilized world were influenced by two distinct forces: the steppe barbarians, forever battering at the gates, countered by the Iranian example of how to organize effective defense against barbarian attack. A somewhat closer look at the course of events will show how this see-saw worked across each of the exposed frontiers of the civilized world.

The Huns and the Western Steppe

‡‡‡ The nomad peoples of the Eurasian steppe may be likened to molecules of gas in a very leaky bottle. Pressure at any point spread rapidly through the entire system. Any groups of nomads displaced from traditional pasture grounds either perished or quickly seized a neighbor's pasturage by force of arms. Within a few seasons, therefore, any important disturbance of pasturage rights spread from one end of the grasslands to the other, neighbor nudging neighbor, until the weakest or least well-organized groups either died, fled into the inhospitable forest land lying north or west of the steppe, or else penetrated civilized defenses to the south, where they might become masters of agricultural populations.

We have already seen how the rise of the Hsiung-nu confederacy just before 200 B.C. started one such wave of migration (above, p. 171). Soon after A.D. 350 a similar confederation centering once more in Outer Mongolia took form. The Chinese called it Juan-juan. At its height, this war confederation exerted authority all the way from Manchuria to Lake Balkhash. As Juan-juan power swept westward along the steppe, whole tribes and peoples fled before them.

One such group was known in European history as Huns. They appeared in southern Russia in A.D. 372 and immediately defeated the Ostrogoths, who had been ruling that region for more than a century. Fear of the Huns persuaded the neighboring tribe of Visigoths to seek refuge inside Roman frontiers, where that wandering horde of warriors lived off the country, alternately quarreling and making alliances with the Roman authorities. After sacking the city of Rome in A.D. 410 the Visigoths moved westward to Spain, where they set up a kingdom that lasted until A.D. 711. Several plundering German tribes soon followed the Visigoths; others submitted to the formidable Huns.

Meanwhile the Huns had set up their headquarters in the Hungarian plain, from which vantage point they raided southward into the Balkans and westward into Italy and Gaul. Yet in A.D. 453 when Attila, their last great war captain, died, the Hunnic confederacy broke up even more rapidly than it had arisen. Quarrels among rival leaders combined with rebellion on the part of some of the subjugated peoples to destroy almost overnight what had been a territorially vast empire.

The overthrow of the Huns' empire failed to bring any sort of order to western Europe. Some of the Germanic peoples who had been subjugated by the Huns fled south and west to Roman territory, and set up new kingdoms in north Africa (Vandals), Gaul (Burgundians), and Italy (Ostrogoths). Simultaneously, a quite different and much more lasting German advance took place in Britain and the Rhineland. Here German-speaking plowmen took over new and fertile acres which had formerly been thinly occupied by Roman (i.e. mostly Celtic) populations. This agricultural settlement proved lasting, whereas states set up by roving bands of German-speaking warriors were all short-lived, like the similar barbarian regimes of north China and eastern Iran.

Steppe Peoples of the East

‡‡‡ The migrations and political changes precipitated in western Europe by the sudden appearance of the Huns were matched by similar disturbances accompanying the almost simultaneous eruption of the Ephthalites (sometimes termed Ephthalite Huns or White Huns) into

eastern Iran. From this base, the Ephthalites raided northwest India, and eventually set up a predatory empire of their own, which spanned the mountains just as the Kushan empire had done before. The disorders loosed upon India by the Ephthalites brought the Gupta age and dynasty to an end. But the invaders were no more able than the Huns of Europe to establish a stable regime over the lands their bows and horses had conquered. Ephthalite power in India disintegrated into endemic civil war by A.D. 549. North of the mountains the horde was finally destroyed at about the same time (A.D. 554).

The fundamental weakness of these barbarian states was everywhere the same. Their rulers tried to do two incompatible things. On the one hand, the victorious chieftain and his followers wanted to retain the traditional ways and manners of their warlike past. On the other, they sought to enjoy the luxuries and delights of civilized living by squeezing goods and services from their new subjects. But the more civilized the conquerors became, the less did old tribal and war band traditions hold up. Easy living and vice regularly undermined barbarian vigor and warlike effectiveness within a generation or two.

Civilized peoples as a rule disliked their barbarian masters. When opportunity offered they were predisposed to welcome a liberator who proclaimed his loyalty to old traditions and ideals. The Chinese and Persians had the greatest success in rolling back the barbarian tide in this fashion. In A.D. 552 the Juan-juan confederacy was destroyed by Chinese armies co-operating with Turks who promptly created a new steppe empire as formidable as the Juan-juan had been. Yet a dynastic quarrel within the ruling family of the new empire led in A.D. 572 to the division of the Turkish confederacy into eastern and western hordes, each jealous of the other and torn by internal quarrels.

With the threat and pressure from the steppe reduced in this way, a new Chinese dynasty, the Sui, swept away the last of the barbarian states of north China and reunited the entire country in A.D. 589. China's military and cultural dominance over the adjacent barbarian peoples was promptly re-established.

Almost the same rhythm of events manifested itself along the eastern frontier of Iran. Persian monarchs of the Sassanian dynasty combined with the Turks in A.D. 554 to overthrow the Ephthalites. The quarrel between the two branches of the Turkish confederation which ensued in A.D. 572 allowed the Sassanians to push the frontier of the

Persian empire to the Oxus river once again, thus reuniting the eastern marchlands with the rest of the Iranian lands.

Weakening of the Roman Empire

‡‡‡ The Romans, however, were not so successful. During the first prolonged and bitter crisis of civil war and invasion (A.D. 235–84) the Roman imperial government had become an undisguised military despotism. Such a regime was not very popular since officials often behaved in a violent and tyrannical fashion. Moreover, the will of the soldiery was fickle. A general, elevated to supreme power through a soldiers' revolt, might find himself deposed without warning if, for any reason, he proved incapable of pleasing the armies that had put him in power. Fictitious election to office by the "Senate and people of Rome" no longer meant anything more than ceremonial validation of naked military usurpation.

The Emperor Constantine (ruled A.D. 306–337) changed Roman government in two important respects. He established a new capital at Byzantium, which he renamed Constantinople, and he made Christianity a favored state religion. The new capital was well situated both for trade and for defense, since it was relatively easy to supply the city from the far-flung coastlands of the Black and Aegean seas. The uninterrupted survival of Roman (often called Byzantine) imperial government until 1204 was made possible by this fact.

Christianity also lent important support to the imperial Roman government from Constantine's time onward. Most of the Christian bishops proved eager to co-operate with the emperor, and regarded Constantine and his successors as chosen by God to rule the empire. Here was a simple but persuasive idea that could really clothe the nakedness of military usurpation with the garment of legitimacy. The Emperor Theodosius (d. A.D. 395) carried the alliance between throne and altar to its logical conclusion by prohibiting all rival faiths, thus making Rome officially Christian.

Yet this commitment raised another acute problem, for Christians did not agree with one another on doctrine. Soldier emperors and politic bishops found it hard to handle such issues in an age when theoretical questions of theology became popular rallying cries around which all sorts of discontents against constituted authority quickly gathered.

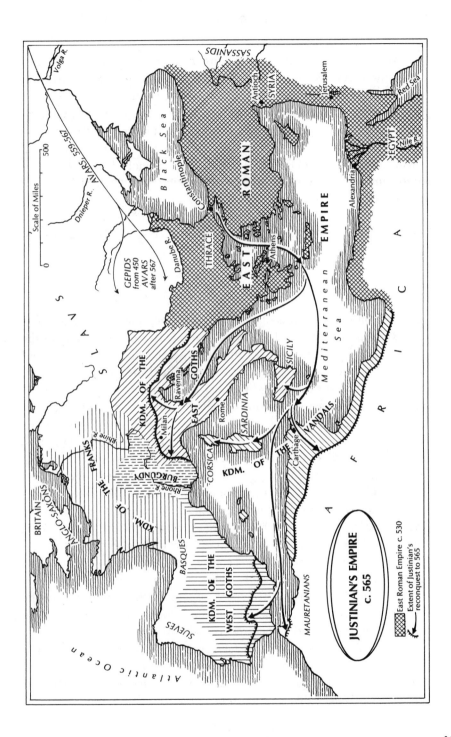

Scale of Miles

0   500

Volga R.

Dnieper R.

AVARS 559-567

Black Sea

Constantinople

THRACE

Danube R.

GEPIDS
from 450
AVARS
after 567

SLAVS

Rhine R.

KDM. OF THE

EAST   GOTHS

Ravenna

Milan

Rome

BURGUNDY

Rhone R.

CORSICA

SARDINIA

KDM.   OF   THE

BRITAIN

ANGLO-SAXONS

KDM. OF THE
FRANKS

BASQUES

SUEVES

KDM. OF THE
WEST GOTHS

Atlantic Ocean

MAURETANIANS

Carthage

VANDALS

A   F   R   I   C   A

SASSANIDS

Antioch

SYRIA

Jerusalem

Red Sea

EAST   ROMAN   EMPIRE

Athens

SICILY

Mediterranean   Sea

Alexandria

EGYPT

Nile R.

JUSTINIAN'S EMPIRE
c. 565

East Roman Empire c. 530

Extent of Justinian's
reconquest to 565

Most of the Germanic kingdoms of western Europe confronted similar problems. Nearly all the German kings accepted a variant form of Christianity known as Arianism. This made them foul heretics in the eyes of most of their Roman subjects. The Emperor Justinian (A.D. 527–65) therefore had good ground for hoping that if he could overthrow the German kings' military forces he could expect a majority of the local inhabitants to rally to his side. He accordingly launched a series of campaigns into the western Mediterranean, seeking to re-establish the unity of the Roman empire. He was only partly successful; and nearly all the gains he won in north Africa, Spain, and Italy had to be given up immediately after his death, when new invaders attacked the Roman frontiers.

Reactions to the Barbarians in China and Iran

‡‡‡ The differing degrees of success with which the Chinese, Iranians, and Romans re-established the unity and security of their states in the sixth century provide an index of the adequacy of their political and military institutions in the face of the barbarian challenge.

China had the advantage that her traditional imperial institutions had themselves been shaped in the days of the Han to cope with the barbarian threat offered by the Hsiung-nu. Hence the Sui emperors and their successors of the T'ang dynasty (A.D. 618–907) were able to conform faithfully to ancient imperial precedent while re-establishing an effective frontier guard against the Turkish confederacy. Diplomacy, subsidy, and the use of Chinese commanders to control barbarian mercenary troops guarding the frontier, all came into play. Behind the reconstituted defenses the Sui organized an efficient, rather ruthless, bureaucratic regime, whose greatest accomplishment was the completion of a canal linking the Yangtse with the Yellow river. This canal speedily became a major artery of China's imperial economy. Products from the fertile south could be sent north via the canal to the imperial capital where officials and soldiers stood ready to consume the enlarged supply that thus became available to them. Close control of the entire Yangtse valley and a far greater concentration of goods at imperial headquarters became possible after the opening of the Grand Canal, as this waterway was called. Hence the reconstituted imperial China was stronger than in Han times, able to mobilize more men and

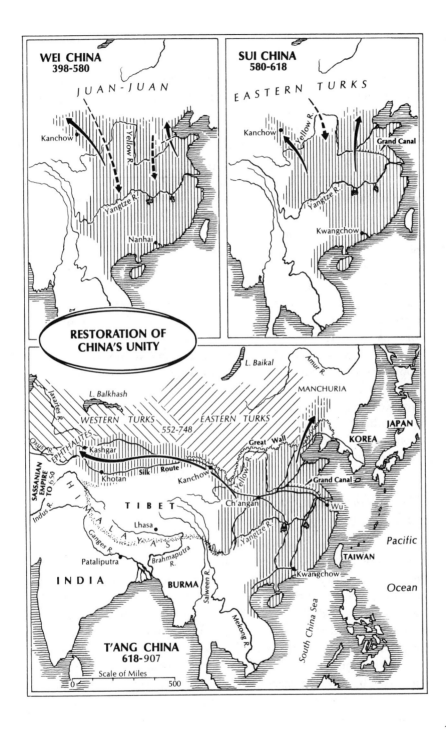

WEI CHINA
398-580

JUAN-JUAN

Kanchow

Yellow R.

Yangtze R.

Nanhai

SUI CHINA
580-618

EASTERN TURKS

Kanchow

Yellow R.

Grand Canal

Yangtze R.

Kwangchow

RESTORATION OF CHINA'S UNITY

L. Baikal

Amur R.

L. Balkhash

MANCHURIA

Jaxartes R.

WESTERN TURKS

EASTERN TURKS

552-748

JAPAN

Oxus R.

EPHTHALITES

Kashgar

Great Wall

KOREA

SASSANIAN EMPIRE TO 650

HIMALAYAS

Khotan

Silk Route

Kanchow

Yellow R.

Grand Canal

Indus R.

TIBET

Ch'angan

Wu

Lhasa

Pacific

Ganges R.

Brahmaputra R.

Yangtze R.

TAIWAN

Pataliputra

INDIA

BURMA

Salween R.

Kwangchow

Ocean

South China Sea

Mekong R.

T'ANG CHINA
618-907

Scale of Miles

0   500

material for warlike or peaceful enterprises than ever before. Barbarian raiding, therefore, quickly lost its terrors in the face of the organized imperial might of reunited China.

The Iranians had a rather more complex problem. No new resources lay easily at hand, as in China, to reinforce the imperial, central power. To be sure, the technology of heavy armored cavalry was familiar enough. The difficulty lay in creating a system of society that could support a sufficient number of suitably armored and trained cavalrymen near enough to the frontier to provide effective and continual protection against steppe raiding. The Parthian monarchs had allowed (perhaps they even encouraged) the growth of a military class of landowners who equipped themselves as heavy cavalrymen and were perpetually on the alert to protect their own lands from destruction. But the Parthian monarchs were usually unable to exert anything like an effective central power over the Iranian baronage. The Parthian royal government seems to have favored cities and towns, whence came their supply of ready cash. But the towns of Iran and Mesopotamia failed to supply enough money to the king to permit him to maintain a strong enough standing force of heavy cavalry to be able to over-awe his powerful subjects. Hence the price of an effective frontier guard against the steppe had been a continual welter of local rebellion and disobedience which constantly weakened the central authority of the Parthian government.

The Sassanian Empire

‡‡‡ In A.D. 226 one such rebel, Ardashir, supplanted the Parthian regime entirely. The Sassanian family to which Ardashir belonged remained on the throne of Persia and Mesopotamia until A.D. 651. Sassanian royal power underwent many spectacular crises during these centuries, and not all the kings followed the same policy. Nevertheless, the principles laid down by Ardashir (reigned A.D. 226–240) were never abandoned for long. For the founder of the Sassanian state based his power squarely on the Iranian baronage. He cultivated a consciousness of the Persian imperial past, and in particular supported and was supported by a reorganized Zoroastrianism. Appeal to Persian imperial greatness and to the faith of Zoroaster apparently had the effect of persuading most of the barons of the countryside to support the Sassanian

monarchs, at least in times of crisis. The central power therefore remained alive and vigorous, a formidable rival for the Roman empire.

Zoroastrian doctrine depended on local traditions that had been treasured by priestly and aristocratic families like that from which Ardashir himself had sprung. But there were embarrassing divergences from shrine to shrine. The Sassanian kings therefore ordered that a standard version of the Zoroastrian scripture, the *Avesta*, should be established. They further decreed that the Zoroastrian heritage should be enriched by suitable borrowings from Greek and Indian authors. But the revamped faith, despite the coherence and completeness with which its scriptures were thus endowed, never took root in the cities of the Sassanian realm. The baronage, however, appears to have been well enough pleased, since rebellion, usurpation, and royal assassination—which constituted the order of the day in Rome—remained comparatively rare in Persia. Throne and altar, in other words, appear to have made an effective alliance in Sassanian Persia almost a full century before Constantine inaugurated a similar alliance within Roman boundaries.

The real importance of the Sassanian experiment lay not in details of doctrine, which were lost soon after the Moslem conquest ended Persian cultural independence. Rather, it was the fact that the supernatural sanctions invoked by official religion and an organized priesthood effectively reconciled the conflict of interest between militarized landowners and the central royal authority. A numerous and formidable fighting class of heavy armored cavalrymen could thus protect the land from raids without at the same time threatening to tear civilized society apart through incessant civil war. No other part of the civilized world was so successful at inventing new institutional forms. The Sassanian example, therefore, had a powerful effect on Byzantium, and through Byzantium on western Europe.

Sassanian Religion

‡‡‡ Nevertheless, the alliance of king, barons, and Zoroastrian priesthood was not without its cost. The cities of Mesopotamia, from which the Parthian rulers had drawn their strength, were more or less excluded from the Sassanian scheme of things. Perhaps for this reason, the Sassanian period was one of unusual religious effervescence in Mes-

opotamia. The greatest figure was the prophet Mani (*c.* A.D. 215–273). King Shapur I (reigned A.D. 240–271), son and successor of the founder of the Sassanian dynasty, appears to have looked favorably upon Mani, perhaps hoping to balance the proud rural Zoroastrianism of his father against Mani's new revelation, which appealed mainly to the urban inhabitants of his realm.

Mani was a most self-conscious prophet. He set out to purge all existing religions of the corruptions which time had worked in the divine message, which, he held, had everywhere been the same, even when delivered through such diverse lips as those of Jesus, Buddha, and Zoroaster. To guard against similar corruption of his own revelation, Mani personally wrote his message down and emphatically prohibited careless copying of his inspired texts. As a result, Manichean scripture always remained scarce, and modern scholars cannot reconstitute Mani's texts from the scraps and paraphrases (often recorded by religious rivals) which alone survive. Mani's precautions against error thus backfired. So did the excessive precision with which he established his church and organized missionary enterprise. Having foreseen and prohibited all sorts of mistakes and vulgarizations, Mani in effect limited his doctrine to an elite of specially trained and disciplined souls.

Despite this limitation, during his lifetime Mani met with wide acceptance in Mesopotamia and in other urban centers, both east and west. Yet at home, the Zoroastrian priesthood was not kindly disposed to a prophet who accused them of having corrupted the truth originally entrusted to them by Zoroaster. Hence, when Shapur I died (A.D. 271) Mani was exposed to the anger of outraged Zoroastrian orthodoxy. As a result he spent his last years in prison and his followers suffered severe persecution. This did not prevent the survival of the faith, but did make the Manicheans into opponents of the Sassanian regime.

Three hundred years later a more definitely revolutionary faith was preached in Persia by a prophet named Mazdak. An emphatic egalitarianism seems to have been central to Mazdak's message, although details cannot be recovered from the shocked denunciations of his opponents who accused the Mazdakites of advocating community of property and of women. For a while, Mazdakism enjoyed royal tolerance; but when Chosroes I (reigned A.D 531–79) came to the throne, he embarked upon a policy of violent suppression which destroyed the sect.

As it happened, none of these Iranian-Mesopotamian religious movements led to the establishment of a world-girdling faith. Instead, Islam invaded Iran and gave the Sassanian world a religion suited to urban needs and at the same time able to over-awe the countryside. Because of this, not much is known about Sassanian religion or cultural life at large. Yet, if one remembers that, despite its late start, Manicheism constituted the most formidable competitor Christianity had to face in the Roman empire, and realizes that the oases of central Asia as far as the Chinese frontier became provincial outposts of Sassanian culture, then the strength and vitality of the Sassanian civilization can be better appreciated.

Art also offers some indication of the importance of the Sassanian accomplishment. Some of the features of Byzantine architecture appear to have originated in Sassanian Persia. But unfortunately the piles of dusty brick which alone survive today can give us no real idea of what the royal palaces were like. Their exteriors may never have been particularly impressive, but the domed and vaulted interiors, where glazed bricks once made the light shimmer in brightly colored patterns along the walls, must have been splendid indeed.

The Byzantine Empire

‡‡‡ Other things, too, the Romans borrowed or adopted from Persian models. Symbols of royalty, for instance—crown and scepter—and rituals of court ceremonial were deliberately borrowed by the Emperor Diocletian (reigned A.D. 284-305), in the hope of clothing his person in an aura of mystery that would inhibit the sort of squalid assassination that had destroyed so many of his predecessors. Most important of all, after the time of Constantine, the Romans also made heavy armed cavalrymen the backbone of their imperial field army. No other kind of force was capable of meeting Persian attack on the one hand and barbarian harassment on the other.

The Romans, however, were unwilling to adapt their social structure to the Sassanian "feudal" style. The elaborate body of legal principles and practices that had grown up piecemeal across the centuries inhibited any really drastic alteration of the urban-centered social and political order. Justinian's (A.D. 527-65) codification of Roman law was therefore not merely a matter of administrative convenience; it also constituted a reassertion of continuity with a distinctively Roman and fundamentally urban antiquity.

To solve the immediate military problem of defense the Byzantine emperors tried to keep a standing force in being, preferably near their own persons, ready at a moment's notice to travel to any threatened frontier or revolted province and there enforce the imperial will. But tax income was not sufficient to maintain a large force of expensively equipped and armored cavalrymen. When Justinian attempted to re-conquer the lost provinces of the western Mediterranean, for example, he resorted to the practice of allowing his general Belisarius to raise a company of 5000 heavy cavalrymen privately, in the expectation of paying them from booty and plunder. Belisarius' long campaign in Italy (A.D. 535–549) therefore involved ruthless and prolonged plundering, which turned out to be more damaging to local inhabitants than any of the previous barbarian invasions had been.

Inevitably, when the principal armed force of the state remained near the imperial person, the frontiers were seriously exposed. Time and again small-scale raids from beyond the Danube, for instance, went scot-free since the imperial bodyguard could not leave Constantinople to chase down every little band of marauders. As a result, the Balkan hinterland lay at the mercy of small bands. Only a few coastal cities, strong behind their walls, remained safe. Nothing remotely resembling the vigorous Sassanian local defense system protected Roman frontiers.

The exposure of the borderlands to barbarian raids and infiltration was, in a sense, the price paid by the urban populations of the empire for their continued dominance of society. An armed, rural aristocracy would have challenged that dominance, as had happened in Iran and Mesopotamia with the establishment of the Sassanian empire. The em-perors and people of Constantinople chose instead to let the remote and barren inland regions of the empire go, if need be, while defending the vitals of the state with a small mobile standing army, technically equipped in the Persian manner, but maintained by taxes and booty rather than by grants of land.

Heresy and Orthodoxy

‡‡‡ The urban, and in certain basic tenets also democratic, character of Christianity reflected and sustained this emphasis within late Roman

and early Byzantine society, just as the aristocratic Zoroastrianism of Sassanian Persia reinforced rural predominance in the militarily more successful regime of Iran. Thus, in refusing to imitate the Sassanian military model in its entirety, the Byzantines asserted the socio-political difference between their sea-centered empire and a purely land power such as Persia. The development of Christianity and clearer definition of church organization and doctrine also underlined the differences between the two rival empires.

Even before Constantine made Christianity a legal religion, teachers in Alexandria had tried to organize Christian doctrine into coherent form. The great pioneer was Origen (d. *c.* A.D. 254), who, inevitably, when attempting to speak about ultimate realities, fell back upon the vocabulary of Greek philosophy. Thenceforward, argument about points of Christian doctrine was couched in a philosophic, and sometimes extremely abstruse, Greek. As soon as the pressure of official persecution was removed (A.D. 312) a series of bitter disputes broke out among Christians. Donatism in North Africa and Arianism in Egypt attracted Constantine's personal attention; and when remonstrance failed to bring reconciliation among the warring theologians, the Emperor summoned the first ecumenical council of the Christian church at Nicaea in A.D. 325. There the doctrine of Arius concerning the relation between Father and Son of the Trinity was anathematized, and a concise creed was approved as orthodox. This did not suffice to convince Arian Christians, however. Subsequent councils, summoned to deal with yet other heresies, succeeded only in defining orthodoxy more and more precisely, and in expelling from the church those who thought otherwise on disputed points.

The major and enduring doctrinal splits that developed among Christians tended to conform to deep-seated ethnic and cultural lines of demarcation. The Coptic church in Egypt and the Syriac church in western Asia voiced secular and ethnic as well as theological dissatisfaction with rule from Constantinople. Disaffection was so widespread that when Moslem Arabs invaded Egypt and Syria, they were often greeted as liberators from a heretical and oppressive yoke.

Relations between Greek- and Latin-speaking Christians were more complex. Rome was the seat of the pope, i.e. the bishop of Rome. Tradition held that the church of Rome had been founded by the Apostle Peter. The popes therefore considered themselves to be successors to Saint Peter and claimed primacy over the entire Christian church on the ground that Peter had been specially appointed by Christ as prince of the Apostles. Other major bishoprics of the Christian world resisted the pope's claim and preferred to rely on a council of all the bishops to settle matters of common concern. When the Council of Chalcedon (A.D. 451) accepted Pope Leo the Great's formulation of trinitarian doctrine (thereby repudiating the "monophysite" view popular in Egypt and Syria) a headlong collision between the two theories of church government was postponed but not, of course, resolved.

Debate over points of doctrine and church discipline occasioned a great outpouring of polemical and expository works, together with numerous commentaries on scripture and a few ventures into speculative theology. The bulk of this literature was written in Greek, and it gave exhaustive definition both to orthodoxy and to mutually opposing heresies. In the Latin world, the role of the church fathers was different, for they were less concerned with refuting heresy than with making the truths and basic documents of Christianity available to Latin readers. St. Jerome (d. A.D. 420), for example, translated the whole Bible into Latin—the so-called *Vulgate*, which became the standard version for later generations of Latin Christians. His contemporary, St. Augustine of Hippo (d. A.D. 430), produced a shower of sermons, biblical commentaries, and apologetic writings. His greatest work, *The City of God*, sketched a universal Christian history, extending from creation to the day of judgment, which remained fundamental to the world view of western Europe. His *Confessions* offered a vivid autobiography of his conversion to Christianity and ended with a penetrating philosophic inquiry into the nature of time and eternity. Taken together, Augustine's works gave later Latin Christians a philosophically sophisticated statement of their faith and imparted a distinctly Platonic coloring to it.

As the Germanic invasions and attendant disorders (A.D. 378–511) disrupted the urban centers of the Latin West, monasteries became the most active centers of Christian piety, education, and culture. The earliest Christian monks took to the deserts of Egypt and Syria, where each pursued holiness in his own way. Church administrators soon felt the need to regulate and control extreme forms of behavior that some of the monks went in for. In the Greek-speaking half of the church, the rule of St. Basil (d. A.D. 379) set a pattern for monkish conduct that was widely followed in later centuries. Latin monasticism received its lasting definition when St. Benedict of Nursia (*c.* A.D. 529) drew upon his personal experience as abbot of a monastery at Monte Cassino to create his *Rule* for the governance of monks' lives. Both Basil's and Benedict's rules made prayer and worship central. Labor, reading, and other activities were all subordinated— at least in principle—to the adoration of God. In a violent and barbarous age, communities of monks, devoted to the service of God, were small islands of calm in a stormy world. Especially in the Latin West, monasteries became the main institution that preserved a minimum of intellectual culture during what are often called the Dark Ages.

With the decay of imperial administration in the western, Latin-speaking provinces of the empire, the church inevitably assumed a fairly independent attitude vis-à-vis secular authorities, who were more likely to appear as ravaging plunderers than in any other guise. The conversion of Clovis, king of the Franks, to the orthodox form of Christianity in A.D. 496 did bring the most powerful German kingdom officially within the pale of papal Christianity; but the conduct of Clovis and his successors was barely tinged by Christian precepts. Impoverishment and political chaos brought to Italy by Justinian's long-drawn-out wars of conquest weakened the authority the pope was able to exert outside of Rome itself. By contrast, the Eastern church, under the administration of the patriarch of Constantinople, remained closely in touch with the imperial authorities. In many cases the Greek church operated almost as an arm of the government, yet in other instances, patriarchs boldly opposed imperial decrees as heretical.

A Christendom so deeply divided between Greek, Latin, Syriac, and Coptic churches was clearly in no very favorable position to withstand the assault of Islam, especially since the Arab conquest from the south coincided with renewed attacks from the north where disturbances on the steppe once again set whole peoples in motion across Christendom's ill-defended frontiers.

The changed balance of the world resulting from the explosion of Islam will be the theme of the next chapter.

CHAPTER 13

The Rise of Islam

In A.D. 636 an Arab army defeated the Roman (Byzantine) garrison of Syria and Palestine, and permanently eliminated Roman power from those two provinces. Shortly thereafter, other Arab expeditionary forces overran Mesopotamia (A.D. 641) and Egypt (A.D. 642), and by A.D. 651 Iran had also been annexed to the new Islamic empire created by these victories. The fervor of fresh religious revelation vouchsafed to the prophet Mohammed (d. A.D. 632) inspired these extraordinary victories. Even more remarkable was the fact that the religious conviction Mohammed aroused enabled crude Arab conquerors and their descendants to weld a new and distinctively Islamic civilization from the various and often discordant elements Middle Easterners had inherited from a past that reached all the way back to the first beginning of civilization.

The Life of Mohammed

‡‡‡ In Mohammed's time, Arabia was divided between warlike tribes, some nomadic and some settled at agricultural oases or in trading towns. Judaism and Christianity had made some inroads into Arabia, but Mecca, the city of Mohammed's birth, remained pagan. As a young man, Mohammed probably traveled with caravans carrying goods to towns along the Palestinian border. Then at about the age of

forty he began to fall into trances and hear voices, which he presently recognized as visitations from the angel Gabriel, instructing him in obedience to the will of Allah. Under the impulsion of these experiences, Mohammed began to preach the unity and omnipotence of Allah, the impending day of judgment, and the necessity of complete obedience to Allah's will. He summed up his message under the rubric "Islam," that is, "submission" to Allah. Prayers five times daily, almsgiving, pilgrimage to Mecca at least once in a lifetime, abstention from wine and pork, and a month-long fast from sun-up to sun-set every year were the principal obligations Mohammed imposed upon the faithful. Obedience to Allah, the Prophet revealed, would be rewarded by a place in Paradise, whereas idolaters and other wicked men were destined to suffer eternal fiery torment. Bodily resurrection on the Last Day was another point upon which Mohammed put much emphasis.

Initially, the Prophet assumed that Jews and Christians would recognize his preaching as the last and most perfect revelation of God's will. For Allah, Mohammed believed, was the same deity who had spoken to Abraham, Moses, Jesus, and all the other Hebrew prophets. Since Allah could not contradict himself, differences between Mohammed's own revelation and the tenets of the older religions were simply attributed to human error in preserving the authentic divine message.

A few Meccans accepted Mohammed's warnings, but the great majority declined to give up their traditional worship, which Mohammed denounced as idolatry. Then, in A.D. 622, Mohammed fled from Mecca to Medina, where he had been invited by one faction of that strife-torn oasis city in the hope that an outsider could settle their quarrels. From this time onward, Mohammed became a political leader and lawgiver. At Medina, Mohammed had his first direct encounter with Jews, who declined to accept his authority. Mohammed therefore drove them out, and took their land for his own followers. A little later, Mohammed conquered another Jewish oasis. This time he left the inhabitants in possession of their land on condition that they render tribute in the form of a head tax. These first encounters were of great importance because they became binding precedents, defining the relation between Moslem rulers and their Jewish (and later also Christian) subjects.

While at Medina, Mohammed attracted a steady flow of new re-

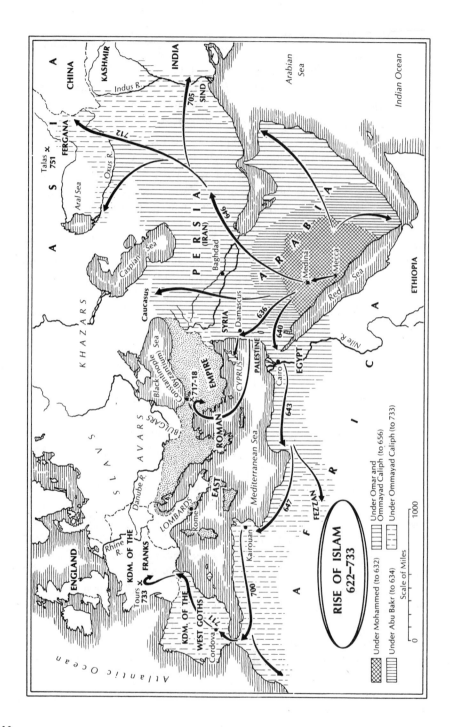

RISE OF ISLAM
622–733

Under Mohammed (to 632)
Under Abu Bakr (to 634)
Under Omar and Ommayad Caliph (to 656)
Under Ommayad Caliph (to 733)

Scale of Miles

0   1000

cruits and converts. As a result, the community of the faithful was soon hard pressed to find a livelihood in the narrow confines of the Medinan oasis. An obvious solution was to raid caravans owned by the Meccans. The first raids were successful; others soon followed until resistance in Mecca crumbled. Mohammed returned in triumph and then went on to unite all of Arabia under the banner of Islam, partly by war, but mainly by diplomacy and negotiation.

Scarcely had this been accomplished when Mohammed died (A.D. 632), leaving no son to succeed him. One of the Prophet's old friends and close companions, Abu Bakr, was chosen as caliph (i.e. successor) to lead the Moslem community. He immediately had to face a widespread withdrawal of allegiance by Arab chieftains, who felt that their submission to Mohammed did not obligate them to the community of the faithful as a whole. But when it came to fighting, the enthusiasm and conviction of the hard core of Mohammed's converts once again prevailed, and the Arabian chieftains were forced to unite once more behind the banner of the new faith. Abu Bakr died as soon as this crisis was past (A.D. 634). Leadership passed next to Omar (caliph A.D. 634–644), who proved himself not only pious and devout, but also a very successful general and administrator.

Arab Conquest and the Ommayad Caliphate

‡‡‡ The unification of all Arabia prefaced the amazing series of Arab conquests that brought the whole of the ancient Middle East (except for Asia Minor) as well as the desert region of the lower Indus valley (by A.D. 715), North Africa, and even Spain (A.D. 711–715) under Moslem control. No military change accounts for these victories. Arab armies were neither very numerous nor particularly well equipped, but the conviction that God was with them, the belief that death in battle assured a blissful life in Paradise, and Omar's effective leadership sufficed to give the Arabs superiority over their enemies.

After A.D. 715, however, easy victories stopped. The city of Byzantium withstood a hard and prolonged siege (717–18). This major defeat was matched by failure in a series of frontier skirmishes in central Asia, where a Turkish force pushed the Moslems out of eastern Iran by 715. A little later, the Franks defeated a Moslem raiding party at the battle of Tours in central Gaul (A.D. 732).

These defeats, together with the inevitable waning of the first flush of religious excitement and conviction, created acute problems within the Moslem community. During the first generation or two, the Arab warriors had remained more or less insulated from their subjects. Omar set up special garrison cities, where the Arabs settled down under their tribal leaders. Each warrior received pay derived from the taxes collected from the population at large by traditional Roman and Persian bureaucratic methods. This system worked pretty well at first, and remained effective even when the leadership of the Islamic community passed into far less capable hands than those which had guided its first years.

The first test came in A.D. 644, when Omar was assassinated. A chieftain of the Ommayad family then succeeded to the caliphate and the office remained in that family until A.D. 750. The Ommayads made Damascus in Syria their capital. The power of the Ommayad caliphs depended upon maintaining a delicate balance between three very different roles. The caliph had first of all to balance rival Arab chieftains and tribes off against one another. He had also to manage the bureaucracy inherited from his Roman and Persian predecessors and use it to tax the population at large. Then, in the third place, the caliph somehow had to serve as religious head of the Moslem community.

Of these three roles the one the Ommayads failed to fill adequately was the last. Serious and devout men, seeking to know the will of Allah and to do it faithfully, found no satisfaction in the spectacle offered by Ommayad administration. As long as military success continued uninterruptedly, such discontents were politically ineffective. But after A.D. 715, when the Moslems suffered their first serious defeats, the pious opposition, which demanded a worthy, God-chosen caliph, became a serious matter.

As administrators of the population at large, the Ommayads also ran into increasing difficulty. Numerous Christians and Zoroastrians and followers of other religions found the theological simplicity, legal precision, and practical success of Islam perfectly convincing. On principle, such converts were welcome to join the community of the faithful. But when conversion meant relief from taxation—as at first was the case—religious success meant acute fiscal embarrassment. Moreover, the Moslem community was still organized by tribes, and the tribes could not or would not welcome masses of strangers into their ranks. Arabs looked scornfully upon the new converts and treated them as less than fully equal members of the community of Islam, despite the plain injunctions of Mohammed's revelation.

All these strains came to a head in A.D. 744, when a disputed sucession precipitated civil war. Fighting ended with the overthrow of Ommayad rule (except in Spain, where a descendant of the Ommayads made good his claim to power). The privileged position of Arab garrison troops also disappeared when the victors, an Arab family called Abbasid, set up their capital at Baghdad in Mesopotamia. The backbone of their military support came from Persian converts. It is not, therefore, surprising that Abbasid policy from the start smacked strongly of Sassanian precedent. Arab tribal groups, which had been so important before, disintegrated because tribal garrisons no longer received pay through their chiefs, as in Ommayad times. In Arabia proper, where the old style of nomad life continued, tribal ties remained unchanged. But in the settled parts of the empire the Arabs blended into the general population, usually as landowners or in other privileged positions, and soon forgot their tribal identity and discipline. Instead, bureaucracy of the familiar imperial model took over all ordinary administration, while Iranian and Turkish or other mercenaries more and more constituted the core of the caliph's armed forces.

These reversions to very ancient imperial precedents met the demands of the non-Arab converts to Islam, who were now, like everybody else, the subjects of a distant, unapproachable caliph. But these changes did nothing to meet the demands of the pious Moslems who were bent upon realizing God's will on earth in all its specificity. The solution Abbasid statesmen found for this difficulty was of fundamental importance for all subsequent Islamic society. Instead of trying to combine religious authority with military and political leadership as previously, the Abbasids tacitly agreed to transfer jurisdiction in all matters of religious importance to experts in the lore of Islam—men known collectively as *ulema*.

Moslem Scripture and Sacred Law

‡‡‡ The *ulema* had developed spontaneously. Pious men, confronting a problem of conduct, wished to know what God's will in the matter might be. The way to find out was to seek for precedents in the words

or deeds of the Prophet. But ordinary men were not familiar with these deeds and words, and had to ask experts who were. As the first generation of the Prophet's companions died, this called for systematic study. Naturally enough, Medina was the first seat where the details of Mohammed's career were studied. Here his inspired utterances were collected and put carefully in order just a few years after the Prophet's death. The resulting scripture, the Koran, has ever since constituted the ultimate repository of religious authority for Moslems.

Many matters for which the Koran offered no direct guidance had somehow to be coped with also. For answers to such questions, experts in the lore of Islam resorted at first to reports about Mohammed's everyday words and deeds emanating—really or fictitiously—from companions of the Prophet. When this failed, the conduct of men closely associated with Mohammed might be helpful. When even these "traditions" could not be brought to bear on a case, the *ulema* admitted the use of analogy to decide a difficult point. If analogy failed to offer convincing guidance they fell back ultimately upon the consensus of the faithful, arguing that Allah would not permit the entire community to err, however faulty individual judgments might be.

Using these methods, the learned men of Islam rapidly built up an elaborate system of law, which they believed expressed the will of Allah. The sacred law was, of course, unchangeable, since Allah did not change. It was also rather detailed and specific, since the whole effort was aimed at making unambiguously clear what Allah wished men to do in particular situations. As a result, the sacred law of Islam later proved a heavy burden for Moslem society to carry, since it could neither be repudiated nor altered.

Under the Abbasids, however, the sacred law still glistened like newly minted gold. Allah's will for men seemed surely there revealed, and it behooved the faithful to bend every effort to conform to its clear and definite prescriptions. This was not hard to do since learned men, respected for their exact knowledge of the Koran, the Traditions, and the details of the Sacred Law, sat in the market place of every considerable town, ready to pass judgment on matters of conscience brought before them. Much of the business of government affecting private persons and individual lives was thus transferred to the jurisdiction of these religious experts. Pious Moslems could therefore feel that in everything that really mattered, the best and wisest men were in control. By comparison with this, who happened to be running the central government, collecting taxes, guarding the frontiers, and enjoying the luxuries of palace life did not matter so very much.

The early ideal of a totally holy community, led by a worthy successor to the Prophet and dedicated solely to obedience to Allah, was thus somewhat reluctantly surrendered by the majority of Moslems. But not by all. Some stubborn idealists clung to the original vision and thereby became heretics. Many of them came to hold that only descendants of Ali, the son-in-law of the Prophet, were worthy of heading the community of the faithful. When Ali's direct line died out in the twelfth generation, some argued that the true successor to the Prophet had withdrawn from an irremediably wicked world but would return in the future and turn his terrible avenging wrath against those who had betrayed the truth and been false to Allah's commands. Extreme sects split into numerous sub-groupings. Some of them nursed a fiercely revolutionary intolerance for Abbasid, or indeed for any constituted authority that fell short of their utterly unyielding ideal. Such groups are termed Shi'a. The majority, who were willing to live within the framework accorded by Abbasid policy, are known as Sunni Moslems.

The Sunni-Shi'a split has continued to run throughout Islam right down to the present day. Equally, the restrictions the Abbasid compromise placed upon the jurisdiction of secular government affected the policy of all Islamic states ever since.

An important corollary of the autonomous administration of the Sacred Law was that Moslem political authorities expected the leaders of other religious communities to guide and legislate for their flocks in all personal and religious matters just as the *ulema* guided the lives of Moslems. Far-ranging autonomy for Christian and Jewish communities was thereby assured.

A second important implication of the Moslem legal code was that a man had to accept Islam in its entirety or reject it utterly. No halfway house was possible. Either Mohammed was Allah's latest and only authoritative prophet, and the Sacred Law in every jot and tittle was the true expression of Allah's will for men, or else these claims were false. No middle ground could be found in logic, and very little was discovered in fact. Islam, in short, shared the doctrinal intolerance of its Judaic and Christian forerunners to the full.

The religious aspiration that found expression in Islam very soon set a powerful stamp upon the daily lives of millions of men in the Middle East and north Africa. Cultivation of the Arabic language as the necessary vehicle for all religious discourse become part of piety. As a result, a rather rapid linguistic shift went hand in hand with the propagation of Islam, as Arabic displaced Greek and/or Aramaic as the everyday speech of the Middle Eastern peoples. Persian, however, retained its currency in Iran, although for a while it ceased to be used for literary purposes.

Arabic Court Life and Culture

‡‡‡ Poetic records of tribal and individual prowess were an important part of the culture of pre-Islamic Arabia. Mohammed had looked with disfavor upon these rivals to the poetry of his own inspired utterances. Nonetheless, Arab warriors continued to cultivate a taste for poetry and rhythmic prose in spite of the Prophet. The warrior's ideal expressed in such poetry was reinforced by the ease and leisure the first Arab generations experienced, when they began to live upon the taxes collected from their new subjects. As a result, a courtly style of gentlemanly life developed among Arab fighting men which stood in conscious opposition to the ideals of the pious Moslems. Wine drinking, for example, was part of the gentlemanly code of behavior despite Mohammed's prohibition. More generally, a warm appreciation of the sensory joys of the world, refinement of manners, and delicacy of sentiment in matters of pride, hate, and love, fitted awkwardly with the pious drive for complete obedience to Allah. Only in high political circles, pre-eminently in the court of the caliph himself, could this secular, leisured, and essentially aristocratic style of life flourish freely.

A second element inherited from the past also stood stubbornly in the way of energetically pious champions of Islam. The speculative habit of mind, so persistently cultivated among the Greeks, could not be entirely suppressed. In matters of religion, to be sure, the *ulema* resolutely and on the whole successfully resisted temptation by refusing to entertain questions of speculative theology. They held it to be a self-evident truth that everything a man needed to know was provided by the Koran and Traditions.

Nevertheless, there were two professional services the Moslems —or at least the rich among them—were not prepared to do without: the prediction of the future by astrologers and the curing of illness by doctors. Astrology and medicine were, of course, deeply imbued with Greek thought. In taking over these professions, the Moslems, therefore, inevitably imported into their own learning a generous share of the Greek inheritance. And once Moslem minds began to reason about things, it was hard to call a halt. Before long, curiosity spread to other matters not directly related to either medicine or astrology. Some of the Abbasid caliphs even became patrons of learning and organized systematic translation of Greek and Indian works of science and philosophy. In this way much of Greek knowledge and some Indian learning (e.g. the decimal-place notation system) passed into Arabic and fired the curiosity of a handful of courtiers and professional men.

The ease and precision of arithmetical calculation, which the decimal system allowed, stimulated Arab mathematicians to generalize arithmetical processes and relationships into what we know by its Arabic name as algebra. This carried mathematical understanding of numbers in quite new directions, and away from the geometrical style of Greek mathematical thought.

A second fruitful direction in which scientific curiosity turned was toward alchemy. Many of the ideas and some of the skills alchemists acquired seem to have originated among Taoists in China. But the Arabs took up the search for the philosophers' stone with enthusiasm and tried long and hard to transmute base metals into gold. In the process, devices for distillation, heating, dissolving, and in other ways altering the physical state of matter were invented or improved; and a number of chemical compounds were synthesized successfully, despite radically erroneous ideas about how chemical reactions occur. Another science in which Arab work surpassed anything known to the Greeks was mathematical optics—a result of the skill the Moslems acquired in grinding lenses of glass to fit a mathematical curve. But such improvements did not shake the general authority of such authors as Galen in medicine and Ptolemy in astronomy. Except in mathematics, Arab science remained always faithful to the Greeks in fundamentals and departed from their authority only in detail.

The Abbasid Empire

‡‡‡ Under the Abbasids, therefore, the traditions of Greek rationalism and science, the aristocratic warrior ideal cherished by pre-Islamic Arabic tribesmen, and the radical striving for holiness characteristic of pious Moslems, all found shelter under the roof of an imperial bureaucracy and armed establishment that drew its main inspiration from Persian prototypes. The amalgam created a richness and complexity of civilization that surpassed anything then known in Europe and rivaled the efflorescence of T'ang China far to the east.

Two points of weakness remained. At home, the dissent of Shi'a groups, feeding upon ethnic and perhaps also upon economic divisions within Moslem society, led to recurrent revolt. After A.D. 800, various break-off states that drew some of their strength from just this sort of religious-social discontent began to eat into the imperial structure. Secondly, along its northern frontier the Abbasid empire was not able to cope for long with the relentless pressure from the steppe. As a result, Turkish soldiers and adventurers, filtering in from the steppeland, gradually took over political control even in Baghdad. But they continued to cloak their usurpation of effective authority by keeping members of the Abbasid family on the throne until A.D. 1258. Long before that time, however, the combination of provincial rebellion and palace *coup d'état* led to the breakdown of central control even in the Mesopotamian-Syrian heartland of the empire.

Thereafter, new strands within Islam, arising from the infolding of Turkish tribesmen from the steppe and the increased scope allowed to mystic seekers after forms of religious enlightenment for which early Islam had made no room, gave the Moslem world a markedly different character. The date A.D. 1000 roughly accords with the onset of these transformations and corresponds also to important alterations in relations between the Moslems and their Hindu and Christian neighbors. But before pursuing these matters further we must retrace our steps in time to survey the reactions of other civilized peoples to the rise of Islam and to the new style of civilization that Islamic conquerors so successfully created at the ancient Middle Eastern crossroads of the Old World.

CHAPTER 14

China, India, and Europe

A.D. 600-1000

 Because Islam quickly became a coherent and legally defined way of life, neighbors had either to accept or reject it *in toto.* This tended to divide the civilized world into more nearly watertight compartments than had been true in earlier times, when dogmatic religion had not played so central a part in civilized life. Nevertheless, stimulus across cultural frontiers remained negatively important. In resisting Islam both Hindustan and Christendom had to define their own distinctive traits more emphatically than before.

A second general characteristic of the centuries between A.D. 600 and 1000 was the spread of semi-civilized styles of life throughout broad borderlands both north and south of the earlier zone of civilization. In the Far West, for example, Celtic, Germanic, and Slavic tribes were all brought within the fold of Christendom by the year 1000. With Christianity came at least the rudiments of high culture and civilized social order. In eastern Europe and central Asia, Turkish tribes entered the fringes of civilization at the same time. The best-organized Turkish states did not accept a religion established already among their civilized neighbors, but preferred Judaism (in the case of the Khazars) or Manicheism (in the case of the Uighurs). They thus retained greater spiritual and cultural independence.

The fact that pastoralism, war, and caravan trade continued to dominate the life of Turkish tribesmen of the steppes made it easy for them to keep religiously and culturally apart from their civilized contemporaries, who were all fundamentally agriculturalists. Further west, however, there was no such gap between barbarian and civilized communities. Instead, a major improvement of agricultural techniques permitted German and other barbarian peoples to transform the forests of the north European plain into fields. As a result, civilization could now penetrate the forested lands of the European Far West in a fuller sense than was geographically or socially possible on the steppe grasslands. The key change was that German cultivators invented a new type of heavy mouldboard plow, capable of draining wet low-lying lands and strong enough to penetrate even the heavy clay soils that covered much of northern Europe. This mouldboard plow made it possible to cultivate for the first time lowland forested areas where the light, scratch plows familiar to Mediterranean and Middle Eastern farmers had been completely ineffective. No comparable technical change came to the steppe to transform the conditions of life in that region. Hence the northward extension of civilization to German and Slavic peoples involved far more radical changes than did the simultaneous northward movement of familiarity with aspects of civilized life which occurred among the Turkish tribes living to the east of them.

In the Far East the situation was again different. A slow, painstaking extension of the garden-style of cultivation, which had been developed by the Chinese centuries before, continued. Nameless pioneers ditched and diked and pumped and piped water from innumerable little streams into new fields. No technical innovation was involved, just a vast expenditure of human effort. And while the Chinese slowly brought the Yangtse valley to the south into high cultivation, Koreans and Japanese, on the northeastern flank of the original center of Chinese life, painstakingly carried through another geographically substantial expansion of the area of Far Eastern agricultural civilization by raising the cultivation of their respective homelands to the Chinese level.

Like their Uighur contemporaries, the Korean and Japanese peoples maintained their cultural distinctiveness vis-à-vis China by sticking to their separate languages and by espousing a religion different from that prevailing in the center of the civilization with which they were in contact. Thus the Koreans made Buddhism into a state religion and clung to it all the more emphatically after the Chinese disestablished that faith in A.D. 845. Japan, on the other hand, was far enough away from China not to feel the risk of complete absorption into the Chinese culture sphere. Hence, between A.D. 600 and 1000 the Japanese welcomed Buddhism, Confucianism, and every other aspect of Chinese culture they could import. They did so with an energetic enthusiasm for things foreign, which, recurring in later times, gives Japanese history a jerky character all its own. Thus during the Nara period (A.D. 645–784) the Japanese emperors very quickly and systematically created a miniature model of the great T'ang court in China. The precocious sensibility of Japanese courtly life is delightfully illustrated by Lady Murasaki's delicate love story, *The Tale of Genji*, written soon after A.D. 1000. But it was a much cruder style of life, sustained by baronial patrons in their provincial castles, that really nourished Japan's cultural independence. As the political and military power of such warlords grew at the expense of the imperial administration—a feature of Japanese life that became very prominent after 1000—the unique nature of Japanese cultural development came to be assured.

On the southern flank of the civilized world a similar string of new peoples and states arrived at a level of life properly termed civilized during the same period of time. Yunnan became a cultural satellite of China, as Annam (modern North Viet Nam) had done earlier. Tibet took advantage of its intermediate position between China and India to combine elements from each, taking its religion from India and secular aspects of culture mainly from China, but retaining always a strong local individuality. Tibet's religion, for example, mingled native "Bon" rites with Buddhist motifs to create what is known as Lamaism. On the southern flank of the Himalayas, Bengal and Kashmir became important frontiers of Indian culture, where powerful local states arose that dominated the political life of the north Indian plains, although neither was ever able to unite the Ganges and Indus valleys into a new "universal" empire. Arabia's sudden eruption into the Middle East we have already noted. Across the Red Sea, Ethiopia and Nubia in east Africa and Ghana in west Africa became seats of local states that boasted many of the trappings of civilization. Ethiopia and Nubia accepted a form of Christianity (monophysite) declared heretical in Rome and Constantinople. Ghana remained pagan.

The enormous geographic expansion of civilized styles of life and the increased variety of local blends and combinations of disparate cultural elements that occurred all along the northern and southern flanks of the civilized world after A.D. 600 recapitulated, but on an enlarged scale, the development of regional sub-cultures and variants around Mesopotamia that had occurred when civilization first became attuned to survival on rain-watered land about 2000 B.C. The intrinsic attractiveness of civilized accomplishments was of course centrally responsible for both spreads. In both cases, also, a much enhanced export of commodities from the civilized world in the form of plunder and tribute as well as trade made it possible for barbarian chieftains, kings, captains, and potentates of every description to initiate the exposure of their peoples to the seductions of civilization. After A.D. 600 the various civilized communities of the Old World were in a position to export more goods than before because their own internal economic and technical development everywhere underwent significant advance in the course of what has traditionally been called the "Dark Age" of Europe's history.

To appreciate better the increasing reach of civilized societies, we shall consider each in turn.

China

‡‡‡ Not long after the reunification of China (A.D. 589) by the Sui dynasty, a brief round of war brought a new dynasty, the T'ang, to power (618–907). The T'ang, in turn, after a longer interregnum were succeeded by the Sung (960–1279). Actually, the realities of Chinese government do not precisely correspond to the traditional dynastic pattern. Within the four centuries (600–1000) with which we are concerned, strong central government lasted only until 755 and was followed by a period of weakened imperial power, local war-lordism, and dependency upon a powerful Turkish confederacy headed by the Uighurs of central Asia. The overthrow of the Uighurs in 840 simply substituted other barbarian masters, who took over direct administration of north China during the later decades of the T'ang rule. The Sung dynasty also failed to displace these barbarian rulers from the northeastern region.

Yet the disruption of central power after 755 did not seriously check the economic development of China. Particularly in the south the labor of millions of peasants gradually extended their rice paddies up the hill slopes from the river edges to make a continuous carpet of fertile and carefully tended fields, producing rice in quantities great enough to maintain a much enlarged urban population of craftsmen, landlords, and officials. Trade was often in foreign—especially Uighur and Arab—hands. Confucian doctrine held merchants to be social parasites anyway. Hence, despite a substantial growth of foreign trade and of interregional exchanges within China, the urban classes did not challenge the traditional dominance of the landowning gentry. Instead, the ingenuity and skill of Chinese artisans and of foreign and Chinese merchants were directed mainly toward satisfying the tastes of the landlord-official class, whose members, being educated in classical Chinese learning, strove to practice the arts and decorum appropriate to gentlemen.

The gentlemanly idea underwent considerable elaboration in the T'ang and early Sung periods. Painting, for example, which became the principal fine art of China, assumed classical forms in this period, although no authenticated works survive. Poetry also assumed its classical form with the work of Li Po (A.D. 705–62) and Tu Fu (A.D. 712–70) whose verse patterns elaborated rhythms of popular songs and snatches, and in doing so established conventions that became binding for subsequent generations. The freshness and autobiographical poignancy characteristic of Li Po's verses was more difficult to imitate than his prosody, so that those who are capable of judging agree that Li Po was not only the pioneer but also the greatest of Chinese lyric poets.

Buddhism assumed an almost official status in early T'ang times, but ran into systematic persecution after A.D. 845. The emperor's desire to confiscate the lands that Buddhist monasteries had accumulated from gifts of the pious may have triggered these persecutions. But the basic factor was the distrust, indeed antipathy, Confucians felt toward an alien faith that taught disregard of all the obligations and duties Confucians held to be central to the good life. After the persecutions of the ninth century, Chinese Buddhism survived only in comparatively humble walks of life.

Yet Buddhism contributed a great deal to Chinese culture. Confucians, for example, learned from the Buddhists how to read new meanings into old texts by analogy and symbolic interpretation. More-over, many of the new meanings they discovered in the classics of the Confucian canon dealt with metaphysical and cosmological questions which had first been brought to Chinese attention by Buddhist teach-ers. For their part, the Taoists chose to combat Buddhism by borrow-ing not merely aspects of doctrine but the pattern of monastic organi-zation and a system of schooling from their rivals. Hence even in its official defeat, Buddhism left a large heritage behind—a fact nicely illustrated by the manner in which later Chinese painters used repre-sentational and narrative techniques, taken over from Buddhist art, in order to illustrate secular and Confucian subjects.

The elaborated and philosophically sophisticated reinterpretation of the classics is called Neo-Confucianism. Its full development came after the period we are now considering, but the school was well launched before A.D. 1000. The policy of the early Sung rulers, who enthusiastically championed everything they felt to be authentically Chinese and rejected consciously all that was felt to be foreign, assured the victory of Neo-Confucianism in official circles. Gentry dominance of society went hand in hand with this cultural policy. By operating together, these factors gave China a remarkably uniform history, as compared with the stormier developments of western Asia and Europe.

Another factor contributing to China's stability was the examina-tion system for recruiting talented individuals into the imperial bu-reaucracy. This became the normal way of entering government serv-ice under the Sung dynasty. Candidates were required to demonstrate their familiarity with the Confucian classics in written examinations. Those who received the best marks became eligible for official appoint-ment and could hope to rise to the highest posts of government. Years of study were needed to prepare for the examinations and, naturally, nearly everyone who passed came to share a common outlook and sys-tem of values inculcated by the classics. As a result, the officials of the Chinese empire became a remarkably homogeneous group, and the manner of their recruitment assured a high level of competence.

Humble origins were not an insuperable barrier to advancement. Bright young boys, even from very poor families, sometimes made it into the ranks of officialdom. Occasionally whole villages clubbed to-gether to support a promising candidate during his years of preparation. Success, if it came, assured the village of a protector in high places, and this seemed worth the cost to all concerned. The net effect was to assure China of significant social mobility. Office brought wealth as well as status; but sons of even the wealthiest had to win their way into the ranks of officialdom to assure continuance of high status and efficient protection of their inherited wealth. Probably, too, recruitment by examination helped to legitimize official authority in the eyes of those who had to submit to it, since the men who exercised command had personally won the right to do so.

India

‡‡‡ Islam offered no direct military challenge to the Chinese. There were skirmishes in central Asia, but the loss of a few distant oases to Moslem warriors after A.D. 751 (Battle of Talas) was of no great importance. In the decade immediately following this defeat, disasters far closer to home disrupted the T'ang imperial power; and soon thereafter the Uighur Manicheans interposed themselves as an effective cushion between the Moslem and Chinese worlds. India was far more exposed. Moslems conquered Sind in northwest India by 715 and soon thereafter seized primacy on the seaways of the Indian Ocean as well. Hence it came to pass that followers of Mohammed, who regarded Hinduism, at least in principle, as abominable idolatry, cut India off from her former cultural dependencies in southeast Asia.

The caste organization of India, with the political-military weaknesses that inevitably resulted from such a system of society, meant that Hindus were unable to repel the Moslems by force. Their response was therefore peaceable, aimed at conserving the Hindu heritage that Moslems found so offensive. On the one hand, a handful of Indian philosophers set out to systematize the intellectual tradition of the Upanishads. This allowed the learned to rebut effectively Moslem reproaches against the idolatrous practices traditional to Hinduism by explaining that all such rites, if properly understood, helped simple men along the path to a pure and transcendent theological monism. The philosophic system created by Shankara (788–850) became standard for later Hinduism. Shankara justified even the crudest traditional religious practices by claiming that they encouraged humble intellects to reach toward knowledge of the Absolute residing behind every sensory experience. As a good Hindu, he was even prepared to argue that

Moslem rites had value for those who could see no further into the Truth than Mohammed had done.

Turning the tables on Moslem teachers in such a dexterous fashion was all very well in theoretical discussions. At the more practical everyday level Indian sentiment hardened against foreigners. Like the Chinese of later T'ang and Sung times, popular Indian culture set out to reject systematically everything felt to be of alien inspiration and to defend and acknowledge all that seemed their own. In the process, much that had been hidden and primitive in Indian life entered the literary record for the first time. In particular, extremely varied cult practices known collectively as Tantrism came into the open and underwent vast elaboration. Tantric adepts sought to achieve the supernatural powers popularly attributed to holy men and ascetics by using magic charms and incantations. Tantrism therefore constituted a short cut to holiness, allowing quite ordinary men to attain the ascetic's goals without undergoing the pains and tribulations of ascetic discipline. Such a bargain had wide appeal and tended to undercut all forms of asceticism.

Tantrism was always a mainly private system of rites, although small groups might make magic together. On the more public side, temple services supplemented by occasional spectacular festivals in honor of one or another deity of the Hindu pantheon continued as before, and may even have become more elaborate. In Gupta times, the court provided patronage and an audience for writers and artists. After the collapse of the Gupta imperial peace, no comparable courtly center arose. Temples therefore took over first place. The more secular, intellectual aspects of Hindu civilization suffered from this transformation. In particular mathematics, which had made such a promising start in the Gupta age, simply fell into oblivion; it had no function in a temple-centered high culture. Courtly poetry like that of Kalidasa was supplanted by anonymous hymns which sometimes celebrated the love between God and his worshippers in vivid and very fleshly language. Dancing and hymn singing amid crowds of onlookers and participants could and did generate high emotional excitement. Millions found that through such ceremonies they could experience a sense of communion with the divine power they believed to lie behind everyday happenings. Hinduism thus retained deep roots in popular feeling, making it pretty well proof against the arguments of Moslem (and later of Christian) missionaries.

Information about the social and economic life of India in this age, and even about the political units into which the land was divided, remains very imperfect. A generally high level of activity certainly continued, and in such border regions as Bengal and the high Himalayan valleys of Kashmir, important geographical expansion of Indian society occurred. In these regions, jungle and swamp, hillside and forest, gave way to cultivated countryside. The total mass of Indian society therefore continued to increase, despite the loss of the border provinces along the Indus to Islam. Yet these continued successes do not suffice to counterbalance the fact that in general the Indian reaction to the Moslem threat appears to have been an indrawing of sensibilities, concentrating upon what was clearly and unambiguously Indian, rejecting alien stimuli, and in so doing abandoning or de-emphasizing some of the more active and successful developments of the preceding Gupta age.

Europe

‡‡‡ Europeans, too, remained on the defensive until the very end of the period we are here considering. But the European defensive was military first and foremost, and only in a secondary sense intellectual and emotional. Thus, in contrast to India, the primacy of politics over other bases of human association which classical Greece had first so emphatically declared was reasserted by the warlike barbarians and struggling Christians of Europe's "Dark Age."

It is useful to group the disturbed events of Europe's political history during this period into three successive waves of barbarian invasion, separated from one another by two periods of short-lived stabilization. We considered the first wave in Chapter XII. This was the movement of peoples triggered by the Hunnic invasion of central Europe that brought Goths, Burgundians, Vandals, Franks, Anglo-Saxons, and other Germanic peoples to Roman soil between A.D. 378 and about 450. The consolidation of a Frankish monarchy in Gaul under the descendants of Clovis (d. 511), and the reassertion of Roman administration in North Africa, Italy, and parts of Spain by the Emperor

Justinian (d. 565), constituted a shaky stabilization of civilized (or, in the Frankish case, semi-civilized) administration in the wake of this first great barbarian advance.

A second wave developed immediately after the death of Justinian, when a new band of nomads, known as Avars, drove westward from southern Russia into the Hungarian plain, and like Attila before them, began to raid far and wide into the agricultural lands lying south and west of their new headquarters. Avar power was near its height when the Moslems besieged Constantinople in the years 717–18. Yet the walls of Constantine's capital on the Bosphorus held. A new emperor, Leo III, the Isaurian (717–41), came to power and proceeded to reorganize and strengthen the Byzantine armed establishment. He did so by making extensive land grants to fighting men who undertook to guard the frontiers in return for the lands thus assigned to them. In Asia Minor this policy soon rolled back the attacking Arabs and proved capable of checking them permanently at about the line of the Taurus mountains. In Europe, however, Leo and his successors failed to stem a massive Slavic infiltration which gradually transformed all the northern and central regions of the Balkan peninsula into a predominantly Slavic-speaking countryside. In a similar fashion, after 568 the German tribe of Lombards displaced the Byzantines from control of all the inland parts of Italy.

Stabilization of a sort came to Europe with the recovery of Byzantine power in Asia Minor (after 718) and the consolidation of two barbarian states: the first Bulgarian empire on the lower Danube (after 679) and the Carolingian empire in the Far West (after 687). The Bulgar kingdom folded Slavic manpower into a Turkish war-band organization. It proved powerful enough to become a serious military rival to the Byzantine empire. In the process, attributes of civilized government and administration penetrated among the Balkan Slavs, even before the Bulgar khan's conversion to Christianity (865) opened the floodgates to civilization in its Byzantine form.

Among the Franks a somewhat similar pattern of events unfolded. The kingdom had become officially Christian in the time of Clovis (A.D. 496). Despite savage quarreling among his descendants (the Merovingians), traces of old Roman life remained precariously alive in Gaul. Then in 687 Pepin of Heristal won effective control over both the halves into which Clovis' kingdom had divided. Pepin came from the eastern and more purely Germanic (Austrasian) portion of the Frankish lands, where he was Mayor of the Palace to a do-nothing Merovingian. Pepin granted extensive new estates in the more Romanized parts of Gaul to his own followers and supporters on a scale sufficient to constitute a second wave of Germanic invasion. In 752 the power of Pepin's family was officially recognized when his grandson (also named Pepin) took the title King of the Franks. In the next generation Charlemagne brought the power of the newly constituted Carolingian dynasty to its peak. He conquered all of Germanic and Roman Europe, save for Scandinavia and England. He converted Saxons and other pagan German tribes to Christianity by main force. He destroyed the Avar camp in Hungary and asserted a somewhat shadowy control over a fringe of Slavic lands in central Europe. In recognition of his power, in 800 the pope crowned Charlemagne Emperor of the Romans. A few years later, the imperial master of Byzantium ratified the pope's action, thus in legal form reconstituting a Roman empire in the west to match the Roman (Byzantine) empire in the east.

Co-operation between Byzantines and Franks was never close. Political distrust was exacerbated by persistent religious friction, centering on the proper role of images in Christian worship. Emperor Leo III, the Isaurian, having saved Constantinople from the Moslems by breaking the siege of 717–18, wanted to purge the Christian church of image worship. He therefore banned icons. He may have been responding to Moslem reproaches of idolatry. Undoubtedly there were many Christians who believed that the military setbacks they had suffered at Moslem and barbarian hands were due to God's displeasure at idolatrous practices. But the pope in Rome and many ecclesiastical leaders in Constantinople resisted the emperor's iconoclastic policy. Each denounced the other as heretical. This quarrel with the Byzantine emperor put the pope in an awkward position. Rome was still officially under Byzantine administration, but the Lombard invaders were constantly expanding their control in Italy and threatened Rome itself. Under these circumstances, in 754, Pope Stephen II traveled to the Frankish court where Pepin has just assumed the royal title and invited him to come into Italy with his armies to protect the papacy. Pepin did so, and after defeating the Lombards transferred a belt of territory in central Italy to papal administration. The papal states thus created lasted until 1870, and the alliance between the papacy and the Carolingian monarchy lasted as long as the Carolingians did.

In the end, the Byzantine emperors gave in to the will of the people of Constantinople and restored icons to the churches (A.D. 843). This officially ended the grounds of quarrel between the popes and the rulers of Constantinople. But in practice, the gap between the eastern and western parts of Christendom continued to widen. As a result of the Slavic infiltration of the Balkan hinterland, Latin all but disappeared from the streets of Constantinople after Justinian's time (d. A.D. 565). Long before, Greek had been forgotten in the west, where knowledge of Latin itself was only precariously maintained in a few monastic and cathedral schools. Popular speech was evolving rapidly away from classical forms, toward the various Germanic and romance languages of medieval and modern times.

It was therefore a culturally and politically divided Christendom that met the third and last wave of barbarian invasion. Once again, a new war band, fleeing from southern Russia, penetrated to the Hungarian plain and began raiding from that base. This time the invaders were named Magyars or Hungarians. They crossed the Carpathian passes in A.D. 896. A little later, Moslem states in north Africa abruptly reversed the balance of power in the Mediterranean by almost destroying Byzantine naval strength. A series of large-scale piratical raids followed, directed against the entire northern coastline of the Mediterranean. A similar and even more ruthless harassment was simultaneously launched by Viking pirates, whose base of operations lay in Scandinavia.

A fundamental reversal of western Europe's relations with its neighbors occurred about A.D. 1000. This was signalized by the rise of Italian shipping which presently was able to exchange blow for blow with the Moslems in the Mediterranean, and by the conversion to Christianity of Russia (989), Hungary (1000), and the three Scandinavian kingdoms of Denmark, Sweden, and Norway (between 831 and 1000). In every case, conversion signified the emergence of an ambitious royal authority which welcomed Christianity as an aid in taming the unruliness of subordinates and in establishing such necessary adjuncts of civilized life as literacy and organized religion among their still barbarous subjects.

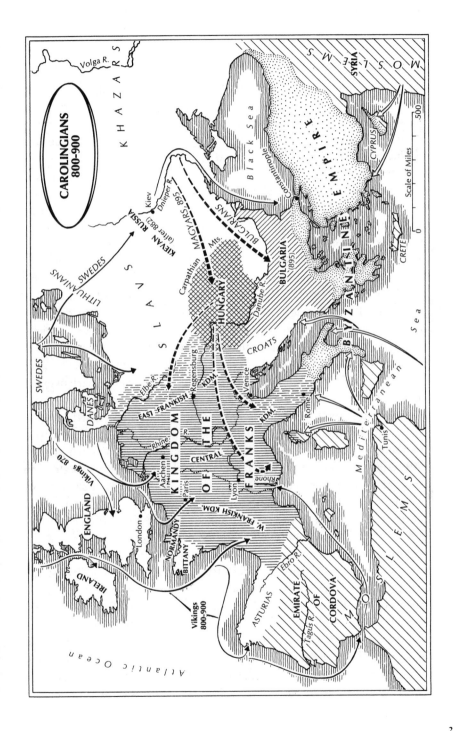

CAROLINGIANS
800–900

Volga R.

KHAZARS

SWEDES
LITHUANIANS

SLAVS

KIEVAN RUSSIA (after 882)

Kiev

Dnieper R.

MAGYARS 895

Carpathian Mts.

HUNGARY

CROATS

Black Sea

Constantinople

BULGARS

BULGARIA (895)

Danube R.

BYZANTINE EMPIRE

SYRIA

MOSLEMS

CYPRUS

CRETE

Scale of Miles

500

0

SWEDES

DANES

ENGLAND

Vikings 870

London

IRELAND

Atlantic Ocean

NORMANDY

BRITTANY

Paris

Aachen

Rhine R.

Elbe R.

EAST-FRANKISH

KINGDOM

CENTRAL

Regensburg

KDM.

KINGDOM OF THE FRANKS

KDM.

Venice

Rome

Tiber R.

Mediterranean Sea

CENTRAL

W. FRANKISH KDM.

Lyon

Rhône R.

Vikings 800–900

ASTURIAS

Ebro R.

EMIRATE OF CORDOVA

Tagus R.

MOSLEMS

Tunis

233

The Beginnings of Feudalism

‡‡‡ The taming of the northern barbarians by spontaneous acts of conversion was at least in part a tribute to the much enhanced effectiveness which Europe's institutions began to demonstrate under the hammer blows of Magyar, Viking, and Arab raids. In the east, the Byzantine empire at length transformed itself in the fashion pioneered so long before by the Persians. A feudal system developed, whereby princely landowners maintained retinues of heavy armed cavalrymen along the frontiers of the state, ready for local self-defense against raiding neighbors of whatever sort. The risk involved in this transformation was real enough. The greatest Byzantine conqueror, Emperor Basil II (ruled A.D. 976–1025), who finally succeeded in overpowering the Bulgar empire and was able to push his frontiers to the Danube and the upper Euphrates, was twice nearly toppled from his throne by rebellions of feudal magnates. Moreover, the emergence of great warrior-landowners in the countryside eroded urban dominance of society as a whole—a fact perhaps related to the eclipse of Byzantine sea power which had unleashed Arab raiding in the Mediterranean.

In the west, central administration did disintegrate. Charlemagne's empire proved quite incapable of defending itself from Viking and Magyar raids. Instead, military and political leadership passed into the hands of rough-and-ready local lords and men-at-arms, who equipped themselves as heavy armored cavalry, or knights. But Western knights differed in one very important respect from heavy armored cavalrymen of other parts of the world. Apparently from the time when this sort of expensive armament was first introduced into the Far West, i.e. in the time of Charles Martel (ruled A.D. 714–741), Frankish knights relied upon a fundamentally new tactic. Instead of shooting arrows at opposing troops as their Persian and Byzantine counterparts did, the Franks relied upon a heavy lance. By charging headlong against the foe, they could put the full momentum of horse and rider behind the lance point and thus exert a comparatively enormous force that could easily break through any other sort of military formation.

Stirrups were essential to this invention. Without stirrups to stand in, leaning the entire body forward at the moment of impact, the shock of contact would sweep the rider ignominiously from his horse's back. Unfortunately, the origin and diffusion of stirrups is quite unclear. But

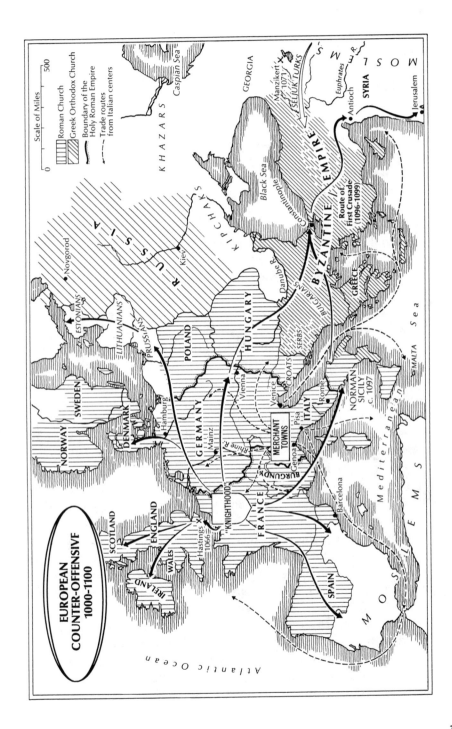

EUROPEAN
COUNTER-OFFENSIVE
1000-1100

Atlantic Ocean

Scale of Miles
0   500

	Roman Church
	Greek Orthodox Church
	Boundary of the Holy Roman Empire
	Trade routes from Italian centers

SCOTLAND
IRELAND
WALES
ENGLAND
Hastings 1066 X
"KNIGHTHOOD"

NORWAY
SWEDEN
DENMARK
Hamburg
GERMANY
Mainz
Rhine R.
MERCHANT TOWNS
BURGUNDY
FRANCE
Genoa
Pisa
ITALY
Rome

SPAIN
Barcelona

ESTONIANS
LITHUANIANS
PRUSSIANS
POLAND
Vienna
HUNGARY
Venice
CROATS
SERBS
BULGARIANS
Danube R.
NORMAN SICILY c. 1097
MALTA

Mediterranean Sea

MOSLEMS

KHAZARS
Caspian Sea

RUSSIA
Novgorod
Kiev

KIPCHAKS

Black Sea
Constantinople
BYZANTINE EMPIRE
GREECE

GEORGIA
Manzikert X 1071
SELJUK TURKS
Euphrates
Antioch
SYRIA
Jerusalem

Route of First Crusade (1096-1099)

MOSLEMS

235

it does seem certain that early in the eighth century the Franks combined stirrups, armor, big horses, and a heavy lance to produce a style of fighting man whose equal, man for man, could be found nowhere else. As long as their numbers remained very few the newfangled knights were unable to stop barbarian raiding. But need for local defense was acute and pressing. Consequently, partly by legal grant from the king or from some other public authority (duke, count) and partly by local usurpation and informal arrangement, more and more agricultural land was assigned for the support of knights. As a result, well before the year 1000 most villages of western Europe had come under the control of a professional fighting man who was equipped with a horse, lance, and armor, and a generous store of brute ferocity. The knightly class which thus came into existence proved able not merely to turn back attack but quickly took the offensive across every frontier of western Christendom.

Two other fundamental changes gave additional reach and power to the emerging medieval system of Europe's society. One was the spread of the heavy mouldboard plow, mentioned earlier (see p. 222). Agriculture based on such a plow provided the economic support needed to maintain enough knights to make Europe truly formidable. The second was the development of trade in Europe's northern seas. Pirates and sea rovers quickly discovered that trade might be advantageous when ravaging was no longer safe. Bands of itinerant merchants, seamen, and part-time pirates often found it convenient to settle down at some more or less permanent headquarters, wherever lines of communication and safe harborage created a suitable site. In this way the kernel was fashioned from which medieval town life later arose in northwestern Europe. It was most significant for the future development of Western civilization that the first European townsmen were accustomed to running their own affairs and defending themselves against all comers. This gave the middle classes of northwestern Europe a very different, more assertive style of life than was habitual among townsmen of the other civilizations, where deference to social superiors and polite catering to landowners and officials prevailed.

The combination of knighthood, the heavy plow, and a morally independent not to say aggressive mercantile population gave the Far West a set of local institutions and techniques that were both new and quite distinct from any contemporary civilization.

In this sense the "Dark Age" of European history was in fact very fruitful. New sources of mechanical power were tapped by the construction of windmills and watermills. These were not new inventions: the earliest windmills seem to have been made in central Asia to send prayers to Buddhist bodhisattvas by turning a wheel, and water mills were installed in the Tiber river near Rome in the third century to grind wheat for the populace of Rome. But Latin Christians built more of them and improved their design so that tasks that once had to be done with human or animal muscles could often be accomplished by mechanical means. Another important improvement was the horse collar, which for the first time allowed a horse to put his full strength into pulling a heavy load without choking himself. The horse collar—and horseshoes, which kept brittle hooves from splitting on hard surfaces —made it possible for European peasants to use horses as work animals; whereas in earlier times the horse had been used strictly for military purposes. Since horses move nearly twice as fast as oxen—the main alternative draught animal—use of horses for plowing and other tasks allowed a single man to accomplish nearly twice as much in the same amount of time.

The Decay of Learning

‡‡‡ Yet in another sense the Dark Age deserves its traditional name. On the European mainland, men were too busy struggling against one another to devote much energy to literature or art. In Ireland and Britain, however, a remarkable upsurge occurred which, under other circumstances, might have developed into an independent civilized style of life. The first landmark of this history was the conversion of Ireland to Christianity by St. Patrick (d. A.D. 461). Thereafter, in a number of Irish monasteries pagan traditions of oral schooling were fertilized by Latin and even Greek letters and learning. Missionaries sailed to Scotland and England; thence others visited the mainland, where they played a conspicuous part in converting the Germans, and everywhere brought a higher level of intellectual culture to the scene than anything preserved in Gaul or Germany itself. The Venerable Bede (d. A.D. 735), whose greatest work was an ecclesiastical history of England, represents one of the finest flowers of this tradition of learning. Soon after his death, Vikings destroyed the monastery where he had lived

and worked. The same fate befell all the other centers of Irish and English learning, so that by the year 900 almost nothing remained. Ireland, together with the rest of Celtic Europe, relapsed into the status of a marginal and backward participant in the wider European world.

Summary

‡‡‡ If one tries to compare Chinese, Indian, and European responses to Moslem and barbarian pressures, it seems clear that by far the most radical changes came within Europe. China, in effect, was untroubled in essentials and went its own way, returning, after a Buddhist interlude, to a restored and enriched Confucian heritage. India was more deeply affected, but reacted by withdrawing within its indigenous religious tradition. Europe, on the contrary, fought back, and in doing so transformed its most fundamental institutions and improved its techniques in a fashion that proved capable of sustaining even greater future achievements. At the time, however, Islam, China, and India far surpassed the level of European civilization, as measured by almost any conceivable standard. The Far West had in fact sunk back toward barbarism, retaining only tattered shreds of classical learning, literature, and art. Fresh creativity in these fields came only after A.D. 1000.

CHAPTER 15

The Impact of Turkish and Mongol Conquests 1000-1500

Close ties between steppe nomads and the civilized world had been a prominent feature of the centuries before A.D. 1000. During the ensuing five hundred years, this led to a series of infiltrations and conquests that brought Turkish and Mongol rulers to China, the Middle East, India, and eastern Europe. Civilized victims and subjects reacted in different ways.

The Moslems altered the emphasis and internal balance of their society and civilization in a far-reaching and strikingly successful fashion. In effect, the Moslems captured the military energy of the steppe peoples for themselves. Turkish and (much less important) Mongol recruits gave Islam a new cutting edge that established it as the ruling faith in all of India and in eastern Europe. Simultaneously, merchants and wandering holy men carried the religion of Mohammed to southeast Asia and through east and west Africa as well, and even penetrated some of China's western provinces.

The Chinese found nothing to admire in the novelties brought to their attention by Mongol conquerors, and at the first propitious moment they rallied to cast off what was always felt to be an alien and barbarian yoke. Hence the episode of Mongol rule (the Yuan dynasty,

1260–1368) left remarkably few traces behind, unless the Ming dynasty's (1368–1644) enhanced determination to value old and authentically Chinese culture can be attributed to their reaction against Mongol rule.

The great majority of Indians and orthodox Christians who found themselves under the government of Islamized Turks remained faithful to their respective religious traditions. Nevertheless, prolonged geographical intermingling provoked a good deal of interchange between the rival religious communities, despite official efforts by guardians of the faith on each side to maintain the purity of their respective versions of theological truth.

The Turkish Infiltration

‡‡‡ Before examining civilized reactions in more detail it will be well to recapitulate the course of world events. In A.D. 1000 Turkish-speaking tribes lived throughout the middle reaches of the steppe, from the Altai mountains as far west as southern Russia. In eastern Iran, extensive interpenetration between Moslem towns and cultivators and Turkish nomads had already occurred, and many Turkish tribes had accepted Islam, usually in a somewhat casual and superficial fashion. The Iranian barons who for so many centuries had held the steppe nomads at bay ceased to be effective after about A.D. 850 or 900. The reasons are obscure, but it seems possible that many moved into towns, acquired a far richer culture than their forefathers had known, and in the process lost their taste for war and hard knocks, leaving that role to Turkish mercenaries, who presently found themselves in a position to hold the Moslem heartlands of Iran, Iraq, and Syria up for ransom.

When, therefore, Turkish mercenaries and tribesmen started everywhere to dominate the political life of Islam (after about A.D. 900) the newcomers already knew a good deal about both Persian and Arab versions of Moslem culture. Yet the Turks maintained their own languages and a certain sense of military camaraderie against the rest of Islamic society. Their rule was disorderly. Detribalized military adventures competed with the unstable power of clan leaders, whose followers regularly deserted tribal discipline after a few years in a civilized environment. Rivalries and alliances among such precariously situated rulers were unusually fragile and created an endless political kaleidoscope throughout the heartland of Islam.

Nevertheless, the newcomers extended Moslem frontiers very substantially. Penetration deep into India began with massive raids launched by Mohammed of Ghazni in the year 1000. Within three centuries only the southern part of that sub-continent had escaped Moslem conquest; and in 1565 the south capitulated also when the empire of Vijayanager fell before a coalition of Moslem princes. Turkish successes against Christendom were also very great. After the battle of Manzikert (1071) the Byzantines lost control of the interior of Asia Minor to Seljuk Turks. Simultaneously other Turkish tribes (Kipchaks) pressed across what is now the Ukraine, where they cut off easy communication between Byzantium and freshly Christianized Russia. These heavy blows helped to precipitate the First Crusade (1096–99); but despite its dramatic success, this and later crusades failed to check the Turkish advance. On the contrary, when the Fourth Crusade actually attacked Constantinople and captured and sacked the city (1204), the weakness of the Byzantine state was advertised to all the world. Partial recovery—there was a Greek emperor again in Constantinople after 1261—was not sufficient to check the force of Italian commercial exploitation on the one hand and Turkish military assault on the other. The Ottoman Turks reaped the ultimate victory. They won their first foothold in Europe in 1354 by crossing the Dardanelles and seizing the peninsula of Gallipoli. After 1389, when they defeated the Serbians at the battle of Kossovo, the Turks won military supremacy in the Balkans. Not until 1453, however, when they conquered Constantinople and made it the capital of their empire, was the last trace of Byzantine power erased from the face of the earth.

The Mongol Conquest

‡‡‡ This vast tide of Turkish advance into India and Europe was punctuated in the thirteenth century by a sudden storm emanating from Mongolia. The founder of Mongol greatness was Genghis Khan (ruled 1206–27). In his youth an all but helpless refugee from local enemies, Genghis succeeded in welding together a vast military confederacy among the peoples of the steppe. He then raided successfully in every direction—southward into China, westward against the

Moslems of Iran and Iraq, and against the Christians of Russia as well. On his death the empire was divided among his four sons. They transformed the massive raiding of Genghis' time into a somewhat more stable form of political rule. For some time, there continued to be effective co-operation among the separate parts of the vast empire. Leadership rested, according to Mongol custom, with Genghis' youngest son and that son's heirs. They ruled Mongolia and China and commanded nearly the whole of the Mongol army.

In Genghis' time the Mongol tribesmen were pagan shamanists. They treated their human victims much as they treated their animals —tending or slaughtering them as convenience might dictate. But once encamped amid more cultivated peoples, the Mongols did what every other nomadic conqueror had done: they quickly took on the color of their subjects' civilization. In the western portions of their empire this meant the acceptance of Islam. In China, matters were different, for the Mongol emperors could not afford to see the armed forces upon which their power depended dissolve into the Chinese mass. The effort to hold themselves aloof from the Chinese led the Mongols to accept Tibetan Lamaism as the preferred religion of state, although a grand mixture of faiths—Christian, Moslem, shamanist, and others— continued to be represented at court. Yet the penalty of remaining distinct from the Chinese was vulnerability to native reaction, which brought the Ming dynasty to power only a century and a half after Genghis had launched his raids.

Mongol rule therefore constituted no more than an episode in China's long history. In the Middle East and Russia almost the same was true, for after an initial anti-Moslem policy the Mongols not only accepted Islam (Russia, 1257; Persia, 1295) but rapidly assimilated themselves to the Turkish community, which was already dominant everywhere on the central and western steppe. There were too few Mongols and their culture was too crude to permit any other result. Hence in the fourteenth and fifteenth centuries Islamized Turkish warriors, often led by captains who claimed descent from Genghis Khan, again pressed forward against Christendom and Hindustan. The Moslem world had by then largely recovered from the set-back wrought by the pagan Mongol conquest of the thirteenth century. Baghdad, however, and the irrigation system that made Iraq fertile, were not restored. Mongol destruction had been too great. As a result, the former seat of the caliphate remained in ruins until the twentieth century.

The Ottoman Empire

‡‡‡ By far the most durable and important of the new states that arose in the course of this renewed Turkish offensive was the Ottoman empire. It originated as a small frontier principality in northwestern Asia Minor. Turkish warriors flocked to the service of the Ottoman sultan from all over the Moslem world, because his raids against Christian territory made religious merit and heroic exercise of violence coincide, as was true nowhere else in the Moslem world. Under these circumstances territorial advance became rapid, especially after 1354, when the Turks made their first permanent lodgment across the straits in Europe. Presently, the Sultan faced difficulty in commanding the loyalty and obedience of his followers, who had been assigned conquered lands on the usual feudal pattern. The Ottoman rulers met this difficulty by expanding their personal household into a standing army. This became the famous janissary (i.e. "new troops") corps. Its members, together with the officers who commanded them, were legally classed as slaves. So were the specially trained and selected men who went out into the provinces as agents of the Sultan and took command of local Moslem landowners and warriors when they were called up for active service with the Sultan in war. Since these special slave commanders were backed up by the janissary corps and by the Sultan himself, their commands were usually obeyed. The Ottoman state therefore had at its disposal both an effective standing army, the janissaries, and an obedient feudal army of Turkish warriors.

Personnel for the Sultan's slave family numbered several thousand. At first, war captives provided most of the needed manpower, supplemented by purchases from commercial slave dealers. But soon this method of recruitment proved inadequate. The Turkish Sultan therefore fell back upon rough-and-ready conscription among the Christian villages of the remote Balkans. Thus it happened that young men born as Serb, Greek, or Albanian peasants in the western mountain zone of the Balkan peninsula provided a strategically decisive element in the military and administrative cadres of the Ottoman empire.

No other Moslem state achieved such a remarkable and effective internal organization; and none played anything like the role in world affairs that the Ottoman empire was to do.

We shall now examine a little more closely the reactions of each of the major civilized communities to Turkish and/or Mongol rule.

Islam—the Sufi Movement

‡‡‡ The Abassid caliphs had become mere puppets and playthings of Turkish mercenary captains long before the Mongols, in capturing Baghdad (1258), put an end to the caliphate and to the pretense of a single jurisdiction over all Moslems. Under such circumstances, the principles and compromises upon which classical Islam rested lost their plausibility. What, indeed, was the use of the entire effort to shape a society in accordance with Allah's express will and command as revealed to Mohammed and his companions if brutal deceit and impiety brazenly flaunted themselves in the seats of the mighty? The private sphere remained, and here the doctors of the Sacred Law continued as before to guide personal conduct by giving opinions on difficult cases in accordance with the elaborate precedents they so carefully gathered and studied. But in all this effort there remained a gaping hole: for the Sacred Law could no longer be stretched by any feat of the imagination to legitimize the political chaos that prevailed almost everywhere in the Moslem world.

Such a logically imperfect and increasingly routine approach to holiness could not sustain the authentic fires of conviction which had fueled the first Moslem centuries. Instead, seekers after holiness increasingly drifted into mysticism. A great variety of holy men—or Sufi as they were termed—cultivated the beatific vision of God. They adhered to diverse disciplines. Followers gathered round a man of unusual holiness and sometimes thereby founded a dervish order that might last for centuries and spread over wide regions of the Moslem world. In other cases such associations disbanded again, leaving no trace. But organizational fuzziness did nothing to obscure the vision of God which, when experienced personally by scores of thousands of men, gave the Sufi movement an emotional force and vivacity which "official" Islam had lost.

Conversion to Islam became comparatively easy when the first step was reverence for and imitation of Sufi holy men who walked familiarly with God. It was no longer the case that acceptance of an elaborate law code and radical changes of private life were needful before becoming a Moslem. Instead, the remodeling of private life to accord with the Sacred Law came along afterwards, and only after Sufi mystics had brought initiates into the Moslem fold. The success with which Asia Minor was made into a Moslem land, the geographically far more extensive conversion of the western and central steppes to Islam, the substantial penetration of India by Islamic sects, the annexation of large parts of east and west Africa to the Moslem world, and, not least, the conversion of nearly all the Christians remaining within the Syrian and Egyptian heartland of Islam all resulted from the new momentum Sufi mystics imparted to Mohammed's creed.

Previously, Islam had been a city religion. Indeed, some of the ritual prescriptions of the Sacred Law could not be met in rural isolation. But when reverence for "saints," homage at their tombs, and a spectator's part in ecstasy-inducing dervish rituals became the first step toward membership in the Moslem community, then simple country folk could share the faith with urban sophisticates. In other words, something like the gradation and variety of religious practice and outlook which had long characterized Hinduism permeated Islam. Indeed, insofar as the mysticism of the Middle East retained traces of Indian origins, one may describe the triumph of the Sufi path as an Indianization of Islam.

Sufism also worked important changes within the fabric of Islamic high culture. Its greatest success was in suffusing the gentlemanly and courtly ideal of early Islam with the delicate ambiguity of heavenly as opposed to carnal love. Persian poetry became the supreme vehicle of this semi-religious, semi-secular sensibility. The three great poets were Rumi (d. 1273), founder of an important Sufi order; Sa'di (d. 1291); and Hafiz (d. 1390). They, with some lesser luminaries, created a body of poetry which soon became part of the education of all cultivated Moslems. Persian thus displaced Arabic as the leading poetic language of the Moslem world. Arabic, however, remained supreme for all sacred matters, while Turkish was reserved for war and administration.

In the intellectual sphere, the impact of Sufism was less happy, though no less great. Men who themselves saw God in visions were not much interested in mere human reasonings. Kings and successful captains continued to need the services of doctors and astrologers, and these professions therefore continued to flourish. Systematization set in with men like ibn-Sina (Avicenna, d. 1037), who wrote a widely used *Canon* of medicine, and al-Biruni (d. 1048), who deliberately sought to synthesize Indian, Greek, and Moslem thought, in the hope of thereby mastering all knowledge. Perhaps the systematizers were too successful. What after all remained for any doctor of medicine to investigate once so comprehensive a professional handbook as that of ibn-Sina had been compiled? Or perhaps, by fastening attention upon mystical penetration of reality the Sufi adepts deprived mere outward scientific investigation of any attraction for men of sensitive intelligence. Whatever the reasons, Moslem science withered after about 1200.

Disinclination from and distrust of reason found its own systematic expositor in the person of al-Ghazali (d. 1111), who used Aristotelian logic to demonstrate the impossibility of discovering the truths of theology by human reasoning. His book, *The Destruction of Philosophy*, as its title implies, expressly repudiated the value of logic as a path toward truth. Yet, mystics could not entirely refrain from talking and writing about their supra-rational experiences. From such discussion there emerged a complex analysis of the stages and nature of mystical reality which had many of the characteristics of a reasoned, theologico-philosophic system. This sort of Sufi learning hardened toward fixed forms after about 1200, in much the same way as the Sacred Law of Islam had done about 350 years before.

As this occurred, Moslem minds encased themselves in twin (and mutually quite incompatible) mausoleums. By remarkable ill fortune, they did so just as men of western Europe were beginning to embark upon the restless investigations and inquiries of medieval and modern times. Thus, by a striking paradox, such rigorous and challenging thinkers as the Spanish Moslem ibn-Rushd (Latin: Averroës, d. 1198) and the Egyptian Jew Maimonides (d. 1204), both of whom found central inspiration in the philosophy of Aristotle, were almost disregarded in the Moslem world, whereas they both had powerful influence upon the emerging Scholastic philosophy of Paris.

In summary, we may say that Sufism succeeded in merging the rationalistic tradition inherited from the Greeks, the genteel tradition inherited from Arab and Persian aristocrats, and the sacred tradition inherited from Mohammed into a single, and far more coherent, whole than had been achieved in Abbasid times. When one adds to this the fact that Sufi missionaries introduced Islam to an area more than twice the size of the Abbasid empire, something of the magnitude and success of the movement can be appreciated, even by those for whom the mystic path has no attraction.

Fine Arts

‡‡‡ The Sufi movement was matched by the rise of impressive and distinctive Moslem styles of architecture and painting. Among Moslems architecture was always more important than painting, since religion itself required the construction of mosques and other public buildings. But because nearly all the important centers of Islamic life have been continuously inhabited to the present, details of the architectural past are often unsure. Buildings have been repaired and remodeled from time to time, and old ruins have sometimes been buried under structures which cannot be disturbed by the archaeologist's spade. Nevertheless, where careful study has established dates and the sequences of style—as, for example, in Cairo—it is clear that the size, magnificence, skill of workmanship, and accuracy of detail, together with the artistic success of the structure over-all, tended to increase throughout the five centuries with which we are now concerned. Islamic architects were no longer, as in the first days of Ommayad rule, dependent on Greek or Persian models, but had a style of their own in which "arabesque" linear decoration played a prominent part.

Pious Moslems always disdained the art of painting since portrayal of the human figure invited idolatry. Nevertheless, a school of illuminators arose in Persia whose miniatures usually illustrated manuscripts of the great Persian poets. The bright colors, minute detail, and linear elaboration of these paintings rank them among the most sophisticated and perfect of the world. The best such work, all anonymous, was done in palace workshops between 1400 and 1600. Other arts—carpet weaving for example—reached a comparable level of refinement and allowed the rulers of the land to surround themselves with a splendor that amazed and impressed the first crude European intruders who encountered it.

India—Changes in Hinduism

‡‡‡ The Moslem conquest of India had a serious impact upon Hinduism. To be sure, the conquerors fitted into the Hindu social system without straining it unduly, becoming another caste, just as earlier conquerors had done. But Islam, being a universal and missionary faith, systematically resisted the Indian caste system. Moslem doctrine held that all men were equally puny before the omnipotence of Allah and equally precious in his eyes. Hence, it is not surprising that itinerant Sufi holy men, preaching Islam, met with considerable success in attracting low-caste urban Hindus to the faith of Mohammed. Along the frontiers of Indian society also, especially in eastern Bengal, newcomers to Indian civilization tended to prefer Islam, with its equalitarian emphasis, to Hinduism, which placed them near the bottom of the caste hierarchy. Moreover, the reproach of idolatry which Moslems leveled against traditional Hindu piety was not easy to meet, even though refined philosophical systems could explain and justify India's age-old multiplicity of cult practices.

Hence the Islamic community in India came to be divided between a thin layer of rulers, warriors, and landowners—many of them Persian in culture and Turkish in origin—and a much more numerous company of poor and humble local peoples, who inevitably brought with them into Islam much of their own local cultural heritage. As a result, Indian Islam remained quite distinct from the Islam of Arabic-speaking Moslems of the Middle East.

Hinduism itself altered in three main directions under Moslem rule. First of all, Moslem invaders pillaged the temples around which Hindu cult practices had begun to crystallize. Moslem rulers usually refused to allow such idolatrous structures to be rebuilt. Hence only in southern India do Hindu temples survive with anything like the splendor and elaboration they once attained all over the land. Driven from the ruined temples, Hindu religious ceremonies took on a more public and plebeian character, often taking place in a public square or forming processions that wound their way through town and village streets. Holy men, enjoying an ecstatic communion with Vishnu, Shiva, or some other member of the Hindu pantheon, became the key figures of Hinduism. Inasmuch as Hindu saints saw God with the same vividness as Sufi mystics, Islam enjoyed no emotional superiority over Hinduism on Indian ground. Hence, in general it was only the fringes of Indian society that were attracted to Islam.

Secondly, a few individuals found the intellectual challenge of Islam too immediate to be passed by merely on the strength of warm emotional attachments to the Hindu pantheon and rituals. Venturesome thinkers attempted to synthesize Hinduism and Islam, repudiating what they felt to be false in each system and retaining the common core of truth that each of the rival faiths had buried under false accretions. The most famous such religious innovator was Kabir (d. 1518). Nanak, who probably was a disciple of Kabir's in his youth, founded the Sikh faith on the basis of a similar blending and "purification" of the Hindu and Moslem traditions.

In the third place, the Sanskrit language in which Hinduism had wrapped itself so enthusiastically during the Gupta age was generally discarded. Vernacular tongues—Hindi and others—came into use for all religious purposes. Sanskrit sank back toward being the precious possession of a learned few; while popular Hindu piety almost lost sight of its ancient Sanskrit base.

These changes all had the effect of bringing Hinduism closer to the population at large, while cutting away courtly and priestly elaboration. This surely helped to assure the survival of Hinduism. It also cost Hindu civilization a great deal, for all the more costly and official aspects of culture became Moslem. From an architectural point of view, India became a province of the Islamic world, nothing more. And without royal and princely patronage, Hindi literature failed to develop a secular counterpart to the hymns and other religious texts which dominate (perhaps disproportionately) our record of India's past.

Orthodox Christendom

‡‡‡ The separation between Latin (Roman Catholic) and Greek (Orthodox) Christendom achieved formal and lasting definition in 1054, when the pope and the patriarch of Constantinople anathematized each other, thus creating a schism which has endured until the present. The occasion of the quarrel was a difference of opinion about the proper phrasing of the Apostles' Creed; but the distinction between the two halves of Christendom ran very deep, and the gap widened when a new and vigorous civilization began to arise in western Europe, in

which the Greek Orthodox had no real share. Instead, as the Latin west increased in wealth, power, culture, and self-confidence, eastern Christendom became one of the victims of Latin expansive energy.

The Orthodox world's loss of Asia Minor and of southern Russia to Turkish invaders was noticed above (p. 241). This two-pronged assault coincided with a similar double thrust from the west. Italian merchant traders came by sea; Norman knights seized southern Italy (by 1071) and Sicily (by 1091) from the Byzantines, and then crossed the Adriatic to march overland against Constantinople. Byzantine diplomacy was able to parry this first thrust from the west by diverting the formidable "Franks" to the Holy Land, where they could expend their ferocity on Byzantium's other dangerous enemy, the Turks. The result was the First Crusade, 1096–99. Later, however, the Greeks were less fortunate. The climax came in 1204 when the Fourth Crusade actually captured the city of Constantine, and left behind a short-lived Latin empire of the Levant.

From the point of view of Orthodox Christians, Moslem Turks were definitely preferable to Latin Christians. The Latins insisted on trying to force the Orthodox Christians to accept their version of Christian doctrine at the expense of the immutable truths of Orthodoxy. The Moslems, on the contrary, were prepared to allow Christians of whatever persuasion to continue to follow their accustomed rites. Moreover, the theologians of the church officially classified Islam as Christian heresy: hence Moslem error was really no worse theologically than Latin schism. In addition, the Ottoman Turks, when they first appeared in the Balkans, were much less oppressive tax gatherers than their Christian predecessors had been. The Turks, indeed, in accordance with the Sacred Law gave their Christian subjects far wider local autonomy that they were likely to enjoy under any Christian ruler. Every consideration, therefore, predisposed the Orthodox Christians to opt for Turkish Moslems against Latin Christians if and when choice between the two became necessary. The option expired in 1453 when Constantinople fell to the Turks. Nearly the same factors applied further north in the Russian forests, where such a ruler as Alexander Nevsky (d. 1263) resisted Latin conquest heroically and then tamely submitted to the Mongols.

Before succumbing to the Ottoman Turks, however, the Greek Christians launched a rather vigorous Hellenic renaissance. Memories of classical Greece and of the pagan age of Rome had never entirely disappeared, but after about A.D. 1000 Byzantine artists and literary men began to cherish the past glories of paganism as never before. Art imitative of classical models and literary composition in every mode established by the ancient Greeks were deliberately revived, with varying degrees of success. The *Alexiad*, a history written in verse by Anna Comnena, daughter of the emperor Alexis (reigned 1081–1118), is one of the most distinguished products of this effort. Very different was the rough border balladry, recounting the deeds of heroes fighting against the Moslems, which provided the raw material for the anonymous epic, *Digenes Akritas*, whose rude heroic spirit appeals to modern taste more strongly than does the somewhat artificial learning of the Byzantine upper classes. The Turkish conquest of Constantinople in 1453 abruptly throttled all varieties of secular Byzantine literature; but echoes of the Hellenic renaissance were felt in Italy, and constituted a significant stimulant to the far more fruitful Italian renaissance, which lagged about two centuries behind the Byzantine revival.

In the ecclesiastical sphere, an interesting change occurred within the Greek Orthodox church just after the Turks established themselves in Europe. A monkish party of mystic visionaries, the Hesychasts, overthrew the "Politicians" who had previously controlled the patriarchate and other high offices of the church. Thenceforward, bishops and all other high ecclesiastical dignitaries were recruited exclusively from monasteries, a practice which was not followed in the Latin church. The victory of the monkish party—inspired by personal visions of God—infused a popular, emotionally powerful spirit into the Orthodox community at the time when the Turks took over control of most of the Balkan hinterland. As a result, conversion to Islam, which had occurred very generally in Asia Minor and had begun to occur also on the European side of the straits, came almost to a halt, thus assuring the survival of a Christian majority in the Balkans.

The northern offshoot of Orthodox Christendom, Holy Russia, underwent a slow but very significant development during the period of Mongol rule (1240–1480). Agriculture crept deep into the forest, back from the river banks where the population had first congregated. Little by little great areas of ground were cleared for farming. This allowed a comparatively numerous, though extremely poor, peasantry to establish itself despite the inhospitable soil and severe climate.

Politically, the Mongols were content to farm out taxes, first to corporations of central Asian merchants and then to native Russian

MOSLEM DOMINATION OF ORTHODOX CHRISTENDOM to 1453

Venetian possessions

■ Trading centers under control of Genoa

- - - - Italian trade routes

SWEDEN

Baltic Sea

DENMARK

ORDER

TEUTONIC

HOLY ROMAN EMPIRE

POLAND

Vienna

HUNGARY

Danube R.

Venice

SERBIA
Kossovo
1389 ✗

Rome

KDM. OF NAPLES

Novgorod

CHRISTENDOM

MOSCOW

Volga R.

Moscow

TURKS AND MONGOLS
(1227-1480)

LITHUANIA
(1263-1386)

Kiev

Dnieper R.

KIPCHAKS

ORTHODOX

Black Sea

Adrianople

Constantinople
✗1453

Brusa

OTTOMAN EMPIRE

ASIA MINOR

Manzikert
1071 ✗

Tigris R.

TURKS (from 1071)

Mediterranean

Sea

CRETE

CYPRUS

SYRIA

Euphrates R.

PALESTINE

SULTANATE

MAMELUK
EGYPT

ARABIA

Nile R.

Red Sea

Scale of Miles

0   500

princes, of whom the Grand Duke of Moscow became the chief. As agent for a harsh though distant taskmaster, the Grand Duke of Moscow created an administrative bureaucracy of tax gatherers. The result was that in 1480, when Ivan III repudiated Mongol suzerainty, he had a ready-made administrative machine at his command. Moscow thus became the only great and independent Orthodox state. Russian churchmen soon developed the idea that Moscow was the Third Rome, succeeding Constantinople as Constantinople had succeeded the first Rome on the Tiber, because only in Russia had Orthodoxy remained pure and undefiled. Ever since then the notion that Russia was uniquely chosen for the special mission of guarding the true faith on earth has never ceased to play a part in Russian public life, not least since the Communist revolution of 1917.

China–the Triumph of Tradition

‡‡‡ As already explained, the outward appearance of Chinese civilization was remarkably little affected by the episode of Mongol domination. Neo-Confucianism attained its full development under the later Sung, when the greatest philosopher of this school, Chu Hsi (1130–1200), flourished. But the whole effort of Chu Hsi and his fellow literati was to remain faithful to the ancients, as Confucius himself had tried to be. Hence innovation was never consciously admitted, whether in thought or in art, in manners or in government.

Nevertheless, in the eleventh and twelfth centuries something approaching the sort of economic development that transformed western Europe after the eighteenth century almost came to pass in China. Thus, for example, the Chinese built up a massive iron industry using coal for fuel some seven hundred years before England did the same. Simultaneously, regional specialization created the basis for an expanding trade within the country; and sea-going ships, sailing for the most part from south China ports, began to develop overseas commerce on a scale never before approached.

Confucian principles, of course, regarded merchants as parasites. Hence when a man got rich from trade, he was tempted to buy land and become respectable. Perhaps for this reason, really large-scale private commercial and industrial enterprises never arose in China; and the beginnings of what might be called a proto-industrial revolution failed in the end to change older social patterns.

Official control of economic activity was another factor inhibiting a really far-reaching transformation of society. Even when officials backed a new form of enterprise, the effect was sometimes blighting in the long run. Thus the iron industry that developed under the Sung seems to have simply ended when government orders for arms ceased. An even more dramatic example of how official control could first encourage and then halt a new sort of enterprise is seen in the history of overseas trade and exploration. Early in the Ming period (1368–1644) long distance sea voyaging was brought under official control. Results were spectacular. Between 1405 and 1433 a court eunuch named Cheng-ho launched a series of expeditions into the Indian Ocean, in the course of which truly imperial fleets of several hundred vessels visited all the strategic gateways to the southern seas—Malacca, Ceylon, Calicut, and even Hormuz at the mouth of the Persian Gulf—and temporarily established Chinese control over most of these places. Then the Ming emperor ordered the expeditions stopped, and forbade Chinese subjects from building sea-going vessels or leaving the country. Court intrigues between rival cliques may have had something to do with this decision, so pregnant for the future commercial and imperial balance of power in Asia. But basically the Ming rulers, from their capital at Peking near the ever-dangerous Mongol border, felt that imperial resources should not be squandered on such distant enterprises when the need for protection against the nomads required all the strength the government could muster.

This deliberate abdication from an active role in the southern seas condemned Chinese overseas colonies to speedy decay. Mastery of the seas passed to Japanese and Malay pirates, who soon made the coasts of China unsafe for peaceable shipping. From time to time they even succeeded in interrupting transport on the Grand Canal by penetrating inland along China's numerous waterways.

The fact that officials could override the self-interest of merchants and seamen in this fashion attests the power of Chinese officialdom in economic and social matters. That power was fundamentally sustained by the fact that the landlord-gentry class, from which most officials came and whose interests Confucianism had long defended, maintained an easy dominance in Chinese society as a whole, even in the centuries when new mercantile wealth developed most rapidly. This was possible because agricultural wealth increased as fast or faster than industrial and commercial activity, even in the eleventh and twelfth centuries. The secret of this agricultural advance was the introduction (about A.D. 1000) of a new variety of rice which could ripen quickly enough to permit double cropping on well-watered land. Even more important, early ripening rice could mature successfully on hilly ground where water was available for the paddy fields only during a short period of the spring run-off. The total agricultural productivity of China was thereby greatly enlarged, especially in the far south, where hilly ground, previously unsuited to rice growing, prevailed. Hence, as trade and commerce prospered, so did the landowning gentry. Their numbers and weight in society presumably increased more or less equally with the increase in the importance of merchants and artisans. Then, with the overthrow of the Mongol rulers who had been special patrons and protectors of merchants (witness Marco Polo), the stage was set for the native Ming dynasty first to organize and then officially to throttle China's overseas trade.

The social dominance of the gentry class meant that even such potentially disturbing inventions as gunpowder (reported in Chinese sources from about 1100), printing (invented 756), and the magnetic compass (first mentioned early twelfth century) were kept under control and used simply to strengthen the existing social order. Printing, for example, widened the circle of Confucian literati; it was not employed to bring unorthodox novelties to public attention, as happened so dramatically in Reformation Europe. Gunpowder, similarly, made suppression of local warlords easier than before and allowed the imperial government to maintain a more or less effective central control over all of China (with only a few brief periods of breakdown) from the time the Ming dynasty completed the expulsion of the Mongols until 1911. Nothing could be more traditional.

Chinese culture and institutions had, in short, attained such inner perfection and balance that nothing short of wholesale social breakdown, of a sort that did not occur in China until the twentieth century, sufficed to make more than a superficial, transitory impression upon the bearers of the Chinese learned tradition. The myth of immutability, so eagerly accepted by nineteenth-century Europeans, fed upon this fact, overlooking earlier times and aspects of Chinese society which continued to alter, even when the government and official culture remained frozen to the ideal of Confucian propriety.

CHAPTER 16

Medieval Europe and Japan

1000-1500

 The self-transformation and expansion of Islam was the most dramatic and conspicuous shift in world history that took place between A.D. 1000 and 1500. A second change, even more significant for the future, was the rise of two new civilizations on the extreme flanks of the civilized world, in northwestern Europe and in Japan.

Both were closely related to adjacent, older, and more sophisticated civilizations: Japan to China and western Europe to Byzantium. Both Japan and Europe also exhibited a pronounced militarism, which penetrated all ranks of society in a fashion elsewhere unknown among civilized peoples. This imparted a degree of formidability vis-à-vis their more polished neighbors that allowed both Europeans and Japanese to borrow whatever they felt good from these same neighbors without surrendering their sense of superiority and cultural individuality by doing so. Unusual flexibility and capacity for growth resulted, so that by about 1500 both medieval Europe and Japan had arrived at a level of culture and style of civilization that in most respects could bear comparison with any other in the world.

Medieval Europe

‡‡‡ By the year 1000 the inhabitants of northwestern Europe possessed a comparatively numerous knightly class whose armament and training gave them man-to-man superiority over any other military force in the world. Manorial agriculture, based upon the mouldboard plow, provided an adequate economic support for society as a whole. There was a further advantage in that it could readily be enlarged by clearing additional woodlands, which everywhere lay close at hand. Finally, energetic and enterprising townsmen, and a church which had inherited an elaborate theological doctrine from antiquity, stood ready to organize and advance economic and cultural life.

Western Europe's improved posture was demonstrated most dramatically by geographical expansion across every frontier confining Latin Christendom. The effective incorporation of Scandinavia and the western Celtic fringe into the European body social was an affair of centuries, but the conversion of Norway and of Iceland (1000) together with the invasion of Wales and Ireland (1171) by Anglo-Norman knights made the ultimate upshot clear. In an eastward direction, German knights conquered and colonized a broad belt of territory east of the Elbe river; others used ships to leap-frog along the Baltic coast, conquering Prussia, Livonia (modern Latvia), and Estonia, but failed (1241–44) in an attempt to penetrate and subdue the Russian interior. Poland and Hungary withstood the German pressure only by imitating the armament of German knights and by importing German (and Jewish) townsmen to provide essential artisan and mercantile services. In so doing, of course, these outposts of Latin Christendom became far more firmly incorporated into western European society than before.

The most significant frontier for Latin Christendom lay to the south and east, for here Moslem and Byzantine neighbors had something more than barbarian hardihood and backwardness to contribute to European civilization. The Norman conquest of southern Italy and Sicily (1059–91) brought formerly Byzantine soil under papal and "Frankish" rule.* A long-drawn-out advance of Christian power in

* All Latin Christians were called "Franks" by Byzantines and Moslems. The term is useful as an indicator of the cultural watershed separating them from their eastern and southern neighbors.

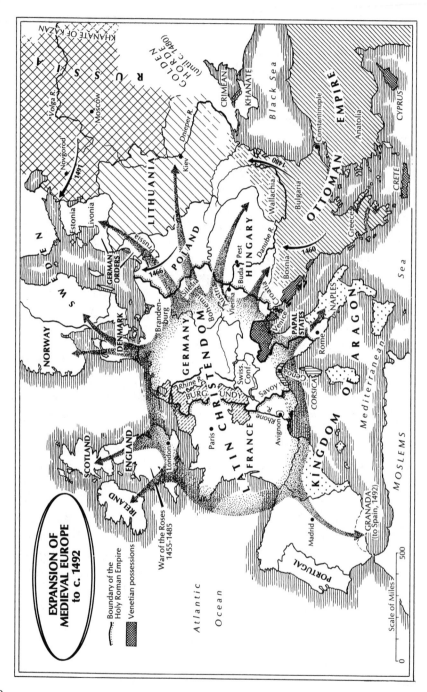

EXPANSION OF
MEDIEVAL EUROPE
to c. 1492

⌇⌇⌇ Boundary of the
Holy Roman Empire

▦ Venetian possessions

War of the Roses
1455–1485

Scale of Miles

0   500

Atlantic
Ocean

SCOTLAND

IRELAND

ENGLAND
London

Paris

LATIN CHRISTENDOM

FRANCE

Avignon

Rhône R.

Savoy

Swiss.
Conf.

BURGUNDY

Rhine R.

GERMANY

Brandenburg

DENMARK

NORWAY

SWEDEN

Estonia

Livonia

GERMAN
ORDERS

Prussia

1466

Novgorod
1491

Volga R.

MOSCOW

R U S S I A

KHANATE OF KAZAN

LITHUANIA

POLAND

Silesia

Bohemia

Austria

Vienna

Buda
Pest

HUNGARY

Styria

Danube R.

Croatia

Bosnia

Wallachia

Bulgaria

Greece

CRIMEA

KHANATE

1480

Dnieper R.

Kiev

GOLDEN
HORDE
(until 1480)

Black Sea

Constantinople

Anatolia

OTTOMAN EMPIRE

1460

CRETE

CYPRUS

Venice

PAPAL
STATES

Rome

Genoa

CORSICA

NAPLES

KINGDOM OF ARAGON

Mediterranean   Sea

MOSLEMS

GRANADA
(to Spain, 1492)

Madrid

PORTUGAL

258

Spain and Portugal also rolled back the Moslem frontier bit by bit, until Granada, the last Moorish stronghold on the European side of the straits, was overrun in 1492. These conquests were more lasting than the spectacular crusading ventures to the Holy Land, the Aegean, north Africa, and Egypt, which led to the establishment of Europe's first overseas empires. These empires, nonetheless, weathered innumerable ups and downs across the centuries until the last of them disappeared in 1797 with the extinction of the Venetian republic by Napoleon Bonaparte.

Geographical expansion abroad was matched by a great work of consolidation at home. Consolidation proceeded in every walk of life, and won spectacular successes, yet never quite sufficed to fix European institutions and cultural patterns in an enduring mold. The unusual mutability of European (more recently of Western) civilization is, indeed, its most distinctive characteristic. No sooner had the restless West worked out a potentially "classic" style of life, as happened for the first time during the medieval period, than with great tribulation that particular ordering of society and culture was discarded. Then, after a time of troubles, another potentially "classic" mould emerged only to encounter the same fate. No other civilization of the world has undergone spontaneous and repeated mutation in this fashion, though as we shall see, the sudden turns and shifts of Japanese cultural history have been quite as drastic and a good deal more abrupt than anything in European experience. The difference lies in the fact that the major shifts of Japanese history came in response to circumstances others had created, whereas Europeans responded mainly to dilemmas and opportunities of their own making.

The geographical reversal which dates from the opening of the oceans to commerce, whereby what had before been remote and isolated extremities of the civilized world became instead strategically open to every sort of foreign sea-borne influence, does much to explain the recent instability of European and Japanese history. Deep-seated discrepancies, producing internal polarities and tensions within the two civilizations, also help to account for what happened.

Europe's Economic Consolidation

‡‡‡ Clearing of forest, founding of new villages, and expansion of the cultivated fields surrounding old ones went ahead rapidly in north-

western Europe from about A.D. 900 until the middle of the fourteenth century. Then, at least in some parts of the continent, the ravages of the Black Death (1347–51), together with more obscure changes in markets, rents, and taxes, halted or even reversed agricultural expansion. By that time, nearly all the easily cultivated land of Europe had been put to the plow. Further agricultural improvements required new crops, ditching and draining, or other expensive innovations which, for a while, were not forthcoming.

Town life exhibited the same general curve. Very rapid upthrust occurred between 1000 and about 1300. Thereafter, growth slowed, or stopped entirely, save in certain special regions, such as along the Baltic coast of Germany or in central and northern Italy, where vigorous commercial exploitation of the new Baltic and Levantine "empires" that had been created by German and Frankish knighthood continued to sustain important urban development until after 1400. Thereafter major economic innovation tended to concentrate more in central Germany and the Low Countries, where mining and the herring fisheries gave a special fillip to increasingly large-scale capitalist enterprise.

The outstanding characteristic of European commerce was the great importance of rude and vulgar commodities. Articles of rather wide consumption, like woolen cloth, grain, herring, and iron, entered interregional trade. Luxuries and fine articles designed for the rich constituted only a minor part of the stream of European commerce. In most of the civilized world, transport was so costly that long-distance trade was pretty much confined to articles of high value in proportion to their bulk. Europeans could afford to move much less valuable goods to distant markets because intrusive seas and long, slow-moving streams made water transport available to very large parts of the European countryside. Shipping was of course, very much cheaper than transport overland, which, in the absence of well-maintained roads, had to be conducted by animal pack trains.

Neither India nor the Middle East had as dense a network of natural waterways as Europe, but China's canals and rivers and Japan's indented coastline offered facilities for water transport about as good as those of the Far West. Nevertheless, as we saw in the preceding chapter, the social structure of China was so dominated by officials and landlords as to prevent the free development of shipping and trade. As for the Japanese, they did not take to the sea on a large scale until after

1300. Then, early in the seventeenth century, after a heroic period of sea roving, the government, as in China, forbade all naval enterprise. Hence it was only in Europe that an aggressive merchant class confronted the technical potentialities of sea transport in a geographically propitious environment without being hampered by hostile officialdom.

From about 1000, Europeans were therefore in a uniquely favorable position to exploit their natural waterways to bring articles of common everyday consumption to market. To be sure, improvements in ship building and navigation were necessary before the stormy and tide-beset waters of northwestern Europe became reasonably safe for shipping. Critical improvements in seamanship were made during the Viking age, when, for example, the much more efficient stern rudder supplanted the steering oar. Thereafter as shipping grew and flourished, all the advantages of economic specialization, which Adam Smith was later to describe in his *Wealth of Nations*, accrued to medieval Europe. Trade and commerce affected almost every rank of society, since peasants as well as townsmen and landowners could afford to buy some of their tools and other necessities from petty traders, artisans, or shopkeepers. In other words, the market penetrated deeper into the tissues of European society than it did in land-fast Asian communities. Correspondingly, European manufactures catered to a cruder level of taste and a cheaper market than was usual elsewhere.

Political Consolidation

‡‡‡ Throughout the Middle Ages a confusing variety of overlapping jurisdictions competed for sovereignty. The Pope in Rome and the imperial heirs and successors of Charlemagne each claimed universal leadership over all Christendom—meaning, in practice, over Latin Christendom alone. National monarchs, feudal princes, local landowners of every degree, as well as towns and (on the fringes of Europe) even clans and free villages, all competed with one another for authority, rights, immunities, and jurisdictions.

We can distinguish three phases of Europe's political evolution between 1000 and 1500. During the first period, the emperor (i.e. the ruler of Germany whose title derived from Charlemagne's usurpation), supported by most German and some Italian bishops, sought to keep all more local sovereignties in check. In practice the kingdoms of

France, England, Spain, Scotland, Scandinavia, Poland, and Hungary were always free to go their own ways. The emperors had more than enough to do in trying to rule Italy and Germany. During the second period, beginning in 1059, the papacy took the lead in seeking to purify and reform the Church. Among other matters, this reform deprived the emperor of his customary right to appoint the bishops of Germany and (parts of) Italy. A long struggle ensued, in the course of which the popes allied themselves with the new-sprung Norman kingdom of southern Italy and with Italian towns of central and northern Italy, in order to find the military strength needed to resist sporadic invasions from the north launched by a succession of indignant German emperors. By 1254, however, the imperial power had utterly collapsed and the papacy was left as the only claimant to the universal government of Latin Christendom.

Papal authority soon collided with the national monarchies of France and England, both of which had before usually stood in loose alliance with the papacy as a form of insurance against the German emperor's claims to supreme authority over Christendom. In 1303 the new balance of power was dramatically demonstrated when agents of the French king kidnapped Pope Boniface VIII, yet met with neither divine nor human retribution. Soon thereafter the popes and kings of western Europe struck a bargain whereby the papacy gave up its claims to appoint bishops without consulting the king, while the king in return agreed to allow papal agents to collect specified taxes and dues from the clergy of the realm. In effect, kings and popes collaborated in reducing the powers and independence of lesser local jurisdictions, specifically seeking to diminish the rights and powers of local nobles, both lay and ecclesiastical.

In Germany and Italy, however, things went the other way. Small city-states and various princely jurisdictions acquired most of the attributes of sovereignty. In 1273, after a long interregnum, Rudolf of Hapsburg was elected emperor. Thereafter, with only a few exceptions, members of the Hapsburg family continued to occupy the imperial office until 1806, when it was abolished. Their power, however, rested not so much on the imperial title as upon hereditary lands, while centered around Austria in southeastern Germany.

Soon after the empire thus limply revived, its victorious rival, the papacy, suffered a serious set-back. Pope Clement V and his successors set up their residence at Avignon in southern France (1307), thereby becoming the close allies and at times almost the agents of the French king. Efforts to remedy this situation resulted in the establishment of rival popes in Avignon and Rome (1378–1417). Unity was restored only by means of a general council of bishops, summoned to meet in the Swiss city of Constance by the Emperor Sigismund (1414–17). Nothing resembling universal papal monarchy could survive such an experience.

Before turning attention to the cultural consolidation of medieval Europe, a word should be said about the development of representative and parliamentary government. This distinctive political institution had two principal roots. On the one hand, canon law held that bishops should be elected by the clergy of their cathedral church, and that matters of general concern should be settled by meetings of church leaders, whether in a local synod or in a general council. Particularly during the fourteenth century, when rival popes claimed supremacy over the Church, ecclesiastical reformers developed elaborate arguments in favor of settling the question through a council. Some went on to argue that all legitimate authority derived from consent of the governed, expressed through designated or elected representatives. Such ideas were readily transferrable to secular government, where the traditional relationships between a ruler and his followers provided a second root from which parliamentary institutions grew. Princes of every degree had to consult their subordinates and servants from time to time, particularly before undertaking any important new enterprise. Originally such consultation served two main functions: the settlement of quarrels among the prince's followers, and deliberation about whether to undertake a particular military campaign. To this was presently added the grant of "aids," i.e. of money payments needed by the prince for some public undertaking.

Aids tended to become more and more important as time passed. Many knights or holders of knights' fiefs (e.g. the young son of a dead knight not yet of age) preferred to pay someone to fight in lieu of making a personal appearance when summoned to war. Knight service was thus sometimes commuted to a fixed money payment. This allowed the king to gather round himself a body of salaried fighting men who were, in the nature of things, more obedient to the royal will than a levy of landholders, scattered far and wide across the kingdom, could ever be.

But as soon as money matters became a major subject of consultation between the prince and his followers, it seemed sensible to bring representatives of the towns to court also, for the townsmen were, of course, the most fertile source of cash. Representatives of the towns usually sat apart from the noble landowners in a separate house or "estate." The upper clergy also constituted a separate estate, since, being also under the pope, they had a special legal relationship to secular authorities. In this somewhat haphazard fashion, it became customary in every important European kingdom for the prince or king to consult representatives of all the major interests of the realm—about tax payments first and foremost, and about other matters of general concern too, since representatives easily discovered that they could withhold approval of a new tax levy until the prince redressed their grievances —or promised to do so.

By means of such representative institutions, important conflicting interests within each European state found more or less effective voice. Peasants were seldom represented and town artisans were likewise left out. But property holders and taxpayers were heard in public matters that most concerned them.

Europe's political consolidation therefore involved the enfolding of the most active elements of society into the political process in a fashion that had no real parallel in other civilized lands. Relatively close collaboration between rulers, landowners, and merchants was thus assured. It is hard to believe, for example, that any European government could have overridden the interests of such a massive group of shipowners and seamen as existed in south China at the time the Ming emperor forbade the further construction of seagoing vessels. A somewhat stumbling but generally effective sensitivity on the part of public administrators to the economic interests of the subjects was built deeply into the fabric of European government. In this sense, therefore, European governments, like European trade and commerce, were unusually vulgar, and by the same token unusually apt to accommodate themselves to new forms of economic enterprise—particularly if the innovation seemed likely to produce additional tax revenues.

Cultural Consolidation

‡‡‡ For more than two centuries, from the time when Europe's recovery commenced until about 1200, eager appropriation of everything

that appealed to Western men in the Arabic and Byzantine cultural traditions, together with bold and vigorous creativity, imparted a youthful brilliance to medieval culture that can only be compared to the ancient Greeks' similar period of apprenticeship to and emancipation from the cultural model of the ancient Middle East.

Both in Spain and in southern Italy, scholars organized systematic translation from Arabic into Latin. A large literature of professional handbooks and encyclopedic information was thus added to the Latin inheritance, which had previously been almost exclusively ecclesiastical. The translation of Aristotle's works into Latin proved particularly influential. Western men found in Aristotle's pages a reasoned, complete, and persuasive view of the entire universe which was, however, pagan. The task of reconciling Aristotelian doctrine with Christian truth became critical for those—and they were many—who refused willingly to surrender any part of their intellectual inheritance, whether it be the new Aristotelian logic or the old Christian faith.

Another dimension of European culture—the inheritance from the barbarian world generally, and the knightly style of life in particular—also called for integration into a Christian mould, for the rough brutality and violence of the tenth century had next to nothing in common with Christian love, hope, and charity.

These challenges were initially met in a spirit of reckless abandon. St. Anselm (d. 1109) and Peter Abelard (d. 1142), for example, seem to have felt that human reason and Christian doctrine would be sure to support one another if reason were resolutely and rigorously pursued. Thus, St. Anselm found it possible to prove the logical necessity of the Incarnation, and Peter Abelard launched a critical inquiry into the conflicts among Christian writers on points of doctrine. Simultaneously, in the field of law the monk Gratian (c. 1140) weightily argued the pros and cons of discordances within the laws of the Church, while Irnerius (d. c. 1130) began the systematic study of Roman law in hope of finding a key wherewith to unlock the prevailing confusions that plagued the local, customary law of Europe. To such men, nothing was too difficult to try.

Western Europe's upsurge after 1000 was demonstrated also by the development of monumental stone building in the style known as Romanesque. Western architects expressly repudiated the Byzantine architectural style, which had previously found a modest footing in western Europe, and preferred to work from models offered by surviving Roman basilicas and early Christian church structures. With the same sort of sublime confidence, barbarian violence was at least partially Christianized through such enterprises as the Crusades (beginning 1096) and by the development of a knightly ideal that asked men-at-arms to aid the weak, serve womankind, and protect Mother Church.

Between about 1200 and 1300 the initial *élan* of medieval Europe's cultural upthrust developed a more complex and troubled yet richer texture. Tensions between Christian faith, ecclesiastical order, and naïve acceptance of the authority of the past on the one hand, and men's rational, secular, and critical faculties on the other, became acute. Yet in diverse and conscious ways these tensions were for a while effectively resolved, thus producing the great climax of medieval culture—the synthesis of the thirteenth century—toward which an important company of sensitive Westerners have ever since nostalgically looked back.

In the field of theology, faith and reason were resolutely reconciled by St. Thomas Aquinas (d. 1274) and St. Albert the Great (d. 1280). Aquinas' *Summa Theologica* arrayed authoritative opinions about and carefully reasoned answers to a vast number of questions of faith and morals. His book very soon came to be recognized as a semi-official statement of Christian doctrine. Aristotelian logic and some of Aristotle's conclusions were thus skillfully harnessed to the task of upholding Christian truth, in accordance with the general principle that while faith and reason could never contradict one another, there were points of theological truth that were simply not accessible to unaided reason and had therefore to be imparted to mankind through divine revelation. Yet Aquinas was not without his critics. The most influential of these distrusted long chains of logical proofs, and preferred the certainty of things divine that came from mystical experience, and the knowledge of things mundane that could be achieved by careful attention to information supplied by the senses. Such thinkers as St. Bonaventura (d. 1274) and Roger Bacon (1294) represented this loosely Platonic (and Franciscan) intellectual tradition, which they consciously opposed to the Aristotelianism of Aquinas and Albert the Great, who were both of the rival Dominican order.

In the field of action, diversity and discrepancy were more apparent than synthesis; but opposing tendencies and ideals were balanced against one another in such a way as to give scope to a wide spectrum of human impulse. Thus, for example, Christian knighthood was countered by a "romantic" ideal that emphasized courtly (i.e. extramarital) love and a code of manners that risked sensuality in the pursuit of sensibility. Or again, heresy which spread widely among weavers and other artisan groups met a counterpoise in the piety of Franciscan and Dominican friars. Unlike monks, the friars lived and worked among laymen, preaching, caring for the sick, aiding the poor and helpless, and in other ways offering a practical demonstration of Christian idealism. St. Francis (d. 1226), founder of the Franciscan order, and St. Dominic (d. 1221), founder of the Dominican order, were the most important leaders of this fresh outpouring of Christian feeling. Yet here too lay a difficulty, for the very intensity of St. Francis' pursuit of holiness pushed him to the verge of heresy. Some of his followers, who criticized the pope and bishops of the Church for failing to imitate Christ and the Apostles by leading lives of poverty (as the friars in principle undertook to do), passed beyond the verge at which their saintly founder had always called a halt. After a long legal process these "Spiritual" Franciscans were condemned as heretics, despite (or because of) their intense piety.

The literary activity of the thirteenth century gave voice to all these diverse strands of thought and feeling, and did so partly in Latin, partly in vernacular languages. Popular tales, often scurrilously anticlerical, and naïvely pious "miracle" plays based on Biblical stories reflected the diversity of life in the towns. Romances and troubadour songs did the same for the aristocracy. The greatest literary figure of the age was Dante, the Florentine exile (d. 1321). His love sonnets, political writings (*De Monarchia*), and above all his Christian epic, *The Divine Comedy*, set forth a world view that more nearly captured the multifaceted life of thirteenth-century Europe than any other man came near to doing.

The history of art shows the same headlong rush toward multiplicity and variety. Gothic cathedrals of the thirteenth century achieved a complex, subtle, and enormously successful solution to the problem of enclosing a large space for Christian worship. Yet the Gothic style quickly evolved toward greater and greater decorative complication, until encrusted tracery obscured the structural simplicity of rib, buttress, and pier. This flamboyance matched the complication and occasional triviality of later Scholastic philosophy and may have corresponded also to a certain weakening of Christian conviction and increased delights in display and luxury which gave point to the "Spiritual" Franciscans' attacks upon the worldliness of ecclesiastical dignitaries.

A general fraying out of the medieval cultural synthesis was characteristic of the period after 1300. In the fourteenth and fifteenth centuries, the competing ideals of holiness and human satisfaction in this world failed to find any really satisfactory resolution. During this time, developments in Italy diverged significantly from the climate of opinion north of the Alps. Italy became the seat of a conscious renaissance of classical antiquity, meaning, in practice, the Roman rather than the Greek past. Many educated Italians discovered that study of the pagan Latin poets and of Cicero offered not only models of literary excellence but fresh and valuable insights into the question of how men should live and conduct themselves. Humanists, as men who cultivated these concerns were proud to call themselves, seldom broke explicitly with Christianity. Indeed, humanistic literary and artistic values often were shared by wealthy clergymen, who ranked among the most important patrons of the movement.

In the milieu of the Italian towns a new art style was born. Like the humanists' Ciceronian Latin, it was deliberately modeled on ancient example. Architecturally, pillars, pilasters, and round arches constituted the elements from which the "renaissance" style was derived. In painting few ancient examples were available, and perhaps in consequence, a more profound originality developed. Aerial and—from about 1430—linear perspective gave the Italian painters a systematic, remarkably rational, and optically persuasive technique for arranging objects in an illusory space. The result was to create a powerful and unique style of painting which matured shortly before 1500. It endured as the fundamental frame for European painting until the end of the nineteenth century.

North of the Alps no such successful and venturesome assertion of novel humanistic and naturalistic interests came to expression. Instead, something of a stalemate between the discordant elements of the European cultural inheritance set in. Florid court chivalry accorded ill with the brutal reality of the Hundred Years' War (1337–1453) between France and England, when bands of mercenary soldiers robbed and burned their way across the fertile fields of France. Popular discontents found expression in a rash of peasant revolts and in the rise of new heretical movements like the Lollards of England and the Hussites of Bohemia.

The medieval frame of European culture was clearly in difficulty, but its eventual repudiation was a painful and prolonged process, decisively launched only by such great events as the opening of the oceans to European shipping and the nearly simultaneous outbreak of the Reformation. Discussion of the genesis of modern Europe will, however, be reserved for the third part of this book.

Japan

‡‡‡ The precocious courtly culture of Japan did not entirely disappear even when the imperial power had become no more than a shadow. But border barons who pioneered the expansion of Japanese society northward through the archipelago were not in a position to share or admire the refined and anti-militaristic cultural ideal which the first Japanese courtiers had imported wholesale from T'ang China. Instead, they developed a code of manners and a warrior ideal of their own, emphasizing courage in battle, loyalty to a chosen leader, and the personal dignity of each and every fighting man, no matter how poor he might be or how desperate his cause. In time the code of the *samurai*, as the Japanese warriors were termed, became strict and binding, and even attained written codification. It arose from the discipline and spirit of successful war bands, recruited by individual captains for their own and their followers' aggrandizement. A successful band of course took possession of a piece of territory and collected dues in kind from the peasant inhabitants. Hereditary possession became usual, but continual vigilance and ready capacity to demonstrate individual and collective prowess in battle were always required to maintain what had been won. Constant local wars were the result, for any quarrel between members of different bands could only be adjudicated by the sword, and, for that matter, it was not always possible for members of a single band to settle differences among themselves peaceably.

Japanese feudalism, therefore, closely resembled the feudalism of early medieval Europe. Even the survival of an ineffective imperial suzerainty in Japan resembled the vague deference paid to the imperial idea by Europeans. In detail there were important differences. For example, the Japanese samurai grouped themselves into clans (real or ficti- tious), whereas European knights were governed by contractual relations—homage and fealty—not by kindreds. Moreover, the style of agriculture which sustained the Japanese fighting class was en- tirely different from that of Europe. As in China, intensive cultivation by hand, in which rice paddies played the central part, prevailed in Japan. Accordingly a densely settled peasantry, producing a smaller food surplus per family than European peasants could do, constituted a very poor but extremely hard-working mass base for Japanese society as a whole.

After about A.D. 1300 a third element began to achieve greater prominence in Japanese society—to wit, townsmen and sailors. Im- portant improvements in naval architecture, pioneered by the Chinese, permitted this development in Japanese society. The compass, adjusta- ble centerboard, keels, cloth instead of slatted bamboo sails, and a gen- eral increase in size and strength of ship construction all spread from China to Japan. This made sea voyaging practicable up and down the Japanese coasts, and across the sea to China, to southeast Asia, and to the nearer islands of the Pacific as well. Fishing soon developed into an important industry. Then, when the Chinese withdrew from the seas in the 1430's, the Japanese rapidly took over naval primacy throughout the southwest Pacific region.

In these circumstances, piracy and sea roving offered a very prom- ising career for poverty-stricken samurai who lacked enough land or had been dispossessed in some local struggle. Japanese pirates, there- fore, quickly became the scourge of the China coast. They brought back rich hauls of booty to their home ports, where town life became more important than before, partly on the strength of the profits of such piracy. An extensive interpenetration between merchants and war- riors produced a warlike, self-reliant middle class, whose only parallel in the civilized world was in Europe, where piratical origins had also helped to define the townsmen's ethos.

The rise of towns in Japan meant also the appearance of new so- cial milieux in which the polarity between Chinese civility and Japa- nese reality could work itself out. Townsmen speedily created a more elaborate Japanese high culture than the spartan ideal of rural samurai allowed. Drama based on episodes from struggles among samurai clans and war bands was one of the products of this interaction. The development of a Japanese style of painting, related to yet distinct from Chinese styles, was another. The refinement of samurai manners by such elegancies as the "tea ceremony" and the use of silk clothes was still a third.

Japan's religious history reflects the same development toward local independence of Chinese examples. Zen Buddhism was initially imported from China, but on Japanese soil Zen became intertwined with the samurai ideal in a fashion totally alien to Chinese precedent. Aged or defeated samurai not infrequently retired to Zen monasteries, where they found in the metaphysical doctrine of sudden enlightenment a needed supplement to the bleak militarism of their secular life. From about 1200, Pure Land Buddhism became prominent in Japan. This sect appealed to a wider public. It was organized on congregational lines and expressly repudiated reliance upon priestly or monkish mediators between ordinary men and salvation. Both Zen and Pure Land Buddhists occasionally resorted to violence. Zen monasteries, indeed, were often important landholders and therefore found themselves compelled to defend their property like a samurai clan. Pure Land Buddhists, on the other hand, provoked a number of large-scale peasant risings. These broke out after 1400, but were nowhere successful for long.

The cult of the Sun Goddess from whom the imperial family claimed descent underwent an important transformation in the fifteenth century. Previously this cult had been almost entirely confined to the imperial court and family, and had been assimilated to Chinese patterns of ancestor worship. After 1400, however, priests of the Sun Goddess's principal shrine began to develop elaborate interpretations of traditional myths. The cult thus acquired a metaphysical theology comparable to Buddhist doctrines. This remodeled cult, or Shinto, could and did appeal to an emerging Japanese sense of national identity and uniqueness—a sense greatly stimulated by the enlarged contacts with the outside world their successful sea roving inaugurated.

By 1500, therefore, Japanese society and culture had become comparable in complexity, formidability, and sophistication to other civilized communities of the Old World. A comparatively small and isolated geographical range and the comparatively great ethnic homogeneity of the bearers of Japanese culture cramped the full development of this new civilization. Or perhaps one should rather say that before Japanese civilization had time to spread beyond the confines of the Japanese islands and attract other peoples (e.g. the Filipinos and Amerindians) into its sphere of influence, rival sea-borne civilizations, to wit, the Islamic and European, pre-empted the ground and effectually fenced Japanese culture in, so that it could not spread among new peoples in the way more favorably situated new civilizations had always done. Japan, nevertheless, achieved civilized status in time to preserve full cultural and political autonomy in modern times, as the less advanced peoples of Africa, Australia, and the Americas, whose cultural development we will glance at in the next chapter, were unable to do.

CHAPTER 17

The Fringes of the Civilized

World to 1500

By A.D. 1500 only a slender zone of tundra and Arctic shoreline in the Old World remained unaffected by the development of civilized styles of life. A few reindeer herders continued to carry on a traditional existence, and an Eskimo culture, skillfully adapted to survival in the special environment of the Arctic shoreline, came into being without any perceptible relationship to what men had done in more favored regions of the earth.

South of the belt of civilized communities that extended all the way across Eurasia, geographical conditions and cultural relationships were far more complicated. Yawning gaps remain in our information about the history of such a vast and varied region of the earth as Africa, and what is known presents almost as many historical puzzles as it solves. Only a very tentative summary of what appear to be the main lines of development is possible in a book such as this. The reader should be aware that much of what follows rests on nothing more solid than shrewd guesswork.

In A.D. 1500 Africa south of about the Zambesi river, as well as the whole of Australia and adjacent islands like Tasmania and New Guinea, remained entirely untouched by civilization. Wandering peoples there pursued a Stone-Age life similar, so far as we can tell, to that of the earliest human hunters.

Southeast Asia and the South Pacific

‡‡‡ North of these two major refuge areas, however, the transforming force of civilized styles of life had everywhere been felt. In southeast Asia and the islands of Indonesia, societies familiar with root agriculture and adept in the arts of primitive seamanship existed before either Indian or Chinese explorers penetrated the river mouths of that part of the world. Then, as we have already seen, beginning about the Christian era, massive acceptance of Indian culture occurred. After about A.D. 600 links with India weakened, largely as a result of the replacement of Hindu by Moslem shipping in the Indian Ocean. The various Hindu (and some Buddhist) courts of southeast Asia were therefore thrown back upon their own local resources. The results were occasionally magnificent. Java, for example, became the seat of a Hindu empire which built the great temple of Majapahit, while the lower Mekong became the seat of a similar state, the Khmer empire, whose monument is the vast and impressive palace-temple-city of Angkor Wat.

Beginning about A.D. 1200 two outside forces attacked the Indianized court civilizations of southeast Asia. Thai tribes descended from the north, overthrew the Khmer empire, and substituted their own more warlike and more tumultuous dominion in the Mekong valley. Missionaries in time converted the Thai to a form of Buddhism bearing a Burmese-Tibetan rather than an Indian stamp. Simultaneously, Moslem missionary enterprise gathered headway as a result of the internal changes in the Islamic community which we have already noticed. Accordingly, Malaya, Sumatra, and presently Java and distant Mindanao in the Philippines became the seats of Moslem regimes. Sooner or later Hindu cults disappeared everywhere, save in the island of Bali, where something of the older life survived until modern times.

During these same centuries, Polynesian navigators were carrying their high barbarism far across the Pacific. Their culture was at least loosely related to the cultures of southeast Asia. Ancestors of the Polynesians probably came from somewhere on the Asian mainland, but their great dispersion occurred only after the invention of outriggers permitted a canoe made from a single hollowed log to travel in safety

Mukteśvara Temple, c. A.D. 950, general view. Bhuvaneśvara.

PLATE 17

Mukteśvara Temple, detail.

PLATE 18

Photo, Gunvor Moitessier

Woman with a mirror, 11th cent. A.D. Decorative detail from a temple at Bhuvaneśvara or Khajurāho.

PLATE 19

View of the Great Temple Compound, 8th-13th cent. A.D. Bhuvaneśvara.

PLATE 20

Caṇḍi Puntadewa, c. A.D. 700. Dieng Plateau, Java.

TEMPLES OF SOUTHEAST ASIA

Temples built along Indian lines to house religious ceremonies deriving in large part also from India extend across a wide segment of Asia, from Tibet in the north to Java in the south, and as far east as Cambodia. In each of these regions, amalgamations took place between local religious and political traditions on the one hand and Indian cultural and religious practices on the other, so that no simple copies of Indian prototypes can be found. Yet the impact of India's religious architecture is plain to see. The acculturation of barbarian peoples to an Indian style of civilized life, here demonstrated through architecture (Plates 21-24), parallels the process we saw visually attested by the spread of Greek styles of sculpture (with appropriate modification) to Rome and western Europe (Plates 4-7).

PLATE 21

Stupā, showing the eyes of the Buddha, possibly 8th or 9th cent. A.D. Near Kāthmandū, Nepal.

PLATE 22

The temple of Shiva, late 9th cent. A.D. Lara-Djonggrang, Prambanan, Java.

PLATE 23

Angkor Wat, early 12th cent. A.D., air view from the northeast. Cambodia.

PLATE 24

Chinese, Mongol, Persian, and Mughal Painting

Ma Yüan. Two Sages and an Attendant Under a Spreading Plum Tree, Sung dynasty.
Museum of Fine Arts, Boston.

CLASSICAL CHINESE PAINTING

This and the three plates following have been chosen to suggest the wide variety
of effects Chinese gentlemen were able to achieve with the restricted means they
chose to employ: paper, brush, and ink. All these works date from the Sung dynasty
(960-1279), when Chinese painting attained its classical forms. Authentic earlier work
scarcely survives, and subsequent artists were nearly always content to work within
one or other of the genres established by the Sung masters. They sought refinement
and perfection and eschewed the ostentatious vulgarity of personal innovation. As
a result, the history of Chinese art lacks sharp changes of style. Delicate economy of
means devoted to maintaining an elegant and multifold stability made Chinese
painting a faithful mirror of the structure of traditional Chinese society.

PLATE 25

Ma Fen (attributed). The Hundred Geese, Sung dynasty,
section of the scroll. Honolulu Academy of Arts, Hawaii.

PLATE 26

Liang K'ai. The Poet Li T'ai-po, Sung dynasty.
Formerly Count Matsudaira Collection, Tokyo.

Mu Ch'i. Persimmons, Sung dynasty.
Ryūkōin Temple, Kyoto.

PLATE 27

Tung Yüan. Clear Weather in the Valley, Sung dynasty, section of the scroll. Museum of Fine Arts, Boston.

THE IMPACT OF CHINESE ART ON PERSIA: I

The hunting scene opposite illustrated a Persian poem—a subordination of art to literature entirely strange to Chinese practice. Moreover, the innumerable tiny patches of brilliant color that irradiate the original (but must here be left to the imagination) contrast utterly with the low tints characteristic of Chinese painting. Nevertheless, the mountain in the upper left of this picture is clearly Chinese (compare above) and attests the impact of Chinese styles—first brought to Persian attention by the Mongols, who ruled both lands in the thirteenth century—upon an already highly skilled school of palace art.

PLATE 28

Photo, The Asia Institute

Bihzād. King Darius Reproved by His Herdsman, from a "Būstān" MS, 1488, Iran. Royal Egyptian Library, Cairo.

PLATE 29

THE IMPACT OF CHINESE ART ON PERSIA: II

Comparison of the tree shown here with the plum tree of Plate 25, and of the leaves with the bamboos of Plate 26, shows once more how Persian artists picked up motifs from Chinese masters and put them to their own—sometimes incongruous—uses. Contrast the partial and controlled use of Chinese motifs by these Persian artists with the wholesale appropriations of foreign styles characteristic of barbarian peoples, illustrated above in Plates 4-7 and 21-24.

Courtesy, The Art Institute of Chicago

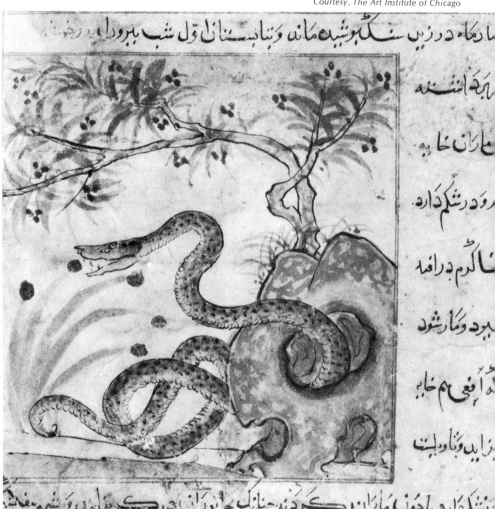

Serpent, from a ''Manafi Al-Hayawan'' MS, Mongol, c. 1300, Iran.
The Art Institute of Chicago.

PLATE 30

Illustration from the Romance of Amir Hamzah, Mughal, 16th cent.
The Metropolitan Museum of Art, New York. Rogers Fund, 1923.

FROM CHINA TO INDIA BY WAY OF PERSIA

The Mughals carried their Persian culture with them into India, as demonstrated by
this painting, which was produced during the first part of the reign of Emperor Akbar
(1556-1605). By that time in Persia itself religious reformers had stamped out all
figure art as dangerously idolatrous; but this did not prevent motifs that had originated in China some five hundred years before from appearing now in India. In
the process of transmission we see (compare Plate 28) that what had been mighty
mountains dwarfing humanity have shrunk so small as to become a strangely shaped
peacock perch. Yet, however misunderstood by the Mughal artist, the odd and eye-
arresting shape of the Chinese original unmistakably survives.

PLATE 31

Prince Dara Shikuh and His Son, Mughal, 17th cent. Staatliche Museen, Berlin.

THE POMP AND SPLENDOR OF IMPERIAL ISLAM

Three great empires, ruled by the Ottoman, Safavi, and Mughal dynasties, consolidated their control over most of the Moslem world during the sixteenth century. These mighty states found it relatively easy to expand their power at the expense both of a squabbling Christendom in Europe and of a disorderly Hindustan in India.

These political facts find faint echo in this painting of a magnificently caparisoned elephant, gay yet stately, whose mighty tread dwarfs the landscape. The scene may also be read as an indication of how Persian ways (the carpet and riders' dress) mingled with older Indian traits (the elephant's anklets) to produce a new and distinctive Mughal style, both of art and of life.

PLATE 32

across the open ocean. When this critical breakthrough had been made (sometime between A.D. 1 and A.D. 600) Polynesians spread across the vastnesses of the Pacific within a few hundred years—a fact attested by the close affinity of their languages in regions as distant from one another as New Zealand and Hawaii.

Sub-Saharan Africa

‡‡‡ Africa was probably the original cradle of mankind, and that continent has preserved until our own time a greater ethnic variety than any other part of the earth. Peoples as widely different in their physical appearance as Bushmen, Hottentots, Dinka, and Masai cannot be found elsewhere. In times past some of these peoples held much larger territories than they do today, whereas other populations—Bantu-speaking Africans in particular—were once confined to a small portion of the ground they now occupy. The naïve idea that Africa is and has always been inhabited by a more or less uniform Negro population is completely unfounded; but the truth is too complicated and too ill-recorded to be easily reconstructed.

The Sahara desert effectually divides Africa in two. The northern coast shared in the classical and medieval history of the Mediterranean and does not concern us here. Sub-Saharan Africa, however, is far from uniform geographically. The Congo rain forest is bordered north, east, and south by savanna—that is, landscapes of grass dotted by occasional clumps of trees. But the mountains and great lakes of central east Africa interrupt the arc of the savanna, so that it is not a continuous belt, but divides into two major parts: west Africa, bisected by the curved course of the Niger river, and east Africa, running down the east spine of the continent all the way to the Cape of Good Hope. Scant pasture lands, fringing the southern Sahara, skirt the northern face of the mountain barrier. This miniature steppe therefore linked the two major productive regions of east and west Africa.

The geographical compartmentation of Africa helps to account for the restricted reach of ancient Egypt, whose influence does not appear clearly outside the Nile valley itself, and then only as far south as Nubia. During the Christian era, or perhaps shortly before, an important Indonesian component was brought into Africa. At that time, the island of Madagascar was colonized by a people who arrived by sea

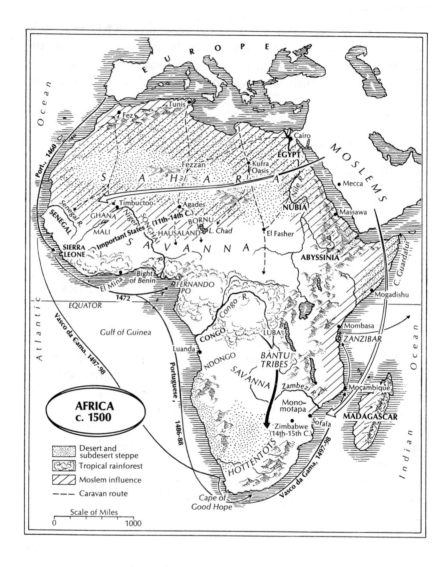

from one of the islands of Indonesia, perhaps from Borneo, where their closest linguistic relatives live in modern times. Other Indonesian settlements probably once existed along the eastern coast. The surest evidence of this is that a number of root crops native to Indonesia and therefore well suited for rain-forest cultivation established themselves as staples of African agriculture. The new crops had their major im-

pact on west Africa where cultivators began to penetrate into the vastnesses of the Congo rain forest about this time, perhaps because the
new Indonesian crops first made agriculture in that environment practicable. The initial expansion of the Bantu-speaking peoples, whose
original homeland and point of dispersion lay in west Africa, not far,
perhaps, from the Bight of Benin, may have depended on their successful exploitation of the new Indonesian crops.

About A.D. 300 trans-Saharan camel trains began to bring influences from the Roman world to bear upon west Africa. On the
strength of a growing caravan trade, whose main commodities were
gold, salt, and slaves, Ghana, the first major west African state, began
to take form sometime between A.D. 300 and 600. Meanwhile in east
Africa the kingdoms of Nubia and Abyssinia entered into much closer
relations with the Roman world. Both became Christian at an early
date, but Abyssinian and Nubian Christianity soon diverged from doctrines accepted in both Rome and Constantinople, so that links with
the Mediterranean world became slender. Abyssinia for a while controlled the straits of Aden and exercised considerable power in Arabia.
But the rise of Islam and Mohammed's unification of Arabia drove the
Abyssinians back across the straits. Thereafter, the Christian culture of
Abyssinia was always on the defensive. Islam quickly planted itself in
east Africa and Moslems soon took over all the coastline, confining the
Christians to the highlands, where they still exist.

The Arab conquest of Egypt (A.D. 642) and of all north Africa (by
711) gave both east and west Africa Moslem instead of Christian neighbors. The further fact that Moslem shipping speedily took over primacy on the Indian Ocean meant a further exposure of Africa to Moslem infiltration. Until after the year 1000, however, Islam made only
modest headway south of the Sahara. Thereafter, its advance became
much more rapid. Ghana, for example, was overthrown in 1076 by a
Moslem conqueror. Thereafter Moslem states dominated west Africa.
The most important of the early Moslem empires was Mali. In east Africa, the effort required to resist Islamic assault actually generated
something of a "golden age" in Abyssinia's cultural history, but Nubia
succumbed to Moslem conquerors in the fifteenth century. After the
conquest of Nubia Arab nomad tribes began to move all the way
across the African continent, skirting the southern edge of the Sahara.
When these migrants reached west Africa they harassed, burnt, and

plundered the farming villages so harshly that the frontier of cultivation shrank back a considerable distance southward.

The history of east Africa south of Cape Guardafui is still quite
unclear. At some time between 700 and 1400 large-scale mining occurred at several sites in what is now Rhodesia. Extensive rock-built
ruins at Zimbabwe and nearby attest the scale of this enterprise. Another important event was the spread of cattle nomads southward.
Once again, the pioneers were Bantu-speaking tribes who had presumably acquired the art of cattle rearing from some more civilized
people—perhaps from Nubia. Bantu cattle nomads drove out the
Hottentot hunters who had previously occupied a large part of east
Africa. By 1500 the frontier of Bantu expansion had reached the Zambesi river.

Before Europeans circumnavigated the Cape of Good Hope,
therefore, nearly all of Africa had felt the influence of more advanced
societies in attenuated but unmistakable form. Numerous local versions
and variants of civilized patterns of life had taken root in both west and
east Africa, wherever suitable agricultural land existed.

The Americas

‡‡‡ The Americas had meanwhile become the seat of complex societies
that fully deserve the epithet "civilized." Generally speaking, the level
of mastery over the environment attained in Mexico and Peru by 1500
seems very similar to what the ancient Mesopotamians and Egyptians
had achieved by about 2500 B.C. A four-thousand-year lag was far too
great for the Amerindians to make up when the Spanish conquistadors
burst in upon their seclusion. Since the higher culture of the Aztec and
Inca empires left only limited traces behind, we can afford to be quite
cursory in our consideration of the Amerindian civilization.

Cultivation of food crops began in the New World at about the
same time that neolithic farmers began their experiments with wheat
and barley in the Old. But the fundamental food crop of the New
World, maize, literally had to be invented by selection from various
natural crossings between a plant known as teosinte and various other
wild species. (The exact genetic ancestry of modern maize is still under
investigation.) This took a long time, and not until about 2500 B.C. did a
sufficiently productive form of the plant appear to provide the basic

sustenance of human populations. Until then, the yield of food plots had to be supplemented by hunting and gathering. Human populations had to remain correspondingly sparse.

A second disadvantage confronted Amerindians: the near absence in the New World of domesticable animals that could serve human purposes and enrich human food resources. The llama, dog and guinea pig, which were domesticated in the New World, constituted a poor equivalent to the array of domesticated animals that played such a central role in the life of Old World cultivators and nomads.

For these reasons, it was not until shortly before the Christian era that more complex societies that we can properly call civilized began to develop in the Americas. The evidence for this change is archaeological. A number of monumental religious centers, featuring temples built of stone atop artificial pyramidal bases, were built in Guatemala (Mayan) and the central Mexican plateau. During the next centuries, improvements in skill were rapid. Finer carving, larger structures, more precise layouts of the temple precincts appear in both the Mayan and Mexican centers. What archaeologists term the "classic" stage of the Amerindian cultures of Central America emerged by about A.D. 300 and lasted for some six hundred years. During this time, Mayan and Mexican temples attained vast size and systematic elaboration. The Mayas developed an accurate calendar and a form of writing which scholars today can partly decipher. Priestly control and management of society seem clear; but the details of the ideas and myths, religious principles, and administrative organization by which the effort of ordinary farmers was mobilized to raise the great temples, and how expert stone masons and other artisans were maintained, cannot now be known.

Peru may have lagged somewhat behind the Mexican and Guatemalan development, but the "classic" period of the three major cultures of Peru is thought to coincide fairly closely with the classic ages of the Mayan and Mexican temple states. Potatoes and the llama were important resources of the Andes slopes not available in Mexico. In addition, the Peruvian societies of the coastal area depended on a very skillful irrigation, whereas in Central America maize was grown on rain-watered land. At some date between A.D. 500 and 1000 all of the Peruvian valleys that plunge down to the Pacific were overrun by an art style originating in the high Andes at Tiahuanaco. Perhaps this attests military conquest, though it may represent some religious movement. Whatever its nature, centralization did not survive for long. When the Incas began to develop a new empire from a center in the high Andes, their expanding power met and overcame a series of local city and tribal states (fifteenth century). The Incas imposed a very strictly centralized regime upon all of Peru. Their empire was linked together by roads, officials, and a religion of the sun, of which the Great Inca was chief priest. The resemblance to the religio-political centralization of ancient Egypt is striking.

The Mexican area was more various and may be compared in this respect to ancient Mesopotamia. About A.D. 900 Mayan and Mexican priest-led communities broke down. The reasons are not clear. In the central valley of Mexico it seems probable that barbarian invasion from the north destroyed the priestly regime. Further south, traces of military assault are lacking, and it is possible that some withdrawal of belief, whereby the Mayan farmers ceased to find it necessary to support the priestly centers in order to assure the fertility of their maize fields, accounts for the abandonment of the temple sites. Nevertheless, more militaristic regimes did come to the Mayan lands. First Chichén Itzá in Yucatán and then Mayapan seem to have created a sort of lose empire among the Mayans, but by the time the Spaniards arrived, even this sort of political unity had vanished. Despite their past, attested by the great temple centers, Mayan agriculturalists were living in simple village communities when the Spaniards first appeared and had no elaborate military, political, or even priestly organization.

Further north a number of waves of invasion may have occurred before the Aztecs (arrived in central Mexico A.D. 1325) asserted a loose hegemony over all of central Mexico. Aztec military operations were directed toward the capture of prisoners whose hearts were then offered to the gods daily throughout the year. We may presume that the victims were not pleased with their fate. No really effective loyalty or political unity therefore existed among the millions of inhabitants of the central Mexican valley when Cortez led his handful of ruffians to Montezuma's palace in 1519.

Other Indian societies had begun to move toward agricultural elaboration before the European discoveries. In the southeastern United States, for example, a number of cult centers arose, simpler than those of Mexico but influenced by them. Similar proto-civilizations existed in

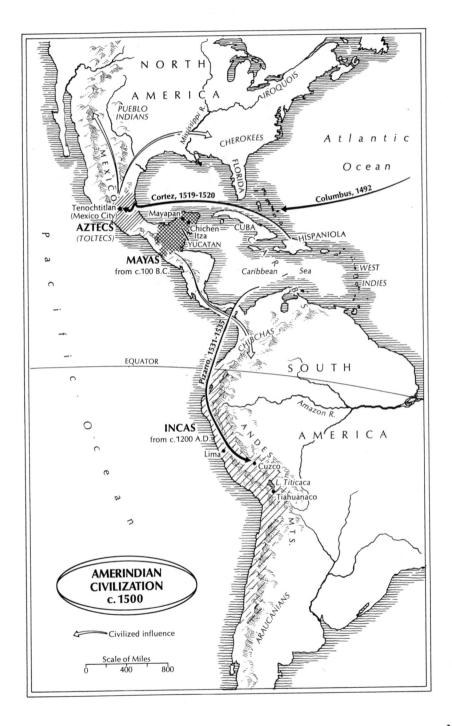

NORTH

AMERICA

PUEBLO
INDIANS

IROQUOIS

Mississippi R.

CHEROKEES

FLORIDA

A t l a n t i c

O c e a n

MEXICO

Cortez, 1519-1520

Columbus, 1492

Tenochtitlan
(Mexico City)

Mayapan

AZTECS
(TOLTECS)

Chichen
Itza
YUCATAN

CUBA

HISPANIOLA

MAYAS
from c.100 B.C.

Caribbean   Sea

WEST

INDIES

P   a   c   i   f   i   c

CHIBCHAS

Pizarro, 1531-1535

EQUATOR

S O U T H

A   N   D   E   S

Amazon R.

INCAS
from c.1200 A.D.

A M E R I C A

Lima

Cuzco

L. Titicaca

Tiahuanaco

O   c   e   a   n

M   T   S   .

AMERINDIAN
CIVILIZATION
c. 1500

ARAUCANIANS

Civilized influence

Scale of Miles
0   400   800

what is today Colombia and Chile. Still further afield, the Indians of Virginia and New England knew how to raise maize, and a people like the Iroquois had begun to construct a formidable political-military confederation even before they came into contact with white men.

A much debated issue is whether or not Amerindian cultures owed anything important to trans-oceanic voyagers, whether from across the Atlantic or the Pacific. Some striking resemblances between a few art motifs in Central America and southeast Asia, together with the pre-European distribution of cultivated plants in the Pacific islands, suggest that some sort of relationship existed among the cultures on the two sides of the Pacific from a fairly early time. Nevertheless, many scholars emphatically deny that Amerindian civilizations profited significantly from contact with the rest of the world. The matter must remain open and cannot be firmly settled without more careful archaeological study than has yet been made.

Bibliographical Essay, Part II

As I conceive world history, the entire span of time between 500 B.C. and A.D. 1500 belongs together, as a sort of inflated "Middle Ages," sandwiched between the constitutive age of civilization building and the age of Western dominance that set in after 1500. Such a classification runs counter to the traditional periodization of our history, which divides what is here treated together, at about A.D. 400, into a classical and a medieval segment. The traditional chronological pattern fits the histories of other parts of the world very awkwardly, however, and it therefore seems best to list titles by region alone, and not to undertake any chronological ordering.

EUROPE. Most classical authors have been translated into English and published in the Loeb classical library, with opposing pages in the original Greek or Latin. In addition, the more important authors have been translated elsewhere and often, and I lack sufficient knowledge to be able to recommend particular editions of authors like Aeschylus, Sophocles, Aristophanes, Herodotus, Thucydides, Plutarch, Livy, Tacitus, Plato, Aristotle, Cicero and others of similarly enduring popularity. Any curious student should, however, be invited to turn to these authors at once, for they constitute one of the taproots of western civilization.

Among the moderns, choice becomes arbitrary and difficult. Two fine standard texts are: J. B. Bury, *History of Greece to the Death of Alexander the Great*, 4th ed. (London, 1975); and Max Cary, *History of Rome Down to the Reign of Constantine the Great*, 2nd ed. (London, 1954). Gisela M. A. Richter, *Sculpture and Sculptors of the Greeks*, rev. ed. (New Haven, 1950) is another standard authority; and Moses Hadas, *History of Greek Literature* (New York, 1950) surveys his subject gracefully. For economic history see F. M. Heichelheim, *Ancient Economic History*, 3 vols. (New York, 1958); M. I. Rostovtseff, *The Social and Economic History of the Hellenistic World*, 3 vols. (Oxford, 1941); the same author's far more impassioned *Social and Economic History of the Roman Empire*, revised by P. M. Fraser, 2nd ed., 2 vols. (Oxford, 1957); Tenny Frank et al., eds., *An Economic Survey of Ancient Rome*, 5 vols. (Baltimore, 1933-40); A. H. M. Jones, *The Greek City: From Alexander to Justinian* (Oxford, 1940); .K. D. White, *Roman Farming* (Ithaca, N.Y., 1970); M. I. Finley, *The Ancient Economy* (Berkeley, 1973); and Ernst Badian, *Publicans and Sinners: Private Enterprise in the Service of the Roman Republic* (Ithaca, N.Y., 1972). On special aspects of military and political affairs, the following are particularly interesting: A. R. Burn, *Persia and the Greeks: The Defence of the West* (New York, 1962); H. W. Parke, *Greek Mercenary Soldiers* (Oxford, 1933); A. H. M. Jones, *Athenian Democracy* (Oxford, 1957); Sir Ronald Syme, *The Roman Revolution* (Oxford, 1939); J. R. Hamilton, *Alexander the Great* (London, 1973); F. E. Peters, *The Harvest of Hellenism: A History of the Near East from Alexander the Great to the Triumph of Christianity* (New York, 1970); Ernst Badian, *Roman Imperialism in the Late Republic* (Oxford, 1968); Fergus Millar, *The Emperor in the Roman World, 31 B.C.–A.D. 337* (Ithaca, N.Y., 1977); Ramsey Macmullen, *Roman Social Relations, 50 B.C.–A.D. 284* (New Haven, 1974). Three other books that can be recommended are: Marshall Clagett, *Greek Science in Antiquity* (New York, 1956); W. W. Tarn and G. T. Griffith, *Hellenistic Civilization*, 3rd ed. (London, 1952); and Georges Dumezil, *Archaic Roman Religion* (Chicago, 1970).

Early Christianity is a subject by itself. Two excellent works by classicists are C. N. Cochrane, *Christianity and Classical Culture* (New York, 1944); and Arnaldo Momigliano, ed., *The Conflict Between Paganism and Christianity in the Fourth Century* (Oxford, 1963). William A. Chaney, *The Cult of Kingship in Anglo-Saxon England: The Transition from Paganism to Christianity* (Berkeley, 1970) sheds light on the continuities as well as the discontinuities of an important period of transition. Good general treatments of early Christian history are: Kenneth Scott Latourette, *A History of the Expansion of Christianity I: The First Five Centuries* (New York, 1937); Robert M. Grant, *Historical Introduction to the New Testament* (New York, 1963); and Rudolf Karl Bultmann, *Primitive Christianity in its Contemporary Setting* (London, 1956). More specialized themes of interest are dealt with by A. D. Nock, *Conversion, The Old and the New in Religion from Alexander the Great to Augustine of Hippo* (London, 1933); J. M. Allegro, *The Dead Sea Scrolls and the Origins of Christianity* (New York, 1957); Jean Doresse, *Secret Books of the Egyptian Gnostics* (New York,

1960); and Peter Brown, *Augustine of Hippo* (Berkeley, 1967). Salo W. Baron, *A Social and Religious History of the Jews*, 2nd ed., 8 vols. (New York, 1952–58), is a very useful counterpart to the study of early Christianity. Medieval histories divide almost always between the Latin and Greek halves of Christendom, and Slavic Europe often constitutes still a third compartment. Similarly, relationships with Islam are neglected or treated in isolation from general narrative. The result is to emphasize, more than perhaps the facts really warrant, the compartmentalization of relationships in the medieval period within Europe—not to mention Eurasia as a whole. Hugh Trevor-Roper, *The Rise of Christian Europe* (London, 1965); Gustave E. von Grunebaum, *Medieval Islam: A Study in Cultural Orientation*, 2nd ed. (Chicago, 1955); and Robert S. Lopez, *The Birth of Europe* (New York, 1967); transcend this sort of narrowed vision; as does Lynn White Jr., *Medieval Technology and Social Change* (Oxford, 1962).

Recent work on medieval economic history has turned very largely upon the "Pirenne thesis" as set forth in Henri Pirenne, *Mohammed and Charlemagne* (New York, 1955) and affirmed in a larger context in his *Economic and Social History of Medieval Europe* (New York, 1937). *The Cambridge Economic History of Europe*, 3 vols. (Cambridge, 1941–63), reflects expert consensus; and C. S. and C. S. L. Orwin, *The Open Fields*, 2nd ed. (Oxford, 1954) brings practical experience with farming to bear upon elucidation of the much disputed matter of manorial land patterns. Recent works of synthesis by distinguished scholars include: M. M. Postan, *The Medieval Economy and Society: An Economic History of Britain, 1100–1500* (Berkeley, 1972), and Robert S. Lopez, *The Commerical Revolution of the Middle Ages* (Englewood Cliffs, N.J., 1971).

In political matters it seems best to settle for a list of the books that are more interesting or important than most; Marc Bloch, *Feudal Society* (Chicago, 1961); Carl Stephenson, *Medieval Feudalism* (Ithaca, N.Y., 1942); Sir Steven Runciman, *A History of the Crusades*, 3 vols. (Cambridge, 1951–54); Charles Homer Haskins, *The Normans in European History* (Boston, 1915); Geoffrey Barraclough, *The Origins of Modern Germany*, 2nd ed. (Oxford, 1947); and P. H. Sawyer, *The Age of the Vikings* (New York, 1962).

A similarly arbitrary principle for cultural history suggests the following: R. W. Southern, *The Making of the Middle Ages* (New Haven, 1953); Christopher Dawson, *The Making of Europe* (London, 1932); Johan Huizinga, *The Waning of the Middle Ages* (London, 1924); L. J. Daley, *The Medieval University* (New York, 1961); Charles Homer Haskins, *The Renaissance of the Twelfth Century* (Cambridge, Mass., 1927); C. H. McIlwain, *The Growth of Political Thought in the West* (New York, 1932); David Knowles, *The Evolution of Medieval Thought* (London, 1962); Ernst

Kitzinger, *Early Medieval Art in the British Museum*, 2nd ed. (London, 1955); Erwin Panofsky, *Gothic Architecture and Scholasticism* (Latrobe, Pa., 1951); Paul Oskar Kristeller, *Renaissance Thought: The Classic, Scholastic and Humanist Strains*, rev. ed., 2 vols. (New York, 1961); and Ernst Cassirer et al., eds., *The Renaissance Philosophy of Man* (Chicago, 1948). David Talbot Rice, ed., *The Dawn of European Civilization* (London, 1965), provides a general and well-illustrated introduction to the art of Europe and the Near East during the first millennium. Two general works trace important themes in European culture: Clarence Glacken, *Traces on the Rhodian Shore* (Berkeley, 1967), which deals with European ideas of nature, and Herschel Baker, *The Dignity of Man* (Cambridge, Mass., 1947, new title, *The Image of Man*, New York, 1961).

Eastern Europe has less in English, but the following can be recommended: Archibald R. Lewis, *Naval Power and Trade in the Mediterranean, A.D. 500–1100* (Princeton, 1951); Sir Steven Runciman, *Byzantine Civilization* (London, 1933); William H. McNeill, *Venice: The Hinge of Europe, 1081–1797* (Chicago, 1974); Norman H. Baynes and H. St. L. B. Moss, eds., *Byzantium* (Oxford, 1961); Peter Charanis, *Studies on the Demography of the Byzantine Empire: Collected Studies* (London, 1972); O. M. Dalton, *East Christian Art: A Survey of the Monuments* (Oxford, 1925); N. P. Kondakov, *The Russian Icon* (Oxford, 1927); George Vernadsky, *A History of Russia*, 5 vols. (New Haven, 1943); and Jerome Blum, *Lord and Peasant in Russia* (Princeton, 1961).

THE REALM OF ISLAM. This is an elastic term because Islam continued to make converts and expand its territorial base throughout the first thousand years, and in fact continues to do so today. Moreover it is convenient to consider the Parthian and Sassanian empires under this general heading, since in many respects they were precursors of the Abbasid caliphs. In general, studies of Iran are few. Two brief general works are Richard N. Frye, *Heritage of Persia* (Cleveland, 1963), and Roman Ghirshman, *Iran from the Earliest Times to the Islamic Conquest* (Penguin, 1961). For the Parthian and Sassanian periods see: Neilson C. Debevoise, *A Political History of Parthia* (Chicago, 1938); for those who read French, Arthur Christensen, *L'Iran sous les Sassanides*, 2nd ed. (Copenhagen, 1944); Roman Ghirshman, *Persian Art, The Parthian and Sassanian Dynasties* (New York, 1962); and Arthur Upham Pope and Phyllis Ackerman, eds., *A Survey of Persian Art*, 7 vols. (London and New York, 1938–39) are excellent. On religious history, F. C. Burkitt, *The Religion of the Manichees* (Cambridge, 1925), and two books by Robert Charles Zaehner, *The Dawn and Twilight of Zoroastrianism* (New York, 1961), and *Zurvan: A Zoroastrian Dilemma* (Oxford, 1955) are available.

Among the numerous general accounts of Islam the following are especially good: H. A. R. Gibb, *Mohammedanism: An Historical Survey*, 2nd ed. (London, 1953); Bernard Lewis, *The Arabs in History* (London and New York, 1950); Marshall G. S. Hodgson, *The Venture of Islam: Conscience and History in a World Civilization*, 3 vols. (Chicago, 1974); Gustave E. von Grunebaum, *Medieval Islam: A Study in Cultural Orientation*, 2nd ed. (Chicago, 1955); T. W. Arnold, *The Caliphate* (Oxford, 1924); and T. W. Arnold, *The Preaching of Islam*, 2nd ed. (London, 1913). On Mohammed's career, Tor Andrae, *Mohammed: The Man and his Faith* (New York, 1956), W. Montgomery Watt, *Muhammad at Mecca* (Oxford, 1953) and W. Montgomery Watt, *Muhammad at Medina* (Oxford, 1956) are excellent. Many translations of the Koran exist; none seems to capture in English the literary power of the original, and I lack the capacity to choose which is best. Eric Schroeder, *Muhammad's People* (Freeport, Me., 1955) is a striking pastiche of translations from Arabic poetry, mostly pre-Islamic. William Polk, *The Golden Ode* (Chicago, 1974) translates an important work of pre-Islamic Arabia and discusses it as an introduction to Arab society. Utterly different in tone is Ibn Khaldun, *The Muquaddimah: An Introduction to History*, tr. Franz Rosenthal, 3 vols. (New York, 1958). W. Montgomery Watt, tr., *The Faith and Practice of Al-Ghazali* (London and New York, 1953), an autobiography of a famous Moslem theologian, offers an insight to still a third dimension of Moslem civilization.

For the great change that came to Islam with the Sufi movement, A. J. Arberry, *Sufism: An Account of the Mystics of Islam* (London, 1950) and Reynold Alleyne Nicholson, *Studies in Islamic Mysticism* (Cambridge, 1921) are recommended. Edward G. Browne, *A Literary History of Persia*, 4 vols. (London and Cambridge, 1902–24), is a classic deserving its reputation; and T. W. Arnold, *Painting in Islam* (Oxford, 1928), and Richard Ettinghausen, *Arab Painting* (Geneva, 1962) are useful.

More specialized themes are capably handled by: George Fadlo Hourani, *Arab Seafaring in the Indian Ocean in Ancient and Early Medieval Times* (Princeton, 1951); Andrew S. Ehrenkreutz, *Saladin* (Albany, N.Y., 1972); W. Barthold, *Turkestan Down to the Mongol Invasion*, 2nd ed. (London, 1928); Paul Wittek, *The Rise of the Ottoman Empire* (London, 1938); Halil Inalcik, *The Ottoman Empire: The Classical Age, 1300–1600* (New York, 1973); Franz Babinger, *Mehmet the Conqueror and His Time* (Princeton, 1977); J. K. Birge, *The Bektashi Order of Dervishes* (Hartford, 1937); and Marshall G. S. Hodgson, *The Order of Assassins* (The Hague, 1955).

CENTRAL ASIA AND THE STEPPE. The Eurasian steppe has usually not been treated as a whole. René Grousset, *The Empire of the Steppes* (trans. New Brunswick, 1970), is one of the few books that does try to link happenings east and west into a single conspectus. William M. McGovern *The Early Empires of Central Asia* (Chapel Hill, 1939), and Owen Lattimore, *The Inner Asian Frontiers of China* (New York, 1940), treat the eastern portions of the steppe. W. W. Tarn, *The Greeks in Bactria and India*, 2nd ed. (Cambridge, 1951), A. K. Narain, *The Indo-Greeks* (Oxford, 1957), deal with a particularly dramatic episode of central Asian history. No comparable work on the Kushan empire is known to me, nor is there any satisfactory treatment of the Sassanian penumbra that spread through Central Asia in the time of the Uighur Manichees. Sir Aurel Stein, *On Ancient Central Asian Tracks* (London, 1933), records his finds, but fails to weave the record into a history.

The westerly portions of the steppe are better treated by historians. M. I. Rostovtseff, *Iranians and Greeks in South Russia* (Oxford, 1922) and Tamara Talbot Rice, *The Scythians* (London, 1957) were mentioned in the bibliographical essay for part I. Mortimer Wheeler, *Rome Beyond the Imperial Frontiers* (New York, 1955); E. A. Thompson, *A History of Attila and the Huns* (Oxford, 1948); Otto Maenchen-Helfen, *The World of the Huns* (Berkeley, 1973); and D. M. Dunlop, *The History of the Jewish Khazars* (Princeton, 1954) cover major phases of steppe history very satisfactorily as far as relations with Europe are concerned. R. A. Stein, *Tibetan Civilization* (trans. Stanford, 1972), is a standard treatment of the subject. Two books about the Mongols are particularly good: H. Desmond Martin, *The Rise of Chingis Khan and His Conquest of North China*, ed. Eleanor Lattimore (Baltimore, 1950), and Christopher Dawson, ed., *The Mongol Mission* (London and New York, 1955). Michael Prawdin (pseud. for Michal Charol), *The Mongol Empire: Its Rise and Legacy* (London, 1940), is a highly readable, but undocumented, account.

INDIA AND SOUTHEAST ASIA. A. L. Basham, *The Wonder That Was India*, rev. ed. (New York, 1963), is the best general introduction to Indian civilization. A recent general survey is Stanley Wolpert, *A New History of India* (New York, 1977). K. A. Nilakanta Sastri, *A History of South India from Prehistoric Times to the Fall of Vijayanagar*, 3rd ed. (Madras, 1966), and E. H. Warmington, *Commerce between the Roman Empire and India* (Cambridge, 1928), present interesting data on the interrelations of the Mediterranean and Indian Ocean worlds.

For Indian thought and letters, standard works are: Surendranath Dasgupta, *A History of Indian Philosophy*, 5 vols. (Cambridge, 1932–55); A. B. Keith, *A History of Sanskrit Literature* (London, 1928); and A. B. Keith, *The Sanskrit Drama in Its Origin, Development, Theory, and Practice* (Oxford, 1924). Indian art is well portrayed by Heinrich Zimmer and Joseph

Campbell, *The Art of Indian Asia*, 2 vols. (New York, 1955); Benjamin Rowland, *The Art and Architecture of India* (Penguin, 1953); and Calambur Sivaramamurti, *The Art of India* (New York, 1977). Among available translations of Indian literature, V. R. R. Dikshitar, ed. and tr., *The Lay of the Anklet* (Silappadikāram) (Oxford, 1939); Johannes A. B. van Buitenen, *Tales of Ancient India* (Chicago, 1959); Franklin Edgerton, ed. and tr., *The Bhagavad Gita, translated and interpreted* (Harvard Oriental Series, Cambridge, Mass., 1944); and N. A. Nikam and Richard P. McKeon, eds. and trs., *The Edicts of Ashoka* (Chicago, 1958) are particularly interesting. Johannes van Buitenen's important translation of the *Mahabharata* multivolume, (Chicago, 1973–) has been mentioned in part I of this essay. Two excellent works provide a good introduction to Indian religion: Robert C. Zaehner, *Hinduism* (Oxford, 1966) and Mircea Eliade, *Yoga: Immorality and Freedom,* 2nd ed. rev. (Princeton, 1969).

Southeast Asian history may be pursued with help from D. G. E. Hall, *A History of Southeast Asia* (New York, 1955); John F. Cady, *Southeast Asia: Its Historical Development* (New York, 1964); H. G. Quaritch Wales, *The Making of Greater India: A Study in Southeast Asian Culture Change* (London, 1950); J. C. van Leur, *Indonesian Trade and Society* (The Hague, 1955); B. H. M. Vlekke, *Nusantara: A History of the East Indian Archipelago* (Cambridge, Mass., 1943); and G. Coedes, *The Indianized States of Southeast Asia,* trans. (Honolulu, 1968).

THE FAR EAST. L. C. Goodrich, *A Short History of the Chinese People,* 3rd ed. (New York, 1959) and Charles O. Hucker, *China's Imperial Past* (Stanford, 1975) are good general histories of China. George B. Sansom, *Japan: A Short Cultural History* (New York, 1962) and John Hall, *Japan: From Prehistory to Modern Times* (New York, 1970) play the same role with respect to Japan. For Korea, M. Frederick Nelson, *Korea and the Old Orders in Eastern Asia* (Baton Rouge, 1945); Homer B. Hulbert, *The History of Korea,* rev. ed. by C. M. Weems, 2 vols. (Hillary, N.Y., n.d.; first published, Seoul, 1905); and Woo-kuen Han, *The History of Korea* (Seoul, 1970) are available. E. O. Reischauer, John K. Fairbank, and Albert Craig, *East Asia: Tradition and Transformation* (Boston, 1973) treats the Far East as a whole.

Special themes in China's long political and social development are dealt with by: Derk Bodde, *China's First Unifier: A Study of the Ch'in Dynasty as Seen in the Life of Li Ssu* (Leiden, 1938); Michael Loewe, *Crisis and Conflict in Han China* (London, 1974); Arthur F. Wright, *Buddhism in Chinese History* (Stanford, 1959); Kenneth Ch'en, *Buddhism in China: An Historical Survey* (Princeton, 1964); Arthur Wright and Denis Twitchett, *Perspectives on the T'ang* (New Haven, 1973); Edwin G. Pulleyblank, *The Back-*

ground of the Rebellion of An Lu-shan (London, 1955); Edward A. Kracke, Jr., *Civil Service in Early Sung China, 960–1067* (Cambridge, Mass., 1953); Shiba Yoshinobu, *Commerce and Society in Sung China*, trans. (Ann Arbor, 1970); James T. C. Liu, *Reform in Sung China: Wang An-shih and his New Policies* (Cambridge, Mass., 1959); Charles O. Hucker, ed., *Chinese Government in Ming Times* (New York, 1969); and J. J. L. Duyvendak, *China's Discovery of Africa* (London, 1949). Raymond Dawson, ed., *The Legacy of China* (Oxford, 1964) includes concise introductory essays on many aspects of traditional Chinese civilization, written by the leading authorities in their fields.

Chinese art and thought may be approached with the help of: Osvald Siren, *Chinese Painting: Leading Masters and Principles*, 7 vols. (New York, 1956–58); Lawrence Sickman and Alexander Soper, *The Art and Architecture of China* (Penguin, 1956); James Cahill, *Chinese Painting* (Cleveland, 1960; reissued in paperback, New York, 1977), the best introduction to the subject; Feng Yu-lan, *A History of Chinese Philosophy*, tr. Derk Bodde, 2 vols. (Princeton, 1952–53); and Wing-tsit Ch'an, *A Sourcebook in Chinese Philosophy* (Princeton, 1963). Wing-tsit Ch'an, tr., *Reflections on Things at Hand: The Neo-Confucian Anthology Compiled by Chu Hsi and Lü Tsu-ch'ien* (New York, 1967), and Tu Wei-ming, *Neo-Confucian Thought in Action: Wang Yang-ming's Youth* (Berkeley, 1976), deal with two sides of the Neo-Confucian thought that dominated later imperial China. *Historical Relics Unearthed in New China* (Peking, 1972) and *Murals from the Han to the T'ang Dynasty* (Peking, 1974) provide color photographs of many of the most important objects discovered by contemporary Chinese archaeologists. Joseph Needham, *Science and Civilization in China*, multivolumed (Cambridge, 1954–   ) and T. F. Carter and L. C. Goodrich, *The Invention of Printing in China and Its Spread Westward*, 2nd ed. (New York, 1955) are the best authorities for their respective subjects. Two of China's most famous historians may be studied through Burton Watson, tr., *Records of the Grand Historian of China*, 2 vols. (New York, 1961) and Homer H. Dubs, ed. and tr., *The History of the Former Han Dynasty by Pan Ku* (Baltimore, 1938–55). Arthur Waley, tr., *The Poetry and Career of Li Po, 701–762 A.D.* (London, 1951) deserves mention.

Donald L. Philippi, tr., *Kojiki* (Tokyo, 1968), makes available the most important source on archaic Japan. Murasaki Shikibu, *The Tale of Genji*, tr. Arthur Waley (Boston, 1935), is the best introduction to Heian culture. Several works are useful for the study of pre-modern Japan: Ivan Morris, *The World of the Shining Prince* (New York, 1964); Jeffrey Mass, *Warrior Government in Early Medieval Japan: A Study of the Kamakura Bakufu,*

Shugo and Jito (New Haven, 1974); and Alfred Bloom, *Shinran's Gospel of Pure Grace* (Tucson, 1965).

AFRICA. Roland Oliver and John D. Fage, *A Short History of Africa* (Penguin, 1962) is now standard, but Philip D. Curtin, *African History* (Boston, 1978) may well challenge the older book. Regional accounts of general interest include: Zoë Marsh and G. W. Kingsnorth, *An Introduction to the History of East Africa*, 2nd ed. (Cambridge, 1961); John D. Fage, *An Introduction to the History of West Africa*, 2nd ed. (Cambridge, 1960); E. W. Bovill, *Caravans of the Old Sahara: An Introduction to the History of the Western Sudan* (London, 1933); J. Spencer Trimingham, *A History of Islam in West Africa* (London, 1962); A. H. M. Jones and Elizabeth Monroe, *A History of Abyssinia* (Oxford, 1935; reissued as *A History of Ethiopia*, 1955); and Nehemia Levtzion, *Ancient Ghana and Mali* (New York, 1973). Roland Oliver, ed., *The Cambridge History of Africa, III: from c.1050 to c.1600* (Cambridge, 1977) reflects the current state of scholarship on its subject.

THE AMERICAS. Gordon R. Willey, *New World Prehistory*, Smithsonian Institution Report for 1960 (Washington, D.C., 1961) and H. E. Driver, ed., *The Americas on the Eve of Discovery* (Englewood Cliffs, N.J., 1964), are good general introductions to the Amerindians. G. H. S. Bushnell, *Peru*, rev. ed. (New York, 1963); J. Eric S. Thompson, *The Rise and Fall of Maya Civilization* (Norman, Okla., 1954); G. C. Valliant, *The Aztecs of Mexico* (Penguin, 1950); and Friedrich Katz, *The Ancient American Civilizations* (New York, 1972), are also very useful. On the disputed question of trans-Pacific contacts with the New World before Columbus, see M. W. Smith, *Asia and North America: Trans-Pacific Contacts*, Society for American Archeology, Memoir No. 9 (1953), and Andrew Sharp, *Ancient Voyagers in the Pacific* (Wellington, N.Z., 1956).

PART III

The Dominance
of the West

T HE year 1500 serves better than most historical landmarks as a divide between modern and pre-modern times. This is true in European history, for the great discoveries, quickly followed by the Reformation, gave the coup de grâce to medieval Europe and inaugurated a century and a half of desperate effort to achieve a reasonably stable new pattern of thought and action. As a result of these efforts, a new balance for European civilization attained a hazy sort of definition after 1648. The year 1500 marks an important turning point in world history also. The European discoveries made the oceans of the earth into highways for their commerce and conquest. They thus created a new cultural frontier along every habitable coast that rivaled, and in the end eclipsed, the importance of the land frontiers where the civilizations of Asia had for centuries stood guard against steppe nomads.

Little by little all the non-Western peoples of the earth found it necessary to do something drastic about the intrusive Europeans with their restless, disturbing ways. The rise of the West to this position of dominance all round the globe is, indeed, the main theme of modern world history.

Nonetheless, changes such as these take time to ripen. For a full two hundred years after Christopher Columbus (1492), Vasco da Gama (1498), and Ferdinand Magellan (1519–22) sailed across the oceans of the earth, the old established civilizations of Asia reacted sluggishly to the new sea-borne challenge constituted by Europe's growing wealth and power. In the Americas, and in the less highly developed lands of northern Asia, the European impact was much more drastic. Local cultures withered when confronted by the missionary spirit and technical superiority of European pioneers in both these great regions of the globe. As a result, a European type of society expanded both east and west from its original focus and center, penetrating deep into Siberia and across the Atlantic into the New World.

After 1700, however, the Islamic peoples together with the Hindus and Buddhists of Asia found themselves unable to stave off the Europeans. Old institutions and attitudes hallowed by centuries of reli-

A.D.	AMERICAS	EUROPE	RUSSIA

A G E O F R E C O N N A I S S A N C E

Ivan III repudiates Ta[tar]
rule

Columbus

1500 E U R O P E A N ——————— O C E A N I C

| | | RENAISSANCE / REFORMATION | |

Cortez
Pizarro

Leonardo da Vinci — *Luther*
Machiavelli

Empire of Charles V

Henry VIII

Catholic reformation — *Calvin*
Michelangelo *Copernicus* — *Loyola*
Dutch *Vesalius* — *Xavier*
revolt
Philip II of Spain
Montaigne

Hawkins brings first
African slaves

Ivan IV cap[tures]

Livonian war — Rus[sia]

1600
Virginia, Quebec,
New Amsterdam,
Massachusetts
established

sugar plantations fix Negro
slavery upon New World

Dutch driven from New
Amsterdam

Shakespeare Henry IV of France *El Greco*
Bacon
Cervantes *Kepler* **THIRTY YEARS' WAR**
Galileo *Cyril Lukaris*
English civil wars
Milton *Descartes* *Rembrandt*
Harvey Louis XIV
Glorious revolution *Molière*
Newton *Spinoza* Frederick the Great
Locke *Hobbes* decay of Swedish

Time of Troubles
Polish assault

NIKON AND
CHURCH REF[ORM]

PETER THE GRE[AT]

1700
Leibniz rise of Austria
Mabillon — empire
Bach Newcomen's engine
Voltaire South Sea Bubble
Rousseau **SEVEN YEARS' WAR**
Watt's engine

British gain Canada
abolition of trade
monopoly in
Spanish empire

AMERICAN WAR
OF INDEPENDENCE *Mozart* partition of Poland

Linnaeus
Adam Smith **FRENCH REVOLUTION** *Hume*
Kant
NAPOLEON
Herder

St. Petersburg new
capital

nobles exempted
state service
CATHERINE
THE GREAT
Pugachev revolt

1800
Latin American
independence

Congress of Vienna

Hegel

Alexander I
Pushkin
Nicholas I

C R I M E A N

1848-49 revolutions
Darwin
United States
Civil War
railroad building *Marx* Cavour
Napoleon III Bismarck
Nietzsche Papal infallibility
automobile
radio rival alliance systems

abolition of serf[dom]

Dostoyevsky

railroad buildin[g]

1900
Panama Canal
Wilson airplane

Einstein *Freud* *Picasso*

W O R L D
D E P R E S S I O N

F. D. ROOSEVELT *Atomic energy:* CHURCHILL HITLER MUSSOLINI
W *Fermi* O R L

Russian revolut[ion]
1905 W A[R]
RUSSIAN REVOLUT[ION]
OF 1917 LEN[IN]
STA[LIN]

(left margin vertical labels: AGE OF RECONNAISSANCE · OLD REGIME · NEW REGIME · CONTEMPORARY)
(right column vertical labels: DYNASTY · ROMANOV)

296

ISLAM	SOUTH ASIA	EAST ASIA	PACIFIC AND AFRICA
		Cheng-ho	
e of Constantinople			

V O Y A G E S _____ **O** _F_

ISLAM	SOUTH ASIA	EAST ASIA	PACIFIC AND AFRICA
SAFAVI n-French alliance AN THE LAWGIVER	da Gama Moslem control of Java Babur ——► India *Chaitanya*		Magellan
Astrakhan		Macao founded	Portuguese ——►Japan Spanish ——► Philippines
er Sibir bbas the	fall of Vijayanagar to Moslems AKBAR, MUGHAL EMPIRE	Hideyoshi invades Korea	
	Dutch and English East India companies	Ricci ——► Peking Russians reach Pacific	Dutch ships ——► Japan
revival of Ottoman re	Taj *Mahal* *Tulsi Das*	*Tibetans convert Mongols to Lamaism*	Japan closed to foreigners
seige of Vienna	Aurangzeb, last strong Mughal emperor	MANCHU CONQUEST OF CHINA	West African slave trade
f Karlowitz; loss of ary		treaty of Nerchinsk	
	Nadir shah	*rites controversy* treaty of Kiakhta	Bering's voyages
Wahhab	battle of Panipat British expel French from India	Chinese control in Tibet, Mongolia, Turkestan	Captain Cook's voyages
war huk Kainardji			Spanish found San Francisco Australia colonized
and Greek revolutions med Ali of Egypt ts Sultan and Wahhabis	Consolidation of British control in India	abolition of East India Company monopolies	New Zealand colonized
anal	British-Afghan wars	opium war	Perry opens Japan
	Ram Mohan Roy Sepoy mutiny	Taiping rebellion	Livingstone's explorations
		Europeans capture Peking Sino- Japanese war	Meiji restoration colonial scramble in Africa
		Boxer rebellion ——Russo-Japanese war— Chinese Republic Japan rules Korea	
		Sun Yat-sen	
ha Kemal d	GANDHI	Japanese in Manchuria and North China	
			African states become independent

TOKUGAWA SHOGUNATE

(D I S C O V E R Y)

L   U   T   I   O   N
W   A   R   N

(Indian independence — Chinese Communists to power)

gion could no longer stand up to the new power western European peoples had been able to generate. Successive demonstrations of this fact in India, the Balkans, and the Middle East caused a stunned paralysis to descend upon nearly all Moslems and most Hindus. Yet decisive breakdown of traditional ways and institutions did not occur before about 1850, when with an extraordinary suddenness the Ottoman, Mughal, Manchu, and Japanese empires within a single decade either collapsed or found themselves compelled to venture forth from the shelter of familiar ways in the hope of being able to beg, borrow, or steal from the Westerners the secrets of their strength.

This effort at conscious modernization (i.e. selective and partial Westernization) still continues to command the central place in the aspirations of all the non-Western peoples of the world. The pace of social change accelerates steadily, and the effort to manage society so as to achieve goals set by some directing clique or party seems to gain force with every passing year.

After 1500, however, divisions of European history do not match the bench marks of world history very closely. This is no more than what we should expect, for if it is correct to say that the main theme of modern history is the rise of the West to dominance over the globe, there should be a time lag between successive stages of Europe's own development and the impact upon other peoples and distant continents.

Hence it seems well to bracket the history of the non-Western world down to 1700 with Europe's domestic history until 1648 as a period when the Far West first decisively and definitely challenged all the other cultures of the earth by demonstrating important superiorities in such fields as military organization and technology, natural science and inquisitiveness. The period of world history between 1700 and 1850 may similarly be bracketed with Europe's Old Regime, 1648–1789, when a potentially classic reorganization of European civilization emerged from the struggles and confusion of the preceding period. By the same logic, world history since 1850 may be paired with Europe's history since 1789, when the twin movements of industrialization and democratization began to transform Western institutions fundamentally, and imparted to them the irresistible force to which the other civilizations of the world bowed only after 1850.

The chapters that follow are therefore arranged in two tiers: A survey of Europe's self-transformation 1500–1648 precedes discussion of the development of each of the major regions of the world in the period 1500–1700. Then chapters on Europe's Old Regime and on the colonial expansion of European society in the years 1648–1789 set the stage for a second tour of the rest of the world, surveying its development in the period 1700–1850. The awkwardness of such a plan will, I believe, be counterbalanced by the fact that its chronological irregularity underlines and illuminates the central reality of early modern world history.

CHAPTER 18

The Great Discoveries and

Their World-Wide Consequences

 Prince Henry of Portugal (d. 1460), nicknamed "the Navigator," prepared the way for the dramatic voyages of oceanic discovery that opened the entire circuit of the habitable globe to Europeans within a time span of no more than two generations. What he did was to bring the best available theoretical knowledge into contact with traditional rule-of-thumb seamen's and shipbuilders' skills, in order to improve the seaworthiness and navigability of his ships. Prince Henry had in view the rounding of Africa, hoping thereby to link up with the half-mythical Christian champion, Prester John, and thus outflank and eventually overwhelm the realm of Islam. Profit from trade in slaves and other commodities to be picked up along the African coast helped to sustain the enterprise, but this was not a central motive.

Navigation remained inexact, for until the invention of a satisfactory marine chronometer (1760) no precise method for determining longitude (east-west) was known. Latitude (north-south) could be measured by finding the angle of the sun above the horizon at noon. With the help of tables of the sun's declination at known latitudes for each day of the year, a sea captain could establish his position north or south of the equator within some thirty miles or so, even when using comparatively crude sighting instruments. The trick lay in compiling accurate tables. This task Prince Henry assigned to specially selected astronomers and mathematicians who, after lengthy calculation, provided Portuguese sea captains with the necessary information. By guessing how far east or west they had gone, explorers could then make charts of the African coast, permitting later navigators to travel long distances across the open ocean and yet steer their ships toward an expected landfall at a precisely established latitude. In 1497, for example, Vasco da Gama spent ninety-seven days out of sight of land, and yet steered accurately for the Cape of Good Hope, despite the fact that the Cape had not been visited by any European since it had first been discovered by Bartolomeo Diaz nine years before.

Da Gama's method was the same as that used by all early European oceanic sailors. He knew the latitude of his target—in this case the Cape of Good Hope—because Diaz had measured and recorded it on his voyage of discovery. By sailing far out in mid-Atlantic, where dangers from shoals were nil and winds blew stronger and more regularly than close in shore, da Gama got to the latitude of his intended landfall safely and much quicker than he could have by following the coast. Then, turning due east, he sailed till the expected shoreline came up over the horizon. As long as the ship's captain knew the latitude of his destination, he could find it easily enough by sailing far from shore to the right point north or south, and then heading due east or due west along the appropriate line of latitude until sight of land allowed exact pilotage into harbor.

European shipbuilding made equally important advances. The Portuguese took the lead, multiplying the number of masts and fitting at least the larger central masts with more than a single sail. This allowed sailors to trim their canvas to fit different conditions of wind and wave, and made the ship much more maneuverable and seaworthy. This in turn permitted the construction of larger vessels; but large vessels required stouter hulls. As a result, by 1500, the mighty keel, heavy ribs, and double oak planking of a European vessel were able to withstand the recoil from heavy cannon. Vessels of lighter construction, such as those familiar in the calmer waters of the Indian Ocean, could not fire such weapons without shaking themselves apart.

These developments of European shipbuilding entirely outmoded prevailing methods of sea fighting. Ramming and boarding—

standard tactics of earlier times—could seldom be brought into play against vessels capable of smashing enemy ships with cannon fire at a distance of as much as 200 yards, and capable also of rapid and agile maneuver to bring enemy ships under fatal bombardment. Hence, when Columbus, Vasco da Gama, Magellan, and numerous less famous but no less daring captains opened the oceans of the entire globe to European navigation, their ships enjoyed a crushing technical superiority over vessels built elsewhere and designed for less stormy waters than those of the North Atlantic. Chinese and Japanese junks offered the only competition. They usually lacked enough heavy guns to come near to matching European ships. Gun metals remained comparatively scant in the Far East, whereas Europe's cruder but much larger-scale metallurgical industry allowed Europeans to arm their vessels far more lavishly than Far Eastern shipbuilders could ordinarily afford to do.

These technical facts help to explain the rapidity of Europe's initial expansion along the seaways. Vasco da Gama completed the first round trip to India in 1499. Ten years later the Portuguese defeated a numerically much superior Moslem fleet off the port of Diu in the Arabian Sea, and thereby fastened their naval supremacy on the Indian Ocean. Without delay they established naval stations at the key strategic points of Goa (1510), Malacca (1511), and Ormuz (1515). A Portuguese expedition penetrated to the Spice Islands in 1511–12, and an individual merchant reached Canton in 1513. A generation later, missionary and trade relations were opened with Japan (1545) and a permanent Portuguese settlement was established along the south China coast in 1557 at Macao. Here Portuguese expansion lapped up against the rival imperial power of Spain, which fastened itself upon the Philippines via Mexico in 1571.

As far as the Asian civilizations were concerned, Europe's naval supremacy after 1500 did not make much difference. From the point of view of the Chinese imperial government, for example, it was not in the least important whether or not sea trade passed into the hands of a new set of barbarians. Moslems from southeast Asia, Japanese pirates, and the beak-nosed "south sea barbarians" from Europe seemed all alike to Peking. In India also the rulers of the land were little concerned with mercantile matters, and after the defeat at Diu (1509) made no concerted effort to oppose the Portuguese presence. Instead, Moslem trading vessels simply evaded Portuguese patrols, which always remained scant because of the vast distances from the homeland. Light, small ships soon were able to conduct trade almost as before. The occasional loss of a vessel to the Portuguese became for Moslem traders and shipowners a mere inconvenience.

In the Americas, however, the arrival of Spanish conquistadores in Mexico (1519–21) and Peru (1531–35) brought sudden and irreparable disaster to the Amerindian high cultures. The complete collapse of the Aztec and Inca regimes opened the way for the creation of a vast land empire, ruled by Spaniards and dedicated both to the saving of Indian souls and to the export of silver and gold from American mines. With remarkable docility, the Amerindians submitted to Spanish leadership. Earlier religious and cultural ideals survived only at the village level, or in remote regions of the rain forest, mountain, and desert, where Spanish power and missions failed to penetrate. Thus a new type of society, Spanish in form and Catholic in religion but based upon the labor of millions of almost mute Amerindians, arose in the New World.

Europe's new naval supremacy had no remotely comparable result in the Old World. Nevertheless, three major consequences of the opening of the world's oceans to European shipping affected every civilized society and transformed conditions of life for many barbarous and primitive peoples as well. These were (a) the price revolution resulting from the flow of massive quantities of silver and gold from the Americas, (b) the spread of American food crops, and (c) the spread of diseases. Each of these deserves a little elaboration.

The Price Revolution

‡‡‡ The price revolution affected Spain first and most drastically, but spread to other parts of Europe with only small delay and modest diminution of its force. The Ottoman empire in the eastern Mediterranean was affected too, and so was distant China, where Mexican silver provided a far more abundant coinage than had been available before. As for India, nothing is known. The economic and social consequences of the price revolution in Turkey and China have not been studied, and may not have been as important as they were in Europe, which felt the first and strongest impact, since it was to European—specifically to

Spanish—ports that the treasure first came. Careful investigation has shown that within a century, prices in Spain multiplied about four times over. Less drastic price rises occurred elsewhere in Europe, but everywhere the changes were enough to disturb traditional economic relations profoundly. Persons with fixed incomes suffered severe loss of purchasing power, while those engaged in business often prospered, since the prices of their goods tended to increase.

All the certainty inherent in an established routine of life defined by traditional socio-economic relationships crumbled in an age when prices changed as sharply as happened in Europe between 1500 and 1650. Governments universally found their accustomed sources of income insufficient, and were compelled to find new devices for raising revenue. Even the humblest artisan or the poor peasant selling his few eggs in the market place felt the force of the price revolution. No one of course understood the relationship between increased supplies of silver and increased prices. But when all society was affected, so that some prospered while many were deprived and everyone—rich or poor—suffered from uncertainty as to the future, most men concluded that greater greed and wickedness were loose in the world than ever before. This conviction fed the extraordinary bitterness of religious and political controversy which set this age off from both earlier and later periods of European history.

American Food Crops

‡‡‡ American crops were botanically altogether different from those familiar in the Old World. Some of them proved to be extremely valuable supplements to what European, Asian, and African farmers had previously known. American corn, or maize, for example, spread rapidly to southwestern China, Africa, and southeastern Europe. In China the potato proved to be less important than the botanically unrelated sweet potato, which flourished abundantly on hillsides and other previously waste lands, where rice could not be grown. In Europe the relationship was reversed, for a cooler climate suited a plant native to the high Andes, whereas European summers were not warm enough to allow sweet potatoes to mature.

The reception of American food crops increased local food supplies, and usually provoked a corresponding increase in population.

This certainly occurred in south China. American crops also permitted a dramatic multiplication of population in Africa, especially in west Africa, whence came most of the millions of slaves who worked the plantations of the New World in the seventeenth and eighteenth centuries.

Details of the American food plant migration are not well established, and it is likely that the major impact of the new crops came after rather than before 1650. This was certainly the case in Europe, where it took time for illiterate cultivators and tradition-bound peasantries to discover the advantages of and to learn how to raise the new crops.

The Spread of Diseases

‡‡‡ The spread of disease did not wait upon human initiative, but proceeded, like the price revolution, despite human intention and without being understood at the time. Indeed, all details remain obscure, since the records of pestilential attacks, whether among Indians in America or in some city of Europe, are so imprecise as to make accurate medical diagnosis impossible. In general, however, it is clear that as ships began to ply the oceans they carried germs as well as goods from one port to another. Consequences for human life were sometimes important. European vessels, for example, transferred a number of diseases —including in all probability such scourges as yellow fever and malaria—from Africa to the New World, where these mosquito-borne infections made parts of Central and South America almost uninhabitable. In addition, diseases long established among the populations of Europe proved devastating when loosed upon the Amerindians who had no inherited or acquired immunities to such infections as smallpox, measles, or typhus. Perhaps the Amerindians reciprocated by transmitting syphilis to the Old World, although the American origin of syphilis is not certain.

Despite these ignorances, we may discern some of the over-all consequences of the diffusion of disease germs by ocean-going ships. First of all, previously isolated populations suffered drastic losses. It has been calculated, for example, that the population of the regions of America eventually incorporated into the Spanish empire in the New World stood at about 50 million in 1500, and fell to a mere 4 million by about

1650, and this despite Spanish immigration! Similarly drastic depopulation occurred in small islands of the Pacific and elsewhere, whenever new diseases encountered locally dense, previously isolated, and therefore unresistant populations.

Civilized populations, however, had long been exposed to a wide variety of infection. Indeed—with the possible exception of syphilis —no important new disease seems to have found large numbers of victims awaiting its ravages among the civilized inhabitants of the Old World. On the contrary, diseases that had been known previously in epidemic form gradually became endemic. As a result, by 1700 epidemic pestilence ceased to play any important role in checking population growth. Very likely the modern upward spurt of civilized populations dates from this change in the nature and incidence of diseases. Available statistics certainly seem to show that in Europe, China, India, and in at least some regions of the Middle East, population growth set in at previously unheard-of rates some time between 1600 and 1750. By then the epidemiological effects of oceanic shipping had had time to make themselves felt and American food crops had begun to come into their own. Modern scientific medicine, on the other hand, had little influence upon human populations before about 1800 even in Europe, much less in China or India, and cannot be held responsible for the early phase of modern population growth.

Clearly, the effect of the new oceanic dissemination of diseases redounded strikingly to the advantage of Europeans. Their home populations suffered no irreparable loss and soon began to multiply at a hitherto unparalleled rate, while in the Americas, and in other remote parts, the sudden ravages of disease crippled native resistance to European dominion. Even in the Old World the destruction (1757) of the last nomad confederacy in central Asia successfully to oppose civilized arms was the work not of guns but of smallpox.

European Knowledge and Inventiveness

‡‡‡ On an entirely different plane, too, the consequences of the great European discoveries worked strongly in Europe's favor as against all the rival cultures of other parts of the earth. For new skills and knowledge garnered from all over the habitable world became available to enrich and enlarge European technology and culture. As was the case

with their forefathers of the feudal age, when the techniques of knightly warfare had given western Europeans a short-lived military superiority on land, naval supremacy in the early modern age imparted such a sense of security to European seafarers that they found it possible to examine all they met with a naïve yet confident curiosity, eager both to know and to discover, and ready to borrow anything that pleased them in the tool kit of others. An upsurge of European inventiveness and ingenuity, feeding upon their enlarged knowledge of the world and its variety, both natural and human, was the inevitable and admirable result.

No other civilization responded to the new possibilities opened by ocean travel with anything remotely resembling European venturesomeness. Toying with foreign novelties did occur, most notably in the Far East, but nothing inimical to ancient and well-established tradition ruffled the mind of Chinese mandarins for very long. Moslem and Hindu reaction was even more emphatically negative. Anything conflicting with ancient truths was simply repudiated and neglected—or not noticed at all.

How different was Europe's response, where the convulsions of the age of Renaissance and Reformation shook European society to its core and shattered the medieval frame of European civilization entirely! The stimulus of the discoveries, and their subsequent exploitation, was not the sole cause of this transformation of Europe. Deepseated and long-standing tensions within European civilization contributed at least as much as anything from the outside. To an examination of these internal forces and their interplay we must therefore devote the next chapter.

CHAPTER 19

Europe's Self-Transformation

1500-1648

Despite tremendous complication in detail, it is not difficult to discern the main thrust of European development in the field of politics between 1500 and 1648. As compared with the tangle of overlapping jurisdictions that had prevailed in medieval times, power tended to concentrate at relatively few centers. The European landscape came to be partitioned into a series of well-consolidated states, each controlled by a central and usually monarchical government. In the most successful cases, the scale of consolidation was nation-wide: France, Spain, England, Sweden. In central Europe, smaller units seized sovereignty: city states, princely states, and ecclesiastical states. But even here, each separate state gathered authority and power toward a single center in the same way that the larger nation states were doing. In eastern Europe the pattern became weaker, for there, in some cases, noble and town privileges remained embedded in national monarchies. This was true, for instance, of Poland and Hungary. In other cases—Russia and Turkey—political centralization ran beyond the limits of a single nationality, subjecting peoples of diverse language and religion to a single imperial rule.

Within the borders of each successful state, the powers of government expanded radically. Matters which had once been strictly local came within the cognizance of agents of the central government. Kings and princes also acquired authority in matters of ecclesiastical administration and patronage, even in countries that remained Catholic and continued to recognize papal headship of the church. Noble rights and immunities together with town and village autonomies suffered drastic curtailment. Every sort of local authority based on inherited personal status crumbled before demands made in the name of a distant sovereign by officials whose power depended on royal or princely appointment.

This process of political consolidation may be looked at in a number of different ways. In one sense, it amounted to the application north of the Alps of techniques of government which had been first worked out in Italian city-states. Thus, for example, the merging of noble and burgher classes into a single (if tumultuous) body politic had been pioneered in Italian cities like Florence about two hundred years before French and English kings began to make much progress in that direction. Or, again, the use of standing professional armies to back up the will of the ruler was commonplace in Italy long before 1500, but became practicable in Spain and France only after that date. In the important instances, of course, state-building north of the Alps proceeded on a much enlarged territorial scale as compared to anything Italy knew. With this territorial enlargement the effective power of the leading European governments increased enormously, and the whole scale of interstate politics underwent corresponding magnification.

From another point of view, however, the complex overlapping jurisdictions of medieval political life were dissolved far more by the violent deeds and emotions connected with the Reformation than by slow seepage of Italian political practices north of the Alps. Assuredly, the effort to renew the church and make it holy had an enormous and immediate impact upon politics. Sustained and serious effort to make human life conform to God's will as revealed in the Bible changed men's minds and altered their behavior. Wholesale violence sanctified by dogmatic differences quickly erupted, and for more than a century Europe was convulsed by wars fought in the name of Christian truth —though scarcely in accordance with its precepts.

Amid all the violence and bloodshed, secular sovereigns unceasingly inched their power forward. In the principal states that became Protestant the government took over most of the properties formerly owned by churchmen, and acquired the right to appoint, or at least to approve the appointment of, leading clergymen. Almost the same fate befell the church in countries that retained their allegiance to the pope. The fact that land and other property was not confiscated outright did not prevent Catholic rulers in Spain, France, and Austria, for example, from appointing the dignitaries and taxing the lands of the church within their domains.

From still a third viewpoint, the consolidation of political power in a comparatively small number of centers reflected the rapid elaboration of military technology. As weapons became more complicated, the exercise of organized violence became prohibitively expensive for local nobles and impossibly complex for universal authorities. The medieval knight, once he acquired a horse, armor, and training, was almost self-sufficient, or, more accurately, wherever he went he could find what he needed in the way of food and minor repairs to his equipment without much difficulty. If threatened by some superior force he could retire behind castle walls, where, if the castle were well provisioned, he could wait safely enough until the enemy went home. But when artillery and infantrymen armed with pikes and guns drove the knight first from his castle and then from the battlefield—a process lasting from about 1350 to 1550—military organization became vastly more complicated. Supplies of powder and shot, transport for heavy guns, the arts of discipline, and money to pay for everything an army needed were not within the reach of most merely local authorities and, as it proved, were too disparate for any universal monarch to muster effectively across the whole of Europe.

Dependence upon a growingly complex system of land armaments also tied governments to the sources whence such complicated devices came: that is, to artisan shops and manufactories, mining and metallurgical entrepreneurs, capitalists, bankers, and generally, to the urban element in society which alone could assemble the necessary raw materials, produce the weapons, and deliver them to the soldiery in the right assortment and at the right time. Hence, really powerful governments were those in whose territories a sufficient urban development had occurred to sustain the complex demands of the new military technology. Territorially great states like Poland, for example, in which such a development failed to occur, were unable to take advantage of their size to become correspondingly powerful.

Each of these three points of view is surely valid. Their interplay over a century and a half, acting amidst the innumerable unpredictable acts of individual men who found themselves in critical situations facing new and unparalleled choices, gives the political history of this period an unusually intense, chaotic quality.

At the time, the eventual victory of the royal and princely governments over both local and universal rivals for sovereignty was far from obvious. In some of the eastern and northern parts of Europe, for example, aristocrats and clan chieftains retained or even enhanced their liberties. This was done both in the name of Calvinist reform of church and state, as in Hungary and Scotland, and in the name of a restored and reinvigorated Catholicism, as in Poland and Lithuania.

In the Dutch provinces and in England similar political developments proceeded from very different causes, for there the royal power was dismantled by townsmen and commercial farmers who found in legal precedent and Calvinist doctrine suitable justification for their defiance of the centralizing authority.

The Dutch revolt against Philip II of Spain began in 1568 and attained definite success by 1609, when a truce was concluded that ended large-scale campaigning. The rebel provinces worked out a loose federal union in the face of the exigencies of the war against Spain. The union survived the war, and, despite recurrent friction between urban and rural elements, sufficed to make the Dutch into a world power of the first rank.

In the next generation the English civil wars (1642–48) also ran counter to the trend toward monarchical absolutism. It was the parliamentary opponents of modern, efficient royal bureaucracy who prevailed. Like the Reformation itself, the parliamentary cause was radically reactionary, for it rested both on a reaffirmation of the traditional liberties of Englishmen (Magna Carta and all that) and upon relentless Puritanical striving after a government of saints. But like other successful revolutionaries, the Puritans in power were compelled to betray their program. English liberties and a government of saints degenerated after the execution of King Charles I (1649) into an open military dictatorship under Oliver Cromwell (d. 1658). His earnest efforts to re-establish a parliamentary form of government ran afoul of the stubborn fact that the vast majority of Englishmen repudiated the Puritanical ideal that inspired Cromwell's armies. After Cromwell died, King

Charles II's restoration (1660) resolved the impasse; but the new king did not attempt to build up royal power as Charles I had done. Sovereignty remained with Parliament; and the English Parliament managed to balance local and national interests in such a way as to make the central government reasonably responsive to changing circumstances.

Yet, however pregnant English parliamentarianism and Dutch federalism may have been for later times, they were exceptional and entirely atypical of the age. By giving political expression to the stubborn localism of landowners and burghers, the English and Dutch governments seemed to be defending a lost cause. Only the fact that their security vis-à-vis other states rested on naval rather than on land forces explains how it was that these two maverick nations were able to play roles as great powers without submitting to the bureaucratic centralization which in other lands proved to be the price of military strength, or indeed of political survival.

International Politics

‡‡‡ The most spectacular aspect of European politics between 1500 and 1648 was not the incessant wearing down of local jurisdictions by representatives of some central authority. However important, administrative centralization proceeded by means of innumerable petty local quarrels and decisions. Far more dramatic was the conflict at the other end of the political scale, which pitted the two great universal institutions of Latin Christendom—papacy and empire—against the emerging territorial sovereigns of western and central Europe. It seems clear, at least in theory, that Renaissance rationalism and the Reformation effort to apprehend and enforce a complete truth that could save men from uncertainty and error might both have been harnessed to support a universal state and a single church—if any single sovereign had been able to exploit the increasing technical complexity of warfare in order to organize a power so strong as to overwhelm all political rivals and hunt down all heretics.

Nothing of the sort happened. Yet in 1519, when Charles V of Hapsburg added the title and powers of Holy Roman Emperor to his already magnificent inheritance, it certainly seemed that universal monarchy might indeed prevail. For through a fortunate marriage alliance, Charles V inherited not merely his family's lands in Austria and nearby regions of Germany, but a magnificent Burgundian inheritance as well that extended southward from the Low Countries in an irregular strip of territory lying between France and Germany. In addition, he fell heir to the Spanish crown in 1516. To this was soon added the vast new empire of the Americas, which emerged before Europe's startled eyes as first Cortez (1521) and then Pizarro (1535) unlocked the dazzling wealth of the New World. As though this were not enough, Charles's brother Ferdinand, whom he entrusted with the administration of his Austrian possessions, inherited the crowns of Bohemia and Hungary in 1526, when his brother-in-law, the Hungarian king, died without heirs when fleeing the Turks after the disastrous battle of Mohacs.

Charles's enemies were as numerous as his subjects, however, and his subjects never united for any sort of prolonged common effort. The result was therefore first stalemate, and then weakening of the imperial power, even in Germany. But a long and stormy passage intervened between the time of Charles's coronation as Holy Roman Emperor (1519) and his descendants' reluctant acknowledgment in the Treaty of Westphalia (1648) of the sovereignty of local German princes.

The king of France and the sultan of Turkey were the most consistent opponents of the Hapsburg imperial power. (Their treaty of alliance, 1536, though seldom effective in the field, was a constant reproach to the Most Christian King of France.) In addition, Charles tangled violently with the papacy, and his soldiers sacked Rome in 1527. From the 1560's, however, after Spanish arms and Spanish piety had invaded Italy, captured the papacy, and inspired the Counter Reformation, the popes began to co-operate with the Hapsburgs. The resulting alliance between empire and papacy proved capable of reconverting nearly all the inhabitants of the Austrian, Hungarian, and Polish lands which had briefly proved hospitable to Protestantism.

In Germany, however, the Reformation enormously strengthened and intensified the opposition of local princes to any consolidation of the imperial power. After initial hesitation, Charles V declared himself firmly against Martin Luther and his followers; but wars with the French and Turks, fought mainly in Italy and the Mediterranean, kept him so busy that he never had time to marshal his full force against the

Lutherans. He confessed his inability to restore religious uniformity to Germany by making peace with the Lutheran princes in 1555, guaranteeing them the right to protect Lutheran forms of worship and doctrine. In the next year, Charles abdicated, transferring Spain and its empire together with the Burgundian lands to his son, Philip, but endowing his brother, Ferdinand, with Austria and the imperial title.

Yet even this division of the inheritance did not, in the end, permit consolidation of either part. Germany remained divided and its princes nursed a lively suspicion of Hapsburg imperial ambitions. For a long time Ferdinand and his heirs followed a cautious policy, while the greater power of Spain under Philip II struggled vainly first to consolidate and then to hold dominion over the Low Countries. The success of the Dutch revolt (1568–1609) and the English victory over the Spanish Armada in 1588 did not prevent the Spaniards from retaining the rest of the Burgundian lands in Europe and dominating most of Italy while staving off the Turks in the Mediterranean, establishing their empire over a vast region of the Americas, and even, for a while, annexing Portugal and the Portuguese empire (1580–1640).

Only after Philip's death (1598) did Spanish predominance begin to fade. France had been distracted by a series of religious wars which pitted rebellious Protestants against the royal authority, but emerged again as a strong and united state under Henry IV (1589–1610). Meanwhile industrial stagnation or even retrogression diminished Spain's capacity to equip the armies and navies needed to maintain her imperial position. As a result, leadership of the Hapsburg and Catholic cause in Europe passed to the Austrian branch of the family, descended from Charles V's brother Ferdinand I. His namesake, Ferdinand II (reigned 1619–37), was a far more energetic and ruthless monarch than his predecessors had been. His agents set out in the name of Catholic restoration to overthrow local rights and immunities. The result was to fan a revolt in Bohemia (1618) into thirty years of violent war that convulsed most of Europe. The collision between Protestant and Catholic forms of Christianity envenomed the conflict, but just as much at stake were the conflicting princely and imperial claims to sovereignty. When Ferdinand's forces seemed likely to win, first the Danes, then the Swedes, and finally the French intervened against the Hapsburg imperial cause. Brutal devastation of parts of Germany ended with the

Peace of Westphalia (1648), which guaranteed the emptiness of the imperial title by recognizing the sovereignty of the separate German princes. Thenceforward, for more than two hundred years, Germany remained divided among scores of local rulers whose courts and governments imitated but could not rival the really great power that emerged from the Peace of Westphalia—that is, France.

European Colonization and Trade

‡‡‡ The upshot of Europe's political, military, and religious history between 1500 and 1648 was, therefore, almost as confused as the events themselves. Plural sovereignties still divided the landscape, and their relations were complex and changeable as ever. Papal power remained real in much of Europe; Spain retained most of her empire both in the Americas and in Europe; and even the imperial power of the Austrian branch of the Hapsburg family found ample scope in consolidating and strengthening its administrative control over hereditary lands in Austria, Bohemia, and Hungary. The French dominance that emerged in 1648 was therefore very limited, even on the continent of Europe. When one considers naval power and overseas empire, French preponderance disappears, for England and the Dutch had both become formidable sea powers, superior to the French. They used their ships to encroach upon the Spanish and Portuguese overseas empires, dispatching traders to the Indian Ocean and colonists to the Americas.

The establishment of the Dutch and English East India companies (1600, 1601) gave a lasting and effective mercantile organization to the enterprises of these two nations in Indian and Far Eastern waters. At first it was the Dutch who won the most spectacular successes. From an initial venture in 1594, within a mere fifty years they drove the Portuguese from Malacca and Ceylon and established their power in Java, thus becoming the masters of the spice trade. Early English lodgments along the west coast of India were relatively modest.

In the Americas, however, the balance was reversed, for the English colonies in Virginia (founded 1607) and Massachusetts (founded 1620) soon outstripped the Dutch colony at New York (founded 1626). French colonization of Canada started almost simultaneously at Quebec (founded 1608). But by far the most lucrative European ventures across the Atlantic in the seventeenth century were directed toward the smaller islands of the Caribbean, where sugar plantations, worked by slaves imported from Africa, provided a commodity in high demand at home. By the 1640's, English, French, and to a lesser extent Dutch entrepreneurs had taken the lead in this trade, overtaking the Portuguese and Spaniards, who had first experimented with sugar along the Brazilian and Caribbean coastlines.

This very rapid expansion of European settlement and trade attested the restless growth of European power vis-à-vis other less volatile peoples and civilizations. All the futilities and confusions of European politics, the brutal clash of arms, and the impassioned struggle after theological certainty which constituted the stuff and substance of European experience in these years were not entirely in vain. Men seldom accomplished what they desired, but their struggles did very greatly increase Europe's capacity to mobilize wealth, manpower, and ingenuity for political and economic purposes. The consolidation of sovereignty and the expansion of the scope of governmental activity constituted one important aspect of this evolution. The rise of joint stock companies like the Dutch and English East India companies— and of other large-scale business enterprises—was another. Equally, in the intellectual and artistic realms, a reckless pursuit of truth and of beauty, enhanced and sometimes stimulated by advances of technology (e.g. printing, the telescope), imparted to European culture a greater variety and toughness than the comparatively parochial outlook and limited knowledge of the medieval age had allowed. We must consider these changes next.

The Renaissance

‡‡‡ The twin yet rival movements of Renaissance and Reformation emphasized different aspects of the European cultural inheritance. Men inspired by the ideal of giving rebirth to the knowledge, skills, and elegance of pagan antiquity magnified the Greco-Roman constituent of Europe's past, whereas believers anxious to reform religion on Biblical lines drew their main inspiration from the Judeo-Christian component of Western civilization. A few single-minded advocates in either camp sought to repudiate the other entirely; yet this was unusual, for a complex cross-play always existed between the two movements. Some of the greatest reformers were skilled classical scholars and found the

techniques which had been developed for establishing the correct texts of pagan authors applicable to Biblical studies too. Similarly, the artists and men of letters of the Renaissance remained deeply concerned with religion and questions of theology, not least, when, as with Machiavelli (d. 1527), they expressly renounced the Christian faith.

The Renaissance had, of course, taken form in Italy, from about 1350. A return to antiquity, with its memories of Roman greatness, naturally had strong appeal to Italians. More than that, Italian towns harbored secularly minded commoners and princely patrons who deliberately turned their attention toward things human and away from things divine.

The Italian Renaissance reached its peak just about the year 1500. Leonardo da Vinci's (d. 1519) restless probing of the natural world through his art and through minute observation of men and things, together with Niccolò Machiavelli's ruthless analysis of the nature and use of political power based upon personal experience and study of classical authors, well represents its culmination. Only a little later, Michelangelo Buonarroti (d. 1564) and Nicholas Copernicus (d. 1543)— who though he died in Poland drew his intellectual stimulus from the University of Padua where he had been trained—gave up the radical reliance on human rationality which seems implicit in the work of both da Vinci and Machiavelli. Michelangelo suffered torments of doubt about practically everything, even about the value of his art; and Copernicus' heliocentric system of astronomy, which assumed a circular instead of an elliptical orbit for the planets, was inspired by neo-Pythagorean number mysticism and actually flew in the face of observational data.

The attractions of the Renaissance ideal of beauty as created by human skill and of truth to be discovered by untrammeled exercise of human faculties were not lost on the rest of Europe. Aristocratic and courtly circles were particularly receptive north of the Alps; but wherever urban growth had created a substantial middle class—as in Holland, the Rhineland, England, and France—commoners, too, were soon attracted by local efforts to imitate or surpass Italian models. The result was the development of distinct national schools of literature and to some extent also of painting. Thus, for example, *Don Quixote* by Miguel Cervantes (d. 1616) and the plays of Lope de Vega (d.

1635) gave literary definition to the Spanish language. Modern French acquired its literary form through the labors of three utterly diverse men: François Rabelais (d. 1553), who mocked what he could not alter, John Calvin (d. 1564), who strove relentlessly to reform and sanctify all human life, and Michel Eyquem, seigneur de Montaigne (d. 1592), who recommended an aloof moderation in the face of human short-comings. English owes its literary definition to Elizabethan writers—William Shakespeare (d. 1616) above all—and to the King James Bible (1611). Modern literary German is the creation of Luther's trans-lation of the Bible. Most of the other tongues of Germanic Europe (Dutch, Danish, Swedish) took form also as a by-product of Protestant translations of the Bible into the vernacular.

The Reformation

‡‡‡ The other leading characteristic of Europe's cultural life in this age was the reassertion of religious concerns despite the charms of rampant secularism toward which the thought and sensibility of Ren-aissance Italy seemed to be moving.

Reform and reinvigoration of the Roman Catholic Church had been undertaken repeatedly in medieval Europe. By their very nature such movements challenged constituted ecclesiastical authorities, who were always tempted to declare their critics heretical. This had been the fate of John Wycliffe (d. 1384) in England and Jan Hus (d. 1415) in Bohemia, each of whom nevertheless attracted a considerable body of followers. The healing of the Great Schism in 1417 through the res-toration of papal monarchy at the Council of Constance made it harder for heresy to flourish in the following century. In Spain, particularly, religious conformity and political loyalty tended to coincide. The cru-sading spirit, fanned by centuries of war against the Moors (driven from Granada only in 1492), continued to inspire the Spanish imperial effort both in Europe and overseas. A uniquely close relationship be-tween church and state resulted. Elsewhere, pope and monarch usually collaborated in taxing the clergy, but were otherwise as often at odds as in alliance.

The papacy itself claimed sovereignty over part of Italy, and some popes allowed their pursuit of political advantage in the peninsula to outweigh the spiritual headship over Christendom their predecessors had so vigorously asserted. Elsewhere in Italy and Germany bishops and abbots often followed the pope's example.

Amidst such a tawdry religious scene, Martin Luther's (d. 1546) conviction, based on poignant personal experience of how a sinful man might still win through to salvation, flashed like the sword of an avenging angel. Luther initially challenged the validity of the sale of indulgences. Sales of these documents, which purported to relieve suffering souls from the torments of Purgatory, had been organized in a thoroughly commercial spirit as part of a campaign to raise money to build a new St. Peter's cathedral in Rome. According to the conventions of traditional scholastic debate Luther publicly denied the value of indulgences by posting 95 theses on the church door at Wittenberg in 1517. But instead of remaining a matter of academic controversy, Luther's views spread like wildfire through Germany. Public debates with champions of the papacy rapidly drove Luther toward more radical and complete exposition of his convictions. Three eloquent pamphlets written in 1520—*An Appeal to the Nobility of the German Nation, The Babylonian Captivity of the Church,* and *The Freedom of a Christian Man*—defined the heart of Lutheranism. Subsequent controversy developed numerous differences in doctrinal formulation between Catholics, Lutherans, and other kinds of Protestants. At the center of this theological strife was the question of the source of religious authority. Luther rested his case on the Bible and his own personal experience of what he felt to be the freely given grace of God. He further denied that the clergy had any necessary mediating role between the individual sinner and God, and boldly proclaimed the priesthood of all believers.

The printing press spread Luther's views rapidly and widely through Germany and adjacent lands. His protest speedily gathered other discontents behind the banner of church reform. Luther's attack on the papacy, for example, attracted many in Germany who felt aggrieved at being taxed and exploited by foreigners; but this expression of German nationalism was soon stifled by the refusal of the emperor, Charles V, and of other important rulers in Germany to become Lutheran.

Instead, therefore, of becoming German, the Protestant movement became European, particularly after John Calvin established his headquarters in Geneva (1541) and made it the center of a vigorous propaganda. England, for example, broke with the pope in 1534, but the Church of England became Protestant in doctrine only by degrees, very largely under stimulus from Geneva. Simultaneously the Dutch and Scots made Calvinism dominant in their countries. In France, on the contrary, the government remained Catholic. French Protestantism, after a promising start, lost its *élan* about 1600. In Italy, Protestantism never commanded wide support and withered quickly when the force of revived Catholicism became apparent. Scandinavia, on the other hand, became Lutheran, along with almost half of Germany. Local nationalisms, which were beginning to emerge all over Europe, played important parts in determining each of these results.

Social and economic protest also made a brief appearance in Lutheran dress. But when rebellious peasants took Christian liberty to mean relief from dues and rents, Luther denounced them violently (1525). Thereafter, social unrest and religious radicalism found expression among Anabaptists and other sects. These groups met severe persecution, and survived mainly among the poor, and often as secret or semi-secret groups.

The drastic nature of the social and economic changes that came to Europe between 1500 and 1648 contributed powerfully to religious controversy. Yet it would be wrong to forget that the search for an absolutely certain religious truth gathered enormous energy behind it simply because of the inherent attractiveness of a definite and coherent world view. Peace of mind required authoritative and adequate answers to the uncertainties that daily experience thrust so remorselessly upon a large proportion of Europe's population. Luther was sure about how he himself had gained God's grace. This was one of the secrets of his success, since others wished desperately to achieve a similar state of inward grace and assured salvation. When a man did achieve certainty, he naturally wished both to communicate the saving truth to others and to denounce error in all its guises. A great outpouring of preaching and writing, aimed at such explication, was soon supplemented by systematic schooling in carefully drawn-up catechisms. Defenders of the papacy presently developed Roman Catholic counter-propaganda. All across Europe a far greater knowledge of Christian doctrine and an emotionally deeper commitment to chosen or inherited forms of the faith resulted.

One of the ironies of Protestantism was its tendency to split into sects and sub-sects. The reformers never abandoned the ideal of a single Catholic church embracing all Christians. But the Bible—their sole source of religious authority—was capable of diverse interpretation. Truths that seemed self-evident to one man did not always seem so to others who were just as sincere and equally eager for the certainty of salvation. In such a case each was compelled to denounce the other as a preacher of false doctrine, and often did so with more vigor than charity. Yet as the white heat of the first generation of reform receded, efforts to build a church organization and enforce doctrinal conformity met with success in most parts of Protestant Europe. In

REFORMATION AND
COUNTER-REFORMATION

- - - - Stabilized Religious Frontier
⇒ Protestant Reform
→ Catholic Reform

Scale of Miles
0   500

England the process was more drawn out. Piecemeal reform under the Tudors (1534–1603) failed to satisfy a powerful group of rigorists, or Puritans. Their effort to make over all human life in accordance with God's will did not exhaust itself until after the utter failure of the government of saints under Oliver Cromwell (1658).

The Roman church reacted slowly to the Protestant challenge. At first many hoped that reconciliation could be achieved. Pious and educated Catholics, who were best capable of meeting the Protestant movement on its own terms, often hesitated to divide Christendom even more deeply by counter-attacking against the Lutherans. Yet the passionate drive for theological certainty which armed the Protestants could also be harnessed to the Catholic cause. St. Ignatius Loyola (d. 1556) did so. After a conversion experience as poignant as Luther's, he set out to preach the truth as a soldier of the pope. He soon collected a group of like-minded young men around himself and then organized them into the Society of Jesus, which speedily became a most effective agent for the defense and propagation of Catholicism, both in Europe and overseas. When the Jesuit order was still in its infancy, the Council of Trent (1545–63) assembled. After lengthy and thrice-suspended sessions, it succeeded in decreeing a number of practical reforms and defined disputed points of doctrine in a firmly anti-Protestant sense.

Thereafter the initial ambiguity of the appeal for church reform faded, and men everywhere in Europe were confronted by the spectacle of a comparatively well-organized, united, and reformed Roman Catholic church locked in combat with an equally determined but not nearly so tightly organized Calvinist movement, while Lutherans and conservative churchmen in England looked on with a general distaste for both of the protagonists. Eventually, the failure of pope and emperor in the Thirty Years' War (1618–48) and the almost simultaneous failure of the Puritan revolution in England (1640–60) turned many men's minds away from religious controversy, which, in the course of both conflicts, had often become a transparent disguise for ignoble political and economic interests.

The Growth of Science

‡‡‡ As a matter of fact, throughout the Reformation period a small but important company of men had not permitted the quest for theo-

logical certainty to eclipse other, more mundane concerns. Galileo Galilei (1564–1642), for example, lived through the height of Europe's religious conflicts, yet found it preferable to devote himself to physical and astronomical investigations. His defense of Copernican astronomy on the basis of telescopic observation and mathematical reasoning, and his ingenious efforts to give mathematical expression to carefully recorded observational data, inaugurated lines of inquiry which physicists and astronomers have not yet exhausted. René Descartes (d. 1650) was another who deliberately turned his back on theological controversy and instead set out to create a mathematically rigorous philosophy which would, with sublime impartiality and on the basis of reason alone, provide answers to metaphysical as well as to all other questions about which men had quarreled so bitterly and desperately since the time of Luther and before.

Other intellectual traditions were active and fruitful too. Paracelsus (1541), Andreas Vesalius (d. 1564), and William Harvey (d. 1657) successfully challenged the authority of Galen in medical matters, as much on mystical and neo-Platonic grounds as upon the basis of more exact observation of human anatomy. Similarly, a superstitious mystic, Johannes Kepler (d. 1630), strove vainly to discover the harmonic ratios among the orbits of the planets, but did, after vastly laborious computation, discover a mathematical formula that exactly described the elliptical motions of each separate planet in its orbit—thus, incidentally correcting Copernicus and removing one of the most important objections to the Copernican hypothesis. Still another tradition, optimistic and empirical, was represented by Francis Bacon (d. 1626), who argued that careful observation and systematic collection of information would allow men to unlock nature's secrets without the help of either religious revelation or mathematical reasoning.

Invention of a number of new instruments, particularly the telescope (c. 1608) and the microscope (c. 1590), the pendulum clock (c. 1656), thermometer (c. 1654), and barometer (c. 1643), gave the observations and experiments of the small company of natural philosophers much greater precision than had been possible in earlier ages. This, together with the vast influx of miscellaneous information flooding into Europe from overseas, provided a rich diet for those who preferred such studies to the controversies of theologians. Hence, when (after 1648) hostile religious camps came to be widely discredited among reflective men, the natural philosophers were ready and primed to offer a world view less complete perhaps but scarcely less fascinating than the rival theologies that had dominated the attention of earlier generations.

Yet it would be wrong to suggest that science supplanted religion. On the contrary, the Reformation age left behind a heightened religious concern in all walks of life. Science and other secular inquiries did not expressly oppose the claims of religion, which had been pitched so very high by reformers of both Protestant and Catholic persuasions. Rather, secular investigation grew up and throve in the interstices of knowledge which were treated as matters of indifference by theologians. Later, after about 1650, scientific investigation attained enough respectability that scientists and men of learning—at least those who lived in the most active centers of European civilization—no longer had seriously to worry about how their discoveries would fit into the frame of official theology. Quarrels continued to arise. But neither clergymen, defending Christian truth, nor scientists, arguing some new idea, were able to suppress or overthrow those who disagreed with them. Both appeal to force and appeal to the necessity for universal agreement on matters of importance, which had seemed self-evident and necessary in the Reformation age, slowly ceased to carry much conviction to politicians and the public.

Emergence of Cultural Pluralism

‡‡‡ Thus the upshot of Europe's long travail between 1500 and 1648 was strangely contrary to what almost all the great men of the age had desired. Instead of discovering and enforcing a universal truth, Europeans discovered that they could agree to disagree. Intellectual pluralism established itself on European soil more flagrantly than ever before. No official hierarchy of knowledge provided a complete scheme for understanding the world—as had been the case, in theory if not in practice, in medieval times. Each separate church, nation, and profession was in a position to pursue truth according to its own lights. Such diversity assured the continued and very rapid development of European thought down even to our own time.

Art and letters also exhibited an increasing pluralism. The rise of the vernacular which had occurred at the beginning of our period created separate national schools of literature. Painting, too, tended to diverge from the pattern established by the great Italians, so that Spanish (Velasquez, d. 1660; El Greco, d. 1614), Dutch (Rembrandt, d. 1669), and Flemish (Rubens, d. 1640) schools, each with distinctive traits, developed within the general European tradition. Architecture remained less variable. In all of Catholic Europe a baroque elaboration of Renaissance styles prevailed, whereas in most Protestant lands variations upon Gothic held the ground.

The trauma of emergence from the medieval mould was enormous. Never since have Europeans faced more agonizing or more pervasive uncertainties. Yet the severity of the experience called forth human genius and individual achievement on a most unusual scale. Columbus and Cortez, Luther and Loyola, Leonardo da Vinci and Descartes, Copernicus and Galileo—to name only a few of the greatest —were makers of the modern world in a more profound sense than were men of earlier or later generations who did not confront, as these men did, the challenges of a new world—both literally and metaphorically—opening before their startled eyes. The surpassing success with which these and scores of thousands of other Europeans rose to meet this unprecedented opportunity is best attested by the subsequent career of Western civilization, of which we and all the world are heirs.

CHAPTER 20

Europe's Outliers:

Russia and the Americas

1500-1648

At a time when China, India, and the Middle East found it unnecessary to make more than trifling accommodation to the European presence along their shores, Russian and American populations were already deeply entangled with western Europe. Paralyzing collapse came to Amerindian higher cultures, and the new institutions planted on American soil by the conquistadors in every case derived directly from Spain. Russian institutions were much tougher and did not crumble like Amerindian institutions at the first approach of armed strangers. Yet Russia, too, found it hard to shift from resisting traditional pressures from the steppe to resisting the quite novel challenges coming from western Europe. Severe strain in both church and state registered the difficulties of this about-face, which was quite as profound as western Europe's simultaneous struggle to emerge from its medieval chrysalis.

The Rise of Moscow

‡‡‡ Until 1480 most of the Russian lands remained under the suzerainty of the Khan of the Golden Horde, whose capital was at Kazan on the Volga river. The Golden Horde descended from one of the four segments into which the Mongol empire of Genghis Khan divided. But by the fifteenth century, the Khan of the Golden Horde and his warriors spoke Turkish, followed the Moslem religion, and were commonly referred to as Tatars. In the Russian lands that fell within his jurisdiction, the khan entrusted tax collection to the Grand Duke of Moscow, who did not always find it necessary to remit what he collected to his suzerain. Hence when Ivan III formally renounced his allegiance and assumed the title of tsar (1480), the act had more symbolic than practical significance. The really important fact was that the Tatars were unable to do anything about it. Military supremacy no longer rested securely with the cavalry archers of the steppe. The Kremlin, a citadel impregnable to anything short of prolonged siege, secured Moscow from capture. The artillery pieces defending it announced with their every discharge that the end of steppe nomad supremacy was at hand.

One should not, however, exaggerate the rapidity with which the new technical possibilities of warfare could be applied effectively on the ground. As late as 1571, for example, an unusually large Tatar raiding party burned the outskirts of Moscow. By that time infantry fire power had already become decisive on the battlefield, but the problem was how to bring elusive raiders to battle. Not until a string of fortified frontier posts had been constructed, manned by horsemen (Cossacks) as speedy as the Tatars themselves and better equipped with weapons than they, could steppe raiding be entirely halted. This occurred only after 1648.

Yet while satisfactory frontier defense against hit-and-run raids continued to exceed Russian military capability, the central fact remained: from about 1500, horse archers could no longer overcome well-equipped infantry. The trading and agricultural society of Russia could and did equip infantry regiments with guns, the master weapons of the age, whereas the nomad societies of the steppe, which had for so long enjoyed a fundamental military superiority over settled agriculturalists, refused to dismount in order to exploit the new technical possibilities of gunpowder. The radically new balance of power which resulted was not long in manifesting itself. In 1552, Ivan IV, the Terrible, captured Kazan. Four years later his soldiers completed the conquest of the lower Volga by taking Astrakhan. An enormous territory thereby came under Moscow's rule, and a line of river communication with Persia by way of the Caspian opened up. Russia's southern flank still remained exposed to raids by the Tatars of the Crimea. But their power depended on political alliance and commercial relations with Constantinople. A fully independent nomad empire could no longer survive in the face of civilized musketeers.

In the next generation, Russian pioneers crossed the Urals, overthrew the Moslem khanate of Sibir, and by 1587 had established themselves along the middle reaches of the Ob river. Once across the Ural mountains, their long-established skill as river boatmen (in winter, sleighdrivers) allowed Russian adventurers to cross the easy portages separating one Siberian river system from the next. As a result, in 1638 the first Russian explorers reached the Pacific at Okhotsk. Native hunters and gatherers who inhabited the grim and forbidding Siberian swamps and forests were few in number and politically weak. Hence, when Russians demanded tribute in furs, they set their hunting and snaring skills to work for their new masters and soon provided them with a commodity that was in great demand both in Europe and in China. Income from the export of furs was, in fact, especially important to the Russian state, since it allowed the import of European armaments and other manufactures on a scale that would have been impossible otherwise.

Withdrawal of the long-standing pressure exerted by the military superiority of the steppe peoples had, however, its disruptive side. As long as the Grand Duke of Moscow had to appease a distant but terrible suzerain in Kazan by delivering tributes punctually, the Russian people saw the necessity of obedience and submission to the Grand Duke's tax collectors. But, after the Tatar danger had gone, emigration into the new lands along the Volga or in the Ukraine became a practicable alternative to paying taxes; and many restless young men did in fact escape into the wilds. Rough and ready Cossack communities in the Ukraine and along the lower Don recruited their members in this way. Farther east, in the Volga and Ural regions, individual settlers and pioneers broke away even from the loose discipline of Cossack life and developed a style of isolated small-family existence very similar to that familiar on the North American frontier.

This sort of leakage extended Russian settlement to new ground rather rapidly. Loss of manpower could be borne by the central authority so long as enough peasants and townsmen remained behind to pay taxes. The discontents of the noble (boyar) class were far more dangerous. The fact that right next door in Poland-Lithuania, great nobles enjoyed effective independence from any sort of royal administration was a constant reminder of how easy it would be to live without the Muscovite autocracy. Religious distaste for the Catholicism of their western neighbors, was, perhaps, the strongest factor inhibiting a mass transfer of loyalty to Lithuania. The Muscovite autocrats, however, did not view treason lightly. Ivan IV acquired his sobriquet, the Terrible, through the bloody violence with which he attempted to destroy boyar opposition to his rule. He did, in fact, kill off so many of the old families as to make the creation of a noble republic on the Polish-Lithuanian model impossible. This became evident during Russia's Time of Troubles (1604–13), when despite breakdown of political legitimacy the old boyar families proved unable to seize and hold power in the name of aristocratic liberty on the Polish model. Instead, by common consent, autocracy was soon restored.

Western Influence—Political Turmoil

‡‡‡ The main reason that the Muscovite centralized and autocratic regime survived was the appearance of a new foreign threat, coming this time from the west rather than from the steppe. Western pressure had two dimensions: military-political and religious-cultural. Militarily, Ivan IV had found it impossible, despite very strenuous efforts, to avoid losing territory to Sweden and Poland. Ivan began the Livonian war (1557–82) with high hopes of matching his new-won Caspian coastline with a window on the Baltic. Instead, the war strained Muscovy to the limit and ended in failure. A generation later, during the Time of Troubles, when usurpers ruled and civil strife spread all through the Russian lands, Poland-Lithuania took the offensive. A Polish army occupied Moscow in 1608 and set up a puppet government. But a great revulsion against the foreigners soon developed among all classes of Russians. Simultaneously, civil disturbances in Poland weakened the invaders. In 1613, accordingly, the invaders withdrew and the Patriarch of Moscow was able to proclaim his son, Michael Romanov, tsar. The Romanov dynasty remained on the Russian throne until 1917.

Autocratic Russia's military and political survival—helped, incidentally, by the diversion of Swedish power into Germany during the Thirty Years' War and by Polish concern for the outcome of that struggle—remained precarious as long as Russian technology and wealth lagged a long way behind the levels attained farther west. Yet, by a supreme irony, deliberate and strenuous efforts to close the gap and overtake the West required wholesale resort to force. This, in itself, emphasized differences already dividing Russian from Western institutions and social relationships. Ivan IV's secret society of aides, bound to the service of the autocrat by common participation in orgies and crimes, constituted a strange caricature of Western bureaucracy, even though the "service nobility" he created performed the same functions that Western officials and army officers performed for their sovereigns. Moreover, at the bottom of Russian society serfdom was being fastened upon the peasantry precisely at the time when in more westerly lands peasants (along with the rest of society) were beginning both to suffer from and to enjoy greater personal freedom and independence.

The reason for this development is clear enough. In Russia the tsar lacked enough money income to pay salaries to officials and army personnel. He had, therefore, to reward his servants with grants of land. But land without peasants to work it was useless. To prevent peasants from running away, it seemed therefore necessary to pass laws authorizing landholders to chase after and capture runaways. By 1649, when a new-law code systematized previous enactments, a theoretically rigid frame had been imposed upon Russian society, whereby each man was required to remain at his post, in the place and walk of life to which he had been born. Russian reality never conformed to this legal prescription. Runaways continued to make good their escape to the frontiers, pushing the fringe of Russian society and settlement ever deeper into Asia and the Ukraine. Others, who happened to catch the eye of some powerful man, might rise from humble beginnings to the very top of officialdom—but always by exception.

Western Influence—Cultural Change

‡‡‡ The abrasive effect of contact with Westerners upon Russian religious and cultural life was almost as troublesome as these military-political tribulations. Russians badly needed a sense of national mission in

order to be able to counterattack and devalue the all-too-evident superiority of Western wealth and technique.

After the fall of Constantinople to the Turks in 1453, therefore, the Russians easily convinced themselves that their branch of the Orthodox church was the last stronghold of true Christianity. This flattering view came under severe attack after 1565, when Jesuit missionaries established themselves in Poland and, having quickly routed their Protestant opponents, turned serious attention to the task of converting Orthodox Christians to the papal obedience. At that time, the Polish-Lithuanian state embraced a broad band of west Russian lands whose Orthodox inhabitants recognized the ecclesiastical jurisdiction of Kiev. When, therefore, in 1596, the Metropolitan of Kiev together with most of his subordinate bishops accepted the papal definition of Christian doctrine, the shock in Muscovy was sharp. The fact that the Ukrainian or "Uniate" church was permitted to retain a Slavonic ritual for church services did nothing to diminish Orthodox dismay.

Yet effective rebuttal to Jesuit arguments for Roman Catholic doctrine was difficult. Russian church books were not everywhere precisely the same, and some copyists' and translators' errors had crept into the most familiar of all sacred texts, the ritual phrases of the Eucharist. As long as no unfriendly critic called such anomalies to their attention, Russian churchmen had found no trouble in adhering to traditional formulas, despite minor local variations. But once Jesuit scholars had pointed an accusing finger at such irregularities, how, indeed, could Orthodox Russia's claim to a monopoly of Christian truth be sustained? Worse yet, how could the real truth, the authentic sacred phrase, be recognized amid the confusing textural variants that in fact had been inherited from the past? The traditional learning and piety of the Russian church was quite unable to cope with this problem.

Nevertheless, the Russians could fall back on one undoubted fact: Greek Christianity was older and therefore presumably more authentic than the Latin Christian tradition so ably represented by the Jesuits. Yet, to alter Russian liturgical books in order to bring them into accord with Greek models constituted a confession of past error, which the Russian church found hard to stomach. Salvation itself, they felt, depended on correct ritual. Error—or at least its admission—endangered the whole structure of Orthodox dogma.

Religious scholarship and propaganda were not, of course, the only guises in which western European cultural achievements came to Russian attention between 1500 and 1648. Ivan III initiated the importation of Italian workmen and architects to beautify and dignify Moscow with buildings of stone. Italian stone-masonry and decorative motifs when crossed with older Russian styles of wooden church architecture, and livened also with a dash of Persian elegance, produced the famous Cathedral of St. Basil, which adorns Moscow's Red Square. This amazing and remarkably successful structure was built for Ivan IV to celebrate his victory over the khanate of Astrakhan in 1556.

Russian icon painting, also, reached its climax during this period. The artists harnessed painters' skills derived from Italy and Byzantium to the expression of the mystical piety that sustained the Russian Orthodox church through the long decades when its spokesmen could find no effective reply to Roman Catholic criticism. Until 1648, this emotion allowed Russian Orthodox civilization to remain spiritually independent, despite constant contact with the parts of Europe where the cultural mutation of early modern times was proceeding so powerfully.

Spanish America

‡‡‡ The traumatic experiences of Holy Russia, due to its uncomfortable geographical proximity to western Europe, were slight in comparison to the shocks suffered by Amerindians who had to confront the same challenge with a far weaker cultural inheritance to rely on. As a matter of fact there was no organized, prolonged struggle to preserve the pre-Columbian ways of life. Instead, a catastrophic collapse of Amerindian cultural leadership allowed the Spaniards—few in number though they were—to substitute themselves for the vanished priests and warrior clans of the Aztec and Inca realms. Within little more than a generation, all the important inhabited locations of Mexico and Peru had become at least superficially Christian. Soon thereafter, wherever the needful labor power and architectural skill could be mobilized, huge baroque churches arose. In details of decoration they sometimes betray the hand of an Indian artist only imperfectly familiar with European prototypes; otherwise they look as though they had been translated bodily from Spain.

In cities and towns, legal forms and relationships were promptly recast in a Spanish, as well as Catholic, mould. The mines, too, whence came the flow of silver that so disturbed the world's price system, were promptly organized along European technical lines. But the great peasant majority at first lived much as before. The new masters with their religion and laws played the same limited role in their lives that the vanished rulers of the Aztec and Inca past had done. This simple relationship was soon upset by the fact (see p. 306) that diseases cut deeply into village manpower. As depopulation proceeded, the old subsistence agriculture broke down, for the Spaniards badly needed the village labor that did remain to feed the towns and to work in the mines. To be sure, Spanish law did not permit enslavement, and official policy, as laid down in Madrid, protected Indian rights very thoroughly. All the same, the needs of Spanish settlers came first, and when they required Indian labor they got it, usually by allowing the Indians to incur debts and then enforcing a creditor's perfectly legal rights against insolvent debtors. Such debts became hereditary; and Indian debtors were put to work under the direction of the Spanish settlers to perform whatever tasks the Spaniards needed done.

After the first rush of gold-hungry conquistadores subsided, Christian missionaries took over their role as pioneers along the frontiers of the Spanish domains. Jesuits, Franciscans, and others labored both to save souls and to civilize their charges by teaching them the useful arts of Europe. A remarkable mission society arose in Paraguay, for example, where Jesuit priests exercised a truly benevolent despotism to create a large and prosperous Indian community among tribes that had previously been quite primitive. Skillful management made the mission pay for itself through export to European markets of the product of the Indians' labor. Before long the Jesuits were in fact able to make substantial profit from their enterprise.

Other European Colonists

‡‡‡ Jesuit efforts within the framework of a mission society to transform native behavior along rational economic lines were interestingly intermediate between the paternalistic and protective policy officially adopted by Spanish authorities toward the Indian villages of Mexico and Peru, and the ruthlessly rational slave-staffed plantation economies that developed along the Caribbean and Brazilian coasts and in some of

the Caribbean islands. In these regions, the native Indian population died away quite rapidly. But labor power was needed; slaves imported from west Africa filled the gap. An Englishman, John Hawkins, piloted the first slave ship to Spanish waters in 1562–63; but until sugar cultivation became firmly established (after about 1630) Negro slavery and agricultural plantations were not of great importance. After that date this inhumane mode of exploiting the land of America with the labor of Africa rapidly assumed a vast scale, and directed to the New World a stream of migration from Africa almost as large as the migration from Europe itself.

The entrepreneurs of the slave economy in the New World were mainly Portuguese, English, French, and Dutch, not Spanish. With their arrival on the scene, the Amerindians confronted considerably more ruthless intruders than the Spaniards had been. Missionary concern for the welfare of the bodies as well as the souls of their converts had always been a real factor in limiting Spanish exploitation of their Amerindian subjects. No comparable inhibitions checked the behavior of Portuguese, English, and Dutch settlers and traders. The French, like the Spaniards, attempted to organize missions and to protect the Indians of Canada from the ill effects of too rapid exposure to European civilization. Success was small, because unlike the situation in Paraguay, where the Jesuits maintained a strict quarantine against any but authorized movement into and out of their domain—to control spiritual rather than bacteriological infection—the Canadian missions were not proof against destructive epidemics of smallpox and similar diseases. Hence French benevolence, as much as English and Dutch indifference, had the effect of disrupting and destroying pre-existing Indian societies along the east coast of North America. In Brazil, the Portuguese colonization, which dated from 1530, had similar consequences.

Until after 1648, of course, European settlement in North America as well as in Brazil remained very near the coast. The vast interiors of the two continents were only indirectly affected by the arrival of white men. But indirect effects could be important, as, for example, the development and spread of a Plains Indian culture across the North American prairie. This nomadic, hunting style of life was based upon the use of horses to hunt buffalo—horses which had, of course, first been introduced into America by the Spaniards.

Thus, even in regions where European settlement had not yet penetrated and in parts of the continent where no European foot had yet trod, the impact of the West's civilization was sometimes felt. Just as the Russians could no longer afford to disregard the stimuli and challenges emanating from the lands that lay across their western frontier, so also the Americas had clearly become an outlier of the civilization of western Europe. In 1648, no other parts of the world had yet suffered anything like so drastic a shift of cultural climate.

CHAPTER 21

The Realm of Islam, with Its Hindu and Christian Subject Communities, 1500-1700

 Local and temporary set-backs notwithstanding, the realm of Islam had tended steadily to increase ever since Mohammed first established the holy community of the faithful at Medina. This age-old process did not come abruptly to a halt after A.D. 1500, despite the Far West's new dominion of the seas. On the contrary, India, southeast Asia, Africa, and Europe all continued to be theaters for Moslem expansion. Indeed, if one estimates millions of square miles or numbers of new subjects brought under Moslem rule between 1500 and 1700, these two centuries would certainly rank among the most successful of the entire Moslem era.

In India, for example, a flow of refugees and adventurers from north of the mountains supplied Moslem rulers with enough fighting manpower to allow them to overwhelm the last important independent Hindu state in south India, the empire of Vijayanagar, in 1565. And just at the close of our period almost the whole of Peninsular India was brought under the single sovereignty of the Mughal emperor Aurangzeb (1658–1707).

In southeast Asia, a coalition of Moslem coastal states combined to overthrow the Hinduized empire of Java between 1513 and 1526. Both before and after this conquest, successful missionary activity, conducted by merchants and itinerant Sufi holy men, continued to spread Islam throughout the ports and coastal districts of southeast Asia as far as Mindanao in the Philippines and Borneo in Indonesia. Penetration of Africa continued, operating overland rather than by sea, and substituting caravans for ships. In both these great regions, the development of trade and market relations went hand in hand with an acceptance of Islam by those elements in the local population that were most active in the new sorts of economic activity such trade provoked. Subsequently, military operations and administrative pressures were often applied to bring the countryside and remoter parts into the Moslem fold. Thus a series of imperial Moslem states arose in west Africa—Bornu, Morocco, Timbuctoo, and Sokoto—whose policy toward pagans resembled that which Charlemagne had followed in northwestern Europe nearly a thousand years before when he converted the stubborn Saxons to Christianity by force.

In Europe itself resistance to Islam was better organized than in India, Africa, or southeast Asia. Yet there too, Moslem power advanced at the expense of Christendom. By 1543 most of Hungary came under Turkish administration. Thereafter recurrent border wars tended, as late as 1683, to favor the Turks as against both the Poles and the Austrian Hapsburgs. Ottoman military inferiority vis-à-vis the Europeans first became unmistakable during the long war, 1683–99, which began with the second Turkish siege of Vienna and ended with the transfer of most of Hungary from Ottoman to Austrian hands. Yet a provincial variant of Ottoman society continued to expand and consolidate itself in Rumania long after 1699, though it is true that Turkish power in this region of the empire was exercised only indirectly through Greeks of Constantinople.

Only in the western and central steppelands of Eurasia, did Islam suffer permanent territorial setback before 1700. Russia's advance at the expense of the successor states to the Golden Horde, the Moslem khanates of Kazan, Astrakhan, and Sibir, has already been mentioned. Farther east on the steppe, Islam suffered another equally serious defeat. Between 1550 and 1650 a revivified Tibetan Lamaism (the "Yellow Church") forestalled Islam in Mongolia and displaced it in the regions of central Asia around the Ili river.

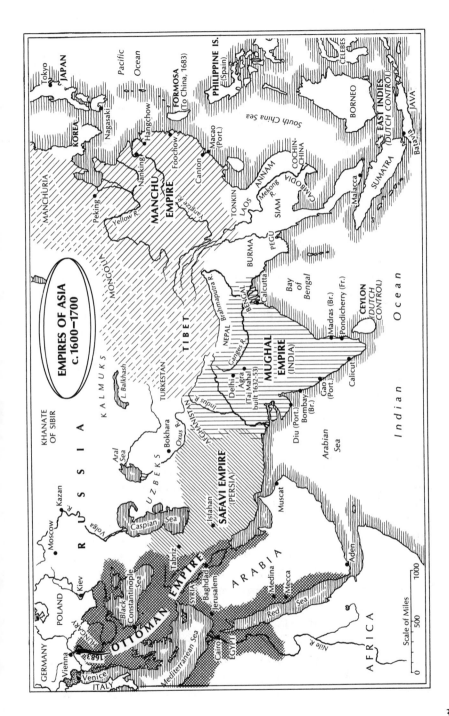

EMPIRES OF ASIA c. 1600–1700

GERMANY
POLAND
Moscow
Kiev
Kazan
Vienna
1683
Venice
ITALY
HUNGARY
Black Sea
Constantinople
OTTOMAN EMPIRE
Mediterranean Sea
Cairo
EGYPT
Jerusalem
SYRIA
Baghdad
Tabriz
ARABIA
Medina
Mecca
Red Sea
Aden
Muscat
Nile R.
AFRICA

RUSSIA
Volga R.
Caspian Sea
Aral Sea
Oxus
Bokhara
UZBEKS
Isfahan
SAFAVI EMPIRE (PERSIA)
AFGHANISTAN
KHANATE OF SIBIR
KALMUKS
L. Balkhash
TURKESTAN
TIBET
MONGOLIA

Arabian Sea
Diu (Port.)
Bombay (Br.)
Indus R.
Ganges R.
NEPAL
Brahmaputra R.
Delhi
Agra
(Taj Mahal built 1632–53)
MUGHAL EMPIRE (INDIA)
Goa (Port.)
Calicut
Madras (Br.)
Pondicherry (Fr.)
CEYLON (DUTCH CONTROL)
Bay of Bengal
Calcutta
BENGAL

Indian Ocean

MANCHURIA
Peking
MANCHU EMPIRE
Yellow R.
Nanking
Hangchow
Foochow
Canton
Yangtze
Macao (Port.)
KOREA
Nagasaki
JAPAN
Tokyo
Pacific Ocean

FORMOSA (To China, 1683)
PHILIPPINE IS. (Spain)
South China Sea
BURMA
PEGU
TONKIN
LAOS
ANNAM
SIAM
CAMBODIA
COCHIN-CHINA
Mekong R.
Malacca
SUMATRA
Batavia
JAVA
EAST INDIES (DUTCH CONTROL)
BORNEO
CELEBES

Scale of Miles
0   500   1000

The steppe, however, was in itself poor and unpromising country. When trade routes ceased to run across the grasslands (being diverted north along the Siberian rivers and south through the oceans), Moslem merchants and holy men, who had long been the principal missionaries of Islam, simply ceased to frequent these lands. The remarkable successes of Tibetan Lamaism on the steppe therefore owed something to the withdrawal of Moslem competition.

Inroads of European Commerce

‡‡‡ On the seas, matters were more complex. On both the Mediterranean and the Indian Ocean, Spanish and Portuguese fleets challenged and in critical battles defeated Moslem sea power. Yet the naval resources of the two Iberian states were never great enough to allow them to drive Moslem shipping from the seas. Hence a long series of Mediterranean struggles ended in 1578 with Turkish sea power dominant in the eastern Mediterranean, just as it had been in 1511 when the contest began. In the Indian Ocean, also, small and light Moslem ships recovered most of the trade they had lost to the Portuguese. Before the end of the sixteenth century the Portuguese even decided to admit Moslem vessels to ports under their control because they needed revenue from harbor tolls.

After 1600, however, a new regime began to assert itself upon the seas. Dutch, English, and French vessels supplanted Spanish and Portuguese as the principal merchantmen of the Indian Ocean and Mediterranean Sea. In the short run, this shift certainly looked like a victory for the Moslem cause. In each case the newcomers established their first footholds by virtue of special treaty arrangements with Moslem rulers, and refrained from any sort of Christian missionary activity. This represented a sharp change in policy. Missions had been as important as trade for the Portuguese and Spaniards, whereas the new Dutch, English, and French traders left the field of religious propaganda exclusively to the Moslems.

Nevertheless, the economic activities of the newcomers proved in the long run a much more powerful solvent to traditional Moslem styles of life than Iberian religious propaganda had ever been. Moslem minds, after all, were effectively closed against even the most eloquent and learned Christian missionary by the assurance, central to all Islamic learning, that Mohammed's revelation had corrected and therefore superseded the partial and distorted truths of Christianity. But Moslem society was by no means proof against economic rationalization and the expansion of market relations, especially when repercussions of the European price revolution lapped over into the realm of Islam.

Inland regions were, of course, least affected. At any great distance from salt water, age-old patterns of caravan trade and artisan production, peasant-town exchanges and interregional trade in luxury objects, remained almost unaffected by the business practices, organization, and energy of Europeans. But along the coasts far-reaching changes had begun to manifest themselves by 1700. In the Ottoman empire, for example, commercial agriculture made rapid advances, based in part on maize and tobacco brought from the Americas and on cotton come originally from India. The peasantries of Roumania, Bulgaria, Thrace, and Macedonia, together with others living in Anatolia, began to feed themselves and their animals on maize, and were able to export much larger quantities of wheat and cattle than before because the new American crop was so much more productive than older crops had been. The coastal lands of the Black Sea and the north Aegean were the main theaters of this development.

The rise of commercial agriculture in the Ottoman empire did not stimulate manufactures. Artisan guilds clung to traditional processes. They possessed powerful allies in the janissary corps, whose members intermingled with the artisans of all the main cities of the Ottoman empire after 1572, when these formidable soldiers were first legally permitted to marry. Entrepreneurial energy was diverted from industrial and commercial channels by the superior gains to be had by tax farming and making loans at high interest rates to aspirants for high office. Officials repaid such loans by squeezing money from the public in both legal and extra-legal ways. Thereby, of course, they made new industrial or commercial ventures nearly impossible, since anyone who could afford to invest in a new enterprise became an obvious target for tax collectors and bribe-seeking local officials. The absence of technical advance in manufactures and the restrictions upon entrepreneurial energy in trade meant that Ottoman exports tended to become almost exclusively agricultural. This resembled what had happened in the last centuries of Byzantine independence, when Italian cities took over the commerce of the Levant. The parallel augured ill for the economic health of Ottoman society.

In the Indian Ocean, European merchants also began to alter Asian economies by their systematic and organized pursuit of profit. The great European trading companies were under constant home pressure to export more goods to India and thus reduce the outflow of silver. But woolen cloth and other European manufactures were generally too coarse to command much sale in the warm climates that prevailed on the shores of the Indian Ocean. Dutch and English merchants had, therefore, to try to develop profitable carrying trade between Asian ports, for this alone would allow them to pay for the goods of Asian origin that they brought back to Europe without having to ship large quantities of gold and silver to India in exchange. They did so with very considerable success.

The English, for example, organized cotton cloth manufacture in western India by advancing small sums of money to the spinners and weavers. In return, they specified the sort of cloth they wished to have produced, and by regulating the scale of such advances could also affect the amount of cloth reaching the market. The "calicos" thus made to English specification were sold up and down the African and Asian coasts, wherever purchasers could offer anything of commercial value in exchange. This sort of trade stimulated rapid development of many parts of the southeast Asian coastlands, where relatively simple, subsistence societies had previously dominated the scene. Under such a regime, the coasts of Burma and Siam, for example, and the Philippine Islands, together with Java and Sumatra, underwent very rapid commercial development—mainly agricultural. East Africa, however, found it easier to export men. The African coast became the seat of a series of slave-raiding principalities and port cities supplying slaves to the Moslem world on a scale that rivaled but never equaled the west African slave trade with the Americas.

The areas of the spice islands which fell under Dutch control witnessed an even more intensive and systematic economic transformation. For the Dutch early embarked upon a policy of military conquest, and found it possible to pay the costs of administration by compelling local princelings to deliver specified quantities of agricultural commodities that could be sold on the world market. In this way the Dutch made local notables into plantation overseers, and reduced the cultivators to a sort of semi-serfdom. New crops were systematically introduced. Coffee from Arabia, tea from China, and sugar cane from India were all imposed upon the Javanese by the imperious demands of the Dutch, whose policy was based on calculations of how to maximize profit by securing the best assortment of commodities to suit an ever-changing market demand.

Moslem political sovereignty, exerted in India and southeast Asia through traditional administrative forms, was obviously far less important for the lives of Indian weavers and Javanese cultivators than was the new, market-oriented, capitalistic enterprise directed by English and Dutch agents of incorporated companies whose headquarters were in London or Amsterdam, and whose owners were identified only by the possession of pieces of embossed paper called stock certificates! Yet, in 1700 this was not easy to recognize. A Moslem statesman or religious expert could very reasonably congratulate himself upon how successfully the tried and true institutions of Islam had withstood the Iberian crusade which, at the beginning of our period, had seemed as serious a threat as the medieval Crusades had been in a still earlier time. In both cases, the crusading movement had been blunted and then turned back successfully, while the realm of Islam had continued to expand. What better proof of Allah's favor and of Islam's superiority to all other faiths could be asked?

The Shi'a Revolt

‡‡‡ The smug self-satisfaction which such a frame of mind induced was the more remarkable because at the very beginning of the sixteenth century Islam had experienced a profound religious shock. Moslem lands had long been hospitable to various religious sects, divided into the two general camps of Sunni and Shi'a. Many Shi'a groups conformed outwardly to Sunni forms of piety, but taught a secret doctrine to trusted initiates that was sometimes, as among the Bektashi order of dervishes, fundamentally hostile to all forms of organized religion. Most Moslem rulers supported the Sunni position officially and tolerated dissenting groups as long as they made no overt attack upon the official religious establishment.

This *modus vivendi* was rudely shaken in the year 1502, when, after a series of rapid victories, a fanatical Shi'a sect of Turkish tribesmen saw their leader, Ismail Safavi, crown himself shah in Tabriz. In quick succession Ismail conquered Baghdad (1508) and then secured his eastern flank by administering a crushing defeat to the Uzbeks of Bokhara. In 1514 his forces met the imperial muster of the Ottoman empire at Chaldiran; but despite defeat in the field Ismail had the satisfaction of seeing the victorious sultan withdraw because the Ottoman janissaries refused to press forward.

Shah Ismail's military career was not so very remarkable in itself, for Tamerlane (d. 1405) and other central Asian captains had previously been able to create great states almost as speedily. What made the establishment of the Safavi empire so disturbing to the Moslem world was that the shah's unlettered followers thought him to be Allah incarnate; and even his more learned and theologically erudite supporters, in whose ears such a claim was sacrilege, argued that, as a descendant of the seventh of the twelve legitimate rulers of Islam, Shah Ismail was rightfully the head of the entire Moslem community.

Such claims, advanced with the full fanaticism of complete conviction and sustained by a series of striking military victories, introduced a profoundly disturbing element into the realm of Islam. For if the Safavi claims were correct, all other Moslem rulers were of course usurpers. In many parts of the Moslem world there were important groups of Shi'a sectarians who were prepared to listen sympathetically to such ideas. Indeed, Shah Ismail's supporters provoked a large-scale rebellion in Anatolia in 1514, defying Ottoman authority with fanatical zeal.

The Ottoman response was swift and effective: the sultan, Selim the Grim (ruled 1512–20), defeated the rebels of Anatolia and mercilessly hunted down remnants of the disaffected communities afterwards. This discouraged other Shi'a groups in other parts of the Ottoman empire from open revolt. He then pressed forward against Ismail himself but, as we have seen, failed to destroy the root of the trouble because the janissaries refused to march onward against the heretical shah. In subsequent campaigns Selim annexed Syria, Egypt, and Arabia, thus forestalling an alliance between Ismail and the rulers of these lands and gaining control over the religiously strategic centers of Mecca and Medina. His successor, Suleiman the Lawgiver (ruled 1520–66), concentrated upon combatting Shi'a heresy by organizing Sunni orthodoxy at home. He instituted state support for Sunni religious colleges and state control of religious functionaries in all the important towns of the empire. Such a policy would have excited the liveliest resistance in earlier ages; but the Sunni doctors accepted Suleiman's regulations without demur, partly because of the attraction of state salaries, and partly because they feared the fanaticism and disorder that Shah Ismail's religious revolution threatened to spread throughout Islam.

From about 1514, Shah Ismail himself found that the fires of religious revolution needed control. He summoned doctors of Shi'a law, of the Twelver sect, from all over the Islamic world, and with their help set out to purify his lands of all traces of erroneous belief. In pursuit of this end he persecuted Sunni and dissenting Shi'a groups and confiscated their properties. Simultaneously, the vigorous popular propaganda upon which Ismail's power had originally been based was directed into more nearly orthodox channels. Precise equivalents of the "shorter catechisms," which Protestant teachers were at the same time imprinting upon the minds of their followers, spread familiarity with the tenets of the Twelver sect among nearly all of Ismail's subjects.

The duel between the Sunni and Shi'a versions of Islam, embodied so spectacularly in the collision between the Safavi and Ottoman monarchs, presented all the other Moslem states and peoples with an often embarrassing choice. Everywhere long-standing and traditional local arrangements between Sunni and Shi'a sects threatened to erupt into bitter struggles. Religious principles tended to become an index of political loyalty. The Mughals of India were particularly embarrassed. At low points in their fortunes, both Babur (d. 1530), the founder of the Mughal dynasty, and his son Humayun (ruled 1530–56) publicly professed the Shi'a faith in hope of securing much-needed aid from the shah. Later when their position in India seemed stronger, they proclaimed their independence of the Safavis by renouncing the Shi'a form of Islam in favor of Sunni doctrine. Akbar (ruled 1556–1605), under whose administration Mughal power became for the first time securely established, preferred to claim independent religious authority for himself. He experimented with Hindu and Christian as well as Moslem forms of piety, to the agonized scandal of Roman Catholic missionaries, who convinced themselves more than once that the emperor was on the point of conversion.

Under Shah Abbas the Great (ruled 1587–1629) the power of

the Safavi state reached its peak, but the fires of religious conviction had dimmed—at least in court circles—by that time. Ottoman fears correspondingly relaxed, and in 1638, the sultan's government concluded a lasting truce with their former enemy. Religious tensions were, indeed, so much reduced that after 1656, when a reform administration achieved power in Constantinople, the new Grand Vizier, Mohammed Kuprili, actually allowed crypto-Shi'a groups to operate freely again in Ottoman society. One interesting result was that for the first time in more than two hundred years conversion from Christianity to Islam again assumed an important scale in Crete, Albania, and southern Bulgaria, where heterodox dervish communities became especially active.

Intellectual Retreat and Artistic Advance

‡‡‡ The cultural repercussions of the Sunni-Shi'a split within Islam were as far-reaching as its political-military consequences. Persian poetry dried up at its source, since delicate ambiguities between divine and human love upon which that poetry turned were anathema to the stern sectaries who followed Ismail. More important, perhaps, the learned men of Sunni Islam failed, in a fundamental sense, to fulfill their social responsibility. The doctors of Sunni Islam did not meet the Shi'a challenge on its own terms—that is, as a religious doctrine claiming to be true. Instead, they fell back on the secular arm and everywhere repressed their rivals and critics by force. When, therefore, at a later time European ideas and knowledge clearly called much traditional Moslem lore into question, the learned class of the Ottoman empire was in no position to investigate the new ideas responsibly. Having avoided one challenge by sheltering behind the police power of the Ottoman state, the experts in the Sacred Law also declined to grapple seriously with the second challenge, perhaps for fear of exposing their flanks to religious attack from within the Islamic community while trying to cope with Christendom's intellectual novelties. Better, they felt, to repeat the Koran and to memorize commentaries upon the Sacred Law and thus assure Allah's good favor. As long as Moslem military power remained great enough to meet all comers on equal terms, such resolute conservatism and anti-intellectualism was, of course, a tenable posture. Its eventual costs became clear only after

1700, when Moslem state power everywhere proved unable to resist new-sprung rivals.

Intellectual stultification, induced very largely by official policy, did not imply artistic decay. On the contrary, the rise of great empires in the Moslem world assured ample and comparatively stable patronage for architects and artists of all varieties. Isfahan, for example, was constructed as a garden city by order of Shah Abbas the Great. It is one of the most impressive monuments of architectural and city planning in the world. On a smaller but still very grand scale, the Taj Mahal of India was built to suit the Mughal emperor's taste between 1632 and 1653. Persian art, likewise, continued to flourish into the seventeenth century. In India new growth occurred when painters applied Persian techniques to Hindu religious themes. Such paintings appealed to "Rajput" landowners, whose Persianate culture and service to the Mughal empire did not wean them from the Hindu faith of their forefathers.

Indeed, by any standard except that set by the contemporary pace of cultural development in western Europe, Islam was in a flourishing condition between 1500 and 1700. Not decay, therefore, nor yet stagnation, but vigorous growth is the right phrase with which to describe Islamic society in this period. It is ironic to reflect—with benefit of hindsight—that precisely during these years of success Islam failed to grapple with or even to notice vital challenges which Europeans were beginning to present both on the economic and on the intellectual level.

Other Religions Under Moslem Rule

‡‡‡ Before turning from the Moslem to the Far Eastern cultural domain, something should be said about the history of the Hindus and Buddhists who found themselves under Moslem rule or on the edges of an expanding Islamic world. Likewise, the fate of the Orthodox Christians of the Balkans, who constituted an important part of the Ottoman body politic, deserves attention.

Between 1500 and 1700 Hinduism underwent a revival in India. Moslem conquest deprived Hinduism of state support, though the new rulers tolerated most traditional rites. This in effect forced the religion into the streets, where a company of holy men and poets provided India's ancient and amorphous faith with vibrant new forms of adoration.

The saint and revivalist, Chaitanya (d. 1527) was believed by his devotees to be a living incarnation of Krishna. He gathered around himself a following of enthusiasts who repudiated caste distinctions and other outwardnesses of religion in favor of intensely emotional public ceremonies. In Bengal, where Chaitanya spent most of his time, the new sect effectively stopped conversion to Islam. This meant that as Indian society slowly advanced eastward and tamed the jungles beyond the Ganges delta, conversion to Hinduism rather than to Islam became again the hallmark of incorporation into civilized society. The present-day division of Bengal between Bangladesh, a Moslem state, and India is, of course, the direct result, for, as we saw, Islam had previously met with solid success along this frontier.

Two important poets, Sur Das (d. 1563) and Tulsi Das (d. 1623), did even more than Chaitanya to revivify Hinduism, since their influence was not confined to a single sect. Both used Hindi verse to develop themes from the rich tradition of Hindu mythology. They thus created a stock of chants and hymns suitable for religious celebrations that could be understood by the general public of northern India where Hindi was spoken. Tulsi fastened attention on the figure of Rama, Sur preferred Krishna: but both these deities were viewed as incarnations of Vishnu. Thus there was no clash of doctrine, between the two great renovators of Hindu piety. Save for the followers of Chaitanya, there was not even any repudiation of ancient Sanskrit piety or of Brahmanical ritual. But Sanskrit was left to professionals. Daily religion found expression in the Hindi vernacular. The warm emotion generated by the adoration of a divine yet human deity, with whom the pious devotee could enter into mystic union in moments of public religious excitement, made popular Hinduism entirely proof against the arguments of both Moslem and Christian missionaries. Political eclipse after 1565 therefore altered the form but entirely failed to destroy the spirit of Hinduism. The overwhelming majority of Indians remained, as always, true to the protean religion of their ancestors.

Buddhism survived among three smaller peoples as a religion of state: the Singhalese of Ceylon, the Burmese of Burma, and the Thai of Siam. In each case Buddhism served as a national identity marker, protecting each of these peoples against the encroachment of polyglot, cosmopolitan faiths: first Islam, then Christianity. Those nations welcomed Christians at first, partly at least as counterweight to long-standing Moslem pressures, but as soon as the European presence seemed to threaten traditional ways in any important fashion, each instituted a policy of isolation and withdrawal. Not until the nineteenth century did the barriers thus erected against outsiders fall before renewed European thrusts.

The Orthodox Christian subjects of the Ottoman empire inevitably shared many of the experiences of their Turkish masters. Prejudice against the Latin west was as deep among Greek Orthodox Christians as among the Moslems themselves. Hence it is not surprising that when the Patriarch Cyril Lukaris (d. 1638) inaugurated discussion of issues raised by Calvinists and Catholics from the west, his efforts met with little success. The overwhelming majority of Orthodox churchmen felt well content with the doctrinal formulae they had inherited from the church fathers and the ecumenical councils of the fourth and fifth centuries. Medical men, however, kept in touch with new ideas coming from Italy and other centers of European science. The most competent Greek doctors were trained at the University of Padua, and in the course of their student days they absorbed familiarity with many aspects of Western culture. Such individuals provided a slender but strategically important transmission belt by means of which intellectual contact between the separated halves of Christendom was maintained.

An important change in the relationship between the Ottoman government and the subject Christian communities came when the Sultan ceased to recruit members of his slave family from Christian villages of the Balkan wild west. As long as the highest officials and military leaders of the empire spent the first twelve to twenty years of their lives as peasant boys in remote, usually impoverished, mountain villages, a general sympathy for the Christian peasantry pervaded the Ottoman administration. A very different bias prevailed when these posts came to be filled by the sons of placeholders—a transformation that came about gradually between 1572, when legal marriage was first permitted within the sultan's slave family, and 1638, when recruitment from Christian villages was discontinued.

When the high officials of the empire came to be city folk, born and bred, they began to exploit the villagers and to wink at the dubiously legal actions of others who sought to use peasant labor to establish commercial farming. Radical worsening of the villagers' lot was often the consequence. The cost was a widespread disaffection among the Christian populations.

A deep alienation between town and country—a fissure which approximately, but only approximately, coincided with the religious line between Christian and Moslem—had thus become a serious and fundamental weakness for Ottoman society by the end of the seventeenth century. Yet peasant disaffection was normal in most Christian states, and of itself should not be exaggerated into a sign of inevitable decay. It was the unwillingness—nay, the inability—of Moslem minds to modify traditional attitudes and institutions to take account of challenges from within and from without that presaged decay, despite all the outward splendor of Moslem art, the complexity of Moslem learning, and the might of the Ottoman, Safavi, and Mughal empires.

CHAPTER 22

The Far East 1500–1700

 In 1513 when the first Portuguese merchant visited the south China coast, the Ming regime was already beginning to show the ills typical of decaying Chinese dynasties. Heavy and inequitable taxation together with court and clique intrigues provoked sporadic uprisings in the provinces, and raids from the steppe and from the sea were becoming serious. The Ming armies were numerous and well enough equipped. When well led they were capable of giving a good account of themselves. Between 1592 and 1598, for example, Ming troops helped Koreans to halt two formidable invasions from Japan, despite the best efforts of the Japanese war lord Hideyoshi. On the sea, Ming naval forces also won some notable victories, even over Portuguese ships. Yet the land-minded administration in Peking never authorized the creation of a permanent naval force, and disbanded sailors often took part in piratical enterprises, thus justifying the official distrust of seamen.

The final collapse of the Ming government came in a thoroughly traditional way. Acting in concert with a Ming general, a powerful and well-disciplined barbarian war band from Manchuria entered Peking in 1644 under the pretext of helping to suppress a domestic rebellion. Once in possession of the capital, the Manchus refused to co-operate with the Ming dynasty any longer. Their own leader claimed the title the Son of Heaven, thus founding a new dynasty, the Ch'ing. It took more years of war before the Manchus consolidated their hold over all of the Chinese mainland. Taiwan, the last refuge of a self-styled champion of the Ming cause, did not submit to Peking's authority until 1683.

The Manchus already had a fairly intimate acquaintance with Chinese civilization when they entered China as conquerors. No alien taint from western Asia, such as had colored Mongol culture at the time of their victories over the Chinese, prevented a smooth and rapid appropriation of all outward trappings of Chinese civilization by the new masters of the land. Nevertheless, the Manchu emperors distrusted the loyalty of native Chinese, and sought to keep military power in the hands of their own people. Garrisons of Manchu soldiers were therefore stationed at strategic points all over China. They maintained their own distinctive native dress and manner, for it became a matter of policy to keep the soldiers from mingling too freely with the Chinese population. The civil administration, however, employed Chinese as well as Manchus, and traditional methods of recruitment to the bureaucracy by state examinations based upon knowledge of the Confucian classics continued in force without more than local and temporary interruption.

Such a smooth transition from one dynasty to the next had seldom occurred before in China's long history. Moreover, the behavior of the Manchu emperors was completely traditional. They directed their main attention and the bulk of their forces to securing the land frontier of China against the steppe nomads and such restless neighbors as the Tibetans. In this they were extremely successful, thanks to the growing superiority of civilized armament over the old-fashioned horse archers of the steppe. Yet there was a novel aspect to the Manchu pacification of China's land frontier, for they had to deal not merely with nomad tribes but with the expanding agricultural empire of Russia as well. Russian fur traders, it will be recalled, had extended their operations right across Siberia in the early seventeenth century, reaching the Pacific at Okhotsk in 1638. Russian agents then sought, not without some success, to enter into relations with the steppe peoples lying southward of the Siberian forests. In addition, they opened a trade in furs with China, where ermine was as much admired as it was in Europe.

After some sparring for advantage, in 1689 the two civilized nations agreed to the Treaty of Nerchinsk. According to this treaty the main portion of the steppe, in Outer Mongolia and farther west in central Asia, was to be a no-man's-land, insulating the two empires from one another. The treaty also provided for a regulated caravan trade, built around the exchange of tea and silk for furs. This settlement was unstable, however, because the Mongols and the Kalmuks, who inhabited the buffer zone, were not willing to play the neutral and passive role China and Russia had assigned to them. Instead, they entered into religious and diplomatic relations with Tibet. This aroused Chinese fears of a new barbarian league, potentially as dangerous as the never-to-be-forgotten hosts of Genghis Khan. To forestall such a possibility the Chinese embarked again upon a forward policy, and, since the Russian armies were then deeply engaged against the Ottoman Turks, the tsar's representative had to stand quietly by while the Chinese, after some severe fighting, conquered Outer Mongolia and Chinese Turkestan. Tibet then came obediently to heel. These campaigns were not completed until 1757, when the Kalmuk confederacy collapsed before Chinese armies and a smallpox epidemic. The remnant secured asylum in Russian territory and was planted near the Volga where their descendants still exist. Thirty years previously, in the Treaty of Kiakhta, the Russians had formally registered their acquiescence in this very substantial advance of Chinese power across almost half of the Eurasian steppe.

The Manchu emperors were equally successful in settling the problem of sea defenses. In 1636, for reasons of its own, the Japanese government forbade its subjects to sail the high seas, and stopped the construction of ocean-going vessels. This cut off the main source of the piratical raids that had plagued the China coast for more than a century. Agreement with the Europeans, concluded informally between local representatives of the Chinese administration and no less haphazardly appointed spokesmen for the Portuguese merchant community, had the effect of taming the ravages and controlling most of the illegal activities in which the first European merchant ships had freely engaged. Hence, the need for any departure from traditional methods of guarding the sea coast disappeared just when governmental stability returned to China. As was to be expected, therefore, the Manchus did nothing to build a navy or to improve their coastal defenses. They saw no need for such steps, and in fact there was none.

Prosperity and Conservatism in China

‡‡‡ The restoration of peace and regular administration throughout the vast Chinese mainland provided propitious conditions for a great upthrust of prosperity. Population began to grow rapidly. The new American crops—especially sweet potatoes and maize—allowed the agricultural community to expand *pari passu* with the growth of artisan manufactures and the expansion of commercial activity. Trade with European merchants became brisk. Portuguese ships long enjoyed an effective monopoly of the carrying trade between China and Japan, since neither government allowed its nationals to construct sea-going vessels. In addition, export of tea and porcelain and of a host of other Chinese wares to distant European drawing rooms steadily increased in scale. To supply these markets, Chinese entrepreneurs developed mass production of certain cheaper types of porcelain. But such changes merely strengthened traditional China by increasing its already enormous bulk without in the least straining the traditional structure of society.

Cultural life demonstrated the massive conservatism of Chinese attitudes. Nothing in the Chinese experience between 1500 and 1700 failed to fit into the frame of inherited learning and sensibility. To be sure Europeans brought some intriguing novelties to the attention of the learned world. New geographical information, improved astronomical skills, and such delightful devices as pendulum clocks were accorded the recognition they deserved. In 1601 a Jesuit mission headed by a learned Italian, Matteo Ricci, was even admitted to the court at Peking, but only after the Christian missionaires had acquired a decent veneer of Confucian learning so as to be able to communicate with the scholars of the court. The change of dynasty did not permanently disturb the Jesuit position in Peking. On the contrary, between 1640 and 1664 the head of the mission, Johann Adam von Schall, established a remarkable friendship with the young Manchu emperor, and exercised some influence upon the conduct of the imperial government. Yet for all their position at the imperial court, the Jesuits seem to have made rather little impression upon the circle of learned mandarins with whom they associated, and their efforts to evangelize the population at large met with no success.

Instead, Chinese scholars and gentlemen fastened their eyes resolutely upon the classics and sought, by using the most careful critical methods they could invent, to establish the true meanings of old Confucian texts. A sparer, more philologically rigorous "Han school of learning" thus came into vogue, discouraging the bold flights of allegorical interpretation in which earlier generations of Neo-Confucianists had freely indulged.

No explanation is needed to understand why the Chinese declined to take seriously the learning and alien modes of thought professed by the "south sea barbarians" from distant Europe. When home institutions were working well, why indeed should wise, sober, and responsible men waste time on such trifles? And when the empire was formidable abroad, peaceful at home, rich, cultivated, and elegant, organized according to the principles of Confucian teaching, and properly decorous toward those who had spent long years of hard labor mastering the classics—when all this was true, why indeed should anyone pay more than passing attention to things foreign? Almost without exception, therefore, the Chinese followed the dictates of sound common sense, and took no more than casual notice of the novelties the Jesuit missionaries brought to China.

Hideyoshi and the Tokugawa Shoguns of Japan

‡‡‡ Japan's history during these two centuries was totally at variance with the majestic continuity of Chinese life. At the beginning of the period, Japan was suffering from endemic civil war. Local samurai, monkish strong-arm bands, urban-based pirates, and footloose adventurers of every stripe, fought and double-crossed one another, while paying lip service to the fiction of an imperial administration. The arrival of the Portuguese in the 1540's brought a significant change to the scene.

The Japanese were impressed by many aspects of European civilization. A vogue for European styles of dress and for baptism into the Christian religion spread rapidly and widely through the islands. Of course not all approved such novelties, but few failed to recognize the uses of European guns. Local lords eagerly traded supplies of metals and other valuables for arms imported by the Portuguese. But just as in Europe, when cannon and muskets became the decisive instruments in war, the increased cost of armaments meant that only large territorial sovereigns could afford what it took to win victories. Rapid political consolidation was the result. Within less than half a century after the first Portuguese ship touched at Japan, the entire Japanese archipelago had been effectively united under a great war lord, Hideyoshi (d. 1598). Hideyoshi's authority was based upon successful leadership in the field, for he was of humble birth and had served as a groom when a boy. His government rested upon alliances between a number of samurai clans, whose members were assigned income from particular villages in return for military services to their immediate chief, and through him to Hideyoshi himself.

Having consolidated his power over all Japan, Hideyoshi attempted to turn Japanese military energies outward. He organized two great attacks upon Korea, intending, if his manifestos are to be believed, to conquer the entire world! But, as we have seen, Hideyoshi's troops failed to win decisive success on the mainland, and when he died, the Japanese withdrew, since a fresh outbreak of civil war threatened. After a single battle, one of Hideyoshi's companions, Ieyasu of the Tokugawa family, succeeded in asserting his supremacy.

Japan's new ruler was a much less reckless and expansive character than Hideyoshi had been. He abandoned all thought of overseas conquest and instead set out systematically to guard himself against real or potential domestic rivals. This meant, first of all, controlling the sea rovers, for a samurai clan leader, dispossessed in the wars at home, might always recoup his fortunes by a successful piratical cruise, and might even return home rich enough to try his hand at regaining what had been lost in earlier struggles. Such risks the Tokugawa shoguns —as Ieyasu and his successors are called—were unwilling to face. Accordingly, they first regulated and then forbade sea roving entirely, with the happy consequences for China's coastal security that we have already noticed.

The substantial Christian community of Japan also seemed dangerous to the shoguns. Hideyoshi himself had issued an edict in 1587 banning foreign missionaries from Japan, but had not seen fit to enforce his own decree, perhaps because he feared that the Portuguese would retaliate by breaking off trade with him. After 1609, when Dutch ships first appeared in Japanese waters, the Japanese had an alternative channel through which they could supply themselves with whatever they needed from Western arsenals. It therefore became safe to launch spo-

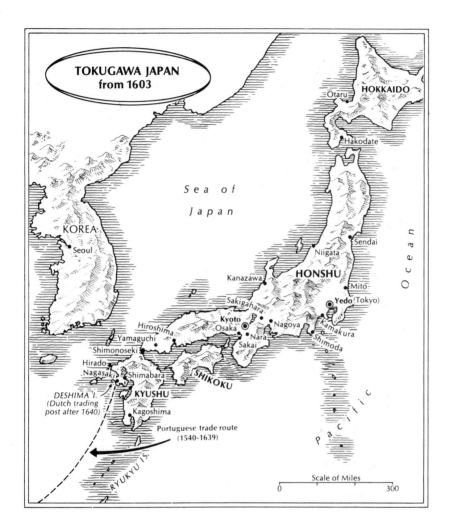

TOKUGAWA JAPAN
from 1603

HOKKAIDO

Otaru

Hakodate

S e a   o f

J a p a n

KOREA

Seoul

Sendai

Niigata

Kanazawa

HONSHU

Mito

O c e a n

Yedo (Tokyo)

Sakigahara

Kyoto

Kamakura

Hiroshima

Osaka

Nagoya

Yamaguchi

Nara

Shimonoseki

Sakai

Shimoda

Hirado

Nagasaki

Shimabara

SHIKOKU

DESHIMA I.
(Dutch trading
post after 1640)

KYUSHU

Kagoshima

Portuguese trade route
(1540-1639)

P a c i f i c

RYUKYU IS.

Scale of Miles

0   300

radic persecutions against the Christian community in Japan. Then in
1637 Christians revolted in Kyushu, and the shogun determined upon
their entire destruction. A full year was required before the last Christian stronghold was taken. The struggle was to the death. All captured
Christians, whether Europeans or Japanese, were executed out of hand.
A few Christians survived in secret, but they were weak and without
influence. Almost the entire Christian population of Japan was destroyed, bringing to a bloody and disastrous end a venture that had

been by far the most successful Christian mission in any civilized Asian country.

For more than two hundred years thereafter the Tokugawa shoguns continued to rule Japan. Yet for all the outward rigidity of their government, important changes in the economic and cultural life of the country continued to keep Japanese society and civilization under severe though hidden strain, far different from the serene stability Chinese life seemed to have attained by 1700. The core of the problem was that the samurai found themselves without a meaningful occupation as soon as warfare ceased. They could waste time in a genteel way by elaborating the code of the warrior, engaging in various ceremonies appropriate to their station in life, while waiting endlessly for the summons to action which never came. Or else they could plunge into the expensive delights of town amusement quarters, where a vigorous, sensuous, and entirely unofficial cultural life quickly developed.

Many samurai in fact went bankrupt and sold or mortgaged their legally assigned right to collect rice from the villages. Merchants who bought such rights usually transported the rice they had acquired to town markets. Consequently, a bustling market economy insinuated itself between the peasant and landholding classes, and reached far down into the interstices of Japanese society, affecting almost the entire population. Against such forces, the best efforts of the shogun's government to reinforce traditional patterns of samurai life met with very imperfect success. Instead Japan presented the spectacle of a profound duality between the vigorous vulgarity of the towns and the austere decorum of official culture.

This duality continued to prevail in Japan as long as the shogunate lasted. Perhaps the two modes of life were really complementary, the attractions of the one remedying the deficiencies of the other.

CHAPTER 23

The Old Regime in Europe

1648-1789

 The volcanic passions loosed in Europe by the Reformation and Counter Reformation subsided after 1648. Leaders of both church and state recoiled from the attempt to enforce total conformity to theological or any other sort of truth. Carefully skirting both the heights and depths of human passion, the leaders of European society preferred to rely on the competence of trained professionals, whose grasp on truth could only be partial and whose temper was seldom fanatic. Tepid professionalism therefore found new scope at every strategic position in society: in barracks, pulpits, law courts, universities, schools, government bureaus, and even in the offices of such new-sprung instruments of power as chartered companies and banks. By providing a secure niche and useful function for these and still other specialized professions, European society opened wide the door for pluralism of thought and sensibility as never before. Each profession, pursuing its own limited vision of the truth, advanced and elaborated upon the work of earlier generations, and felt no pressing need to erect or conform to any overarching grand synthesis of all truth and knowledge. So long as their own professional autonomy and dignity were not called in question, Europe's men of affairs found it

perfectly possible to let others in other walks of life think and, within limits, act as they pleased.

Pluralism and compromise had of course been present in European as in every other civilized society from the time civilization first began. Indeed, one definition of civilization is a society in which occupational specialization exists. What was new in the second half of the seventeenth century in Europe, therefore, was not so much the fact as its recognition, and a willingness to tolerate discrepancies and divergencies which the most strenuous reforming efforts of preceding generations had been unable to remove. Moderation, balance, manners: these could replace the impassioned striving after metaphysical certainty which had for so long inspired Europeans to denounce and destroy one another. Logic certainly suffered from such compromise, but common sense and the fact that it worked supported the new professionalized piecemeal approach to problems of truth and morals.

Limited Wars

‡‡‡ Moderation, balance, and manners even infected interstate relations. Something approaching a code of professional conduct for diplomats and soldiers defined itself in the decades after the close of the disastrous Thirty Years' War. Formalization of warfare reached its peak, perhaps, at the battle of Fontenoy (1745), when French and English officers courteously offered one another the privilege of firing first. Thereafter, the intensity of European warfare tended again to increase. Weapons became more destructive and the political stakes larger, until French revolutionary leaders once again armed and unleashed popular passions upon the battlefield.

Between 1653 and 1689 France enjoyed a definite superiority over her rivals. In his boyhood, King Louis XIV (reigned 1643–1715) witnessed the failure of the last aristocratic effort to assert noble rights against the king by armed rebellion (the so-called Fronde, 1648–53). As a grown man, he set the victorious royal armies the task of winning for France the "natural boundaries" of the Rhine and Pyrenees. His initial successes at the expense of the tattered Spanish empire ground to a halt when the Dutch and English (1689) entered into alliance with the Hapsburgs to check French aggression. Thereafter, England and France conducted a series of wars in which dominion over North

America and India were at stake, while on the European continent the Austrians reaped the major fruit of the final dismemberment of Spain's European empire by taking over Spain's position in Italy and the southern Netherlands (Wars of the Spanish Succession, 1701–14). By 1763 England (become Great Britain through union with Scotland and Ireland in 1707) won decisive victory overseas in India and Canada—a success only partly undone in the next generation when French aid (1778–83) allowed rebellious British colonists to make good their effort to establish an independent nation in North America.

While western Europe experienced these tumultuous yet limited actions, eastern Europe witnessed a more drastic realignment of power. After 1648, Poland and Sweden, like the Dutch in western Europe, ceased to be able to defend their status as great and imperial powers. Instead, Austria, and a new-sprung German state, Brandenburg-Prussia, competed with Russia for Swedish and Polish territories (1648–1721). Later the same three powers wiped the Polish Kingdom from the map entirely by partitioning Poland between them (1772–95).

Central Europe remained a sort of bridge (and not infrequently a convenient theater of war) between Europe's western and eastern balances of power. The small states into which Italy and Germany had been divided by the Treaty of Westphalia (1648) continued to incline either to a French or to an anti-French alliance, depending on local conditions and rivalries, dynastic ties, and—at least sometimes— upon straightforward sale to the highest bidder.

Balancing Intranational Interests

‡‡‡ Within each of the sovereign states of Europe, the government recognized no legal limits to its freedom of action in matters of foreign policy. Yet in fact calculations of the balance of power restricted any one ruler's freedom of maneuver within rather narrow bounds. Similarly, each European monarch, even when claiming absolute power over his subjects, was in fact limited by a tangle of countervailing interests and privileges, traditionally distributed among different groups and classes. Moreover, these diverse interests usually had some sort of corporate organization that could and did give them effective political weight.

Thus the stately grandeur of Louis XIV's court and his proud

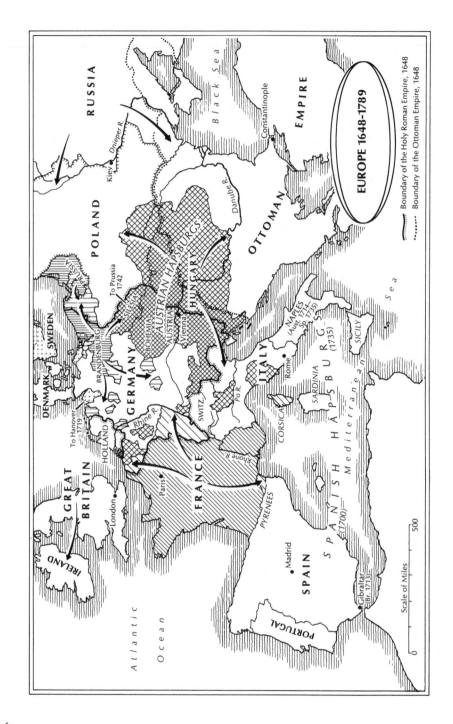

EUROPE 1648-1789

Boundary of the Holy Roman Empire, 1648
Boundary of the Ottoman Empire, 1648

RUSSIA

Black Sea

Constantinople

OTTOMAN EMPIRE

POLAND

Dnieper R.

Kiev

Danube R.

AUSTRIAN HAPSBURGS

HUNGARY

Vistula R.

To Prussia 1742

SILESIA

SWEDEN

DENMARK

BRANDENBURG

BOHEMIA

AUSTRIA

Vienna

GERMANY

To Hanover 1719

HOLLAND

Po R.

SWITZ.

ITALY

Rome

NAPLES (Aust. 1714 Sp. 1735)

SARDINIA

CORSICA

SICILY

SPANISH HAPSBURGS (1735)

Mediterranean Sea

GREAT BRITAIN

IRELAND

London

Rhine R.

Rhone R.

FRANCE

Paris

PYRENEES

(1700)

Atlantic Ocean

SPAIN

Madrid

Gibraltar (Br. 1713)

PORTUGAL

Scale of Miles

0   500

boast, "*L'état, c'est moi,*" disguised a very different reality. Even in Louis's youth, when energetic officials in his service sought to carry through a systematic centralization of French administration, the countervailing force of corporate privileges, some of long standing (e.g. the provincial representative assemblies or "Estates" of France), and others newly established (e.g. the French East India Company), severely limited the practical success French bureaucrats achieved. Nevertheless, royal policy attained its central aim: the taming of the aristocracy. But King Louis XIV secured this end as much through a judicious distribution of pensions and court offices, as by direct suppression of noble rights and privileges.

After Louis XIV's death, the French aristocrats set out to reclaim some of their former independence, but did so by legal process and argument rather than by attempting, as their forefathers had so often done, to resort to force. Military and civil administration had advanced to such a point that any other course had become wildly impractical. For ordinary men, the effective reduction of violence and the establishment of a regimen of law in the countryside were the central and basic achievements of the Old Regime in France, and in other west European countries.

The precise equilibrium between competing interests and corporate groups varied from state to state and from time to time, creating an ever-changing pattern of politics. Generally speaking, the Hapsburg lands, both in Spain and Austria, lagged perceptibly behind the French. In these lands the centralizing drive of bureaucratic reform, seeking to reduce or eliminate local differences, found its main expression not in the seventeenth century, as in France, but in the eighteenth. The Church retained far greater independence in the lands under Hapsburg jurisdiction than was the case in France, where Gallicanism—that is, the doctrine that there was and should be a separate French church within the Roman Catholic fold—had prevailed from medieval times. In practice, Gallicanism meant a close subordination of bishops and other dignitaries of the French church to the royal government.

English Parliamentarianism

‡‡‡ Toward the outer edges of western Europe, two quite atypical governments assumed distinctive form between 1640 and 1688. By a re-

markable coincidence it was precisely during these years that English parliamentarianism on the one flank and Prussian militarism on the other achieved their decisive formulations. The English civil wars (see above) were the crucible from which parliamentary sovereignty emerged; but a workable adjustment between old-fashioned localism (so vigorously represented by the squires and burgesses of the House of Commons) and the requirements of national policy was made only after the Glorious Revolution of 1688. During the reigns of Charles II (1660–85) and his brother James II (1685–88), the restored Stuart monarchs not unnaturally found it difficult to trust Parliament, and, in fact, accepted subsidy from France to allow them to get along without too slavish a dependence on parliamentary grants. Successful national policy could scarcely be conducted under such conditions.

Circumstances changed abruptly with the Glorious Revolution of 1688, which brought James's sister, Mary, and her husband, William of Orange, jointly to the English throne. William was also Stadholder of Holland, and his interests focused on the Continent where he became leader of the diplomatic-military coalition forming against Louis XIV. He was perfectly prepared to leave the government of England to Parliament, if parliamentary leaders would supply him the necessary means for keeping Louis XIV in check. Thereafter, until George III mounted the throne in 1760, no English monarch attempted to evade or control parliamentary leaders, who thus developed the habit of and created the needful institutions for governing the country with a nice respect for the competing demands of local, national, and international concerns.

To meet these requirements, English politicians and parliamentarians developed two important new institutions, cabinet government and the national debt. The cabinet was appointed by the crown, to be sure, but was responsible to Parliament. The cabinet's ability to pass legislation by securing the votes of a parliamentary majority was based upon a loose but real clique-and-party system of alliances among the members of Parliament. Despite occasional fumbling and frequent rumblings of dissatisfaction on the part of the worsted party, this system of government had the virtue of being able to register incessant changes in the assortment of interests represented in Parliament. No centralized bureaucracy of the eighteenth century could adjust so sensitively to social changes. In this lay the essential superiority of parliamentary government as practiced in eighteenth-century England. It was not in the least a democratic regime, for the unpropertied majority together with religious dissenters had no representation at all. Rotten boroughs and political patronage allowed men of wealth and birth to dominate Parliament completely.

The success of parliamentary government in England after 1688 also owed a great deal to the invention of a new instrument of credit, the national debt. This allowed public borrowing to meet emergency expenses on very advantageous terms. The key idea was to make Parliament responsible for repayment. Previously, governmental borrowing had been in the king's name, and his debts were treated as personal obligations, to be repaid, if at all, by the king in person by whatever means he could find. In 1694, however, Parliament established the Bank of England. One of its most important functions was to lend money to the government on the understanding that repayment would be guaranteed by Parliament and by whatever taxes Parliament might decide to levy. In this way the costs of a war could be spread out over many years. More important, interest rates went down as the assurance of repayment increased, and the English government became able to borrow from foreigners as well as from its own subjects. Other governments, lacking the Parliamentary guarantee of repayment, were seldom able to borrow on such favorable terms. The rapid rise of England's power was enormously facilitated by this fact.

Brilliant success against the French in the Seven Years' War (1756–63) proved how formidable such a government might be. Correspondingly, the failure of King George III's effort to control Parliament by developing a King's party that would rise above petty and selfish interests was sealed by his embarrassing defeat in the War of the American Revolution (1776–83). Hence, by piecemeal and entirely unsystematic evolution, the pattern of English (after 1707, British) government diverged increasingly from the norm of bureaucratic monarchy which prevailed on the continent. Particularly after 1763, there were Frenchmen and others on the continent who came to believe that British parliamentarianism, which had seemed an archaic and disorderly survival from a medieval past in 1640 and 1688, might in fact provide a useful model for the reorganization of their own more rigid governmental system.

Prussian Militarism

‡‡‡ Prussia's development was very different. Under stern and unremitting prodding from Frederick William, the Great Elector (ruled 1640–88), the scattered territories he had inherited from his Hohenzollern ancestors were welded together into a tightly centralized and strictly disciplined state. The drastic experience of the Thirty Years' War, when Brandenburg (which lay at the heart of the Hohenzollern possessions) had been repeatedly subject to devastation by Swedish and other foreign troops, disarmed local resistance to the Great Elector's policy. He aimed to achieve sufficient military strength to repel attack and was prepared to pay almost any price. The cost was certainly high, for his lands were poor and not very thickly inhabited. Yet, he was able by severest parsimony and unremitting care to create a standing army powerful enough not only to defend, but to enlarge his territories. His successors carried on the same policy, with no less success though with an increasingly relaxed temper. At his death, Frederick II, the Great (reigned 1740–86), left a much enlarged and territorially consolidated state, the kingdom of Prussia, which had become one of the great powers of Europe, rivaling Austria in the Germanies and dealing with Russia, the colossus of the east, on even terms.

Hohenzollern rulers showed systematic concern for economic development. Prussia's kings well knew that manufactures and population provided the sinews of victory in war. So successful were they in developing the unpromising sandy soils and limited mineral resources under their administration that Prussia began, by the end of the eighteenth century, to assume more of the social complexity familiar to more westerly lands. Artisans, merchants, professional men, and other urban classes became more numerous and influential. As this occurred, the barracks atmosphere, which had been so distinctive in the time of the Great Elector and his immediate successors, faded. Yet it did not disappear from Prussian life. It merely retreated within the narrower circle of the professional officer corps, which was recruited mainly from among younger sons of the landowning squirearchy ("Junkers") of East Prussia and adjacent Baltic lands.

Advances in Agriculture and Technology

‡‡‡ Europe's economic life underwent continued rapid escalation throughout the period of the Old Regime. Agriculture remained basic, and the great majority of the population continued everywhere to work as farmers, even in the most highly urbanized countries. In wide regions customary patterns of cultivation continued. Wherever the manorial style of collective cultivation had rooted itself, there were great obstacles to making any important changes in familiar routines, since overlapping property rights were likely to require unanimous (or nearly unanimous) consent for any important alteration. Nevertheless, even within old rhythms of work great increases of harvest could come from such simple procedures as systematic seed selection, or by improvements in plow design.

Some important departures took place in westernmost Europe. New crops like clover and turnips came into use, providing adequate winter fodder for horses and cattle—always the vulnerable point of medieval agriculture. Turnips required careful cultivation, which eliminated weeds from the fields just as efficiently as plowing a fallow field had traditionally done. In this way fallowing could be eliminated entirely and agricultural productivity expanded proportionately. In addition, clover helped to improve soil fertility by the fixation of nitrogen on its roots. The spread of potatoes was, however, the single most important change in European agriculture, for it very greatly enlarged food-producing capacity. On the sandy soils and in the cool climate of Baltic Germany, for example, as much as four times the number of calories could be had from a crop of potatoes as from grain. This permitted a dramatic upthrust of German population and prosperity, which began to manifest itself from about 1750, when potatoes first became important in central Europe. Maize played a similar role in the Balkans and in Hungary; but northern Europe was too cool for maize to thrive, and western Europe too wet.

Manufactures and communications saw a similar improvement. France took the lead in developing all-weather roads and a system of canals that linked all the important river systems of the country into a single network. Only after 1750 did the English begin to catch up. In manufactures, however, the relationship tended to be reversed, for private enterprise and empirical inventiveness found freer scope in Britain than in the more tightly regulated economies of the continent. In addition, English coal fields were abundant and easily exploited. The invention of coking (*c.* 1709) permitted the use of coal for smelting iron ores. Then in turn, a more abundant supply of iron and steel allowed the substitution of metal for wood in the working parts of many machines.

The most significant departure, however, was the development of powerful engines, using steam pressure derived from the burning of coal to produce mechanical energy. As early as 1712 Thomas Newcomen invented a crude steam engine to pump water from mine shafts. It depended on atmospheric pressure working against a partial vacuum produced by the condensation of steam. In 1769 James Watt patented a much-improved engine, which used live steam to drive a piston in a closely fitted cylinder. Since Watt's engine did not require alternate heating and cooling as Newcomen's had done, it was vastly more efficient. Very quickly it was put to work providing power for factories and mines, and before long for transportation too.

Among the most spectacular uses for Watt's steam engine was the driving of textile machinery, whose size and complexity had grown rapidly throughout the eighteenth century. The result was a tremendous increase in the amount of cloth that could be produced in a given period of time and the rapid cheapening of the final product. By 1789, indeed, English mills using cotton grown in India and imported to England around the Cape of Good Hope were able to undersell the Indian handweavers in India itself! No more startling demonstration of the technological advance brought by England's eighteenth-century success in harnessing coal, iron, and mechanical ingenuity could be conceived, for the skill of Indian weavers and the cheapness of their labor had previously excelled all rivals in the entire world.

Changes, sometimes small, sometimes fundamental, came to nearly all the traditional crafts of Europe. In addition, new crafts were created by systematic and deliberate imitation of the products of other lands. The most spectacular instance of this enrichment of European skills was the way in which craftsmen, scientists, entrepreneurs, and government officials collaborated to duplicate Chinese porcelain. The Chinese guarded their trade secrets well, and it was only after prolonged trial and error that Europeans learned how to produce porcelain almost indistinguishable from the Chinese.

At least as important as any of these technical improvements was the simultaneous development of organizational forms that permitted Europeans to mobilize greater and greater resources for undertakings requiring long exertion and the co-operation of large numbers of persons. The importance of chartered companies for European overseas operations was mentioned above, p. 316. In addition, such important fiscal devices as central banks and national debts were introduced during the Old Regime, thus beginning to free economic relations from restrictions imposed by limitations on the supply of gold and silver, and introducing an initially ill-understood and very violent cyclic fluctuation into the price system. Indeed, the first runaway credit boom (South Sea Bubble, 1718–20) so discredited joint stock companies that they were made illegal in all leading European countries—a situation that continued to prevail until the nineteenth century.

Europeans also explored the potentialities of another powerful device for co-ordinating industrial processes by learning how to supplement craftsmen's manual skills with the precision of mathematical measurement. The boring of cannon and of musket barrels required close accuracy, if the finished weapon were to fire properly. Equally, Watt's steam engines required a close fit between pistons and cylinder walls, and a general matching up of gear wheels, screw threads, bearings, and other moving parts. Clocks, watches, telescopes, and microscopes could only be made by specialists who were able to cut parts to specified dimensions so that the separate pieces could be assembled into a whole that really worked. This required dexterity of hand and eye, but also depended on a more and more precise mathematical definition of each task and accurate measurement of the product at each stage of manufacture.

These aspects of European economic organization remained rudimentary in 1789, and found their major application only later. Nevertheless, the start had been made, the idea was known, its practicability had been demonstrated. The possibilities of radical rationalization of manufacturing processes had been foreshadowed, to Europe's enormous advantage and further enrichment.

Mathematics and Sciences

‡‡‡ During the second half of the seventeenth century, Europe's intellectual energies, which had been concentrated on religious debate for more than a century, shifted focus rather abruptly.

Mathematics had been undergoing rapid development throughout the Reformation age, when men like Johannes Kepler (d. 1630) and Galileo Galilei (d. 1642) were active. New notations helped to broaden and simplify calculations and induced new concepts. In particular, the sciences of geometry and algebra, which had been studied separately since the time of the Arabs, began to merge, thereby creating analytic geometry. Analytic geometry in turn gave rise to "fluxions," or the calculus, which enlarged the scope and refined the power of mathematical reasoning, and had important applications in the study of physics.

So great was the vogue for mathematics that many men felt sure that appropriately rigorous and careful application of the techniques of mathematical reasoning to any and all questions of the human condition might reach true and universally acceptable conclusions. René Descartes (d. 1650) was the first influential man to make this bold attempt. His deductive reasoning from axioms and self-evident first principles, in the manner of the geometricians, was so persuasive that a school of enthusiastic Cartesians rapidly developed in France and elsewhere. They vigorously popularized and defended Descartes's views. Others were fired by the same vision of mathematical certainty, but, alas, came to different and mutually incompatible conclusions. Baruch Spinoza (d. 1677) in Holland and Thomas Hobbes (d. 1679) in England were among the most famous of these philosophers. In the next generation, Gottfried Wilhelm Leibniz (d. 1716) nourished the same ambition.

These philosophers lacked any satisfactory way of settling their differences, for there was no empirical test by which disinterested experts could choose between their rival views. The matter was otherwise with the magnificently elegant analysis of physical and astronomical motions developed by Isaac Newton (d. 1727) in his book *Philosophiae Naturalis Principia Mathematica*, published in 1687. Like his predecessors, Newton sought to reduce observed multiplicity to mathemtatical order. To explain the behavior of moving bodies, both in the heavens and on earth, he hypothesized a mysterious force— universal gravitation. This he supposed operated in space according to an absurdly and delightfully simple mathematical formula— diminishing between any two bodies with the square of the distance.

Some of Newton's contemporaries boggled at the mystical implications of a force acting at a distance. Newton's efforts to clarify the issue by speaking of an ethereal substratum and, in another passage, of space as "the mind of God," did not help much to relieve such anxieties. But what did convince almost everyone was the fact that Newton's theory could be tested empirically. Newton's laws of motion had originally been generated through his effort to express mathematically the motion of the moon. But there were innumerable other moving bodies that could be used to test the accuracy of his formulas. On the basis of such observations and measurements it soon appeared that the formulas did work. Reality in fact conformed to Newton's laws of motion.

In our own time, scientific prediction and the operation of natural law are usually taken for granted. It requires, therefore, an act of the imagination to understand how extraordinary and exciting such discoveries were when they were new. Men who had been brought up to conceive the universe as ruled by a very active, personal God, who might intervene in any situation at any moment to work a miracle of conversion or to forgive a past transgression, found the Newtonian vision of the universe both liberating and frightening. God, it appeared, was a mathematician and had chosen to create the universe accordingly. In such a universe it seemed almost beneath God's dignity to work a miracle, for that would involve the local and temporary cancellation of his own decree, and a confession of the inadequacy of natural law to achieve all good and necessary aims. A starker contrast with the world view of Luther or Loyola, which turned upon an intensely personal and completely unpredictable relationship between God and each single human soul, could scarcely be imagined.

Yet most men, even after they had been persuaded to accept a Newtonian view of the natural universe, remained Christian. Newton himself wrote Biblical commentaries in which he attempted to discover hidden meanings in Holy Writ; and his long lifetime (1642–1727) was particularly prolific of new religious movements that emphasized personal relation with and experience of God. Within Protestantism, for example, the Quakers and Methodists of England and the Pietists of Germany got their start while Newton was still alive. Among the Roman Catholics, Jansenism and Quietism achieved their greatest influence in Newton's time. Official reprobation by the papacy resulted in the eventual disappearance of both these schools of piety, but the three Protestant movements, despite all intervening changes, continue to flourish today.

Other sciences proved rather less amenable to definitive mathematical formulation. Much was done to collect information about the various forms of plant and animal life, and new knowledge about distant human societies, both civilized and savage, poured into Europe as missionaries and other men of learning recorded their observations. Yet a mathematical formulation of the biological and social sciences failed to emerge from the cloud of new information. To be sure, a Swedish botanist, Carl Linnaeus (d. 1778), hit upon a system of classifying plants which has remained standard since, and a school of "physiocrats" in France, with Adam Smith (d. 1790) in Scotland, did attempt, with rather impressive success, to deduce what would happen to trade and industry if governments refrained from interfering with individuals' natural behavior. Believing that men were motivated by rational self-interest, they concluded that wealth as well as liberty would be advanced by such a policy. Unlike Newton's laws of motion, such laissez-faire theories were never put to the test of experience, since governments and men persistently declined to behave rationally.

Political Theories, Historiography, and Empirical Philosophy

‡‡‡ Two other dimensions of social thought underwent very significant change. First, a new theory of political legitimacy had to be developed by men who no longer could take it for granted that God did intervene in everyday human affairs. A king claiming to rule by divine right was a mere usurper unless God had in fact chosen him for his office from among all available candidates. Men who accepted the Newtonian view of the universe certainly found it hard to believe the older theory, particularly since so many kings seemed grossly unfit for their office. Solution to this problem was found in the idea of a social contract whereby tacitly or in some more active and definite way all the human beings living within a particular state were assumed to have reached agreement as to the forms and powers of government. Obviously, by assigning different terms to such a contract very different practical conclusions could be drawn. Thomas Hobbes, for example, argued that men, being nasty and brutish by nature, had been able to establish civil society only by delegating unlimited power to an absolute sovereign. John Locke (d. 1704) on the contrary held that the contract lay between the public and the ruler, so that if the

Christ Pancrator, c. 1148. Cathedral at Cefalù, Sicily.

GOD INCARNATE, RULER OF ALL

The quest for certainty that can plausibly be read into late Roman sculpture (see Plate 8) has here come majestically to rest. Although this mosaic was made in Sicily when that island was under Norman rule, the style is Byzantine. In the restless West, however, even so powerful a style as this provided a chrysalis from which to emerge rather than a frame within which to exist, as the following pages will show.

PLATE 33

Giotto di Bondone, 1266-1337. The Resurrection of Lazarus. Arena Chapel, Padua.

PLATE 34

DEFINITION OF A FAR WESTERN ART STYLE

Between the fifteenth and twentieth centuries, mathematically exact perspective, creating an illusory third dimension, became the West's stylistic hallmark. Its emergence is illustrated here. Giotto's figures serenely inhabit a shallow depth in the foreground, but his landscape is on a different scale. A century and a half later, Piero della Francesca knew how to organize foreground and background into a single coherent illusory space. But his painting, too, is divided, for the resurrected Christ bespeaks the Christian past, whereas the foreshortened limbs of the sleeping soldiers both mock and proclaim mastery of a new, secular this-worldliness.

Piero della Francesca, 1416-1492. Resurrection of Christ. Galleria Comunale, Sansepolcro.

PLATE 35

Albrecht Dürer, 1471-1528. Self-Portrait. Alte Pinakothek, Munich.

MAN INCARNATE, RULER OF SELF

Albrecht Dürer's portrait of himself at age twenty-eight sufficiently resembles the traditional mien of Christ Pancrator (Plate 33) to make one wonder whether such a dip into the penumbra of blasphemy was deliberate. In any event, a proud self-consciousness and delight in technical virtuosity for its own sake (observe the contrasting textures of fur, hair, and beard) pervade the work. The humanist conception of the self as a work of art to be moulded to full manhood by conscious cultivation of the arts of life stares starkly back at us from Dürer's mirror.

PLATE 36

THE CHRISTIAN PILGRIMAGE THROUGH LIFE

Dürer's knight, averting his gaze from the menacing figure of death (with the hourglass) and turning his back upon the Devil (here dressed up as the great beast of the Book of Revelation) is headed for the fair city high upon a hill in the background. The engraving is thus an allegory of the Christian life as understood in Germany on the eve of the Reformation. Like Luther, the Christian knight of Dürer's engraving pursues salvation through the private heroism of an individual act of faith. Dürer here combines old sentiments—veritable clichés—and new techniques of realistic draftsmanship. With the same radical ruthlessness, Luther sought to recover old truths by applying the latest devices of humanist scholarship to the Bible.

The links and tensions between Renaissance and Reformation seem quintessentially summed up in the resemblances of and differences between these two products of Dürer's hand.

Courtesy, Museum of Fine Arts, Boston

Albrecht Dürer, 1471-1528. Knight, Death, and the Devil.
Museum of Fine Arts, Boston.
Gift of Mrs. Horatio Greenough Curtis, in memory of her husband.

PLATE 37

St. Nicholas the Wonder Worker. School of Rublev, Moscow, 15th cent.
Collection, George R. Hann, Sewickley, Pennsylvania.

CONSERVATISM IN THE EAST

The reckless plunge toward modernity illustrated in the two preceding plates was
not shared everywhere and at once, even within Europe. Muscovy in the east clung
close to Byzantine tradition, and the Holy Orthodox Church remained immune from
catastrophic reformation until the seventeenth century. This icon bespeaks the conservative stability of Russian culture and society. Yet the stimulating presence of the
West may be glimpsed in details such as the use of shadow to give an illusory third
dimension to St. Nicholas's face and hand—a technique pioneered in Italy not long
before some anonymous monk painted this work.

PLATE 38

El Greco, 1541-1614. St. Jerome. The Frick Collection, New York.

CONSERVATISM IN THE WEST

In Spain, almost two centuries later, the stranger from Crete whom Spaniards called El Greco—that is, "The Greek"—painted in a style that preserved unmistakable echoes of the Byzantine icons he had known in his youth. But St. Jerome's elongated face and hands, his intense gaze, and the pyramidal garment he wears—elements deriving from Byzantine iconography—here appear decked out with the full virtuosity of Italian Renaissance technique. This is well illustrated by the way in which Jerome's hair and beard attain optical realism—at the expense, surely, of saintly otherworldliness. Similarly incongruous juxtaposition of strictly traditional with radically new elements characterized Spanish society as a whole in the age of the conquistadors and of the Counter Reformation.

PLATE 39

Rembrandt van Rijn, 1606-1669. Syndics of the Cloth Guild. Rijksmuseum, Amsterdam.

THE OLD REGIME IN ART

Sober, serious, and self-satisfied burghers, careful of their money, jealous of their rights, and eminently capable of looking after their own interests, here confront a slender aristocrat, delightfully decorative and sweetly debonair. The two classes, whose contrasting styles of life find powerful expression in these paintings, dominated the Old Regime and by their prudent moderation gave Europe a modicum of stability after the wracking storms of Renaissance and Reformation.

PLATE 40

Jean Baptiste Perronneau, 1715-1783. Madame de Sorquainville. Louvre, Paris.

PLATE 41

Jacques Louis David, 1748-1825. Une Maraichère. Musée de Beaux Arts, Lyon.

PLATE 42

LIBERTY, EQUALITY, FRATERNITY

The keen, suspicious glance of a Parisian market woman that stares at us from David's painting, and Goya's record of how Napoleon's soldiers dealt with Spaniards who rebelled against being liberated from tyranny and superstition give visual shape to some of the conundrums raised in revolutionary France, 1789-1815, by resolute pursuit of a sanctifying, democratic, yet strangely elusive General Will.

Anderson-Art Reference Bureau

Francisco Goya, 1746-1828. The Third of May, 1808. Prado, Madrid.

PLATE 43

Honoré Daumier, 1808-1879. The Third-Class Carriage. The Metropolitan Museum of Art, New York. The H. O. Havemeyer Collection.

PLATE 44

THE NEW REGIME

Daumier's painting on the left records the fact that nineteenth-century industrialism brought even peasant women to market and allowed them to mingle demurely with city folk while returning home third class. Thus at the lower end of the social scale, age-old distinctions between town and country diminished, while, at the other extreme, the dividing line between bourgeois and noble also blurred, as Sargent's portraits of a self-made businessman of London and his high-born wife suggest.

John Singer Sargent, 1856-1925. Asher Wertheimer and Mrs. Asher Wertheimer, Tate Gallery, London.

PLATE 45

Ben Shahn, 1898- 1969. Liberation. Collection, James Thrall Soby, New Canaan, Connecticut.

PLATE 46

TWENTIETH-CENTURY LIBERATION

On the eve of World War I, a small band of iconoclasts deliberately repudiated the conventions of European painting which, despite all the intervening changes, had held up since the fifteenth century, when Italian artists first discovered the mathematical rules for creating illusory three-dimensional space in their pictures. Humanity at large quickly followed the artists' example by cutting adrift from tradition of almost every sort and in almost every society. Primitive impulse and abstract, depersonalizing intellectuality oddly collaborate in the uncharted landscape this wholesale liberation from the past opened up, as Miró's painting (below) may perhaps symbolize. Shahn's work commemorates both the destruction wrought by World War II and humanity's ruthless renewal amid the ruins.

Collection, The Museum of Modern Art, New York

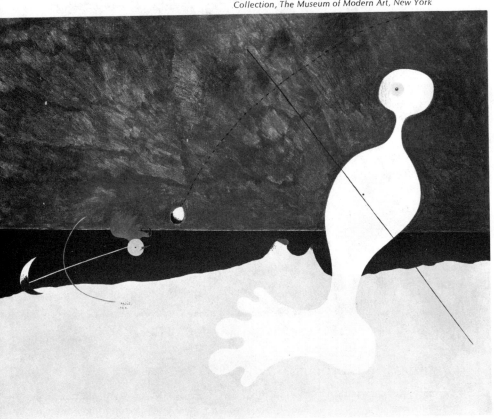

Joan Miró, 1893-   . Person Throwing a Stone at a Bird. Collection,
The Museum of Modern Art, New York.

PLATE 47

University of Chicago

Henry Moore, 1898-   "Nuclear Energy," University of Chicago.

THE PAST IS PROLOGUE

This brooding presence, a monument in Chicago at the place where men first created a controlled and self-sustaining nuclear reaction, gives visual form to the hopes and fears with which we contemplate our fate—sentiments based today on new premises, yet presumably of no greater poignancy than in times past, since then as now life and death hung daily in the balance and no man knew (or knows) what the morrow will bring forth.

PLATE 48

ruler overstepped specified bounds the people were justified in rebelling against his usurpation. In this way Locke was able to defend the Glorious Revolution of 1688, which had driven an undeniably legitimate monarch from the English throne to the scandal of many Englishmen who clung to old-fashioned ideas of Divine providence and feared a new outbreak of the recently concluded civil wars. Across the Channel a far more radical view was propounded in the next century by Jean-Jacques Rousseau (d. 1778), who held that the social contract justified rebellion whenever the sovereign failed to satisfy the people, in whose Common Will resided inalienable and indefeasible sovereignty.

The other major change in men's view of themselves was a by-product of the patient labors of numberless philologians, numismatists, historians, and other scholars. Their perseverance in sorting out Europe's complex heritage of literary and historical manuscripts, discovering how to translate dates from one calendrical system to another, and arranging reigns, battles, and other historical events into a reliable chronological sequence, gave a depth and accuracy to historical knowledge which had never before been approached. The greatest single figure in this world of scholarship was Jean Mabillon (d. 1707), who established a sophisticated knowledge of the different types of handwriting used in different ages and at different monasteries and royal chanceries in the early Middle Ages so that it became possible to discover—sometimes at a glance—where a given manuscript came from and approximately how old it was. The same expertness of course allowed detection of the numerous forgeries which had been inserted into the historical record at various times in the past for various purposes, and provided European scholarship with tools and concepts which were later to be applied to the study of other civilizations. Just at the end of the eighteenth century, the first exciting fruit of this venture came to public attention, when William Jones (d. 1794) discovered that Sanskrit, the sacred language of India, was closely related to the languages of Europe, and so very old that it promised to provide an eager European world with fresh insight into the nature of their own most primitive ancestors!

These scholarly labors allowed men to write far more accurate and fuller histories than ever before. Edward Gibbon's *History of the Decline and Fall of the Roman Empire* (published 1776-88), is the most famous instance of what had become possible; but other historians, like Voltaire (d. 1778) and David Hume (d. 1776) were almost as popular at the time. By inserting between their own age and the time when Christianity had first been established a long and complex human history, with all its variety of episodes and fluctuations of moral as well as of theological standards, the historians in their way also dampened the fires of religious controversy. For with a fuller vision of the historical past in mind, an immediate return to apostolic conditions in church and state—which had been the great hope of the Reformation age —ceased to seem possible or, perhaps, in view of the conduct of some of the Roman emperors, desirable!

While political theory and history flourished mightily, metaphysics passed through the needle's eye of empirical criticism and emerged strong and healthy, if a bit abstruse and far removed from day-to-day concerns. The confident deductive reasoning of Descartes and his fellow seventeenth-century philosophers came under the scrutiny of a group of English empiricists. First John Locke (d. 1704) and then David Hume (d. 1776) asked the embarrassing question of how sense experience is related to human ideas, and came up with the conclusion that certain knowledge about anything is impossible. Immanuel Kant (d. 1804) accepted Hume's conclusions, but turned his critical logic around by arguing that careful analysis of the structure and capacities of the human mind would give us accurate and necessary knowledge about the nature of all possible sensory experiences, since the unknowable thing-in-itself could only come to consciousness by conforming to human sensibilities and modes of thought. In this fashion Kant opened the door wide for nineteenth-century German philosophers to anatomize the Spirit, whose creative role in defining knowable reality Kant had so persuasively pointed out.

The Arts, Classical and Romantic

‡‡‡ By comparison with the progress of natural and social science, which inaugurated a new era in the second half of the seventeenth century, the fine arts, with the exception of music, remained conservative. Styles came and went, national schools rose to eminence or suffered comparative eclipse, and all along the way a tendency to add to an already richly various cultural inheritance manifested itself. But nothing

as radically novel as the Newtonian world view emerged from such vigorous, but traditional, activity.

At the end of the seventeenth and the beginning of the eighteenth centuries, the prestige of French culture reached its height. Admiration for the power and grandeur of Louis XIV's government mingled with an equal or greater admiration for French literature, manners, taste. Classicism, which rested upon a belief that rules for artistic excellence could be discerned and should be followed, prevailed in both the visual and literary arts. In the hands of a great artist, such rules were no hindrance. Architect Christopher Wren (d. 1723) in London, or the three great classical dramatists of France, Pierre Corneille (d. 1684), Molière (d. 1673), and Jean Racine (d. 1699), for example, conformed with grand effect to rules of correctness, which in lesser hands became heavy baggage indeed.

In the eighteenth century, European music entered upon one of its greatest periods. New or newly perfected instruments and a physico-mathematical analysis of musical pitch gave musicians new technical range and variety. With so much that was new to digest, the "classical" rules of harmony and composition did not act as hampering limitations, as such rules sometimes did in literature, but instead stimulated creativity by focusing attention on a manageable range of variables. The work of Johann Sebastian Bach (d. 1750) and of Wolfgang Amadeus Mozart (d. 1791) established a norm for subsequent European music which became almost as fundamental, though not so enduring, as the norm created for European painting by the invention of linear and aerial perspective in the fifteenth century.

In literature the classical ideal tended to wear thin after the middle of the eighteenth century, particularly in Germany and England. Researches into the national and medieval past, and persuasive investigations of the palpitating flux of feeling nicknamed the human heart, combined to persuade many Germans and some Englishmen that true literary greatness could only be achieved by giving free rein to spontaneous impulse. This romantic point of view was associated with a new valuation for the language of the common folk and of the nation. Johann Gottfried Herder (d. 1803), for example, argued with passion that Germans could achieve national and literary greatness only by using German, not French. A similar interest in the national springs of literature inspired Thomas Percy (d. 1811) to compile and publish traditional English and Scottish ballads in his book *Reliques of Ancient English Poetry* (published 1765).

Yet it would be erroneous to put too much weight upon the traditional classification of Europe's cultural history into a classical followed by a romantic age. At all times a great diversity of taste and artistic creativity prevailed. In the history of English literature, for example, John Milton (d. 1674) wrote his great Christian epic *Paradise Lost* precisely when William Wycherley (d. 1716) was producing bawdy Restoration comedies; and toward the close of our period the artful simplicity of Robert Burns (d. 1796) confronted with equanimity the periodic sentences of Dr. Samuel Johnson's (d. 1784) sesquipedalian prose. Similarly, Luther's Bible and Shakespeare's plays never passed out of fashion in their respective countries, while the classical literatures of ancient Rome and Greece irradiated the separate national literatures of Europe by providing all educated men with a common stock of knowledge and range of sentiments upon which writers and artists could play, knowing that casual allusions to the Greek and Latin classics would be easily and immediately understood.

Roots of Europe's Dominance

‡‡‡ Richness, variety, vigor, and a readiness to grapple with any novelty that might swim within man's ken distinguished the cultural life of Europe in the days of the Old Regime. No other part of the world exhibited anything like such an adventurous spirit. For the first time, therefore, Europe began conspicuously to pull ahead of the other, more conservative civilizations of the Old World—not merely in matters technological and military, but in science, philosophy, history, and scholarship. Where unabashed and untrammeled application of reason to the matter in hand was not decisive—as in the realm of fine arts generally—Europe cannot be said to have enjoyed any clear and unmistakable superiority. Indeed, the refinement and stylistic coherence of Chinese and of Moslem artistry remained greater than anything Europeans ever managed to produce with their restless multiplicity of styles.

Yet the rise of the West to world dominance had clearly begun. In the following chapters we must trace the fashion in which Europe's new-found superiority undermined and in the end overthrew the cultural autonomy of other great civilizations of mankind.

CHAPTER 24

The Americas and Russia

1648-1789

In 1648, colonial America and Orthodox Russia were still outliers of Europe, and did not fully share in European civilization. By 1789 this was no longer true. The former outliers had become active participants in what we should no longer call European but rather Western civilization. A European type of society had planted itself firmly in the Americas, and American ideas and institutions, proudly trumpeted to the world by the newly independent United States of America, threatened Europe's Old Regime as it had never been threatened before. In Russia, too, by 1789, the ruling clique had mastered the refinements of European high culture, and Russian state power had started to play a major part in European war and politics. Russia's enormous size and autocratic government also threatened the comparatively small states of western Europe. This threat, in its way, was no less real than that presented by the American example of democratic revolution. Hence it seems better in this period to classify the two great offshoots of Europe as part of the expanding body social of Western civilization. The important peculiarities which still, of course, marked off American and Russian society from one another and from the life patterns of the European heartlands were not so great as to indicate the emergence of separate civilizations. Instead, increasingly intricate interaction across the Atlantic and across the Russian frontier tended to close the gap between western Europe and its Russian and American outliers.

The fundamental factor that distinguished society in both Russia and the Americas from that prevailing near the center of Western civilization was a comparative abundance of land and a shortage of manpower (or at least of trained and skilled manpower). In any such situation two responses are possible. All the elaborate interlocking of skills, ranks, services, and patterns of deference which holds civilized society together and provides a workable pattern of relations between social classes and specialist groups may dissolve toward anarchic equality and cultural neo-barbarism. The Cossacks and many Siberian pioneers in Russia lived in just such a fashion. So did French *coureurs de bois* in Canada, English-speaking pioneers in the United States, Brazilian *bandeirantes*, Argentine *gauchos*, Australian swagmen, South African *voortrekkers*, and Alaskan sourdoughs. Unless restrained by some neighboring and hostile state, an expanding civilized society probably always tends to fray out toward just this sort of rudely equal, roughly violent neo-barbarism.

In other cases, however, an extreme polarization between masters and servants may arise in frontier societies. This is so because outside pressures—economic, political, and military—sometimes require a more elaborate social organization than frontier equality permits. In such circumstances, no impersonal law of the labor market compels one man to work for another, and it is not physically difficult for a man at the bottom of the social scale to run away into the wilds and thus make good his freedom. Hence, only strenuous resort to legal and sometimes to physical force can prevent this from happening. The slavery of the New World and the neo-serfdom of the Old were therefore quite as characteristic of the frontier as was the freedom and equality which a pious national tradition in the United States has tended to equate with frontier living.

On the whole, and with important exceptions, it is true that the equalitarian and libertarian response to manpower shortage dominated the social and political development of North America and of parts of South America, whereas the repressive response to the frontier's labor shortage prevailed in Russia. Yet in the richest and most developed parts of America, those occupied by Spaniards, a sharply graded society prevailed until long after 1789; whereas in Russia an anarchic, libertarian spirit has run (and continues to run) very near the surface of public life. Seeming opposites, in other words, have much in common.

Competition for the Americas

‡‡‡ As the tiny colonies established by French, Dutch, and British adventurers at the beginning of the seventeenth century took root and began to flourish, the Americas came to be divided into national spheres of influence. As a result, the wars of Europe were faithfully mirrored (and sometimes provoked) by colonial struggles, in which Indian warriors, European soldiers, and colonial militiamen all took part.

The first decisive bench mark of these struggles was the exclusion of the Dutch from any leading part in American colonization. This occurred between 1654 and 1664, when the Dutch first lost Brazil to local insurgents who proclaimed their (somewhat conditional) loyalty to Portugal, and then New Amsterdam to the British, who renamed it New York. The second major turn came in 1763, when the French surrendered Canada to the British after an unprecedentedly severe, globe-encompassing war. This overwhelming success (the British simultaneously won supremacy in India) was quickly followed, however, by quarrels with the American colonists who felt aggrieved at being taxed by the British government. When danger no longer threatened from Canada, the colonists felt that British redcoats along with British revenue officers were quite superfluous. The result was first controversy, then war (1775–83), won by the colonists with the potent help of the French, who took revenge for their earlier defeat by intervening decisively against the British between 1778 and 1783.

Along the Pacific coast of the Americas, Europe's international rivalries also affected events. Between 1728 and 1741, the Russian naval captain Vitus Bering discovered Alaska as well as the strait that bears his name. Russian fur traders soon followed this up by establishing small settlements in the Aleutian Islands and on the Alaskan mainland. This news stimulated the British Hudson's Bay Company to explore and lay claim to all of Canada west to the Rockies. This was accom-

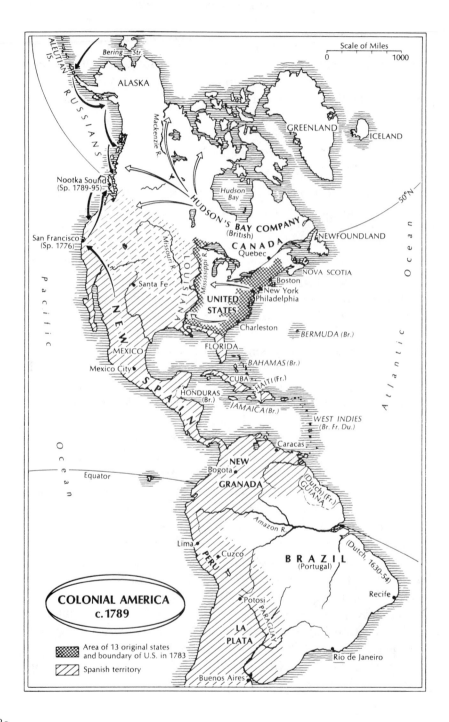

Scale of Miles
0   1000

ALEUTIAN IS.

Bering Str.

ALASKA

RUSSIANS

Mackenzie R.

GREENLAND

ICELAND

Hudson Bay

Nootka Sound
(Sp. 1789-95)

HUDSON'S BAY COMPANY
(British)

50°N

San Francisco
(Sp. 1776)

NEWFOUNDLAND

CANADA

Quebec

Missouri R.

LOUISIANA

Mississippi R.

NOVA SCOTIA

Boston

Pacific

Santa Fe

UNITED
STATES

New York
Philadelphia

NEW

Charleston

BERMUDA (Br.)

SPAIN

MEXICO

FLORIDA

Mexico City

BAHAMAS (Br.)

CUBA

HAITI (Fr.)

HONDURAS
(Br.)

JAMAICA (Br.)

*WEST INDIES
(Br. Fr. Du.)*

Ocean

Caracas

NEW

Atlantic Ocean

Equator

Bogota

GRANADA

GUIANA
(Dutch) (Fr.)

Amazon R.

(Dutch, 1630-54)

Lima

Cuzco

B R A Z I L
(Portugal)

PERU

Recife

COLONIAL AMERICA
c. 1789

Potosi

PARAGUAY

Rio de Janeiro

LA
PLATA

Area of 13 original states
and boundary of U.S. in 1783

Spanish territory

Buenos Aires

plished by 1789. The Spaniards reacted to the Russian advance by pushing farther up the coast, establishing missions at San Francisco (1775) and Nootka (1789).

The net result, therefore, of Europe's power struggles was to carve up all of the New World into more or less clearly delimited imperial fragments. Social reality never caught up with claims of course, for the advance of settlement in North America had barely reached the Appalachian mountains at the time of the American Revolution, and nowhere else had white men established a European type of society very far inland.

The Magnificence of Spanish America

‡‡‡ Given the economic and political relations that prevail today, it is difficult for citizens of the United States to keep an historically correct perspective on colonial times. Yet by almost any standard, the poverty and rustic simplicity of the Massachusetts backwoods or of the Virginia piedmont in the eighteenth century paled before the viceregal splendors of Lima and Mexico City. Indeed, in 1793, the 100,000 inhabitants of Mexico City made it larger than any European city except London and Paris.

The decay of the Indian population, which had been so disastrous in the sixteenth and early seventeenth centuries, came to a halt about 1650. Thereafter, Mexico and other parts of the Spanish empire witnessed an increasingly rapid population growth. Presumably Amerindians acquired the necessary immunities to the European and African diseases which had destroyed so many of their predecessors. Growing populations, in turn, provided the setting for a general upthrust of commercial prosperity, particularly after the relaxation (1774–78) of monopolistic regulations which had prohibited coastal trade among the American ports of the Spanish empire, and had funneled all colonial exports and imports through the single city of Cadiz, Spain.

Ancient universities and aristocratic traditions of culture allowed individual savants of the Spanish empire to participate in the cultural and intellectual life of Europe, even before the renewal of economic expansion in the late eighteenth century created a small but vivacious middle class of professional men, merchants, and officials who developed a lively interest in the latest fashions and ideas emanating from a newly "Enlightened" Spain.

Two features blunted the further development of Spanish American society despite such a big head start over anything yet achieved among English-speaking colonists farther north. First, the Indian peasantry, upon whose stolid labors the society depended, shared scarcely at all in the high culture of Spanish colonial life. Second, intellectual and moral sloth prevailed in the church and made its extraordinary economic dominance within colonial society indefensible. But when, as soon occurred, secular-minded liberals attacked the church they shook the only institutional link that gave the Indians an emotionally vital share in Spanish civilization and bound them to submission. Any serious move against the church therefore opened the door to Indian revolt and social chaos. Such a by-product of their convictions appalled liberal-minded men. Profound inner uncertainties promptly beset the Spanish elite—a state of mind that gave self-interested adventurers and political rakes unusually wide scope.

Such comments become plausible in the light of nineteenth- and twentieth-century developments in Spanish America. But up until the end of the eighteenth century, the future weaknesses of Spanish imperial society were not yet evident. Instead, like the Chinese empire on the other side of the Pacific, Spain's American empire towered like a great oak, standing high above all adjacent states, peoples, and cultures.

Backwardness Versus Precocity in the Colonies

‡‡‡ Brazil, on the Spaniard's southeasterly flank, remained politically chaotic even after the Dutch had withdrawn. The vigor of backwoodsmen's exploitation of placer gold, the ruthlessness of their attacks upon the Jesuit Indian preserve of Paraguay, not to mention the vitality of transplanted African cultures among the slaves of Brazilian plantations—all these seemed squalid when compared with the dignity and pomp of the well-ordered, peaceable, and reasonably well-administered Spanish vice-royalties. Nevertheless, far-ranging local self-government allowed the common people of Brazil to prosper in much the same way that commoners prospered in the English colonies of North America.

Like Brazil, the English colonies never rivaled Spanish grandeur. To

be sure, in the ports of Boston, New York, Philadelphia, small-scale rep-
licas of the society and cultural life of England arose. Religious differences among the various colonies and, before long, within each colony
as well, made enforcement of religious conformity impractical after
1700. Secularism perhaps found easier expression as a result of the
breakdown of church authority; but the discomfiture of established religion also opened a path for emotional religious revivalism, which became a very prominent feature of colonial life.

In many respects the English colonies lagged behind the contemporary development of Europe. But in some ways the evolution of
North American society outstripped that of the Old World. The
American War of Independence gave by far the most important expression to this phenomenon. To be sure, the ideas which the colonists
used to explain and justify their rebellion against King George III and
the British Parliament drew heavily upon traditional definitions of the
"rights of Englishmen." In addition, however, more radical definitions
of the "Rights of Man" played their part and rescued the American
Revolution from a merely local importance. Many Europeans actually
persuaded themselves that the Rights of Man as realized in the United
States of America constituted a model toward which benighted and
backward peoples of Europe, like the French, might hopefully strive.
Through the force of its example, therefore, the American War of Independence and the constitutional settlement that emerged from the
war entered powerfully upon the stage of world history. The liberal
principles professed by men who had but lately ranked as poor and remote country cousins of the English catapulted American affairs into
the forefront of European politics.

The Modernization of Russia

‡‡‡ In joining the mainstream of European history, American colonists
suffered no psychological wrench. On the contrary, they were re-
covering a fuller share in the cultural traditions their ancestors had left
behind when they first emigrated from England. No conversion was
called for. Russia, however, had first to repudiate its own special style
of life, built around the Orthodox claim to monopoly of Christian
truth, and upon obedience to an absolute tsar. To abandon such a past
was difficult; yet this is what the Russians—or more correctly what

the Russian rulers—did between 1654, when the Patriarch Nikon launched his official reform of the church's liturgical books, and 1725, when Tsar Peter the Great died.

Nikon sought to base the manuals used in all the services of the church upon authentic and indubitably correct Greek texts. Only so could uniformity be secured throughout Russia, and only so could the painful reproaches of Roman Catholic propagandists, who pointed to errors in existing Russian texts, be silenced. Leaders of secular government as well as of the church fully accepted this reasoning, so that even after Nikon had quarreled with the tsar (1658) and was dismissed from his patriarchal office (1666), his reform policy continued to prevail.

But many poor and humble Christians felt that official tampering with the familiar words of the church ritual had inaugurated the reign of Anti-Christ. Who else would dare to alter the sacred phrases necessary for salvation? As a result, communities of dissenters—the "Old Believers" of subsequent Russian history—came into existence and stubbornly, sometimes heroically, refused to submit to official coercion. Efforts to break up such communities by force occasionally led to mass suicide on the part of the beleaguered defenders of the old ways. Sometimes too, dissent ran into hidden channels so that peasants who outwardly conformed to the new order of church worship secretly listened to teachers who viewed the unholy alliance of a corrupted church with a secularized state as the work of Anti-Christ, tokening the imminent end of the world.

It is impossible to know how widely such opinions spread among the Russian people. It seems plausible to believe that massive peasant discontents which under other circumstances might have found political forms of expression were most effectually diverted into religious channels, as long as secret and persecuted groups exhorted one another to await the miraculous opening of the skies that would announce the Second Coming of Christ. This psychological safety valve was probably what permitted Peter the Great and his immediate successors to revolutionize Russia as ruthlessly as they did without provoking a crippling revolt. For Peter's reforms were the work of a tiny clique that he created from among his personal acquaintances and boon companions, reinforced by captured Swedes and kidnapped Dutchmen, and by other flotsam and jetsam from the European world of the West that drifted within the tsar's reach.

Peter came to the throne in 1689 while still a boy, and did not begin his revolutionary assault upon old Russian life until after returning in 1698 from an anonymous (but well-advertised) trip to western Europe. Thereafter, he never rested from frantic and sometimes erratic efforts to build an army and navy as good as any in the world, supported by all the industrial, administrative, and intellectual skills that might be necessary. A vigorous and violent personality certainly helped Peter to achieve as much as he did, but his orders could only become effective through the actions of subordinates, educated to submit to his hectoring commands. He found these subordinates, in large measure, among the rank and file of the Guards Regiments, which he had personally created while still a mere child. Later he reinforced their ranks by requiring nobles' sons to enter the Guards Regiments as privates, where, if they did well, he might presently notice them and promote them, assigning them to any sort of task, civil or military, diplomatic or judicial, depending on the needs of the moment.

The system worked. Young men from the country houses of Russia came to court and there, as members of the Guards Regiments, were converted to a new set of manners, before being sent off to do the tsar's work in peace and in war. Philip of Macedon and the great Ottoman sultans had used the same device for creating an obedient military and administrative corps, capable, like Peter's friends, of carrying through a revolution from above on the word of command precisely because each of them had first been cut off from his past by the seductive glitter of a radically novel style of court culture.

Peter's death in 1725 presented his associates with a serious problem, for they recognized no clear principle of political legitimacy. How then could succession to the throne be regulated, particularly since the revolutionary tsar had killed his own son and left no male heir? Resulting uncertainties bred intrigue and ugly palace *coups d'état.* The most spectacular of these put a German princess on the throne of Imperial Russia, in 1762, after the murder of her royal husband. She took the title Catherine II. Despite her dubious claim to power, Catherine ruled long and prosperously and, like Peter, soon earned the sobriquet "the Great." A stabilizing factor was that whenever quarrels and intrigues among the ruling clique threatened to get out of hand, all concerned drew back because they realized how few and weak they were when measured against the vast, resentful peasant mass of Russia. The further fact that the Russian economy experienced a prolonged boom with the opening of the Ukraine to commercial farming in the latter part of the eighteenth century also helped to maintain workable cohesion among the masters of the Russian land.

Russia Arrives as a Great Power

‡‡‡ In military and diplomatic matters Peter met with incomplete success. He defeated the Swedes in a long and difficult war (1700–1721) and was able to secure a short coastline on the Gulf of Finland. With extraordinary ruthlessness, he then built a new city, St. Petersburg, on swampy land at the mouth of the river Neva, and made his new creation into the capital of Russia. Against the Turks, on the other hand, Peter fared much less well. Despite an initial success in 1696, he had to surrender all he had won a few years later (1711). In the last year of his life, however, victory over his other Moslem neighbor, the shah of Iran, allowed the tsar to advance his frontiers to the southernmost part of the Caspian Sea.

Peter's successors regularly committed Russian troops to Europe's struggles. The most dramatic demonstration of Russia's power occurred during the Seven Years' War (1756–63), when a change of ruler in Russia shifted Russian strength from one side to the other, literally overnight, and saved Frederick II of Prussia from what had seemed certain disaster. In addition, the Russians fought two inconclusive wars against the Turks before Catherine the Great launched what proved to be a decisive war against the sultan (1768–74). To be sure, her grand plan for overthrowing the Turks and establishing a new Byzantine and Orthodox empire under her imperial protection was not realized. But Russia did annex the Black Sea coast as far as the Dniester river, and, as a sop for her restraint vis-à-vis the defeated Turks, the Prussians and Austrians agreed to permit Catherine to occupy a large part of Poland in the first partition of that hapless country (1772). In each of the two subsequent partitions, too, Russia secured a share (1793 and 1795), advancing the Russian frontier west to the Vistula.

While Russia thus became an active and respected member of the exclusive company of the great European powers, at home the progress of settlement southward into the Ukraine together with a rapid upswing of manufactures and trade began to give Russian society a more European aspect. The peasant majority remained "deaf and dark," living in a world apart from that of their masters, who more and more imitated the manners and acquired the legal rights possessed by the aristocracies of other more westerly lands. In 1762, for example, the legal require-

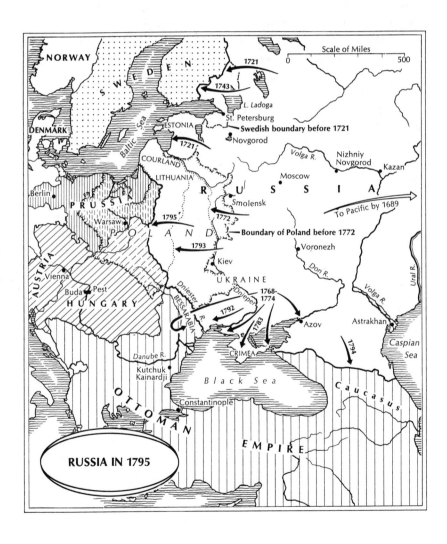

RUSSIA IN 1795

ment that nobles must serve the tsar was canceled, and many did in fact withdraw to their estates. By that time, enough men had been trained to fill and more than fill available posts, and the government's tax income had become large enough to allow payment of modest salaries in lieu of the land grants upon which Ivan the Terrible and Peter the Great had mainly relied.

Serfs, whose legal obligations to the landowners were tightened rather than relaxed, certainly felt deep grievance at the privileges thus accorded their masters. Why should the poor and humble not also be freed from the burden of forced service? A great uprising led by Emilian Pugachev and centering in southern and western Russia, where memories of the free frontier days were still fresh, gave vent to these feelings. It was brutally repressed (1773–75). Thereafter peasant discontent reverted to religious dissent and drunkenness. Most of the nobles, on the other hand, set out eagerly to try to equal or overtake France and the other great nations of Europe. For at least a generation after Catherine's time they found ample scope for their idealism and energies (as well as for self-interest) in forwarding the agricultural, commercial, and administrative advance of their country. In spite of peasant disaffection, servants of the autocracy were sure that they were acting in the true interests of all, making Russia rich and great and respected among the nations of the world. Whatever compulsion was necessary to make the lower classes of Russian society play their part seemed amply justified by Russia's solid successes in war and diplomacy.

CHAPTER 25

Asian Reactions to Europe's Old Regime 1700-1850

 In Moslem eyes, the Peace of Karlowitz (1699), whereby the Ottoman empire surrendered nearly all of Hungary to the victorious Austrians, ran completely against the grain of history. What was far more embarrassing, such a serious defeat also conflicted with fundamental theological principles, for ever since Mohammed's followers at Medina had attacked and overcome the scoffers of Mecca, victory in battle had been recognized as a sign and seal of divine favor. This being so, how could Allah favor Christian dogs and unbelievers, who were increasingly untrue even to their own mistaken faith?

The full force of this puzzle confronted the Moslem world only toward the end of the eighteenth century. Between 1768 and 1774 the Russians defeated Ottoman armies utterly and were prevented from capturing Constantinople and destroying the sultan's power more by the intervention of European diplomats than by any inherent strength of the Turkish regime. Even so, the treaty of Kutchuk Kainardji ("Little Fountain") ending the war was ominous for the future. It invited Russian intervention in Ottoman affairs by according the tsar a vaguely worded protectorate over Orthodox Christians under Turkish rule. The Russians also acquired important territories along the Black

Sea coast, together with rights of unrestricted navigation on that sea and passage through the straits. The sultan's palaces and Constantinople itself thus came within easy range of Russian naval guns.

To be defeated by the Holy Roman Emperor, who ranked in Moslem eyes as the political leader of Christendom, was as nothing compared to defeat at the hands of a ruler whose predecessors had been obedient subjects to the Khan of the Golden Horde, and whose Orthodox Christianity classed them with the sultan's own Christian subjects in the Balkans. Moreover, by 1774, Moslem supremacy over India was also clearly in danger, and the Safavi empire had dissolved, turning Iran and Turkestan into a cockpit where rival military captains tore civil society apart.

To pious Moslems, who accept the principle that divine favor and military success are closely linked, world events since 1699 remain an unsolvable conundrum. Total apostacy seems the only alternative to blind faith—a faith that can only await the turning of the tide, when Allah's inexplicable reversal of the pattern of world history will in its turn be reversed. In the meanwhile, resentful passivity, supported by a doctrine of fatalism, has characterized Moslem reaction to Europeans throughout the period of Western ascendancy.

Some, however, were not content passively to await Allah's intervention. Two obvious remedies offered themselves: (1) to surpass their rival's power by appropriating from the "Franks" the technical basis of their military success or (2) to regain Allah's favor by purifying Islam from all traces of the corruptions that had crept into Moslem lives. Champions of each policy made their voices heard early in the eighteenth century; but it was Islam's misfortune—unlike, for example, the Japanese—that the two remedies seemed almost always diametrically opposed to one another. Reformers' efforts therefore tended to cancel out, leaving the mass of Moslem society more confused and frustrated than ever.

The Wahhabi Movement

‡‡‡ The most important champion of religious purification was Mohammed ibn Abdul Wahhab (1691–1787), who lived in the Arabian desert and relied upon princes of the house of Sa'ud to protect his followers and promulgate his teachings. Abdul Wahhab's aim was clear:

to restore the faith of the Prophet in all its pristine purity. This meant in practice a strenuous and unbending rejection of saint worship and other corruptions that Sufi holy men had brought to Islam. It meant also insistence upon strict observance of all the rules of personal conduct laid down in the Koran. Wine drinking, for example, and other religiously prohibited acts were sternly punished by the Wahhabis, who inclined, whenever a point of doubt legitimately arose, to adopt the severer and stricter view.

The Wahhabi community in Arabia grew from very small beginnings in almost exactly the same fashion as the original community of Islam had grown. By the time of Abdul Wahhab's death, his followers controlled most of Arabia, but soon thereafter the movement met a crushing military setback, when Egyptian troops, trained and equipped on the European model, collided with the old-fashioned warriors of the Arabian desert and defeated them decisively (1818). But defeat in battle did not destroy the Wahhabi movement. On the contrary, when Wahhabism ceased to be so closely tied up with the military-political fortunes of the Sa'ud family, it actually widened its appeal by attracting pious and serious-minded Moslems in India and the Ottoman empire.

The delicate balance that had long prevailed in most Moslem lands between the legalism of early Islam and the mystical Sufi piety of later ages could not survive the effect of Western skepticism on the one hand and Wahhabi incandescence on the other. Intellectual rigidity, sheltering behind familiar phrases safely transmitted from generation to generation by rote memorization, had been characteristic of Sunni learning ever since the time of Suleiman the Lawgiver. Wahhabi zealots, by taking the words of the Koran with deadly seriousness and seeking to apply them anew to every condition of human life, made this sort of mindless conservatism impossible. Yet the heirs of Moslem learning and civilization knew more of the complexities of the world and its ways than was ordinarily vouchsafed to the Bedouin tribesmen among whom Abdul Wahhab found his first followers. Urban sophisticates therefore usually found it difficult to believe that all would come right again if only the faithful would conform exactly to Wahhabi prescriptions. Hence the Wahhabi movement failed to provide the ground for resumption of vigorous and successful intellectual life within Islam, and, indeed, made fundamental departure from ancient formulas and rules of conduct more difficult than ever.

The Failure of Reform

‡‡‡ Reformers who sought to strengthen Moslem states by borrowing European techniques met with small success prior to 1850. In the eighteenth century, very few Ottoman officials took such an idea seriously. Moreover, any success in war had the ironical effect of reducing the apparent need for further tampering with ancient practices. For example, after 1699 a group of Ottoman officials did set out to reform and re-equip Turkish artillery units with guns like those the Austrians had used so effectively against Ottoman troops in the long war of 1683–99. Later, after another disastrous war with the Austrians (1716–18), military reform spread to a few infantry units as well. When both Austria and Russia attacked the Turks, 1736–39, these new units helped to administer unexpected defeats to the Austrians. The Austrians soon withdrew from the war, whereupon the Russians did the same. Yet this striking vindication of the policy of military reform did not persuade the Ottoman government to persevere. On the contrary, military victory was interpreted to mean that no further military changes were needed, and, in fact, during the long peace that ensued the new units were gradually allowed to wither into ineffectiveness. When Catherine II of Russia attacked the Ottoman empire in the war of 1768–74, the Turks therefore found themselves hopelessly outclassed by the Russian troops which had been freshly tempered and tested in the Seven Years' War (1756–63).

The shattering defeat of 1774 revived the effort to modernize Ottoman armies, but not until 1826 did a decisive breakthrough come. The reason was that the severity of the disaster which Russian armies had inflicted seemed to demand a thoroughgoing reorganization of all Ottoman institutions. In such circumstances conservatives felt that the whole Islamic character of the state was in danger. Even very modest steps toward reform of the armed forces therefore sufficed to rouse fanatic resistance. Not until a further series of military disasters had occurred, including successful revolt on the part of the sultan's Serbian and Greek subjects, did the reforming cause prevail. Even then it did so at enormous cost, for the sultan had to order his artillerists to mow down the rebellious janissaries and the Constantinople mob supporting them. Such a bloody and violent step did indeed destroy conservatism's armed strength but failed entirely to replace the old army with a new one capable of protecting the empire. Fresh humiliation therefore lay in store for the Ottoman empire at the hands of the European powers and of upstart rebels like the formidable tyrant of Egypt, Mohammed Ali (d. 1849).

By 1850, therefore, most Turkish officials and men of affairs concluded that imitating European uniforms and guns was as ineffectual as standing fast. No solution seemed to offer itself, and the policy makers of the Ottoman empire relied instead on a certain low cleverness in diplomatic intrigue, seeking to divide the European powers and compel one or another of them to come to the rescue of the "Sick man of Europe."

British Control of India

‡‡‡ The Mughal empire survived in name until 1857, but only in name. No European balance of power came to its rescue. Instead, the struggle for trade and influence in India tipped decisively in favor of the British after 1763. Thereafter the turbulent political stage in India allowed—indeed invited—continued encroachment, so that after 1818 only Sikhs of the Punjab and tribesmen of the remote northwest frontier remained truly independent of British authority.

The decay of Mughal power became apparent even before the Emperor Aurangzeb died in 1707. Although his conquests in southern India brought the empire to its greatest territorial extent, before he died a number of serious revolts had already begun to undermine the imperial authority. In particular, Hindu hillsmen in central India—the so-called Marathas—launched a guerrilla war which the slow-moving Mughal forces could not counter. Later, Sikhs also revolted and set up a territorial lordship in the northwest. In time many local governors made themselves independent of the central administration, until even the immediate environs of Delhi, the capital, sometimes ceased to obey the imperial command.

Under these conditions, the agents of the European trading companies found it necessary to protect themselves. They did so by enlisting Indian soldiers ("sepoys") under European officers, equipping and training such forces in a European manner. Very soon it became evi-

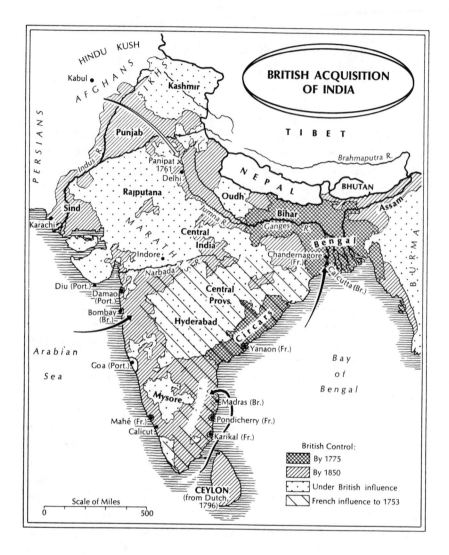

dent that these troops were in fact superior to any other type of armed force known to India. Local rulers, and adventurers wishing to make good their claim to a piece of territory, obviously had deep interest in securing such troops for their own uses, and began hiring Europeans to command "sepoy" armies. This in turn stimulated rivalries among the European powers, for a local European military commander could be assumed to favor the cause of his fellow nationals at the court of his employer. In the confusion which resulted, the French, who were seeking to build up a powerful India company, and the British, whose trading activities in the Indian Ocean dated from 1600, became the principal rivals. But the superior strength of the British navy meant that in case of war between the two countries, British forces in India could be moved to and fro by sea and be sure of supply from home, whereas the French, who risked being cut off, lost strategic mobility, save insofar as they could march their forces cross-country overland. When, therefore, all-out struggle was joined between France and Great Britain in 1756, it is not surprising that the British in India won decisive success, and after the end of the war (1763) effectually excluded the French from further participation in Indian political and economic affairs.

While the struggle between French and British companies was still in progress, an Afghan invading force ravaged northwestern India and administered a crushing defeat to the Maratha armies at Panipat, near Delhi (1761). From this time onward, therefore, the local princes of India found themselves caught between two equally aggressive foreign powers: the British coming from the sea and the Afghans coming from the north. When choice became necessary, most preferred the British. Without very much fighting, therefore, almost all Indian states had by 1818 concluded treaty arrangements establishing a binding alliance with the British. British control was usually exercised by a resident at court, who acted as a sort of watch dog to guarantee the faithful performance of treaty agreements. Part of India was directly administered by the British East India Company; but only when a native ruler stubbornly resisted offers of alliance or proved unusually incompetent did the company actually displace him from his throne.

The directors of the East India Company, sitting in London, almost invariably disapproved of territorial advance. They disliked military adventure on the grounds that it cost money and interfered with trade. Their whole aim was to earn as much as possible as cheaply as possible. This meant, among other things, refraining from any attempts to convert Indians to Christianity or in any other way altering their accustomed ways of life and government. Indeed, many of the company's officers were convinced that a mere handful of Britishers could never govern India or maintain their favored position in the sub-continent by any other policy.

As long as genuinely independent states continued to exist in India this argument had considerable force. After 1818, however, when the last Maratha war ended in an easy British triumph, no military rival remained. Missionary pressure from home and the demand of a handful of Hindus for legal and humanitarian reform mounted. Moslems, on the other hand, whose quarrels and political-military weakness had invited the westerners into India in the first place, only wished to be left alone.

Iran and Turkestan

‡‡‡ In Iran and Turkestan, too, Moslem political and economic life suffered humiliating decay, when measured against the mounting power of Europe. To be sure, the military exploits of Nadir shah (ruled 1736–47), who deposed the last of the Safavis and raided India victoriously, and the no less spectacular career of the Afghan chieftain Ahmed shah Durani (1747–73), conformed admirably to the warrior tradition of their predecessors. The difficulty was that these great conquerors now encountered armies trained and equipped in the European fashion whenever they ventured far from home, and, in fact, depended themselves in no small measure on the import of guns, powder, and shot. Judicious distribution of subsidies by civilized neighbors who had access to abundant supplies of powder and shot could, under these circumstances, raise up a rival or bring down the mighty at the very zenith of his success. Hence, from the beginning of the nineteenth century, the political life of Iran and Turkestan began to turn less upon local factors than upon British and Russian subsidies and punitive raids, such as that which brought British troops to the Afghan capital Kabul in 1839.

No Moslem could look with satisfaction upon the sad state into which the once proud realm of Islam had descended by 1850. No cultural rebirth or intellectual awakening relieved the somber political scene; while on the economic front, European machine-made goods had begun from about 1830 to reduce traditional artisan communities of the Moslem world to penury. Where, indeed, in such a world was Allah?

Hindu Reform

‡‡‡ Hindu and Christian subject communities of the Moslem world found the new order considerably easier to adjust to. Hindus could not get very excited at the spectacle of another invader destroying the alien Mughal (that is Persian and Turkish) dominion over India. Similar changes of master had occurred too often in the past for this to seem strange or particularly important. For a long time, therefore, the European presence in India provoked no very obvious repercussions within the Hindu communities. Hindus simply treated the Europeans as another caste.

Moreover, as we have seen, official British policy sought to minimize shocks to established social institutions and relationships. Thus, for example, the language of administration remained unchanged until 1837, so that any young Hindu aspiring to a government job had to learn Persian, the language of his old Moslem masters, not English.

After the beginning of the nineteenth century, however, initiatives both from the British and from the Hindu side began to enlarge the range of interaction between Western and Hindu culture. Missionary colleges, established initially in open defiance of the British East India Company's policy, introduced an important new element onto the scene. A number of energetic missionaries, arriving privately in India, proceeded to translate European books into the vernaculars spoken in various parts of the country. This provided a powerful stimulant to the literary development of the modern Indian languages, as well as opening a window upon important aspects of Western culture to Indian readers.

Few Indians ever became Christians since Hinduism proved just as much proof against Christian as against Moslem preaching. But the widened access to knowledge of European civilization which missionary activity in India allowed did not fail to stimulate a few Indians to the effort of trying to understand the strange outside world inhabited by their British rulers. This effort was pioneered by Ram Mohan Roy (d. 1833), whose inquiries into Christian and Moslem religion convinced him that all world religions conveyed fundamentally the same message—ethical unitarianism. He and others easily convinced themselves, as well as a few eager disciples in the Western world, that

Hindu philosophers had discovered these universal truths long before any other people. Hence, proud and pious Hindus could feel that even wholesale borrowing of European techniques might be acceptable, since Indians had such precious spiritual insight to give in return. Western scholars assuredly did have much to learn from the Upanishads and the Vedas and, especially in the early nineteenth century, showed a considerable enthusiasm in undertaking the task.

Energetic researches into early Indian texts, however, produced an unexpected backlash. Existing Hindu practices had little or no relation to the Vedas. This opened a door for Hindu reformers, who, by judicious selection from the vast religious literature of Hinduism, could find ample authority for the sorts of liberal and humanitarian reforms many of the Christian missionaries and a few of the company's officials had begun to advocate. The test case was the custom of *suttee*, i.e. the custom of burning a widow on the funeral pyre of her dead husband. There was no Vedic authority for this practice. Ram Mohan Roy launched a series of pamphlets condemning *suttee* and urging British authorities to prohibit it. In 1829 they did so. Six years later they also decided to introduce a school system for Indians that would be conducted in English and would have a European curriculum. This, too, had been advocated by Ram Mohan Roy as needful if Indian youths were to acquire knowledge of scientific truth.

Once such tampering with traditional customs and institutions had been started, there was no stopping. The British authorities soon found that each reform generated a demand for others. As a result, administrative action failed to keep up with demands for more and more resolute and radical transformation of the traditional social structure. A handful of educated Hindus were among those who clamored for faster action. The great majority, of course, remained passive, only vaguely aware of the concerns and aspirations of their reforming fellows. Nevertheless, the contrast with the Moslem community of India was fundamental, for Hindu leadership acquiesced when it did not demand reform, whereas Moslems of high and low degree were as one in deploring everything that was happening around them. This difference between the two main religious communities of India remains until today, and has helped, more than anything else, to make India again a Hindu land.

The Christian Balkans

‡‡‡ In the Balkans, on the other flank of Islam, the Christian populations also found it comparatively easy to welcome the decaying fortunes of their Ottoman masters. To be sure, there were groups of Christians in Constantinople who had benefited greatly from their position as bankers and advisers to the Turks and were not anxious to see the imperial fabric, upon which their wealth depended, fall to pieces. But strategically situated sophisticates—merchants and professional men in particular—fell under the spell of the secularized version of Western culture which goes by the name of the Enlightenment, and looked forward to change. Old theological quarrels about the wording of the Nicene Creed seemed irrelevant to readers of Voltaire and Rousseau. Moreover, civil liberties and natural rights had no announced geographical or cultural limits. Hence, insofar as Orthodox Christians of the Balkans took such ideas seriously, they not unnaturally aspired to create free and modern national states of their own to supersede the decaying Ottoman regime.

This spirit, combined with not a little old-fashioned Balkan banditry, gave the Serbian (1803–15) and Greek (1821–30) revolutions a character of their own, and made them the first step toward a more perfect incorporation of those nations into Western society. Difficulty soon arose from the fact that the Christian nations of the Balkans cherished conflicting territorial ambitions. But until after 1850 this was hidden by the confident anticipation of a future brotherhood of free men everywhere which infected revolutionary circles.

Christian Missions in China

‡‡‡ In the Far East, no events as dramatic as the British conquest of India or the Russian advance against Ottoman Turkey disturbed the calm of the Confucian world. Throughout the eighteenth century, China remained great and powerful and Japan persevered in a rigorous policy of isolation. After about 1775, however, changes in both countries began to undermine—at first imperceptibly—the basis upon which peace and prosperity rested. By the middle of the nineteenth century, therefore, when European powers began to surge against the

Far Eastern citadel with an energy reinforced by the industrial and democratic revolutions, Chinese and Japanese capacity to resist had been drastically reduced.

Until the end of the eighteenth century, Chinese government remained so successful and so traditional as to require little description here. Europeans found much to admire in a society which lacked both revealed religion and hereditary aristocracy. Many "enlightened" spirits of the Far West advocated just these things in their own countries, and easily persuaded themselves that the virtuous Chinese had already created a working model for the society of which they dreamed. The Chinese, however, did not return the compliment. Indeed they seem to have been rather less interested in European knowledge and skills during the eighteenth century than they had been when such matters were still novelties. This was partly due to the fact that a bitter "rites controversy" broke out among the Christian missionaries in China, discrediting Europeans generally, and, in particular, reducing the intimacy and scale of contact between learned men of the two cultures.

The issue at stake in the rites controversy was fundamental for Christian missions. The Jesuits, who had pioneered the penetration of China, followed a policy of accommodation to local customs and ritual observances insofar as such rites did not unmistakably conflict with Christian teaching. In China, for example, they had decided that rites honoring ancestors and Confucius were civil ceremonies, not religious worship, and need not be forbidden to a Christian convert. Less politic missionaries, especially Franciscans, were shocked by this Jesuit policy and complained to the pope. Another point at issue was whether the Chinese word for "heaven" was suitable as an equivalent for "God," or whether its pagan associations were too close to make such a translation correct.

Clearly, the pope was in no position to decide how the term "God" should be translated into Chinese, and for a long time the papal court sought to compromise. This proved impossible, however, and eventually (1715) the papacy decided against the Jesuits. But the Emperor of China, to whom the question had also been referred, had already decided in their favor. The Son of Heaven, not unnaturally, felt that the papal decision flouted his authority in his own land. He therefore forbade any Christian missionary to enter China who did not subscribe to the Jesuit position. After 1715 obedient Catholics could no longer do so. Missions therefore had either to close down or become illegal. Some illegal entry did occur, but the missionaries who succeeded in evading the imperial authority in this manner could appeal only to the poor and humble classes. Accordingly, Christianity ceased to be at home in the court and among highly educated Chinese, and became instead a small, seemingly unimportant secret society, tinged with antigovernmental or even openly revolutionary sentiments. A handful of Jesuits remained at court as astronomers, and when the Society of Jesus was dissolved by the pope in 1773 this professional function was transferred to the Lazarist order. But the rites controversy had dramatized for the Chinese the extent to which Christian missionaries were agents of a foreign power. Loyal and obedient officials of the empire reacted by keeping the royal astronomers at a distance.

Opening China to European Trade

‡‡‡ Until the last quarter of the eighteenth century, China's political and economic order functioned so well that there seemed no reason for any concern with things foreign. After about 1775, however, the traditional signs of dynastic decay began to appear and multiply. Most fundamental was the fact that in many parts of China the population had grown so great that peasant farms had been subdivided into plots upon which a family could not produce enough to survive in a poor season. Indebtedness then led to loss of ownership of the land. Usurers thus tended to concentrate landed wealth in their hands, while peasant debtors accumulated grievances that burst out sporadically in violent risings. The first serious rebellion began in 1774. Revolts became increasingly widespread during the following decades, building up toward the catastrophic Taiping rebellion, which broke out in 1850.

These internal strains were accompanied by troubles across the frontier. Throughout the early nineteenth century, China's northwest frontier remained stable. The military power of steppe peoples had been completely broken in the eighteenth century by Chinese and Russian arms. But this unusual security was counterbalanced by the fact that novel and unprecedented difficulties arose on the southern coast, where trade with the "south sea barbarians" from Europe concentrated. This trade had long been conducted on monopolistic lines, between an association of Cantonese merchants on the one hand and the British East India Company, which had largely supplanted its European rivals, on the other. In 1834, however, the British government abolished the East India Company's legal monopoly of the China trade, and sought to introduce at Canton the patterns of commerce normal to European ports. This the Chinese opposed, since the Chinese government was trying to tighten official regulation of trade. From the Chinese point of view indeed, the development of the Canton trade in the early nineteenth century was thoroughly deplorable. Large numbers of Chinese had begun to smoke opium, and the British and other Euorpeans gladly supplied the drug, which was produced mainly in India. When Chinese officials forbade the import of opium, European traders resorted to smuggling and bribery, so that trade began again to assume the extra-legal forms it had had in the first period of European activity along the China coast.

In 1839 the Chinese sent a special commissioner to Canton with instructions to clamp down on illegal trade and stop the importation of opium. His efforts were quite effective even before a quarrel over how to punish British sailors who had murdered someone on shore provided the occasion for the outbreak of war between the British and Chinese governments. To the surprise and dismay of the Chinese, British gunboats proved capable of overwhelming Chinese coastal defenses. The Treaty of Nanking (1842), which ended the war, gave the British nearly all they asked. Four ports in addition to Canton were opened to European trade, Hong Kong was ceded to the British, and British consuls were admitted to all the treaty ports. Other Western nations soon demanded and received the same privileges, and indeed, improved upon the original British terms by demanding extra-territoriality (i.e., exemption from Chinese law) for their nationals living on Chinese soil. The Chinese were enormously affronted by what had happened, but found themselves quite unable to do anything to drive the foreigners back.

China's decline from the heights of its eighteenth-century imperial grandeur was sudden, yet quite in accord with ancient precedent. Other dynasties had also decayed in precisely the same fashion. Until after 1850 therefore, the old, traditional frame of Chinese life remained essentially intact. Foreign disaster, however unpleasant, was traditional too, and therefore seemed to require no more than traditional remedies.

Social Tensions in Japan

‡‡‡ Japan's history was very different. Japan remained at peace throughout the eighteenth century when Chinese armies were winning empire in central Asia. Japanese population remained almost constant so there was no unusual push toward excessive subdivision of peasant farms as in China. In addition, Japan escaped foreign harassment until 1854.

Nevertheless, Japanese society was in travail between 1700 and 1850. The samurai class had lost its traditional military occupation. Idleness induced extravagance; extravagance fastened a heavy load of debt on nearly all of Japan's military class. This introduced a persistent discrepancy between the distribution of political and of economic power. Japanese culture reflected the same sharp duality, putting the spare aesthetic of samurai ceremonial side by side with a lascivious urban "floating world" of geisha girls and purse-proud upstarts.

The barriers between these two worlds tended to lessen as time went on. Samurai families sometimes adopted a merchant's son, thus refreshing their fortunes and admitting a few commoners to the ranks of the aristocracy. Intermingling of art styles, as artists experimented with elements from Chinese, Western, and Japanese autochthonous traditions, reflected a similar blurring of what had formerly been separated.

More significant for the future was the fact that a handful of Japanese intellectuals overcame great obstacles in order to study Western as well as Chinese learning. The Tokugawa regime had made Neo-Confucianism official, and even prohibited the study of other philosophies. But a few individuals, who felt disaffected toward the regime in greater or lesser degree, could not be prevented from pursuing the foreign learning which filtered into the country through the medium of books brought by the single Dutch ship that was officially allowed to enter Nagasaki harbor each year.

There were still other Japanese who opposed the Tokugawa regime on Neo-Confucian and patriotic grounds. For if the supreme virtue was obedience to superiors, as Neo-Confucians taught, what was the proper relation between the shogun and the Emperor? No rewriting of the record could make the shogun's position look like anything but a usurpation, and some Japanese scholars dared to say so, even at risk of their lives. Others abandoned Neo-Confucianism in favor of the ancient Shinto, and piously sought to elaborate that still somewhat cloudy body of myths and rituals into a more systematic and impressive doctrine.

The really important fact about these currents of intellectual dissent and opposition is that they tended to flow together and support one another. For Western learning could be valued not only for its own sake but also because it pointed up hitherto unsuspected deficiencies in Neo-Confucian doctrine. Thus, opposition to the shogun, reverence for the emperor, Japanese patriotism, and enthusiasm of Western learning, all came together to form a sort of intellectual underground. Particularly in outlying parts of the Japanese archipelago, where the so-called "Outside Lords" remembered the time when their ancestors had been rivals, not subjects, of the Tokugawa family, such ideas met with the protection of the powerful. Hence when in 1854 the shogun reluctantly decided to abandon the policy of isolation, there existed in Japan a small but vigorous body of men who had alternative policies for their nation clearly in view.

The opening of Japan, in other words, was like the release of a trigger. It did not of itself revolutionize the country. It did allow opposition groups to come to power, who, in the name of a restored emperor and ancient legitimacy, initiated a wholesale appropriation of Western technology. No other Asian people was anything like so well prepared to take advantage of the opportunities offered by contact with European civilization, for no other people had previously known the duality of culture and tensions between rival ideals which prevailed in Japan throughout the Tokugawa period.

Bibliographical Essay, Part III

After the great European discoveries, interrelations among the far parts of the globe became closer than before, and a number of histories reflect this fact by taking up interregional and transcivilizational themes. Among those of special interest are: John H. Parry, *Europe and a Wider World, 1415–1715* (New York, 1949); John H. Parry, *The Age of Reconnaissance: Discovery, Exploration and Settlement, 1450–1650* (New York, 1963); P. M. Ashburn, *The Ranks of Death: A Medical History of the Conquest of America* (New York, 1947); Donald F. Lach, *Asia in the Making of Europe*, multivolume (Chicago, 1965–); A. Grenfell Price, *The Western Invasions of the Pacific and Its Continents: A Study of Moving Frontiers and Changing Landscapes, 1513–1958* (Oxford, 1963); J. H. Elliott, *The Old World and the New, 1492–1650* (New York, 1970); Alfred W. Crosby, Jr., *The Columbian Exchange: Biological and Cultural Consequences of 1492* (Westport, Conn., 1972); Niels Steensgaard, *Carracks, Caravans, and Companies: The Structural Crisis in the European Asian Trade in the Early Seventeenth Century* (Lund, Sweden, 1973); Carlo M. Cipolla, *Guns, Sails and Empires: Technological Innovation and the Early Phases of European Expanion, 1400–1700* (New York, 1966); Walter D. Wyman and Clifton B. Kroeber, eds., *The Frontier in Perspective* (Madison, Wisc., 1957); Robert R. Palmer, *The Age of Democratic Revolution: A Political History of Europe and America, 1760–1800*, 2 vols. (Princeton, 1959, 1964); Hans Kohn, *The Age of Nationalism: The First Era of Global History* (New York, 1962); W. S. and E. S. Woytinsky, *World Population and Production: Trends and Outlook* (New York, 1953); and Barrington Moore, Jr.'s provocative *Social Origins of Dictatorship and Democracy, Lord and Peasant in the Making of the Modern World* (Boston, 1966).

EUROPE AND THE WEST. The plethora of books makes for confusion. A very popular and well written general text is Robert R. Palmer and Joel Colton, *A History of the Modern World*, 5th ed. (New York, 1977). The great European empires are treated by: Charles R. Boxer, *Four Centuries of Portuguese Expansion, 1415–1825* (Chester Springs, Pa., 1961); C. H. Haring, *The Spanish Empire in America* (New York, 1947); W. B. Willcox, *Star of Empire: A Study of Britain as a World Power, 1485–1945* (New York, 1950). No comparable essay in English about the fourth great European empire, the French, is known to me, but for an overview, see D. K. Fieldhouse, *The Colonial Empires* (New York, 1966). The following throw some special light on Europe's internal political evolution: Crane Brinton, *Anatomy of Revolution*, rev. ed. (New York, 1952); Peter Gay, *The Enlightenment, an Interpretation* (New York: 1966); J. R. Pole, *Political Representation in England and the Origins of the American Republic* (New York: 1966); and Eric J. Hobsbawm, *The Age of Revolutions 1789–1848* (Cleveland, 1963). On the French Revolution, Georges Lefebvre, *The French Revolution*, 2 vols. (Cambridge, 1965) may be compared with contrasting views of two leading experts: Albert Soboul, *The Parisian Sans-culottes and the French Revolution, 1793–94* (Oxford, 1964) and Alfred Cobban, *The Social Interpretation of the French Revolution* (Cambridge, 1964). On the other dominating transformation of modern times, Phyllis Dean, *The First Industrial Revolution* (Cambridge, 1965); John Clapham, *The Economic Development of France and Germany, 1815–1914*, 4th ed. (Cambridge, 1936); David Landes, *Prometheus Unbound* (London, 1969) and Walt W. Rostow, *The Stages of Economic Growth* (Cambridge, 1960) are recommended. Peter N. Stearns, *European Society in Upheaval* (New York, 1967) and George Mosse, *The Culture of Western Europe: The Nineteenth and Twentieth Centuries: An Introduction* (Chicago, 1961) are standard surveys of their respective themes. A distinctive French school of history arose between the two wars which is represented now in English translation by Fernand Braudel, *The Mediterranean and the Mediterranean World in the Age of Philip the II*, 2 vols. (New York, 1972–73)—a masterpiece—and Lucien Fevre, *Life in Renaissance France* (Cambridge, Mass., 1977).

Books of more than routine interest treating European science, technology, and economy include: Alfred Rupert Hall, *The Scientific Revolution, 1500–1800* (Boston, 1954); Herbert Butterfield, *The Origins of Modern Science, 1300–1800* (London and New York, 1957); Abraham Wolf et al., *A History of Science, Technology and Philosophy in the Sixteenth and Seventeenth Centuries*, 2nd ed. (New York, 1951); Sir Eric Ashby, *Technology and the Academics: An Essay on Universities and the Scientific Revolution* (London, 1958); John Francis Guilmartin, Jr., *Gunpowder to Galleys:*

Changing Technology and Mediterranean Warfare at Sea in the Sixteenth Century (New York, 1975); Fernand Braudel, *Capitalism and Material Life, 1400–1800* (New York, 1973); John U. Nef, *Industry and Government in France and England, 1540–1640* (Philadelphia, 1940); W. W. Rostow, *British Economy of the Nineteenth Century* (Oxford, 1948).

It seems futile to suggest readings from the store of modern European and American authors: all the classics of our modern languages fall within such a scope. Similarly, no large-scale histories of the cultural development of modern times illuminate the subject so well that they should be preferred to a direct plunge into the original texts.

Russian history perhaps should have special attention, since most readers of this book will probably know less of the Russian past than of that of other parts of the western world. Michael T. Florinski, *Russia: A History and Interpretation*, 2 vols. (New York, 1953–54), is a good text. Jane Harrison and Hope Mirrlees, trs., *The Life of the Archpriest Avvakum by Himself* (London, 1924) offers a precious and concise insight into the consciousness of an Old Believer. Other volumes of unusual interest are: James Billington, *The Icon and the Axe: An Interpretive History of Russian Culture* (New York, 1966); Otto Hoetzsch, *The Evolution of Russia* (New York, 1966); Raymond H. Fischer, *The Russian Fur Trade, 1550–1700* (Berkeley, 1943); W. E. D. Allen, *The Ukraine: A History* (Cambridge, 1940). Jerome Blum, *Lord and Peasant in Russia* (Princeton, 1961) has been mentioned in part II of this essay. Two very interesting works trace the relations between Russia and China from their beginnings: John F. Baddeley, *Russia, Mongolia and China*, 2 vols. (London, 1919) and Michael N. Pavlovsky, *Chinese-Russian Relations* (New York, 1949).

AFRICA. Aside from general histories of Africa mentioned in the bibliography to part II, two books treat the European slave trade vividly: Basil Davidson, *Black Mother: The African Slave Trade* (Boston, 1961) and Eric Williams, *Capitalism and Slavery* (Chapel·Hill, N.C., 1944). Philip D. Curtin, *The Atlantic Slave Trade: A Census* (Madison, Wisc., 1969) dispelled earlier exaggerated estimates of the number of Africans carried to the New World. Leopold Marquard, *The Story of South Africa* (London, 1955) is a simple, well-written account. Robert W. July, *The Origins of Modern African Thought* (New York, 1968) and Philip D. Curtin, ed., *Africa and the West: Intellectual Responses to European Culture* (Madison, Wisc., 1972) deal with African "Third World" ideas.

THE REALM OF ISLAM. Modern historiography of the Islamic world remains in a quite unsatisfactory state of development. The following general essays are helpful: H. A. R. Gibb and Harold Bowen, *Islamic Society and the West*,

I: Islamic Society in the Eighteenth Century, 2 parts (London, 1950, 1957); Wilfred Cantwell Smith, *Islam in Modern History* (Princeton, 1957); Gustave E. von Grunebaum, *Modern Islam: The Search for Cultural Identity* (Berkeley, 1962); H. A. R. Gibb, *Modern Trends in Islam* (Chicago, 1947); and Gustave E. von Grunebaum, ed., *Unity and Variety in Muslim Civilization* (Chicago, 1955). Marshall G. S. Hodgson's monumental *The Venture of Islam*, 3 vols. (Chicago, 1974) was listed in part II. Clifford Geertz, *Islam Observed* (New Haven, 1968) offers an analysis of the interplay between Islam and local traditions at the extremities of the Islamic world. For the separate areas of Islam, consult: George Antonius, *The Arab Awakening* (London, 1938); Zeine N. Zeine, *The Emergence of Arab Nationalism* (Beirut, 1966); Bernard Lewis, *The Arabs in History*, new ed. (London, 1966); Bernard Lewis, *The Emergence of Modern Turkey* (New York, 1961); Wilfred Cantwell Smith, *Modern Islam in India: A Social Analysis*, rev. ed. (London, 1947); Percy Sykes, *A History of Persia*, 3rd ed., 2 vols. (London, 1952); and Peter Avery, *Modern Iran* (New York, 1965).

INDIA. Percival Spear, *India: A Modern History* (Ann Arbor, 1961), and his revision of Vincent A. Smith, *The Oxford History of India*, 3rd ed. (Oxford, 1958) offer good general guides. K. M. Panikkar, *A Survey of Indian History*, 3rd ed. (Bombay, 1956), gives an Indian point of view. Stanley Wolpert, *A New History of India* (New York, 1977) was mentioned in part II. Percy Brown, *Indian Painting under the Mughals*, A.D. 1550 to A.D. 1750 (Oxford, 1924) offers an insight into Indian culture in the days of the Mughal empire's greatness. I know of no good history of that empire, but its founder's memoirs, Annette S. Beveridge, tr., *Babur's Memoirs*, 4 vols. (London, 1912–21) are delightful. Two books by W. H. Moreland, *India at the Death of Akbar: An Economic Study* (London, 1920), *From Akbar to Aurangzeb, A Study in Indian Economic History* (London, 1923); and M. Athar Ali, *The Mughal Nobility under Aurangzeb* (New York, 1966) are helpful. See also, Richard G. Fox, *Kin, Clan, Raja and Rule: State-Hinterland Relations in Preindustrial India* (Berkeley, 1971).

CHINA AND JAPAN. E. O. Reischauer, J. K. Fairbank, and A. M. Craig, *East Asia: Tradition and Transformation* (Boston, 1973) and George M. Beckman, *The Modernization of China and Japan* (New York, 1962) offer general surveys of the modern history of the Far East. Immanuel Hsü, *The Rise of Modern China*, 2nd ed. (New York, 1975) is the best general treatment of recent Chinese history. Charles R. Boxer, *Fidalgos in the Far East, 1550–1770* (The Hague, 1948) treats the Portuguese role skillfully. For Christian missions see: Kenneth Scott Latourette, *A History of Christian Missions in*

China (New York, 1929) and Arnold H. Rowbotham, *Missionary and Mandarin: The Jesuits at the Court of China* (Berkeley, 1942). On government see: Franz Michael, *The Origin of Manchu Rule in China* (Baltimore, 1942) and Etienne Balazs, *Political Theory and Administrative Reality in Traditional China* (London, 1965). Jonathan Spence, *The Death of Woman Wang* (New York, 1978) is a graphic depiction of life among the lower orders of society in late imperial China. Ping-ti Ho, *Studies on the Population of China, 1368–1953* (Cambridge, Mass., 1959); the same author's *The Ladder of Success in Imperial China: Aspects of Social Mobility, 1368–1911* (New York, 1962); Chung-li Chang, *The Chinese Gentry: Studies in their Role in Nineteenth Century Chinese Society* (Seattle, 1955); and Hsiao-t'ung Fei, *Peasant Life in China: A Field Study of Country Life in the Yangtze Valley* (New York, 1946) all cast light on aspects of China's social order and disorder in recent centuries. For technology there is Sun E-tu Zen and Sun S. C., *Chinese Technology in the Seventeenth Century* (University Park, Pa., 1966). Theodore de Bary, ed., *Sources of Chinese Tradition* (New York, 1966) is a useful collection of translated documents arranged chronologically and thematically. John K. Fairbank, ed., *Chinese Thought and Institutions* (Chicago, 1957) explores Chinese intellectual history; John K. Fairbank, ed., *The Chinese World Order: Traditional Chinese Foreign Relations* (Cambridge, Mass., 1968) is also enlightening.

Osvald Siren, *A History of Later Chinese Painting*, 2 vols. (London, 1938), offers the best available sampling of modern Chinese art. Students can also acquaint themselves with the texture of Chinese society by sampling traditional Chinese fiction. Two of the most important examples are available in English translation: Wu Ching-tzu, *The Scholars* (New York, 1972) and Ts'ao Chan, *Dream of the Red Chamber* (New York, 1958).

For the study of Japan's recent history see: George B. Sansom, *The Western World and Japan* (New York, 1950); Donald Keene, *The Japanese Discovery of Europe* (New York, 1954); Charles R. Boxer, *The Christian Century in Japan, 1549–1650* (Berkeley, 1951); Conrad D. Totman, *Politics in the Tokugawa Bakufu, 1600–1843* (Cambridge, Mass., 1967); Robert N. Bellah, *Tokugawa Religion* (Glencoe, Ill., 1957); Maruyama Masao, *Studies in the Intellectual History of Tokugawa Japan* (Princeton, 1974); William R. Braisted, tr., *Meiroku Zasshi: Journal of the Japanese Enlightenment* (Cambridge, Mass., 1976); Hugh Borton, *Japan's Modern Century* (New York, 1955); and Tetsuo Najita, *Japan* (Englewood Cliffs, N.J., 1974). Thomas C. Smith, *The Agrarian Origins of Modern Japan* (Stanford, 1959), is a distinguished work which illuminates much of early modern Japanese society.

Peter C. Swann, *An Introduction to the Arts of Japan* (Oxford, 1958) is a helpful treatment. Ichitaro Kondo, ed., *Hiroshige, The Fifty-three Stages of the Tokaido* (Honolulu, 1965) provides images of late Tokugawa society as interpreted by one of Japan's greatest artists. Howard Hibbet, *The Floating World in Japanese Fiction* (New York, 1959) is a good introduction to the earthy fiction of Tokugawa Japan.

PART IV

The Onset of Global Cosmopolitanism

*B*EGINNING *in the late eighteenth century, European society entered upon twin transformations.*

*Political revolution, centered in France, broke through the
complex corporate privilege of the Old Regime, and thereby unleashed
the energies of innumerable individual citizens. Government and people entered into a closer partnership than before. By guiding and at the
same time following the will of the people—expressed through elections
and in riots, demonstrations, journalism, and, not least, by acquiescence
in existing leadership—government became vastly more powerful. Millions were mobilized for war—more or less willingly. Scope for innovation in economics and politics was enlarged; legal obstacles to individual
initiative withered.*

*This "democratic revolution" spread haltingly but inexorably from
France to other countries of Europe. In time, new forms of corporate
privilege arose in France itself; and various half-way houses between
liberal, democratic theory and actual practice arose in other European
lands. The New, or as we may better call it, the Bourgeois Regime, inaugurated so hopefully in 1789, thus grew old; and new socialist challenges to prevailing institutions gathered force as the nineteenth century
drew toward its close.*

*At the time when France entered upon profound political revolu-
tion, the economy of Great Britain had begun to alter through the
application of mechanical power to manufactures. Steam-driven machines
for spinning and weaving cotton were the most spectacular early instances of the new technological resources that ingenious mechanics and
eager entrepreneurs began to exploit. This "industrial revolution" also
spread, haltingly but ineluctably, to other countries of Europe, and in
time to lands beyond Europe as well. Fresh invention, systematically
harnessed to scientific theory from about 1870, added ever new dimensions to the industrial revolution. Under these circumstances, the wealth
and power—military as well as economic—at the disposal of Western
industrialized nations increased by leaps and bounds.*

*During World War I and World War II these two fundamental
changes flowed together. That is to say, the enhanced power of govern-*

*ments, sustained by democratic forms, reorganized the technical pro-
cesses of industrial production to serve political ends. Winning the war
was the initial goal; since 1945 more complex purposes have competed
for priority. Higher standards of consumption rivaled armament, price
stability, capital investment, and, most recently, preservation of the
natural environment as goals of economic-social-political management.*

*The vastly enhanced power that thus came to Western nations
made it easy for Europeans and Americans to beat down traditional obstacles to their activity that other peoples offered. Distance shrank as
transport and communication improved. During the second half of the
nineteenth century all important parts of the habitable earth entered into
a single globe-girdling commercial net. Political and military as well as
intellectual and cultural interrelationships became as inescapable as the
ties of economic interchange. For a few decades, European empires extended over nearly all of Africa and much of Asia; after World War II
these empires shrank back more rapidly than they had grown. But this
did not mean withdrawal or exclusion of the "new nations" from cosmopolitan modernity as it had been defined in the Western world since
1789. Political independence, on the contrary, planted the traits of
modernity deeper in all parts of the non-western world.*

*Such rapid and far-reaching changes in human society involved
much violence and sharp political as well as ideological changes. The
old and famous states of Europe dominated the scene throughout the
nineteenth century: Great Britain, France, Prussia (Germany from 1871),
Austria, and Russia. In 1917 the Communist revolution in Russia
and the proclamation of a rival American remedy—"national self-determination"—for the world's ills, brought powerful new political ideologies to the fore. But both the United States and Russia deliberately withdrew from world affairs in the 1920's, until new upheavals, centering in
Germany and Japan, provoked World War II and a massive reassertion
of Russian and American power. Since 1945 these two super-powers
have continued to dominate the world's political and military scene.
Yet the stubborn efforts to achieve fuller political and cultural autonomy
by other nations, particularly by the Chinese and other anciently civilized peoples of Asia, kept world politics from any simple polarity between Communist and non-Communist regimes.*

*Science, technology, and the natural desire of weaker states and
peoples to borrow from richer and stronger nations the secrets of their*

power tended to unite the world. Geographical differences, linguistic barriers, and the wish to preserve local cultural traditions acted in the opposite sense. How varied and how uniform subsequent generations may become remains, therefore, an open question. In all parts of the world, local cultural continuity with past generations has been profoundly challenged. Changes in everyday life with urbanization, industrialization, bureaucratization, and automation are so far-reaching and still so new that no one can yet expect stable human adjustments to the new conditions of life to emerge.

Such an age of swift and fundamental change may be uncomfortable to live through; but in time to come men will probably look back upon these centuries as a period of extraordinary achievement, when global cosmopolitanism first became a reality.

CHAPTER 26

The Transformation of Western Civilization by the Industrial and Democratic Revolutions 1789-1914

 Until about 1870, the industrial revolution had its primary seat in Great Britain. Then Germany to the east and the United States to the west began to catch up with British industrial technology. After 1789, the primary seat of the democratic revolution was in France, where the defects of royal bureaucratic government and the critical temper of the public combined to provoke a long-drawn-out, impassioned, and deliberate effort to remake traditional political institutions in accordance with reason and the (presumed) will of the people. Each of these great movements tended to spread from its primary center throughout the Western world, and, ere long, beyond the borders of Western civilization also.

As this occurred, older patterns of society, culture, and government altered drastically—so much so that some observers are inclined to treat modern industrial civilization as different in kind from anything that went before, whether in Europe or anywhere else. On the other hand, one may regard this vast alteration in the way men live as the most recent in a long series of self-transformations of European

(Western) civilization. Both views are plausible, and we of the twentieth century simply lack sufficient depth of time perspective to be able to choose firmly between them, if a choice must be made.

We begin, however, to be far enough removed from the interval between the outbreak of the French Revolution in 1789 and the beginning of World War I in 1914 to see some of the main lines of Western man's development during this period. Throughout the 125 years involved, the Western nations of Europe and overseas were able to expand their power and wealth enormously. This was partly due to continuation of older processes of colonization and trade expansion that had started as long ago as the year 1000. Thus, for example, millions of pioneer farmers pressed westward through the North American continent—some coming from Europe, some from the eastern parts of the United States and Canada. In this fashion, the entire breadth of the North American continent was brought firmly within the body social of Western civilization by the close of the nineteenth century.

Similar colonization took place in parts of South America (Argentina, Chile, Uruguay), in South Africa, Australia and New Zealand. But these movements overseas were considerably less massive in scale than the eastward and southward movement of Russian peasants and pioneers that populated vast regions in the lower Volga basin, the lands between the Black sea and the Caspian, as well as parts of Siberia all the way from the Ural mountains to the Pacific. By the end of the nineteenth century most good agricultural land in Central Asia as well as in European Russia had been broken to the plow, just as was happening at the same time in North America. As they pushed southward from northern forests, Russian settlers met expanding Chinese-, Korean-, Turkish-, Persian-, or Rumanian-speaking agriculturalists, and sometimes intermingled with these populations. Similarly in New Mexico, American settlements lapped up against Spanish and Indian farming communities and intermingled with them without driving them from the land. More primitive hunting and gathering folk, in Siberia no less than in the Americas, melted away before the advance line of settlers without offering any effective resistance.

The upshot of this vast movement of colonization, therefore, was that the geographical base of Western civilization expanded from the core region in western Europe literally round the earth, for the American westward movement met the Russian eastward movement in Alaska, which was transferred from the Tsar's sovereignty to that of the United States by purchase in 1867.

To be sure, both Russia and the United States retained important marks of their frontier position. In particular, oppressive systems of compulsory labor continued to exist in both countries until the Russians abolished serfdom in 1861 and the United States abolished slavery in 1863. The struggle over slavery was acute in the United States. President Lincoln, in fact, issued the Emancipation Proclamation in the midst of a bitter civil war (1861–65) that pitted the slave-holding Southern states against the rest of the country.

The elimination of slavery from the United States that resulted from the victory of the Northern forces in the Civil War was part of an anti-slavery movement that affected the entire Western world. The first great victory for this movement came in 1833, when Great Britain abolished slavery in all territory under British rule; the last Western country to follow suit was Brazil, where slavery became illegal in 1888. In the more conservative Moslem countries—Yemen for example—slavery lasted until very recently, but in most parts of the world rapid population growth in recent times means that there are plenty of willing hands available to do even the nastiest work. Unskilled individuals scraping a living in a crowded labor market may not be much better off than slaves were in former times. Nevertheless, the legal prohibition of slavery quite properly counts as one of the positive achievements of the past two centuries.

The continuing territorial expansion of Western types of society was sustained and hastened by truly revolutionary changes taking place in the heartlands of Western civilization. A surge of technological improvements, that became particularly dramatic in the second half of the eighteenth century, has come to be generally known as the "industrial revolution," ever since an English historian coined the term in the 1880's. In addition, Western governments and nations underwent far reaching internal reorganizations. These changes can be summed up as a "democratic revolution," although this phrase is newer (invented in the 1950's) and less well established than the older term. But the industrial and the democratic revolutions deserve to be paired with one another all the same, because both of them allowed Westerners to mobilize men and materials on an ever-increasing scale and across longer periods of time and greater distances than had ever been possible before.

No other peoples underwent any remotely comparable kind of transformation. Hence the preponderance of the West as against other civilizations of the world, which had existed already under the Old Regime, became so great in the course of the nineteenth century that after about 1850 all traditional barriers against Western penetration collapsed. Westerners took advantage of their new-found power to surge into every part of the habitable globe. The world thus for the first time in human history entered upon an adventure in global cosmopolitanism. We in the twentieth century still flounder amidst its early phases.

*　　*　　*

It is convenient to analyze the transformation of Western civilization from the Old to the Bourgeois Regime under three heads: (1) economic, (2) political, and (3) intellectual. But any such scheme is artificial and imperfect, tending to obscure relationships that run across these classifications. There is, for example, a sense in which both the industrial and democratic revolutions were simply applications of human reasoning power to economics and politics respectively. But, conversely, the industrial revolution provided a greatly increased margin of wealth which allowed more men to spend more time in intellectual and artistic pursuits than had been possible previously; and the democratic revolution, by breaking through status barriers, opened careers in business, politics, and the arts to anyone with requisite talent. Thus economic, political, and intellectual changes interpenetrated each other in a very complex and intimate fashion, so that all three aspects of the Western experience in fact constituted a single whole.

The Industrial Revolution

‡‡‡ In the eighteenth century, spectacular technological improvements in Great Britain centered especially in the textile trades and, after 1769, when Watt's first patent was granted, in the development of steam engines powerful enough to drive the new machinery of textile mills. During the nineteenth century, radical technological changes not only

spread to almost every established branch of manufacture, but also created vast new industries and products which had no traditional existence whatever.

There were two phases. Until about 1870, practical invention was mainly the work of ingenious mechanics and hard-driving entrepreneurs who relied more on common sense and traditional skills than on systematic research or theoretical science. This was the age of coal and steam, when the railroad conferred a new speed and efficiency upon overland transport, and when improvements in ocean shipping led to the substitution of steel hulls and steam-driven water screws for wood and sail. This was also the age when British leadership in every phase of technology and industry remained unquestioned. Textile machinery and steam engines, railroads and steamships, together with the coal and steel industries that provided the necessary basis for the new technology, all were first introduced or attained their earliest large-scale development in Great Britain.

The rise of the chemical industry, swiftly followed by the development of electrical technologies, marked a change in the character and direction of the industrial revolution. To be sure, the old sort of haphazard invention continued. In the United States, for example, Henry Ford introduced his automobile (1903) and the Wright brothers built an airplane (1903) after prolonged and ingenious tinkering. But this sort of isolated, individual invention more and more gave way to systematic research, conducted in well-appointed laboratories by staffs of engineers and scientists who kept in close touch with scientific theory on the one hand and with technological processes on the other.

Germany was the country where linkage between theory and practice first became habitual. Germany's flourishing school and university system assured a flow of well-trained theorists; an artisan tradition provided abundant practical skills. The rewards were sometimes very great. By the beginning of World War I, for example, Germany had become the sole supplier of many industrial chemicals, and the German electrical industry likewise led the world in technological ingenuity and efficiency. Elsewhere, and in older, better-established industries, it still seemed quixotic for a firm to pay out good money to maintain a body of men whose job was to make the machinery and techniques on which the profits of the company depended useless. As a result, systematic interplay between scientific theory and technological practice had barely begun to show its potentialities before 1914. Deliberate invention first came decisively into its own during the two great wars of the twentieth century, not before.

Nevertheless, the rush of technical discoveries and improvements in the nineteenth century was tremendous when compared to changes that had occurred at any earlier time. Such familiar aspects of our twentieth-century lives as photography, bicycles, typewriters, sewing machines, telephones, electric lights, automobiles, phonographs, and motion pictures were all invented in the nineteenth century, though later improvements and changes in design make the earliest models of these devices scarcely recognizable today. Radio and airplanes achieved the same pioneer status before 1914 too, but their major development took place only during World War I and after.

Each important new product characteristically required or allowed other new industries to get started. The automobile, for instance, revolutionized the rubber business by the demand for tires; and the electrical industry did the same for copper, which became the usual conductor for electrical current.

As industries multiplied in this fashion, older manufacturing processes also underwent fundamental changes. Generally speaking, what happened was that handicrafts gave way to machine production. This involved standardization in the machinery of production and in the end product; standardization, too, of the workers in the sense that everybody had to get to work at the same time and perform his assigned part in the production process at the proper speed to allow the whole factory to work smoothly. Any tie-up or breakdown, whether of machinery or of men, became far more costly than before. Relatively vast quantities of raw material, capital, and labor had to be assembled for the new mass production, and a stoppage immobilized everything.

But the increased vulnerability of complex machine manufacturing processes to interruptions was more than made up for by increased productivity when everything went right. The flow of goods became a torrent, sweeping away old handicrafts, not only in the Western world but in other societies and civilizations too. All over the globe, weavers, metalworkers, and innumerable other artisans quickly found that they could not compete with cheap mass-produced machine-made goods.

Thus the first and most obvious characteristic of the industrial revolution was a vast expansion of scale. More power, more raw material, more end product, more waste, more transport, more clerks to keep track of the industrial and commercial processes, more consumers to buy and more salesmen to sell, and bigger firms with larger capital and larger work forces, all came rapidly into action. Older, simpler forms of manufacture were superseded by the cheapness and, sometimes, also by the improved quality of factory production.

Escalation of the scale of industry required enormous intensification of transport and communication. Distant supplies of raw materials and distant markets for the end products were vital to the success of machine mass-production. Improvements in roads and canals were important in many parts of Europe and the United States of America. But the construction of a railroad net, which got under way in the 1840's, reached boom proportions in the 1850's and 1860's, and continued to absorb large sums of capital until the eve of World War I (trans-Siberian railroad completed 1903; Berlin-to-Baghdad railroad under construction in 1914 and never since completed), far eclipsed all other forms of land transportation. The railroads opened up inland regions, and allowed transport of bulk materials like iron ore and coal across comparatively long distances. The coal fields of Silesia and of Pennsylvania were among the first to expand production because of the new possibilities opened by overland railroad transport. Other coal fields located deeper in the American and Russian interiors came into large-scale operation at somewhat later periods—a process continuing in western Canada and in central Asia as recently as the 1950's.

Revolution in oceanic transport came rather more slowly. Robert Fulton built the first successful steam boat as early as 1807, but for a long time their wasteful use of coal meant that steam vessels could not compete with sailing vessels on the long ocean runs. Not until after about 1870 did better boilers and larger steel hulls allow steamships to come into regular use for transoceanic cargo carrying. One result was the flooding of Europe with grain raised (with the powerful help of new machines) on the broad and fertile plains of North America, Argentina, and Australia.

The shape of the habitable world was altered, quite literally, by the opening of the Suez Canal in 1869, and of the Panama Canal in 1914. Air transport, on the other hand, was no more than an exercise of the imagination before World War I.

Communication was almost as important as transport in linking together the participants in the newly intensified industrial process. The establishment of the public penny post in Great Britain (1840) pioneered the development of modern mail systems. National mail delivery systems achieved trans-national integration as a result of the International Postal Agreement of 1875. The electric telegraph was invented in 1837. Since stringing wires from place to place required relatively modest expenditure, telegraph systems spread very rapidly throughout the Western world (first trans-Atlantic cable, 1866). Wireless telegraphy by radio also very rapidly achieved practical importance for long-distance communication after its first practical demonstration by Guglielmo Marconi in 1895. Improved communication provided a flow of news that sustained mass circulation newspapers, which came into being during the 1850's. This in turn affected politics and diplomacy, making it necessary or advantageous for statesmen to play upon and respond to public opinion as generated and expressed in the pages of newspapers.

Consequences of the Industrial Revolution

‡‡‡ In general, the industrial revolution greatly increased the wealth of the Western world, and allowed fundamental improvement in standards of cleanliness, health, and comfort. In its initial stages, to be sure, the crowding of factory hands into new industrial towns and the rapid growth of older cities created social problems with which traditional institutions could not cope. This provided the basis for Karl Marx's (d. 1883) vision of a proletarian mass growing ever poorer in the midst of plenty until a socialist revolution solved the problem. In 1848, when Marx first clearly formulated his main idea, such a view was indeed plausible. Revolutionary violence, drawing its strength from the urban poor, had in fact been an effective force in Europe's political experience since 1789, when a mob assault on the Bastille in Paris had ignited the torch of the great French Revolution itself.

In 1848–49, however, a series of similar crowd risings ended in failure. Soon thereafter, a variety of social inventions began to control and ameliorate the hardships and ugliness of early industrial society. Such an elemental instrument of modern public order as the urban police force came into existence only during and after the 1840's. No less important were sewer systems, garbage collection services, parks, hospitals, health and accident insurance schemes, public schools, labor unions, orphanages, asylums, prisons, and a great variety of humanitarian and charitable enterprises aimed at relieving the sufferings of the poor, sick, and unfortunate. Throughout the second half of the nineteenth century these and other inventions came into operation almost as fast as the swelling towns created the need for them. As a result, revolutionary feeling tended to recede in the most highly industrialized countries, and remained vivid only along the expanding edge of industrialism— most spectacularly in Russia, where tsarist bureaucracy reacted slowly and unsympathetically to the needs of an industrializing society.

A second basic feature of the industrial revolution was the accelerated growth of population. In Europe, for example, the population of the entire continent in 1800 was about 187 million. By 1900 it had increased to about 400 million, despite the fact that nearly 60 million had emigrated overseas during the nineteenth century and an unnumbered host had also crossed the Urals from European Russia into Siberia and central Asia. A drastically reduced death rate was the main factor promoting such rapid multiplication of population; and this in turn depended partly on improvements in medical science and public sanitation, partly on the enlargement of the food supply, and partly on a general improvement in the material conditions of life.

Before World War I only Great Britain saw a majority of its population leave the land and enter urban occupations. In every other important state the age-old tie to the soil and the rhythms of planting and reaping continued to govern the lives of the majority until after 1914. Nevertheless, the shift from field to factory and from village to city had made itself manifest everywhere in the Western world. This implied a shift away from a mode of life whose basic rhythms had been established in neolithic times, and toward a new pattern of life whose potentialities and limits we are still trying to discover.

It seems likely that the change in ordinary everyday human experience and habit implied by wholesale flight from the fields will alter society as fundamentally as it was altered when men ceased to be simple predators and began to produce their food. If so, it is difficult to overemphasize the historical importance of the industrial revolution and impossible to believe that the social organization and styles of life that will eventually prove to be best attuned to industrialized economies have yet clearly emerged.

The Democratic Revolution in France

‡‡‡ The principle that governments derive their just powers from the consent of the governed and from that alone had been trumpeted to the world in 1776 by American rebels against King George III. This democratic notion continued to guide American constitutional experimentation during and after the war of independence. Such an idea had strong appeal in many countries of Europe—not least in Great Britain itself, where ever since 1688 parliamentary supremacy had meant the supremacy of a limited body of property holders who had the right to vote for members of Parliament. But it was in France that the new political doctrines stimulated dramatic revolution against royal absolutism.

During the eighteenth century, French government became hidebound. The king remained absolute in theory; but in fact almost all efforts at administrative reform were stopped in their tracks by the opposition of one or another special interest, operating usually from within the bureaucratic machine itself. Failures in war matched this dismal record at home; and when in 1778–83 the French did succeed in humbling British pride and helping the Americans toward independence, the result was to thrust the government into hopeless insolvency. This was not surprising, for in the absence of administrative changes, tax income remained inelastic whereas the expenses of warfare kept on multiplying with the elaboration of armaments.

Louis XVI (reigned 1774–92) sympathized in a small way with the idea of governmental reform, and agreed that a closer link between his government and the people at large would be desirable. When his efforts to increase tax receipts met with the usual crippling resistance, he therefore decided to revive the ancient representative assembly of France, the Estates-General, in hope of persuading that body to authorize new taxes and thus relieve the government's financial embarrassment. But when the Estates-General met on May 1, 1789, many of its members felt that before any new taxes were authorized far-reaching reform in government should be carried through. Their general aim was to make the French government responsible to the people, meaning, in practice, to property holders.

Reform sentiment was strongest among the representatives of the third estate, i.e. commoners. But a few clergymen and nobles favored the reform program also, and, in the absence of firm and consistent royal policy, this tipped the balance. Accordingly, during the month of June the Estates-General transformed itself into the National Assembly and undertook the task of preparing a constitution for the kingdom of France.

Advocates of reform soon generated widespread popular excitement. Rumors that the king was preparing to suppress the National Assembly precipitated a mob attack on the Bastille (July 14). This event was later celebrated as the birthday of the Revolution. Thereafter, Paris organized a revolutionary government—the Commune. Its leaders rested their power directly on the people of Paris, whom they summoned to mass demonstrations in times of crisis. The Paris crowd was frequently able to over-awe anyone who opposed or seemed to oppose the majesty of the people, with whose voice they claimed to speak.

From Paris, excitement spread to the countryside. During the months of July and August peasants began to burn noble châteaux and refused to pay traditional dues and rents. The National Assembly reacted by annulling feudal rights and obligations in a burst of emotion on the night of August 4, 1789. This had the effect of winning a majority of the peasants for the cause of revolution—a fact of fundamental importance in the following years.

The task of making a new constitution for France proved difficult, and the Assembly frequently interrupted its work to deal with pressing immediate problems. In particular, the financial bankruptcy of the government called for remedy. The assembly decided to issue a paper currency—*assignats*—against lands confiscated from the church, with the idea that as these lands were sold the *assignats* would be retired from circulation. In fact, however, more and more paper currency was printed, and prices spiraled upward. Wages, as always, lagged behind. Real economic suffering thus gave a cutting edge to the crowd demonstrations in Paris, since it was easy to persuade poor wage-earners that higher prices were the work of "enemies of the people."

By 1791 the new constitution was ready. It established a limited monarchy, resting supreme authority in a Legislative Assembly, to be elected by all active citizens, i.e. those paying more than a certain amount of money annually in taxes.

The most enduring aspect of the constitution of 1791 was the abolition of innumerable local administrative peculiarities which had long hampered the French government. Instead, France was divided into new geographical units of roughly equal size, called *départements*. Administrative, judicial, and ecclesiastical jurisdictions were made everywhere to coincide with the new and quite artificial *département* boundaries.

The most controversial aspect of the constitutional settlement of 1791 was the arrangement prescribed for the church. Bishops and priests were to receive salaries from the state, and were to be elected by the citizens of each diocese and parish, quite like any civil magistrate. The pope and most bishops and priests denounced this departure from canon law and demanded the return of confiscated church property. Thereafter the "Civil Constitution of the Clergy," as the laws affecting the church were called, divided Frenchman sharply between those who supported the new ideas and those who adhered to the ancient traditions of the Roman Catholic Church.

The constitution's greatest weakness, however, lay in the fact that it entrusted extensive powers (suspensive veto, appointment of army officers, etc.) to King Louis XVI, who had long since lost all sympathy with the revolutionary cause. He had, in fact, begun to conspire actively with foreign courts (Austria, Prussia) and with émigré nobles who had fled from France. War against Austria and Prussia broke out in April 1792 and the French armies suffered initial defeats. This aroused suspicion against the king, until in August 1792 the Paris crowd intervened decisively again, and induced the Legislative Assembly to suspend Louis XVI from the exercise of his constitutional powers. A new assembly, the Convention, was elected, and charged with the task of making another constitution.

This inaugurated a second and much more radical phase of the Revolution. The Convention declared France a republic, executed King Louis, and instituted a reign of terror against "enemies of the people," in the course of which several thousand persons were summarily judged guilty and beheaded with scientific efficiency, thanks to Dr. Guillotin's machine for cutting off human heads. Executive authority was concentrated in committees of the Convention, the most important of which became the Committee of Public Safety. Energetic efforts to enlist all able-bodied citizens for the defense of their country soon began to produce results, and French armies presently reached the Rhine, spreading revolutionary principles into Belgium and western Germany as they advanced.

Simultaneously, an impassioned and effective propaganda was organized within France as rival political cliques sought to justify and consolidate power. In 1793 and the first half of 1794, the most successful of these groups was the Jacobin Club, where active and ambitious revolutionaries gathered to hear the impassioned oratory of Maximilien Robespierre (1758–94) and others who sought in the name of republican principles to inaugurate a reign of Virtue. Rival factions were not content to settle their differences by words and votes on the floor of the Convention. Mob demonstrations and the guillotine were called upon to assist Robespierre and his allies to defeat and destroy one group of "traitors" after another. But as the revolutionary armies rolled back the foreign invaders, justification for such high-handed violence faded. The members of the Convention reacted to the new tone of public affairs in July (Thermidor by the revolutionary calendar) 1794, when an unexpected vote in the Convention led to Robespierre's arrest and death. Though some at least of Robespierre's enemies had not intended it, the removal of the man who had become a symbol for revolutionary extremism triggered a widespread reaction, and the Committee of Public Safety was soon disbanded.

The Convention finally completed the task of drawing up a new constitution for France in 1795. The Directory, which thus came into existence, governed the country for the next four years. In 1799 a *coup d'état* brought a successful young general, Napoleon Bonaparte (1769–1821), to power. He engineered a series of constitutions, each of which gave him greater and more absolute authority than its predecessor. Even after he crowned himself Emperor of the French in 1804, Napoleon continued to claim that his power rested on the will of the people and he took considerable pains to prove his popularity by holding plebiscites to ratify each of his successive constitutions.

In fact, Napoleon was in many respects a true heir to the revolution. He completed the reorganization of the laws of France (*Code Napoléon*) which translated into everyday legal practice many of the principles enunciated in general terms by revolutionary orators, e.g.

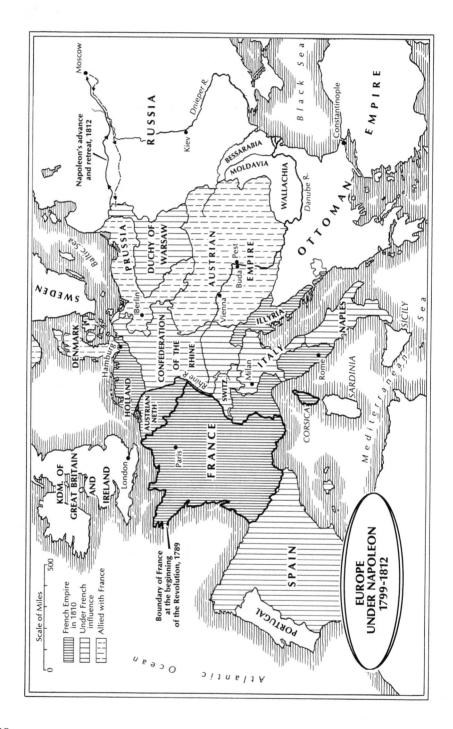

Scale of Miles

0   500

▦ French Empire
  in 1810
▨ Under French
  influence
▦ Allied with France

Boundary of France
at the beginning
of the Revolution, 1789

**EUROPE
UNDER NAPOLEON
1799-1812**

Napoleon's advance
and retreat, 1812

KDM. OF
GREAT BRITAIN
AND
IRELAND

London

PORTUGAL

SPAIN

FRANCE

Paris

HOLLAND

DENMARK

Hamburg

AUSTRIAN
NETH.

CONFEDERATION
OF THE
RHINE

Rhine R.

SWITZ.

ITALY

Milan

Rome

CORSICA

SARDINIA

NAPLES

SICILY

Mediterranean Sea

Atlantic Ocean

SWEDEN

Baltic Sea

Berlin

PRUSSIA

DUCHY OF
WARSAW

AUSTRIAN
EMPIRE

Vienna

Buda Pest

ILLYRIA

RUSSIA

Moscow

Kiev

Dnieper R.

Black Sea

Constantinople

OTTOMAN

EMPIRE

BESSARABIA

MOLDAVIA

WALLACHIA

Danube R.

freedom of contract, civil marriage and divorce, and abolition of class differences before the law. The *Code Napoléon* offered a convenient model for legal reform in other lands as they were brought under French influence by the victories of Napoleon's armies. Once such changes had simplified the daily routines and legal relationships of a region or country it proved practically impossible to restore the complications and special privileges of the Old Regime.

Democratic Revolution in the Rest of Europe

‡‡‡ Hence, even when Napoleon at length met with defeat at the hands of a coalition of almost all the powers of Europe (1812–15), traces of the revolutionary upheaval through which Europe had passed could not be removed. Indeed, by 1815 the revolutionary imprint had stamped itself upon Napoleon's most inveterate enemies. For it was only after the monarchs of Europe had learned how to stir patriotic enthusiasm by imitating the French and appealing to the sentiments and interests of their subjects that their armies and peoples became capable of meeting and overthrowing Napoleon's forces.

To be sure, the peace settlement that emerged from the Congress of Vienna (1815) failed to unite Germany into a single state, as many German patriots had hoped, and put a politically divided Italy under Austrian and papal influence once again. Prince Clemens von Metternich, chancellor of Austria and one of the principal architects of the Vienna settlement, tried to balance defeated France against insurgent Russia, whose tsar, Alexander I (ruled 1801–25), toyed with the thought of reorganizing Europe even more drastically than Napoleon had done. Metternich was successful in thwarting Tsar Alexander's radical aspirations, and within a few years convinced him that careful restraint was required to prevent popular revolution from once again disturbing the peace of Europe.

Yet liberal and revolutionary aspirations remained alive, particularly among educated men of the middle class. In 1830 and again in 1848–49, popular risings overthrew constituted authority in important parts of the continent. Yet the revolutionaries failed to create either a united Germany or a united Italy as they had hoped to do. France became a republic again (1848–52) until Napoleon III imitated his uncle the great Napoleon by converting his election as president into a personal empire, guaranteed by plebiscite. Great Britain escaped revolution, but launched upon a policy of piecemeal reform, expanding the franchise by degrees between 1832 (Reform Bill) and 1884, when almost complete manhood suffrage was introduced.

The failure of the revolutions of 1848 led many to despair of achieving really fundamental political change by reliance upon the will of the people. Yet Napoleon III in France (governed 1852–70) as well as a number of influential British statesmen felt that export of liberal and parliamentary government to other peoples of Europe was a good thing and ought to be encouraged. After 1848, Russia became the main prop of the political status quo in central Europe. When the Russians blundered into war with Turkey (1854), France and Great Britain came enthusiastically to the Turks' rescue, and defeated the Russians on their own ground in the Crimea.

This demonstration of an unexpected weakness in the tsarist autocracy allowed two daring political gamblers, Count Camillo Cavour (d. 1861) of Sardinia and Count Otto von Bismarck (d. 1898) of Prussia, to unite Italy and Germany around their respective monarchies between 1859 and 1871. Bismarck's success was achieved by means of three brisk, victorious wars against Denmark (1864), Austria (1866), and France (1870–71). The first two left no enduring scars; but the Franco-Prussian war of 1870–71 and the peace terms the victorious Germans dictated (transfer of Alsace and Lorraine from France to Germany) left all patriotic Frenchmen eager for revenge. As long as Bismarck remained in control of German policy, however, the French were unable to find allies on the continent of Europe; and party struggles weakened the Third French Republic which had arisen from the debris of Napoleon III's defeated empire.

In Italy a constitutional monarchy prevailed despite unrelenting opposition from the pope, who resented his loss of territorial sovereignty over central Italy. In Germany, however, Chancellor Bismarck established a constitution for the new imperial Germany (1871–1918) which combined incompatible political ideas in an ingenious but, as it turned out, unstable fashion. Democratic principles were accepted in the form of a Reichstag, elected by universal manhood suffrage, to which budgetary authority was granted. Yet the autocratic principle (rule by divine right) was not surrendered. The German King-Emperor retained full authority over the army and foreign affairs; and the chief minister, the Chancellor, was responsible not to the Reichstag but to the Emperor alone.

Unlike their Prussian rivals, the Hapsburg emperors of Austria found it impossible to come to terms with nationalism and the liberal demand for popular representative government. The numerous nationalities inhabiting their empire quarreled with one another so bitterly that no democratic consensus could emerge. Nevertheless, in 1914 some sort of parliamentary elective body existed in every important European country, even in Russia (from 1906); and every government tried to establish effective partnership between official policy and "public opinion" as expressed and generated through newspapers and political parties.

On the surface this constituted a tremendous victory for the ideals of popular government, ideals which in 1789 had seemed to most men of affairs to be no more than wild and impractical dreams. But in reality as they spread across Europe, liberal and democratic principles suffered drastic dilution by admixture with elements from the Old Regime. This was especially true in central and eastern Europe, where bureaucratic control from the top remained a far more vigorous reality than the parliamentary trappings of the Austrian, Russian, and German governments suggested. Major changes in east European society usually came as a by-product of official actions, e.g. the abolition of serfdom (Austria, 1848, Russia, 1861) and the establishment of wide political autonomy for Hungary (1867). Railroad building and major mining and industrial developments, which became important in Russia from the 1880's, also depended in very large measure on official initiatives and/or on special concessions arranged by the government.

In the more truly liberal countries of western Europe, a wide variety of special interests—corporations, cartels, labor unions, political parties, churches, special occupational groupings like army officers, bureaucrats, lawyers, and others—grew up in the course of the nineteenth century in such a way as to hedge round the theoretical sovereignty of the people as effectively as the theoretical sovereignty of the king of France had been hedged around on the eve of the Revolution itself by a similar tangle of vested interests. As this occurred, of course, the revolutionary drive for liberal, democratic government which had inspired so many bright hopes at the beginning of the nineteenth century wore itself out. The democratic ideal and the tarnishing realities of power had rubbed off on one another. Special privilege, far from fearing revolutionary unmasking by champions of the people, was more likely to have learned, like Bismarck, how to extend and entrench its power by manipulating the levers of democratic mass politics from behind the scenes.

Revolutionary ardor (or at least revolutionary rhetoric) passed therefore from liberal into socialist channels after the middle of the century. In 1848, Karl Marx (1818–83) and Friedrich Engels (1820–95) proclaimed in the *Communist Manifesto* their vision of how an international revolutionary proletariat was destined to seize power and thereby inaugurate true liberty and equality. However attractive in itself, Marx's vision proved difficult to realize. Tumultuous quarrels accompanied the early stages of the international socialist movement, and it was not until after Marx's death that a somewhat more stable organization, the Second International Workingmen's Association (established 1889), came into existence.

But the emergence of large and relatively well-disciplined socialist parties meant that these organizations, too, began to settle toward a *modus vivendi* with the parliamentary regime of the age. Hence in 1914 when war came to most of Europe, German and French socialists rallied to their respective national colors and fought against one another despite professed internationalism. Only a tiny fringe of extremists refused to violate the principles of international class solidarity to which the whole socialist movement was officially committed.

Deliberate Social Change and Popular Government

‡‡‡ Looking at this political evolution as a whole, it seems clear that the French revolutionaries and their liberal heirs accomplished two things.

First, the revolutionaries demonstrated beyond all reasonable doubt that governments were indeed man-made, and could be altered and manipulated more or less according to plan. The older idea that government was divinely instituted, and that some men were appointed by God to hold dominion over others, seemed less and less plausible in the face of the success that came to regimes professing to derive their powers from the will of the people. The idea that social reform was an ongoing process grew out of the liberal political outlook. More and more men began to feel that if hardship or injustice existed, steps could and should be taken by deliberate action to remedy the situation. Society thus came to be looked upon as indefinitely pliable, to be altered bit by bit as changing standards of propriety and need came to be recognized.

All this was very different from older notions. Before 1789, most people had taken it for granted that they lived within a stable social structure whose institutions had been established by God's will and which, therefore, neither could nor should be altered. Hence, as the new liberal frame of mind spread, effective response to the social needs created by rapidly industrializing societies tended to come faster, and aroused less strenuous resistance than before.

Second, the political experience of the French revolution itself and of all European governments in succeeding decades showed that if political leaders were skillful enough to win the support of the majority of the population under their control, then government could command far greater power than rulers of the Old Regime had been able to do. Universal military service was the most striking example of the way in which a government enjoying the sympathy of the population as a whole could conscript manpower on a scale no monarch of the Old Regime ever dreamed of doing. A steadily mounting scale of taxation was an almost equally striking demonstration of the enlarged scope available to popular governments as against those which failed —as happened, for instance, in Austria—to establish an effective rapport with their subjects.

Enhanced political flexibility and expanded power were thus the upshot of Western civilization's democratic revolution. It therefore constituted a true twin of the industrial revolution, which in its own sphere also enhanced flexibility and vastly enlarged the power available to Westerners. Taken together, the result was to raise the power and wealth of the Western style of life so far above those familiar to other civilizations as to make resistance to Western encroachment no longer possible.

Intellectual and Cultural Revolutions

‡‡‡ The secret of Western preponderance over the rest of the world was not solely a matter of material superiority and political organization—important though these were. In addition, during the nineteenth and early twentieth centuries the intellectual achievement of Western science together with the artistic expression of Westerners' aspiration after truth and beauty attained a depth, power, and sophistication unmatched elsewhere.

The scale and variety of cultural activity in the Western world between 1789 and 1914 make a brief summary unusually difficult. This is particularly true of art and literature, where among the romantics of the early part of the nineteenth century personal self-expression and originality came to be prized for its own sake. Interest in the unique historic past of each nation and region of Europe fed and was fed by the nationalistic movements of the age; and a rising valuation of national distinctiveness tended to divide literature into separate national schools.

Science, on the other hand, remained international and public, and perhaps for this reason it is easier to detect the main lines of its development. Two rival and basically incompatible outlooks upon the world underwent extraordinary elaboration during our period. Then shortly before the outbreak of World War I a series of conundrums and paradoxes began to make men aware of the defects and limitations of each of the two rival world views.

The first of these was basically Newtonian. Four fundamental terms—matter, energy, space, and time—seemed capable of explaining all the phenomena of physical nature. The effort met with startling success. Indestructible matter, composed of molecules, atoms, and (after 1897) sub-atomic particles, was paired with an equally indestructible energy and it seemed as though all chemical and physical changes could be explained as the result of combinations and recombinations of these two indestructibles within a uniform, infinite matrix of time and space.

Many phenomena that had previously seemed unrelated to one another fell into place as part of this grand scheme. In particular, the processes of chemical change came to be understood in terms of interactions among molecules, atoms, and electrons, absorbing or giving off energy with each change. As we have seen, this sort of understanding often allowed chemists to control and alter natural processes, thereby creating new industries and improving old products at an unprecedented rate. Similarly, such seemingly diverse phenomena as visible light, infrared, and ultraviolet rays, radio waves, X rays, and still higher energy radiation came to be viewed as parts of a continuous electromagnetic spectrum whose control and manipulation also began to extend human powers in dramatic ways just before the outbreak of World War I.

Yet toward the close of the nineteenth century, unsuspected weaknesses began to cloud the elegant clarity of this vision of the universe. Matter lost its solidity as first molecules and then atoms dissolved into tiny particles vibrating in comparatively vast emptinesses. Energy, too, sometimes seemed to come in particles, or quanta. But what was most surprising and distressing of all was the strange results of experiments intended to measure the speed of the earth through space. For Albert Michelson (d. 1931), using very sensitive instruments, discovered that light appeared to travel with uniform velocity in every direction, even when launched from the rapidly moving platform of the earth. This result, first attained in 1887, seemed entirely incompatible with Newtonian notions of absolute space and time, for light launched in the direction of the earth's motion ought, by all ordinary logic, to move faster than light sent in the opposite direction, since in one case the speed of the earth should be added and in the other it should be subtracted from the absolute speed of light.

In order to bring mathematical order to this surprising result, Albert Einstein (1879–1955) proposed in 1905 that space and time should be collapsed into a single space-time continuum whose nature was such that changes in the relative motion of any two bodies affected measurements of one taken from the other. Laymen and not a few scientists found this wrenching from familiar intuitive ideas of space and time hard to accept. Equally, the discovery of various subatomic particles and of energy quanta which began to occur very rapidly during the first decades of the twentieth century brought the elegant simplicity of earlier theory into disrepair. What had seemed about 1890 to be a well-understood, absolute system of scientific truth, tested by experiment, validated by innumerable practical applications, and lacking the elucidation of only a few small corners of reality to achieve complete adequacy, crumpled suddenly before a confusing welter of inconceivably tiny and unimaginably vast phenomena that failed to fit the familiar Newtonian scheme.

The second world view of nineteenth-century Europe emphasized the fundamental character of time and saw all reality—natural, biological, social—as part of an unending, developmental flux. Men who pursued this vision of reality did not look for absolute, universal laws such as those proposed by physicists and chemists, but sought to comprehend patterns of evolutionary innovation in particular circumstances and under given conditions. Such men believed that reality, in whichever of its manifestations especially interested them, was capable of seizing upon unique strategic moments when some new possibility opened to create what had never been created before—thereby, perchance, preempting the ground and inhibiting, or at least obstructing, any later efforts to do still better.

Georg Wilhelm Friedrich Hegel (d. 1831), the German philosopher, pioneered the effort to view all reality as a process of unending change. Subsequently, geologists, biologists, archaeologists, and historians combined to open before men's startled eyes a vista of terrestrial history unimaginably vast by comparison with anything previously dreamed of. Geologic eons, organic evolution (first clearly proposed by Charles Darwin in 1859), and human history all seemed to belong together. Even Christian doctrine and the unchanging stars were presently brought within the scope of this evolutionary view. Theologians examined the Bible with the tools of historical and philological criticism that had been sharpened by generations of work on classical and medieval texts. The result was to make the Scripture appear to be the work of many different minds, each reflecting distinct views about God and religion appropriate to different ages and circumstances. The certainties of traditional doctrine tended to dissolve under such scrutiny; and when astronomers began to speculate on the birth and death of stars and galaxies, the eternity of the heavens, too, began to dissolve before men's puzzled eyes.

Such an all-encompassing flux was just as difficult to reconcile with the ordinary human scale of experience as was the inconceivably tiny world of sub-atomic physics which simultaneously opened beneath men's feet. Human values tied to a particular place and time seemed dubious indeed in a world where everything changed, and where nothing—unless change itself—remained absolute and eternal.

Revolutions in the Arts

‡‡‡ Art did not fail to mirror the expanding range of uncertainty that characterized European thought on the eve of World War I. A handful of painters, living mainly in Paris, twisted and then entirely discarded the use of perspective as an organizing principle of their art. Instead, Pablo Picasso (1881–1973), Georges Braque (1881–1963), and others employed disjointed elements of optical experience, together with shapes only vaguely if at all reminiscent of observable reality, to create a pattern and suggest a mood. They repudiated, above all else, the idea of using painting as a vehicle to portray something outside or beyond the work of art itself.

Literature, being tied to language, was less international than painting and less radical in rejecting traditional forms. In Russia, however, the tension between the old Russian, Orthodox cultural traditions and new-fangled Western styles of thought and sensibility drove a handful of writers like Feodor Dostoyevsky (d. 1881), Leo Tolstoy (d. 1910), and Anton Chekov (d. 1904) to create a new moral universe, each for himself. This characteristic of nineteenth-century Russian literature lends its best productions a special relevance for many readers of the twentieth century who face a similar problem themselves. Outside of Russia, however, the literatures of Western nations continued to flourish within familiar and well-tried modes of thought and sensibility, along lines that had been fundamentally laid down in the age of the Renaissance.

Despite the comparatively conservative character of Western literatures, the changes that came to science, thought, and art, together with the drastic upheavals in routine resulting from the industrial revolution, and the changes in political and social structure ratified by the progress of the democratic revolution were so deep-going and massive that some men argue that Western civilization was in fact on the verge of breakdown in 1914—when Europeans proceeded, of course, to complete the job by plunging into an unprecedentedly strenuous war. Yet one may just as well take a more optimistic view and believe that such discrepancies are no more than the signs of growth toward some new and as yet unachieved resolution of the diverse tendencies of our time. Future events may perhaps decide between the two interpretations.

In the meantime it is already clear that the difficulties into which Western civilization plunged at the beginning of the twentieth century entirely failed to hamper the spread of Western influence to other parts of the world, at least in the short run. Instead, vast new springs of power made the West overwhelming to others everywhere. A survey of how the major stems of mankind reacted to such an unprecedented confrontation will therefore be the theme of the next chapters.

CHAPTER 27

Asian Reactions to Industrialism and Democracy 1850–1945

The military, economic, and intellectual power at the disposal of Western diplomats, soldiers, merchants, and missionaries increased enormously as the industrial and democratic revolutions took hold and began to transform the nations of Europe. A critical tip point came in the decade 1850–60, when each of the major civilizations of Asia proved unable to stave off Western intruders by traditional methods.

The public events that marked the collapse of Asian defenses against the West followed close upon each other. First came the outbreak of the Taiping rebellion in China in 1850. This was a vast peasant rising, led by men whose ideas had been shaped in part by contact with Christian missionaries. To be sure, the Christian element in the Taiping movement tended to fade with the passage of time, particularly when it became clear that the Western powers were not going to aid the rebels against the imperial Chinese government. But in their effort to put down the rebellion, which lasted fourteen years and affected more than half of China, the imperial authorities had to give greater scope than ever before to Western-type armaments, and to the diplomats, traders, and missionaries associated with these vital new military instruments.

Under the circumstances, China's traditional way of handling foreigners as tributary barbarians became a hollow farce. Western adventurers swarmed into the treaty ports opened to foreigners after the Opium War, 1839–41. They restlessly set out to make their fortunes by selling machine-made goods to the Chinese, and flatly refused to play the humble role assigned to foreign merchants by Confucian tradition. Worst of all, from a Chinese point of view, these upstart merchants could count on Western guns and diplomats to back them up in almost any quarrel with Chinese officials. This struck educated Chinese as profoundly immoral and unjust; but for a long time they could not persuade themselves to redress the balance by abandoning Confucian ways. China therefore remained weak and ineffectual in dealings with the West until the twentieth century, not so much because of inherent limits upon the nation's strength and power as because the leaders and rulers of Chinese society could not bring themselves to abandon the ways that had served their ancestors so well for so long.

China's inability to resist Western pressures served as an object lesson to the Japanese. The policy of rigorous seclusion, in effect in Japan since 1638, could no longer be enforced against the will of the Western naval powers, because Japanese shore defenses had become insufficient to stop well-armed warships. A few Japanese were tough-minded enough to recognize this fact from the time of China's humiliation in the Opium War. Most Japanese, however, simply reacted by intensifying their dislike of foreigners. The matter became critical in 1853 when the United States sent four warships to Japan under the command of Commodore Perry, and requested the right to use Japanese ports for trade and as coaling stations for ships traveling between San Francisco and Shanghai. The Tokugawa Shogun hesitated; then accepted (1854) the American terms. This stirred up a hornet's nest of opposition among patriotic, discontented clan leaders who felt that the Japanese government had been unforgivably weak in submitting to foreign demands. Many malcontents fastened their hopes upon the Emperor; and when additional failures against foreign navies discredited the Tokugawa government even further, the Emperor's power was in fact restored in a *coup d'état* (1868). But by a supreme irony, those who overthrew the Shogun's government in the name of the Emperor concluded, once they were in power, that the only way the West could be staved off was to learn the Westerners' technical and political secrets. A few Japanese had set themselves this task even before Commodore Perry "opened" Japan in 1854; after that date an ever increasing number of patriotic Japanese systematically set out to master the skills and knowledge that made the Western nations so powerful. To defend their land they thus deliberately revolutionized it.

No other people responded to Western predominance so vigorously or so successfully as the Japanese thus started to do. The three great Moslem empires, the Ottoman, the Persian, and the Mughal, were particularly ineffectual. The Crimean war (1854–56), in which the Ottoman Turks, fighting side by side with French and British forces, won a victory over the Russians, ironically cost the Turks more than earlier defeats at Russian hands had ever done. Previously, the Sultan had lost territory, but remained sovereign within his own land. But during and after the Crimean war, the Turkish government found it necessary to defer to advice given by Western diplomats for the "reform" of traditional Ottoman institutions along liberal, and of course, Western lines. The Sultan and his ministers, not to mention the ordinary Moslem subjects of the empire, could sometimes sabotage distasteful reforms; but for the most part they could only sulk and grumble at changes that seemed to benefit only the Christian subjects of the empire and always violated the principles of Islam. Yet the Sultan could not break away from the unwelcome Western tutelage, because the survival of the empire clearly depended on the support of one or another of the European Great Powers. Until the 1870's, Great Britain played the role of primary protector of the Turks; later (by the 1890's) the Germans became the principal patron to whom the Sultan looked for support.

The fate of the Mughal empire in India showed what could happen to a great Moslem state in the absence of outside assistance. In 1857 news of the Turkish victory over the Russians reached the ears of Indian soldiers serving the British in India. This helped to set off a widespread rising against their foreign masters among the "sepoys." These soldiers—some Moslem, some Hindu—briefly threatened to drive the British into the sea; but they lacked a clear political goal and never mobilized the general population of India behind them. The British government was thus able to send reinforcements from home and defeat the mutineers. Afterwards, Parliament decided to suppress the East India Company, which had been the legal instrument of the British power in India, and substituted direct rule through a Viceroy, appointed by the Cabinet in London. As for the Mughal empire, it too was formally declared at an end. With it, Moslem claims to rulership over India evaporated, and the Hindu majority confronted the British ruling clique directly.

The situation in Iran was no less disquieting for Moslems. British and Russian agents competed for influence at the Persian and Afghan courts, alternately supplying arms or sending expeditionary forces to invade the region. Nothing within the power of local rulers allowed them to escape from the role of helpless puppet of one or the other foreign patron.

To be sure, the weakening of all these Asian empires was not wholly a matter of superior Western force and economic pressure. The Ottoman, Mughal, and Manchu empires were all suffering from thoroughly traditional internal ills at the time when the Western presence became so critical for each of them; and the Shogunate in Japan, too, had lost the hard cutting edge characteristic of the first Tokugawa rulers. Westerners on the spot were always very few in number, even in India. The extraordinary ease with which a few gunboats or a column of Cossacks could enforce the will of a distant European government on the great empires of Asia in the decades after 1850 was due as much to Asian internal weakness as to inherent Western strength.

It is worth remembering that the Manchus, Mughals, and Ottoman Turks were foreigners in the eyes of the majority of their subjects. This made any appeal to national and cultural in-group feeling very dangerous to the constituted authorities. They would clearly endanger their own variety of foreign rule by making such an appeal. But only by such means could the population as a whole be mobilized to resist Western incursions. Hence the imperial regimes of China, India, and the Middle East were in no position to rouse effective mass resistance to Westerners. Where rulers and people were of the same nationality, as in Japan and Afghanistan, a far more effective opposition to Western pressure manifested itself, even when, as in Afghanistan, the material basis for the preservation of national independence was not particularly impressive.

A second problem that convulsed most of China, parts of India, and the Ottoman empire arose from overpopulation. Peasant numbers had started to increase in nearly all parts of the civilized world between 1650 and 1750, and the increase continued year by year. Farms that had to be divided and subdivided, generation after generation, sooner or later became too small to support a family. Chronic indebtedness and semi-starvation were the normal result. Such conditions could, and often did, provoke political violence that could cripple even a great empire. This is what happened to China with the outbreak of the Taiping rebellion. Only after that vast movement had run its disastrous course, involving millions upon millions of deaths, did the desperate circumstances that had provoked the rising begin to disappear. For when enough people had been killed or had died of disease and starvation, the survivors could expect to find sufficient land to allow them to earn a living. As this became obvious in one devastated region of China after another, much of the steam went out of the revolt, and the eventual victory (1864) of the imperial regime became far easier. A similar cruel rhythm can be detected in parts of European Turkey (Peloponnese especially) where population pressure fomented rebellions, and rebellions, ruthlessly put down, thinned the population for about a generation until the process repeated itself once more.

Western populations also grew rapidly, but in most Western lands new job opportunities created by the industrial revolution and/or migration to one of the expanding frontiers of settlement available to Western nations made the steady increase in population a source of strength rather than of weakness. Asian societies, with the exception of Japan, could not respond in this fashion. Asian cities were suffering an economic crisis of their own because traditional artisan trades, especially those connected with the manufacture of textiles, could not compete against Western machine-made products. Cities and towns, heavily burdened with dispossessed artisan groups, could not absorb large numbers of immigrants from overcrowded villages into economically productive activity. But Asian cities attracted migrants from the countryside all the same. Millions of poverty-stricken ex-peasants migrated to the towns and cities because they had no means of livelihood at home. They either died or eked out a miserable existence by performing part-time work, offering marginal services, begging, or stealing. Even those who found regular employment were badly paid. The entire, vast class of urban poor thus tended to become a discontented, disappointed, and politically inflammable mass.

Asian societies' political, social, and economic weaknesses were remotely related to the Western presence. Population growth, which did so much to upset traditional social relationships, was probably a response to the changed distribution and character of diseases resulting from intenser communication across long distances; and this, in turn, was a result of the opening of the oceans by European shipping in the sixteenth century. Moreover, the imperial political structures of China, India, and the Middle East had all come into existence with the help of heavy artillery when big guns for the first time gave the central power an easy superiority over local rivals, who could no longer withstand lengthy seige behind fortified walls. And the spread and early development of heavy artillery also owed a great deal to the sea communications opened by Western explorers and traders from 1500 onwards. It was Asia's bad luck, perhaps, that the two to three centuries that had elapsed since the Manchu, Mughal, and Ottoman empires attained their prime was long enough for the traditional ills of a bureaucratic imperial regime—corruption, inequitable taxation, hidebound routines, and an overdose of ordinary stupidity in high places—to manifest themselves acutely just at the time when Western pressure upon Asia attained a new intensity as a result of the industrial and democratic revolutions.

All the same, it is worth pointing out how very recent and comparatively superficial the Western impact really was. Four to five generations have passed since the mid nineteenth century, when each of the great Asian civilizations began to find that traditional political and military arrangements were not enough to meet the challenge of the West. At first only a small number of Asians were directly affected. The great peasant majority continued until quite recently—in India until the 1930's, in China until the 1950's—to live in ways that had altered very little. In Japan and among the Moslem states the traditional patterns of rural life began to break down earlier; but throughout Asia the majority of the population has felt the impact of Western ways only in the last two or three generations. Such a length of time is very brief in the history of societies numbering hundreds of millions. It would be foolish to suppose that stable relationships or patterns likely to endure for very long have yet emerged from the clash of cultures since 1850.

Islam's Reactions to Western Dominance

‡‡ The dilemma confronting the heirs of Islamic civilization from about the middle of the nineteenth century was starkly simple: how to be Moslem without being a Moslem. That is to say, Islamic political and intellectual leaders had somehow to maintain a Moslem cultural identity vis-à-vis the West while at the same time escaping the intolerable rigidities of the Islamic Sacred Law which, for so many centuries, had constituted the controlling uniformity of Moslem civilization.

The only response that has so far (1978) won much support was to borrow the Western notion of linguistic nationality as a basis for creating modern, secularized nation-states. But this has the unfortunate effect of splitting the Moslems into a number of comparatively small nations, no one of which is likely to be great enough to regain the proud position Islam so recently occupied in the world. Nationalism has the further disadvantage of being incompatible with Islam's universalism. Any modern, secular-minded government ruling over a Moslem community cannot, therefore, command the wholehearted support of its people, since the teachers and preachers of Islam must of necessity deplore a regime that no longer even tries to conform to God's will as revealed through Mohammed. Hence nationalism has remained an ill-fitting garment, almost as awkward to wear as the Sacred Law itself, whose incompatibility with modern government and habits of mind lies at the root of Islam's crippling difficulty in coping successfully with the Western disruption of its traditional world.

Even after the helplessness of the old-fashioned, imperial Moslem states had become crushingly apparent, their response to the Western challenge remained weak and lethargic. After all, Moslems firmly believed that Allah ruled the world, and if it pleased Allah to overthrow Moslem empires and to force the followers of Mohammed to submit to infidel rule, then there was nothing for a pious man to do but wait patiently for God's mysterious purpose to emerge. It was only logical to argue that any change, if change there had to be, ought to be a stricter observance of the precepts of the Koran, that is, a return to the puritanical rigor of early Islam. This was the argument put forward by

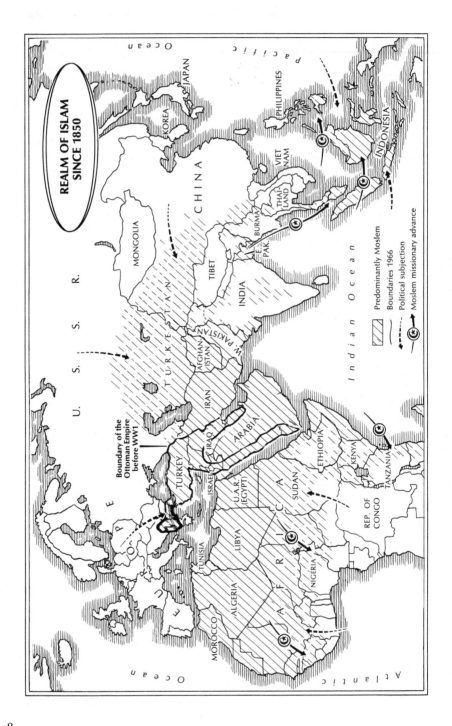

REALM OF ISLAM SINCE 1850

Predominantly Moslem

Boundaries 1966

Political subjection

Moslem missionary advance

Boundary of the Ottoman Empire before WW1

Wahhabi reformers, who had been based in Arabia ever since the eighteenth century. Given the basic commitments and assumptions of Islam, the argument was, in fact, irresistible. Many sensitive and serious Moslems in India and elsewhere were influenced by this line of thought, though practical implementation of Wahhabi reform on anything more than a private, personal level was politically out of the question everywhere except in desert Arabia.

The opposite point of view had some adherents, of course. Reform, which meant imitation of Western military, legal, and constitutional patterns, had become official policy in the Ottoman empire since 1839, and began to make some real difference in everyday affairs from the 1850's. A few Turks really believed in this way of responding to Western pressures; but they could never reconcile their chosen line of policy with the principles of Islam. Only a man who no longer really believed Mohammed's message could advocate deliberate imitation of foreign, non-Moslem ways. As a result, reformers lacked support in Ottoman society; they were always (or always seemed to be) the puppets and playthings of Western ambassadors.

Between 1878 and 1908 Sultan Abdul Hamid tried a different tack. He rejected reform and harked back instead to the autocratic power of the first Ottoman sultans. His efforts to mobilize Moslem sentiments behind the Ottoman state never became very effective however, because a pious Moslem could not take Abdul Hamid's claim to be caliph (that is, legitimate successor to Mohammed) seriously. Moreover, his efforts to modernize the army backfired. Young officers who had learned some Western skills (mathematics for artillerymen, medicine for army doctors, etc.) wanted to share power themselves. One such circle—the Young Turks—organized a *coup d'état* in 1908 that resulted in Abdul Hamid's overthrow. Soon thereafter the empire lost nearly all the remaining Ottoman territory in the Balkans as a result of the Balkan wars (1912–13) and World War I (1914–1918).

The political fortunes of Islam reached their low point at the close of World War I when the Ottoman empire was partitioned among the victors. Before this final catastrophe, the western provinces of the Islamic world in the Balkans and in Africa had all been sheared away, either by the rise of new independent Christian states in the Balkans or by the establishment of European colonial regimes in Africa. The same fate had also befallen Islam's eastern marches. Americans in the southern Philippines, the Dutch in Indonesia, the British along India's north-west frontier, and the Russians in central Asia had all closed in on Moslem states and peoples and forced them to accept a humiliating subjection. Hence, by 1914 only a slender band of states lying athwart the historical heartland of Islam retained even a tattered claim to independence: Afghanistan, Iran, and the Ottoman empire itself.

Yet the disaster of World War I presaged at least a partial political recovery. Outraged Turkish feeling stubbornly rejected the victors' peace terms. Under the leadership of Mustapha Kemal (1881–1938), a resolute general and charismatic political leader, the Turks succeeded in defending their Anatolian homeland, and by 1923 had won the assent of the European powers to the repossession of Constantinople itself. The new, revolutionary regime of the Turkish republic that Mustapha Kemal fashioned in the heat of battle was secularist, nationalist, and completely indifferent to liberal scruples against an indefinite expansion of governmental authority at the expense of private property and individual rights. Drastic internal reform, including the disestablishment of Islam, shift of the capital from the incurably cosmopolitan city of Constantinople to Ankara, and compulsory changes of manners—e.g. the unveiling of women—shook traditional life to the core. Such enactments were accompanied by strenuous and organized propaganda, which attempted to plant a fierce pride in Turkishness and a sympathy for the regime among all ranks of society.

Official effort did succeed in overcoming peasant indifference and cultivating a sense of nationalism among the Turks. On the other hand, a lingering attachment to Islam remained beneath the surface; and the government's efforts to develop modern industry met with only slight success prior to 1945. The trouble was this: insofar as the Turkish republic succeeded in really stirring up popular support and participation in public life, attitudes and values based partly on Islam, partly on the Turkish warrior tradition, came to the fore. But these attitudes and values were generally out of tune with industrialism, and tended therefore to hamper further efforts at modernization and economic development.

This dilemma was even more acute in Iran and the Arab lands. A usurper, Reza Pahlevi, seized power in Persia in 1925 and started secularist reform from the top along lines like those Mustapha Kemal was pursuing in Turkey at the same time. But the new shah's power remained brittle and the Islamic faith remained far stronger in Persia, with the result that modernization advanced more slowly than in Turkey. The same was true of Afghanistan, which nevertheless regained a more effective independence after World War I than it had enjoyed for some decades previously.

Among the Arabs, however, there was a different reaction to the upheaval of World War I. The peace settlement of 1919 assigned the richer and more settled portions of the Arab world to French and British colonial administrations. The peoples of Iraq, Syria, and Palestine baulked a little, but soon submitted. In Arabia itself, however, the puritanical Wahhabi reform movement came to power through the victories of Abdul-Aziz ibn-Saud (1880–1953), whose family had been the principal political and military protector of the Wahhabi reformers from the time the movement began in the eighteenth century. By 1925 ibn-Saud had conquered most of the Arabian peninsula and in particular had gained control of the two holy cities of Mecca and Medina.

Yet by a supreme irony, ibn-Saud used his new-won power over the Holy Places of Islam not to realize the Wahhabi's ideal of creating a society and government truly pleasing to Allah, but to introduce such instruments of centralization as roads, airplanes, and telegraphic communication among the cities under his rule. Then, within less than a decade after the establishment of ibn-Saud's power, Western businessmen discovered enormous reserves of oil in Arabia, and by paying royalties on oil taken from the ground, began to shower the ruling dynasty with fantastic riches. Under these conditions the moral energy of the Wahhabi movement rapidly dissipated itself, betrayed by the new wealth that flowed from oil.

Secularism made rapid gains also in Egypt, Syria, and Iraq. Above all else, this spirit took the form of agitation for political independence from the French and British who had divided the Middle East between them after World War I. Iraq won independence—at least on paper—in 1932; but genuine independence did not come to the other Arab lands until after World War II. Arab nationalists dreamed of a return to the glories of early Islam when all Arabs had been firmly united under the banner of the true faith. But such a pan-Arab, Islamic ideal cut across efforts to work within existing political boundaries, which had been imposed by France and Britain after World War I. The pan-Arab ideal remained (and remains) impractical because of

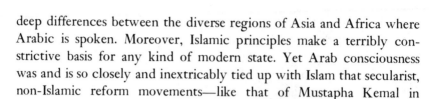

deep differences between the diverse regions of Asia and Africa where Arabic is spoken. Moreover, Islamic principles make a terribly constrictive basis for any kind of modern state. Yet Arab consciousness was and is so closely and inextricably tied up with Islam that secularist, non-Islamic reform movements—like that of Mustapha Kemal in Turkey or of Reza Shah in Iran—could not gain wide support.

Such a political record was dismal at best, and nothing in the intellectual or economic histories of the Moslem peoples between 1850 and 1945 did much to relieve the picture. Traditional Moslem educational systems continued to exist side by side with new-fangled school systems in which Western subjects were taught. This institutional compartmentation corresponded to a kind of mental compartmentation. Most of the Moslems who were exposed to Western ideas strictly segregated Moslem ideas and principles from those implicit in the skills and knowledge derived from the West. Real creativity or inward self-assurance are difficult to attain under such circumstances, and no Moslem figures of world renown did, in fact, emerge between 1850 and 1945.

In economics, likewise, modern industry failed to take vigorous root in Moslem lands. What new businesses and technical improvements there were—and by comparison with earlier times the pace of such innovation was high—tended to be introduced by foreigners. European administrators, for instance, reorganized the irrigation systems of both Egypt and Iraq, with the result that new land came under cultivation and the peasant populations of both these countries could, for a while, find new soil with which to support their increasing numbers. Similarly, the oil industry, which began to assume major proportions all round the Persian gulf in the 1930's, was directed and managed by foreigners. Independent Moslem initiative, whether governmental or private, was of minor importance.

Nevertheless, Islam did not decay. The faith of Mohammed remained a living faith for millions, and religious observances that marked Moslems off from unbelievers were generally maintained, even among the most westernized. The age-old rivalry between Islam and Christendom made it especially difficult for an heir of the Moslem civilization to abandon his religion, for such an act seemed not only religious but cultural apostasy.

Moreover, in some important parts of the world, long standing processes of conversion to Islam continued throughout the nineteenth and early twentieth centuries. This was true in parts of central and west Africa, for example, where teachers of Islam competed with very considerable success against Christian missionaries, who suffered from too close an association with European colonial rule. In India and parts of southeast Asia, too, Moslems attained a greater self-consciousness and internal discipline after they had ceased to be ruling cliques and had to submit, like their Hindu or Buddhist neighbors and ex-subjects, to European political control.

Among the one-seventh of mankind that recognizes Mohammed as Prophet of God, neither the industrial nor the democratic revolutions of modern times made much progress before 1945. In contrast, the two principal communities once subject to Moslem rule—the Christians of the Balkan peninsula and the Hindus of India—were each able to respond far more successfully to the challenges inherent in the West's Bourgeois Regime.

The Balkan Christians

‡‡‡ Balkan Christians won independence from Ottoman rule through a series of revolts and diplomatic crises, extending from 1803, when the Serbs rebelled against Turkish authority, until 1912–13, when the Turks were driven from all but a small bridgehead in Europe through the combined efforts of Bulgars, Serbs, and Greeks. Virulent and conflicting nationalisms, appealing to peasants as well as to townspeople, made the Balkans a political cockpit throughout the nineteenth century.

Unlike the Moslems, the Balkan Christians felt no serious incompatibility between their traditional Orthodox religion and the dictates of modernization along Western lines. Accordingly, economic and social development was fitfully but deliberately pursued by nationalistic governments in the nineteenth and early twentieth centuries, for it did not take much wisdom to realize that, as a minimum, national strength and security demanded local arms factories and a communications net that would allow rapid movement toward any threatened frontier. It was, however, only after World War II that efforts of this nature attained solid success. As this took place Balkan society welded itself to the West, perhaps more securely than ever before, since even in Roman times the cultural gap between the Greek- and Latin-speaking halves of the empire always remained enormous.

The Hindus

‡‡‡ The relation of the Hindu population of India to Western civilization was very different from the Balkan Christians'. After the shock of the Mutiny, which for a brief period in 1857 seemed to endanger British power in India, a benevolent but fundamentally autocratic civil service, whose members were recruited almost entirely from British universities, imposed a long series of reforms upon India. Their own liberal principles inhibited these civil servants from using governmental powers for any sort of forced-draft economic development; all forms of trade and manufacture, the British felt, were best left in private hands. Yet they did build a coherent railroad network that tied the entire sub-continent together as never before. In addition, British authorities organized an educational system which taught almost the same subjects as were taught in British schools and universities and used the English language for all higher instruction. The vast majority of Indians had no access to such schools. Even so, the schools and universities did create a numerically small but very influential group of Anglicized Indians, most of whom found positions in government offices where they first assisted and then gradually took over responsibility from British officials.

Within this framework, India's reaction to Western civilization proceeded peacefully and comparatively quickly. Economic innovation rested very largely with outsiders: Parsis, Greeks, Britishers and others. Few Hindus were ready to risk private capital in new industrial or commercial ventures, preferring to use any surplus funds they might accumulate for old-fashioned village usury or for the purchase of land. During World Wars I and II, however, partial disruption of supply lines from Great Britain presented the administrators of India with a sudden need to find alternative sources of supply for thousands of needed items. Efforts to start new industries or expand existing ones therefore became urgent. Lines between private and state enterprise blurred or even disappeared under these wartime conditions. As a result, when independence came to India in 1947, a semi-socialistic economic regime was easily developed by building upon wartime emergency measures.

In the sphere of politics, Indian response to the British presence was striking and unique. As we saw above, early in the nineteenth century, Ram Mohan Roy (d. 1833) used British ideas and rhetoric to agitate for a number of legal reforms in India. By 1885 enough Indians had been educated in British-style schools and universities to provide a sounding board and effective support for the Indian National Congress, which was organized in that year with the aim of pressing for eventual Indian self-government. After World War I, leadership of the Congress passed into the hands of Mohandas Karamchand Gandhi (d. 1948), nicknamed "Mahatma," i.e. "Great Soul," by his followers and admirers. Gandhi had been trained in the intricacies of English law, and as a political leader he combined the shrewdness of a lawyer with a direct appeal to India's religious traditions. In particular, he used the principle of nonviolence to organize massive civil disobedience campaigns (1919–23, 1930–34) in which India's urban millions and even some of the villagers took part. British authorities were unable to suppress Gandhi's movement without violating their own ideas of the proper restraints upon the arbitrary use of power.

Mahatma Gandhi, a Vaisya by birth and thus himself of an upper caste, also tried to overcome traditional Hindu discrimination against the so-called "Untouchables" and other low-caste groups. He was less successful in this than he was in mobilizing Hindu India against the British. He lived in a style modeled on that of Indian holy men, and more than once started to fast "unto death" to compel the British authorities to yield on some disputed point. He thus combined traditional and distinctive Indian patterns of leadership with a very shrewd mastery of the impact of modern mass communications upon the political and psychological attitudes of his British opponents. The combination of old and new, Indian and British methods proved extraordinarily effective, and led directly to Indian independence after World War II.

On the other hand, as Gandhi and his followers mobilized larger and larger numbers of Hindus around the Indian National Congress, the Moslems of India became uncomfortable. An independent India in which Gandhi's principles prevailed would make Indian Moslems into a relatively small religious minority. Few of them were willing to accept such a prospect. Hence, when the Moslem League (organized 1905) proclaimed its goal to be the establishment of a separate Moslem state of Pakistan (1940), nearly all Indian Moslems fell in line. The result was a direct and violent clash between Moslem and Hindu brands of Indian nationalism.

Thus Gandhi's appeal to ancient Hindu patterns of leadership had the effect of generating a rival Moslem movement within the Indian body social based directly and exclusively (as Gandhi's movement never was) upon religion. Independence, when it came in 1947, therefore involved the partition of India, despite the fact that neither Hindus nor Moslems had initially wished to divide the land of India between them.

China's Response to Western Dominance

‡‡‡ The massive continuity and prolonged success of their civilization across so many centuries made it peculiarly difficult for Chinese officials to believe that uncouth foreigners could have anything really important to teach them. Hence, even after the imperial government found it necessary to hire foreign military experts to help suppress the Taiping rebellion, only a few mandarins dared or cared to take the lesson of China's weakness to heart. Their efforts to create the basis for a more efficient army and navy soon petered out, partly because of conservative opposition but also because the reformers themselves were half-hearted, and recoiled from any action that really affected traditional Chinese social patterns. The creation of a technically up-to-date military force would have required massive technological, educational, and administrative changes. This the Chinese reformers of the nineteenth century were not prepared to undertake. The inevitable result was further military humiliation. In 1860 a French and British expeditionary force actually seized Peking and burnt the emperor's summer palace in retaliation for China's imprisonment of their diplomats. In the same year, the hard-pressed imperial government ceded the land beyond the Amur river to the Russians, who thus secured a new outlet on the Pacific at Vladivostok. French possession of Indo China (1885)—Viet Nam, Cambodia, Laos—and British control over Burma (1886) also sheared off regions which the Chinese imperial government had been accustomed to regard as tributary dependencies. Such defeats were bad

enough; in addition, foreign control over Chinese customs (1863), postal services (1896), and foreign concessions for the construction of railways (beginning 1888) seemed to point toward an eventual breakup of Chinese sovereignty. But what stung Chinese pride to the quick was not these humiliations at the hands of Europeans. Rather it was success that came to Japanese arms in Korea (1894–95). China looked upon Korea as another dependent kingdom, more important than others because it lay close to the imperial capital itself. The Japanese, however, became interested in Korea during the 1870's, and eventually reduced the Korean government to puppet status. When the Chinese tried to intervene, their forces were crushingly defeated by the Japanese, whose own army and navy had barely had time to adjust to the new-fangled Western weapons and pattern of organization. Peace terms compelled China to withdraw entirely from Korea, and to transfer Formosa (Taiwan) and some smaller islands off the Chinese coast to Japan. The Japanese also secured a base on the Chinese mainland proper (Liaotung peninsula) and collected an indemnity as well.

Japan thus joined the European imperial powers as one of China's tormenters, and simultaneously began her own imperial expansion in the Pacific area. Korea became a bone of contention between Russian and Japanese agents after 1896, and friction between the two rival imperial powers led to the outbreak of war in 1904. To almost everyone's surprise, the Japanese were again successful, defeating the Russians handily. The peace treaty ending the struggle assigned Korea exclusively to the Japanese sphere of influence. When Korean nationalist resistance developed the Japanese deposed the last Korean king and annexed the peninsula (1910).

Realization that Japan within a single generation had been able to equip its army and navy so as to outclass Chinese and Russian armed forces came as a severe shock even to the most conservative mandarins. Yet efforts to cope with the problem of China's weakness remained ineffective, partly because agents of the rival European powers and of Japan began to swarm in upon Chinese officials, seeking special concessions and other advantages. To many Chinese, the government's concessions to foreigners looked like a cynical betrayal of the national interest. Hence, secret societies aimed at the overthrow of the Manchu dynasty and the establishment of an authentically Chinese and presumably more patriotic government began to proliferate widely, especially among students and other youth groups. This revolutionary, nationalist point of view gained fresh impetus when the Emperor experimented briefly with radical reform (1898) only to be overthrown by a clique of Manchu courtiers who feared loss of their privileged positions. Another tumultuous response to China's helplessness took the form of a bitterly anti-foreign semi-secret society. Westerners nicknamed the members "Boxers" because they engaged in calisthenic exercises. When the Boxers attacked missionaries and other hated foreigners the Western powers sent an international expeditionary force that occupied Peking (1900) and dictated a settlement whereby China agreed to pay an indemnity for all the damages the Boxers had inflicted.

The multiple failures of the Imperial Chinese government discredited Manchu rule so much that in 1911, when revolutionary activity came out into the open, the dynasty found few supporters. A Chinese republic therefore came into existence without much bloodshed (1912); but no effective agreement could be achieved as to who should run the new government. Confusion was increased after the outbreak of World War I, when the Japanese tried to take advantage of the fighting in Europe to increase their own special privileges in China (Twenty-one Demands, 1915). The Chinese hemmed and hawed, and the United States set out to keep Japan's ambitions in check; but the diplomatic situation was not cleared up until 1922.

By then, Japan was ready to draw back, faced on the one hand by mounting American opposition and on the other by a restored Russian presence in the Far East. Russian administration of Siberia and the Maritime Provinces had been interrupted by the civil wars after the Bolshevik revolution; Moscow's control over Vladivostok was only restored in 1922. The new balance of forces was registered at the Washington Conference (1922) which arranged a general settlement in the Pacific area comparable to the settlement for Europe which had been worked out in Paris in 1918–19.

Even though foreign diplomatic intervention thus staved off Japan's effort to gain special privileges in China, internal upheavals continued to keep China in turmoil. Rival warlords built up private armies in several provinces and the central government could therefore only exercise nominal control over many parts of the country. Constitutional and other far-reaching reforms were put on the books, but both before and after the abdication of the last Manchu emperor in 1912, tinkering with forms of government did not at first effect basic changes. A rising level of violence and disorder in the provinces largely nullified official initiatives. Rising violence also had the effect of checking Western economic penetration. Railroads that did not run because of rebellion somewhere along the line, and modern mines that operated only sporadically for similar reasons, obviously were far less efficacious instruments of Westernization than the same physical plants might have been in time of internal peace. Moreover, by discouraging foreign investment outside the limits of the zones actually administered by foreigners in Shanghai and other port cities, civil violence tended to preserve a thoroughly traditional social and economic order through-out China's interior.

Peasant discontent, based on land shortages, debt and heavy rents and taxes, fed civil disorder. Earlier Chinese dynasties had repeatedly passed from the scene amid just such disasters. But in the twentieth century, these throughly traditional manifestations of dynastic decay were transformed. The thrust of revolution inside China changed in character because new kinds of ideas began to attract the loyalty of China's educated class. Since 1905, when the ancient imperial examina-tions were abolished as the avenue of recruitment into the imperial bu-reaucracy, China's intellectual and political leaders have almost unani-mously turned their backs upon Confucianism. Students, who in earlier times would have mastered the classics, swarmed instead into Western schools. Many enrolled in Japanese educational institutions and others traveled to the United States or Europe. Missionary schools in China itself expanded rapidly and new secular institutions were also set up. Hence a comparatively large number of young men and women en-countered and enthusiastically embraced Western learning without al-ways fully understanding it.

Sun Yat-sen's (d. 1925) naïve mixture of moral exhortation, social utopianism, and nationalism faithfully reflected the utter confusion prevalent among the first generation of Chinese students who sought to digest the intellectual culture of the West at a single gulp. Yet despite his intellectual confusions and extremism, Sun Yat-sen became the founder of the Kuomintang party. Between 1911 and 1949, this party struggled for the control of China against local war lords, Japanese puppets, and Communist rivals. Sun Yat-sen's revolutionary movement suffered at first from divided counsels and inexpert organization. It began to assume a different aspect after 1923 when Russian veterans of the Bolshevik movement arrived in Canton and began helping the Chinese to construct a well-disciplined, ideologically self-conscious, and militarily competent revolutionary party.

Soon after Sun Yat-sen's death in 1925 the Kuomintang party leadership set out to extend its power northwards. Chiang Kai-shek, the military commander, soon quarreled with his Russian advisers; and when he decided to attack the Chinese Communists, who had hitherto co-operated closely with the Kuomintang, the breach with the Russian instructors became final. The Chinese Communist party (organized 1921) survived by withdrawing to rural areas, where the Communists organized peasants against landlords and usurers. Even after Chiang Kai-shek and the Kuomintang succeeded in gaining control of most of China from local warlords (1928) they were unable to destroy their Communist rivals. Civil war, though conducted only sporadically, continued to afflict China throughout the period between World Wars I and II.

In the 1930's China's troubles were complicated by a revival of Japanese expansion. The Japanese first occupied Manchuria (1931); then invaded China itself (1937) and forced Chiang Kai-shek to retreat far up the Yangtse river to Chungking. He remained there throughout World War II while the Japanese controlled all the coastal regions of China. The Communists, under Mao Tse-tung, based themselves in the northwest, close to the Russian border. As a result, when the Japanese met defeat (1945) and began to withdraw their troops from the Chinese mainland, Chiang Kai-shek and the Kuomintang faced the formidable rivalry of Mao Tse-tung and the Chinese Communists. Open fighting between the rival Chinese regimes, which had been muted during the years of Japanese occupation, flared afresh after the end of World War II. Warfare ended on the Chinese mainland only with decisive Communist victory in 1949.

The breakdown and repudiation of Confucian orthodoxy opened a path for radical intellectual and literary change. A handful of Chinese eagerly mastered Western science and technology, but in general the political and military insecurity of the country made technical progress very difficult. Radical simplification of the literary language, bringing it closer to the speech of the common people, was pioneered by Hu Shih (d. 1962). The new literary medium won rapid acceptance from the time of its introduction (1917), and a vast outpouring of journalistic writing followed, designed to bring China into touch with all of the most up-to-date currents of thought to be found anywhere in the world. China's intellectual elite thus entered into easy contact with foreign ideas and ideals at a time when the main bulk of Chinese society remained overwhelmingly rural, bogged down in a vicious circle of political instability, overpopulation, and oppressive poverty. Insofar as the enormous peasant mass of China is concerned, real contact with new ideas and techniques came only after 1949 and therefore bore a Marxist rather than a Kuomintang stamp.

Japan's Self-transformation

‡‡‡ China had first to experience a far-reaching breakdown of social order and good government before the Chinese were ready to pay much attention to foreign ideas or techniques. Japan followed an opposite course.* The traditional social order survived in Japan in some important respects at least until World War I, while the leaders of the country used their power to revolutionize one aspect of Japanese life after another. Eventually they undermined their traditional basis for leadership—but not before new political symbols and values had arisen that were capable of sustaining effective internal cohesion among the Japanese.

Once the Shogun agreed to allow foreign ships to put into Japanese ports (1854) there was no turning back. The samurai clans that opposed the Shogun and eventually overthrew his power (1868) wanted to drive the foreigners out; but their leaders were able to see that this goal could only be attained if the Japanese had ships and guns capable of meeting and defeating the warships that the foreigners possessed. Building a modern navy and army thus became the first goal. The Japanese wasted no time getting started. They imported experts and sent missions to buy modern warships and coastal artillery. But the Japanese from the start aimed at being able to produce the sinews of

* So did Siam, where King Rama IV (1851–68) inaugurated a drastic and in the end fairly successful adaptation to the demands made by European merchants and soldiers. As a result, Siam (renamed Thailand in 1939) retained its independence uninterruptedly until the present.

modern war within their own islands. This obviously required all kinds of new factories, mills, and mines. In other words, the effort to become strong militarily very quickly impelled the rulers of Japan to launch their own industrial revolution.

They were strikingly successful. To be sure, there were many difficulties in training managers, engineers, and workmen. Some of the first factories did not work efficiently and some turned out shoddy goods. But the Japanese never stopped trying to improve their performance. Usually they began by copying as closely as possible some foreign product. Little by little they succeeded. World War I gave them a great opportunity. European-made goods almost disappeared from Asian markets when British and other Western nations turned to war production. The Japanese were thus able to capture Asian markets for textiles and other light consumer goods. After the war, when European goods became available once more, the Japanese products proved able to hold their own. Cheap labor and efficient new machinery turned out low-cost goods at a price that other nations could no longer match.

The government played a very active, central role in the industrial development of Japan. In the early stages, many new factories were built by government funds and turned over to private management only after the initial costs of construction and start-up had been met. Later on, when a substantial private industry had come into existence in Japan, the wishes and policies of the government still carried great weight. Making a profit never came to be an end in itself. Japanese firms always sought honor, prestige; factory managers felt it was their duty to serve the nation, to obey their superiors, and to discipline and protect their inferiors. Such attitudes derived directly from the spirit of the samurai clans that had dominated Japan for centuries. The old warrior virtues of courage, endurance, and loyalty found ample scope in the tasks of creating and then managing new steel mills, textile plants, ship-building docks, and similar installations.

Within a firm or factory, too, patterns of human relations tended to model themselves on the age-old relation between samurai and peasant. That is, the industrial managers commanded and instructed; the workers obeyed, but in return were supported and looked after all their lives. In time of economic depression, men were not fired; new jobs were found instead, or the work was shared out among many men. In return, absolute loyalty and strict obedience were expected and almost unfailingly secured. Strikes and other forms of industrial unrest, which so often disturbed European countries, were almost unknown in Japan.

In addition, pre-existing artisan shops and small family enterprises were ingeniously mobilized for the production of new goods by a "putting out" system. This meant that a big firm might provide blueprints and perhaps raw materials, power tools, and credit to an artisan family, and in addition would undertake to purchase the product at a price that would allow the family to live modestly. Traditional reciprocal obligation between high- and low-ranking individuals and families assured the smooth functioning of this system.

Appropriate modification of ancient clan patterns of deference and obligation thus introduced a remarkable efficiency into industrial relations. Radically new and ever changing technologies could be and were introduced without disrupting the chain of command and obedience because these were sustained by vividly sensed mutual obligations and responsibilities that were enough like those of traditional Japanese life to make all concerned ready to accept them without much questioning.

Industrial, technological, and scientific advances which brought Japan fully abreast of Western countries by the middle of the twentieth century were therefore not necessarily connected with liberal, democratic ideas or parliamentary government. In the initial stages, indeed, the policy of opening the country to foreign contact and changing familiar ways was generally unpopular. A democratic regime could not possibly have carried such a policy through. It was only by appealing to traditional loyalty to the emperor, and by emphasizing the nationalistic appeal of Shinto—a religious cult that treated the emperor as a god—that the Japanese revolution from above was able to surmount the troublesome first stage when the rank and file of Japanese society could not yet glimpse eventual success, and saw around them only a wanton destruction and disregard of traditional ways.

The Western-style army and navy created by the Japanese government also combined old and new elements in a very effective manner. By ancient and jealously guarded principle, only samurai born to that rank had the right to bear arms. Nevertheless, in 1872 the samurai clique that had engineered the restoration of the Emperor four years earlier decided to introduce universal military service. They were influenced by contemporary French and German practices, for at this time everything European carried great prestige among Japan's upstart rulers. But the decisive consideration was this: they needed a military weight to counterbalance the numerous rival clans of disgruntled samurai who had been thrust from power by the *coup d'état* that "restored" the Emperor. The government had already destroyed the clan structure of land ownership and abolished feudal duties and privileges —not so much from any abstract sense of social justice as because they wished to break up potential rivals and opposition groups. It was, therefore, only logical that they overlooked the traditional difference between samurai and commoners in building up the new model armed forces.

The long-range result was to make the armed forces a powerful school of patriotism and a very significant social escalator. The navy remained comparatively aristocratic, and became more deeply Westernized, more complexly technical. But the army offered ordinary peasant boys a chance to rise to officer rank by pursuing appropriate training. Few other walks of life allowed such a change of status, since higher education remained expensive in the sense that a student had to forego earning power for years to achieve higher degrees— something an ordinary peasant's son could ill afford to do. But a man who chose to make the army his career could count on a secure if modest subsistence, and could in principle rise as high as his abilities would carry him. Samurai traditions and values were consciously cultivated among the new officer class, though many of them came from humble peasant homes. As in the case of industrial organization, the Japanese armed services were able to modernize and westernize their techniques without surrendering a uniquely Japanese spirit.

By comparison with these deep-seated continuities in Japanese life, the political changes that came with the restoration of the Emperor and subsequent constitutional legislation remained superficial. The Emperor Meiji (1868–1912) promised on his accession that he would set up a deliberative assembly and rule with due respect for public opinion. In 1889 he gave this promise lasting institutional form by promulgating a constitution, modeled in large part on the pattern of Bismarck's Germany. Nevertheless, universal male suffrage for elections to the Diet introduced a popular, democratic element into Japanese politics that was capable of considerable development during the decades that followed. From 1889 on, clan leaders and other high-ranking individuals could only retain political power by winning some kind of popular support. After World War I it even became possible for individuals who lacked high inherited rank to attain political power on the strength of support in the Diet.

In this way something more or less resembling the Western democratic revolution also came to Japan. But the popularly elected Diet had only restricted powers under the constitution, and an inner circle of "elders," descended from the clique of clan leaders that had carried through the original Meiji restoration, continued to exercise very important authority behind the scenes until the 1930's. By that time a new rival for power developed among ambitious young army officers who felt that the civil government was not eager enough to back them in an aggressive policy on the mainland of Asia. These men formed semi-secret patriotic societies, and on several occasions they assassinated statesmen who opposed their views. As a result, the home government in Tokyo came to be the army's half-willing, half-reluctant partner in the conquest first of Manchuria (1931) and then of most of China (1937–41).

Once launched on the path of military conquest, Japan began to collide with American interests in the Pacific. Efforts by the United States to hinder Japan's conquests by trade embargoes on such vital supplies as oil and scrap iron (both of which Japan had to import) persuaded the Japanese to risk a surprise attack on the American fleet (1941) in the hope of paralyzing the United States long enough to allow Japan to seize the oilfields of Borneo and to construct an economically self-sufficient "Co-Prosperity Sphere" in southeast Asia and the southwest Pacific.

The attack on the U.S. fleet at Pearl Harbor was extremely successful; the Co-Prosperity Sphere became a military reality; but the speed and force of American counteroffensives took the Japanese by surprise and completely upset their original plan. By 1945 American bombing raids, and the American submarine offensive which had sunk a large part of the Japanese merchant marine, had made a shambles of the Japanese home economy. In August 1945 the Japanese government sued for peace after the United States dropped atomic bombs on Hiroshima and Nagasaki. World War II thus came to an end, and the American occupation regime started Japan's society and economy upon yet another burst of drastic self-transformation.

By any standard, the Japanese achieved truly remarkable successes in reacting to the industrial and democratic revolutions between 1854 and 1945. Culturally and intellectually, too, the nation underwent extraordinary changes. Western ideas and styles were imported wholesale, especially in the early phases of Japan's self-transformation. Missions were dispatched to Europe and America to study and bring back anything and everything that seemed useful. Students were sent abroad to master one or another aspect of Western learning; then they returned home as experts, and set out, no less systematically, to transmit the knowledge they had acquired to other Japanese.

The government early decided to put major emphasis on developing a primary school system, so that every Japanese child could become literate. On top of this, various technical schools and a number of universities, built on Western lines, gave advanced and specialized training. As a result, by the 1930's Japanese scientists working in Japanese institutions had begun to make active contributions to the world's knowledge, and Japanese technicians and engineers were capable of competing on even terms with any in the world.

Yet cultivation of distinctively Japanese arts did not disappear. Indeed, during the 1930's, the fierce patriotism centered in the army tended to emphasize everything Japanese and downgraded foreign styles and manners. Traditional art, drama, and domestic architecture, together with a popularized form of Shinto religion, remained vigorous.

Over-all, the adjustment between old and new in Japan's intellectual and cultural life remained awkward and unsettled. The myths of Shinto, which claimed that the Emperor was directly descended from the Sun Goddess and therefore divine, accorded ill with the sophistication of Japanese biological laboratories. In the arts, one and the same person could often perform either in Japanese or in Western styles, but effective synthesis, or fresh creativity that combined the two traditions, was seldom or never achieved.

*   *   *

What stands out from a survey like this is the variety of reactions that Asian peoples exhibited to Western civilization during the three generations that elapsed between the effective breakdown of traditional defenses (about 1850) and the end of World War II. The history of our own age, and of ages yet to come, is and will be built upon the processes of cultural interaction which first assumed massive scale in this period.

CHAPTER 28

Africa and Oceania 1850–1945

At the beginning of the nineteenth century Africa was still the "Dark Continent" to Europeans, while Australia and New Zealand, together with the widely scattered islands of the Pacific—lands conveniently grouped together by the term Oceania—had only been superficially explored by European seamen. Throughout recorded history these lands had always been on the fringes of civilized life. But after 1850 both Africa and Oceania felt the expansive force of civilization as never before, and they were rapidly brought into the circle of interacting human societies that more and more embraced the entire globe.

The reasons for the age-old isolation and backwardness of Africa and Oceania were basically geographical. Oceania consists in part of coral atolls—tiny specks of land scattered across the immensity of the Pacific. Until 1759, when the invention of an accurate marine chronometer allowed European navigators to measure longitude as well as latitude, it had been impossible for a ship to be sure of finding any of the smaller atolls. This meant that systematic charting of the Pacific was delayed until the second half of the eighteenth century; and only in the 1820's, when oil derived from the sperm whales that congregated in the higher latitudes of the Pacific became a valuable element of commerce, did European and American ships begin to traverse the south seas in any numbers.

As for Australia, most of the continent was barren desert. The eastern coast, which did have enough rainfall to give the land a more attractive aspect, was guarded for the most part by a vast coral reef that made it impossible for ships to approach close to shore. The native inhabitants, who lived as Stone-Age hunters and gatherers, had nothing to offer European seamen in trade, so that ships steered away from Australia for centuries. When the British navy set out to chart the Australian coastline systematically in the second half of the eighteenth century, however, promising territory south of the Great Barrier Reef was discovered on the east coast. Accordingly, in 1788 the British government sent shiploads of convicts to Sydney harbor, in the hope of relieving English jails and permitting the prisoners to make new and better lives for themselves at the other side of the earth from their homeland. Half a century later, in 1840, the more distant but also more attractive islands of New Zealand were also settled, as part of a charitable scheme to relieve poverty and overcrowding in the British Isles. At the other extreme of Oceania, the Polynesian islands of Hawaii had by 1850 been deeply affected by American missionaries on the one hand and by whalers on the other. The Polynesians, Australian aborigines, and other peoples of Oceania were in no position to oppose further Western encroachments. In fact, they all risked extinction, because they proved extremely vulnerable to diseases brought by visiting ships' crews.

Africa in 1850 presented a far more complex and varied scene. North Africa, fronting on the Mediterranean, had played a part in civilized history from the age of the Pharaohs. Ethiopia and the upper Niger valley in west Africa had also supported civilized states and empires for a thousand years or more. Traders from India, the Middle East, Indonesia, and Europe had operated along the African coasts for hundreds if not thousands of years, and flourishing ports existed in east Africa as far south as the Zambesi river. Scores of kingdoms existed inland, some of them organized systematically for war and slave trading, others more peacefully inclined.

Yet in spite of these facts, and in spite of the general proximity of Africa to the earliest centers of civilized development, the continent as a whole lagged behind both Europe and Asia. Three geographical conditions explain why this was the case.

First, African soils and climate generally are not very good for farming. A large part of the continent suffers from scant rainfall. The vast Sahara desert is almost incapable of supporting human life. Its sandy wastes served to divide the sub-Saharan lands and the Mediterranean coastland; only camel caravans could cross the desert barrier with any ease. Another large chunk of the continent in the southwest is also desert—the Kalahari. Both these deserts are bounded by wide stretches of semiarid land, which can only be used as grazing for cattle. There are, of course, well watered regions in Africa, as in the Congo basin and coastal west Africa where the opposite extreme prevails. Daily rain in these parts supports tropical rain forests. Clearing such forests is a heavy task, and the soils are usually poor, since so much rain leaches certain minerals required for plant growth from the topsoil. Only the east African highlands (Ethiopia, Kenya, Tanzania) and coastal regions in South Africa (Natal, Cape of Good Hope) have really favorable agricultural land—a small part of the continent as a whole.

An additional handicap was that the crops available to early African farmers were not as productive as those developed in Europe and Asia. The arrival of root crops from Indonesia (about the beginning of the Christian era) and of American crops (about 1500) redressed the balance in large part. Maize from America became particularly important. Spreading from the west coast, it allowed a very substantial increase in population to take place wherever suitable soil and rainfall for its cultivation existed.

A second general reason for Africa's backwardness was the prevalence of debilitating diseases over large parts of the continent. Malaria, sleeping sickness, and yellow fever were particularly widespread. Sleeping sickness is caused by a parasite that is transmitted by the tsetse fly. The disease affects both men and cattle, and until recently it kept otherwise fertile and attractive lands vacant of human inhabitants. It was, indeed, the tsetse fly that prevented humans from destroying the big game of Africa long ago. The fly normally feeds on the blood of antelopes, and it does them no great harm, because the wild herds can tolerate the parasite which is fatal to men and cattle. Human hunters, so vulnerable to an infection that was widespread among the antelopes, could not long survive by preying upon the antelope herds. In tsetse fly districts men had therefore to surrender the role of predator in chief to lions.

Fortunately for the African branches of humankind, the tsetse fly does not infest all parts of the continent. Malaria, spread by the anopheles mosquito, was much more widespread; but the Negroid populations of Africa developed a high level of toleration for the disease. This was due to a genetic mutation (sickle-cell anemia) that offers the malarial parasite less favorable breeding grounds than normal red cells do. This allowed Africans to survive in malarial country where Europeans and other strangers died off rapidly. On the other hand, inheritance of the trait from both parents was fatal; only individuals with half normal, half sickle-shaped genes can enjoy the resistance to malaria that the mutation confers.

Yellow fever was still a third insect borne disease that had rather wide distribution and very serious consequences for African populations. Considering these diseases, it is not strange that sub-Saharan Africa as a whole remained thinly populated well into the nineteenth century, at least in comparison with geographically more favored lands of Europe and Asia.

A third geographical handicap under which Africa had to labor was the difficulty of transport and communication. Most of the continent is raised high above the sea, so that rivers must drop over considerable scarps near their mouths. This interrupted river transport and made it difficult for goods coming by sea to move inland more than a few miles. The Nile and the Niger are exceptions. Falls occur only fairly far inland on each of these rivers. It was not accidental that Africa's earliest and most highly developed civilizations arose in the Nile and Niger valleys. Along these rivers large-scale movement of goods by boat over comparatively long distances could be organized with ease; this allowed rulers to concentrate relatively large quantities of food and raw materials at places where specialists could then develop the skills we commonly recognize as civilized.

In regions where animal pack trains or human porters were the only available means of moving goods, it was prohibitively expensive to gather large stocks of food and materials in one place: little could be kept as surplus for the use of specialists. This, therefore, made the rise of flourishing civilizations impossible in most of Africa. To be sure, wherever some unusually precious commodity like gold, salt, or copper was to be found, rather large settlements could arise. This was probably the case, for example, at the mining center of Zimbabwe in Rhodesia, where there are extensive ruins which puzzled early investigators.

The harsh limitations which African geography imposed on the rise of powerful states and on far-ranging movement of traders allowed the survival of a wider variety of cultures, languages and physical types than occurred elsewhere in the world. In addition to the Mediterranean populations of north and parts of east Africa, who physically resemble southern Europeans and Arabs of the Middle East, Africa is the home both of Pygmies, who inhabit the Congo rain forest as hunters and gatherers, and of the tallest people known in the world, the Masai, who live as herdsmen in the region of the African Great Lakes. Closely related to each other and very different from other peoples of the continent are the Bushmen, who live in the Kalahari desert and adjacent regions, and the Hottentots, who survive (often mixed with white blood) around the Cape of Good Hope.

The most widespread African physical type is commonly termed Negroid. Within this general category, physical variations from tribe to tribe or village to village remained very great. This was so because before 1850, local African communities had been able to maintain effective biological as well as cultural isolation from strangers most of the time. This allowed each community to develop its own distinctive physical norm. Civilized conditions of life, on the other hand, bring strangers together regularly and frequently. A natural result is mingling of genes and the formation of wide ranging genetic pools within which variations are less than existed between different African local communities.

African peoples spoke hundreds of different languages, and this reinforced the difficulty of communication which geographical and technological conditions already imposed. Arabic in the north and along the east coast did constitute a language of trade and civilization. Arabic also reached deeply into the savanna zone of west Africa, which lies south of the Sahara and north of the coastal rain forest. In this relatively favored region, agriculture had long been established, and there were well-developed states. These came under strong Moslem influence after 1050 A.D. Thereafter, local kings and princes regularly imported experts in Islam to teach in the sacred language of Mohammed. But Arabic remained a learned language in sub-Saharan

Architecture in the Industrial Era

Théâtre de l'Opéra, Paris. Charles Garnier

The Houses of Parliament, London. Sir Charles Barry

TRADITIONAL GRANDEUR

When European architects set out to design important public buildings in the mid 1800's, they had two divergent traditions upon which to draw: the Greco-Roman, as modified and embellished by Renaissance and Baroque builders, and the Gothic. The first of these traditions is here represented by the Paris Opera (1861-75); the second by the British Houses of Parliament, completed in 1857. These structures architecturally embody the pride Europeans felt in their cultural and political accomplishments during the height of liberalism and national self-confidence.

PLATE 49

NEW TECHNIQUES IN THE SERVICE OF COMMERCE

Joseph Paxton, gardener turned architect, triumphantly explored new principles of construction for the Crystal Palace which housed the Great Exhibition of 1851 in London's Hyde Park. New materials — iron girders and glass — allowed light to flood all parts of the interior. These technical possibilities were later exploited to lighten the interiors of the two big department stores illustrated on the opposite page: GUM in Moscow and Carson Pirie Scott & Co., Chicago, both constructed in the late nineteenth century. The steel frame of the Chicago store allowed the construction of large windows to let in light; in Moscow a different solution, more reminiscent of the Crystal Palace, was employed — a glassed-in roof. But in their exterior decoration, both stores still paid tribute to older ideas of architectural grandeur.

The Crystal Palace, London. Joseph Paxton

PLATE 50

GUM, Moscow

Carson Pirie Scott & Co., Chicago. Louis Sullivan

PLATE 51

Hedrich-Blessing

Wainwright Building, St. Louis. Louis Sullivan

AMERICAN ARCHITECTS AND BUSINESSMEN REACH FOR THE SKIES

In the decades just prior to World War I, the technical possibilities of steel frame construction (plus the development of high speed elevators) allowed architects to reach for the skies. The early development of skyscrapers was peculiarly American, here illustrated by the relatively modest Wainwright Building, St. Louis (1891) and by the far more pretentious Woolworth Building, New York (1913). Yet amid such rapid and spectacular exploitation of new techniques and materials, traditional European conceptions of architectural magnificence still asserted their hold on men's imaginations in the form of decorative trimmings.

PLATE 52

Woolworth Building, New York. Cass Gilbert

PLATE 53

FORM FOLLOWS FUNCTION APPLIED TO TWO FACTORIES

The "Bauhaus" style that flourished in post-World War I Germany expressed a conscious break with earlier cultural and architectural traditions. The stark structural simplicity of steel, concrete, and glass construction, illustrated on the right, defined a new "functional" standard of taste, which scornfully rejected anything that smacked of mere decoration for its own sake. After World War II, the American architect Frank Lloyd Wright had absorbed and transformed the starkness of the Bauhaus aesthetic (left), combining the sheer glass of the tower with softened geometric forms and traditional textures of brick construction in the lower portions of the building.

The Bauhaus, Dessau. Walter Gropius

PLATE 54

Johnson Wax Research Tower, Racine, Wisconsin. Frank Lloyd Wright

PLATE 55

Interior Department, Washington, D.C.

THE HEAVY HAND OF THE STATE APPLIED TO ARCHITECTURE

From the days of ancient Mesopotamia, an important function of architecture has been to express a ruler's pride and a people's collective sense of greatness. In the 1930's, Franklin D. Roosevelt's New Deal embodied itself in the form of vast office buildings needed to house the bureaucrats who flocked to Washington. One example is that of the Department of the Interior, shown here. Simultaneously, Stalin planned Moscow State University (not completed until 1953) as a sort of personal monument and training ground for future state officials, while Hitler sought to fortify his "Thousand Year Reich" by building a vast rallying ground for faithful party members in Nuremberg.

PLATE 56

Moscow State University

Luitpold Hall, Nuremberg. Albert Speer

PLATE 57

Seagram Building, New York. Ludwig Mies van der Rohe and Philip Johnson

THE INTERNATIONAL STYLE

In the 1950's an international style spread all round the world, transforming the sky-lines of cities on every continent. It derived its power from a watered-down version of Bauhaus aesthetic principles and the fact that rectilinear glass and steel construction allowed the enclosure of maximal space at minimal cost. These photos show the impact of the style when it was new: posing the Seagram Building in New York against contrasting, older skyscrapers; silhouetting the apartment houses of Kalinin Prospect, Moscow, against an almost empty skyline; and projecting the new government buildings of Brasília against a still empty hinterland.

PLATE 58

Kalinin Prospect, Moscow

The Congress, Brasília. Oscar Niemeyer

PLATE 59

United States Pavilion, Expo '67, Montreal. Buckminster Fuller

Palace of the Assembly, Chandigarh, India. Le Corbusier

PLATE 60

ARCHITECTURAL GRANDEUR WITH NEW MATERIALS

The aseptic geometry of the International Style never lacked rivals. Among them were the three buildings illustrated here, all completed in the 1960's. Buckminster Fuller's Geodesic Dome, erected in Montreal for Expo '67, clearly harks back to the Crystal Palace of 1851 by using new and startling structural principles to enclose a temporary exhibition in a sphere of light. Le Corbusier's Palace of the Assembly, Chandigarh, India, and Eero Saarinen's TWA Terminal Building, Kennedy International Airport, New York, achieve in their contrasting ways a new definition of architectural grandeur, uninhibitedly using glass, steel, and concrete to achieve vast and dramatic effects. Thus after a full century of restless development, what in the 1860's appeared utterly antithetical turned out in the 1960's to be eminently compatible: architecture in a grand style with the use of cheap, man-made materials.

Ezra Stoller

TWA Terminal Building, New York. Eero Saarinen

PLATE 61

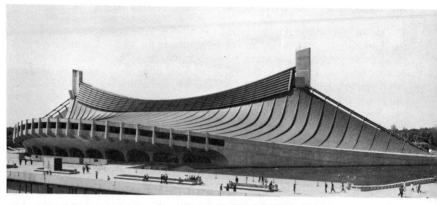

National Gymnasium, Tokyo. Kenzo Tange

Museum of Anthropology, Mexico. Pedro Ramírez Vazquez

PLATE 62

OLD STYLES WITH NEW MATERIALS

Steel, concrete, and glass also sometimes revitalized older, local architectural styles. These three photos show ways in which this has been done in Japan, Mexico, and North Africa. Kenzo Tange's Gymnasium (built for the Tokyo Olympics, 1964) used the technology of a suspension bridge to enclose a large unobstructed space; Tange also managed to create a roof line reminiscent of traditional Japanese temple architecture. The Museum of Anthropology, Mexico City, deliberately re-created an Aztec temple courtyard, yet the central umbrella structure, supported by a 40-foot column carved in bronze, positively flaunts innovative techniques of modern design. On a more modest scale, Roland Simounet's public housing at Djennan-el-Hassan, Algeria, effectively fits concrete shapes to North Africa's age-old housing patterns.

Housing, Djennan-el-Hassan, Algeria. Roland Simounet

PLATE 63

Midtown Manhattan, New York

MAN MADE MAZE

This aerial view of midtown Manhattan portrays the amazing miracle of a contemporary metropolis where people scurry to work in offices piled one on top of another, story upon story, and still find their way safely home at night. Such a collective creation dwarfs any single human being; it epitomizes the entire structure of modern civilization which, like this urban landscape, is almost wholly artificial — the glorious and dreadful work of man's hand.

PLATE 64

Africa, just as Latin did in Medieval Europe. It served as a common denominator for communication among speakers of different local languages.

The other great language family of Africa is Bantu. It is spoken, with relatively minor variations, by tribes scattered throughout all of central and most of south Africa. Close kinship among the different Bantu languages points to the relatively recent dispersal of these peoples. They seem to have started from somewhere near the Bight of Benin, perhaps about the time of the Christian era when they got hold of Indonesian root crops and iron tools and suddenly became able to penetrate the Congo rain forest as slash and burn farmers. Later some Bantu-speaking tribes emerged onto the grasslands that lie to the east of the Congo rain forest. There they acquired cattle. Then they dispersed north and south through the grassy highlands of east and south Africa. Tolerance of malaria due to the sickle-shaped red cell mutation may have been one of the principal advantages the Bantu peoples enjoyed. In the rain forest they intruded upon pygmy populations; on the grasslands the Hottentot-Bushmen melted away before their advance.

In the shore cities of the east coast, a trade language, Swahili, developed from intermixture of Arabic and Bantu. Semitic languages other than Arabic were spoken in Ethiopia and adjacent regions. But in most of West Africa and especially in the Upper Nile and Great Lakes region, a linguistic crazy quilt divided the population into mutually unintelligible, linguistically almost unrelated groups.

*   *   *

By about the middle of the nineteenth century, powerful forces of change were working upon Africa. Moslem influences pressed upon Africa from the north and east; Europeans did the same from the west and south. But these external elements were only part of the story. Inside Africa itself, dramatic and drastic state building was in full career, partly assisted and partly checked by the Moslem and European presence on the fringes of the continent.

Two economic changes help to explain the nineteenth-century spate of state building in Africa. The more basic remained almost unrecorded, so that details of when and where American crops—maize, peanuts, sweet potatoes—were first introduced to the different regions of Africa are almost unknown. But we can be sure that wherever the new crops became established, food production increased very substantially. This allowed population to grow, and denser populations in turn enlarged the resources available for the support of soldiers and other specialists required for the rise of really strong states.

A second economic change working along parallel lines was the suppression of the slave trade and the increase in demand for African products such as ivory and palm oil. The west African slave trade reached its peak in the eighteenth century; but humanitarian feeling, spearheaded by evangelical Christian reformers in Great Britain, checked (1807) and then almost eliminated (1833) the export of slaves from west Africa. After 1833 the British government stationed a naval squadron in west African waters with instructions to intercept slave ships. Whenever a slaver was captured, his human cargo was brought to the British naval base at Sierra Leone and set free there. This produced a most unusually mixed and, before long, an enthusiastically Christian population in that part of Africa.

The east African slave trade was carried on by Arabs. It continued to expand until the 1860's, when British diplomatic and naval pressure first restricted and eventually (1897) abolished slavery in that part of Africa also.

While it flourished, the slave trade allowed certain coastal rulers to build up substantial states, for example, the kings of Dahomey in west Africa and the Sultan of Zanzibar in east Africa. Nevertheless, slave raiding was fundamentally destructive of wealth and population, so that its suppression must have helped to establish a stronger economic base for later state building.

Exchange of European machine-made cloth and other products for various African raw materials tended to increase as the slave trade withered. Organizing and taxing this kind of trade offered a much less destructive basis for state building; on the other hand, European traders also found it profitable to export firearms to Africa. With the new guns, hunters were able to slaughter elephants for the growing ivory trade. Guns also gave an enormous advantage to rulers and captains who were able to get hold of the new weapons for their soldiers. Older military systems, including some remarkable ones like the spear-wielding Zulu war bands of Natal and the armored horsemen of Bornu in west Africa, became obsolete with the spread of efficient firearms. This, of course, introduced a profoundly disturbing factor into all African political systems.

Such far-reaching changes in agriculture, trade, and armament were upsetting enough for African societies. Religion was another factor. The activity of Moslem enthusiasts and of a growing number of Christian missionaries added another dimension of change which was to have vast consequences in the decades after 1850.

Moslem missions in Africa were almost as old as Islam, and the continued expansion of the faith of Mohammed into new regions proceeded throughout the nineteenth century and into the twentieth in ways not fundamentally different from before. In much of east and west Africa rulers of substantial states found Moslem ideas of law extremely helpful in organizing and extending their power. The well-organized Ashanti kingdom (in modern Ghana), for example, had a body of Moslem legal experts at court to help the ruler manage his affairs, though many of the customs of the land remained pagan, and Islam did not penetrate the Ashanti villages in any but the most superficial ways.

Collision with Europeans sometimes generated fanatical Moslem movements that expressed the anger and desperation some Africans felt when confronted by the superior force Europeans were almost always able to bring to bear. One such movement was the dervish brotherhood of the Sanusi, founded near Mecca in 1837 by a native of Algiers. Sanusi lodges spread throughout the oases of the eastern Sahara, where they spearheaded the prolonged resistance the nomadic inhabitants offered to French and Italian efforts to annex these desert territories. In the Sudan, another Moslem holy man, Mohammed Ahmed, announced to his followers in 1881 that he was the Mahdi, i.e. the restorer of Islam. He started a rebellion against Turkish-Egyptian authorities who had recently established their control in the upper Nile valley. But religious enthusiasm was not enough to stand up against gunfire; and in 1896–98 British troops, acting in concert with Egyptian authorities, reconquered the Sudan and destroyed the Mahdi's forces.

Moslem movements of this sort did not add anything fundamentally new to the African scene, since fanatical religious brotherhoods had often before transformed religious revival into territorial conquest, as both the Sanusi and Mahdist movements did in the nineteenth century. Christian missionaries, however, did bring much that was new: schools, hospitals, literacy in African tongues, and a general acquaintance with the intellectual and technical bases of Western civilization. The scale of Christian missionary activity mounted steadily throughout the nineteenth century. Mission schools gradually created a group of Africans who had been formally educated in Western ways and ideas. Frequently this involved alienation from traditional patterns of life, whatever they had been. Hence, as Western types of schooling advanced, the hold of ancestral social and political structures crumbled.

Looking back upon African history from the vantage point of 1978 it is clear that individuals educated along Western lines were destined to play a critical role in the second half of the twentieth century. Yet in 1850 or even in 1875 the impact of European education and other forms of influence upon African society was not nearly so obvious. Up to that time, native African political systems controlled most of the African continent, as they had done for centuries. European penetration of sub-Saharan Africa remained very modest, except in the far south, where Boer (Dutch) pioneers, fleeing from British control at Cape Colony (established in 1815), collided with the advancing power of Bantu tribesmen at about the line of the Orange river in the 1830's. Elsewhere, ancient states like the thousand-year-old kingdom of Bornu near Lake Chad, and upstart creations like the Zulu military despotism (founded 1817*) controlled most of the interior. Yet in some quite well-populated regions nothing that can be properly called a state existed because familial and village ties sufficed to meet all the needs of the inhabitants, and no powerful outsider had yet appeared to demand taxes on a regular basis.

By 1914 the political and economic picture had altered dramatically. Except in Ethiopia, native rulers and states survived only as clients and dependents of foreign imperial administrations, and no part of the continent had escaped at least formal incorporation into one or another state structure. How and why did this occur so quickly?

One factor was technological: the industrial revolution made it possible for European intruders to overcome some of the obstacles to

---

* Its founder, Shaka (1787–1828) revolutionized military tactics by arming his warriors with heavier spears, which were used at close quarters, instead of being thrown, as had been traditional. The result was very like the introduction of the phalanx tactics among the ancient Greeks; indeed, the organization of Shaka's army into age groups, kept under arms in barracks for years on end, resembles nothing so much as ancient Sparta under the Lycurgan constitution.

transportation and communication that had always before hampered the spread of civilized styles of life in Africa. Steamboats on the Congo, above the falls near the river mouth, could move up and down the river freely. When linked to railways that went around the falls, the new transportation system made the exploitation of rich copper mines far in the interior a practicable proposition for Belgian capitalists. Where navigable rivers were absent, railroads cheapened overland

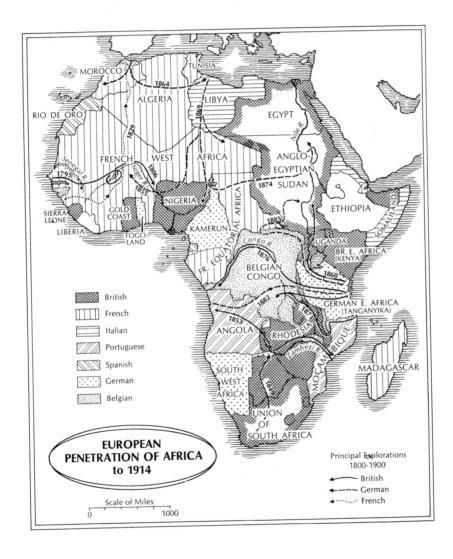

EUROPEAN
PENETRATION OF AFRICA
to 1914

transport enormously. They allowed access to gold and diamond mines in south Africa and to coffee plantations in Kenya, which British capital and colonists set out vigorously to exploit.

African diseases, too, lost some of their terrors when scientific study of how they spread allowed Europeans to take measures to escape mosquito and tsetse fly bites. But anything approaching effective control of malaria and sleeping sickness among the African populations as a whole came long after the establishment of European colonial administrations, and for the most part waited until World War II.

When all due allowance is made for technical and economic conditions, however, it still seems clear that the most important change that kicked off the penetration of Africa by Europeans was in the psychology of the leading colonial nations. Missionary enterprise was of great importance; and British interest in African missionary work was enormously enhanced by the well-publicized explorations undertaken by the famous missionary, David Livingstone. Between 1849 and the time of his death in 1873 Livingstone dramatized the adventure of African exploration for millions of Englishmen and Americans. His disappearance into the African interior and "discovery" by the second famous explorer of Africa, Henry M. Stanley (d. 1904), echoed through newspapers all across Europe. But Stanley was more interested in the economic potential of Africa than in saving souls, as his later career in the Congo demonstrated.

Actually, Europeans saw no conflict between the two types of enterprise. Quite the contrary, spreading trade and spreading Christianity seemed to go hand in hand. The benefits of Western civilization were self-evident to Europeans, so that they easily convinced themselves that it was a moral duty to bring Africans (and other backward peoples) into the circle of civilization—even, perhaps, by force. Millions of well-meaning Europeans and Americans thus became enthusiastic imperialists. Toward the end of the nineteenth century European governments therefore became more and more ready to send soldiers anywhere in the world to support their missionaries and merchants whenever and wherever these standard-bearers of civilization got into trouble with local rulers.

It was this combination of attitudes that triggered the sudden European advance into the interior of Africa. And once the movement started, any step forward on the part of one imperial government impelled others to follow suit for reasons of prestige and rivalry. Various special interests quickly clustered around the imperial adventure: army officers who wanted glory and an escape from the routines of barracks life; politicians in search of a cause; capitalists in search of sudden riches; engineers, administrators, and technicians who found that they could have servants and a better life abroad than at home—all these and many others joined forces to push the imperial adventure ahead.

A good deal of hypocrisy and brutality entered into imperialist attitudes, and an even larger dose of race feeling and smug ethnocentrism. Yet in an age when the tides of popular feeling all run the other way, it is perhaps worthwhile to insist on the idealism that accompanied the hypocrisy. When investigation showed that agents working for King Leopold of Belgium in the Congo were using brutal and inhumane methods, much resembling slavery, to hurry along the economic development of that land, European public opinion was genuinely shocked. Leopold was compelled to give up his personal venture, and the Belgian government took over responsibility for governing the Congo in 1908.

European reaction to the revelations about forced labor in the Congo were particularly strong because the abolition of slavery had been, from the beginning of the nineteenth century, one of the driving forces behind their armed intervention in African affairs. The advance into the interior had been justified, over and over again, by the argument that European control was essential for the final suppression of the slave trade.

Yet the European moral, humanitarian sense had sharp limits. Slavery was abhorrent, along with pagan religion and arbitrary justice as administered by the executioners and bodyguards of African kings; but wage labor, entered into by Africans who scarcely understood the terms offered them and were in no position to bargain or even to seek alternative employment, seemed perfectly all right. Indeed, the advance of civilization required African labor; and since direct resort to force through slavery was wrong in European eyes, imperial administrators commonly resorted to a kind of elaborate charade. They required Africans to pay taxes in money. But most Africans could only pay the new taxes by working for cash wages offered by European employers, who were thus assured of a supply of labor for whatever projects they wished to carry through, whether public or private.

The two leading nations in the contest for opening up Africa to European civilization were France and Britain. France first acquired African territory by undertaking the conquest of Algeria in 1830. Efforts to safeguard the open desert frontiers of that colony soon led adventurous French soldiers deep into the Sahara, where they linked up with other French imperial representatives based in Senegal. The French army, together with French missionaries, developed dreams of civilizing Africa and at the same time making France great by building a vast empire across the northern half of the continent, from the Atlantic to the Red Sea.

This imperial ambition collided with British schemes for a "Cape to Cairo" railway. The great champion of this vision of Africa's future was Cecil Rhodes (d. 1902), who made a fortune in the South African diamond mines and then turned to politics. Rhodes tried hard to develop popular support for his African policy in Great Britain itself, where, in the latter part of the nineteenth century, the old-fashioned evangelical Christian missionary spirit had to compete with a new "hard boiled" school of thought which considered the survival of the fittest to be the key to all history and human life, and believed that the future of the Anglo-Saxon race depended on how much of the earth they could seize and settle with British colonists.

Germans, inspired by British ideas of the struggle for survival, arrived late on the scene (1884) but made up for this by a more ruthlessly aggressive attitude both in Africa (Tanganyika, South West Africa, Cameroon) and in Oceania (Caroline and Marshall islands). Italians also sought to follow the French and British example, but, after moderate successes in the Red Sea region, they met with humiliating defeat at the hands of a revivified Ethiopian empire in 1896—the only case in which an African state was able to drive back European invaders. The Belgian king, Leopold, organized an international association to "explore and civilize" the Congo basin in 1876. This soon turned into a private instrument for the exploitation of the area's resources. The Portuguese, too, revived old claims to African territory in Angola and Mozambique.

Clashes among the eager European imperialists were of course inevitable. The principal rivalry at first lay between France and Britain. Crisis came in 1898 when a French colonel occupied Fashoda, a desolate village on the banks of the upper Nile. French control of the upper Nile seemed a clear threat to Britain's indirect control over

Egypt (acquired in 1882) and also interrupted the projected route of the Cape to Cairo railway. The British had in fact anticipated the French advance toward the Nile by marshalling an army in Egypt both to settle old scores with the fanatical Moslem followers of the Mahdi, who were in control of the Sudan, and to head off the French advance toward East Africa. It took a considerable British force to reconquer the Sudan for Egypt; but having started before the French reached Fashoda, a superior British force arrived on the scene not long after the tiny French garrison had established itself there. Following a tense few weeks, when war between the two nations seemed imminent, the French withdrew and the Fashoda crisis ended.

In the next few years, the two principal European imperial powers settled all important outstanding territorial issues peaceably between themselves. This was because the situation in Europe impelled France and Britain to ally against the rising power of Germany. Thereafter, clashes over Africa tended to consolidate the Anglo-French rapprochement. The Germans first antagonized the British by expressing sympathy for the Boers, whom the British attacked and defeated in a hard-fought war (1899-1902). Then the German government irritated the French by making empty gestures of support for the Sultan of Morocco (1905, 1911), who was resisting French efforts to increase their authority over his country. These imperial quarrels contributed greatly to the international tensions that led to World War I.

Although European colonial administrations grew rapidly between 1875 and 1914, they remained quite superficial in most of Africa. There were substantial populations of European settlers in South Africa and in Algeria; but elsewhere there were few European settlements, and in many regions the Europeans acted only as distant overlords, whose rules and regulations rarely applied to the routines of everyday life.

Two different theories of empire had some impact upon colonial administrations. The British, in general, preferred indirect rule. This was based upon patterns of Indian administration, where British advisers, stationed at the court of native rulers, had long sufficed to control all important matters. Application of this pattern to Africa meant that pre-existing chieftains and kings remained in office, subject to occasional interference and a shower of advice from British official residents.

The French preferred direct administration. That is, they appointed local officials to conduct affairs in accordance with the instructions of the central government of the colony. Such officials were sometimes white, sometimes black; in theory and to some degree also in practice it was not skin color but education and skill that made a man eligible for office.

French policy implied cultural assimilation as the ultimate goal of colonial government: Africans educated in French schools, at least in principle, became Frenchmen who happened to have black skins. British preference for indirect rule left more room for the preservation of local cultural traditions. Indeed, it eventually came to be the case that British colonial authorities sometimes found themselves propping up old and decaying political and social structures at a time when most politically conscious Africans had withdrawn their support from discredited chiefs and corrupted kings.

Theory, however, had only a small part in determining the actual character of colonial administration. A constant problem was finance. Africa was poor, and tax income never sufficed for the projects European administrators wished to carry out. Anything that promised to increase tax income was therefore eagerly welcomed. This meant encouraging anyone willing to invest in Africa. Mining enterprises were particularly attractive, both to European investors and to colonial administrators, for the exploitation of gold, copper, and other minerals offered the surest profit and the best available tax source. Local African interests were therefore brushed aside whenever they happened to conflict with mining and similar developments.

Yet native Africans regularly did object to the activities of the Europeans. In some cases, chiefs and kings mobilized the resources at their command to try to oppose or roll back European power. The Berbers of the Atlas mountains were up in arms against the French for decades; and the Ashanti kingdom of west Africa fought the British four times, and was not definitively annexed to the Gold Coast (modern Ghana) until 1901. Similarly, in south Africa, the Zulus did not submit to British indirect rule until after the power of the paramount chief had been broken on the battlefield (1879).

These and other parallel efforts all failed, with the single exception of Italy's defeat at the hands of Emperor Menelik II of Ethiopia in 1896. Many African rulers realized the futility of armed resistance to European soldiers, and came to terms with the colonial administrators more or less willingly. It was in such cases that the pattern of indirect rule was most effective. Sometimes, indeed, an African ruler was able to strengthen and consolidate his power under the shadow of a European administration. This was the case, for example, in the kingdom of Buganda. In other cases, European colonial administrators rescued an African state threatened with disruption and propped it up by recognizing the ruler's legal rights to territory and his various traditional perquisites. This was the case in Basutoland, where English colonial administrators intervened in 1868 to save the tribe from destruction at the hands of Boer settlers.

Even in its most bureaucratic manifestations, direct administration did not wipe out older social structures. Kinship groups, village communities, and tribal ties persisted, and colonial administrative officers had to deal with the population through such structures. The difference between direct and indirect rule is therefore easy to exaggerate. Everything depended on the territorial scale of the native social structures which the colonial administrators recognized and utilized. Policy in such matters had only a limited scope. Colonial officials usually dealt with whatever kinds of native leadership the local situation afforded. They were not in sufficient control of the local scene to be able to do much else. Thus, for example, the French, however much they might have preferred uniform bureaucratic administration in theory, often in practice had to settle for their own version of indirect rule. This was the case in Tunis and Morocco, for instance, where European diplomatic entanglements required them to maintain native Moslem rulers in office.

Despite the fact that on a day-to-day basis European colonial government remained quite superficial, its establishment still made a big difference in Africa. First of all, once definite boundaries had been settled, and all the European powers had agreed to accept them, the scale of violence sharply decreased. Up to 1900 or so, bloodshed remained widespread. Africa had been soaked in blood in the decades before Europeans penetrated the interior. The most famous African states had, in fact, been built for war and waged it almost every year. But once European expeditionary forces had proved how unequal head-on clashes between native African armies and European troops had become— thanks to European arms, discipline, and supply systems—the scope for organized and large-scale violence shrank drastically. Former enemies had to live side by side, often within the same colonial administrative structure. Cattle rustling and slave raiding, which had given focus to the life of the warrior peoples of Africa, was quite effectively suppressed. This involved far-reaching changes in social patterns and moral values. Sometimes the balance of forces between two different African peoples was dramatically reversed by the ending of war and violence. This was the case in Kenya, for instance, where the Masai, who had been cattle-raisers and warriors, lost their traditional occupation and main *raison d'être*, while the agricultural Kikuyu increased their population and soon vastly outnumbered their enemies, the Masai.

Suppression of organized large-scale violence hastened the increase of population generally. So did a variety of agricultural improvements: more extensive irrigation works in the Nile valley, and new cash crops, such as cacao and peanuts in west Africa, cloves and coffee in east Africa, sugar cane and oranges in south Africa, etc. Before long, in parts of the continent, rural over-population threatened to become a problem, and people began to move into cities. Individuals who made the move from rural simplicity to the sophistication of new sprung cities, built on a generally European pattern, faced difficult problems of adjusting custom and habit to the urban environment.

Up to 1914, however, the breakaway from traditional molds of African life had not become very general. World War I brought only minor disturbances to the continent. German colonial possessions were overrun without too much difficulty by the British and French, and these were apportioned among the victors after the war, again without serious controversy. From many points of view, World War I marked the high water mark of European imperialism in Africa as well as elsewhere. The ideas and ideals that had sustained the imperialist thrust weakened after 1918; and the expected profits which enthusiastic promoters had promised greedy European investors were seldom realized. Indeed, it seems to be true that imperialism as a whole never paid off in hard cash. The costs of administration and development in African colonies probably exceeded the value of goods exported from Africa to Europe. Individual mines and other enterprises, of course, sometimes made spectacular profits for their owners and managers; but other ventures failed, and public investment was seldom entirely paid for from local resources. Everything depends on what costs are taken into account; but the idea that white men gained great wealth by plundering Africa can only be supported by biased and naïve accountancy.

Between the wars, Africa presented an outwardly peaceful appearance. Colonial administrators faced few rebellions, and friction between the different colonial powers was minimal. Three independent states existed: the Union of South Africa, Liberia, and Ethiopia. The first of these was a self-governing dominion under the British crown. Set up in 1908, it gave full political autonomy to the white population, Boer and British alike. Liberia had been established on the west coast in 1847 as a homeland for ex-slaves returned from America. It was governed as a republic with a constitution modeled on that of the United States.

Ethiopia's rulers, beginning with the Emperor Theodore (reigned 1855–68) were remarkably energetic, ambitious, and ruthless men, who welded together the unruly peoples of the Abyssinian plateau partly by main force and partly by appeal to the ancient cultural traditions embodied in the Christian church of Abyssinia. In 1934, however, the Italians attacked, largely in order to wipe out the sting of their defeat in 1896. This time, with the help of airplanes and poison gas, they drove Emperor Haile Selassie from his throne and made Ethiopia the kingpin of a short-lived empire in northeast Africa.

This belated manifestation of European imperialism was counterbalanced, in a sense, by the beginnings of British withdrawal, symbolized by the grant of legal independence to Egypt in 1922, followed in 1936 by a treaty that promised speedy withdrawal of all British troops from the Nile valley.

The most important aspect of African history during the interwar period was not so much political as economic and psychological. Between 1918 and 1945 the Africans' exposure to new experiences of many different kinds weakened all traditional forms of society profoundly. Men who served in European armies, especially during the two World Wars, learned new skills and saw new sights which made them unwilling to go back to village life. Children who attended mission schools often had similar reactions, particularly when they were able to attend secondary or higher institutions of learning. Far more numerous were those who left their native communities to work in some mine or in town. Hundreds of thousands of such persons experienced a completely new pattern of life at new jobs in a new environment where old customs for the most part simply did not fit. When strangers from many different tribes rubbed shoulders with each other day by day all concerned had to find a new basis of mutual accommodation. Kinship and tribal rules of conduct were all too obviously inapplicable.

In such situations, the models offered by European law and manners had great advantages. Urban and industrial living were nothing new to Europeans; and both schools and government administrators propelled African towards closer conformity with European norms. The only available alternative model for urban life was Islamic. In the parts of Africa where Islam had been established for many centuries, the people clung fast to their inheritance. In most of sub-Saharan Africa, however, even in those regions where Islamic rulers had previously exercised state power (e.g. northern Nigeria), the Islamic model for civilized life was not very successful when it had to compete with Western models. Indeed, in these regions Islam tended to falter because it was associated with old-fashioned, outmoded political structures which the modern Africans of the cities blamed (along with European exploitation) for Africa's weakness and poverty.

These processes created a numerically small but strategically well placed group of Africans who shared sufficiently in Western knowledge and skills to wish for political independence. Their number and level of self-conscious organization differed from colony to colony, but they were present everywhere, ready to take over control from the hands of European administrators when, after World War II, one imperial government after another decided to relinquish the burdens of African colonial administration.

*   *   *

The native peoples of Oceania met a far harsher fate. In all the smaller islands of the Pacific, and in Australia, disease and a disruption of traditional social structures followed upon the arrival of the white men. The natives came near extinction. White settlers took over the land in Australia and in much of New Zealand. These lands, like South Africa, became self-governing dominions of the British Commonwealth of Nations in 1901 and 1907, respectively. Like other Polynesians, the Maoris of New Zealand experienced a period of drastic population decline after the first contacts with white men, but they began to increase in numbers after about 1900. Since then, the Maori population has grown very rapidly. They remain largely rural, and depend on potatoes for food. This was a new crop in New Zealand, introduced by the white settlers, which derived ultimately from South America.

In the other big island group of Polynesia, Hawaii, the native population barely survived. From 1810 the islands were united under a native dynasty, but men from the United States engineered a *coup d'état* in 1893 and arranged for the annexation of the islands by the United States in 1898. Before and after this transfer of sovereignty a succession of immigrants arrived in the islands to work on plantations set up by American entrepreneurs. Of these the Japanese became the most numerous; but a wide spectrum of races and peoples came to reside in the islands. The original Polynesian communities broke up, and survivors became a small minority.

In some of the Pacific islands, for example, in parts of New Guinea, primitive life persisted almost unchanged, mainly because Westerners found nothing there that attracted them. In still others, like the Philippines, native populations adjusted very successfully to foreign rule, first Spanish (from 1571) then United States (from 1898). Only in a few (Tasmania) did complete and total extinction of native populations occur. But everywhere the effect of the Western intrusion was to reduce the sharpness of local cultural and racial peculiarities by mingling the fragments of previously isolated peoples with in-migrants, who often came from quite diverse parts of the earth.

The same process went on in all the other parts of the earth (southeast Asian highlands, northern Siberia, the rain forest of Brazil), where primitive peoples had managed to maintain themselves until the nineteenth century. Over-all, therefore, the effect of the expanded outreach that civilized men achieved by the new means of transport and communication acquired in the industrial revolution was to accelerate the homogenization of mankind. This is a process as old as civilization. Homogenization has always depended on the long distance movement of people and goods across cultural, geographic, and genetic pool boundaries, which civilized societies both permit and require.

What happened was therefore not new, though its scale and speed were without earlier parallel. Moreover, the dominating role played by Europeans and men of European descent, who everywhere

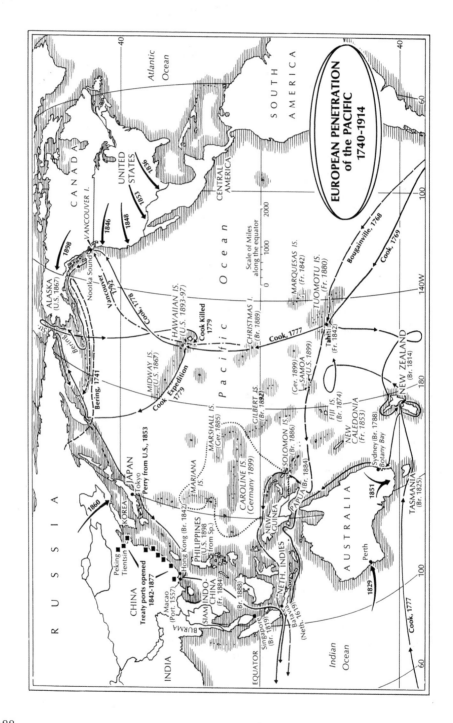

EUROPEAN PENETRATION of the PACIFIC 1740-1914

Scale of Miles along the equator

0   1000   2000

Bougainville, 1768

Cook, 1769

Cook, 1777

Cook, 1778

Cook Killed 1779

Cook Expedition 1779

Bering, 1741

Vancouver, 1792

Nootka Sound

Atlantic Ocean

SOUTH AMERICA

CENTRAL AMERICA

CANADA

UNITED STATES

1806

1827

1853

1848

1846

1898

VANCOUVER I.

ALASKA (U.S. 1867)

MIDWAY IS. (U.S. 1867)

HAWAIIAN IS. (U.S. 1893-97)

CHRISTMAS I. (Br. 1889)

MARQUESAS IS. (Fr. 1842)

TUOMOTU IS. (Fr. 1880)

Tahiti (Fr. 1842)

Pacific Ocean

Bering

Str.

RUSSIA

KOREA

JAPAN

Tokyo

Perry from U.S., 1853

1860

CHINA

Peking
Tientsin

Treaty ports opened 1842-1877

Macao (Port. 1557)

Hong Kong (Br. 1842)

PHILIPPINES (U.S. 1898 from Sp.)

INDO-CHINA (Fr. 1884)

SIAM

BURMA

INDIA

Singapore (Br. 1819)

Batavia (Neth. 1619)

NETH. INDIES

EQUATOR

Indian Ocean

MARIANA IS.

CAROLINE IS. (Germany 1899)

MARSHALL IS. (Ger. 1885)

GILBERT IS. (Br. 1892)

NEW GUINEA

PAPUA (Br. 1884)

SOLOMON IS. (Br. 1886)

NEW BRITAIN (Ger. 1899)

SAMOA (U.S. 1899)

FIJI IS. (Br. 1874)

NEW CALEDONIA (Fr. 1853)

AUSTRALIA

Perth

1829

Sydney (Br. 1788)

Botany Bay

1851

TASMANIA (Br. 1825)

NEW ZEALAND (Br. 1814)

Cook, 1777

488

acted as the principal agents of innovation, had no historical parallel from the time when multiple centers of civilization first arose in Europe and Asia.

To complete our survey of world history it is appropriate to turn in the final chapters to a closer examination of seminal transformations that occurred in the Western world itself between World War I and World War II as a preface to some parting observations about the heightened pace of world-wide cosmopolitan interaction that dominates the contemporary scene.

CHAPTER 29

The Western World 1914-1945

Two World Wars, 1914–18 and 1939–45, separated from one another by a brief and uneasy peace, acted like a vast pressure cooker to hasten social change in Europe and the Western world generally. The two wars also channeled Western society into directions which it might otherwise not have taken. In particular, obstacles to the mobilization of human and material resources for waging war were swept away in the heat of conflict; and, as governments discovered how powerfully wartime "command economies" could concentrate effort on the attainment of particular goals, a new range of possibilities for deliberate manipulation of human societies for peace as well as for war came into view. Accordingly, such diverse regimes as Stalin's Russia, Hitler's Germany, and Franklin D. Roosevelt's United States all tried their hand at redirecting human and national effort according to plan. World War II reinforced and confirmed the discovery that economy and society, like government, were man made, and could be remade (at least within broad limits) if enough human beings could be persuaded or compelled to act in accordance with someone's commands.

Between 1815 and 1914 a different ideal and practice defined what we may appropriately call the "bourgeois era" of European and Western history. The American and French revolutions and the liberal constitution-making of the nineteenth century showed clearly enough that political systems were neither natural nor God-given, but man made, and could be changed if enough people agreed upon the change to be desired. On the other hand, both liberals and conservatives of the nineteenth century agreed that society and economy were natural and therefore beyond conscious control. They assumed that in-born human nature and the impersonal relations of the market defined these aspects of human life in ways that could only be marginally affected by public taxation, education, or other governmental actions. Only socialists foresaw the possibility of wholesale and deliberate re-ordering of economic relations through governmental action; but socialist expectations of what a post-revolutionary society would be like only faintly resembled what twentieth century governments have in fact achieved.

World War I was, therefore, a watershed of unusual import for the history of Europe and the West. During four years of fighting, new and powerful forms of socio-economic mobilization were explored, fumblingly and almost desperately, by the belligerent governments. The war effort undermined class and regional distinctions, so that the outlines of a new, post-bourgeois style of mass society clearly emerged by 1918, not only in Russia but in all the leading industrial nations of the West.

Men's ideas were profoundly shaken too. No one had expected four years of stalemate and the brutal butchery of industrialized war. It was easy enough to reject belief in progress and rationality—ideals which had already been called into question before 1914. But what sort of vision of the human condition to substitute for these outworn, eighteenth century faiths was more difficult to agree upon. No recognizable consensus emerged during the first half of the twentieth century, despite the emergence of new totalitarian ideologies—Communist, Fascist, Nazi.

World War I

‡‡‡ World War I broke out by accident. No European government wanted a general war; on the other hand, all the major European powers except Italy preferred to fight rather than back down in the face of diplomatic provocation from their rivals.

The pattern of alliances which divided Europe into two rival camps made each side less flexible than otherwise might have been the case. To back down risked alienating allies who might be needed for some future confrontation. Thus Germany backed Austria against the Serbs not so much because the Serbs (or the Balkans as a whole) interested Germany, but because the Hapsburg monarchy was the only ally Germany could count upon to help counterbalance the threat of encirclement by the Triple Entente—France, Russia, and Great Britain. Similiar calculations required the French to rally to the side of Russia. Only by proving herself a loyal ally when French interests were not centrally engaged could the French count upon Russian help against Germany in some future crisis.

The second factor that swept Europe into the war was the rigidity and clumsiness of the mobilization plans that had been worked out by each major army. According to these plans, millions of reservists had to be called up from civilian life, issued uniforms and weapons, and then transported to the frontier—and all as quickly as available transport allowed. The irony of the situation was that the more carefully every last railway car had been put to use by the mobilization plan, the more costly any modification of the plan became. When everything had been smoothly meshed with everything else, to call a halt part way through would simply create chaos; and chaos invited military defeat—exactly what the mobilization plan was supposed to prevent.

Hence, once the Russians ordered general mobilization (and they "had to" because they needed more time to gather their forces at the frontier than their enemies did) Austrian, French, and German mobilization orders followed in quick succession, each triggered by the other. Automatism displaced policy; military leadership supplanted civilian leadership; mobilization plans transmuted themselves into war plans —without anyone really deciding to do so—as the rival armies plunged across the frontier "according to plan."

This kind of sleepwalking along lines laid out carefully in advance did not last long. Only the German "Schleiffen" plan stood the test of practice. This required the Germans to concentrate most of their army against the French, with especially strong forces gathered in the north, near the sea. The aim was to encircle Paris and defeat France within the first few weeks of the war, in order to be able to concentrate later against Russia on the east. But the Germans figured that to achieve such a success they would have to march through Belgium: the French-German border was too restricted to allow the necessary mass of German troops to pass through speedily enough to win the victory as planned. It was inconvenient that a treaty of 1839 declared Belgium perpetually neutral. But a mere "scrap of paper," especially such an old one as this, seemed a small obstacle to the German armies in 1914. On the other hand, Germany's violation of Belgian neutrality, more than anything else, provided the British government with a decisive argument for intervening in the war against the Germans. It also made it easier for the Italians, who, in 1914, had a defensive alliance with Germany and Austria, to decide that they were not obligated to join the fighting because the Germans and Austrians had not been attacked.

In the first few weeks of the war, however, these considerations seemed unimportant. German armies pressed deeper and deeper into northern France. By the fifth week of the war they were close to Paris; but the men and horses were tired out, and the French will to resist had not wavered, despite all the setbacks they suffered. A decisive turn came during the second week of September, when a French counter offensive, launched with the aid of taxicabs requisitioned to carry soldiers from the Paris railway stations to the front, penetrated a gap that had opened between two of the advancing German armies. After a confused battle, the German High Command decided to withdraw behind the Marne river. Their plan for quick victory had failed. Everybody else's plans had failed too.

When the rival armies vainly tried to outflank one another, stalemate set in. A tangle of trenches and field fortifications soon stretched all the way across France, from the English Channel on the north to the Swiss border in the south. In the ensuing months shovels almost replaced guns as the primary weapons of the war. Soldiers set to work deepening and improving the trenches, strengthening gun emplacements, protecting supply lines, preparing fields of fire, designing rear trenches into which to withdraw in case of assault, and in other ways making the front practically impregnable for either side.

Slowly and reluctantly, the rival generals realized that machine guns deployed in a system of mutually supporting trenches could not be overrun by infantry assault. The cure, they decided, was to increase the scale of preliminary artillery bombardment so as to knock out enemy machine guns before the attack. This called for more and more big guns; and artillery bombardments, lasting for days—indeed, for years—called for shells in hitherto unimagined numbers. New factories had to be built, new supplies found for all the raw materials required for manufacturing shells and guns. In the meantime millions of men had to be fed and supplied in the trenches; and other millions trained and equipped to take their place as shells and machine guns cut them down.

To create and supply armies on such a scale required drastic changes on the home front. Labor had to be found for armaments plants as well as for other essential industries; food, fuel, and raw materials had to be allocated so that everything needed for the war effort could be provided in suitable quantities. This soon created civilian shortages. By the end of the war, food and clothing had become scarce in many parts of Europe, while less essential supplies had in some cases disappeared entirely.

In the first weeks popular enthusiasm for the war inspired every combatant nation. But as casualty lists lengthened and the hardships of the war multiplied, that enthusiasm rapidly waned. This was particularly true in Russia, where the government was unpopular to begin with, and failed to administer the war effort very successfully. The shortcomings of the Russian state were dramatized by the ebb and flow of the eastern front during 1915 and 1916. In France, where elaborate supply systems supported every mile of trenches, vast effort, involving the expenditure of millions upon millions of shells and the loss of millions of soldiers' lives, only shifted the battle line slightly. For three long years, a few miles' advance across utterly devastated landscape was all that either side achieved.

On the Russian front, however, supply from the rear was too thin to sustain intense fighting for any length of time. Instead, a comparatively small margin of superiority in manpower and supplies here allowed one side or the other to win victory in the field, whereupon the defeated army had to withdraw for scores or even hundreds of miles, until such time as the supplies available to the victorious advancing forces ran out. The result, therefore, was a violent seesaw. Russian initial advance into East Prussia in 1914 soon gave way to a general retreat; but on three later occasions Russian armies again took the offensive and recovered substantial territories. By the spring of 1917, however, the Russians had been driven far back from the prewar frontier. Severe shortages of food and other supplies hampered war production and fostered radical discontent in the Russian cities, especially the capital, Petrograd.

Intensification of the war effort among the principal belligerents was matched by efforts to spread the war by engaging new allies in the struggle. Turkey joined the Central Powers (Germany and Austria) almost at the beginning; Italy rallied to the Allies' side (France, Britain, Russia) in 1915; Bulgaria assisted the Central Powers in overrunning Serbia later in the same year, but Rumania and Greece saw fit to adhere to the Allies. Arabs rebelled against the Turks with British encouragement, while in the Pacific area Japan took the opportunity to seize distant German colonial possessions.

The complicated negotiations that brought these nations into the war committed the Allies to a series of secret treaties that partitioned Ottoman and Austrian territories among the signatories. This proved embarrassing later, but at the time the expansion of the war fronts into Italy and the Balkans effectively encircled the Central Powers by land, while by sea the British navy, with some French help, cut Germany and Austria off from access to the rest of the world very effectively. The Allied naval blockade was administered in such a way that even the remaining neutrals like Switzerland and Holland were not allowed to import supplies for transshipment to Germany. The war thus turned into a kind of vast seige. The Allies controlled the seas, and could bring supplies from America and elsewhere; the Central Powers were cooped up inside Europe, dependent on local resources.

With each month of war, resources of manpower and material available to each side became scanter. The war became a matter of slow attrition. In any such contest, Imperial Russia was the weakest link, for administrative and technical skills available to the tsar were less than among the other great powers. By March 1917, discontent provoked revolution; the tsar abdicated and a provisional government attempted both to carry on the war and to lay the groundwork for a new constitutional system for Russia. The short-term effect was disastrous. Russian armies melted away as soldiers responded to radical socialist agitation. The Central Powers were able to advance almost at will, and food became even scarcer in the Russian cities as peasants ceased to send their crops to market. In November 1917, when a second revolutionary *coup d'état* brought the Bolshevik faction of the Social Democratic Party to power, Russia officially withdrew from the war. This allowed the Germans to concentrate their remaining resources for a final push on the western front.

Russia's withdrawal coincided with America's involvement. The United States Congress declared war against Germany on April 6, 1917. The occasion was a dispute over the rights of neutrals at sea. Germany had declared a blockade of Great Britain, relying upon submarines to enforce it. The United States refused to recognize the legality of such an action and continued to send ships carrying war and other supplies to Great Britain. Some of them were sunk; and the Americans chose to treat this as an act of war, requiring full scale American intervention in the struggle. The whole issue was largely a smoke screen. A more fundamental reason for the United States' entry into war was fear that German victory would organize the entire continent of Europe under a government unfriendly to the United States.

It took time to mobilize American resources for war, and even longer to deploy American troops in France. In the meanwhile, in the spring of 1918, the Germans started a vast offensive, using new tactics of infiltration without announcing an assault by a prolonged artillery barrage as before. As in 1914, the front began to surge toward Paris: to war-weary Germans victory seemed finally within their grasp.

But by that time the war had changed character. Military discipline, equipment, and supply systems were no longer the sole determinants of success in battle. Instead, new and powerful ideologies, proclaimed both by Lenin, leader of the Russian Bolsheviks, and by Woodrow Wilson, President of the United States, had begun to affect the behavior of nations and armies. Lenin summoned the proletariat, particularly in Germany and other advanced industrial countries, to revolt against capitalist oppressors. Wilson called upon the peoples of Europe and the world to settle the war by democratic processes of political self-determination, without annexations or indemnities. In cases of dispute, majority vote, presumably, would decide, peaceably and reasonably.

Both Lenin's socialist ideal and Wilson's democratic ideal were revolutionary in the sense that action in accordance with either program clearly involved the overthrow of existing governments and social structures in part (Wilson) or all (Lenin) of Europe. Both, too, had real appeal to the war-weary peoples of the continent. By comparison, the German, Austrian, and Ottoman empires lacked any really persuasive, powerful ideals to justify the final effort required to win the war.

This altered psychological climate played a decisive part in tipping the balance against the Central Powers in the last months of battle. In addition, American troops began to arrive in France in vast numbers during the first part of 1918, and this dimmed the prospect of German military success. Hence, when the momentum of the German spring offensive finally spluttered out in July 1918, the Central Powers rapidly lost all hope of victory. Subject nationalities in the Ottoman and Hapsburg empires embarked upon open preparations for independence; by October the German and Austrian governments officially accepted President Wilson's famous Fourteen Points as a basis for peace, but haggling over details postponed the end of hostilities until November 11, 1918. By then, revolutionary movements had toppled both the German and Hapsburg emperors from their thrones, and all of central and eastern Europe was in economic as well as political turmoil.

The overthrow of the German, Austrian, and Ottoman empires was a golden opportunity for socialist revolution, or so Lenin and the Bolsheviks in Russia believed. Fear of proletarian revolt soon became a major preoccupation among the victors, who found themselves supporting a variety of upstart regimes in eastern Europe whose claims to respectability rested, often, more on their anti-Bolshevism than on any authentically democratic support they commanded. The fact was that democratic self-determination was an unworkable ideal in most of central and eastern Europe under the chaotic conditions that prevailed in 1918–20.

Active civil war broke out in Russia and its borderlands in 1918 and continued to rage until 1920. Nationalist movements in the Ukraine and the Caucasus eventually failed; and these regions joined in a federal arrangement with Russia to constitute the Union of Soviet Socialist Republics. In Finland, Estonia, Latvia, Lithuania, and Poland, however, nationalist movements won out against the Soviet appeal. By 1921 new independent states had come to terms with the Russians in each of these lands.

Events in Russia and its borderlands were governed by naked military force. But armed force in turn depended on psychological and sociological conditions. In these respects, throughout the heartland of Russia the Bolsheviks enjoyed a fundamental advantage. The vast peasant majority believed that Lenin's party would allow them to keep the land which they had seized from landlords in 1917–18 with the blessing of the Bolsheviks. No matter what Lenin's rivals said, the peasants suspected that they would try somehow to give the land back to its former owners. Hence, whenever the choice had to be made,— and it was often—the majority of peasants regularly opted for the Bolsheviks. This is why Lenin's followers won out in the end; but they only won after Russia had been brought to the verge of economic collapse.

The peace conference that met in Paris in January 1919 did not even attempt to deal with the situation in Russia. Instead the victors contented themselves with dictating terms to the defeated German, Austrian, and Ottoman governments. Agreement on boundaries proved difficult to achieve, especially since the Italians wanted all the territory they had been promised by the secret treaties that brought them into the war in 1915, whereas President Wilson felt that his sacred principle of national self-determination should override secret and disreputable bargainings to which the United States was, in any case, not a party.

A second difficult issue was how to make sure that Germany would never be able to renew the war. President Wilson hoped that a League of Nations would keep the peace by legal processes. The French had little faith in the League and wanted military alliances with Britain and America, as well as German disarmament and the right to station French troops on German soil.

The result was compromise. Wilson got his League of Nations, though the United States later refused to join. France got German disarmament, but never succeeded in making Germany pay the costs of the war, as the treaty prescribed. Boundaries for the new states of east central Europe—Poland, Czechoslovakia, Rumania, Hungary, and Yugoslavia—were established by paying lip service to national self-determination while keeping a wary eye on Europe's military and administrative power balances.

The peace conference saw the break up of the alliance that had won the war. Italy withdrew when it became clear that her territorial ambitions would not be satisfied. France and Britain quarreled over how to distribute Arab lands and other issues. The United States soon began to lose interest in Europe's problems, so that, in 1920, the United

States Senate actually refused to ratify the Treaty of Versailles, of which President Wilson had been a principal architect.

The Interwar Years

‡‡‡ America's withdrawal from active concern with Europe was confirmed by the elections of 1920, which brought a new president, Warren G. Harding, to office. His campaign promised return to "normalcy." Normalcy for most Americans meant a return to prewar simplicity when perplexing foreign problems scarcely mattered, and when private efforts to make a fortune could proceed with little concern for what the government was doing. A boom soon developed in the United States, where by 1920 a majority of the population had become urban dwellers and were eager to possess cars, radios, and other new consumer goods. Installment buying allowed even expensive items like automobiles to find a mass market for the first time.

Britain, too, tried to allow prewar patterns of life to resume operation unhampered by governmental regulation. But prosperity stubbornly refused to return. Instead chronic unemployment depressed the coal fields and some other segments of British industry. In France, the massive public expenditure which was required to restore the devastated regions of the country prevented the French government from following American and British examples. In Germany, and further east in Europe, no automatic resumption of prewar patterns of social and economic life was possible, because the war and its immediate aftermath had bitten too deeply into older social structures.

Italy, where the war left all segments of the nation dissatisfied, constituted a special case. Rising political agitation led to a *coup d'état* which brought a new Fascist regime to power in 1922. The Fascists aimed at making the state great and respected by overriding special class and individual interests in the name of the nation as a whole. Led by an ex-socialist, Benito Mussolini (d. 1945), Fascism exalted the military virtues and indulged freely in bombast. Yet, unlike the governments of France and Britain, the Fascist regime of Italy was willing to experiment with peacetime mobilization of national resources along lines that had proved so successful during the war years. In this sense, as Mussolini proudly boasted at the time, his government did represent "the wave of the future."

The other postwar movement that proudly claimed to have the future on its side was international Communism. In 1919, as civil war was rising toward its crisis inside Russia, Lenin summoned a conference of foreign sympathizers to found a new International. In the next months, all European socialist movements split between those who accepted Bolshevik (re-christened Communist) leadership and those who resisted Communist take-over. This split was especially fateful in Germany, where the prewar Socialist movement had been particularly strong. Quarrels with the Communists drove the majority of German socialists into closer collaboration with "bourgeois" parties than their leaders might otherwise have been willing to accept. The socialist revolution that broke out in Germany in 1918 was thereby blunted. A series of coalition governments took office under a new constitution devised, according to irreproachable democratic principles, at Weimar in 1919. Such a government was ill-equipped to resist the rash of revolutionary threats that stemmed from both left and right. Nonetheless it survived, thanks to a tacit alliance with the remnant of the old officer corps of the German army, which put decisive military force at the disposal of the government. However, this left the tiny army permitted by the Versailles Treaty in the hands of men who lacked all sympathy for the new regime. Yet after 1924 even this weakness seemed supportable. Booming prosperity returned, helped by loans from the United States.

The rapid upthrust of German economic activity that developed in the late 1920's contrasted with a slower and much more difficult economic recovery in Russia. After the civil war came to an end, Lenin decided that the effort to establish communism all at once would have to be postponed. As a matter of fact, his calculations had always rested on the assumption that the highly industrialized countries of western Europe would also undergo socialist revolution, thus bringing substantial proletarian experience and numbers to bear upon the problems of building a communist society in Europe and the world. When communist revolutions failed to develop outside the boundaries of Russia, plans based on help from German and other foreign proletarians had to be shelved. Russia, willy-nilly, was thrust back upon her own resources. Lenin responded by announcing a New Economic Policy

(NEP) in 1921. This allowed peasants and small traders to buy and sell freely. Only the "commanding heights" of the Russian economy remained in state hands: banks, factories, foreign trade, and transportation.

Many idealistic Communists felt that NEP was a betrayal of true socialism—an unworthy concession to selfish economic behavior characteristic of the unenlightened peasantry. Outside of Russia, NEP was generally greeted as proof that communism could not work. In fact, however, the urban sector of the Russian economy remained essentially under state management, just as Lenin said it would. His death in 1924 provoked a hidden but fierce struggle for supreme power. Not until 1927 did Stalin emerge as Lenin's successor. By then, the difficulty of running an economy part free (i.e. managed by innumerable private persons, mostly peasants, who responded sluggishly to market prices) and part directed (i.e. managed by state officials who responded—also sluggishly—to directives from their political superiors and paid little attention to market prices) had become acute. The supply of food and raw materials to the cities was inadequate to support the projects for industrial development which the government wished to launch. Stalin therefore decided to abandon NEP and use force to make the villages contribute the food and raw materials needed for expansion of the urban and industrial sector of the economy.

This was done by compulsory collectivization of agriculture. Peasants were compelled to pool their land and draft animals to equip collective farms; and each collective farm was required to deliver part of its harvest to the state as a kind of tax before distributing anything to the peasant members as payment for their work. The Russian peasants resisted collectivization; they even slaughtered their animals rather than transfer them to the new collective farms. This created a severe agricultural crisis in the early 1930's. But Stalin decided to requisition grain from the collective farms anyway, even if it meant starvation or near starvation for the uncooperative peasantry.

The food and raw materials gathered by main force from Russia's collectivized peasants supported vast work forces that built factories and dams, opened new mines, and made other capital improvements. A long list of tangible goals were set forth in a Five Year Plan. The Russians organized their efforts to meet these goals and even to surpass them, exactly like a military campaign. Men and materials were assembled and work was conducted on the principles of a military chain of command. Even the terminology was military: newspapers and speeches resounded with appeals and warnings to shock brigades, front line workers, class enemies, and the like. By 1932, Stalin was able to announce overfulfillment of the first Five Year plan in a period of only four and a half years. In spite of the heavy cost of collectivization, Russia's planned mobilization did in fact result in rapid industrial expansion.

By 1932 this achievement echoed widely through the capitalist world. The boom of the 1920's had come abruptly to an end in 1929 when the stock market in New York collapsed. Panic spread from country to country, leaving mass unemployment in its wake. Unemployment reduced purchasing power, and this made the depression worse. But Russia's expanding economy had somehow liberated itself from this vicious and seemingly inescapable circle. To many Western observers, the high costs of forcible collectivization seemed easy to forgive when contrasted with the futility and suffering generated by the great depression.

Marxist predictions of the breakdown of capitalism seemed confirmed by the depression; yet the long-expected socialist revolution failed to appear in any of the highly developed industrial countries of the West. France and Britain staggered along, unable or unwilling to take drastic governmental measures for restoring the economy. Germany and the United States, on the other hand, generated far more energetic responses to the depression crisis.

In the United States, President Franklin D. Roosevelt inaugurated a "New Deal" in 1933. This amounted to a partial return to patterns of economic mobilization that had been used during World War I. Emergency programs of public works and efforts to regulate prices and agricultural production never attained sufficient scale to end unemployment; yet the impact of the depression was blunted, and a workable public consensus supporting New Deal innovations in economic management maintained itself precariously until the onset of World War II introduced a new and very different set of problems.

Germany experienced a more drastic change of regime when Adolf Hitler came to power in January 1933. Hitler was leader of the National Socialist (Nazi for short) German Workers' Party. He believed in will and heroism; and he thought that the Germans had been stabbed in the back in 1918 by Jews, Marxian Socialists, and other "traitors" to the nation. The comradeship of the trenches was a fond memory for Hitler and most other Nazi leaders; only in the ranks of their party could they find a similar outlet for their aggressive as well as for their comradely emotions. Belief in the natural superiority of blond, racially pure "Aryans" was a particularly nasty aspect of Nazi doctrine. It justified attacks against, and an eventual effort to destroy, Jews and other supposedly inferior peoples.

Hitler's policy on taking office was first to secure dictatorial power by transforming the constitution and eliminating rival parties and political leaders. Then he set out to make Germany great once again by rebuilding the armed forces, putting men and machines back to work, and engaging in shrewd and daring diplomatic maneuvers. Neither France nor Britain was able to resist Hitler's action effectively. The United States and Russia did not even try. Hitler was therefore able in an amazingly short time to make Germany once more the dominant power on the continent of Europe, while at home, by persecuting Jews and ending unemployment, he consolidated his popularity among the majority of Germans. The secret of his success lay in his wholesale resort to the pattern of economic mobilization that had been worked out by Germany during World War I. Nazi practices fitted the wartime mould smoothly, since, from the start, rebuilding the armed forces in preparation for war constituted an overriding priority for Hitler's domestic policy.

Until 1938, Hitler's announced foreign policy was to undo the injustices of the Versailles Treaty. This meant not merely rearmament to make Germany again the equal of France and other powers; it also meant bringing all Germans under a single political roof. Hence the annexation of Austria (March 1938) and of the German-inhabited parts of Czechoslovakia (September 1938) did not seem completely unreasonable to most British statesmen, who took self-determination seriously.

Hitler, however, was not content with annexing regions already inhabited by Germans. He believed that a life and death struggle for living space was the stuff and substance of history. The future of the Aryan race could only be assured, he argued, by seizing broad territories in the east and settling them with Germans. This was a policy that neither France nor Britain would passively accept. Yet Stalin, who had most to lose, actually allied the U.S.S.R. with Hitler when the Nazis set out in 1939 to extend German power eastward by reducing the Polish state to subservience. Hitler's attack upon Poland, September 1, 1939, started World War II, for at that time, a reluctant France and Britain honored their promises to help the Poles and declared war. Until June 1941 Stalin continued to help Hitler in economic and diplomatic matters, thus assuring the Germans (once Poland had been crushed) of a war on only one front—a luxury Germany had not enjoyed in 1914. To be sure, Stalin had something to show for it, since Russia not only annexed about half of Poland, but also occupied the three small Baltic states of Estonia, Latvia, and Lithuania. Finland resisted the same fate in a winter war (1939–40), but had to yield some border territory to Stalin.

World War II

‡‡‡ France and Britain were neither materially nor morally able to oppose Hitler successfully in 1939. As a result, Germany, with her allies, Italy (from 1940) and Japan (from 1941), won a series of dramatic victories during the first three years of the struggle. Poland was overrun within four weeks, and divided between Germany and Russia. In the spring of 1940, the Germans conquered Denmark and Norway as a preface to a smashingly successful attack upon France, Belgium, and Holland. Once again, resistance crumpled after only a few weeks. Hitler had done what imperial Germany had failed to accomplish: almost all of the European continent lay at the feet of the victorious German army. America remained neutral; Russia cringed. Britain alone fought on, mounting a successful air defense against German bombers and keeping the sea lanes open despite German submarine attacks. But no one supposed that Britain's resources would suffice to overthrow the German colossus that bestrode Europe triumphantly.

In the fall of 1940, the technical difficulty of invading England without first winning air and naval superiority persuaded Hitler to turn his armies against Russia instead. Living space for the Aryan race, of which the Nazis spoke so freely, was to be found in the east. Moreover, Hitler despised the Communists on ideological grounds, and he believed that the destruction of Stalin's regime would be easy. Almost every outside observer agreed with him, for the Russian army had

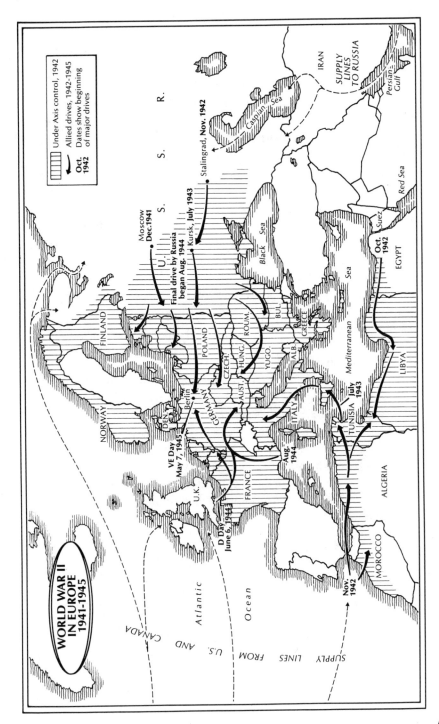

WORLD WAR II
IN EUROPE
1941-1945

Under Axis control, 1942

Allied drives, 1942-1945

Oct. 1942 — Dates show beginning of major drives

suffered wholesale purges of its officer corps in the 1930's, and, when put to the test, attacking Russian armies had been held at bay for months on end in 1939–40 by numerically inferior Finnish troops.

Before invading Russia, the Germans launched still another brilliantly successful "lightning war" into the Balkans, overrunning Yugoslavia and Greece in a matter of three weeks. Russia's turn came next, and on the night of June 22, 1941, Hitler's armies attacked without the formality of declaring war. Strangely enough, Stalin was caught by surprise. The advancing German armored columns captured millions of Russian soldiers. Yet despite initial wavering, the Russians' will to resist did not break and, as winter approached, actually hardened. German supplies and machinery began to run down; the pace of the advance slackened, and then cold weather set in, halting the Germans in their tracks.

Being confident of speedy victory, the Nazis had made no preparations for the Russian winter. German machines and men could not function in sub-zero temperatures, whereas the Russians, familiar with winter cold, succeeded in driving back the most advanced portions of the German line near Moscow and in some other places. Hitler thus met his first fundamental setback, although it was not clear until another full year had gone by that the Russian armies would ever be able to conduct a general offensive against the invading Germans.

The first German withdrawal on the Moscow front occurred on December 6, 1941. On the next day, Japan attacked the United States fleet at Pearl Harbor, thus bringing the Americans into war. For a few days it was uncertain whether the United States would declare war on Germany as well as on Japan. Hitler solved this problem for the American government by declaring war on the United States. This presumably relieved his irritation at the long series of acts "short of war" by which the Americans had already helped Great Britain to resist the Germans.

After entering into full-scale belligerancy, it became American policy to concentrate major effort first against Germany, on the ground that Germany was a more formidable opponent than Japan. This implied co-operation with Britain and Russia, as well as with such lesser allies as gathered around the Big Three. By degrees a remarkably effective co-ordination of effort was devised between Britain and America. Russia remained always apart, although deliveries of civilian

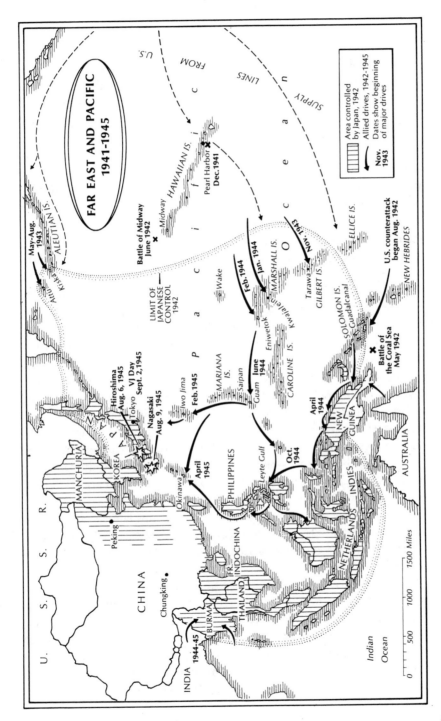

FAR EAST AND PACIFIC 1941-1945

Battle of Midway June 1942

May-Aug. 1943

ALEUTIAN IS.
Kiska
Attu

Pearl Harbor **Dec. 1941**
Midway
HAWAIIAN IS.

U.S.

FROM

SUPPLY LINES

Ocean

Pacific Ocean

LIMIT OF JAPANESE CONTROL 1942

Wake

Feb. 1944

Jan. 1944

MARSHALL IS.
Kwajalein
Eniwetok

Nov. 1943

Tarawa
GILBERT IS.

ELLICE IS.

NEW HEBRIDES

U.S. counterattack began Aug. 1942

CAROLINE IS.

June 1944

MARIANA IS.
Saipan
Guam

Feb. 1945

Iwo Jima

Hiroshima **Aug. 6, 1945**
Tokyo **VJ Day Sept. 2, 1945**
Nagasaki **Aug. 9, 1945**

JAPAN
KOREA

April 1945

Okinawa

PHILIPPINES

Leyte Gulf

Oct. 1944

SOLOMON IS.
Guadalcanal

April 1944

NEW GUINEA

Battle of the Coral Sea May 1942

MANCHURIA

Peking

U. S. S. R.

CHINA

Chungking

INDIA
1944-45

BURMA

THAILAND

FR. INDOCHINA

NETHERLANDS INDIES

AUSTRALIA

Indian Ocean

0   500   1000   1500 Miles

Legend:
Area controlled by Japan, 1942
Allied drives, 1942-1945
Dates show beginning of major drives
Nov. 1943

supplies and war material from Britain and the United States certainly helped the Russians in important ways. But difficulties of delivery were great in the first critical months, and Russia never revealed enough information about her own resources to allow accurate dovetailing of Anglo-American strategic and production plans with those of the U.S.S.R.

By the fall of 1942, American war production was beginning to mount to flood proportions. The early victories of the Japanese had by then been contained, and a more or less stable front in the Pacific and in Asia had been defined. In November 1942 the first Anglo-American counteroffensive was launched in North Africa. The Germans and Italians were driven from North Africa by May of the next year, whereupon Anglo-American troops landed in Sicily and then in southern Italy. As a result, Mussolini fell from power (July 1943). The Italian government officially withdrew from the war, though Italy remained a battlefield until the end of hostilities in Europe.

For the Germans, operations in the Mediterranean were little more than a side issue. Major fighting concentrated on the Russian front throughout 1942 and 1943. In the summer of 1942 the Germans renewed their offensive on a grand scale and penetrated to the Volga river, at Stalingrad. There they halted. Between November 1942 and February 1943 the Russians turned them back and then cut off the entire attacking army. When the Germans attempted to resume the offensive in the summer of 1943, the Russians quickly turned the tables. Thereafter, the Germans remained on the defensive, withdrawing mile by mile from Russian soil. In late summer 1944, Russian armies crossed the prewar frontiers and pressed onward toward Berlin.

In the same summer, Anglo-American troops landed on the coast of Normandy (D-Day, June 6, 1944) and drove successfully toward the Rhine. Allied plans called for the defeat of Germany before the end of the year, but German resistance proved more stubborn than anticipated, and it was not until April 1945 that Russian and American troops met near the Elbe river in Germany. With defeat a certainty, Hitler committed suicide (May 1, 1945), and a week later German surrender was formally signed by representatives of the German High Command. As for the Nazi government, the victors refused to treat with it, and instead divided Germany into zones of military occupation, where each occupying power (Russia, Great Britain, United

States, France) was at liberty to set up whatever kind of local authority it saw fit. Efforts to concert Allied policy for Germany as a whole soon broke down, and eventually the country came to be divided in two: a larger western portion, the Federal German Republic, comprising the former British, American, and French zones of occupation, and a smaller eastern German People's Republic, formerly the Russian occupation zone, which passed under Communist rule.

As in 1918, Europe in 1945 was devastated. Massive air raids had shattered German and other European cities; communications were badly damaged; economic paralysis was general. Yet recovery came far more smoothly after 1945 than after 1918, mainly because all concerned realized that spontaneous return to normal was out of the question. As a result, techniques of social and economic management that had been developed during the two World Wars and in response to the depression of the 1930's were used to reconstruct postwar Europe.

Economic recovery became apparent from 1949 onward. Within an amazingly short time, almost all of the damage caused by the war had been repaired. Europe went on to achieve greater productivity and prosperity than at any time before the war—this despite the loss of almost all colonial possessions overseas. No more striking demonstration of the peacetime uses of the kinds of socio-economic management which the wars had pioneered could be imagined. Europe's recovery, no less than Europe's war-making powers, showed how much could be accomplished by co-ordinating the efforts of millions of skilled persons for goals that commanded nearly universal support. In this, more than anything else, lay the key achievement of the Western world in the twentieth century, an achievement shared by Communist and non-Communist regimes alike. Only Japan made comparable advances in concentrating effort on a mass scale; the rest of the world lagged far behind.

Thought and Culture

‡‡‡ We do not know which events of the twentieth century will stand out as the truly important innovations in Western thought and culture. Traditional values and assumptions have certainly been challenged; many have been discarded. Perhaps Western civilization as defined by our medieval and modern predecessors is breaking down in

somewhat the same way as other civilizations broke down in the nineteenth century, when Chinese, Indian, and Moslem minds found their traditional habits of thought and action incapable of coping with Western intruders.

On the other hand, it is possible to argue that what is new and strange in twentieth century art and thought constitutes another self-transmutation of Western culture similar to past transmutations that we know as "Renaissance and Reformation," or the "Enlightenment," or by some other familiar historical label. Until more time has passed, and the elements of change and continuity can be better distinguished, it is really impossible to pass definite judgment between these opposite views.

A factor that weighs heavily in favor of breakdown and discontinuity is this: until the twentieth century the vast majority of men in the Western world, as elsewhere, were farmers. As such, their lives were regulated by age-old rhythms of the seasons. Attitudes toward work, family relations, and the world outside were all fundamentally shaped by farming routines. This norm has faded fast from industrialized societies in the twentieth century. Urban patterns of daily experience are bound to differ profoundly from those of the rural past. How this will affect culture and society remains to be seen. But the impact seems likely to be great, and may be so great as fundamentally to sever post-industrial civilization from anything men have previously known.

The scope of mass media in urban communities may mark the onset of such a new phase of culture. Radio and movies became influential during the 1920's, and had an impact on politics as early as the 1930's. Television, which is far more powerful, came only after World War II, but it has worked along parallel lines. The effect of such media has been to break through distinctions of class and locality. Everyone within reach of the mass media networks tended to be brought closer to a common level. By-passing the written in favor of the spoken word (reinforced on TV with visual stimuli), these channels of communication evoked responses akin to those which have always existed in face-to-face contact.

This opened wide the gate to new kinds of conscious manipulation of human behavior. Most advertising depended on arousing subliminal responses, associating an emotionally charged object with some product or other. Powerful political movements, like Hitler's, also resorted, quite consciously, to deceit and lies, and deliberately aimed at arousing emotion.

World War I, in fact, made millions aware as never before of the irrational dimension of human conduct. Sigmund Freud's (d. 1939) effort to plumb the unconscious level of the mind therefore attracted many followers after the war among intellectuals and in artistic circles of Germany and, before long, in France, Britain, and the United States as well. But Communists and Nazis refused to tolerate Freudian ideas, so that, after 1939, this school of thought flourished mainly in the English-speaking world.

This was indicative of a deeper difference. In French and English circles, art and literature continued to be regarded as primarily an individual product, addressed to other individuals and dealing, usually, with private and personal rather than with public and official themes. Insofar as artists and writers set out to explore a world uniquely their own, they ran the risk of becoming unintelligible to others. Only small circles of initiates cared, for instance, to make the effort needed to understand the more arcane poetry of T. S. Eliot (d. 1965) or to penetrate the verbal acrobatics of *Finnegans Wake* by James Joyce (d. 1941).

Interestingly enough, the visual arts experienced a widening of their public even when some artists cut loose from creating recognizable images of reality. This was because improvements in the methods of photographic reproduction allowed a (perhaps attenuated) experience of a work of art to multiply indefinitely. When the whole range of historical art styles thus became available to the general public, stimuli of the most diverse origins began to inspire artists. African art and other primitive models became influential; personal styles proliferated wildly; and still the camera kept up, feeding a wider public than had ever existed before with an enormously expanded range of visual art.

A different view of art dominated the scene in Communist Russia and Nazi Germany. To be sure, in the first days of the revolution, Russian artists rejected old restraints, but under Stalin they were organized to serve the state and the party, and told what kinds of themes and styles to use. Art, in short, was treated as an instrument for affecting public attitudes and action, and only those works that seemed likely to forward causes approved by the government were permitted to see the light of day. Hitler followed a similar policy, though he put more effort into persecution of dissenters than into definition of an acceptable style.

Preoccupation with personal helplessness and irrationality was often characteristic of "capitalist" art and literature. Such emphasis accorded strangely with the continued triumphs of science. No fundamental new insight changed the shape of the natural sciences between 1914 and 1945, although quantum mechanics, developed in the mid-1920's by Werner Heisenberg (d. 1976), Erwin Schrödinger (d. 1960), and others, offered a powerful new mathematical and conceptual tool for dealing with extremely small sub-atomic events. Other applications and ramifications of Einstein's relativity as well as of older scientific ideas multiplied at a prodigious rate. The penetration of the very small was matched by an entirely new sophistication of astronomic studies. Detailed calculations of how the stars could convert matter into energy (in accordance with Einstein's formula) yielded very convincing explanations of how the stars shone.

Theoretical advances were only a small part of the over-all effort of natural science. Chemists turned out a host of new synthetic materials, some of which had important application (nylon, ethyl gasoline) in consumer goods and industry. Physicists built new and powerful machines that could accelerate electrons to very high speeds in order to smash atoms. Even atom-smashing skills were harnassed to the task of producing a uniquely powerful and destructive kind of consumer goods during World War II: the first atomic or nuclear bombs.

The controlled release of nuclear energy which wartime scientists achieved was an example of a general and very important change that came to the process of invention. Before 1914, most important inventions were made by individuals working more or less on their own. The inventors or some intermediary often had to work hard to convince others of the value of what they had invented before it could be put into practical operation. But during World War I and, even more dramatically, during World War II, this traditional relationship between invention and application was reversed. Men first decided what kind of a machine or weapon they wanted; then they assigned experts the task of designing something that would meet the desired specifications. Invention thus became a deliberate and in some degree even a controlled process. It became possible to speak with assurance of a time when tanks or airplanes would travel further and faster with bigger loads, and even to estimate in a rough way how long it would take to solve the problems connected with designing and manufacturing such improved models.

The technique of deliberate invention resembled the techniques of socio-economic management which found such wide scope during the war and depression years. Men first analyzed the process into component parts. Then they looked for bottlenecks where some expansion of scale or change of method would be required if the process as a whole were to behave as the planners desired. Effort and ingenuity were then focused on the critical points until some new idea, put to the test of practice, worked well enough to raise the horizon of the possible for the process as a whole. Engineers and designers of large industrial installations had worked in this fashion for a long time. What was new was first the scale—not one plant but an entire industry became the normal unit for planning purposes—and second, the assumption that existing performance patterns and material limits could always be improved by taking thought. The effect was extraordinary: invention accelerated and moved purposively toward solving specific technical problems with a speed and certainty never equalled before. It was as though a blind man, groping his way through a strange room, had suddenly acquired sight.

The invention of deliberate invention was an enormous triumph of human rationality. In other fields, not least the social sciences, rationality also won some notable victories. Economics, for instance, advanced enormously through the work of John Maynard Keynes (d. 1946) and others. Reflecting on the depression that afflicted Great Britain throughout the interwar years, Keynes recognized that governmental policies affecting supply of money and credit were a major factor in fixing the level of economic activity, even in a free market economy. This insight, supplemented by increasingly elaborate statistical data about details of economic action, gave economists the ability to advise government officials on how to adjust tax and monetary policies so as to damp down if not altogether suppress the alternation of boom and bust which had proven so costly in the interwar (and earlier) years. Such indirect controls promised, indeed, to surpass Communist command techniques of economic management, in the sense that a finer adjustment of demand and supply seemed attainable through skilfully managed market mechanisms.

The continued triumphs of human rationality in science and social management stand in strange opposition to twentieth-century awareness of irrational levels of individual motivation and action. In principle, rational calculation can perhaps allow for irrational behavior, at least when dealing with statistically significant numbers rather than with single events. It is only this that makes the science of economics possible. Managers can also use rational calculation in launching appeals to irrational levels of the human psyche in order to change behavior—whether it means persuading people to buy a new soap, inducing the public to vote for a particular candidate, or training recruits to become obedient soldiers.

A wider and more systematic application of these techniques to society would divide mankind between managers and managed, sheep and shepherd, elite and mass. Communist society more or less explicitly accepted such an ideal by putting responsibility for leadership in every walk of life upon the shoulders of party members. Fascist doctrine emphasized will and courage more than reason, but was also elitist. Democratic theory, inherited from the eighteenth century, denied any basic difference between rulers and ruled, but administrative and professional practice in the democratic states of the Western world fits an elitist pattern too. Mass vs. elite, irrationalism vs. reason, spontaneity vs. control are different aspects of an apparent contradiction that runs throughout twentieth-century Western experience.

On a different plane, the historical vision of temporal process which attained such power during the nineteenth century continued to expand its domain as archaeology and the historical study of non-Western societies made world history for the first time a genuine possibility. Oswald Spengler (d. 1936) and Arnold J. Toynbee (d. 1975) were the two most influential scholars who treated other civilizations as equivalent to their own. The vision of history which put European or Chinese or some other part of mankind's total experience squarely in the center and neglected or dismissed all the rest began to lose ground; but no generally accepted alternative model for understanding the human past emerged. The Marxian model of progress—from slavery to serfdom, capitalism, socialism, and eventual communism—froze into dogma in the Soviet Union; elsewhere no consensus arose.

Discrepancies of viewpoint, multiplied enormously by the intellectual autonomy of a steadily widening number of professions, was thoroughly in accord with the pluralism of earlier Western tradition. With sufficient time perspective we may even discover unifying traits amidst what, to contemporaries, seems rampant confusion. Few societies have been as innovative as the Western world was in the first half of the twentieth century. Continued innovation in thought and practice, in science, art, and technology, in social and political organization, and in economic management, supported the continued predominance of Western styles of life throughout the world, and made Europe and its overseas extensions the heart and center of the world-wide cosmopolitan culture that increasingly bound all men into an interacting whole in the second half of the century.

CHAPTER 30

Global Rivalries and

Cosmopolitanism Since 1945

Before World War II, international politics centered in Europe. Old and famous nation states of that continent—France, Germany, Great Britain, and Italy—dominated the scene. In the Far East, Japan's imperial ambitions and China's internal disorders created a second, largely independent, storm center. The vast bulk of the U.S.S.R., and the only slightly smaller bulk of the United States, separated the European cockpit from the Far Eastern power struggle. These sleeping giants, as a matter of ideological principle, took only marginal parts in interwar political maneuvering. Colonial governors and officials kept the peace in Africa and southern Asia; Latin America fretted in the shadow of United States' economic power; while the British Commonwealth countries—Canada, Australia, New Zealand, and South Africa—were content to let others worry about international affairs.

This pattern was utterly disrupted by World War II. The U.S.S.R. and the United States emerged from the war as the two dominant powers of the globe. Strangely enough, the same ideological principles which before the war had made each of these countries unwilling to engage freely and as equals in the League of Nations and in other aspects of interwar diplomacy impelled both the Russians and the

Americans to interest themselves in the affairs of all parts of the post-war world. As Marxist-Leninists, the Russians felt called upon to be-friend communist movements which rose to prominence in Asia, Europe, and some other parts of the world; while the Americans, in defense of the Wilsonian vision of democratic self-determination, felt themselves called upon to halt the global spread of communism.

To be sure, it took a while for this "Cold War" alignment to de-fine itself. Most Americans at first expected to repeat in 1945 what their fathers had done in 1918: bring the troops home and disarm. The United Nations, sustained by a Great Power consensus, would take over the task of peacekeeping. The difficulty was that Great Power consensus was just as much lacking after 1945 as it had been after 1918. Efforts to agree upon terms for peace treaties with Germany and Japan proved futile; as a result, by 1947 the United States government con-cluded that withdrawal of its soldiers from Europe and Japan would have to wait until the expansive ambitions of Stalin's Russia had been "contained."

Exactly how Stalin saw matters in the postwar years remains a matter for speculation. He had a low opinion of foreign Communists and in 1945 perhaps did not expect Communist parties in China or eastern Europe to be able to take power. Yet he made it easy for American and other observers to believe that the Russians were master-minding a world-wide movement aimed at establishing Communist governments everywhere. Stalin reasserted Marxist orthodoxy in post-war Russia, and this doctrine predicted world revolution. He set up coalition regimes in the part of eastern Europe overrun by the Russian armies in 1944–45, and all these regimes became Communist party dictatorships within two years. He also tried half-heartedly to gain control of the Straits at the mouth of the Black Sea, and showed signs of wishing to expand into Iran. In Asia, meanwhile, Communists began to win control over China, and Communist-led guerrilla movements strove to seize power in several other Asian countries. In western Europe, Communist parties were also strong and talked much of revolu-tion. All this presumably seemed natural, necessary and desirable to the Russians—the working out of Marx's predictions of world revolu-tion. It seemed to Americans and many Europeans to be the result of a world conspiracy, centered in Moscow, stirring up revolution and civil war wherever postwar difficulties or social inequities allowed.

When a Communist guerrilla movement broke out in Greece, and threatened to overthrow the government there, the United States decided to intervene against the guerrillas. President Truman took the occasion, in March 1947, to urge Congress to approve a policy of opposing Communist movements whenever and wherever they resorted to force in an effort to seize power by revolutionary means. After three years the American effort in Greece proved successful; but a world-wide policy of nipping Communist revolutionary movements in the bud was more than the power, wealth and will of the United States could carry through.

In Europe, America's Cold War policy proved very successful. In 1948, the separate governments of western Europe worked out a European Recovery Plan. Congress made American funds available, and by 1953, when the program officially came to an end, economic prosperity and political stabilization had in fact been achieved in all parts of Europe that were not under Communist control. During the same years, economic plans, modeled on the Russian five-year plans, came into force in each of the east European countries under Communist rule. The result was relatively rapid economic development in all of eastern Europe. Efforts to develop trans-national markets and economic co-operation were spectacularly successful in western Europe; in eastern Europe separate national plans proved difficult to co-ordinate. Partly for this reason, the economic growth and continued technical advancement of western Europe outstripped the very considerable achievements of eastern Europe during the 1960's.

In other parts of the world, however, neither the Russian nor the American view of what was happening in the world and how to cope with it fitted the facts very adequately. From the Russian point of view, as Communist movements in western countries subsided after 1948, a fundamental discrepancy between expectation and experience grew ever greater. For revolutionary Marxism took hold not in lands where an industrial proletariat existed (as Marx and Lenin both had expected) but in countries where the overwhelming majority of the population were peasants, and where modern industry was only beginning to develop.

A second awkward point was that the international brotherhood predicted by Marx did not seem to result from revolutionary victories. New Communist governments did not show much desire to co-operate

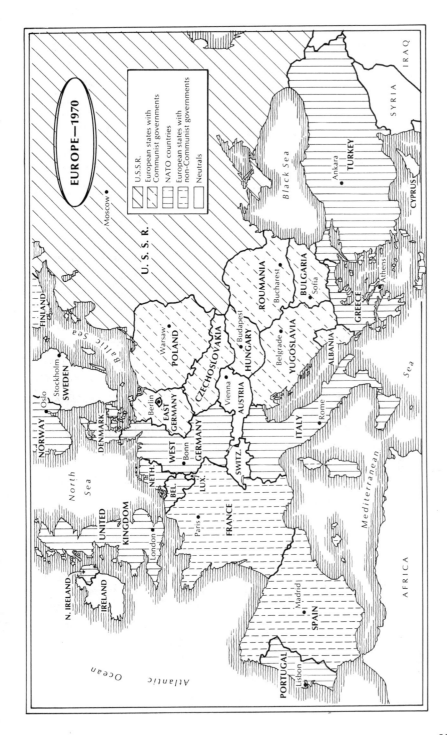

EUROPE—1970

U.S.S.R.

European states with
Communist governments

NATO countries

European states with
non-Communist governments

Neutrals

U. S. S. R.

Moscow

FINLAND

NORWAY

SWEDEN

Stockholm

Oslo

Baltic Sea

North Sea

DENMARK

Atlantic Ocean

N. IRELAND

IRELAND

UNITED KINGDOM

London

NETH.

BEL.

LUX.

WEST GERMANY

EAST GERMANY

Berlin

Bonn

POLAND

Warsaw

CZECHOSLOVAKIA

AUSTRIA

SWITZ.

Vienna

HUNGARY

Budapest

FRANCE

Paris

PORTUGAL

Lisbon

SPAIN

Madrid

ITALY

Rome

YUGOSLAVIA

Belgrade

ALBANIA

ROUMANIA

Bucharest

BULGARIA

Sofia

GREECE

Athens

Black Sea

TURKEY

Ankara

CYPRUS

SYRIA

IRAQ

Mediterranean Sea

AFRICA

519

with the Russians. This was particularly true of the Chinese, but the first public demonstration of a split in the Communist camp came when Stalin tried to assert control over Yugoslavia in 1948, and provoked instead a public denunciation of his domineering policy. Behind such strains lay the fact that nationalism and racial-cultural pride were not wiped away by Communist revolutions. On the contrary, Asian Communist movements were as much nationalist as Communist, and in attacking white imperialism also appealed to race feeling that was as much anti-Russian as anti-French or anti-British.

Still a third discrepancy between Russian ideology and the realities of the non-American, non-Russian world was the way in which European colonial empires were dismantled after World War II. The British led the way by withdrawing from India in 1947. Distrust between Moslems and Hindus had become acute, and the British decided to partition the country into a Moslem Pakistan and a Hindu India, as nearly as possible in accordance with the principle of majority rule. As British troops withdrew, massive riots broke out between the two religious communities, thousands were killed, and many more fled across the new borders to find refuge with their co-religionists. Despite this inauspicious start, after 1947 India and Pakistan enjoyed self-government. India (but not Pakistan) maintained a parliamentary, democratic form of government in spite of illiteracy, poverty, and regional differences. Almost as soon as India's independence had been achieved, the British also withdrew from Ceylon and Burma, although they remained in Malaya for a few years longer.

Once the British decided to withdraw from colonial administration as soon as local leaders could be found to take over the tasks of government, the process of decolonialization gathered headway very rapidly. Other colonial powers found it prudent to follow the British example. Thus, the first African colony to become independent was Ghana (former Gold Coast) in 1957. Within no more than five years, nearly all the other European colonies of Africa had also become independent, with the exception of Portuguese Angola and Mozambique.

To be sure, the European colonial powers were not always eager to withdraw. The Dutch tried briefly, for instance, to restore their rule in Indonesia but, when confronted by armed resistance, decided to yield (1949). The French tried much harder to restore their colonial position, but military resistance in Syria, and especially in Viet Nam, together with British colonial policy, eventually frustrated French efforts.

By far the most painful struggle occurred in Algeria, where large numbers of European settlers had made their homes. When Algerian Moslems began to agitate and presently to fight for independence, the settlers fought back. At first French opinion supported them, but as years of fighting dragged on, sentiment divided more and more sharply, until France came close to civil war. This provoked the return of General Charles de Gaulle to power in 1958. De Gaulle had led the Free French movement during the war and had briefly headed the restored French government, 1945–46. Upon his return to power he revised the constitution to give more authority to the head of state, and then as elected head of state, he used his powers to make peace in Algeria. In 1962, after seven years of fighting, France accepted the result of a popular vote that registered overwhelming support for Algerian independence.

Such a speedy and, in most cases, more or less peaceable dismantlement of European colonial empires resulted partly from changes in outlook among the European governments. For instance, the Labour Party of Great Britain, which came to power in 1946, disapproved of imperialism on principle and wanted to disentangle Britain from colonial responsibilities not only in India, but everywhere. A second factor was the rise of political consciousness among the various colonial peoples themselves. Independence movements roused resistance against foreign rule and at the same time created political structures that could take over the task of administration from European colonial officials. Ironically enough, populations that had to overcome initial resistance to independence were usually better prepared for self-government than lands like the Belgian Congo, where independence came almost as a gift.

In southeast Asia, ancient cultural and political differences reasserted themselves when French Indo China split apart into separate states: Viet Nam, Cambodia, Laos. Elsewhere, however, nearly all of the borders drawn by European administrators remained in existence. The reason was that in all of the newly independent states the tasks of government fell into the hands of new men, who had been educated in European types of schools. Traditional tribal groups, pre-European princely states, and the like were unable to break away from the political-administrative control exercised by the native-born successors of white colonial administrators. Efforts to do so, e.g. the Biafran revolt in Nigeria in the late 1960's, uniformly failed.

Both the United States and the Soviet Union approved the disappearance of European colonial empires. This was one of the reasons why the movement went ahead so rapidly once it got started. Yet neither of the great powers could be quite satisfied with the consequences. For one thing, a large number of "new nations" won a place in the United Nations General Assembly. There they constituted a "third world" bloc that on most issues refused to line up solidly with either the Communist-led or the American-led side of the Cold War. Moreover, Russian and American ideological expectations failed to be realized. The breakup of colonial empire did not hasten socialist revolution in the industrial countries of Europe. Ex-colonial powers prospered without their colonies. This exploded Lenin's explanation of why revolution had not come to western Europe when it should. (Lenin had accused the Western proletariat of sharing in the profits of imperialism, thus becoming exploiters of the colonial peoples and delaying the development of revolutionary consciousness in Europe.) From an American point of view, however, the development of independent Africa and Asia was not very reassuring either. Independence did not bring democracy and liberal institutions; on the contrary, one-party regimes and military dictatorships predominated.

From a strictly ideological point of view, it was often hard to see how Communist governments were further from American democratic ideals than many of these regimes. Yet the idea that a world-wide Communist conspiracy, controlled from Moscow, sought to undermine the peace and security of all the non-Communist world continued to command much support in the United States. This opinion, which had justified use of American resources to stabilize Europe between 1947 and 1953, had been powerfully reinforced by events in China, where American efforts to prop up the government headed by Chiang Kai-shek proved unavailing in face of Communist military victories.

Scarcely had the Chinese Communists taken power (1949) when a Communist government in North Korea attacked South Korea (1950). Americans saw this as one more step in the Communist plan of expansion. Since the Russians were boycotting its sessions at the time, the United States was able to get the United Nations Security Council to vote sanctions against the aggressor. American troops, together with smaller contingents from other members of the United Nations, thereupon intervened against the North Korean Communists. When the North Koreans were about to meet defeat, the Chinese came to their aid and soon drove the United Nations forces back to a line very close to the original demarcation between North and South Korea.

Stalemate on the battlefield eventually gave way to a truce (1953) which left both sides disgruntled by the upshot of their efforts. Japan, however, profited greatly from the Korean war, becoming a principal supplier of commodities needed by the United Nations forces. This expanded demand provided all the stimulus Japanese industry needed to recover from the devastation of World War II and start upon an upsurge that soon surpassed the economic recovery that was taking place at the same time in Germany.

International relations were deeply affected throughout the period of the Cold War by the fact that both the United States and the U.S.S.R. possessed nuclear weapons capable of devastating whole cities instantaneously. In 1945, atomic bombs were brand new and only the United States possessed them, thanks to secret wartime research. But Russia spared no effort to redress the balance. Technical secrets gathered by spies helped, but Soviet scientists and engineers surprised most Western experts by the speed with which they were able to duplicate the Americans' atomic weaponry. After the first Russian atomic explosions took place (1949) the United States government decided to start work on a far more powerful kind of nuclear warhead, the so-called H-bomb, whose energy derived from the same process of hydrogen fusion which fueled the sun and other stars. The Russians must have made the same decision at almost the same time. At any rate, they were only a few months behind the Americans in exploding the first hydrogen warheads (1953–54).

This drastic escalation of destructive capacity was promptly followed by another secret contest to see which side could first develop rockets capable of delivering nuclear warheads, if need be half way round the globe. By the early 1960's both Russia and the United States had rockets poised and ready to fire which were capable of devastating the others' cities within a period of about half an hour from the time someone decided to press the launch button. The balance of terror produced by this unprecedented situation clearly challenged the technical skills of the two nations to devise means for intercepting attack-

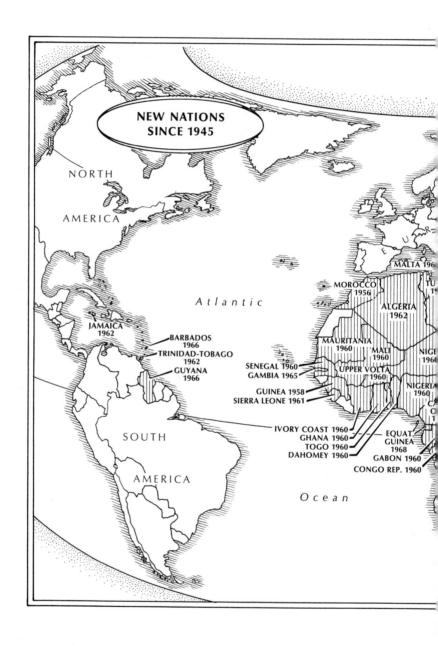

NEW NATIONS
SINCE 1945

NORTH

AMERICA

EUR

MALTA 196

Atlantic

MOROCCO
1956

TU
1

ALGERIA
1962

JAMAICA
1962

BARBADOS
1966

TRINIDAD-TOBAGO
1962

GUYANA
1966

MAURITANIA
1960

MALI
1960

NIGE
1960

SENEGAL 1960
GAMBIA 1965

UPPER VOLTA
1960

GUINEA 1958
SIERRA LEONE 1961

NIGERIA
1960

C
O
1

SOUTH

IVORY COAST 1960
GHANA 1960
TOGO 1960
DAHOMEY 1960

EQUAT.
GUINEA
1968

GABON 1960

AMERICA

CONGO REP. 1960

Ocean

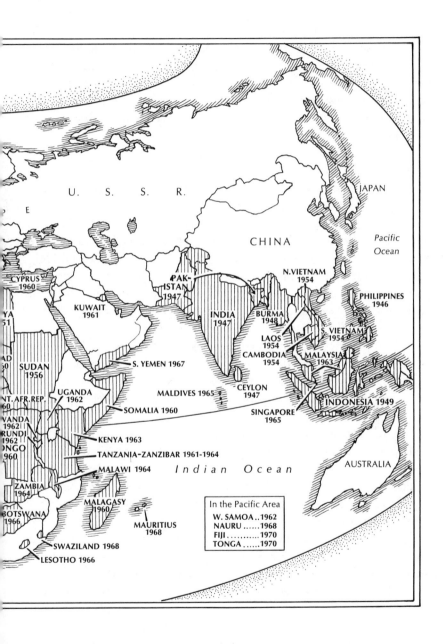

U. S. S. R.

E

CHINA

JAPAN

Pacific
Ocean

CYPRUS
1960

N.VIETNAM
1954

PAK-
ISTAN
1947

KUWAIT
1961

PHILIPPINES
1946

YA
51

INDIA
1947

BURMA
1948

LAOS
1954

S. VIETNAM
1954

AD
50

S. YEMEN 1967

CAMBODIA
1954

MALAYSIA
1963

SUDAN
1956

UGANDA
1962

MALDIVES 1965

CEYLON
1947

NT.AFR.REP.
60

INDONESIA 1949

SOMALIA 1960

SINGAPORE
1965

VANDA
1962
RUNDI
1962
NGO
960

KENYA 1963

TANZANIA-ZANZIBAR 1961-1964

MALAWI 1964

Indian Ocean

AUSTRALIA

ZAMBIA
1964

BOTSWANA
1966

MALAGASY
1960

MAURITIUS
1968

In the Pacific Area
W. SAMOA .. 1962
NAURU 1968
FIJI 1970
TONGA 1970

SWAZILAND 1968

LESOTHO 1966

ing rockets in flight at such a point in their trajectory that no damage would be done to the defending country. Countermeasures against interception included multiple warheads and rocket trajectories that could be altered in flight to dodge interceptors. As the decade of the 1970's began, this unremitting semi-secret struggle to win or retain technical advantage continued to demand a very considerable proportion of the national resources of both powers. Yet each technical escalation failed to guarantee either side a defense against the possibility of sudden, devastating, and total disaster.

Even in the 1950's, the threat of nuclear war probably had a restraining effect on both Russian and American policy. The two great powers more than once shied away from confrontations that threatened to bring nuclear weapons into action. Thus, the United States refrained from bombing China during the Korean war for fear that the Russians would come to the aid of the Chinese and thus provoke World War III. For the same reason, the United States did nothing in 1956 to aid Hungarian insurgents when they revolted against the Communist regime of that country. Similarly, the Russians backed away in 1962 when the United States discovered that Russian rockets were being installed in Cuba (where Fidel Castro had brought a revolutionary anti-American regime to power) and demanded that they be withdrawn. After a few tense days, the Russians decided to yield. To the bitter disappointment of the Cubans, who had hoped to encounter the United States armed as an equal, the Russians dismantled the missile sites and brought their technicians back home.

A remarkable by-product of the armaments race between Russia and America was the exploration of space. Rockets capable of carrying warheads half way round the earth were also capable of launching artificial earth satellites. The Russians were the first to accomplish this feat, in 1957. Four years later they achieved another breakthrough when Yuri Gagarin orbited the earth and descended safely. These Russian achievements provoked the American government to put great resources into space technology. As a result, in 1969 American space ships twice carried men to the moon and returned successfully to earth.

These spectacular technical achievements were only a small part of the exploitation and exploration of space. Unmanned rockets, equipped with various sensory instruments, ranged through the solar system to explore other planets circling the sun. In addition, a large number of artificial satellites were positioned far above the earth's atmosphere where they performed various functions: relaying radio and TV messages, photographing weather conditions, observing military installations. By 1970 spy satellites had penetrated much of the military secrecy which both Russians and Americans had once stressed. Oddly enough, this may have tended to reassure the rivals. Unannounced surprise attack became less likely when satellite observation systems could record the opening of each of the underground storage pits in which intercontinental rockets were emplaced.

An almost paralyzing fear of utter devastation in case of all-out war between the United States and the Soviet Union was another unexpected by-product of the armaments race. After both super powers had demonstrated their unwillingness to risk final confrontation with the other, their allies drew the conclusion that the dreadful nuclear weapons were not likely to be used against them either. The French, accordingly, withdrew in 1966 from the American-led military alliance, NATO (North Atlantic Treaty Organization, established 1949), while the Chinese reproached the Russians for their betrayal of true revolutionary Marxism. In 1961 the Russians responded by withdrawing technicians who had been helping the Chinese to build new factories.

Before long the Chinese-Russian quarrel echoed throughout the Communist world. Some European Communist governments leaned toward the Chinese as a way of escaping from too close Russian control; others flirted with Western liberalism. It became obvious that the Russians were unable to control Communist regimes in other countries. Behind and only imperfectly obscured by ideological argument about the "true" Marxist-Leninist line, long standing national, cultural, and racial antipathies found abundant expression within the Communist camp. A similar development occurred among the ranks of America's Cold War allies. Obviously, the Cold War line-up between a Russian-led coalition and an American-led coalition had worn itself out even in Europe, where the Cold War had started, and where, during the 1950's, it had fitted the political facts far better than anywhere else in the world.

In Africa, Asia and the Middle East, the rivalry between the United States and the Soviet Union impinged upon other deep-seated differences that did not fit in well with the simplicity of a capitalist-communist or liberal-Marxist ideological polarity. Ever since World War II, old lines of cultural differentiation, dressed up in new nationalist and revolutionary (often Marxist) language, and usually exacerbated by race and/or religious feeling, gave the politics of Africa, Asia and the Middle East a distinctive and frequently violent tone.

The Russians collided with this reality in their quarrel with China after 1961. The United States had a far more painful encounter with it in Vietnam between 1964 and 1973. The American government initially began sending troops to Vietnam in order to help a non-Communist regime in south Vietnam defend itself against Communist subversion from the north. To begin with, it looked like Korea all over again, and American Cold War principles called for help to any government that tried to defend itself against forcible Communist takeover. But the realities in Vietnam were utterly different from those of Korea. Where Korean nationalism had in fact been mobilized behind the United Nations effort and against the Russian puppets in the north, in Vietnam this relationship was reversed. In the eyes of most Vietnamese, the rulers of South Vietnam were puppets in the hands of white foreigners—first the French (until 1954) and then the Americans. Hence after 1964, nationalistic and racial chauvinism combined to support a revolutionary effort to throw out the new American imperialists. When heavy fighting broke out, Russian military supplies helped to counterbalance the otherwise crushing superiority of American equipment.

For a long time, American officials deceived themselves about the political realities of Vietnam. Only when a large proportion of the American public began to challenge the rightfulness of the country's action did President Richard Nixon decide to withdraw the United States' armed forces from Vietnam in 1973. Repudiation of Cold War interpretations of international realities became general in the United States after 1973, but no clear consensus replaced that idea. Contrary impulses—to withdraw within national frontiers on the one hand, or to settle all the world's problems by a deal with the Russians (and/or with the Chinese) on the other—vied for dominance; a mood of irritable indifference toward the continuing upheavals in Asian, African, and even Latin American lands tended to prevail.

There were plenty of such conflicts. Hindu India and Moslem Pakistan remained at loggerheads, and when East Pakistan revolted and established itself as the independent state of Bangladesh in 1971, it did so with the armed support of India. In Africa, race conflict in Rhodesia and South Africa between whites and blacks provided an ominous background for struggles amongst the newly independent states of Africa and of factions within such states that often boiled over into local violence. The vain effort of Biafra to secede from Nigeria between 1967 and 1970, armed contests for control of the copper-rich southern province of Zaire in 1960 and 1978, and the bitter warfare between Ethiopian and Somali populations in east Africa in 1977–78 were among the more massive of these disturbances. Without exception, they reflected ethnic more than ideological rivalries; but the great powers had difficulty staying out because of their roles as suppliers of arms for the contestants.

Another region of the world where the Communist vs. non-Communist line-up failed to fit very well was the Middle East. In 1947 the Jewish state of Israel came into existence through armed action, directed partly against the British (who had administered Palestine since World War I) and partly against Arabs, who had lived in Palestine since the time of the Moslem conquest. The Jews were inspired by nationalistic and religious sentiment which had been enormously inflamed by the effort Hitler made during World War II to destroy the Jewish population of Europe. Millions of Jews were in fact uprooted from their homes in Europe, and millions whose labor the Nazis did not need were killed in gas chambers designed for the purpose. At least six million Jews—men, women, and children—died at the Nazis' hands. Those who survived found it hard to resume life in Europe. Large numbers of European Jews therefore decided that migration to Palestine, the Holy Land where Judaism first had taken form, was the only way to escape from being a persecuted minority. But the establishment of a Jewish majority and of a Jewish state in Palestine required large-scale displacement of the Arabs who were living there. And when the Jews took matters into their own hands and set up the new state of Israel by force, the Arabs in neighboring countries as well as those of Palestine itself felt deeply affronted. National pride as well as the injunctions of the Koran (which provided a tolerated but subordinate status for Jews as well as for Christians within Moslem society) were irreconcilable with the rise of Israel. No Arab government was therefore ready to accept the existence of an Israeli state, even when the United Nations decreed (1947) that Palestine should be divided between Jews and Arabs. Efforts to strengthen the Arab position by creating a United Arab Republic met with little success. Syria and

Egypt did unite in 1958, but the other Arab states held back, and Syria broke away again in 1961. Party and regional rivalries as well as poverty and technical backwardness continued to afflict Arab lands; but such shortcomings helped to fire popular hatred both against Israel and against Jews who had lived for centuries as inconspicuous minorities in many Moslem lands. A fresh wave of Jewish immigration from the Moslem world resulted, making Israel less purely a European type of society than it had been originally.

Uneasy truce in the Middle East was punctuated by flare-ups of active war in 1948–49, 1956, 1967 and 1973. In the first three of these wars, the Israelis won; and were able, in 1967, to establish their control over all of Jerusalem while extending their outposts to the Jordan river on the east and the Suez canal on the west. In 1973, however, the fighting was more nearly even and the truce that followed saw an Israeli withdrawal from the banks of the Suez canal, which was reopened for ordinary use soon thereafter under Egyptian management.

Arab-Israeli confrontation got more complicated in the late 1970's when quarrels among Arab factions resulted in the near dissolution of the state of Lebanon, on Israel's northern border. Simultaneously, the Egyptians tried to negotiate some sort of lasting peace agreement with Israel, but despite enthusiastic American encouragement, nothing definite emerged from this initiative in 1978.

Like all the other local conflicts on the face of the globe into which ethnic, tribal and religious antagonisms entered so centrally, the balance of forces in the Middle East depended directly on the supply of arms coming from the great powers. Early in its independent career, Israel got arms from France at a time when the French were also fighting Moslems in Algeria; when French policy reversed itself and began to seek rapprochement with the Algerians and other Moslems, Israel turned mainly to the United States, where pro-Israeli sentiment was strong, especially among American Jews. The Soviet Union undertook to supply Egypt with arms after 1956, when a combined French, British, and Israeli attack on Egypt was checked in its initial stages by United Nations' action. (This, incidentally, was one of the few occasions when the United States and the Soviet Union found themselves on the same side of an international issue in the postwar period.) But Russian-American co-operation in the Middle East was short lived. By the 1960's, the two great powers seemed pitted against each other:

Israel dependent on arms from the United States, the Arab states dependent on arms from the Soviet Union. Then after the 1973 war, the Egyptian government made an about-face and broke with the Russians. Thereafter, the United States found itself in the position of supplying arms to both sides and trying to put some sort of ceiling on the arms race by balancing off deliveries to one side against deliveries to the other.

A new factor in the Middle East situation was the growing dependence of the United States and most of the rest of the non-Communist world on oil imported from the Persian Gulf region. This gave Arab oil-producing lands an enormous influence over the economic life of the industrial countries, a fact dramatically demonstrated in 1974 when the oil exporting countries of the world got together and abruptly doubled the price of oil. The enhanced inflow of funds which the new oil prices brought to the oil-exporting Arab lands widened the gap between rich and poor states in the Middle East, and introduced a new instability into world economic and political relations.

These and other potential trouble spots (Africa, Latin America) promised to keep the peace of the world in jeopardy for an indefinite time. Internal strains within each and all of the world's great states also suggested the possibility of some sudden revolutionary outbreak that might alter the world balance in a sharp and sudden way. Moreover, the apocalyptic vision of nuclear war, destroying cities in an instant and perhaps ending human and all higher forms of animal life on earth, continued to threaten all customary routines and values. As additional states acquired the capacity to build nuclear weapons (Great Britain, France, China, India, and Israel) obstacles to any effective international control became greater, and the possibility of nuclear war presumably increased.

Yet in the years since the first atomic bomb was dropped (1945) the terrible weapon has not again been used, despite all the local wars and constant diplomatic friction that has characterized the post-World War II period. Schemes for disarmament, or at least for an agreed standstill in the development of new and still more costly weapons systems, may some day bring a halt or at least an intermission to the great power armaments race. Efforts in this direction did achieve a SALT (Strategic Arms Limitation Treaty) agreement between the United States and the Soviet Union in 1974, but when this treaty expired in 1977, negotiations for its renewal proved unexpectedly difficult. Obstacles to establishing the level of mutual trust needed to make any agreement work are enormous. Little can be accomplished as long as local political tensions continue to align the world's two greatest nuclear powers almost invariably on opposite sides.

Social and Cultural Changes

‡‡‡ At the close of World War II the social and cultural conditions under which men lived varied enormously from country to country, and within particular countries as well. Nothing since the war has made such contrasts less sharp. Detailed description is impossible; all that can here be attempted is a few general observations on trends that appear to be world wide, or nearly so.

One obvious and overriding fact was the rapid growth of population. Population increased in every country of the world, but most rapidly in the poorer, predominantly peasant countries of Asia, Africa, and Latin America. Elementary public health measures which checked the spread of disease probably accounted for much of the population growth of these countries. In most of the world, traditional family patterns were attuned to maintaining human life under conditions in which as many as half of all children died within their first ten years. As sanitation, innoculation, and the availability of more effective medical aid allowed more of those born to attain childbearing age, population growth quickly became explosive. This is what seems to have happened among all the world's peasant populations since World War II, when new drugs and chemical sprays for the first time allowed public health officials to control many infectious diseases and to reduce malaria and some other endemic afflictions. An enlarged food supply, thanks to better seeds, fertilizers, and distribution facilities, also sustained population growth, though in poorer parts of the world the increase in food supply barely kept up with the increase in hungry mouths. Still a third factor in the increase of human numbers was reduction in deaths by violence. Despite continued warfare, it was probably true that human slaughter became rarer in the world as a whole. After all, modern governments try hard to monopolize lethal violence, and have been a good deal more successful in doing so than was possible before improved communications allowed administrative centralization and control to become as efficient as it is today.

Population growth, however, threatened to become a cause for fresh outbreaks of violence. Increasing numbers made it ever more difficult for poor lands to satisfy mass needs and rising expectations. In the decades after World War II, rural population growth put severe pressure on all traditional peasant societies. Millions of young people, lacking any prospect of making a satisfactory living in the country, migrated to cities, hoping to scrape a living there. Such floating populations of ex-peasants found it hard to prosper in town. They provided tinder for extremist political movements of quite diverse kinds.

Political power passed into the hands of urbanized ex-peasants in most parts of Asia and Africa and in some parts of Latin America after World War II. The rulers of the "new nations" usually came from such backgrounds, and they set out boldly, though not always very successfully, to remake the social structure according to their will. Usually this meant building up an armed force equipped with the best available weapons; sometimes it meant investment in education, and construction of transportation facilities, factories, and other appurtenances of modernity. Always it centered upon a wish to make state, nation, and people strong and respected. The more humiliating recent history was felt to be, the fiercer was the desire to escape from the past.

States where no such revolutionary cliques came to power still saw their leaders undertake wholesale modernization on a vast scale. This was true of the most industrialized European and American countries as well as of Asian (e.g. Japan) and African (e.g. Union of South Africa) states where politically conservative regimes remained in office. And after Stalin's death in 1953, the Soviet Union continued to be dominated by men who sought to modernize the economy and technology of their land at almost any cost.

Modernization more and more meant the concentration of vast human and material resources for achieving politically defined goals. It therefore involved the spread of techniques of mobilization that had been worked out, for the most part, initially during World War I and applied as peacetime measures for the first time in the depression years of the early 1930's. Communist regimes resorted to drastic social mobilization as a matter of course, borrowing methods mainly from the Soviet Union. Capitalist regimes mobilized their populations, and balanced the commitment of other resources among competing goals, by indirect fiscal methods for the most part, although the military establishments of the great powers, not least that of the United States, operated on principles that closely resembled Communist command economies.

In the so-called "Third World," the nations belonging neither to the Communist nor to the technically advanced capitalist bloc, one-party governments and military dictatorships, which everywhere prevailed, used a hodgepodge of methods in pursuit of their chosen socioeconomic, political, and military goals. Such efforts were usually less effective than either Communist or capitalist methods of mobilization, if only because of administrative and technical inexpertness.

Mobilization and modernization everywhere put great emphasis upon the military. The simple military chain of command offered by far the easiest and most obvious pattern for government; and arms races offered by far the greatest scope for mobilizing fresh human and material resources in the service of governments that felt endangered by foreign or domestic foes. This was obviously true of the two great powers, each of which put a large proportion of their entire national product into making and maintaining new and vastly complex weapons systems. Weak African, Asian, and Latin American governments also strained their resources to import armaments from outside suppliers. Sometimes they even traded away the substance of sovereignty by becoming dependent on a single foreign power for the supply of spare parts needed to maintain complicated weaponry. This was dramatically demonstrated in 1965, when Indian and Pakistani tank forces fought one another for a few days, but halted when Great Britain, which had equipped both armies with tanks, refused to supply either side with the spare parts needed to keep the machines in motion for more than a few weeks.

Bureaucratization went hand in hand with modernization and militarization. As government took responsibility for an increasing array of tasks, governmental officials who were appointed, and not elected, took a larger and larger share in making political decisions. But not all bureaucracies were governmental. Big corporations, sometimes operating in many different countries on a globe-girdling basis, also availed themselves of the principles of bureaucracy to co-ordinate the actions of large numbers of men across long reaches of time and space. As long as bureaucracy can in fact achieve such co-ordination—and there is no sign that limits have yet come into sight—the efforts of individuals to assert personal independence by "dropping out," or refusing to recognize official obligations, powers, rights, and privileges, do not seem at all likely to present any effective check on bureaucratic power. Ironically, if protest is to become effective, it, too, must become bureaucratic. Systematic refusal to organize dooms those who repudiate bureaucracy to permanent ineffectiveness.

Technical improvements in data storage and retrieval, which have developed very rapidly since World War II, seem to extend the reach of bureaucracy even further. Electronic computers, first developed during World War II, allow control, at least in principle, not merely of inventories, balance books, and space flights, but of individual lives as well. Even more alarming to men who treasure a perhaps illusory personal autonomy is the possibility of deliberate manipulation of human genetics, which recent advances in biological science suggest may become possible before very long. In 1953 James Watson and F. H. C. Crick developed a model for the DNA molecule that carries genetic heritage from generation to generation in plants and animals. Investigation of the enormously complex DNA structure has since confirmed the accuracy of their model, but exactly how atom-shuffling within the structure can produce differences in full grown organisms has not yet been worked out. When and if such details become known, the next step would be to make deliberate alterations in genetic material so as to produce new organisms, including, perhaps, creatures who would properly deserve the name, Post-human.

Of course, techniques for controlling biological evolution may never become available. Nuclear war may destroy us all instead; industrial by-products may upset the earth's ecology so severely that human life as we know it may become impossible; or the population explosion may create mass famine, bringing down the whole apparatus of scientific research and refined machine technology.

Such visions of catastrophe easily arise when one thinks of the future. On the other hand, in any judicious appraisal of world history one ought to recognize the conservative forces that continue to affect human life. Old demarcations of civilization are still plain to be seen; there is truth in the phrase "Plus ça change, c'est plus la même chose."

The Chinese Communists, for instance, though they repudiated Confucian philosophy, acted very like a new dynasty from China's Confucian past. Similarly, Moslems retain an inherited antipathy to the West which makes it harder for them to imitate European or American skills than it is for the heirs of other cultures. And the political pluralism and ramshackle administration of India derives as much from the Hindu tradition as from anything the Indians learned from their British rulers or any other foreigners.

It is interesting to observe how other civilizations' religious traditions are seeping into the Western world as a kind of heresy, consciously opposed to the mainstream of modern, Western development. Thus, a number of black Americans were attracted to Islam (in altered form, to be sure) because that faith stood so strongly in opposition to things Western. Other dissenters preferred Zen Buddhism or vaguer kinds of mysticism that derived at least part of their inspiration from Indian roots.

From the point of view of conservative Moslems, Hindus, Buddhists, or Confucians, Western cultural traditions played exactly the same role as their own traditions played for the West, but on a more massive and threatening scale. For we should remember that all the groups and individuals in Asia and Africa who wished to attain wealth and power by adopting and adapting Western techniques ranked as heretics in the eyes of their more conservative fellows. It seems probable that mutual interpenetration among the world's traditional civilizations will continue, so that locally dominant traditions will everywhere confront dissenting groups whose inspiration derives, at least in part, from a civilization or cultural tradition which once existed only in some distant part of the globe. The acceleration of communication and greater ease of travel across long distances makes such a development very likely.

Radical rejection of every form of inheritance from the remoter past can hardly become so powerful that cultural survivals and revivals will fade away to triviality. To be sure, disenchanted youth exist in almost every country of the world, and many of them say that they repudiate everything transmitted from their forebears. Drug-induced hallucination can indeed break nearly all bonds with the cultural past (and present); but it seems unlikely that a society could survive even for a single generation if hallucination became chronic and wholesale.

Those who refrain from taking drugs have a far greater chance of surviving and leaving children behind them. It therefore seems unlikely that human beings will "escape" the past. Even those most passionately in revolt against aspects of that past are still its prisoners, in the sense that what they chose to reject and the methods by which their rejection finds expression are governed by the cultural inheritance that lies at their disposal and by the reactions their behavior provokes on the part of defenders of the old order.

Rapid social change, pressing hard against the limits of what people can bear, seems certain to continue to afflict humankind as it has during the past twenty-five years. The whole process may be conceived as a kind of race between the rational, disciplined, co-operative potentialities of humankind, and the urge to destroy, which also lurks in every human psyche. This is not really very new. Humans have always been capable both of love and of hate, of co-operation and of destruction, of thinking and of throwing tantrums. The difference is one of scale, for with the enormously expanded power we now command, the possibilities of irremediable destruction as well as of grandiose construction appear to be vastly greater than in any previous age.

Private lives may become more anxious as a wider range of choices opens, for without firm traditional rules for personal conduct—which everywhere threaten to break down—all kinds of awkward decisions have to be made. But bureaucracy offers an enormously capacious refuge; where religious and other traditional codes to behavior are lacking, official rules and regulations can take over and frequently have done so. New persons, with new styles of dress, new manners, new habits, can be created within a few years. In this way personal isolation and distress seem likely to generate their own cure in the form of party rituals, bureaucratic routines, military codes of conduct, and the like. And even new minted codes of manners have to draw upon elements of the past for their component parts. They often shape their outward manifestations by a conscious opposition to prevailing styles among those whom the innovaters detest. Long hair, for instance, derived part of its charm for young American males in the 1960's from the fact that soldiers were required to crop their hair short, and Russian city folk since 1917 have chosen the Western bourgeois costume of suit and pants as sign and symbol of their escape from peasant status.

Art, Science, and Technology

‡‡‡ It seems impossible to make sensible general statements about world-wide developments in art since 1945. Some styles have been adopted round the world—airport architecture, for example. In terms of quantity, more words have been written and more people have devoted their lives to art in all its different forms since 1945 than ever before. Perhaps future ages will discern greatness amidst the tumult, or perhaps artistic and intellectual synthesis on a grand scale will have to await some future slowing down of social change. For it is arguable that thinkers and artists need an audience that shares a wide range of common presuppositions and experiences with one another and with the artist himself before really great, potentially classical works of art can be produced. Such an audience does not exist today in most of the world.

Science and technology, on the other hand, continue to rush ahead, becoming so specialized that no one can understand or keep up with all discoveries in all the different fields. Significant breakthroughs concentrated especially in molecular biology in the 1950's and 1960's. The decipherment of DNA was only one of many chemical analyses of biological molecules and processes. Complete chemical description of even the simplest organism still remained beyond the reach of science; but the drive to reduce organic phenomena to their chemical manifestations achieved extraordinary successes.

Exploration of the atmosphere and of space, made possible by rockets equipped with delicate mechanical sensors, yielded much new information about earth and its environs. Radio astronomy gained a vast range of new data about the deeper reaches of space; and the first successful moon landings allowed small quantities of moon rock to reach scientific laboratories for analysis and for comparison with materials of the earth.

Altogether, the outreach of man's scientific knowledge continued, in these and other fields, on a scale unequaled in earlier times. A major reason for this fact was that massive government funds were made available to scientists even for abstract theoretical research. Experiments requiring elaborate and costly equipment could thus be undertaken, just in the hope that something interesting might turn up. Anyone who had attained a minimal professional standing among fellow scientists, and who had an idea that seemed at all promising, met with few financial obstacles to testing it experimentally. Scientists had never before commanded such respect or such economic support.

In technology the same was true. Private corporations and governmental officials alike had become convinced by the experience of World War II that systematic search for new techniques paid off. Radar, the controlled release of nuclear energy, and jet propulsion for aircraft, which were developed during the war, all found important applications in peacetime. The most spectacular new developments continued to concentrate in the military field, where hydrogen fusion reactions, intercontinental rockets, and extraordinary communications and control networks were created almost regardless of cost. These were, however, only a small part of the technical novelties of the post-World War II decades. Chemical fertilizers, together with weed and insect killers and scientifically designed animal feeds, seed selection, and animal breeding, changed agriculture drastically in all the industrially advanced countries. An array of new drugs, some of these derived from molds and other organisms, made most infections and some chronic diseases curable. Miniaturization of electronic switches and other parts made complex computers possible and allowed sensitive control devices to fit into corners and crevices of the first space capsules. And on a more everyday level, television invaded millions of homes in Europe and America, and deeply affected and enlarged the daily experience of its viewers. New materials, synthesized in chemists' laboratories, assumed increasingly important roles in industry. Airplanes supplanted railroads and ships as the dominant mode of long-distance travel. Long-distance telephone communication also improved and tended to supplant letters and telegrams for many purposes.

A by-product of the increasing complexity of science and technology was that backward nations and regions of the world found it harder and harder to take any active role in new developments. Relatively vast physical resources and a large pool of skilled manpower were required for scientific and technical research. New developments demanded new equipment and skills which poor and small countries found it next to impossible to supply. Even strenuous efforts to come abreast of modern science and technology often failed to do more than keep the gap between world leaders and backward areas from widening. Small countries often suffered a "brain drain." Their most promising scientists and technicians were easily lured away to major centers of research in other countries, where their aptitudes could find fuller scope than was possible in their native lands.

A second consequence of the development of science and technology was that even in the most industrially advanced parts of the earth, most human beings could not understand what scientists and technicians were doing. They could not even understand how very familiar everyday machines worked. Radio and television sets, for example, remained a mystery to most of those who listened and viewed; industrial processes often remained mysterious even to the men who worked in the plants where they took place. Thus a widening gap between technically advanced and technically backward lands was matched by a widening gap between expert elites (mutually ignorant of one another's skills, of course) and the mass of common people. Admired and favored as scientists and technicians were in the decades after World War II, such a social position was intrinsically precarious. Indeed the position of a modern scientist can best be compared to the role played by priests in early river valley civilizations of the Near East. Barbarian invasions and domestic rebellion more than once endangered the ancient priestly profession; yet new rulers always needed the priests' expertise in dealing with the gods, and they regularly reinstated them. Scientists and technicians today enjoy a similar status in most civilized countries, mediating between humankind and the same mysterious powers and potentialities of nature which ancient priests sought to propitiate by worshipping their gods.

Conclusion

‡‡‡ Anyone reflecting upon the tangled and tumultuous record of human life on earth, even as summarized and abbreviated in this book, is likely to feel distressed at all the brutality and stupidity humans have shown to one another across time. War and preparation for war echoes through all the past. Political power has shifted with changes in military methods and weaponry everywhere and always. Technological advances, too, have often been provoked by men's efforts to kill one another or to guard against being killed.

On the other hand, it is worth pondering the fact that the civilized societies that have flourished and grown great in times past all accepted ethical systems that emphasized kindliness and love. All the major world religions taught such doctrines; and persons who in some measure or other tried to live in accordance with the precepts of their faith were probably more likely to leave descendants than those who rejected kindliness as a principle of conduct.

Cynical rejection of humane and peaceful ideals is therefore as mistaken as the confusion of such ideals with reality. Human life has always existed under tension, between fear and hope. This tension will not disappear in our age. Quite the contrary. But for that very reason wisdom and courage, operating, as usual, between hope and fear, are likely to find more than usual scope, if only because the risks of disaster and the possibilities of advance toward a more humane world society are both so great.

Bibliographical Essay, Part IV

Books which seem worth serious attention that try to explain the over-all direction or significance of mankind's recent and contemporary public experience include: Kenneth Boulding, *The Meaning of the Twentieth Century: The Great Transition* (New York, 1964); Robert L. Heilbroner, *The Future as History* (New York, 1960); Cyril E. Black, *The Dynamics of Modernization* (New York, 1966); Daniel Bell, *The End of Ideology*, rev. ed. (New York, 1962); Filmer S. C. Northrop, *The Meeting of East and West* (New York, 1946); Charles P. Snow, *The Two Cultures, and a Second Look*, 2nd ed. (Cambridge, 1964); Siegfried Giedion, *Mechanization Takes Command* (New York, 1948); Geoffrey Barraclough, *An Introduction to Contemporary History* (New York, 1965); Norbert Wiener, *The Human Use of Human Beings, Cybernetics and Society* (Garden City, N.Y., 1954); and John R. Platt, *The Step to Man* (New York, 1966).

International politics are handled by A. J. P. Taylor, *The Struggle for Mastery in Europe, 1848–1918* (Oxford, 1954); William L. Langer, *European Alliances and Alignments, 1871–1890*, 2nd ed. (New York, 1962), and William L. Langer, *The Diplomacy of Imperialism, 1890–1902*, 2nd ed. (New York, 1951); R. Albrecht-Carrié, *A Diplomatic History of Europe since the Congress of Vienna* (New York, 1958); and G. M. Gathorne-Hardy, *A Short History of International Affairs, 1920–1939*, 4th ed. (London, 1950).

On imperialism, the authoritative Marxist interpretation is Vladimir I. Lenin, *Imperialism, The Highest Stage of Capitalism* (New York, 1939). Joseph A. Schumpeter, *Imperialism and Social Classes* (New York, 1955) and Stewart C. Easton, *The Rise and Fall of Western Colonialism* (New York, 1964) address themselves to the same themes with somewhat different emphasis. On war, Theodore J. Ropp, *War in the Modern World*, rev. ed. (New York, 1962) is recommended. For the prelude to World War I see:

Laurence Lafore, *The Long Fuse: An Interpretation of the Origins of World War I* (Philadelphia, 1965), and Fritz Fischer, *Germany's Aims in the First World War* (New York, 1967). On the war itself see: Marc Ferro, *The Great War, 1914-1918* (London, 1973). Two particularly vivid and revelatory accounts of separate campaigns are Barbara Tuchman, *The Guns of August* (New York, 1962), which portrays the German advance on Paris in 1914, and I. McD. G. Stewart, *The Struggle for Crete, 20 May-1 June, 1941* (London, 1966). Raymond Aron, *The Century of Total War* (Boston, 1955), offers striking opinions about how war is altering society in the twentieth century.

On the Russian Revolution, John Reed, *Ten Days that Shook the World* (New York, 1919) is a famous eyewitness account by a passionately involved journalist. Leon Trotsky, *History of the Russian Revolution*, 3 vols. (London, 1932-33) is a brilliant, analytical history written by one of the protagonists of the revolution. Students should consult the interpretations put forth by E. H. Carr, *The Bolshevik Revolution, 1917-1923*, 3 vols. (New York, 1951-52) and William H. Chamberlin, *The Russian Revolution*, 2 vols. (New York, 1935). Richard E. Pipes, *The Formation of the Soviet Union: Communism and Nationalism 1917-1923* (Cambridge, Mass., 1964); Isaac Deutscher, *The Prophet Armed, Trotsky, 1879-1921* (New York, 1954) and his other biography, *Stalin, A Political Biography*, 2nd ed. (New York, 1967) are thorough, scholarly and more or less detached. Adam Ulam, *The Bolsheviks* (New York, 1965) is also recommended. On the background of the revolution, Donald M. Wallace, *Russia* (London, 1877) and Franco Venturi, *Roots of Revolution* (New York, 1960) are particularly illuminating.

For the great depression of the 1930's see: Charles P. Kindleberger, *The World in Depression, 1929-1939* (Berkeley, 1973) and for the United States, Albert U. Romasco, *The Poverty of Abundance* (New York, 1965). On the Spanish civil war, Hugh Thomas, *The Spanish Civil War*, rev. ed. (London, 1977) is a balanced account. For fascism, F. L. Carsten, *The Rise of Fascism* (Berkeley, 1967); Hanna Arendt, *The Origins of Totalitarianism*, 2nd ed. (London, 1961); Ernst Nolte, *Three Faces of Fascism* (New York, 1968); Alan Bullock, *Hitler: A Study in Tyranny*, rev. ed. (New York, 1962); and Stuart J. Woolf, ed., *European Fascism* (London, 1968) are all respectable works. Adolf Hitler, *Mein Kampf, Complete and Unabridged* (New York, 1939) and the article "Fascism," published originally in the *Encyclopedia Italiana* and often reprinted—e.g. in Benito Mussolini, *Fascism: Doctrine and Institutions* (New York, 1968)—are scarcely respectable (at least in academic circles) but they reveal much about the political climate of the 1920's from which Fascism grew. Albert Speer, *Inside the Third Reich* (New York, 1970) provides an insider's account of Hitler's rule.

The works of Karl Marx, Charles Darwin, Sigmund Freud, John Maynard Keynes, Alfred Kroeber, and their like are by far the best introduction to the major movements of thought and sensibility that have altered the intellectual climate drastically since 1850. Helpful secondary accounts of intellectual and cultural changes and influences include: Jacques Barzun, *Darwin, Marx, Wagner: Critique of a Heritage*, rev. ed. (New York, 1958); three books by Henry Stuart Hughes, *Consciousness and Society: The Reorientation of European Social Thought, 1890–1930* (New York, 1958); *The Obstructed Path* (New York, 1968); and *The Sea Change* (New York, 1975); Ernest Jones, *The Life and Work of Sigmund Freud*, 3 vols. (New York, 1953–57); Leonard Krieger, *The German Idea of Freedom* (Boston, 1957); George L. Mosse, *The Culture of Western Europe: The Nineteenth and Twentieth Centuries* (Chicago, 1961); George P. Gooch, *History and Historians in the Nineteenth Century*, 2nd rev. ed. (London, 1962); Fritz Stern, *The Politics of Cultural Despair* (New York, 1965); Edmund Wilson, *Axel's Castle: A Study of the Imaginative Literature of 1870–1930* (New York, 1931); and Mary M. Colum, *From These Roots: The Ideas that Have Made Modern Literature* (New York, 1937). On the leading ideologies of the nineteenth century see: Guido de Ruggiero, *The History of European Liberalism* (London, 1927) and G. D. H. Cole, *A History of Socialist Thought*, 5 vols. (London, 1953–60). Oron J. Hale, *The Great Illusion, 1900–1914* (New York, 1971) and Raymond Sontag, *A Broken World, 1919–1939* (New York, 1971) cast light on European society in the early twentieth century. André Malraux, *Anti-Memoirs* (New York, 1968) is the personal statement of a man who experienced and reflected upon a wide range of historical events.

World War II provoked an enormous official historiography on the part of the victors. Samuel Eliot Morrison's *History of U.S. Naval Operations in World War II*, 15 vols. (Boston, 1947–62) is a remarkable example of the genre of official history; only slightly less impressive in Wesley F. Craven and James L. Cate, eds., *The Army Air Force in World War II*, 6 vols. (Chicago, 1948–58). The official British *History of the Second World War* also contains some excellent volumes, as does the Royal Institute of International Affairs, *Survey of International Affairs, 1939–1946*. J. V. Stalin, *On the Great Patriotic War of the Soviet Union* (New York, 1945) is interesting for the slant it brings to the subject—very different from American and English views. All earlier efforts at brief interpretation have been left behind by Gordon Wright, *The Ordeal of Total War, 1939–1954* (New York, 1968). A provocative reinterpretation of Hitler's international policies is A. J. P. Taylor, *The Origins of the Second World War* (London, 1961).

The Cold War too has an abundant historiography. Louis J. Halle, *The*

Cold War as History (London, 1967), Norman A. Graebner, *Cold War Diplomacy, 1945–1960* (Princeton, 1962), and André Fontaine, *History of the Cold War,* 2 vols. (New York, 1968–69) are among the more detached accounts. For Asia, see the volume: Akira Iriye and Yonosuke Nagai, eds., *The Origins of the Cold War in Asia* (New York, 1977). Dexter Perkins, *The Diplomacy of a New Age* (Bloomington, 1967), tends to support the official American view that the Russians were centrally at fault in provoking the Cold War; Denna F. Fleming, *The Cold War and Its Origins, 1917–1960* (Garden City, N.Y., 1961) and Guy Alperovitz, *Atomic Diplomacy: Hiroshima and Potsdam* (New York, 1965) are generally critical of official United States positions. For Soviet foreign policy see: Adam Ulam, *Expansion and Co-existence: The History of Soviet Foreign Policy 1917–1967* (New York, 1968). Some of the ideas which underlay American policy during the period of the Cold War were articulated in George F. Kennan, *American Diplomacy, 1900–1950* (Chicago, 1951).

European and American writers and historians have long assumed that movements and revolutions in their own cultural universe are equivalent to world transformations; and, as modern communications and transport have linked the world more and more closely, this assumption becomes less naive than it used to be. Yet the reception and reactions to new ideas and techniques varies infinitely; the books mentioned below show some of this diversity.

AFRICA. In addition to the books listed in the Bibliographies to parts II and III above, the following deserve attention: Ronald Robinson and John Gallagher, *Africa and the Victorians* (London, 1961); T. O. Ranger, ed., *Aspects of Central African History* (London, 1968); and Roland Oliver and Anthony Atmore, *Africa since 1800* (London, 1967). For a poignant literary portrait of life in South Africa see: Alan Paton, *Cry, The Beloved Country* (New York, 1948).

ISLAM. Most of the titles listed in the Bibliography to part III under Islam touch upon the most recent period. In addition, William R. Polk, David Stamler et al., *Backdrop to Tragedy: The Struggle for Palestine* (Boston, 1957) attains a degree of neutrality between Jewish and Arab viewpoints on the most inflamed Middle Eastern issue of our time. Elizabeth Monroe, *Britain's Moment in the Middle East* (Baltimore, 1963); Zeine N. Zeine, *The Struggle for Arab Independence* (Beirut, 1960); George Kirk, *The Middle East, 1945–1950* (London, 1954); Gamal Abdel Nasser, *The Philosophy of Revolution* (Washington, D.C., 1955); Albert Hourani, *Arabic Thought in the Liberal Age* (London, 1962); H. A. R. Gibb, *Modern Trends in Islam* (Chicago, 1947); William R. Polk and Richard L. Chambers, eds., *Beginnings of Modernization in the Middle East: The Nineteenth Century* (Chicago, 1968); and V. J. Parry and M. E. Yapp, eds., *War, Technology, and Society in the Middle East* (New York, 1975) present varying viewpoints on recent developments within the Arab world. Again, one should consult Marshall G. S. Hodgson, *The Venture of Islam*, 3 vols. (Chicago, 1974) for an over-view of the entire realm of Islam from Morocco to Indonesia. Students may get a feeling for the texture of Arab society in the somewhat romanticized, and not altogether reliable account of the World War I revolt in: T. E. Lawrence, *Seven Pillars of Wisdom* (London, 1935).

INDIA. Mohandas K. Gandhi, *The Story of My Experiments with Truth* (Boston, 1957) and Jawaharlal Nehru, *Toward Freedom: The Auto-biography of Jawaharlal Nehru* (New York, 1941) are both poignant and powerful personal statements by the two principal framers of independent India. More formal histories include: Kavalam M. Panikkar, *The Founda-tions of New India* (London, 1963); Ram Gopal, *How India Struggled for Freedom: A Political History* (Bombay, 1967); V. B. Singh, ed., *Economic History of India 1857–1956* (Bombay and New York, 1965); and Hugh Tinker, *Experiment with Freedom: India and Pakistan, 1947* (London, 1967). Milton Singer, *When a Great Tradition Modernizes: An Anthropological Approach to Indian Civilization* (New York, 1972) and James Silverberg, ed., *Social Mobility in the Caste System in India: An Interdisciplinary Sym-posium* (The Hague, 1968) shed light on important aspects of Indian so-ciety. Two novels should be read in conjunction with studies of British India: E. M. Forster, *A Passage to India* (London, 1924) and Rudyard Kipling, *Kim* (London, 1901).

THE FAR EAST. For China see: Immanuel Hsü, *The Rise of Modern China*, 2nd ed. (New York, 1975); Ssu-yü Teng and John K. Fairbank et al., eds., *China's Response to the West: A Documentary Survey, 1839–1923* (Cam-bridge, Mass., 1954); Philip Kuhn, *Rebellion and Its Enemies in Late Im-perial China* (Cambridge, Mass., 1970); Mary C. Wright, *The Last Stand of Chinese Conservatism: The T'ung-chih Restoration 1862–1874* (Stanford, 1957). On the intellectual ferment in modern China see: Benjamin Schwartz, *In Search of Wealth and Power: Yen Fu and the West* (Cambridge, Mass., 1964); Joseph R. Levenson, *Confucian China and Its Modern Fate* (Berkeley, 1958); Chow Tse-tung, *The May Fourth Movement: Intellectual Revolution in Modern China* (Cambridge, Mass., 1960). John K. Fairbank, *The United States and China*, new ed. (Cambridge, Mass., 1958) and Tang Tsou, *Amer-ica's Failure in China, 1941–1950* (Chicago, 1963) treat foreign affairs. The best accounts of Chinese communism are: James P. Harrison, *The Long*

March to Power: A History of the Chinese Communist Party (New York, 1972); Maurice J. Meisner, *Li Ta-chao and the Origins of Chinese Marxism* (Cambridge, Mass., 1967); and two books by Stuart Schram, *The Political Thought of Mao Tse-tung*, rev. ed. (New York, 1969) and *Chairman Mao Talks to the People* (New York, 1975). Dick Wilson, ed., *Mao Tse-tung in the Scales of History* (New York, 1977) reflects current viewpoints on the career of Chairman Mao. Edgar Snow, *Red Star over China*, rev. ed. (New York, 1968) offers a sympathetic appraisal of the Chinese Communists' rise to power. Emily Hahn, *Chiang Kai-shek, an Unauthorized Biography* (New York, 1955) is another journalistic, interesting, if somewhat unkind, account of one of the makers of modern China. Ping-ti Ho and Tang Tsou, eds., *China in Crisis I: China's Heritage and the Communist Political System* (Chicago, 1968), together with its companion volume, *China in Crisis II: China's Policies in Asia and America's Alternatives* summarize academic opinion within the English-speaking world on the subject of Communist China.

Two important works of modern Chinese fiction are helpful in understanding contemporary China, especially when they are compared with the Chinese novels listed in the Bibliography to part III: Pa Chin (pseud.), *Family*, tr. Lu Kuang-huan (Garden City, N.Y., 1972), and Lu Hsun (pseud.), *Selected Stories of Lu Hsun*, tr. Yang Hsien-yi and Gladys Yang (Peking, 1963).

On Japan, in addition to the works listed in the bibliography to part III, there are: Hugh Borton, *Japan's Modern Century* (New York, 1955); Robert E. Ward and Dankwart A. Rustow, eds., *Political Modernization in Japan and Turkey* (Princeton, 1964); E. Herbert Norman, *Japan's Emergence as a Modern State* (New York, 1940) and Marius Jansen, ed., *Changing Japanese Attitudes Toward Modernization* (Princeton, 1965). James C. Abegglen, *The Japanese Factory: Aspects of Its Social Organization* (Glencoe, Ill., 1957), offers fascinating insight into the continuities between pre- and post-industrial social patterns in Japan.

Perhaps the best introduction to modern Japan is through its splendid literature. Many examples are available in English translation: Yasunari Kawabata, *The Sound of the Mountain*, tr. Edward M. Seidensticker (New York, 1970); Naoya Shiga, *A Dark Night's Passing*, tr. Edwin McClellan (Tokyo and New York, 1976); Osamu Dazai, *The Setting Sun*, tr. Donald Keene (Norfolk, Conn., 1956); Yukio Mishima, *Confessions of a Mask*, tr. Meredith Weatherby (Norfolk, Conn., 1958); Kenzaburo Oe, *A Personal Matter*, tr. John Nathan (New York, 1968); and Kobo Abe, *The Woman in the Dunes*, tr. E. Dale Saunders (New York, 1964).

Discussions of the Vietnam War remain largely polemical, but David

Halberstam, *The Best and the Brightest* (New York, 1972) and Frances Fitzgerald, *Fire in the Lake: The Vietnamese and the Americans in Vietnam* (Boston, 1972) are recommended.

EUROPE AND THE AMERICAS. Collective works such as the *Cambridge Modern History*, new ed., 12 vols. (Cambridge, 1956–), and series such as that edited by William L. Langer, *The Rise of Modern Europe*, 20 vols. (New York, 1936–) have long been standard references for more detailed treatment of European history. Textbooks also abound, the current favorite being Robert R. Palmer and Joel Coulton, *A History of the Modern World*, 5th ed. (New York, 1977). United States history is best left alone here, save to refer any inquirer to a standard textbook such as Samuel Eliot Morison and Henry Steele Commager, *A Concise History of the American Republic* (New York, 1977). Mention should be made, however, of Gunnar Myrdal, *An American Dilemma: The Negro Problem and Modern Democracy* (New York, 1944), which has exerted a profound effect on the course of American history.

Latin America is not well served, but Hubert C. and Helen B. Herring, *A History of Latin America: From the Beginnings to the Present*, 3rd ed. (New York, 1968); Harold Blakemore, *Latin America* (London, 1966); John E. Fagg, *Latin America, A General History*, 3rd ed. (New York, 1977); and Robert A. Humphreys, *Tradition and Revolt in Latin America* (New York, 1969) may help a beginner find his way. Hugh Thomas, *Cuba: or The Pursuit of Freedom* (London, 1971) deals with a country that has been at the center of recent world affairs.

Index